TOLD YOU SO
The Big Book of Weekly Columns

TOLD YOU SO

The Big Book of Weekly Columns

RALPH NADER

Introduction by Jim Hightower

Seven Stories Press

NEW YORK

A Seven Stories Press First Edition

Seven Stories Press
140 Watts Street
New York, NY 10013
www.sevenstories.com

College professors and middle and high school teachers may order free examination copies of Seven Stories Press titles. To order, visit sevenstories.com/textbook or send a fax on school letterhead to (212) 226-1411.

Book design by Jon Gilbert

Library of Congress Cataloging-in-Publication Data

Nader, Ralph.
 Told you so : the big book of weekly columns / Ralph Nader ; introduction by Jim Hightower. -- Seven stories press first edition.
     pages cm
  ISBN 978-1-60980-474-9 (pbk.)
 1. United States--Social policy--21st century. 2. Social justice--United States. 3. United States--Social conditions--21st century. 4. United States--Economic policy--21st century. 5. United States--Politics and government--21st century. 6. Corporate power--United States. I. Title.
  HN65.N295 2013
  303.3'72--dc23
                              2013001625

Printed in the United States

9 8 7 6 5 4 3 2 1

Contents

Civil Rights/Civil Liberties/ Civil Justice

Government: Imagination & Stagnation

Global & Labor Concerns

Consumers & the Economy

Observations & Inspirations

Political Games & Shames

Golden Oldies 471

Challenging Wrongdoers, Championing Rightdoers

We progressives were distraught in 1972 after the wretched Richard Nixon was re-elected, but we found some psychic comfort in a common political assumption of that time: "Well, at least it can't get any worse than this."

The "this" of Nixon was plenty bad, including such unforgettable uglies as John Mitchell, Spiro Agnew, CREEP, Henry Kissinger, and Earl Butz. But we couldn't have even imagined what was to come: the happy-go-lucky, union-busting extremism of Ronald Reagan; Daddy Bush's CIA spookism and Willie Horton racism; the welfare-bashing, Wall Street-hugging Clintonista period; the blatant pay-to-play Congress of Newt Gingrich and Tom DeLay; and then the Cheney-Bush Regime of executive autocracy, WMDs, and corporations gone-wild.

In the past three decades, America's top leaders have taken us from Reagan's trickle-down economics to the Koch brothers' *tinkle*-down economics.

Yet, throughout this epoch of plutocratic advance (from Nixon's landslide victory to the present Kafkaesque moment of political absurdity in which Nixon would be rejected by his own party as a liberal), there has been one uplifting, progressive constant: Nader. (Notice that—like Bono or Oprah—Ralph doesn't really need a first name, because "Nader" is the modern-day eponym for a champion of the underdog, someone who's willing and able to confront the Powers That Be on behalf of the Powers That OUGHT to be).

Indeed, let's travel back to Nixon, the Republican who signed the law creating OSHA, an act that (O, progress!) made it at least quasi-illegal for corporations to poison, maim, and kill their workers. Did a president known as "Tricky Dick" actually want this law? About as much as he wanted the painful phlebitis that vexed him later in life. Nader—along with the great (and I mean truly great) labor leader, Tony Mazzocchi—mounted a nationwide organizing, media, and lobbying campaign to force Nixon to do something unnatural for him: The Right Thing.

With deep faith in the power of an engaged citizenry to make a difference, Nader has been out front on nearly every big issue, including product safety, environmental justice, worker rights, fair trade, Wall Street greed, money in politics, war crimes, healthcare for all, whistleblower protection, Pentagon bloat, government secrecy, green energy, Big Pharma, Big Oil, Big Food—you name it. As another activist friend of mine says, "If you're not on the edge, you're not in the action, you're just taking up space." Nader's entire life of civic engagement has been spent on the edge, not only challenging wrongdoers, but, just as importantly celebrating rightdoers—the ordinary citizens and grassroots groups who move our society's ideals of democracy, justice, and the common good forward.

Since 1972, Nader has been writing a weekly column. That's forty years of important history, chronicled in fifty-two informative, sometimes infuriating, often inspiring, and always insightful pieces each year by a guy who's not just witnessing the history, but is in the midst of it.

What you have in your hands is a collection of those thoughtful, spirited, and immensely valuable columns penned by Nader (yes, he writes his own stuff) over the last eight years. What I like about this volume is that it's not merely a screed about how bad things are—due to corporate supremacy, media meekness, and the two-party duopoly—but it's the work of a creative thinker who offers a way out of the mess, inspiring all of us to dare to do something brave, but essential if we are to be a truly-free, self-governing people: AGITATE!

As Nader demonstrates by word and deed, the opposite of courage is not cowardice, it's conformity. This "Book of Ralph" will give you courage, ideas, hope, even some laughs—and the motivation to step up your own fight for justice.

—Jim Hightower

Corporate Power

Combatting corporate abuses requires constant vigilance. Corporations shape America's political process as much as they shape America's economy through PAC contributions and threats to move manufacturing and service jobs to low-wage countries.

Columns in this section catalog the rotten fruit of our diseased political process, including the gigantic growth in corporate welfare (a.k.a. crony capitalism) even as smaller, key social welfare programs are cut; the consolidation of monopoly power while antitrust laws are not enforced; and successive waves of corporate crime.

The Occupy movement's push to get the concerns of the "99 percent" into the political debate was an important milestone. Unfortunately, the agenda of the 99 percent won't be heard over the corporate pleas for more government bailouts and tax cuts, unless "We the People" rise up to tell Washington that we're tired of being shut out of the political process.

Large US corporations lack a patriotic commitment to our country. They receive public services, subsidies and protections in this country, yet they continue to ship jobs overseas, pressuring their suppliers to do likewise, and create tax havens on faraway islands to run away from their tax responsibilities to the United States.

The corporate crime wave that has been continuing for years and that caused the 2008 financial crisis has barely been addressed by lawmakers in Washington. Corporate crimes see little retribution because corporate bosses place the blame on lower-level employees. There is very little corporate accountability. These columns help to inform and encourage the everyday citizen/consumer to push to counter corporate abuses and corporate control of our political economy.

Let Them In!

November 23, 2011

From New York City to Oakland, and several cities in between, the police, on orders from city officials, have smashed the Occupy encampments and evicted the protestors from public parks and spaces. More politicians, from Congress to the state and local level, want the Occupy people OUT!

Well, why don't they start letting them into the places where decisions are being made against their legitimate interests? Let them IN to:

1. Having jobs and affordable housing;

2. Their legislatures without having to pay to play;

3. The courts when they are wrongfully injured or have other grievances without

being blocked by corporatist dogmas and judges;

4. Access to civil lawyers pro bono when they are in dire need, as suggested by Cincinnati attorney Paul Tobias;

5. The dispensing and regulatory agencies with their petitions (without having to face grinding delays and costs);

6. Universal healthcare so they can escape the present avariciousness called "pay or die";

7. Fair contracts, from student loans to mortgages, without fine print and gouging fees and robo-signing type shenanigans that trap them into contract peonage (see FairContracts.org)

8. Fair and clean elections with voluntary public financing and easier ballot access for third party candidates to give voters more choice beyond the two party dictatorship;

9. The media to express themselves on television, radio and in newspapers, so dominated by the plutocratic values of corporatism;

10. Public places to petition and circulate their materials in these large malls that are taxpayer subsidized but considered off limits because they are corporate owned;

11. The political process, with other citizens, with full rights to challenge in courts and by referenda the politicians and their corporate paymasters who unconstitutionally and illegally plunge our country into wars, invasions and occupations abroad;

12. A clean environment where they can breathe clean air, drink clean water and eat safe food by enforcing the existing laws with adequate budgets;

13. The facilities to band together as workers, consumers and taxpayers that exist for commercial companies and their investors;

There would be no need for encampments or street demonstrations if people were allowed IN to these arenas of power, communications and good livelihoods. You don't see corporate executives and managers protesting in the streets. Because they are already IN!

It has been said repeatedly that the Occupy Wall Street movement has no specific agenda. Look at their signs and banners. It is obvious; they want IN. They no longer want to be excluded, disrespected, unemployed, defrauded, impoverished, betrayed and in big and small ways OUT.

They want justice, opportunity and, as the ancient Roman lawyer Marcus Cicero advocated for, the freedom to participate in power.

Repression Expands Resistance
November 16, 2011

From Oakland, California to New York City, the police, ordered by politicians, have smashed through Occupy encampments. Noted for their rigorous non-violence and orderly arrangements—tents with medical assistance, legal aid, libraries, media relations and sanitation controls

—the Occupy protestors are being shoved out of their public places all over the country.

The Mayor of Oakland admitted to the BBC in an interview that mayors, police and other security officials have been in contact with each other regarding how to deal with the removal of the protestors, including an eighteen-mayor conference call she participated in recently.

The police power is always the first response to a mobilized citizen action that refuses to go away. Even a protest against corporate greed and governmental complicity shattering the economy and millions of livelihoods, which has widespread support by the American people, faces police intervention.

How else has the plutocracy of the corporatists and the oligarchy of the politicians who serve them responded? President Obama has remained aloof, as he did earlier this year with the giant Wisconsin labor protests. California Governor Jerry Brown has stayed out of the fray. The Congress is wallowing in its tone-deaf bubble, squabbling over how to reduce the crumbs for the masses while the obscenely-bonused corporate bosses feast on the tables of corporate welfare and privilege.

Chris Hedges, the Pulitzer-prize winning war correspondent, described what entrenched illegitimacy by the power brokers has to offer besides force:

"Our elites have exposed their hand. They have nothing to offer. They can destroy but they cannot build. They can repress but they cannot lead. They can steal but they cannot share. They have no ideas, no plans and no vision for the future."

Except, one may add, for the perpetuation of their autocratic, self-enriching, dominant rule at the expense of the "99 percent." Their outcry is for law and order—clear the tents from the public parks. These are the same corporatists who constantly receive from the corporate-dominated state all kinds of waivers from health and safety regulations, from government contract rules, from fair labor standards and from taxes. And they receive all kinds of loopholes to enhance their profits and executive pay packages. But there are no waivers for orderly encampments non-violently advancing justice for "we the people" by spotlighting the gross inequities and cruelties imposed on tens of millions of innocent Americans.

As the destruction of the Occupy encampments proceeds, this movement will disperse into many locations and become larger and stronger. From the neighborhoods, joining with long-valiant community groups, the Occupy protestors will return by day to these public squares for their ever-more innovative demonstrations.

One protestor told *Democracy Now* that their expulsion from over-night stays in Zuccotti Park will show "how intuitive and ingenious a movement we have." Already the protestors have shown their adaptive creativity. They responded to a ban on bullhorns or other amplifiers with the "human microphone," relaying words through waves of people.

Occupy Wall Street had a 5,000 book library loaning books to residents without access to a nearby city library branch. So taken was the architectural editor of the *Washington Post*'s Phillip Kennicott with Occupy Washington at McPherson Square that he devoted two pages to an aerial view and report of its intricate organization calling it a "vibrant brand of urbanism." The same is true of the other Washington, DC Occupy site at Freedom Plaza. So far City Hall and the National Park Service have left them alone.

With the coming of winter and the Occupy

sites overwhelmed with the hungry and home-less poor—some urged to go there by the po-lice—it was time for stage two. By not being somewhere, the Occupy movement will now be everywhere—in the neighborhoods, on the campuses, in churches and union halls, and marching in the streets toward the edifices of the corporatists and their political lackeys.

Furthermore, this diffusion and magnifica-tion will spread into the established institu-tions themselves as first a few and then more whistleblowers, dissenters and other silent pa-triots do their part to subordinate the corporate structures and political controllers to the sover-eignty of the people. After all our Constitution's preamble starts with "we the people," and ends without a single mention of corporations or po-litical parties.

Becoming stronger from violent over-reac-tion by the police, it will become an "Occupy America" movement with demands for long-overdue revisions of priorities and equities relat-ing to children, workers, consumers, taxpayers, retirees and restricted voters. The sheer volume of Americans coming into the streets with their non-violence will exhaust police resources and police resolve. Already, the city police and local district attorney in Albany, New York refused the governor's order to arrest and remove peace-ful protestors. Why? Because said one police of-ficial "we don't have those resources and these people were not causing trouble," as quoted in the instant new paperback by Yes! Magazine, *This Changes Everything*.

At the University of California at Berkeley demonstration, Daniel Ellsberg said that the official enforcers' "instinct for repression is ir-repressible." That is the dark view, predicted by Aldous Huxley's *Brave New World Revis-ited*—a copy of which was found, ironically, in the debris of the destroyed Zuccotti Park li-brary by Amy Goodman of *Democracy Now*. But the instinct for freedom and justice is also irrepressible. Who are you betting on to prevail this time?

Corporate Tax Escapees and You

July 7, 2011

The all-consuming Washington, DC wrangling over debts and deficits, spending and taxing is excluding a large reality of how these financial problems can sensibly and fairly be addressed. These blinders in Congress and the White House come from fact-starved ideologies—mostly from the Republicans—and fear-fed meekness—mostly from the Democrats. Both are furiously dialing for commercial campaign cash.

Take the gigantic world of corporate tax avoidance. Ronald Reagan signed the Tax Re-form Act of 1986 that was designed to increase corporate tax revenues by over 30 percent. To-day, President Obama wants to diminish or delete some tax loopholes (technically called tax expenditures) for large corporations, but let most of the revenues be cancelled out by low-ering the corporate tax rates. How the world changes.

Obama's mild approach is unacceptable to the big business lobbies and their Republican mascots in Congress.

They want more tax breaks so they can keep trillions of more dollars over the next decade.

Lost in this whirl of vast greed and political calculation are options, which if pursued with a sense of fairness for the people of the country, would go a long way in providing revenues for public works jobs—repairing America—which in turn would generate more consumer demand by these workers.

The ultra-accurate Citizens for Tax Justice (CTJ) publishes precise reports on the effective taxes paid by corporations that make an utter mockery of the 35 percent statutory tax rate for corporations (see CTJ.org).

On June 1, 2011, CTJ released a preview of its forthcoming study of Fortune 500 companies and "the taxes they paid—or failed to pay—over the 2008-2010 period." Judging by the preview, this report should silence those who say that the US taxes corporations more than other industrialized nations.

What do you think the following profitable corporations paid in actual total federal income taxes in that period: American Electric Power, Boeing, DuPont, Exxon Mobil, FedEx, General Electric, Honeywell, International, IBM, United Technologies, Verizon Communications, Wells Fargo, and Yahoo? Nothing!

CTJ reports that "from 2008 through 2010, these 12 companies reported $171 billion in pretax US profits. But as a group, their federal income taxes were negative: $2.5 billion."

CTJ documents that "not a single one of the companies paid anything close to the 35 percent statutory tax rate. In fact, the 'highest tax' company on our list, ExxonMobil, paid an effective three-year tax rate of only 14.2 percent . . . and over the past two years, Exxon Mobil's net tax on its $9.9 billion in US pretax profits was a minuscule $39 million, an effective tax rate of 0.4 percent."

Next time you hear Republicans like Eric Cantor, John Boehner and Mitch McConnell repeat their statement that corporations are overtaxed and need a break, you can tell them that "had these twelve companies paid the full 35 percent corporate tax, their federal income taxes over the three years would have totaled $59.9 billion." CTJ director, Bob McIntyre noted that these twelve companies are "just the tip of an iceberg of widespread corporate tax avoidance."

Of course, most Americans suspect as much, even if they don't have the exact figures. A recent Gallup poll asked the public's opinion on where they stand on the tax cuts for the rich and the tax breaks for the corporations. By a 45 percentmargin, they opposed tax cuts for the rich and by a 55 percent margin, they opposed tax cuts for corporations.

So what are Barack Obama and the Democrats waiting for? They have the undeniable facts and overwhelming public sentiment behind them. Why do they let Cantor, Boehner and McConnell continue to mouth falsehoods without rebuttals of the truth?

It's obvious. The Democrats want big time money from the executives and Political Action Committees of the Fortune 500. The Democrats are willing to let the Republicans fuzz the debate and dare to try and make Medicare and Social Security benefits absorb the sacrifices. Indeed last week, the *Washington Post* headlined Obama signaling to the Republicans that Social Security "is on the table."

Even the meek reporters should no longer fail to challenge the Republican's daily mantras.

Should you have any doubts that the corporate state is in firm control of your government, try this test: If you paid a single dollar in federal income tax in any of the years 2008, 2009 and 2010, you paid more than the giant General Electric (GE) company. In that period GE made $7.722 billion in US profit, paid no taxes and received $4.737 billion from the IRS. As the *New York Times* reported on March 24, teams of

GE tax lawyers and accountants are making sure they avoid taxes altogether, shifting the burden to you.

These big companies are laughing at us all the way to the taxpayer-bailed-out banks. They're even laughing at their own shareholder-owners. The non-financial companies are sitting on about $2 trillion. Inert dollars, producing nothing and earning minuscule interest are better deployed by enlarging the dividend payments to their shareholders. A mere 10 percent of that sum as dividend payments this year would pump $200 billion into an economy needing more consumer demand.

Reporters and columnists need to start addressing these topics at news conferences with members of Congress and White House staffers. The Washington press corps shouldn't behave like sheep!

Stripmining America—Unpatriotically

April 22, 2011

It is time to apply the standard of patriotism to the US multinational corporations and demand that they pledge allegiance to the United States and "the Republic for which is stands . . . with liberty and justice for all." This July 4, 2011 would be good day for Americans to demand such a corporate commitment.

Born and chartered in the USA, these corporations rose to their giant size on the backs of American workers and vast taxpayer-subsidized research and development handouts. When they got into trouble, whether through mismanagement or corruption, these companies rushed to Washington, DC for bailouts from American taxpayers. When some were challenged in for-

eign lands, the US Marines came to their rescue, as depicted decades ago by two-time Congressional Medal of Honor winner, Marine General Smedley Butler.

So what is their message to America and its workers now? It is not gratitude or loyalty. It is "we're outta here, with your jobs and industries" to dictatorial or oligarchic regimes abroad, such as China, that know how to keep their impoverished and abused workers under control.

Note that these company bosses have no compunction replacing US workers with serf-labor, but they never replace themselves with bi-lingual executives from China, India and elsewhere who are willing to work for one-tenth or less of the huge pay packages executives get from their rubber-stamp boards of directors in the US.

Just this week, the *Wall Street Journal* headlined "Big US Firms Shift Hiring Abroad." Veteran reporter, David Wessel writes,

> US multinational corporations, the big brand-name companies that employ a fifth of all American workers, have been hiring abroad while cutting back at home, sharpening the debate over globalization's effect on the US economy. The companies cut their work forces in the US by 2.9 million during the 2000s while increasing employment overseas by 2.4 million, new data from the US Commerce Department show.

While Mr. Wessel acknowledges that other economies, especially in Asia, are growing rapidly, he noted that "The data also underscore the vulnerability of the US economy, particularly at a time when unemployment is high and wages aren't increasing."

Keep in mind that, while receiving all the public services, subsidies and protections in this country, large corporations have been abandoning America by shifting jobs overseas and by making our country perilously and unnecessarily dependent on foreign governments that naturally put their own interests first.

For example, the drug companies no longer have any plant in the US to manufacture essential raw ingredients for important antibiotics like penicillin. In 2004, Bristol-Myers Squibb closed the last such factory in East Syracuse, N.Y. The drug industry always made lots of money here. One of every two Americans are on a prescription medicine. But the pharmaceutical companies want to make more so they have moved their production to Asia.

In 2009, the *New York Times* reported that "the critical ingredients for most antibiotics are now made almost exclusively in China and India. The same is true for dozens of other crucial medicines, including the popular allergy medicine prednisone; metformin, for diabetes; and amlodipine, for high blood pressure.

This flight to Asia raises serious questions. Senator Sherrod Brown (D-Ohio) held hearings because he accurately believed that "the lack of regulation around outsourcing is a blind spot that leaves room for supply disruptions, counterfeit medicines, even bioterrorism."

Industrial scale production of penicillin was developed by the US war production board in World War II and many drug companies made it in US plants until the Chinese government lured the industry there with many freebies and weak safety regulations. A few years ago ninety-five Americans died from a Chinese produced counterfeit ingredient in the drug heparin, an anticlotting drug needed for surgery and dialysis.

As Belgium drug industry consultant, Enrico Polastro, told the *New York Times*: "If China ever got very upset with President Obama, it could be a big problem." The *Times* concluded: "So for

now, like it or not, China has the upper hand."

Who gave China that dominant position? US multinational drug companies, who along with other big US companies, pushed through Congress, with Bill Clinton's support, ratification of both NAFTA's and the World Trade Organization's "pull down" trade agreements. They created the very globalized structure that they now claim they are beholden to in order to meet the global competition. Clever, aren't they?

Other unpatriotic acts include the oil companies who, despite being given a rich oil depletion tax allowance to invest in energy in the US, invested in oil production overseas. The US is now dependent on foreign sources for most of its petroleum. Don't forget the military-industrial giants that thrive on US military expansion abroad and sell modern weapons to many dictatorial regimes which they use to oppress their people and endanger our own national security.

US multinationals that export jobs abroad, show too little regard for our country, or to the US communities that sustained them for decades. Greedy corporate lobbyists continue to press for more privileges and immunities, over those held by real humans, so as to be less accountable under US law for corporate crimes and other mis-behaviors.

If US companies continue to expand their rights of personhood through US Supreme Court's political decisions (eg. the latest being the notorious 5 to 4 Citizens United case opening up the floodgates of corporate cash against or for electoral candidates), then, they should be judged as "persons" and evaluated for their loyalty to their country of creation.

Since corporations are clearly "artificial" entities and not real human beings, narrower civil liberties standards can be applied to the impersonal and massive concentrations of power, capital and technology known as corporations.

Independence Day July 4th presents an opportunity for a national attention to the need for calling out these runaway corporate giants who exploit for profit the patriotic sensibilities of Americans but decline to be held any patriotic expectations or values.

Readers interested in joining such an effort for July 4, 2011 contact info@csrl.org.

Time to Topple Corporate Dictators

February 18, 2011

The eighteen-day non-violent Egyptian protests for freedom raise the question: is America next? Were Thomas Jefferson and Thomas Paine around, they would likely say "what are we waiting for?" They would be appalled by the concentration of economic and political power in such a few hands. Remember how often these two men warned about concentrated power.

Our Declaration of Independence (1776) listed grievances against King George III. A good number of them could have been made against "King" George W. Bush who not only brushed aside Congressional war-making authority under the Constitution but plunged the nation through lies into extended illegal wars which he conducted in violation of international law. Even conservative legal scholars such as Republicans Bruce Fein and former Judge Andrew Napolitano believe he and Dick Cheney still should be prosecuted for war and other related crimes. The conservative American Bar Association sent George W. Bush three "white papers" in 2005-2006 that documented his distinct violations of the Constitution he had sworn to uphold.

Here at home, the political system is a two-party dictatorship whose gerrymandering results in most electoral districts being one-party fiefdoms. The two parties block the freedom of third parties and independent candidates to have equal access to the ballots and to the debates. Another barrier to competitive democratic elections is big money, largely commercial in source, which marinates most politicians in cowardliness and sinecurism.

Our legislative and executive branches, at the federal and state levels, can fairly be called corporate regimes. This is corporatism where government is controlled by private economic power. President Franklin Delano Roosevelt called this grip "fascism" in a formal message to Congress in 1938.

Corporatism shuts out the people and opens governmental largesse paid for by taxpayers to insatiable corporations.

Notice how each decade the bailouts, subsidies, hand-outs, giveaways, and tax escapes for big business grow larger. The word "trillions" is increasingly used, as in the magnitude of the rescue by Washington of the Wall Street crooks and speculators who looted the peoples' pensions and savings.

It is not as if these giant companies demonstrate any gratitude to the people who save them again and again. Instead, US companies are fast quitting the country in which they were chartered and prospered. These corporations, which were built on the backs of American workers, are shipping millions of jobs and whole industries to repressive foreign regimes abroad, such as China.

Over 70 percent of Americans in a September 2000 *BusinessWeek* poll said corporations had "too much control over their lives." It's gotten worse with the last decade's corporate corruption and crime wave.

Wal-Mart imports over $20 billion a year in products from sweatshops in China. About a million Wal-Mart workers make under $10.50 per hour before deductions—many in the $8 an hour range. While Wal-Mart's CEO makes about $11,000 a hour plus benefits and perks.

This scenario has metastasized through the economy. One in three workers in the US makes Wal-Mart level wages. Fifty million people have no health insurance and every year about 45,000 die because they cannot afford diagnosis or treatment. Child poverty is climbing as household income falls. Unemployment and underemployment are near 20 percent levels. The federal minimum wage, adjusted for inflation since 1968, would be $10.00 per hour now; instead, it is $7.25.

Yet one percent of the richest Americans have financial wealth equivalent to the bottom ninety-five percent of the people. Corporate profits and compensation of corporate bosses are at record levels. While companies, excluding financial firms, are sitting on $2 trillion in cash.

On February 7, President Obama showed us where the power is by walking across LaFayette Park from the White House to the headquarters of the US Chamber of Commerce. Before a large audience of CEOs, he pleaded for them to invest more in jobs in America. Imagine, CEOs of pampered, privileged mega-companies often on welfare and in trouble with the law sitting there while the president curtsied.

With Bill Clinton in the nineties, corporate lobbies tightened their grip on our country by greasing through Congress both NAFTA and the World Trade Organization agreements that subordinated our sovereignty and workers to the global government of corporations.

All this adds to the growing sense of powerlessness by the citizenry. They experience hun-

dreds of thousands of preventable deaths and many more injuries every year in the workplace, the environment, and the marketplace. Massive budgets and technologies do not go to reduce these costly casualties, instead they go to the big business of exaggerated security threats.

While the ObamaBush deficit-financed wars in Afghanistan and Iraq have been destroying those nations, our public works here, such as mass transit, schools and clinics crumble for lack of repairs. Foreclosures keep rising.

The debt servitude of consumers is stripping them of control of their own money as fine print contracts, credit ratings and credit scores tighten the noose on family budgets.

Half of democracy is showing up. Too many Americans, despairingly, are not "showing up" at the polls, at rallies, marches, courtrooms or city council meetings. If "we the people" want to reassert our proper constitutional sovereignty over our country—we can *start* by amassing ourselves in public squares and around the giant buildings of our rulers.

In a country that has so many problems it doesn't deserve and so many solutions that it doesn't apply; all things are possible when people begin looking at themselves for the necessary power to produce a just society.

Road to Corporate Serfdom
October 29, 2010

It was Bill Clinton's campaign strategist, James Carville, who in 1992 created the election slogan: "It's the Economy, Stupid." For the 2010 Congressional campaigns, the slogan should have been: "It's Corporate Crime and Control, Stupid."

But notwithstanding the latest corporate crime wave, the devastating fallout on workers, investors and taxpayers from the greed and corruption of Wall Street, and the abandonment of American workers by US corporations in favor of repressive regimes abroad, the Democrats have failed to focus voter anger on the corporate supremacists.

The giant corporate control of our country is so vast that people who call themselves *anything* politically—liberal, conservative, progressive, libertarian, independents or anarchist—should be banding together against the reckless Big Business steamroller.

Conservatives need to remember the sharply critical cautions against misbehaving or overreaching businesses and commercialism by Adam Smith, Frederic Bastiat, Friedrich Hayek and other famous conservative intellectuals. All knew that the commercial instinct and drive know few boundaries to the relentless stomping or destruction of the basic civic values for any civilized society.

When 80 percent of the Americans polled believe "America is in decline," they are reflecting in part the decline of real household income and the shattered bargaining power of American workers up against global companies.

The US won World War II. Germany lost and was devastated. Yet note this remarkable headline in the October 27th *Washington Post*: "A Bargain for BMW means jobs for 1,000 in S. Carolina: Workers line up for $15 an hour—half of what German counterparts make."

The German plant is backed by South Carolina taxpayer subsidies and is not unionized. Newly hired workers at General Motors and Chrysler, recently bailed out by taxpayers, are paid $14 an hour before deductions. The auto companies used to be in the upper tier of high paying manufacturing jobs. Now the US is a low-wage country compared to some countries in Western Europe and the trend here is continuing downward.

Workers in their fifties at the BMW plant, subsidizing their lower wages with their tax dollars, aren't openly complaining, according to the *Post*. Not surprising, since the alternative in a falling economy is unemployment or a fast-food job at $8 per hour.

It is not as if we weren't forewarned by our illustrious political forebears. Fasten your seat belts; here are some examples:

Thomas Jefferson—"I hope that we shall crush in its birth the aristocracy of our monied corporations, which dare already to challenge our government to a trial of strength, and bid defiance to the laws of our country."

Abraham Lincoln in 1864—"I see in the near future a crisis approaching that unnerves me and causes me to tremble for the safety of my country. . . . corporations have been enthroned and an era of corruption in high places will follow, and the money power of the country will endeavor to prolong its reign by working upon the prejudices of the people until all wealth is aggregated in a few hands and the Republic is destroyed."

Theodore Roosevelt—"The citizens of the United States must control the mighty commercial forces which they themselves call into being."

Woodrow Wilson—"Big business is not dangerous because it is big, but because its bigness is an unwholesome inflation created by privileges and exemptions which it ought not to enjoy."

Franklin D. Roosevelt—"The first truth is that the liberty of a democracy is not safe if the people tolerate the growth of private power to a point where it becomes stronger than their democratic state itself. That, in its essence, is Fascism—ownership of Government by an individual, by a group, or by any other controlling private power."

Dwight Eisenhower, farewell address—"In the councils of government, we must guard against the acquisition of unwarranted influence, whether sought or unsought, by the military-industrial complex."

And, lastly, a literary insight:

Theodore Dreiser—"The government has ceased to function, the corporations are the government."

Are you, dear reader, the same now as you were when you began reading this column?

A Win for Whistle Blowers

April 5, 2010

Why would Pfizer, the world's largest drug company, so mistreat and silence one of their top molecular biologists that a federal jury in Connecticut awarded her $1.37 million in damages last week?

The unraveling answer promises to tear open the curtain covering hazards confronting tens of thousands of scientists and assistants in corporate and university labs doing genetic engineering work with viruses and bacteria.

Becky McClain's lawsuit against Pfizer claimed that the company's sloppiness in 2002-3 exposed her to an engineered form of the lentivirus, a virus related to one that could lead to immune deficiencies. Pfizer denied any connection between its lab practices and Ms. McClain's recurring paralysis and other illnesses.

Back and forth over three years came the scientist's claims and Pfizer's denials during which she had to leave her job amidst the increasing retaliatory behavior of her ten-year employer.

Pfizer is known for playing hardball and vio-

lating laws. Last year it had to pay the Justice Department one of the largest fines—half civil, half criminal—for illegal promotion of its drugs for unapproved uses. The fine—$2.4 billion—avoided criminal charges and prosecution, either of the company or officials, and became just another cost of doing business.

Just last week, soon after buying Wyeth Labs for $68 billion, Pfizer's CEO, Jeffrey B. Kindler, told a reporter for the *New York Times* that his company has "invented too few drugs and left its reputation in disrepair after two criminal cases."

That record does not diminish Pfizer's advantage over its imperiled lab workers, which is built on the absence of any available risk assessments, the very nature of possible latent, silent violence, and the cruel refusal to give afflicted employees their own exposure records on the grounds that they are company trade secrets.

Pfizer offered Ms. McClain a paltry sum with a gag order, which she promptly refused. She wanted her freedom of speech and her whistle-blowing rights under federal law. Her lawsuit was filed in 2006 in Hartford.

By dismissing the third count, which might be appealed, in her complaint alleging Pfizer's wanton misconduct, US District Judge Vanessa L. Bryant ruled that the plaintiff did not have available the evidence of causality and it was a worker's compensation matter anyway. Herein started the chicken-egg problem. How could Ms. McClain obtain the evidence in order to prove her case when Pfizer said it was proprietary and secret?

The Council for Responsible Genetics (CRG), started by Harvard and MIT scientists, does not believe laboratory exposure records of workers should be trade secrets. Life, health and remedial rights should trump any such alleged, bizarre property right.

Becky McClain has already exhausted any remedies or assistance from the woeful Occupational Safety and Health Administration (OSHA). This agency has been without any regulations or disclosure requirements about biohazards in laboratories. This inertness might change with the appointment of David Michaels to head OSHA, which should bring the agency closer to its mission of preventing or diminishing tens of thousands of fatalities and injuries each year.

Mr. Michaels told the *Times* that "new biological materials, nanomaterials, there are many things where we don't have adequate information, and we think workers need to have protection." He indicated that OSHA will take another look at the McClain case.

Both Jeremy Gruber, president of CRG, and Steve Zeltzer, chair of the California Coalition for Workers Memorial Day, believe the McClain case will lead to broader scrutiny of biologic laboratories, where research is expanding rapidly with heavy federal funding.

It is well-known that workers in these labs are inhibited from speaking out, either inside or outside their workplace, for fear of losing their jobs. OSHA has long known that companies in old and new industries often do not come close to fully reporting cases of their injuries and sickness either to their insurers or to state or federal job safety agencies. Some have been found to keep two sets of books.

The Bureau of Labor Statistics data are not at all comprehensive. Under-reporting can hide half or three-fourths of the actual traumatic injuries.

Mr. Zeltzer has denounced what he calls "the failure of top company officials to even report to OSHA and other government agencies that many workers were getting sick numerous times in their laboratories although this is required by the law." He called on the US Attorney in Hartford to begin a criminal investigation. (See: workersmemorialday.org.)

As for Becky McClain, this is just the end of the beginning. She says she has lost her career, her health and her health insurance. But she recognizes her case is in the vanguard of many other cases and worker protests to come before enforceable and openly accessible standards and practices become the way of doing business for these labs.

For when it comes to developing materials that are inherently latent, subvisible forms of silent violence, business as usual can become cruel and unusual punishment for innocent, defenseless scientists, lab technicians and other workers.

Such is the weighty responsibility of David Michaels and the new managers of the long moribund, underfunded OSHA in the coming months.

Time to Rein in Out-of-Control Corporate Influences on Our Democracy
January 22, 2010

Yesterday's 5-4 decision by the US Supreme Court in *Citizens United v. Federal Election Commission* shreds the fabric of our already weakened democracy by allowing corporations to more completely dominate our corrupted electoral process. It is outrageous that corporations already attempt to influence or bribe our political candidates through their political action committees (PACs), which solicit employees and shareholders for donations.

With this decision, corporations can now

directly pour vast amounts of corporate money, through independent expenditures, into the electoral swamp already flooded with corporate campaign PAC contribution dollars. Without approval from their shareholders, corporations can reward or intimidate people running for office at the local, state, and national levels.

Much of this 183 page opinion requires readers to enter into a fantasy world and accept the twisted logic of Justice Kennedy, who delivered the opinion of the Court, joined by Chief Justice Roberts, and Justices Scalia, Alito, and Thomas. Imagine the majority saying the "Government may not suppress political speech based on the speaker's corporate identity."

Perhaps Justice Kennedy didn't hear that the financial sector invested more than $5 billion in political influence purchasing in Washington over the past decade, with as many as 3,000 lobbyists winning deregulation and other policy decisions that led directly to the current financial collapse, according to a 231-page report titled: "Sold Out: How Wall Street and Washington Betrayed America" (See: WallStreetWatch.org).

The Center for Responsive Politics reported that last year the US Chamber of Commerce spent $144 million to influence Congress and state legislatures.

The Center also reported big lobbying expenditures by the Pharmaceutical Research and Manufacturers of America (PhRMA) which spent $26 million in 2009. Drug companies like Pfizer, Amgen and Eli Lilly also poured tens of millions of dollars into federal lobbying in 2009. The health insurance industry trade group America's Health Insurance Plans (AHIP) also spent several million lobbying Congress. No wonder Single Payer Health insurance—supported by the majority of people, doctors, and nurses—isn't moving in Congress.

Energy companies like ExxonMobil and Chevron are also big spenders. No wonder we have a national energy policy that is pro-fossil fuel and that does little to advance renewable energy (See: OpenSecrets.org).

No wonder we have the best Congress money can buy.

I suppose Justice Kennedy thinks corporations that overwhelm members of Congress with campaign contributions need to have still more influence in the electoral arena. Spending millions to lobby Congress and making substantial PAC contributions just isn't enough for a majority of the Supreme Court. The dictate by the five activist Justices was too much for even Republican Senator John McCain, who commented that he was troubled by their "extreme naivete."

There is a glimmer of hope and a touch of reality in yesterday's Supreme Court decision. Unfortunately, it is the powerful ninety-page dissent in this case by Justice Stevens joined by Justices Ginsburg, Breyer, and Sotomayor. Justice Stevens recognizes the power corporations wield in our political economy. Justice Stevens finds it "absurd to think that the First Amendment prohibits legislatures from taking into account the corporate identity of a sponsor of electoral advocacy." He flatly declares that, "The Court's ruling threatens to undermine the integrity of elected institutions across the Nation."

He notes that the Framers of our Constitution "had little trouble distinguishing corporations from human beings, and when they constitutionalized the right to free speech in the First Amendment, it was the free speech of individual Americans that they had in mind." Right he is, for the words "corporation" or "company" do not exist in our Constitution.

Justice Stevens concludes his dissent as follows:

At bottom, the Court's opinion is thus a rejection of the common sense of the American people, who have recognized a need to prevent corporations from undermining self-government since the founding, and who have fought against the distinctive corrupting potential of corporate electioneering since the days of Theodore Roosevelt. It is a strange time to repudiate that common sense. While American democracy is imperfect, few outside the majority of this Court would have thought its flaws included a dearth of corporate money in politics.

Indeed, this corporatist, anti-voter majority decision is so extreme that it should galvanize a grassroots effort to enact a simple Constitutional amendment to once and for all end corporate personhood and curtail the corrosive impact of big money on politics. It is time to prevent corporate campaign contributions from commercializing our elections and drowning out the voices and values of citizens and voters. It is way overdue to overthrow "King Corporation" and restore the sovereignty of "We the People"! Remember that corporations, chartered by the state, are our servants not our masters.

Legislation sponsored by Senator Richard Durbin (D-Ill.) and Representative John Larson (D-Conn.) would encourage unlimited small-dollar donations from individuals and provide candidates with public funding in exchange for refusing corporate contributions or private contributions of more than $100.

It is also time for shareholder resolutions, company by company, directing the corporate boards of directors to pledge not to use company money to directly favor or oppose candidates for public office.

If you want to join the efforts to rollback the corporate privileges the Supreme Court made

yesterday, visit citizen.org, movetoamend.org and freespeechforpeople.org.

Purloining the People's Property
August 3, 2009

Every week, Marcia Carroll collects examples of privatization (that is, corporatization of the peoples' assets). Looking at her website, privatizationwatch.org, will either make you laugh helplessly or make your blood boil.

The "off the wall" giveaways at bargain-basement prices of what you and other Americans own eclipses imagination. The latest escapes from responsible government are called "public-private partnerships" and are designed to enable the likes of Morgan Stanley and Goldman Sachs to take over highways, meter-collecting, and public buildings in deals that are loaded with complex tax advantages for the investors.

Here are two of her latest entries. Arizona lawmakers and Governor Jan Brewer are moving to fill a $3.4 billion budget shortfall by selling state-owned buildings. These include not only prisons, but also the House and Senate buildings. That's the state legislature, fellow Americans! Metaphor becomes reality!

The proposed sale has bipartisan support and will require a leaseback by the buying corporation to the lawmakers with the right to repurchase the premises within twenty years.

The *Arizona Republic* reports that the deal, which includes 32 state properties, would bring in $735 million in upfront money and entail state lease payments totaling $60-70 million a year.

"We need the money," State Minority Whip Linda Lopez, a Tuscon Democrat said, adding, "You've got to find it somewhere." Well, why not rent out the backs of the state legislators to their favorite corporate funders? At least the public would get full disclosure of ownership.

"I look at it as taking out a mortgage," practical Arizona House Majority Leader John McCormish, a Republican, told the *Wall Street Journal*.

The second item comes from the *Denver Post*, which reports that the foreign consortium, auto-estradas de Portugal (Brisa), operating the toll road Northwest Parkway under a ninety-nine-year lease, objected to improvements on a nearby public road. Under the complex leasing contract, the company could cite the improvements as an "adverse action" reducing toll revenue and the number of vehicles using the parkway. This action would presumably entitle this foreign company to compensation from Colorado taxpayers.

Last year, Pennsylvania Governor Ed Rendell tried to push through the legislature a complex, seventy-five-year lease of the storied Pennsylvania Turnpike in exchange for $12.8 billion up front. All kinds of tax breaks and trap-door evasions filled the 686-page lease. The Governor was prepared, for example, to agree to pay the consortium of foreign investors if new safety measures or emergency vehicles entered the toll road and affected the flow of traffic. Fortunately, the legislature rebelled and blocked the deal.

The Indiana Toll Road was turned over to private companies in 2006. The seventy-five-year lease was for $3.8 billion, which is a little more than the cost to repair the Woodrow Wilson bridge over the Potomac River between Virginia and Washington, DC.

Tolls on the Indiana Toll Road have already doubled and are expected to double again within ten years, according to the *Dallas Morning News*.

Last year, Mayor Richard Daley of Chicago privatized the city's parking meters. Chicago's inspector general concluded that the meters were worth nearly twice as much to the city as the $1.15 billion that the city received under an agreement rushed through the City Council with no civic input. A fourfold increase in meter rates this year has driven many motorists to residential neighborhoods in search of free parking spaces.

Indiana, a leader in outsourcing governmental functions to private corporations, gave the servicing of the state's welfare program to IBM. According to the *Indianapolis Star*, error rates since corporatization have risen 17.5 percent last November and 21.4 percent in December.

The myth that corporatization is "better, faster, and cheaper" is falling apart. This year, the IRS announced that it will end the use of private tax collectors after consumer groups argued that taxpayers were subjected to immediate payment demands by private collectors while IRS employees would offer citizens an array of options to help pay their tax debt.

Then there are the corporatized water systems where the companies deliver poorer service at higher cost.

Since the 19th century, privatizing public functions has opened the doors to kickbacks, price fixing, and collusive bidding.

New depths of corruption were reached in Pennsylvania recently when two state judges pleaded guilty to taking bribes in return for sending youths to privately-owned jails.

After reading report after report about the vast, relentless waste, fraud, and abuse arising out of corporate contractors to the Pentagon in Iraq, why should readers be surprised at this domestic scene whereby taxpayers pay through the nose for corporations to govern them?

So, you're not surprised. But are you indignant? Are you ready to make sure the politicians hear from you in no uncertain terms, hear from you to stop this recklessness and restore public control of the public infrastructure under accountable government?

If the state politicos try to pull a fast one, demand public hearings with thorough reviews of the proposed contracts or leasebacks. Better yet, in states like Arizona or Colorado, require any such proposals go through the open, state-wide referendum voting process.

Corporatizations such as the above just pass on to our children the burdens that our generation should have assumed itself to run government within its means funded by fair taxation.

Avoiding Corporate Liability

May 27, 2009

Once upon a time early in the nineteenth century, corporations came into existence by state legislatures approving charters, which were granted for a limited period of time and for limited purposes. These corporations—producing textiles and other products in New England—raised capital in part because their investors had *limited liability*. That meant they could not lose any more than their investment if things went wrong.

Since corporations were artificial legal entities and not human, these lawmakers feared that without some strong leashes, they could be creating Frankensteins.

Over the following two hundred years, these ever larger corporations and their attorneys have been driving relentlessly, dynamically to erect systems of privileges and immunities that give the *corporations themselves limited liability*.

Their first big move was to take the chartering authority from the state legislature and place it inside an executive agency where chartering

became automatic, shorn of the conditions the lawmakers once imposed.

Once chartering became automatic, perpetual and open-ended, corporate lawyers moved to have the courts—not the legislatures—turn corporations into "persons" for purposes of constitutional rights.

Their big breakthrough came with the *Santa Clara* case in 1886 when the US Supreme Court allowed its summary headnotes to declare that the railroad in the case was a "person" for purposes of the 14th Amendment. Through elaborations in later Supreme Court decisions, that meant that companies like Aetna, General Electric, Exxon and Lockheed had most of the same constitutional rights as real people like you.

Soon it was off to the races and the promised land of no-fault corporate behavior. Early in the twentieth century, companies erected "no-fault" workers compensation schemes limiting damages for the horrors of worker injuries and workplace diseases in those mines, factories, and foundries.

Then came the steady erosion of shareholder rights and power, notwithstanding the securities acts of 1933 and 1934 which emphasized disclosure and anti-fraud rules. As owners, the shareholders have had little control over the corporations that they "own." The split between *ownership* by the stockholders and *control* by the corporate bosses, and their rubber stamp boards of directors, is now wider than the Grand Canyon.

With the limitless "business judgment rule" and the permissive corporate chartering Goliath ensconced in the state of Delaware, shareholders don't even have a vote as to whether their hired bosses should dissolve their company into bankruptcy.

These investors cannot even determine the limits on the runaway pay packages by and for their supreme executives. Investors cannot even propose their names for election to the boards of directors in these Kremlin-style corporate board elections. Investors are told—if you don't like what we, your bosses, are doing, you're free to sell your shares. And, of course, that exit leaves the rascals more in charge.

Anytime the law is activated on behalf of the "little people," corporate lobbyists move in to weaken or delete these instruments of accountability. For example, tort law giving wrongfully injured Americans their day in court against manufacturers of defective cars, hazardous chemicals or drugs and other products has been weakened by business-backed state and federal laws. More immunity for corporate wrongdoing.

When the early atomic power industry got underway in the fifties, insurance companies would not insure the potentially massive damages a breach of containment disaster might produce. No problem. The industry pushed Congress to pass the Price-Anderson Act in 1957, which greatly limited the utilities' and manufacturers' liability for the human devastation arising from a class nine meltdown.

How about the contracts you sign with credit card, auto dealer, insurance company, bank and other vendors? Over the years by using fine print contracts to avoid many obligations, sellers have disadvantaged consumers who have to sign on the dotted line. Corporate lawyers have turned contract law upside down. And if you don't want to sign, you can't go to a competitor company because the contracts are just as one-sided, taking away your rights page after page, including your right to go to court.

Well, suppose a corporation, like General Motors, is so mismanaged that it is losing sales, profits, creditworthiness and heading toward abject failure. No problem. There is always chapter 11 voluntary bankruptcy to terminate

obligations to creditors, dealers, litigants, and other claimants with pennies on the dollar.

Here is how bankruptcy attorney Laurence H. Kallen described the process in his book, *Corporate Welfare*: ". . . in chapter 11 the megacorporations almost all succeed famously. They dominate the committees and bully the judges. They stay ten steps ahead of any feeble attempts at supervision. They use the bankruptcy laws to force plans of reorganization down creditors' throats. And then the executives of those corporations laugh all the way to the bank."

Speaking of banks, wouldn't you like to have the power to mutate yourself like six large insurance companies did last November to get billions of your tax dollars under the TARP rescue program?

Mired in their risky, reckless investments, including derivatives, these insurance companies qualified for the money simply by a paper restructuring of themselves as bank holding companies. Voilá! The US Treasury declared they qualify as financial firms and will soon be receiving your money. The *New York Times* reports that "hundreds" of other such companies "are still in the pipeline for review."

Whether it is equal justice under the law, equal protection under the law, equal access to the law, or the power to make laws, there is *no contest* between the corporate entity and the real human being.

What Supreme Court Justice Louis Brandeis feared in an opinion he wrote during the thirties is happening. These megacorporations have become Frankensteins—moving to own our genes, the plant seeds of life and taking control of computerized artificial intelligence. Their final conquest is far along—the control of government which is then turned against its own people.

As Paul Harvey used to say: "Good day."

Overpaying CEOs

July 1, 2008

The worst top management of giant corporations in American history is also by far the most hugely paid. That contradiction applies as well to the Boards of Directors of these global companies.

Consider these illustrations:

The bosses of General Motors (GM) have presided over the worst decline of GM shares in the last fifty years, the lowering of GM bonds to junk status, the largest money losses and lay-offs of tens of thousands of workers. Yet these top executives are still in place and still receiving much more pay than their successful counter-parts at Toyota.

GM's stock valuation is under $7 billion dollars, while Toyota is valued at over $160 billion. Toyota, having passed GM in worldwide sales, is about to catch up with and pass GM in sales inside the United States itself!

GM's executives stayed with their gas guz-zling SUVs way beyond the warning signs. Their vehicles were uninspiring and technologi-cally stagnant in various ways. They were com-pletely unprepared for Toyota's hybrid cars and for the upward spiral in gasoline prices. They're cashing their lucrative monthly checks with the regular votes of confidence by their hand-picked Board of Directors.

About the same appraisal can be made of Ford Motor Co., which at least brought in new management to try to do something about that once famous company's sinking status.

Then there are the financial companies. Top management on Wall Street has been beyond incompetent. Wild risk taking camouflaged for years by multi-tiered, complex, abstract financial instruments (generally called collateralized debt obligations) kept the joy ride going and going

until the massive financial hot air balloon start-ed plummeting. Finally told to leave their high posts, the CEOs of Merrill-Lynch and Citi-group took away tens of millions of severance pay while Wall Street turned into Layoff Street.

The banks, investment banks and broker-age firms have tanked to levels not seen since the 1929-30 collapse of the stock market. Citi-group, once valued at over $50 per share is now under $17 a share.

Washington Mutual—the nation's largest savings bank chain was over $40 a share in 2007. Its reckless speculative binge has driven it down under $5 a share. Yet its CEO Kerry Killinger remains in charge, with the continuing support of his rubberstamp Board of Directors. A re-cent $8 billion infusion of private capital gave a sweetheart deal to these new investors at the excessive expense of the shareholders.

Countrywide, the infamous giant mortgage lender (subprime mortgages) is about to be tak-en over by Bank of America. Its CEO is taking away a reduced but still very generous compen-sation deal.

Meanwhile, all these banks and brokerage houses' investment analysts are busy downgrad-ing each other's stock prospects.

Over at the multi-trillion dollar companies Fannie Mae and Freddie Mac, the shareholders have lost about 75 percent of their stock value in one year. Farcically regulated by the Depart-ment of Housing and Urban Affairs, Fannie and Freddie were run into the ground by taking on very shaky mortgages under the command of CEOs and their top executives who paid them-selves enormous sums.

These two institutions were set up many years ago to provide liquidity in the housing and loan markets and thereby expand home owner-ship especially among lower income families.

Instead, they turned themselves into casinos, taking advantage of an implied US government guarantee.

The Fannie and Freddie bosses created another guarantee. They hired top appointees from both Republican and Democratic Administrations (such as Deputy Attorney General Jamie Gorelick) and lathered them with tens of millions of dollars in executive compensation. In this way, they kept federal supervision at a minimum and held off efforts in Congress to toughen regulation. These executives are all gone now, enjoying their maharajah riches with impunity while pensions and mutual funds lose and lose and lose with no end in sight, short of a government-taxpayer bailout.

More than a year ago, leading financial analyst Henry Kaufman and very few others warned about "undisciplined" (read unregulated) and "mis-pricing" of lower quality assets. Mr. Kaufman wrote in the *Wall Street Journal* of August 15, 2007, that "If some institutions are really 'too big to fail,' then other means of discipline will have to be found."

There are ways to prevent such crashes. In the 1930s, President Franklin Delano Roosevelt chose stronger regulation, creating the Securities and Exchange Commission (SEC) and several bank regulatory agencies. He saved the badly listing capitalist ship.

Today, there is no real momentum in a frozen Washington, DC to bring regulation up to date. To the contrary, in 1999, Congress led by Senator McCain's Advisor, former Senator Phil Gramm and the Clinton Administration led by Robert Rubin, Secretary of the Treasury, and soon to join Citibank, de-regulated and ended the wall between investment banks and commercial banking known as the Glass-Steagall Act.

Clinton and Congress opened the floodgates to rampant speculation without even requiring necessary and timely disclosures for the benefit of institutional and individual investors.

Now the entire US economy is at risk. The domino theory is getting less theoretical daily. Without investors obtaining more legal authority as owners over their out of control company officers and Boards of Directors, and without strong regulation, corporate capitalism cannot be saved from its toxic combination of endless greed and maximum power—without responsibility.

Uncle Sam, the deeply deficit ridden bailout man, may have another taxpayers-to-the-rescue operation for Wall Street. But don't count on stretching the American dollar much more without devastating consequences to and from global financial markets in full panic.

Consider the US dollar like an elastic band. You can keep stretching this rubber band but suddenly it BREAKS. Our country needs action NOW from Washington, DC.

NHTSA Stonewalls, People Die
May 12, 2008

Dear President Bush,

You and your White House have been sitting on the National Highway Traffic Safety Administration (NHTSA) since your arrival in January 2001, thus assuring the giant auto companies that NHTSA—toothless under President Bill Clinton and previous administrations—continues morphing even further away from the technology-forcing, life-saving regulatory agency it is supposed to be, to an industry consulting firm.

The result has been tens of thousands of American fatalities and serious injuries that could have been prevented had you and President Clinton simply urged NHTSA to follow its statutory obligations, lately under Congressionally mandated deadlines, with readily feasible, practical safety technologies.

Instead, you stacked the deck with your Chief of Staff, Andrew Card, former president and CEO of the American Automobile Manufacturers Association (AAMA). The rest, as they say, "is commentary."

NHTSA is now set to replace an obsolete motor vehicle roof crush resistance standard that became effective in 1973. You can continue to condemn thousands of Americans to preventable deaths by permitting NHTSA to issue a new, deficient standard, or you can take command and smoke out the corporate lobbyists from Detroit and allow NHTSA to issue FMVSS 216—Roof Crush Resistance at a strength-to-weight (SWR) ratio of at least 4 from the present inadequate standard of 1.5.

Eight models from such companies as Volvo, Saab, Toyota, VW and Honda already meet or exceed the SWR of 4. Note the countries of origin. Note the absence of US manufacturers. The Dodge Ram pickup truck and the Ford F-250 pick-up truck have a SWR down at 1.7.

You may wish to brief yourself about the horrible toll on our country's highways during the past 35 years due to marshmallow structured roofs. The American fatalities and serious injuries alone total more than the entire number of soldiers you have driven to Iraq, many of whom were deployed without adequate body and Humvee armor.

Then there are the quadriplegics and the paraplegics and the thousands of other human beings left defenseless by an auto safety agency under your command that has been at a standstill for years instead of functioning as a law enforcement branch in the Department of Transportation.

You need to see the visuals. You need to see the pictures of the crushed; the pictures of the vehicles whose roofs displaced the "survival space" of the drivers and passengers. You need to speak to the families of the victims who were on the receiving end of such obstinate, criminal negligence by the auto manufacturers' executives who will not let their own engineers put in the simple technical fixes year after year.

Remove the corporatists from your White House schedule for a day and invite some of these suffering citizens, their families and champions. Include Senators Mark Pryor and Tom Coburn who will preside over a Senate hearing on this subject in early June.

Keep in mind that even NHTSA, in its industry-indentured cautious fashion, managed to declare the obvious in 2005:

"In sum, the agency believes that there is a relationship between the amount of roof intrusion and the risk of injury to belted occupants in rollover events. But the agency still mimics the resistance of GM, Ford and Chrysler to any dynamic rollover test that safety advocates favor to assure effective compliance."

A president is not selected or elected to close the doors of state courts to wrongfully injured people who want and need to hold their corporate perpetrators accountable. You must recall your oft-repeated phrase about holding people responsible for their behavior, and actions, with the exception of yourself, and drop your attack on our civil justice system. Therefore, delete the federal pre-emption clause expected in the forthcoming standards that prevent the state judiciaries from hearing product liability suits in this area of vehicle design and construction.

Your legal advisers should point out that in the National Traffic and Motor Vehicle Safety Act of 1966, there is a specific provision that reads: "Compliance with a motor vehicle safety standard prescribed under this chapter does not exempt a person from liability at common law."

Those words were put in the law to prevent just such a federal pre-emption as NHTSA now prepares to facilitate. Twenty-six State Attorneys General opposed pre-emption in a letter to NHTSA back in 2005.

With your invited guests, suggested above, hold a White House news conference. Point to the CEOs in Detroit, and exclaim "Bring 'em on." Remember, you're either with the American people or you're with the big auto bosses.

Sincerely,

Ralph Nader

The Sleeping Professions

November 12, 2007

One of the most noticed photographs in the newspapers last week was that of a well-dressed Pakistani lawyer on the streets hurling a tear gas canister toward the soldiers who were suppressing a demonstration by lawyers protesting the martial law (called "emergency rule") of Gen. Pervez Musharraf.

Can anyone remember anywhere in all of modern history, large numbers of lawyers leading the resistance as they did on the streets of Pakistani cities way ahead of the workers, peasants and even the university students?

Pakistani police and troops rounded up the mass protests of lawyers and pushed hundreds of them into trucks which took them to the prison. Lawyers were willing to go to prison and endure beatings while demanding the re-establishment of the rule of law and the independence of judges right up to the Supreme Court, a rare display of professional courage and duty.

What about lawyers in the United States standing up to the Bush regime's regular violation of our Constitution, the imprisonment of thousands of people without charges and without attorneys, the assault on due process, probable cause, habeas corpus, the spying on Americans without court approval and the defiant, illegal use of torture?

No demonstrations yet. No resolutions by bar associations saying that Bush and Cheney should resign or be impeached.

Except some dozens of active civil liberties' lawyers, law professors, the former head of the American Bar Association, Michael Greco, and the 800,000 or more practicing lawyers have been pursuing business as usual. Given their canons of ethics and their status as officers of the court, looking the other way is not very professional behavior.

Professional behavior also has been in short supply on Wall Street. Once again, the accountants, the corporate lawyers, and the Boards of Directors of such giant companies as Merrill Lynch and Citigroup were either paid to go to sleep on the job or cared less.

Both Merrill Lynch and Citigroup have announced that thus far they are writing off a total of $20 billion on subprime mortgage paper in the housing sector. At the same time, the bosses of these companies, Stanley O'Neal and Charles O. Prince, have been fired and awarded vast golden parachutes totaling $360 million for their mismanagement in taking on reckless levels of risk for short term premiums.

But where were the highly paid watchdogs for these companies in the accounting and legal professions? Professionals are supposed to prevent trouble, not just profit from it. This looks like a repeat of the previous busts during the savings and loan scandals and the dot.com collapses.

Once again, see the bitter fruit of de-regulation or non-regulation by the federal and state governments. It will happen again and again to worker pensions, small investors and the workers, who are laid off, until there is regulatory law and order and the investors are given more dedicated legal authority over the corporations which they own.

This week, a new book titled *Corpocracy* by veteran corporate governance champion, Robert Monks, will be released and shine a bright light on this lack of shareholder rights and the passivity of large institutional shareholders (like pension funds, trusts and university endowments) toward meeting their fiduciary duties.

The gross greed, power and unfairness of this whole rigged system of non-accountability for the top bosses, who mess up big time but leave with the riches of kings, were the subject of a remarkably forthright article in Sunday's *Washington Post* by William S. Lerach—until recently, a very successful litigator against corporate scan artists.

Lerach pleaded guilty last month in federal court to a conspiracy charge regarding payments made to investor-plaintiffs in lawsuits brought against corporations claiming fraud and other misdeeds. For this behavior he will have to pay $8 million in fines and go to prison for at least one year.

Who was damaged by Lerach's crime? The court was misled because it was not told that monetary incentives were given to ready-to-sign-on plaintiffs in the race to the courtroom to become the lead law firm in such class action lawsuits.

Compare this violation with the trillion dollars looted or drained from millions of workers, investors and pension-holders by the corporate crime wave of the past ten years. Lerach and his firm recovered billions of dollars for defrauded investors over that same time span.

Lerach can be forgiven for wondering why so many reckless bosses were rewarded at the expense of shareholders and company profits. Especially, since these big bosses of the huge losses essentially decide what to pay themselves (while they are in their suites and when they leave) through their rubberstamp, selected boards of directors.

Top mismanagement of many US companies—consider the domestic auto manufacturers, for example—is rife with rewards for bad jobs done. Big rewards. In any fair system of corporate governance and SEC regulation, these bosses would have at least had to give up their undeserved pay and cancel their golden parachutes.

Even though O'Neal and Prince have admitted to "mistakes" and "flawed risk models," O'Neal leaves Merrill Lynch with $160 million in addition to over $100 million he received in pay for the past two years.

Reports have Prince leaving with $100 million along with the $100 million he was paid as Citi's CEO. Both companies' stock value has fallen sharply in recent weeks.

In his article, Lerach mused about how the "legal system is a lot tougher on shareholder lawyers than it appears to be on Wall Street executives."

During his time in prison, maybe the determined Lerach can plan his next moves to bring corporate crime, fraud and abuse against all too trusting individuals, institutions and government purchasers to systemic accountability.

Maybe he'll take his strategies to a level far beyond the occasional class action suits that get through all the interference that indentured legislators and conservative judges put in their way.

For if "We the People" do not have a say, we will continue to pay and pay.

Tax Haven Racket

June 12, 2007

Lucy Komisar of the Tax Justice Network USA (taxjustice-usa.org) spoke at last week's Conference on Taming the Giant Corporation about "Closing Down the Tax Haven Racket." Her words were so compelling that the rest of this column is devoted to excerpts from her presentation:

"The tax haven racket is the biggest scam in the world. It's run by the international banks with the cooperation of the world's financial powers for the benefit of corporations and the mega-rich. . . . [M]ost Americans, including progressive activist Americans, don't know what I'm going to tell you. And that's part of the problem.

"Tax havens, also known as offshore financial centers, are places that operate secret bank accounts and shell companies that hide the names of real owners from tax authorities and law enforcement. They use nominees, front men. Sometimes offshore incorporation companies set up the shells. Sometimes the banks do it. Often someone will use a shell company in one jurisdiction that owns a shell in another jurisdiction that owns a bank account in a third. That's called layering. No one can follow the paper trial.

"Offshore is where most of the world's drug money is laundered, estimated at up to $500 billion a year, more than the total income of the world's poorest 20 percent. Perhaps another $500 billion comes from fraud and corruption.

"Those figures fit with [International Monetary Fund] numbers that as much as $1.5 trillion of illicit money is laundered annually, equal to 2 to 5 percent of global economic output.

"Wall Street wants this money. The markets would hurt, even shrivel without that cash. That's why Robert Rubin as Treasury Secretary had a policy, as Joseph Stiglitz told me, not to do any-

thing that would stop the free flow of money into the US. He was not interested in stopping money laundering because the laundered funds ended up in Wall [Street], maybe in Goldman Sachs where he had worked, or Citibank, where he would work.

"Attempts to find laundered funds are usually dismal failures. According to Interpol, $3 billion in dirty money has been seized in twenty years of struggle against money laundering—about the amount laundered in three days.

"The other major purpose of offshore is for tax evasion, estimated to reach another $500 billion a year.

"That's how corporations and the rich have opted out of the tax system.

"They have sophisticated mechanisms. There's transfer pricing. A company sets up a trading company offshore, sells its widgets there for under market price, the trading company sells it for market price, the profits are offshore, not where they really were generated.

"Two American professors, using customs data, examined the impact of over-invoiced imports and under-invoiced exports for 2001. Would you buy plastic buckets from the Czech Republic for $973 each, tissues from China at $1874 a pound, a cotton dishtowel from Pakistan for $154, and tweezers from Japan at $4,896 each!

"US companies, at least on paper, were getting very little for their exported products. If you were in business, would you sell bus and truck tires to Britain for $11.74 each, color video monitors to Pakistan for $21.90, and prefabricated buildings to Trinidad for $1.20 a unit.

"Comparing all claimed export and import prices to real world prices, the professors figured the 2001 US tax loss at $53.1 billion.

"Or a company sets up subsidiaries in tax havens—to 'own' logos or intellectual property.

Like Microsoft does in Ireland, transferring software that was made in America, that benefited by work done by Americans, to Ireland so Microsoft can pay taxes there (at 11 percent) instead of here (at 35 percent). Why is Ireland getting the benefit of American-created software? It's legal. We need to change the law.

"When logos are offshore, the company pays royalties to use the logo and deducts the amount as expenses. But the payments are not taxed or are taxed minimally offshore where they are moved. . . . When Cheney ran Halliburton, it increased its offshore subsidiaries from nine to at least forty-four.

"Half of world trade is between various parts of the same corporations. Experts believe that as much as half the world's capital flows through offshore centers. The totals held offshore include 31 percent of the net profits of US multinationals.

"The whole collection of tax scams is why between 1989 and 1995, of US and multinational corporations operating in the United States, with assets of at least $250 million or sales of at least $50 million, nearly two-thirds paid no US income tax.

"In 1996-2000, Goodyear's profits were $442 million, but it paid no taxes and got a $23-million rebate. Colgate-Palmolive made $1.6 billion and got back $21 million. Other companies that got rebates in 1998 included Texaco, Chevron, PepsiCo, Pfizer, J.P. Morgan, MCI Worldcom, General Motors, Phillips Petroleum and Northrop Grumman. Microsoft reported $12.3 billion U.S income in 1999 and paid zero federal taxes. (In two recent years, Microsoft paid only 1.8 percent on $21.9 billion pretax US profits.)

"During the 1950s, US corporations accounted for 28 percent of federal revenues. Now, corporations represent just 11 percent.

"Those unpaid taxes can buy a lot of politi-

cians and power. When Nixon needed money to pay the Watergate burglars, he got it from some corporate offshore bank accounts.

"The system has given the big banks and corporations and the super-rich mountains of hidden cash they use to control our political systems.

"The offshore system must be dismantled.

"So why isn't the progressive movement doing something about this? This is a case where some people in Congress are ahead of the activists. There are a handful of Democrats like Senators Levin (MI), Dorgan (ND) and Conrad (ND), like Rep. Doggett (TX), who are speaking out and introducing legislation. But there is no movement behind them. And while Obama has signed onto the Levin Stop Tax Haven Abuse Act, Clinton, Biden and Dodd have not."

Ms. Komisar spreads out the proposed strategies at taxjustice-usa.org. One or more are structured so that you can play a part in furthering them toward adoption.

As she concluded: "Let's get the country to tell the corporations that the taxes they are dodging is our money."

Don't Let Wall Street Off the Hook

February 12, 2007

It takes no small amount of hubris for Wall Street hucksters to urge financial services deregulation.

But if there's one thing that the Wall Street power brokers do not lack, it's audacity.

Wall Street leaders have established a series of self-empowered commissions—among them the Commission on Capital Markets Regulation (the "Paulson Commission"), the US Chamber of Commerce's Commission on the Regulation of the US Capital Markets—to peddle a fantasy story to the public and policymakers. This is their fantasy: US competitiveness in financial services is now in grave doubt. Regulation, litigation and prosecution are driving companies to float their IPOs (Initial Public Offerings) on foreign markets. If something isn't done soon, US economic performance is in jeopardy. Give me a break.

In the real world, things look quite different.

First, a disinterested observer might comment that securities regulations exist to protect investors, not to enhance the interests of Wall Street. Wall Street is supposed to serve business and investors, not the other way around.

Second, the much-touted decline in US IPOs is deeply misleading. The regulatory and litigation climate is a small and insignificant factor in the rising percentage of IPOs undertaken outside the United States. The real issue is that other countries' stock markets are strengthening, and most recent IPOs were done by companies outside the United States.

Indeed, a devastating January 2007 White Paper from Ernst & Young looking at every IPO in the first half of 2006 found that 90 percent were conducted in the launching company's home country. Of the remaining 10 percent, only a few were "in play"—most went to regional markets, or were small-caps that went to the London Alternative Investment Market. Of the IPOs in play—a grand total of seventeen for the first six months of 2006—about two-thirds were listed on US exchanges.

Most fundamentally, though, the IPO statistic is a chimera. What matters to the US economy is whether businesses are investing in the United States, not where they undertake IPOs. That's a narrow Wall Street consideration.

Third, although the doom-and-gloom rhetoric of the capital markets commissions might suggest otherwise, Wall Street is in fact doing fabulously well. Goldman Sachs CEO Lloyd Blankfein grabbed a $53.4 million bonus, the largest single annual executive bonus in Wall Street history. Blankfein's bonanza is a sign of the times. Wall Street bonuses totaled $23.9 billion in 2006, according to the New York State comptroller, up 17 percent over 2005. And it is the NYSE and Nasdaq that are buying foreign exchanges, not vice versa.

Sam Pizzigati, editor of the on-line newsletter "Too Much," notes that "Top Wall Street traders, assuming a 60-hour work week, averaged from $17,000 to $33,000 an hour. The typical American household, by contrast, only took home $46,326 in 2005 for the entire year."

Finally, the real problem on the street is too little action from the cops on the beat, not too much. Although the Paulson commission treats the Enron/WorldCom and related scandals as something from a bygone era, they are not even a decade old. And financial wrongdoing is pervasive and ongoing. There is now a new set of financial scandals of even greater breadth than Enron/Worldcom. Researchers estimate that hundreds of corporate executives engaged in back-dating of stock options. And there is strong statistical evidence that insider-trading is rampant—the basis for a just-launched SEC investigation. When companies do get caught cheating, they typically get off with a slap on the wrist—literally a promise not to break the law in the future.

With financial wrongdoing so prevalent, in many cases the best defense for investors is private litigation. So it comes as no surprise that the Wall Street apologists recommend gutting investors' right to sue. In fact, securities lawsuits have declined in recent years, and the overall amounts recovered for investors, despite rampant fraud, are tiny as corporate profits.

A far-sighted Wall Street elite would not seek to reduce regulation, but recognize that the complex, esoteric market innovations are rapidly outdistancing existing systems of control, creating bubbles and huge systemic risk. What is needed is a new theory of comprehensive public regulation and public and private enforcement that responds to present-day realities. These must address the overall risks to financial system well-being, as well as to investor interests, from both innovations in private equity and the long-standing problems and abuses in the traditional publicly traded markets. Otherwise, Uncle Bailout will be asked to pay—if he can foot the bill.

In the meantime, it is vital that the minimal protections against financial crime and wrong-doing now available—regulation, civil litigation and prosecution—be maintained against the encroachments of those who proffer a grotesquely fanciful US financial services competitiveness crisis, when they should be competing with other nations over stability and integrity.

Class Warfare in Reverse

January 12, 2007

The boiling, surging, churning and corporatizing economy of the United States is racing too far ahead for political economists, economists, politicians and the polis itself to understand. Tidbits from the past week add up to this view, to wit:

- The giant, shut-down Bethlehem steel plant in Bethlehem, Pennsylvania will soon become a $600 million casino and hotel complex. With tens of millions of Americans lacking the adequate necessities of food, fuel, shelter, healthcare and a sustaining job, this project is part of a twenty-five-year trend by the economy, moving away from necessities and over to wants and whims. Among the fastest growing businesses for three decades in America are theme parks, gambling casinos and prisons.

- Our Constitution launched "we the people" to "establish justice, . . . promote the general welfare and secure the Blessings of Liberty to ourselves." We're losing ground year after year on all three accounts. Yet to what does Chief Justice John G. Roberts Jr. devote his entire annual report on the federal judiciary this January 1, 2007? He called for a pay raise for judges, calling the current pay ranging from $165,200 to $212,000 (with a great retirement plan) a "constitutional crisis."

- General Motor has introduced yet another prototype electric car—called the Chevrolet Volt—to distract attention from its ongoing engine stagnation and provide a little cover for its gas guzzling muscle cars displayed at the Detroit Auto Show. This procrastinating tactic by GM has been going on since the 1939 New York World's Fair. It keeps people looking far into the amorphous future so as to not focus on the dismal today year after year while gasoline prices sky rocket and oil imports swell. We're still waiting for some of GM's engineering prototypes from 1939 to hit the road in the twenty-first century.

- Just as there are stirrings behind more shareholder rights over the companies they own and more disclosure by management of large corporations relating to executive pay and accounting information, the rapid rise of huge pools of capital controlled by private equity firms and Hedge Funds are buying larger and larger public companies and taking them out of the regulatory arenas into secrecy.

Corporate morphing to escape public accountability has been going on for a long time. Note the coal corporations digging deep under residential streets in Pennsylvania and other neighboring states decades ago. As the homes began to cave in (this is called 'subsidence'), the coal companies disappeared by collapsing themselves only to be succeeded by their next of (corporate) kin.

Today, this corporate morphing is far more ranging and far larger in the economy, drawing trillions of dollars from pension funds and institutional investor firms which themselves are largely closed off from workers and small investors whose money they shuffle around. Corporate attorneys are super-experts in arranging ways for corporate capital to escape not just the tax laws of the US but also the public regulatory frameworks of the Securities and Exchange Commission and other public "law and order" entities.

Independent and academic corporate analysts have barely begun to figure out the consequences of this seismic shift of capital structures.

"Private Firms Lure C.E.O.'s With Top Pay" was the headline in the January 8th edition of the *New York Times*. The subtitle was astonishingly worded as "Less Lavish Packages at Public Companies." The reporters go on to say, in essence, if you think that Home Depot's departed C.E.O., Robert L. Nardelli's $200 million plus take home pay package was a lot, you haven't seen what's happening behind the curtains at the large private equity firms buying up ever bigger public companies. "Public company chieftains are deciding that they no longer want to be judged by their shareholders and regula-

tors, and are going to work for businesses owned by private equity," write the authors.

One such migrant executive, Henry Silverman, went from big riches running the conglomerate Cendant, to making $135 million just from selling one piece of Cendant, Realogy, to a private equity firm. "There is no reason to be a public company anymore," said this happy corporate prophet.

Now go to the other side of the tracks. In the last quarter century the value of the US corporations has risen twelve-fold, according to the *Wall Street Journal*. C.E.O. pay has skyrocketed similarly. But workers today, on average, are still making less, in inflation adjusted dollars, than workers made in 1973—the high point of worker wages!

Citing data from the Center for Labor Market Studies at Northeastern University, *New York Times*' columnist, Bob Herbert, reports that between 2000 and 2006 the combined real annual earnings of 93 million American workers rose by $15.4 billion. That rise is "less than half of the combined bonuses awarded by the five Wall Street firms for just one year."

This is class warfare in reverse. The super-rich and their corporations against the workers, redistributing the workers' wealth into their own pockets and coffers. Mr. Herbert frequently frets about no one in the political parties saying or doing anything about this state of despair. He defines "political parties" as the two major Parties, though knowing full well that there are smaller parties and independent candidates who have campaigned across the country trumpeting the need for economic justice in very specific terms.

So long as most progressive writers ignore these people in the electoral arenas who are laboring to break down the barriers that keep these issues of economic justice over corporate power abuses from moving into elections and government, they will be bellowing in the wind.

Social justice movements in the United States have come from small starts that are duly recognized.

Taking the Cop Off the Corporate Crime Beat
December 1, 2006

It is clear, in the midst of a seven-year corporate financial crime wave, that the business moguls and their academic apologists, who make up the Committee on Capital Markets Regulation (CCMG) have no sense of irony. It is not enough that the CCMG's new report is recommending less law enforcement and accountability after years of Republican regimes addicted to de-regulation. The Big Boys want to make lower standards overseas an argument for starting a race to the bottom, in order for the US financial markets to remain "competitive."

Here are some of CCMG's thirty-two recommendations, expected to be the goal of a big lobbying effort on the Securities and Exchange Commission (SEC) and the Congress next year:

1. Limit how and when state enforcement agencies can pursue cases of financial fraud on investors. This is designed to take care of any future Eliot Spitzers, who take their oath of office seriously instead of ceremoniously. Quite properly, the Governor-elect, present New York Attorney General Spitzer reacted, saying, "To eviscerate the power of the one set of regulators who did anything is absurd."

2. Governments should sue the corporations themselves only as a last resort and instead concentrate on the culpable officials in the company. That will give rise to all kinds of escape hatches and internal scapegoating by clever corporate attorneys. They do demand that companies pay the legal expenses of the accused, however.

3. Make it more difficult to convict defendants by requiring proof of actual knowledge of the specific fraud, which makes it easier for executives to get off the hook for criminal negligence. The "I didn't know" defense is to replace "you should have known."

4. Weaken the post-Enron Sarbanes-Oxley law, including not applying the key section 404 on internal accounting controls to foreign companies if they have to "meet comparable standards" in their home country. What are "comparable standards?" This is a recipe for delay and loopholes. The record of "equivalency negotiations" under NAFTA and the World Trade Organization is enough to give rigorous pause to this slippery move.

5. Stricter cost-benefit analysis to any new SEC rules than are now already in place. This it the time-dishonored technique of producing endless delays in issuing any rules—a device that has devastated updating or declaring new health and safety standards in the consumer, worker and environmental areas. A corporate law firm's gold mine.

6. CCMG wants shareholder approval for any "poison pill" defenses against takeovers that the company officers and Boards institute. Apparently, this change would make

companies more vulnerable to the lucrative business of mergers and acquisitions. But some investor advocates may like this enhancement of shareholder power, along with another proposal requiring a majority vote of shares to elect a company director.

7. In a broader context, CCMG opposes giving shareholders the power to vote on these gargantuan executive compensation packages that often amount to looting company assets and relooting them when the executive is asked to leave by the Board—the so-called "golden parachute."

8. Either cap liability for auditors or give them outright immunity. After major accounting firms profited by looking the other way in big corporate scandals like Enron, WorldCom and the like, it takes a special brand of commercial hubris to stake out this position.

9. Once auditors are immune, the CCMG wants to let outside Directors escape liability for "corporate malfeasance," if they rely "in good faith" on the auditors. It isn't clear what non-good faith reliance would be like.

"If you take every single step on their list," declared Barbara Roper, director of investor protection at the Consumer Federation of America, "you would have made it significantly more difficult to hold corporate criminals accountable for their crimes."

These corporate criminals have looted or drained trillions of dollars from workers, their pensions and millions of investors since 2000. Not even five cents on the dollar have been recovered for their victims. Many of these recoveries have come through private litigation—investor class actions mostly—which the Big Boys want to restrict even more than their restrictive victory—through the Securities Act of 1995. The more crimes, the more they drive for privileges and immunities from the rule of law.

It is not likely that many of these measures will get through the SEC or the new Congress, apart from some leniency for small companies under Sarbanes-Oxley. But they will deter efforts to strengthen the corporate criminal laws and regulations on both the corporations and, in the words of one prosecutor, "their lying, cheating and stealing" executives and accomplices.

For more information, visit corporatecrimereporter.com.

Challenging the Chamber
November 10, 2006

Unlike competing sports teams, adversaries on the corporate and consumer or environment sides rarely square off in public to provide much needed drama and media. They each testify, litigate, petition and conduct press conferences on their own track. Only very rarely do they debate each other.

It is not that the drama is absent. Take the now legendary struggles between the boss—Tom Donohue—of the US Chamber of Commerce—the most avariciously powerful business lobby in Washington, DC and Joan Claybrook, president of Public Citizen.

Claybrook was Donohue's nemesis when he was the head of the American Trucking Association and was pushing for all the states to allow "longer combination vehicles"—namely, double and triple trailers on the highways. At that time—in 1991—about twelve western states allowed these behemoths, notwithstanding inadequate braking systems for their weight and speed, on their highways.

Through Claybrook's leadership and a group she started called Citizens for Reliable and Safe Highways (CRASH), a bill was enacted in Congress freezing any additional states from doing the trucking industry's bidding. Donohue could not believe he and his lobbying battalions lost.

Another battle Donohue lost after he took the helm at the Chamber of Commerce was his drive to open the borders and the entire United States to Mexican trucks following the enactment of NAFTA, so that the US truckers could travel throughout Mexico. One big problem: Safety!

By fiat of the two nation's governments, Mexican and US truck and operator safety standards were deemed "equivalent," but they were not. Mexican trucks up to 180,000 lbs. were allowed on their roads. In the US, the maximum weight, on interstate highways, was 80,000 lbs. Truck driver safety regulations were decidedly weaker in Mexico than in the United States. Truck drivers, in Mexico, could get their license at 18 years of age, did not have to have a special license for the particular rig or the cargo it carried. In the United States truck drivers have to be 21 and obtain a special license for large trucks and know how to handle its cargo.

Six years ago, Claybrook pushed through the Congress standards among which required US trucking inspectors to inspect trucking facilities in Mexico for maintenance and other safety purposes. Mexico refused to allow our inspectors in their country. The result has been that no Mexican trucks or US trucks are coursing each other's highways. The old rule is still in place. Mexican trucks can unload their cargo no further than twenty miles inside the US border.

Now come Claybrook and Public Citizen's latest charge. They filed a complaint with the IRS asserting that since 2000, the Chamber and its Institute for Legal Reform spent tens of millions of dollars "in a stealth campaign to influence federal and state political and judicial elections without declaring this spending on tax returns as required by law."

The Chamber's massive involvement in elections at the state and federal level goes after state supreme court justices, and other state and Congressional candidates, who are not seen as sufficiently subservient to business interests. Money, attack TV ads and other methods have been funded by the likes of Wal-Mart, Home Depot, AIG Insurance Company, Daimler Chrysler and other giant companies.

Public Citizen's complaint (see: citizen.org) declares that the "Chamber's role in elections is mainly hidden because it plays a shell game with state-level front groups to conceal the source of this political money from the public and fails to disclose its grants to local groups on tax forms."

The Chamber's Institute for Legal Reform (ILR) works to block wrongfully injured or defrauded Americans' right to their full day in court. One way it approaches its goals is to contribute and support candidates for the state and federal courts that are "business-friendly."

Public Citizen's complaint to the IRS charges that:

"The Chamber and ILR are two separate legal entities but shared a bank account as recently as Jan. 12, 2005. The ILR reported $38.3 million in revenue in 2004. The ILR also reported that it had no investment or interest income. It is unlikely that an organization with $38.3 million in revenue would not have any investment or interest income. The Chamber reported an income of $90.9 million in 2004, with minimal investment income.

The Chamber's accounting practices could have tax implications.

Electioneering expenditures of Section 501(c) groups, including the Chamber and ILR, are subject to taxes, at the highest corporate rate, on the lesser of: (1) their net investment income for the taxable year; or (2) their aggregate expenditures for non-exempt (i.e., political) functions."

Tom Donohue scoffed at Claybrook's complaint. But Public Citizen does not make charges unless they are meticulously documented. The Treasury Department is not likely to share Donohue's casualness.

And so go the battles over the role of this big business lobby situated in an imposing gray building just opposite the White House across Lafayette Square. More reporters should be visiting the doings of the Chamber instead of simply assuming they are just pushing business interests. The stories are about how, when, where and toward what damaging results this massive combination of corporate greed and power produces.

Mavericks in the Board Room
September 22, 2006

William C. Taylor was a rosy-cheeked Princeton University intern when he began his rise to fame and fortune, working with the *Multinational Monitor* magazine. As a freshly minted Princeton graduate, he worked on the book *The Big Boys: Power and Position in American Business* as a co-author with me. After that it was the Sloan School at MIT, editor of the *Harvard Business Review*, and a co-founder of the sensationally successful Fast Company during the dot-com craze. Now comes the co-author (with Polly LaBarre) of the forthcoming (October) sure-to-be bestseller *Mavericks at Work*.

I've read the galleys and find it a multisplendored information engine about innovative business approaches—so much so that when you get over its exciting, fluid prose, you are left with more questions than the book answers. Which means, given its genre, that it is a very good book indeed, steering you, as it does, to explore your own "maverick" territory.

Taylor and LaBarre take you swiftly through a journey of interviews and insights that reveal the success of "unlearning" of "undoing" traditional business practices, of doing just the opposite of conventional commerce and succeeding. Like Southwest Airlines does.

The opening chapter introduces the readers to the most unlikely banker, the founder of ING Direct USA, Arkadi Kuhlmann. He attacks the banking industries' exorbitant fees, rails against credit card rip-offs and the sales push to get people "to save too little, invest too recklessly, and spend too much." This is sedition, with fast-growing rewards. ING Direct is presently taking in a billion dollars a month in deposits. Now the country's largest internet bank is giving higher interest rates to depositors and charging lower rates to its mortgage customers, say Taylor and LaBarre.

Their treks across the country have produced story after story of maverick behavior in a remarkable range of companies—a construction company, an ad agency, a cable network, little known startups with revolutionary breakthroughs in telecommunications and data-center automation, blazingly creative toy and game designer and vendor. A gold mining company provided formerly confidential data for its internet $500,000 contest invitation to get the world's smartest geologists and scientists helping them find the next 6 million ounces of gold on its lands.

There is the anarchically successful huge annual Edinburgh Fringe Festival for artistic talent in Scotland. Can there be a new idea in selling sandwiches? Try Potbelly Sandwich Works creating a "cauldron of consumer passion" around its aesthetic delights of sound, color, and the unusual décor. Reasonable prices for good food, write Taylor and LaBarre.

The book's description of the state of the art recruitment entrepreneurs, such as Michael Homula of FirstMerit Bank, was one of the most rewarding parts of the book. How to find experienced people by imaginative techniques.

DPR Construction, Inc. out of Redwood City, California catches the reader's eye because it is determined to show how to be "quantifiably different and better, . . . a truly great construction company," declared cofounder and president Doug Woods.

The touted standards DPR sets for itself are breathtaking. Listen to Woods' interview: "This industry hasn't changed the way it does business a whole lot in the last hundred years. We stand for something."

Taylor and LaBarre note that DPR "takes on and remedies some of the most notorious pitfalls of construction, the designed-in headaches that give the industry such a bad name: unreliable price estimates, endless cost overruns, delays and slipped schedules, completed projects with a never-ending list of fixes, lawsuits and recriminations between builders and clients."

I found the least persuasive choice for a Maverick in the book to be Commerce Bank. The authors conceded that the Bank offers lower interest rates in return for personal, wowee service and an atmosphere of exotic friendliness and team spirit by the employees whose official company exclamation is wow!

Commerce Bank culture is indeed spirited and colorful and seemingly in perpetual motion. Some irritating practices like other banks' exploiting your deposited check's float are rejected.

But the Mavericks profiled by Taylor and LaBarre prompt a larger question about the book: If these astute and imaginative ways of doing business are so profitable, what keeps them from diffusing promptly into the canyons of the giant corporations that are mired in mediocrity or the traditional industries that are profitably stagnant? Where is the mimicry if not by copycat, then at least in attitude?

Well, maybe Taylor will cover some of these curiosities on ABC's *Good Morning America* where he is supposed to appear four times in October on the theme—Maverick of the Week—or in both authors' extensive nationwide tour. The last thing they need is a "gee whiz" reception about their selected companies. Maverick readers have to be skeptics and push the envelope not only further—to what benefits for the people—but also deeper too—will these companies be around in ten years?

As Tom Peters learned some years ago after he published his super-best seller *In Search of Excellence*, some "excellence" just didn't have the legs.

Coerced Confessions—A Corporate Abuse
May 19, 2006

In a recent column I wrote about police interrogation tactics that lead a surprising number of people to confess to crimes they didn't commit. It turns out that corporate America has followed suit. Many large corporations take a "loss prevention" approach that utilizes training manuals modeled after the leading police manuals—using the very techniques that cause false confessions. Indeed, the group that produces the leading manual, John Reid and Associates, boasts about its infiltration into loss prevention.

When a large chain finds money missing (which, needless to say, happens often), and is convinced that one of its employees is guilty of theft, in come trained interrogators with well-honed tactics of isolating the individual and cutting off all escape routes until he feels he is better off confessing—even if he's innocent. (The June 2005 issue of *Scientific American Mind* features an excellent discussion of the prevailing interrogative methods and their perils titled *True Crimes, False Confessions* by Saul M. Kassin and Gisli H. Gudjonsson).

It's even worse in the case of private companies than the police, because they don't have to issue Miranda warnings and give employees the opportunity to consult an attorney and remain silent. Instead, they place the defenseless employee in a small, claustrophobic room and systematically break down his will—confronting him with fabricated evidence of his guilt, threatening to fire him instantly (and get the police involved) unless he confesses and promising leniency if he does so.

Last month, we learned more about the way this works from a trial in the Superior Court of San Diego County. A civil jury struck a blow for corporate accountability, socking AutoZone with a verdict of $7.5 million in punitive damages.

The case stemmed from events several years ago, when a store manager became convinced that one of his employees (a loyal worker with a sterling reputation) had stolen $800. The manager followed the playbook. He had a security guard grill the employee in a small office for almost three hours, confronting him with false evidence and threatening his discharge and arrest unless he confessed. If he did confess, he was assured, he could pay the company back and keep his job, and the matter would remain private.

The innocent employee became convinced of the futility of maintaining his innocence, especially since he feared losing his job (and perhaps his freedom) and the ability to support his two young children.

Is it surprising that, under these circumstances, the employee confessed? The more we learn about widespread interrogation tactics, the more we realize that the decision to confess falsely can be rational—a mistake, to be sure, but the product of an understandable cost-benefit analysis made under extreme circumstances—circumstances created by interrogators precisely to make the suspect feel hopeless. AutoZone inculcated such methods in its 200-page handbook for managers. And it isn't just AutoZone—corporations around America have imported the worst aspects of police interrogative techniques.

In the case of the AutoZone employee, the company didn't even keep its coercive promise—it fired him almost immediately after his confession and took the amount he "stole" out of his last paycheck. But Joaquin Robles turned out to be the wrong person to mess with. His lawsuit not only gave him justice, but also shed the spotlight on the corporate coercion industry. The trial exposed the manual used by AutoZone's so-called "loss prevention" managers and produced testimony from other employees about similarly coercive treatment.

The episode exemplifies the grandeur of the civil justice system, with ordinary citizens holding the powerful accountable and establishing that blatant violations of social norms will not be tolerated. Punitive damages play an important role in that process. This case first went to trial several years ago, and a jury found that the AutoZone manager "falsely imprisoned" Robles, and awarded $73,000 in compensatory damages. The trial judge would not allow Robles' attorney to ask the jury for punitive damages. The Court of Appeal of

California, Fourth Appellate District reversed that decision, holding that Robles had the right to argue to the jury that AutoZone's policies were sufficiently outrageous as to warrant punitive damages. The case was finally retried in March of this year. Now, AutoZone is $7.5 million poorer (or at least will be if the verdict survives the inevitable appeal) but perhaps a bit wiser.

AutoZone is not the first company to be called out for its bullying interrogations of employees or customers. (Law buffs can check out 340 F. Supp. 2d 308 and 501 A.2d 561.) But this verdict is comparatively large, and we can only hope that corporations all over America take notice. When they investigate alleged intra-company theft, it isn't asking too much that they follow fair procedures and eschew tactics that predictably lead to the punishment of innocent people.

Robles v. AutoZone was brought to my attention by author Alan Hirsch, whose website www.truthaboutfalseconfessions.com provides a valuable overview about false confessions as well as provocative analyses of both cases in the headlines and cases ignored by the major media.

GM Keeps Fuel Efficiency in the Dark Ages

February 20, 2006

General Motors should be renamed General Wasteful Motors for its decades of destructive resistance to improved fuel efficiency for your motor vehicles.

Never mind that you deserve, after all these years of industry stagnation (the last upgrade in fuel efficiency was 1985), more miles for your gasoline dollars. Never mind that our country is more reliant on imported oil (over 50 percent) than ever before. Never mind that as taxpayers you are being charged billions of dollars yearly for our armed forces safeguarding the flow of oil from the Persian Gulf. And never mind that you are breathing more polluted air from vehicle emissions which are also contributing to global warming.

Giant GM, run by myopic executives, just won't let its engineers and scientists diminish the gas guzzling nature of its infernal, internal combustion engines.

The last legislated standard on fuel economy was in 1975 which declared a phase-in by 1985 of average automobile economy to 27.5 mpg and light trucks to about 20 mpg. Today, average fuel economy overall has been dropping and now comes in at about 24 mpg—the lowest since 1980!

It is reliably reported that General Motors is putting very heavy pressures on its suppliers to lobby Congress against long overdue stirrings by some Democrats and Republicans—most notably Rep. Henry Waxman (D-Calif.), Senator John Kerry (D-Mass.) and Senator John McCain (R-Ariz.)—for higher, mandated fuel efficiencies.

GM is most upset with Senator John Kerry's proposal to boost fuel economy by 50 percent over the next 12 years. Imagine, after assuring decades of delay both before 1975 and after 1985, garnished by futile futuristic promises of new engines and new fuel advances from its exhibit at the 1939 World's Fair in New York to its contemporary propaganda, GM thinks going to 37 mpg by 2014 is not possible. Some automobiles in the nineteen thirties achieved that level. The US Department of Transportation in the mid-seventies said that over 40 mpg average fleet levels could be yours by the year 2000. A few years later, a detailed article in *Scientific American* showed how the average could be in the 80 mpg zone by then. And, of course, Toyota and Honda are already selling thousands of hybrids that average over 50 mpg already.

Talk fuel efficiency and you're sure to evoke from GM its sudden touching concern with auto safety, as if you cannot have both. Clarence Ditlow of the Center for Auto Safety and other engineers have pointed out ad nauseum the corporate fallacy of having either a gasoline efficient less safe car or a safer car that is less efficient.

The stubborn, dug-in-heels of General Motors and its allies have become an ever greater national security, public health and environmental problem. One would think that GM would decide to be a little patriotic and think of our nation's interest for a change.

The attitude of "NYET" is too much even for the leading industry trade journal—Automotive News—whose journalistic integrity under the ownership of the Crain family—evoked the following editorial comment:

"It was a throwback to a darker era. On a Senate witness stand two weeks ago, Greg Dana of the Alliance of Automobile Manufacturers went mute when asked whether a 1-mpg increase in corporate average fuel economy standards during the next decade would be feasible.

"His questioner, Sen. John Kerry, responded 'Don't you think that renders you sort of silly?'

"Indeed, it made the alliance look silly.

"Let's get real. It's time for automakers to deal forthrightly with fuel economy issues. . . . To deny—or refuse to admit—that there is technology that can reduce fuel consumption significantly is ludicrous. The industry's credibility is at stake."

Then *Automotive News* really turned the screw, noting that the $1.5 billion tax dollars that Clinton poured into an engine research partnership with GM, Ford and Chrysler, as an alternative to raising fuel efficiency standards, was used by the Big 3 as a "cover to improve horsepower, not fuel economy."

It is also time for you the motorist to become more demanding of engines and fuel that are more efficient and cleaner. Detroit knows how to do it and has for many years, but once again profits come before patriotism.

Corporations Mortgaging the Future
February 17, 2006

One of the bedrock privileges of commercial corporations is that they create and command the very yardsticks by which their performance is generally evaluated. As economist Milton Friedman once said, the sole responsibility of a corporation is to make a profit for its shareholders. Other corporatists may find this a little too narrow a yardstick without adding compliance with the laws of the land.

Along came the environmental and consumer movements. They added two additional yardsticks but they do not have the primary position that generating profits possesses. So, for example, giant companies can routinely defraud consumers, poison the environment and successfully fight regulatory enforcement, but if they make consistent profits, they are still praised in the *Wall Street Journal*. No individual, no matter how wealthy, can get away with bifurcating his or her behavior in such an irresponsible manner.

The struggle for corporate accountability is basically the struggle for additional yardsticks which public opinion and the law can use to judge corporate behavior and sanctions accordingly. Year after year, global corporations expand their geographical presence, adopt new technologies, develop new ways to shift control or produce capital, maneuver their labor pool across national boundaries, and dominate governments. Their reach into space, time and other peoples' space and time continues unbridled.

So, let us apply an embracing yardstick suitable for their spreading global power—that asks a fundamental question: Do the actions of corporations mortgage the future of oncoming generations, in order to maximize their present day profit?

This can be considered the third corporate strategic objective—the first two being going after the consumer dollar, then the taxpayer dollar (subsidies, government contracts and so forth).

Mortgaging the future environmentally means that companies cut down forests, erode land, contaminate water and soil, deplete the oceans of fisheries and leave certain areas so toxic as to be uninhabitable for centuries. These devastations, along with the horrific global warming trend, deprive our children, grandchildren and their descendants of the enjoyment, use and custody of these life-sustaining natural resources.

Mortgaging the future means burdening unborn generations with the obligation to pay for massive debts and deficits incurred in the present but deferred to the future. These debts and unproductive deficits can also produce inflation, currency devaluation and economic failure on a broad scale. Corporations—the merchants of debt—work overtime to sell products on credit with high interest rates. Consumers just registered the lowest rate of savings—namely zero— since the late 1920s.

As far as government deficits loading up on unborn taxpayers, corporations play a major role. First they work on overtime to reduce their taxes and grab your tax dollars in the form of subsidies, handouts, giveaways and free technology transfers. Second, they are all over Uncle Sam to spend taxpayer dollars on bloated wasteful military budgets and other regular programs disbursing lar-

gess to the corporations, whose lobbyists swarm all over Capitol Hill and the executive branch departments in Washington, DC.

If today corporations were taxed at the same rate as they were in the "prosperous" sixties, the current annual federal deficit would be erased and then some.

Mortgaging the future means unleashing technology whose perils and costs are ignored while their touted benefits are publicized everywhere. Try genetic engineering (changing the nature of nature) and nanotechnology (where you cannot see, hear and see what is around and inside of you for commercial profit).

Then there is the mortgaging of the health of the youth. Look at the accelerating pace of overdosing youngsters with overmedication, overfat food, and over entertainment of the violent, sexual kind in both programming and now advertisements. (Note the ads on the Superbowl.) Day after day, the corporate seduction accumulates with the latest in applied psychology, deception and induced addictions. Dumbing down young minds and damaging their future health.

Would you so mistreat children this way? Of course not. Because you don't look at children as profit centers. We demand more basic human values to children in our society.

Every major religion in the world warned its adherents not to give too much power, too much sway to the merchant classes, the sellers for profit. This common judgment comes from common experience stretching back millennia and across diverse cultures.

Let's apply the yardstick of mortgaging the future of human beings to the runaway corporations that pursue the supremacy of commercial values over the bedrock civic and spiritual values we need to shape the nature of the good society.

Seize the Moment

September 23, 2005

Historians like to speak of special times when leaders "seized the moment" to enact or implement their priorities. Giant hurricanes make these "special times," and no one is moving faster to exploit them than the corporate powers.

Urged on by the *Wall Street Journal*'s editorials, corporate lobbyists are demanding of the federal and state governments (1) taxpayer-funded corporate subsidies; (2) more corporate tax reductions; (3) waivers from worker pay protection laws; (4) a host of waivers from environmental health and land use regulations; and (5) corporate immunity from certain liabilities for harmful conduct. Even the shoreline gambling casinos are pushing for federal monies and getting support from more than a few so-called conservative Republicans.

After every national tragedy, large corporations make moves to cash in on the outcome of those tragedies. They arrange for non-competitive bid contracts so that their cronyism can get them large government contracts awarded with few safeguards to prevent waste, fraud and abuse. They want to give new meaning to New Orleans description as "The Big Easy."

Of course, these companies have their favorite politician in the White House and a Republican Congress marinated in business campaign contributions. Such indentured servants further encourage the corporate supremacists' grab of greed.

This is the president who is supposed to be preparing for mass evacuations in case of attacks or natural disasters. So what did he demand of Congress earlier this year. That the federal budget contribution to AMTRAK be eliminated.

Recall the televised 100-mile traffic jam out of Houston, Texas, fleeing Hurricane Rita, along with all other exiting roadways. Did you see any trains? Unlike Western Europe and Japan, an adequate, modern national railway system, that can lessen congestion on the highways during daily commutes and serve to evacuate efficiently large numbers of people during emergencies, does not exist for large, populated areas of the United States. Billions of tax dollars have gone to the troubled mismanaged airlines, especially after 9/11, but passenger railroads are expected to find their capital expenditures (upgrading roadbeds and equipment) on their own.

On the other side of the political aisle, the forces in Congress for the people can also "seize the moment." They can "seize the moment" for expanding both intercity rail systems and modern in-city mass transit. This will provide more transportation for emergencies, allow lower-income people to get to their jobs or find better jobs, reduce gasoline usage and air pollution, and create good paying construction jobs which serve a very useful public service.

These forces can also "seize the moment" by moving against poverty and opposing all the repulsive privileges, favoritism and freeloading by corporate executives exploiting devastations to innocent people, including real estate takeovers and makeovers for profiteering.

There is not much of any forcefulness on these two objectives yet on Capitol Hill. But Congressman Edward Markey (D-Mass.) and a coalition of Democrats and supportive Republicans, have introduced a very modest proposal to increase the average fuel economy of motor vehicles from the current absurdly low average of 24 miles per gallon (the lowest since 1980) to 33 miles per gallon by the fall of 2015.

Why so little? MIT's *Technology Review* reported that SUVs themselves could reach 40 miles per gallon by 2010. The very modesty of the proposal, at a time of $3 plus per gallon of gasoline, perilous reliance on imported oil, and oceans of gas guzzlers on the highways, is a test of just how arrogant and stubborn are the auto industry's domestic leaders.

Sure enough, the Alliance of Automobile Manufacturers immediately attacked the Boehlert/Markey amendment with specious assertions, imperiously assuring that the industry can do the job by itself.

Sure, just the way the industry has been doing—going backwards into the future with declining average vehicle fuel economy year after year.

Even sales of the hot-selling oversubscribed hybrids by Toyota and Honda for about five years cannot get the lead out of the rear end of General Motors and Ford Motor Company. They are making announcements in newspaper ads that they intend to awaken from their technologically stagnant slumber, however. That's a verbal start. But not anywhere near fast enough for motorists, commuters and national interest.

Bush, Katrina and Big Oil

September 2, 2005

For over two years I have been saying that the Mayor of Baghdad, George W. Bush, should be paying attention to America, including its massively unmet public works needs. But the president, who scheduled five weeks in Crawford, Texas, to assure "a balanced life," is now finding his political status unbalanced and hanging by fewer and fewer threads.

The unfolding mega disasters in New Orleans, Mississippi and Alabama have torn the propaganda curtain away from this arrogant president, and have shown the American people what results for their daily livelihoods from an administration obsessed with the fabricated Iraq War and marinated with Big Oil.

"No one can say they didn't see it coming . . . Now in the wake of one of the worst storms ever, serious questions are being asked about the lack of preparation," writes the conservative New Orleans daily newspaper—the *Times-Picayune*. Nearly one dozen articles in 2004 and 2005 came out of this constantly warning readers and citing local newspapers, citing the Iraq War budget as a training diversion for the lack of hurricane and flood-control dollars, according to Will Bunch of *Philadelphia Daily News*.

A hurricane like Katrina was forecast for the Gulf lowlands and New Orleans more than any predicated natural disaster in American history. No hindsight is involved. This is Bush's country and he paid no attention to the warnings, official and unofficial. In fact, he cut the Army Corps of Engineers budget for the New Orleans area by $71 million this past year, weakened FEMA and steered it and the Department of Homeland Security to a dangerous tilt toward terrorist risks and away from the officially predicted onset of a prolonged period of ferocious hurricanes now and in the next twenty years.

Will this no-fault ruler in the White House ever be held responsible for the consequences of his inattentions, his negligence and his boorish refusal to listen to anyone other than his cronies and patrons? Mr. Perfecto can't even admit to any mistakes although many, many innocents have paid for them on both the American and Iraqi sides.

Let's look at one area of escape from responsibility—the large and ever-merging oil giants whose network has provided Bush with forty-one high administration officials. Reaping profits beyond their dreams of avarice, ExxonMobil and the likes virtually own the Bush regime. They wrote his energy legislation full of subsidies and more tax breaks for this pampered breed, and hover over the Congress showering their campaign money over their keystone legislators.

Gasoline was averaging $1.36 per gallon on January 3, 2000, and is now racing towards $4 a gallon, having soared over $3 per gallon in many localities this week. Oil analysts were not reporting any shortages of supply worldwide, until the rigs and refineries were hurricaned last week in the Gulf of Mexico region raised such specters. OPEC has been pumping oil at record levels. There has been no sudden spike in demand.

But OPEC is no longer the only price-fixer factor in the price of oil. Oil futures in the New York Mercantile Exchange are now where the financial action resides. Oil has now become a big-time speculative commodity. So when you hear about the barrel of oil's price going up, think of the Mercantile Exchange. How does the Bush Government dampen such speculation? One way is to raise margin levels to make borrowing by the speculating traders more difficult. Nothing heard from Bush or the SEC on this point.

If the price of wheat suddenly doubled, why would the loaves of bread in your supermarkets suddenly be marked up or the loaves on their way in transit? The price hike for wheat would not have reached them. Then why does the price of oil and gasoline spike up when these supplies were already purchased at previously lower prices?

A concise answer to this question came from an unlikely source during the state of Hawaii's antitrust suit settled in 2002. Maxwell Blecher, attorney for defendant Tosco Corp. (now Phillips Petroleum) declared in court "High gas prices in Hawaii are the result of a lack of competitive market forces, not collusion. Once you decide it's an oligopoly, you've got an explanation for the phenomenon of the high prices, the

high margins, the high profits, the lack of vigorous price competition. That explains it all."

A compelling report by the Foundation for Taxpayer and Consumer Rights (www.consumerwatchdog.org) described the ever growing joint ownership of production, refining and distribution facilities including pipelines, by the large oil companies that people believe are competing with one another. The Bush and Clinton Administrations' antitrust cops did nothing to stop this merged, joint venture mockery of classical competitive systems.

Nor did Clinton and Bush do anything about the gas guzzling vehicles lumbering on the highways. Worse, they sat by and watched the average in fuel efficiency of the motor vehicle fleet in our country go down, not up, compared to the levels in the 1980s. To make matters worse, Bush successfully opposed a bill in the Senate by Senators John McCain and John Kerry in 2002 to require a one mile per gallon (mpg) increase in average fuel efficiency every year for the next fifteen years. Now the people at the pump are paying the price with the winter heating oil season is around the corner.

Consumer Federation of America reports that if vehicle fuel efficiency in the last fifteen years had increased at the same rate as it had in the 1980s, "our nation would consume one-third less gasoline." Every penny increase in the price of gasoline takes out $1.5 billion dollars from consumers.

In our nation's past, excessive profiteering by oil companies has led to an excess profits tax. The Foundation for Taxpayer and Consumer Rights recommends a "windfall profits rebate."

Tight refinery capacity has been viewed by officials and industry insiders as a factor in higher gasoline and heating oil prices. Why have the oil companies closed down about two dozen refineries in the past twenty years and not built new, cleaner ones on the same sites? Partly because they prefer importing cheaper refined products from abroad, which spell bigger profits.

The oil companies have longer term contracts with oil producers like Saudi Arabia at a fixed price. How extensive are these contracts? And why, if ExxonMobil is getting crude oil at lower prices from these earlier contracts, is their price going up as if they are paying nearly $70 per barrel for all their crude oil?

Such questions are not on the minds of Bush and Cheney, who hail from the oil world. Imagine—experts in the industry that is gouging America that they are, and they keep leaving, America and Americans defenseless.

Maybe Bush and Cheney will be defeated at the gas pumps where they cannot hoodwink so many people, as they did with their cover-ups and distractions during the election of 2004.

The Business Judgment Rule

July 18, 2005

A few years ago Time-Warner's *Fortune* magazine headlined a cover story on the staggering pay spiral of top corporate bosses and why nothing will be done to stop these over-the-top compensation packages. "Whew," I reacted—this coming from one of the nation's premier business publications—is a pretty good confirmation of a century-long silent coup d'etat against the rights of the owners of capital.

The owners are the shareholders, of course. In capitalistic theory, owners are supposed to control what they own. For decades, the managers and the rubber-stamp, pampered boards of directors have seized that control for themselves. Thus, my use of the phrase "corporate capitalism."

The legal innovation that helped strip owners from controlling their large corporation is called the "business judgment" rule accepted by the courts. This rule shields members of the boards of directors from being held personally liable for approving decisions that seriously harmed their company or got their company into trouble, so long as these boards can show they acted in good faith and with due care. Such a showing has often come in the garb of "not knowing" that the books were being cooked or that profits were being secretly inflated by company executives and accounting firms.

It is time to shed the charade and call the "business judgment" rule a cover-up for the irresponsibility or complicity of boards of directors (remember Enron, Health South, Worldcom, etc.). Boards are paid to look the other way in many large companies, as are outside corporate law firms and accounting firms.

Earlier this year, corporate critics and shareholder representatives thought things might be changing. A Delaware Chancery Judge William Chandler III refused to dismiss a case brought by stockholders against the Disney Corporation's board of directors for approving a lavish termination payoff to Disney's president, Michael Ovitz, after less than two undistinguished years on the job.

Plaintiffs charged that the board did not exercise their fiduciary duty to shareholders (the owners) and did not dutifully review and reject Mr. Ovitz's employment contract. A three-month trial produced widely publicized testimony showing how utterly cavalier the board was in letting Michael Eisner give Mr. Ovitz this "golden parachute" to leave the company after a falling out between the two super-rich men. Judge Chandler is expected to render his decision in a few weeks. In the meantime, shudders and shivers have been flitting through America's giant boardrooms to start getting tougher with wastrels in top management and stop being wined, dined and paid into such stupendous stupors.

In 2002, the average pay of the CEOs of the top 300 largest companies in the US came down to $7400 an hour! Imagine Wal-Mart executives making this off of workers earning $7 an hour. Eisner himself in one whopper year made about $1 million a day, assuming a five-day week.

Now comes the venerable New York Stock Exchange firm of Morgan Stanley to show how prophetic were *Fortune* magazine's editors. When Dean Witter and Morgan Stanley merged, CEO Phil Purcell packed the merged company board with his buddies from Dean Witter. Trouble started and the company faltered. A revolt by ex-Morgan Stanley top executives led to toppling Mr. Purcell this year. He took away a package worth about $106 million, including a new $44 million cash bonus. Lots of people would like to be fired that way for not doing a good job.

But it was his protégé's pay package that stunned the usually jaded business press. Look at the terms. One Steve Crawford, hardly in his forties, was appointed by Mr. Purcell and served on the job for three and a half months as co-president. Crony capitalism. He was working in administrative jobs at Morgan Stanley before his windfall elevation.

The board gave Mr. Crawford a guarantee in June 2005 of $32 million in cash compensation over two years or $16 million a year. Then, catch this, the board said that he could walk away with the entire cash hoard if he quit by August 3. Get the idea?

The Morgan Stanley wordsmiths explained these two huge payouts as insuring management stability and not distant from Wall Street's world of the ordinary.

Rewarding Mr. Crawford, payment for his 100 day stint, said the board, was meant to "mitigate the uncertainties that you may be experiencing regarding your future with the company." This was too much even for the *Wall Street Journal's* commentator who acidly said "That's one word for it." Whether they know it or not, millions of investors and thousands of pension and individual trusts will be waiting for Judge Chandler's decision and subsequent court appeals. Delaware law is very influential in matters of corporate governance.

Lo the 47 million full time workers making between $5.15 and $10 an hour, many without any health insurance or sick leave. Lo the poor children living in hovels. Lo the loyal workers whose jobs these executives so readily ship to communist or other dictatorships.

There is pay for real work, pay for real speculation and pay for real cronyism in this country. If the shareholder-investor owners of these companies organized and demanded by law that they must approve or disapprove compensation packages for the top executives managing the companies they purportedly own, obscene crony pay would become a thing of the disgraceful past.

Fighting Corporate Crime
November 25, 2004

In response to corporate crime waves, the government usually passes a series of meek reforms (like the Sarbanes Oxley law of 2002). Over the years, our citizen groups have introduced numerous proposals to crack down on corporate crime, including: the FBI creation of an annual "Corporate Crime in the United States" report; tripling the budgets of the federal corporate crime police; adopting three-strikes-and-you're-out policies for corporate criminals; banning corporate criminals from government contracts; expanding the False Claims Act to include environmental and securities fraud areas; and creative sentencing alternatives, such as sentencing fit coal mine executives, convicted of violating safety laws resulting in casualties, to working with the miners in the mines.

Some of the shrewdest observers of corporate crime come from that former penal colony, Australia. John Braithwaite, who has written many books on corporate crime, argues, "If we are serious about controlling corporate crime, the first priority should be to create a culture in which corporate crime is not tolerated." He believes that "the moral educative functions of corporate criminal law are best achieved with heavy reliance on adverse publicity as a social control mechanism."

"The policy instruments for harnessing shame against corporate offenders include adverse publicity orders as a formal sanction, the calling of press conferences following corporate convictions, encouraging consumer activism and investigative journalism," he writes.

What is needed is political leadership free from negative corporate influence, leadership that will not just talk the talk on corporate crime enforcement, but deliver justice to the American people. For too long people have suffered at the hands of big corporations that defraud consumers; pollute our air, water, and soil; bribe our public officials, injure and destroy the health of workers, and steal from our governments. Creating a culture in which corporate crime is not tolerated in word, law, or deed is long overdue.

This is a citizens' agenda for cracking down on corporate crime:

- Establish a public online corporate crime database at the Department of Justice.

The FBI should also produce an annual corporate and white-collar crime report as an analogue to its "Crime in the United States" report, which focuses on street crime.

- Increase Corporate Crime Prosecution. Budgets of the Securities and Exchange Commission and especially the Department of Justice's corporate crime division have been chronically underfunded. Without proper resources, it is difficult to apply the rule of law to corporate criminals. As a result, government prosecutors and regulators are forced to settle for weak fines and ignore many more violators entirely.

- Ban Corporate Criminals from Government Contracts. Enact a tough, serious debarment statute that would deny federal business to serious and/or repeat corporate lawbreakers. These standards should apply to corporate contracts in Iraq. The federal government spends $265 billion a year on goods and services. Let's make sure taxpayer money isn't supporting corporate criminals.

- Punish corporate tax escapees by closing the offshore reincorporation loophole and banning government contracts and subsidies for companies that relocate their headquarters to an offshore tax haven. Give the IRS more power and resources to go after corporate tax cheats. Require publicly traded corporations to make their tax returns public.

- Restore the Rights of Defrauded Investors. Repeal self-styled securities "reform laws that block defrauded investors from seeking restitution," such as the Private Securities Litigation Reform Act of 1995, which allowed the aiders and abettors of massive corporate crime (e.g., accountants and lawyers) to escape civil liability.

- Grant shareholders the right to democratically nominate and elect the corporate board of directors by opening up proxy access to minority shareholders and introducing cumulative voting and competitive elections. Require shareholders to approve all major business decisions, including executive compensation. Shareholders, after all, are the owners.

- Require shareholder authorization of top executive compensation at annual shareholder meetings. Require that stock options, which now account for about half of executive compensation, be counted on financial statements as an expense (which they are). Eliminate tax deductions for compensation above twenty-five times the compensation received by the lowest paid worker in a corporation.

- Regulate all over the-counter financial instruments, including derivatives, so that they are subject to the same or equivalent audit and reporting requirements as other financial instruments traded on the stock exchanges. Rules should be enacted regarding collateral-margin, reporting and dealer licensing in order to maintain regulatory parity and ensure that markets are transparent and problems can be detected before they become a crisis.

- Enact corporate sunshine laws that force corporations to provide better information about their records on the environment, human rights, worker safety, and taxes, as well as their criminal and civil litigation records.

- End Conflicts of Interest on Wall Street. Reenact structural reforms that separate commercial and investment banking services and prevent other conflicts of interest among financial entities, such as those that have dominated big banks in recent years.

- Corporations must be held more responsible for the retirement security of their employees. At a minimum we need to give workers a voice on the pension board; not require workers to stuff their 401 (k) plans with company stock; and give workers a right to vote for their 401 (k) stock.

- In addition, an Office of Participant Advocacy should be created in the Department of Labor to monitor pension plans.

- Establish a Congressional Commission on Corporate Power to explore various legal and economic proposals that would rein in unaccountable giant corporations. The Commission should seek ways to improve upon the current state system of corporate chartering through federal charters for global corporations and propose ways to correct the evasive legal status of corporations, such as being treated as persons under our Constitution. The Commission should be led by a congressionally appointed expert on corporate and constitutional law, and should hold public citizen hearings in at least ten cities.

If you are in the mood for fun, ask your Member of Congress for an update on what he or she is doing to stop the corporate crime wave.

Maxxam-Pacific Lumber

February 15, 2004

From the failed savings and loan bailout racket to the stately giant redwood trees of Humboldt County, California, the story of the predator corporation Maxxam-Pacific Lumber someday may make a movie on corporate arrogance and abuse. The storyline has taken a bizarre twist today, some years after Maxxam bought out a family-owned lumber company and accelerated, to great opposition, the cutting of these ancient trees.

It seems that a newly elected county district attorney, Paul Gallegos, is irritating the lumber giant for bringing a suit charging Pacific Lumber by filing a false timber harvest plan in order to obtain a global logging permit for their property. The company, he charges, had information about the environmental impact of their logging proposal that they were legally obliged to give to the Californian authorities but did not.

Richard Wilson of the California Department of Forestry publically declared that if he knew about this withholding of material information at the time he signed off on the permit, he would have rejected the permit application.

The owners of Pacific Lumber decided to rid themselves of this prosecution for fraud by starting a recall of the elected Paul Gallegos. So they backed a commercial signature gathering firm which is charging $8 a signature to place this recall on the ballot. It is remarkable what this artificial legal entity, called a corporation, can get away with. Imagine a real person charged with fraud trying to recall the prosecutor.

Well, Pacific Lumber, using fear tactics of mass layoffs, may not get away with this camouflaged campaign charging the D.A. with being soft on crime, when he is actually prosecuting corporate crime. Mr. Gallegos says the polls show he is ahead by 60 to 40. Why so close? The signature gatherers and the propaganda campaign are deceiving people that the petition is about anti-rape legislation or to repeal vehicle license faxes. Over 90 percent of the money for this recall campaign comes from Pacific Lumber.

Known for playing hardball, Pacific Lumber is scaring its hundreds of workers into complaining about the lawsuit and its impact on their jobs. Of course if the workers owned the company, they would realize that a genuine sustainable yield would keep their jobs for a much longer time for themselves and their children.

The recall election is on March 2, 2004. The question in the minds of many in the County is whether the judge will decide this long overdue case before or after that date. Mr. Gallegos is demanding restitution at a level of $230 million for the value of those logged trees and the resultant environmental damage that would not have occurred had the company told the necessary truth to the state forestry officials.

In an interview with the Corporate Crime Reporter, Gallegos said that this is not a "liberal versus conservative issue." It is about "who owns local government. Historically, the feeling has been that it has been owned by a select few. We stand for the idea that it belongs to the people in this community."

He added that Humboldt was a "remote, historically isolated community." So much so that Pacific Lumber owns one town—Scotia—down to every house and the shopping center, he said.

Company towns are not new in our country.

They range from the paper mill towns of Maine to the copper-mine towns of Montana and Arizona to the textile company dominated towns in North and South Carolina.

But Pacific Lumber, as a corporate defendant, is pushing the envelope by trying to recall its prosecutor.

For further information, contact Friends of Paul Gallegos. E-mail: pgallegos@co.humboldt.ca.us.

John Hancock Shenanigans

January 24, 2004

In reading the latest news reports of uncontrollable corporate greed, I recalled the cover of *Fortune Magazine* about two years ago which headlined the runaway compensation packages of the big corporate bosses and why nothing would be done about it.

Also recalled was the *Business Week* cover story in the year 2000 titled "Too Much Corporate Power?" which this leading magazine answered yes! yes! yes! in a long article. The editors took a poll and found 72 percent of the responders believed that corporations had too much control over their lives. And that response was before the corporate crime wave (Enron, Worldcom, Tyco, Wall Street, etc.) that looted or drained trillions of dollars from tens of millions of small investors, workers and pension-holders!

Now comes Jason Adkins, the leading attorney challenging self-enriching conversions of mutual insurance companies to stock companies, to report on the John Hancock shenanigans. With apologies to the American patriot, John Hancock, whose name this company seized and slandered, here is what the top executives pulled off.

First, they rammed a bill through the Massachusetts legislature on a sea of illegally wining,

dining and golfing key lawmakers, to allow the giant mutual to convert to stock. The company bosses rejected assertions that they were readying the stage for enriching their coffers.

In 1999, Hancock converted the mutual to a stock company. Before 1999, Hancock could have merged with the Canadian insurer Manulife Financial when both companies had been mutuals and avoided siphoning off tens of millions of dollars to management. But why choose this approach when unctuous avarice beckons over the horizon?

After a series of backroom dealings, Hancock's officers and rubber-stamp board of directors instead converted and approved the sale of this mutual insurance company to the Canadian firm. Adkins' summary of the wealth transfer that he is challenging in federal court on behalf of a share-holder, Aaron E. Landy, Jr. is worth quoting:

> The top 10 executives of John Hancock stand to make an extra $60 million if the proposed sale of the company to Canadian insurer Manulife Financial goes through. Dozens of other executives will reap additional millions. Alone, Hancock's CEO and chairman, David D'Alessandro, will make a reported $22 million from the deal. This is an addition to his $21.7 million compensation in 2002, which was itself up from his $3.1 million pay in 2000.

By the way, $22 million amounts to almost half a million dollars a week, not counting perks, benefits and expenses!

Hancock's executive greed is also retroactive. Former Hancock CEO and chairman Stephen Brown made $6.7 million in 2002 despite having retired in May 2001, says Adkins. So busy were these executives scheming for themselves that the net income and the company's stock price-to-book-value were down significantly in 2003.

Just read the *Wall Street Journal* every day and see just how out of control companies like Halliburton (overcharges, bribery and pay-and-play deals) are, or the natural gas industry with its driving up your heating bills big time even though, as Senator Joseph Lieberman points out, these "dramatic increases" come despite relatively stable supply and demand.

It was left to *Automotive News'* editorial writers to show just how devastating executive greed can be to losses of jobs by workers at the former Chrysler corporation. When Daimler's CEO, Juergen Schrempp came shopping for Chrysler in 1998, Robert Eaton (Chrysler's CEO) cut a personal compensation deal for $70 million and sold the company to the German auto giant.

As *Automotive News* wrote: "Bob Eaton and Juergen Schrempp cared more about getting the deal done than they cared about the aftermath and its impact on the company and stakeholders. [Schrempp] eliminated skilled Chrysler executives such as Tom Stallkamp after they questioned the wisdom of the deal and the cumbersome bureaucracy that resulted. Eaton took his $70 million and ran."

Is it any wonder that polls are showing more and more demands by the American people for a crackdown on corporate crime, fraud and abuse? Though working longer hours than 30 years ago, American workers are increasingly angry that the economy and the corporate bosses in control are not working for them.

Media & Commercialism

Calvin Coolidge famously declared that "the business of America is business." Surely, there are grander purposes of our collective life than simply measuring the well-being of our society by the size of the gross national product.

The commercial imperative permeates every aspect of our lives. Our food, entertainment, our electoral and political institutions—all of this and much more is controlled by modern-day corporate barons who rarely have time for non-mercantile values.

The commercial juggernaut has moved into area after area once wholly or largely off-limits to commerce, including our schools and colleges, our children, amateur sports, the arts, our holidays and rituals, religious institutions and environment. Our major "public space" is increasingly the corporate shopping mall, which is often hostile toward civic activity like petitioning.

If we take our Constitution and founding ideals seriously, the "business" of America is democracy. A well-functioning democracy requires diverse and vibrant media to ensure a "vigorous, robust, uninhibited democracy." Our country's founders understood that democracy cannot thrive without an open exchange of ideas that includes the ability to receive full information about the workings of government and viewpoints that challenge the official line.

The media is dominated by a handful of interlocking corporations with common political and economic interests, pursued daily by their paid vocalists. The Federal Communications Commission, funded by our taxpayer dollars and rarely responsive to expanding the people's control and use of the public airwaves that "We the People" own.

We own the public airwaves, but the media control what we see and hear. A free and open society needs free and open media about what is going on in this country and the world—media that promote more than the narrow commercial interests.

The columns in this section trace the extent and insidious effects of rampant commercialism and its subjugation of civic values. These columns also detail the media "blackouts" of important events that are relevant to citizens and life in the US such as improving presidential debates and covering people of interest who have contributed greatly to society.

PBS-NPR—Leaning Right

March 14, 2011

The tumultuous managerial shakeup at National Public Radio headquarters for trivial verbal miscues once again has highlighted the ludicrous corporatist right-wing charge that public radio and public TV are replete with left-leaning or leftist programming.

Ludicrous, that is, unless this criticism's yardstick is the propaganda regularly exuded by the extreme right-wing Rush Limbaugh and Sean Hannity. These "capitalists" use the public's airwaves free-of-charge to make big money.

The truth is that the frightened executives at public TV and radio have long been more hospitable to interviews with right of center or extreme right-wing and corporatist talking heads than liberal or progressive guests.

PBS's Charlie Rose has had war-loving William Kristol on thirty-one times, Henry Kissinger fifty-five times, Richard Perle ten times, the global corporatist cheerleader, Tom Friedman seventy times. Compare that guest list with Rose's interviews of widely published left of center guests—Noam Chomsky two times, William Grieder two times, Jim Hightower two times, Charlie Peters two times, Lewis Lapham three times, Bob Herbert six times, Paul Krugman twenty-one times, Victor Navasky one time, Mark Green five times and Sy Hersh, once a frequent guest, has not been on since January 2005.

Dr. Sidney Wolfe, the widely-quoted super-accurate drug industry critic, who is often featured on the commercial TV network shows, has never been on Rose's show. Nor has the long-time head of Citizens for Tax Justice and widely respected progressive tax analyst, Robert McIntyre.

Far more corporate executives, not known for their leftist inclinations, appear on Rose's show than do leaders of environmental, consumer, labor and poverty organizations.

In case you are wondering, I've appeared four times, but not since August 2005, and not once on the hostile Terry Gross radio show.

The unabashed progressive Bill Moyer's Show is off the air and has not been replaced. No one can charge PBS's *News Hour with Jim Lehrer* with anything other than very straight-forward news delivery, bland opinion exchanges and a troubling inclination to avoid much reporting that upsets the power structures in Congress, the White House, the Pentagon or Wall Street.

The longest running show on PBS was hardline conservative William F. Buckley's show—*Firing Line*—which came on the air in 1966 and ended in 1999.

Sponsorship by large corporations, such as Coca Cola and AT&T, have abounded—a largesse not likely to be continued year after year for a leftist media organization.

None of this deters the Far Right that presently got a majority in the House of Representatives to defund the $422 million annual appropriation to the umbrella entity—Corporation for Public Broadcasting (CPB). About 15 percent of all revenues for all public broadcasting stations comes from this Congressional contribution.

Though he admits to liking National Public Radio, conservative columnist David Harsanyi, believes there is no "practical argument" left "in the defense of federal funding . . . in an era of nearly unlimited choices. . . ."

Really? Do commercial radio stations give you much news between the Niagara of advertisements and music? Even the frenetic news, sports, traffic and weather flashes, garnished by ads, are either redundant or made up of sound-bytes (apart from the merely two minutes of CBS radio news every half-hour). If you want serious news, features and interviews on the radio, you go to public radio or the few community and Pacifica radio stations.

Harsanyi continues: "Something, though, seems awfully wrong with continuing to force taxpayers who disagree with the mission—even if their perceptions are false—to keep giving. . . ."

Public radio's popular *Morning Edition* and *All Things Considered* are the most listened to radio shows after Rush Limbaugh's, and any taxpayer can turn them off. Compare the relatively small public radio and TV budget allocations with the tens of billions of dollars each year—not counting the Wall Street bailout—in compelling taxpayers to subsidize, through hundreds of programs, greedy, mismanaged, corrupt or polluting corporations either directly in handouts, giveaways and guarantees or indirectly in tax escapes, bloated contracts and grants. Can the taxpayer turn *them* off?

Here is a solution that will avoid any need for Congressional contributions to CPB. The people own the public airwaves. They are the landlords. The commercial radio and TV stations are the tenants that pay nothing for their twenty-four-hour use of this public property. You pay more for your auto license than the largest television station in New York pays the Federal Communications Commission for its broadcasting license—which is nothing. It has been that way since the 1927 and 1934 communication laws.

Why not charge these profitable businesses rent for use of the public airwaves and direct some of the ample proceeds to nonprofit public radio and public TV as well as an assortment of audience controlled TV and radio channels that could broadcast what is going on in our country locally, regionally, nationally and internationally? (See: Ralph Nader & Claire Riley, Oh, Say Can You See: A Broadcast Network for the Audience, 5 J.L. & POL. 1, [1988])

Now that would be a worthy program for public broadcasting. Get Limbaugh's and Hannity's companies off welfare. Want to guess what their listeners think about corporate welfare?

Wikimania and the First Amendment
December 20, 2010

Thomas Blanton, the esteemed director of the National Security Archive at George Washington University described Washington's hyper-reaction to Wikileaks' transmission of information to some major media in various countries as "Wikimania."

In testimony before the House Judiciary Committee last Thursday, Blanton urged the Justice Department to cool it. Wikileaks and newspapers like the *New York Times* and London's *Guardian*, he said, are publishers protected by the First Amendment. The disclosures are the first small installment of a predicted much larger forthcoming trove of non-public information from both governments and global corporations.

The leakers inside these organizations come under different legal restrictions than those who use their freedom of speech rights to publish the leaked information.

The mad dog, homicidal demands to destroy the leaders of Wikileaks by self-styled liberal Democrat and Fox commentator, Bob Beckel, the radio and cable howlers and some members of Congress, may be creating an atmosphere of panic at the politically sensitive Justice Department. Attorney General Eric Holder has made very prejudicial comments pursuant to his assertion that his lawyers considering how they may prosecute Julian Assange, the Wikileaks leader.

Mr. Holder declared that both "the national security of the United States" and "the American people have been put at risk." This level of alarm was not shared by the public statements of defense Secretary Robert Gates and Secretary of

State Hillary Clinton who downplayed the impact of these disclosures.

The Attorney General, who should be directing more of his resources to the corporate crime wave in all its financial, economic and hazardous manifestations, is putting himself in a bind.

If he goes after Wikileaks too broadly using the notorious Espionage Act of 1917 and other vague laws, how is he going to deal with the *New York Times* and other mass media that reported the disclosures?

Consider what Harvard Law Professor Jack Goldsmith, who was head of the Office of Legal Counsel in George W. Bush's Justice Department just wrote:

> In *Obama's Wars*, Bob Woodward, with the obvious assistance of many top Obama administration officials, disclosed many details about top secret programs, code names, documents, meetings, and the like. I have a hard time squaring the anger the government is directing towards Wikileaks with its top officials openly violating classification rules and opportunistically revealing without authorization top secret information.

On the other hand, if Mr. Holder goes the narrow route to obtain an indictment of Mr. Assange, he will risk a public relations debacle by vindictively displaying prosecutorial abuse (i.e. fixing the law around the enforcement bias.) Double standards have no place in the Justice Department.

Wikileaks is also creating anxiety in the corporate suites. A cover story in the December 20, 2010 issue of *Forbes* magazine reports that early next year a large amount of embarrassing material will be sent to the media by Wikileaks about a major US bank, followed by masses of exposé material on other global corporations.

Will these releases inform the people about very bad activities by drug, oil, financial and other companies along with corruption in various countries? If so, people may find this information useful. We can only imagine what sleazy or illegal things our government has been up to that have been covered up. Soon, people may reject those who would censor Wikileaks. Many people do want to size up what's going on inside their government in their name and with their tax dollars.

Wasn't it Jefferson who said that "information is the currency of democracy" and that, given a choice between government and a free press, he'll take the latter? Secrecy—keeping the people and Congress in the dark—is the cancer eating at the vitals of democracy.

What is remarkable about all the official hullabaloo by government officials, who leak plenty themselves, is that there never is any indictment or prosecution of government big wigs who continually suppress facts and knowledge in order to carry out very devastating actions like invading Iraq under false pretenses and covering up corporate contractors' abuses. The morbid and corporate-indentured secrecy of government over the years has cost many American lives, sent Americans to illegal wars, bilked consumers of billions of dollars and harmed the safety and economic well-being of workers.

As Rep. Ron Paul said on the House floor, why is the hostility directed at Assange, the publisher, and not at our government's failure to protect classified information? He asked his colleagues which events caused more deaths, "Lying us into war, or the release of the Wikileaks papers?"

Over-reaction by the Obama administration could lead to censoring the internet, undermining Secretary Clinton's Internet Freedom initiative, which criticized China's controls and lauded hacktivism in that country, and divert attention from the massive over classification of documents by the Executive Branch.

A full throttle attack on Wikileaks is what the government distracters want in order to take away the spotlight of the disclosures on their misdeeds, their waste and their construction of an authoritarian corporate state.

Professor and ex-Bushite Jack Goldsmith summed up his thoughts this way: "The best thing to do . . . would be to ignore Assange and fix the secrecy system so this does not happen again."

That presumably is some of what Peter Zatko and his crew are now trying to do at the Pentagon's famed DARPA unit. That secret initiative may ironically undermine the First Amendment should they succeed too much in hamstringing the internet earlier advanced by that same Pentagon unit.

Mainstreaming the Extreme Right Wing

October 18, 2010

The strong case that Eric Alterman's book *What Liberal Media?* made in 2003 against the propaganda-style claim by right-wingers, that the mass media has a liberal bias, is an expanding understatement. Just read recent issues of the *Washington Post* and the *New York Times* to see the most extreme reactionaries getting the kind of coverage their publicists love.

Just last Sunday in the October 10, 2010 *New York Times*, two very lengthy features appeared on the rancid Ann Coulter and the blogger Pamela Geller—a grotesque anti-Semite against Arabs who flaunts her sweeping bigotry as a badge of pride. Geller even called herself a "racist-Islamophobic-anti-Muslim-bigot." One

veteran reporter called the sprawling two-page feature, with all of twenty color photos "an advertisement."

Anyone with such open and flaunted hatred against Jews would either be ignored or slammed paragraph by paragraph with denunciations consigning the sick character into media oblivion.

The latest Coulter feature, one of many in the mainstream media over the years, chronicles her efforts to reinvent her shouts since she is being outflanked "on the right by the Tea Party."

The *Times* called her a "conservative," besmirching conservatives, instead of what she really is—a burlesque performer throwing red meat to audiences looking for off-the-wall entertainment. Coulter even denounced the New Jersey 9/11 widows as exploiting their husbands' deaths for enjoyment.

One of the editors at the *New Yorker* wondered what is happening to the *Times* sense of feature-worthiness. I replied that no one on the seriously important Left gets this kind of promotional treatment, no matter how flamboyantly personal they may be. If there are counterparts, calling themselves leftists, who compare with Coulter and Geller, no one knows their names because they don't have the *Times*, Rush Limbaugh, Sean Hannity and Glenn Beck to promote them via the mass media.

National and local talk radio, using our public airwaves free of charge, is dominated by extreme ranting rightwing soliloquists who often pull the plug on the few callers who get by the screeners. Cable political TV, apart from MSNBC (which fired Phil Donahue in 2003 for presenting both sides of Bush's fabricated drive to invade Iraq) is a race between the wildly hysterical Beck-types and Bill O'Reilly exhaustingly trying to out-do Beck, even though O'Reilly knows better.

Take the comparative news and feature coverage of Glenn Beck's rally in Washington, DC on August 28 with the rally at the same place a month later, organized by 400 progressive labor, religious, civil rights, student and environmental groups.

In the *Washington Post*, it was not even close. For the progressive rally of comparable size, representing tens of millions of Americans, the *Post* devoted a short article presaging the event and a regular news story that day on page three, which cited Mr. Beck's preposterous estimate of 500,000 for his meeting (A CBS-retained consulting firm estimated Beck's rally drew just under 90,000).

For the Beck rally, the *Post* went all out. A huge page one story spilled generously onto the inside pages. The Fox network talkers' assembly got articles proceeding and after the gathering. The *Times*, while not so gushing, did manage to give Beck a startling ego-inflating headline—"Where Dr. King Once Stood, Tea Party Claims His Mantle." And Beck is a TV media man promoting political action, a role that formerly was taboo.

The op-ed pages showcase the news media's rightwing bent even more than the news articles. The op-ed pages of the *Post* are overrepresented with war-mongering columnists and contributors. The media watchdog FAIR reported in their monthly magazine *Extra* that, in one nine-month period during 2009, the ratio of op-ed's supporting wars and interventions outnumbered op-ed's by the anti-interventionists by ten-to-one. This in an overwhelmingly liberal Democratic city, no less.

Professor Andrew Bacevich, a former professional soldier and author of acclaimed books, has had five submissions rejected over the past two years or so by Fred Hiatt—the *Post*'s editorial page chief. Hiatt doesn't even bother sending him a rejection, unlike his rejections by the more courteous David Shipley, his counterpart at the *Times*.

On the day President Obama announced the end of combat activity in Iraq, who appears with a lengthy unrepentant op-ed piece on Iraq in the *Times*? None other than a major architect of that illegal, criminal war of aggression—Paul Wolfowitz. John Bolton, the falsehood-prone former State Department wildcatter, whom Secretary Colin Powell could not stomach, managed to get an op-ed in the *Times* and the *Post* on the same day! Other viewpoints are infrequently solicited by the *Times* or *Post*.

The right-moving trend of the mainstream media, absurdly deemed liberal by successfully intimidating corporatists and ideological aggressors, continues year after year. Dissenting groups produce reports and actions that used to make the network television news, but are now shut out. Exposés by civic groups about rampant corporate crime and political corruption are regularly ignored.

Civil rights, women's rights, environment, labor, and consumer issues were once given voice on the *Phil Donahue Show* and occasionally by the *Mike Douglas* and *Merv Griffin* shows. No more. Many of the shows that followed, except for Oprah, showcase crude, violent, aberrant, sadomasochistic personal behaviors.

The media bends over backwards to avoid being called liberal by featuring many corporatist or rightwing think tank views. Media executives should pause to contemplate how their predecessors in the 1960s and 1970s embraced balance and, in so doing, resulted in our country being improved in many ways.

Why not now?

Hammering the Poor and Vulnerable

July 1, 2010

There is a reason why, so many centuries ago, every major religion warned its adherents not to give too much power to the "merchant class." That reason is still here—the commercial drive knows few self-imposed boundaries, especially when it resides in large corporations.

A cruel manifestation of this singular drive for maximizing profit is how companies treat those who are most powerless, most vulnerable or most preoccupied.

Here are some illustrations that highlight the serious failures of law enforcement:

1. Pre-teen children. The direct marketing to children knows no limits of decency. Undermining parental authority with penetrating marketing schemes and temptations, companies deceptively excite youngsters to buy massive amounts of products that are bad for their safety, health and minds. Think junk food—loaded with fat, salt and sugar, that increases obesity, diabetes and predisposition for high blood pressure. (See http://www.cspinet.org.) Obesity produces sickness, death, disability and large medical bills.

Marketers are selling ever more violent entertainment, and soft porn with delivery systems that escape parental review or supervision. Television is no longer the only route to children. Our fourteen year-old, then-startling book— *Children First: A Parent's Guide to Corporate Predators*—now reads as an understatement.

2. The poor. Whether white, African-American, Hispanic or Native American, merchants make the poor pay more. Loan sharks, shoddy merchandise, sub-standard food products and inadequate medical care have plagued the poor

and been the subject of many studies and too few prosecutions.

3. People preoccupied by their bereavement are often preyed upon by the funeral industry. The Federal Trade Commission has an ample file on overcharges and deceptive practices from the unscrupulous merchants in that trade.

4. People with rare diseases often require so called "orphan drugs." Under a 1983 law, drug companies receive a seven year monopoly with no price restraints on these drugs. Drug companies are also given huge tax credits for research and development costs associated with orphan drugs.

The *Wall Street Journal* ("How Drugs for Rare Diseases Became Lifeline for Companies", Nov 15, 2005) called these drugs "lucrative niches." With no competition, these monopoly drugs come with staggering prices for desperate patients.

Here is one story of how your tax dollars are being used for hyperprofit corporate profits. Henry Blair was working on an experimental enzyme under government contract as a researcher at Tufts University Medical School. Working with scientists at the National Institutes of Health, they made the enzyme work as a treatment for Gaucher disease, which swells organs and deteriorates bones.

In 1981, Mr. Blair started the Genzyme company, got the government contract to make the enzyme which he brought to market in 1991. The average price was—get this—$200,000 a year per patient!

In 1992, the Congressional Office of Technology Assessment (OTA) (banished by Newt Gingrich in 1995) reported that Genzyme spent $29.4 million on the drug, with much of the initial research funded and done by government scientists at the National Institutes of Health.

Two years later, Genzyme found a much cheaper way of making the drug. In 2005, the *Wall Street Journal* wrote that the Gaucher drug was still priced at $200,000 per patient each year. The company says it gives the drug at no cost to about 10 percent of the patients. For the rest, either rely on the insurance companies (good luck), or otherwise pay or die.

5. *The Health Uninsured* are charged by hospitals full price, which the *Wall Street Journal* reported "is far more than the prices typically paid by insurance companies." This is the case, the *Journal* added, in spite of an annual taxpayer subsidy of $22 billion to hospitals "to care for the uninsured."

6. Amputees who need prosthetic devices find that the devices in the United States are very highly priced (by comparison with other western countries.) Health insurance companies make these products leading candidates for rising co-payments. This can mean tens of thousands of dollars from the patients or they go without. These shocking co-payment requirements are often in the fine print.

Many of these devices also come about with taxpayer funded research and development. Profit margins are large because of the users' dire necessity to have them for mobility, for work, for human dignity.

7. Low-credit-score credit card holders. The relentless credit card economy requiring plastic to buy more and more things and services. The credit score becomes the hammer. A story recounted by MSNBC's Bob Sullivan in his engrossing new book *Stop Getting Ripped Off* describes: "the card promised an attractive 9.9 percent interest rate.

But there was a catch buried in the fine print: account setup fee: $29; program fee: $95; annual fee: $48; monthly servicing fee: $84 annually; additional card fee: $20 annually." Then this clincher sentence: "If you are assigned the minimum credit limit of $250, your initial available credit will be $71 ($51 if you select the additional-card option)."

No wonder the vendors call them "fee-harvesting" cards. Who needs loan-sharks? These credit card vendors fleece the poor wearing a three-piece suit and sitting in air conditioned skyscrapers.

Such is the fate of the poor or the vulnerable under the boot of commercial avarice.

Breaking With Obama?
December 31, 2009

Those long-hoping, long-enduring members of the liberal intelligentsia are starting to break away from the least-worst mindset that muted their criticisms of Barack Obama in the 2008 presidential campaign.

They still believe that the president is far better than his Republican counterpart would have been. Some still believe that sometime, somewhere, Obama will show his liberal stripes. But they no longer believe they should stay loyally silent in the face of the escalating war in Afghanistan, the near collapse of key provisions in the health insurance legislation, the likely anemic financial regulation bill, or the obeisance to the bailed out Wall Street gamblers. Remember this Administration more easily embraces bonuses for fat cats than adequate investment in public jobs.

Of all the loyalists, among the first to stray was Bob Herbert, columnist for the *New York Times*. He wondered about his friends telling him that Obama treats their causes and them "as if they have nowhere to go." Then there was the stalwart Obamaist, the brainy Gary Wills, who broke with Obama over Afghanistan in a stern essay of admonition.

If you read the biweekly compilation of progressive and liberal columnists and pundits in *The Progressive Populist*, one of my favorite publications, the velvet verbal gloves are coming off.

Jim Hightower writes that "Obama is sinking us into 'Absurdistan.'" He bewails, "I had hoped Obama might be a more forceful leader who would reject the same old interventionist mindset of those who profit from permanent war. But his newly announced Afghan policy shows he is not that leader."

Wonder where good ol' Jim got that impression—certainly not from anything Obama said or did not say in 2008. But hope dims the memory of the awful truth which is that Obama signed on to the Wall Street and military-industrial complex from the getgo. He got their message and is going after their campaign contributions and advisors big time!

Norman Solomon, expressed his sharp deviation from his long-time admiration of the politician from Chicago. He writes: "President Obama accepted the 2009 Nobel Peace Prize while delivering—to the world as it is—a prowar speech. The context instantly turned the speech's insights into flackery for more war." Strong words indeed!

Arianna Huffington has broken in installments. But her disillusionment is expanding. She writes: "Obama isn't distancing himself from 'the Left' with his decision to escalate this deepening disaster [in Afghanistan]. He's distancing himself from the national interests of the country."

John R. MacArthur, publisher of *Harper's* magazine, was never an Obama fan and has been upset with what he calls "the liberal adoration of Obama." In a piece for the *Providence Journal*, he cites some writers still loyal to Obama, such as Frank Rich of the *New York Times*, Hendrick Hertzberg of the *New Yorker*, and Tom Hayden, who are showing mild discomfort in the midst of retained hope over Obama's coming months. They have not yet cut their ties to the masterspeaker of "Hope and Change."

Gary Wills has crossed his Rubicon, calling Obama's Afghanistan escalation "a betrayal." Wills is a scholar of both the presidency and of political oratory (his small book on Lincoln's Gettysburg address is a classic interpretation). So he uses words carefully, to wit: "If we had wanted Bush's wars, and contractors, and corruption, we could have voted for John McCain. At least we would have seen our foe facing us, not felt him at our back, as now we do."

Rest assured the liberal-progressive commentariat has another two years to engage in challenge and chagrin. For in 2012, silence will mute their criticisms as the stark choices of the two-party tyranny come into view and incarcerate their minds into the least-worst voting syndrome (just as they have done in recent presidential election years).

It is hard to accord them any moral breaking point under such self-imposed censorship. Not much leverage in that approach, is there?

No Debate

February 1, 2008

It was billed as the great debate that, in the words of moderator Wolf Blitzer, "could change the course of this presidential race and the nation."

Situated at the packed historic Kodak Theatre—site of the Hollywood Oscar awards, thousands of people, including anti-war protesters, were outside, where tickets were being scalped for $1,000.

The burgeoning excitement swept up Mr. Blitzer into an introduction reminiscent of a heavyweight boxing title fight. Referring to the "glamour on this stage . . . one of the great stages of all time," he declared that "this will be the first time that Hillary Clinton and Barack Obama will be debating face to face, just the two of them, one-on-one." The crowd ROARED!

When it was over two hours later, here is how the reporters, not the columnists, of the *New York Times* described the showdown: "Senators Hillary Rodham Clinton and Barack Obama sat side by side here Thursday, sharing a night of smiles, friendly eye-catching and gentle banter. . . . It was almost as if the battle was to see which of them could outnice the other."

Since neither scored a knockout, a knockdown, and neither stumbled, the audience left without many feeling the pain of their champion being bested. Even the *Times*' critic, Alessandra Stanley, she of the usual barbed pen, could only marvel at the smooth harmony ideology both candidates decided to adopt. She wrote: "They let their eyes make nice. . . . As they stood in front of the audience before the debate, Mr. Obama leaned down to Mrs. Clinton and whispered a few words in her ear, as if continuing the fun chat they had just shared backstage."

The two candidates were unperturbed by any questions from the reporters that they had not answered before or were soft balls they could hit out of the ball park.

As in all debates involving presidential candidates, the reporters were unwilling or incapable of asking the unconventional questions reflecting situations and conditions widely reported or investigated by their own colleagues.

This phenomenon of invincible reluctance should be studied by anthropologists or psychologists. Examples follow:

I called up Chris Hedges, former *New York Times* Middle East bureau chief and author for a question he would have asked. He offered this one.

The Israeli government is imposing severe and continual collective punishment on the 1.5 million people of tiny Gaza, which includes restricting or cutting off food, fuel, electricity, medicines and other necessities. Malnutrition rates among many children resemble the worst of sub-Saharan Africa. Israel's leading newspaper, *Ha'aretz*, has reporters and columnists describing these horrific conditions and concluding that the ferocity of the blockade is detrimental to Israel as well as the Palestinians.

Collective punishment is clearly a violation of established international law. Prominent, former military, security and political leaders in Israel are speaking out against this punishment and calling for negotiations with Hamas. Do you, Senator Clinton and Senator Obama, agree with these Israelis or do you continue to support the policy of collective punishment against innocent men, women and children in Gaza?

The *Nation* magazine's columnist, Alex Cockburn suggested this question:

Senator Clinton, in all your previous debates, you have not criticized the bloated military budget so often documented by the media, Pentagon audits and GAO reports for Congress to be replete with waste fraud and abuse. The Soviet Union is gone. Yet military spending now consumes half of the federal government's operating expenditures.

Specifically, what would you do to significantly reduce the tens of billions of wasted dollars and eliminate redundant weapons systems?

And, further, would you abolish the missile defense project, deemed by the American

Physical Society and other leading physicists to be technically unworkable? It costs about $10 billion a year with a total expenditure of over $150 billion since its inception under Ronald Reagan, without any indication that it can fulfill the function for which it was designed? Please be specific.

□ □ □

Here are a few questions of my own. "Senator Obama, you have taught Constitutional law. Has President Bush violated the Constitution, federal statutes and international treaties during his two terms of office? If so, please elaborate and tell the American people what you think should be done about holding the self-described "responsibility" president accountable under the impeachment authority of Congress and other laws of the land?"

"Senator Clinton, you represent New York, which includes the large banking, brokerage and investment firms colloquially called Wall Street. Eliot Spitzer became Governor of your state largely on his widely reported reputation for prosecuting corporate crooks who fleeced investors, pensioners and workers of hundreds of billions of dollars. He often remarked that the federal criminal laws were too weak and the Securities and Exchange Commission was too lenient.

"As the Senator from New York, what specifically have you done to advance a strong crackdown on corporate crime with tougher laws and larger enforcement budgets? And, specifically, what do you intend to do as president?"

"Senator Obama, you have often spoken about your health insurance plan as a way to reduce costs. Yet you do not discuss three major cost reduction opportunities. The GAO, the investigative arm of Congress, estimates that 10 percent of the entire health expenditures in this country go down the drain due to computerized billing fraud and abuse. This year, that amounts to $220 billion.

"Under a single-payer plan, administrative expenses would be cut by about two-thirds. That would amount to hundreds of billions of dollars a year in savings. And the Harvard School of Public Health study estimates about 80,000 people die every year from medical malpractice in hospitals, estimating costs years ago of $60 billion a year. These are large savings in a $2.2 trillion a year healthcare industry.

"Do you agree and, if so, why have you ignored proposing practical actions in these areas?"

"Senator Clinton, you have long urged more money for children's programs. One way to make this possible is to end or diminish the complex system of corporate welfare—subsidies, handouts, giveaways and bailouts of business corporations. These amount to hundreds of billions of dollars a year, directly and through tax loopholes. Why have you not moved against such spending so that some of the money may go to help needy children? And specifically, what would you do as president to develop standards curtailing runaway corporate welfare programs pushed by corporate lobbyists?"

Is reportorial self-censorship limiting the questions presented to the presidential candidates? You decide.

Covering the Underdogs
December 10, 2007

Gail Collins, the columnist for the *New York Times* has a problem. While regularly writing in a satirical or sometimes trivial way about the foibles of the two major Parties' front-running presidential candidates, she can scarcely hide her disdain for the small starters, the under-dogs.

In a recent column about what she saw as the repetitiveness and small-mindedness of Hillary Clinton (and her spokesman), Barack Obama and John Edwards, she took this unexplained swipe at former Senator Mike Gravel's presence in a debate sponsored by National Public Radio:

"What the heck is Mike Gravel doing back on stage? Didn't we get rid of him ten or twenty debates ago?"

This dismissal may be seen by some readers as a laugh or as an impulsive throwaway line. Not so with Ms. Collins. She has little tolerance for filling media debate chairs with candidates; pundits, like her, believe candidates who are not front runners do not have a chance to overcome their super-low polls.

Nor does she lose any sleep over NBC (a subsidiary of General Electric) keeping the anti-nuclear Mr. Gravel out of its hosted debate in Philadelphia last month because he had not yet raised a million dollars.

Ms. Collins' treatment of the "second tier" candidates in the Democratic Party, such as Mike Gravel and Dennis Kucinich, is remarkable for at least three reasons.

First, although she is a more sand-papered progressive than in her more radical, younger days as a small starter reporting for the Connecticut State News Bureau, I'll bet she agrees with much of the two-time Senator Gravel's record in Congress and his present positions on the war in Iraq, presidential accountability, corporate power and crime and the mistreatment of workers, consumers and uninsured patients.

Second, for several years ending a few months ago, she presided over the *New York Times* editorial page, producing some of the finest editorials in the paper's history. Among many well con-sidered subjects, were included such as: standing up for whistle-blowers, dissenters, the rights of small business and workers and especially, the civil liberties and rights of minority voters afflicted with myriad electoral abuses and obstructions.

Thirdly, she has written a book about the history of women's rights in America—titled *America's Women* (William Morrow, 2003), which must have touched in a sensitive way those lonely self-starters, known as suffragettes, along with those very small parties and even smaller candidates pressing for the female voting franchise. She knows there are many ways to win short of winning an election.

In recent weeks, her paper's editorial page has delivered brilliant excoriations of the similarities in the converging Republican and Democratic parties, taking the latter severely to task on important national issues.

I doubt very much that Gail Collins disagrees with these editorials. In fact, privately she is known to be even more critical of the political status quo in this country. One might surmise that she should therefore welcome more voices and choices to come before the citizenry during election times, including more third party and independent candidates as well.

After all, aren't we all glad that ballot access was so much easier in the nineteenth century, and that small parties like the anti-slavery, women's rights, labor and farmer-populist parties got onto the ballots and pioneered hugely important agendas, ignored by the Democratic, Whig and Republican parties. These small starters never came close to winning the Presidency, except for the populist parties, winning many Congressional elections.

Put Gail Collins back into the nineteenth century and she would be whooping it up for those valiant few voters and little candidates who voted and ran against the grain of the business-indentured, often bigoted major Parties. Here in the twenty-first century, Gail Collins writes the predicates of progressive values and then sprawls to the dead-end conclusions—stay with the least-worst major party candidates.

Just as small seeds need a chance to sprout to regenerate nature and sustain humankind, just as the tiniest obusinesses need to have a chance to innovate in the business world, so too, small candidates need to have the chance. For they can often enrich the political dialogue, move the big boys to overdue recognitions, even if they do not have a chance to win on election day in a rigged, monetized, winner-take all system, bereft of both instant run-off voting and proportional representation procedures.

Columnists such as Gail Collins and her humane colleague, Bob Herbert, abhor going into these fields of political fertility. Instead, their rendition of political and corporate abuses flows into the repetitive, narrow ruts of political servility—not just the two party duopoly ruts but its major candidate groovers.

So progressive columnists, such as there are, wring their hands over why the Democratic Party, its incumbents and its major candidates do not heed their findings, their pleas, their hopes for the American people. They keep on wringing their hands until they encase their minds in a cul-de-sac that categorically disallows even a contemplation that political alternatives in person and party should be given visibility.

Open your mind a little, Gail Collins, and you might learn something about the need for frameworks that enable the sovereignty of the people to be expressed in a variety of practical ways, including national initiatives. You may laugh at Mike Gravel having difficulty explain-

ing his studious proposal for a national initiative during sound-bite debates. Instead, try writing a column on why some noted constitutional law professors believe there is a sound constitutional basis for such a proposal.

This would be a good way to spark a serious debate about the myth of government of the people, by the people and for the people. Such an excursus would help deepen a very shallow presidential campaign and be more becoming to you than wanting to rid Mike Gravel from the so-called debates. And you and the members of your profession, who regularly confess boredom with the major candidates, might actually find some excitement in your daily work.

The Best Editorials Money Can Buy

September 28, 2007

On September 26, 2007, the powerful National Association of Manufacturers (NAM) bought two pages in the *Wall Street Journal* to tout a prosperous, expanding group of member-companies producing products.

It occurred to me as I began reading the copy, that the NAM rarely bought expensive space like this in the *Journal*. Then after going through NAM's introductory message, I realized why they purchased the ad. Month after month in hundreds of loyal editorials the *Journal*'s editorial writers already have been conveying the cravings and demands of this trade association.

The parallels between this revenue-producing two page spread and the *Journal*'s opinion scribes, in contrast to its often sterling news pages, are the stuff of the corporate state.

The editorials argue for more "clean" coal and nuclear power and emphasize expanding production of US oil and natural gas with a token tip to renewables (with plenty of taxpayer subsidies).

So does the NAM.

NAM wants more so-called "free trade" agreements without recognizing, at the very least, that there can be no "free trade" with dictatorships like China. Dictatorial, oligarchic regimes determine wages, prevent free trade unions, and otherwise through grease and no-rule-of-law or access to justice, obstruct market-based costs and pricing.

So do the *Journal's* editorial writers.

In scores of frenzied editorials, the *Journal* assails tort law, tort attorneys and "unreasonable awards." Having read just about all these advertiser-friendly diatribes, I have yet to discern any data to back up their flood of declamations about "frivolous" litigation and "wild" awards.

Neither did the NAM produce any evidence about "lawsuit abuse" because the evidence points to declining product defect and malpractice suits, notwithstanding; that 90 percent of these injured people suffer without any legal claims filed on their behalf. (See: centerjd.org and citizen.org)

The *Journal's* rigid ideologues demand less regulation (read: less law and order for corporations) and the weakening of the Sarbanes-Oxley law enacted to deal modestly with part of the corporate crime wave of the past decade.

So does the NAM.

The NAM wants further reduction of the already reduced corporate tax rate and more taxpayer pay-out to corporations, including super-profitable ones like Intel, GE, Cisco and Pfizer. These latter windfalls are called research and development tax credits. How many Americans know that they are paying these and other super-profitable companies more money to make still more profits? Cisco does not even pay dividends.

So also demands the big business echo chamber on the *Journal's* editorial pages.

The *Journal* has been campaigning for years to end the estate tax which is so diluted that less than 2 percent of all estates have to pay anything to Uncle Sam. Conservative Republican wordsmith, Frank Luntz, in a moment of abandon, called lobbying an effort to end "the billionaires tax."

The NAM wants an end to the estate tax, even though none of its corporate-members ever has to pay an estate tax. For good measure, NAM wants to keep the maximum tax rates on investment income and capital gains at a level half of a worker's maximum tax rate. Far lower taxes on capital than on labor suits the NAM three-piece-suits just fine.

The *Journal* is for brain-draining developing countries. Drain those critical doctors, nurses, scientists, engineers, innovators and entrepreneurs from Asia, Africa and South America. Give them permanent visas and then wonder why those countries are having trouble fielding the skilled leaders needed to develop their own economies. It is easier than training talented minority youths in our country.

The NAM ad calls for "reform of the visa system to attract and retain global talent."

And so it goes. Such a symbiotic relationship! Big business members of NAM pour millions of dollars in ads daily into the Wall Street Journal. In return, the dutiful and gleeful editorial writers deliver the screeds that caress the brows and deepen the pockets of the CEOs.

There is another recurrent message in the insistent materials of NAM and its comrade-in-greed, the US Chamber of Commerce. Enough is never enough.

For over a quarter century, there has been more and more de-regulation (electricity, motor vehicles, coal, drugs, nuclear, occupational safety, pollution, aviation, rail, truck antitrust and more) with detriment to the health, safety and economic well-being of the American people. Still not enough, they say!

In the same period, you the taxpayer have been forced to have your tax dollars pour out of Washington and into the coffers of Big Business in a myriad of ways. Hundreds of billions of your dollars. Not enough, they say! They roar for more coddling.

You want chapter and verse, evidence and data? Get ready to read *Free Lunch*, a riveting new book by the Pulitzer-prize winning tax reporter for the *New York Times*, David Cay Johnston. It will be out in about two months; just in time for your gift-giving season.

GM Courts Talk Radio Hosts

August 10, 2007

Just when one guesses that the standards and practices of national talk radio could go no lower, General Motors comes along to show the way to new lows.

Automotive News (August 6, 2007), the leading trade journal for the industry, reports that GM is wooing the radio stars. Its article led with the headline: "Puff Piece. Rush Limbaugh is one of the radio personalities GM is working with to talk up its vehicles."

Reporter Mary Connelly writes that "GM says it doesn't pay the stars directly for their endorsements, although it advertises on their shows. It gives them new GM cars and trucks to drive for two weeks each month. The company also invites the celebrities to Detroit for private meetings with top executives and VIP tours of GM facilities. The attention is paying off."

Sam Mancuso, GM's director of brand marketing alliances, told Ms. Connelly that his company made contact with seventeen national radio hosts along with numerous local talk show personalities in cities such as Dallas and Los Angeles.

Mr. Mancuso is pleased with the results. The talkers are talking up GM vehicles on their programs—no doubt encouraged by GM's ample advertising budget on those same stations.

He emphasized that GM does not give these radio celebrities any scripts. Which allows for the kind of impromptu creativity that he said reflects a "real emotional connection" with an audience that "knows they are being genuine."

This is just what you need to know about a company's engineered vehicles—words which flow from an emotional connection garnished with free use of vehicles and other freebies!

Take Rush Limbaugh's effusions to his dittoheads: "GM has a ton of momentum," he exhaled, "GM cars and trucks have never been better." This assertion doesn't tell his followers much, however, inasmuch as GM's cars have never been hard acts to follow.

But Rush doesn't stop there. He waxes further: "They [GM] are working hard and they are thinking smart. Believe in General Motors, folks."

Before you can aspire to do that, you have to believe in Limbaugh and all the other talkers—takers of GM's largess. Atom Smasher, a modestly named Dallas disc jockey, was positively oozing on the air: "I am driving around in this Cadillac, and I am not going to want to give it back—the Cadillac SRX. . . . To all the guys at GM: Good job."

His crosstown colleague, Chris Ryan, might as well have been crossing over to his advertising buddies and doing the ad. But this was not ad time. This was program time when he declared: "Have you seen all the cool things that's going on at GM? I have. If you're thinking about a new car, you got to look at GM."

The auto industry has long been brazen when it comes to using its advertising clout. Way back when he was in Dayton, Ohio, Phil Donahue was cut off from car dealer ads after having a program on car dealer deception.

The *Washington Post* found local auto dealers going over to its smaller competitor, the *Washington Star* years ago, after a *Post* columnist tore into car dealer fraud. The dealers made it possible for the *Star* to start an auto puff section with their ads.

More than a few talk show hosts already read their station's ads. That's not enough. GM, viewing the inundation of product placements in movies, is pushing the envelope of advertising integration through talk radio program content.

What is surprising is that GM purportedly enlisted not only the expected suspects like Sean Hannity, Laura Ingraham and Bill O'Reilly but also Bill Press and Ed Schultz, know for their liberal views. Attempts to reach Press, Schultz and Hannity were unsuccessful. Surely, they will be explaining their relationship shortly.

In the radio music disc jockey world, taking such freebies would be considered payola to push songs. Under Federal Communications Commission (FCC) rules, such gifts would be illegal.

So, what about the talk radio arena? Good question. If the freebies are fully and regularly disclosed, then maybe there is a distinction between what is unlawful and what is unethical.

In any event, the FCC needs to investigate. Secretary of Commerce, Herbert Hoover, later to become president in the 1920s, called radio "a public trust." He believed the public airwaves,

being owned by the people, should convey no advertisements whatsoever.

What a gap between the arch-conservative, Herbert Hoover, and today's so-called conservative talk show gabbers!

Auctioning Journalistic Integrity
May 11, 2007

T. Christian Miller works hard year after year as a reporter for the *Los Angeles Times*. He has reported on topics ranging from gross corporate profiteering in Iraq to the production and use here and overseas of older, dangerous pesticides that are either shunned or restricted for use in this country.

Mr. Miller spent months of his life on this latter story. He cares about the well-being of his readers.

Working for the nine daily newspapers and twenty-three television stations owned by the *Tribune* company are hundreds of reporters who sweat the violent streets and neighborhoods, probe the corporate suites, and cover the doings of politicians. They also take some pretty dangerous assignments covering wars, riots and natural disasters in foreign countries.

Together with their editors and support staff, they have a very large stake in their company— both professionally and in terms of their livelihoods.

But they do not have any say about their future. A wealthy real estate speculator, Sam Zell, now has the say. And what he says in the coming months will decide who stays and who has to leave, what will be covered and what will be neglected, what stations and newspapers remain and which are sold off, what is left of any labor contracts, and what powerless new sharehold-ers—namely a corporate tax dodge in which ESOP members have to suffer without any voice.

Finally, Sam Zell has already decreed an ar-rangement that the *Tribune* company, still mak-ing money, will no longer have to pay federal income taxes to Uncle Sam on its profits.

One man, Sam Zell, has all this massive power, thanks to a legal system rigged in favor of capital—borrowed at that—and against labor that puts these newspapers and television sta-tions in front of you seven days a week.

The taking of the *Tribune* company private, via an exotically complex transaction, started with a sluggish stock price that the impatient Chandler family, who sold the *Los Angeles Times* to the *Tribune*, found intolerable. As the largest shareholders, the Chandler family was pressing for a restructuring of the company or an out-right sale.

Sam Zell won the auction in an $8.2 billion deal. Larded with tax avoidance schemes and hefty guarantees for Sam Zell, the new com-pany, if it clears regulatory approvals, will be loaded with huge debts (reaching $13 billion or ten times the *Tribune*'s annual cash flow).

How else could Sam Zell put only $315 mil-lion of his own money into the pot, most of it a loan no less, take control of this media con-glomerate as chairman of the board and retain the right later to buy 40 percent of the stock for only $500 million.

As an "S" corporation with a porous and powerless employee stock ownership plan, or ESOP, "the company is treated, effectively, like a charity. It'll be a tax-exempt entity," declared Robert Willens of Lehman Brothers. See what a bargain Washington is for corporatists making campaign contributions year after year.

Mr. Willens adds "This is going to be the wave of the future." Unless, I might add, work-ers politically organize and campaigns become publicly funded, instead of being offered to the highest cash bidders.

Under Mr. Zell's plan, the employees will no longer receive 401(k) contributions from the company. They will not be permitted to cash in any of their shares for a decade or more—and then only if they retire or have worked for the *Tribune* for at least ten years. They are trapped by Zell who has veto power over all major decisions.

Immediately, there were reports of more staff cuts at the newspapers which already have suf-fered losses of reporters and editors in recent years. The most experienced reporters and edi-tors are usually the first to go.

Sam Zell says he is in this private buyout to make more money, not for pushing any journal-istic ideology. So the questions and the rumors are circulating in the newsrooms.

Will Sam Zell sell off the *Los Angeles Times* or the *Baltimore Sun* or the *Hartford Courant* to local wealthies? What will happen to the workers if that happens, especially if these new spinoffs are loaded further with debt? Will the newsrooms be further stripmined?

Sam Zell will decide. The media has been taken over in the past by larger media, by indus-trial companies like General Electric, by enter-tainment companies like Disney.

Now it is being taken over by tax-avoiding speculators whose monetized mind sweeps aside the fiduciary duties of journalism that is sup-posed to nurture a trust so important that our founding fathers made it the only business pro-tected by the First Amendment.

When Rupert Murdoch's News Corp. re-cently offered to buy the Dow Jones & Co. (publisher of the *Wall Street Journal*) for $5 billion, sharply elevating its share prices, recently retired chairman, Peter Kann, wrote to the majority shareholding Bancroft family applauding their initial rejection of the offer and calling their continued ownership "a public trust.... There is a higher calling to what the people of Dow Jones do each day. They are not merely producing and selling products like corn flakes or computer chips."

Mr. Kann went on to say that the reporters and editors of the *Journal* could have made more money as lawyers or bankers. But they chose to devote their careers "to something more important." So too he urged the Bancrofts to "forego some financial benefits" for other "even higher priorities."

What now with the *Tribune*'s workers and their "higher priorities?" Some are hoping that their newspapers will be sold to local buyers by Sam Zell.

Don't bet on the results if this happens. Ted Venetoulis, speaking for a group of investors in Baltimore, interested in the *Baltimore Sun*, told the *New York Times*, in reaction to Zell's deal: "Why didn't I think of that?"

Outrageous Words, Outrageous Deeds

April 16, 2007

Now that the Don Imus flameout has once again demonstrated that vile words energize many activist groups and many media more than do devastating deeds, it is useful to revisit this strange dimension of public furor.

The latest three word outburst in Mr. Imus' practice of sexist and racist remarks may be compared with the continuing sexist and racist behaviors that civic opponents would argue

should at the very least receive equal time from those who become indignant over cruel, bigoted language.

On March 18, the *New York Times* ran a lengthy cover story in its heralded Sunday Magazine about widespread sexual harassment and rape of female US soldiers by their male colleagues in Iraq. Written by a reporter, Sarah Corbett, the article combined the available official studies, and statements of specialists, with poignant narratives by women soldiers whom she interviewed intensively.

The evidence she amassed included a report in 2003, funded by the Department of Defense (DOD), which declared that nearly one-third of a nationwide sample of female veterans seeking healthcare through the VA said they experienced rape or attempted rape during their service. Of that group, 37 percent said they were raped multiple times, and 14 percent reported they were gang-raped.

A change in DOD policy in 2005 allowing sexual assaults to be reported confidentially in "restricted reports" led to the number of reported assaults across the military rising 40 percent.

There are still many reasons why female soldiers are reluctant to report sexual violence, especially in combat zones. Solidarity is survival. Complaining about your superior or soldiers of comparable ranking ruptures the working hierarchy and its military mission. In addition, it is often the woman's word against the man's word. As one sailor told Ms. Corbett, "You just don't expect anything to be done about it anyway, so why even try?" She said she was raped at a naval base on Guam.

Female soldiers coming back from Iraq relate their fears of even going to the latrines in the middle of the night for the fear of being sexually assaulted.

Sexual violence is often dismissed as fabricated, exaggerated or consensual. It is important not to tarnish many upstanding and respectful male soldiers and sailors with sweeping generalizations.

Abbie Pickett, who is a twenty-four-year-old combat-support specialist with the Wisconsin Army National Guard, told Ms. Corbett: "You're one of three things in the military—a bitch, a whore or a dyke. As a female, you get classified pretty quickly."

Particularly since the Tailhook episode in 1991 which involved sexual violence against women at a naval party, the Pentagon has become more concerned about such assaults. There are far more women in areas of combat now as well. Over 160,000 women have seen active duty in Iraq and Afghanistan already.

Bottom line to all the reports—official and individual—was summarized by the *New York Times* this way: "Many have reported being sexually assaulted, harassed and raped by fellow soldiers and officers." (For more information see democracyrising.us)

Assault and rape are crimes, deeds of devastating impact on the lives of these young women. They are not just vile words. Yet in the month since the *New York Times* article was published, there has been almost no public outrage and no demands for more investigation, more corrective action, more law enforcement.

The members of Congress—women and men—have not mobilized for action. The press did not follow up on the article—"The Women's War" by Ms. Corbett. The National Organization of Women (NOW) condemned Don Imus in no uncertain terms. They have not yet demanded multiple actions to be taken on this continuing violence against women.

Aside from the indifference of the male legislators, Congress is now graced by the largest number of women lawmakers in its history. The Speaker of the House is a woman—Nancy Pelosi. Sure, she has her hands full with the Iraq War. But this is an internal war against many women who need her leadership and her status to spark remedial or preventative action.

Words inflaming more than deeds is also too often the case when racial epithets are uttered by public figures. All those groups and civil rights leaders who conquered and ended the Don Imus media empire should ask themselves what have they done in any sustained manner, given their power and media access, about the brutality of racism by commercial interests in the urban ghettos. Deaths, injuries, disease and loss of livelihood are a daily occurrence, apart from raw street crime and drugs. Little children seriously poisoned by lead, asbestos and other toxics. Whole neighborhoods redlined without adequate corporate police protection. Predatory lending, predatory interest rates, marketing shoddy products and contaminated food proliferate.

Where have been the cries of outrage, the demands for removal of these conditions and prosecution of these crooks and defrauders? The abysmal conditions are daily, weekly, monthly. They have been occasionally reported in gripping human interest terms and statistics and maps.

If only the offenders had used words, instead of committing these awful deeds. Maybe there would have been action, front page headlines and prime time television and radio coverage. If only they had used words!

The Binary Media

JUne 19, 2006

You have noticed, to be sure, how our nation's politics gravitates the binary position year after year. Webster's dictionary defines "binary" as "something made of two things or parts." So, parties, politicians and voters are overwhelmingly either characterized as conservative—right wing or liberal left-wing.

I've never thought the binary approach was very useful; it is too abstract, too far from the facts on the ground, too stereotypical of variations within each category, and too constricting of independent thought that is empirically nourished.

What helps keep binary descriptions going, however, are desires for convenient narratives. So here is one to ponder.

Different aspects of our culture attract either mostly conservatives or liberals or, at least, are identified with one or the other political philosophies or self-characterizations.

Liberals are more identified with popular music—the more risqué or hip-hop, the more the label is applied. So too with movies on abuses of power by corporations and government. *The China Syndrome, Norma Rae, Grapes of Wrath* of years ago. Too many to recount today out of Hollywood.

When it comes to humor, the leaning is liberal whether on the monologues of late-night entertainment hosts, the Jon Stewart, and Stephen Colbert shows, *Saturday Night Live* or the *Al Franken Show*. It's harder to poke fun at established power from a right-wing standpoint.

Documentaries are hands down in the embrace of the liberal-progressive producers. Recent titles include *The Corporation, An Inconvenient Truth, Who Killed the Electric Car?, This Land is Your Land, The Take* and, of course, *Fahrenheit 9/11*.

The larger, more reported political websites seem to lean toward liberal-progressive, the rumor-mill, "Matt Drudge Report" withstanding. *Daily Kos* and the *Huffington Post* are on the ascendancy.

On the other side of the binary, the conservative-corporate worldview dominates radio talk shows and cable talk shows. Just list the hosts—Limbaugh, Hannity, O'Reilly (though less so), and all the way down the ratings ladder.

The most politically motivated and get-out-the-vote people in the neighborhoods, when the chips are down, have been from the conservative communities. Ask the Democrats who had to rely on imported activists (Ohio in 2004) while their Republican opponents relied on people living in the Buckeye State.

Politically-active church pews are filled more with conservatives than with liberals. These are the people who have partially taken over the Republican Party and who supply the motivated cadres before Election Day.

Symbols of patriotism—often shorn of substantive follow-up—belong to conservatives. The flag, singing anthems, parading on the 4th of July, Memorial Day and Veterans Day belong to the people who describe themselves more on the right side of the binary, who would more often describe themselves as conservatives. So too is the case with membership in the American Legion and the VFW. So too as well with membership in the Main Street service clubs—Rotary, Kiwanis and Lions International.

It is fair to say that since 1980, conservative candidates have been winning overall more than have liberal candidates. From the presidency to the Congress to the state legislatures to the governorships, this trend has been much reported.

Moreover, the liberals who do win, like Clinton, Lieberman, Bayh and assorted governors are often more corporatists than liberals on major subjects such as foreign policy, military budgets, the Federal Reserve, corporate welfare, real regulation, tax policy and consumer protection.

It could be that more often than is normally recognized, the self-described conservative voters spend more time personally interacting with one another in situations where "social" can easily move to "political."

More often than the liberal voters, they participate in activities associated with clubs, and churches where person to person conversations abound.

The above areas of liberal domination involve more passive, spectator, celluloid or "cool" internet occasions. And after a while a chronically humorous way of looking at politics becomes a distraction, even though it may be a style that avoids commercial media censorship.

Of course, money in politics comes more easily to corporatist candidates, as does the media. For example, extreme right-wingers get on talk shows, receive media attention or have their own profitable shows like Pat Robertson does. Who are the extreme left-wingers, who receive any press, other than an occasional newspaper picture showing them being dragged away from a protest at the IMF, World Bank or toxic dump site?

The lesson? Politics, even in an age of electronic supremacy, is still strongly moved by the person-to-person, conversational, affinity, communal groupings in our society. Big TV ads cost money and the corporatists can buy them over and over again. But the word of mouth from friend to friend, relative to relative, neighbor to neighbor and worker to worker is not something anyone wants to sell short.

The Dixie Chicks

June 9, 2006

Who would have thought when the Dixie Chicks were selling more than 10 million copies each of "Wide Open Spaces" (1998) and "Fly" (1999) that they would become the most controversial band in America?

Even more improbable was the likelihood that three young women would have the strength of character and personality to stand their ground after the continuing uproar against them by scores of radio DJs and many of their fans.

What provoked the furor was a single sentence by their lead singer—Natalie Maines—uttered onstage in London ten days before Bush's illegal, unconstitutional and fabricated invasion of Iraq on March 20, 2003.

Here is what Ms. Maines, a native Texan, said: "Just so you know, we're ashamed the president of the United States is from Texas."

Those fifteen words must have cost her and her fellow players, Emily Robison and Martie Maguire, at least three million dollars a word so far. Most bands would have retreated, begged for forgiveness and eaten humble pie.

Not these ladies of steel. After taking some time off—Ms. Robison and Ms. Maguire had twins—the Dixie Chicks have come back with their new album, "Taking the Long Way" which has topped the charts in its first two weeks. "We could have pandered," said Ms. Maines to the *New York Times*. They did just the opposite. No apologies. Words of defiance and staying true to themselves flow through the lyrics.

In composing their songs, the remarkable Dixie Chicks told their record company that "We need to approach everything like not one radio station is going to play one single song."

Conviction triumphed over commercialism. Ms. Maines, when asked about country radio, retorted, "Do you really think we're going to make an album for you and trust the future of our career to people who turned on us in a day?"

Well, it's probably what many in the music industry thought they would do. Especially the DJs who boycotted playing their records after "The Incident" in 2003. You can imagine what these DJs thought when they first heard the first single "Not Ready to Make Nice," which cries, "I'm not ready to back down/I'm still mad as hell."

So more furor, more boycotts by DJs, and more backlash in some cities, leading to cancellations due to faltering concert sales. Dropped from their forthcoming "North American Accidents and Accusations Tour" are St. Louis, Oklahoma City, Indianapolis and Memphis.

No doubt, when music fans don't hear the songs on their favorite radio stations, tickets sales will not be as robust. The DJs, a mixed breed apart, were not talking, just boycotting. It was not clear whether they themselves wanted to boycott or whether they were just reacting to outraged emails and calls. Either way, it doesn't deter the Dixie Chicks who are showing they say what they mean and mean what they say.

Now take a larger frame of reference. For the Dixie Chicks it meant not backing down on an issue of free speech. On March 12, 2003, Ms. Maines explained why she spoke the sentence: "I feel the president is ignoring the opinion of many in the US and alienating the rest of the world. My comments were made in frustration, and one of the privileges of being an American is you are free to voice your own point of view."

Lots of Americans were frustrated. Groups representing millions of Americans—veterans, labor, women, students, religionists, business, and others—asked to meet with President Bush before the invasion. The American Caesar turned them all down. He knew it all. Then he blew it all and millions of Iraqis and tens of thousands of Americans are paying a severe price for this pig-headed corporate militarist.

Hundreds of thousands gone or wounded, sickened, homeless in Iraq. Fifty thousand American soldiers wounded, sickened or chronically mentally traumatized. And in the next few days, the 2,500th American soldier will lose his or her life over there.

The Iraq War-quagmire continues its devastating drain on American taxpayers—tax dollars drained away from being used for life and health and other necessities here at home.

The National Council of Churches is now urging its member churches to ring the bells of remembrance on the tragic occasion of the 2,500th fatality. Over 65 percent of the American people are opposed to the war.

Retired Generals, diplomats and national security advisers have spoken against this boomerang war imperiling our national security. But the carnage continues on the orders of the two draft-dodgers George W. Bush and Dick Cheney.

Compare all these cruel Bush deeds to the mild words of the Dixie Chicks. Compare all this, plus the Bush corporation's refusal to stand for the rights of workers and consumers—their health, safety and economic well-being, as he cuts taxes again and again for the wealthy and himself.

Compare the huge taxes that will be paid for the massive Bush deficit by the children of those music fans angry at the Dixie Chicks.

While they keep standing up for George W. Bush, does it ever occur to them to demand that George W. Bush stand up for them?

Time to Impeach

December 23, 2005

Richard Cohen, the finely-calibrated syndicated columnist for the *Washington Post*, wrote a column on October 28, 2004 which commenced with this straight talk: "I do not write the headlines for my columns. Someone else does. But if I were to write the headline for one, it would be 'Impeach George Bush'."

Cohen stated the obvious then. Bush and Cheney had plunged the nation into war "under false pretenses." Exploiting the public trust in the presidency, Bush had persuaded, over the uncritical mass media, day after day, before the war, a majority of the American people that Saddam Hussein possessed chemical, biological weapons and nuclear weapons programs, was connected to al-Qaeda and 9/11 and was a threat to the United States.

These falsehoods, Cohen wrote, "are a direct consequence of the administration's repeated lies—lies of commission, such as Cheney's statements, and lies of omission."

Fourteen months later, no widely syndicated columnist or major newspaper editorial has called for the impeachment of George W. Bush and Dick Cheney. Not even Cohen again. Yet the case for impeachment is so strong that, recently, hardly a day goes by without more disclosures which strengthen any number of impeachable offenses that could form a Congressional action under our Constitution. An illegal war, to begin with, against our Constitution which says only Congress can declare war. An illegal war under domestic laws, and international law, and conducted illegally under international conventions to which the US belongs, should cause an outcry against this small clique of outlaws committing war crimes who have hijacked our national government.

Under established international law—an illegal, criminal war means that every related US death and injury, every related Iraqi civilian death and injury, every person tortured, every home and building destroyed become war crimes as a result.

There are those on talk radio or cable shows who scoff at international law. They rarely tell their audiences that the United States has played a key role in establishing these treaties, like the Geneva Conventions, and the United Nations Charter. When these treaties are agreed to by the US government, they become as binding as our federal laws.

By these legal standards and by the requirements of the US Constitution (Article 1, Section 8, the war-declaring authority), George W. Bush and Dick Cheney are probably the most impeachable president and vice president in American history. An illegal war based on lies, deceptions, cover-ups and their repetition even after being told by officials in their own administration—not to mention critical retired generals, diplomats and security specialists—of their falsity should have prodded the House of Representatives into initiating impeachment proceedings. But then, Bush did not lie under oath about sex.

A majority of the American people have turned against this war-quagmire, against its intolerable human and economic costs, against the increased danger this war is bringing to our nation's interests. They want the soldiers to return safely home. In increasing numbers they sense what Bush's own CIA Director, Porter Goss, told the US Senate last February. He noted, along with other officials since then, that US soldiers in Iraq are like a magnet attracting and training more terrorists from more countries who will return to their nations and cause trouble. Many national security experts have said, in effect, you do not fight terrorists with policies that produce more terrorists.

Now comes the most recent, blatant impeachable offense—Bush ordering the spying on Americans in our country by the National Security Agency. This disclosure stunned many N.S.A. staff who themselves view domestic surveillance as anathema, according to Matthew M. Aid, a current historian of the agency.

Domestic eavesdropping on Americans by order of the president to the National Security Agency violates the twenty-seven-year-old Foreign Intelligence Surveillance Act unless they obtain a warrant from the Foreign Intelligence Surveillance Act (FISA) Court. This court meets in secret and has rejected only four out of 19,000 applications.

So why did Bush violate this law and why does he defiantly say he will continue to order domestic spying as he has since 2002? Not because the FISA Court is slow. It acts in a matter of hours in the middle of the night if need be. The law actually permits surveillance in emergencies as long as warrants are requested within seventy-two hours or fifteen days in times of war.

Bush violated the law because of the arrogance of power. Ostensibly, he believes that a vague Congressional resolution after 9/11 to fight al-Qaeda overrides this explicit federal law and the Fourth Amendment to the Constitution. Bush even claims he can unilaterally decide to domestically spy (from the inherent powers of the presidency) to fight wars. (To him Congressionally-undeclared wars are still wars).

Other than his legal flaks in the White House and Justice Department making such transparently specious arguments as "good soldiers", the overwhelming position of legal scholars is that Bush and Cheney have violated grave laws protecting the liberties of the American people.

The crime, says Professor David Cole of Georgetown Law School, is "punishable by five years in prison." Professor Jonathan Turley of George Washington University Law School said that the president ordered such a crime and ordered US officials to commit it . . . this is a serious felony . . . what happened here is not just a violation of Federal law, it's a violation of the US Constitution . . . an impeachable offense."

It matters not that a Republican-dominated Congress has no present interest in moving to impeach Bush-Cheney. What matters is that impeachment in this case—based on the authority of Congress to charge the president and vice president with "high crimes and misdemeanors"—is a patriotic cause rooted in the wisdom of our founding fathers who did not want another King George III in the guise of a president.

As Senator Russell Feingold said a few days ago: The president is not a king, he is a president subject to the laws and Constitution of the land. Apparently, George W. Bush seems to believe and behave as if his unlimited inherited powers flow from King George III, given the way he has shoved aside both federal law and the nation's Constitution.

Both George W. Bush and Dick Cheney should resign. They have disgraced their office and bled the nation. They have shattered the public trust in so many serious ways that will only become worse in the coming months.

What the Media Misses
December 9, 2005

There are times when unchallenged commercial greed morphs into institutional insanity. I am referring to the overall advertising-saturated, trivialized performance of the media conglomerates' utilization of our public airwaves twenty-four hours a day and their dominance of the ever-expanding scores of cable channels.

Take a test. If you are an average consumer of TV or radio broadcasts or newspapers and magazines, you are ready for your exam. Have you ever seen coverage of the following three long-standing civic organizations which work on fulfilling our society's needs and failures?

Lois Gibbs came out of the struggle over Love Canal's toxified residential neighborhoods to start and lead the nationwide Center for Health, Environment and Justice (CHEJ) in Falls Church, Virginia. Over the years the Center has organized thousands of small but vigorous community groups who are challenging and stopping the presence of toxic chemical particulates and gases in largely lower-income neighborhoods. Gibbs and her associates have trained thousands of ordinary people committed to protecting their families and educated scores of communities about the nature of these toxins and what can be done about them with law, action and exposure.

They have victory after victory to show for their efforts, but so intense and widespread has been the poisoning of America over the decades by corporate polluters that there is always more to discover and do.

Right now, the Center has its community associations "fighting to block local schools from being built on contaminated land in Alabama, New Jersey, Massachusetts, and Rhode Island." CHEJ's new report—"Building Safe Schools: Invisible Threats, Visible Actions"—covers the laws and situations in fifty states. Here is one example of many:

In Birmingham, Alabama, Wenonah High School is being constructed on contaminated soil. The site is also across the street from the largest gasoline storage facility in the state and is adjacent to a railroad track and a junkyard. The site was further contaminated this past July by a gas spill when a train and gas truck collided right in front of the future school.

For more information, see www.childproofing.org.

For an astoundingly-optimistic demonstration of what science can do for the people, consider the Appalachia Science in the Public Interest (ASPI) out of Livingston, Kentucky. Founded in the '70s by one of our former public interest scientists, Dr. Albert Fritsch, ASPI has shown what can be done for peoples' houses, cars, and larger buildings with "proven energy conservation, healthy home and renewable energy solutions." It connects "consumers with marketers of related products and services."

It is the moving force, with state agencies, renewable-energy companies and college institutions, behind the annual Bluegrass Energy Expo. The 2005 event featured, among others, the University of Kentucky College of Engineering Solar Car. The Expo has taught many people in what one writer called "a rich land with poor people" about sustainable forests, water purification and conservation. It is a very hands-on organization that makes you want to obtain its recommended products immediately. See its web site: www.aspi.org.

In Washington, DC another unsung group of Americans is working hard at the National Coalition for the Homeless (NCH).

There are hundreds of thousands of homeless people in our wealthy country. According to the Homeless Coalition, "60 percent are living in emergency shelter or transitional housing, and 40 percent are living on the streets. The majority, 53 percent are single adults, 42 percent are families and 5 percent are homeless/runaway youth."

Hurricanes Katrina and Rita, says NCH, "multiplied the homeless population along the Gulf Coast by as much as a hundred fold." All this is in the face of the Bush regime's proposed slicing of federal subsidies for housing by 40 percent. That proposal, sent to Congress, does not cut the burgeoning budget for the number one occupant of public housing—George W. Bush in the White House.

NCH reports, organizes and lobbies all over the country. They are supporting legislation, introduced by Rep. Julia Carson (D-Ind.), that "tackles the root causes of homelessness and poverty in this nation." For more on NCH, see its web page: www.nationalhomeless.org.

Now back to the mostly maniacal mass media's priorities. Ninety percent of radio and television are devoted to advertisements and entertainment. Often the rest is staccato news, weather and sports repeated throughout the day. There are, of course, the sterling exceptions such as weekly sections of *60 Minutes* or the two-and-a-half minute investigations on the network nightly TV news.

Cable is a widening wasteland, with info-mercials (bracelets and necklaces, etc.), re-run movies, sports and comedy shows, and endless silly drivel. Many new cable channels are added, but there will not be any devoted to the wholesome activities and successes of groups such as the aforementioned to lift up people, get them more active and introduce the young to practical citizenship that solves serious problems.

That is, not until enough people around America become serious about the need for serious media and reassert some control over the public airwaves they own and the rent-free li-

censes given out to radio and television companies by the Federal Communications Commission. Communities that negotiate franchise agreements with cable companies also need to feel the enlightened heat of local residents and neighborhood groups.

It is ours for the demanding. Let's start demanding.

The Corporate Controlled Media
November 25, 2005

The debate between progressives and corporatists over the state of the mass media goes like this—the former say fewer and fewer giant media conglomerates control more of the print and electronic outlets while the latter respond by saying there has never been more choices for listeners (radio), viewers (television) and readers (magazines, newsletters and newspapers combined).

Progressives add that half a dozen big companies, which control so many media, lead to a sameness of entertainment, news and advertisement overload. Corporatists counter by saying that there are more and more specialized media available for just about every taste in the audience.

I want to take a different approach here from my personal experience with the fourth estate and appearing before national audiences. There has been a non-stop decline in access for serious subjects of contemporary importance, especially those topics that challenge corporate power.

Starting in the mid-'60s until the 1980s, the major daytime television entertainment shows were open to people with causes and authors with books. the *Mike Douglas Show* had me and my associates on during programs that featured high-profile entertainers such as John Lennon and the Jacksons. So did the *Merv Griffin Show* and others of a lesser note.

The *Phil Donahue Show* opened to national debate one controversial issue after another—women's liberation, consumer labor, environmental, LGBTQ, anti-war, education, race and verboten diseases. Still Phil managed his share of titillating breakthroughs, including male strippers, along with the staples of fashion shows and celebrities.

No more. Replacing these shows are the sado-masochistic bizzaro shows like Jerry Springer's show or the warm and cuddly Oprah presentations or the middle ground parade of entertainment and celebrity performances such as *Montel Williams' Show*. There is virtually no chance of even getting one's calls returned; the producers have their formulae for shows on a revolving turnstile and need no further suggestions.

Montel Williams used to have a consumer advice show once in a while on matters that shoppers really care about—whether they relate to health, child safety or widely experienced rip-offs in the marketplace. Now, someone as towering and communicative as Dr. Sidney Wolfe of Public Citizen cannot even get on these shows, including Oprah's, when he releases his spectacular new editions of *Worst Pills Best Pills*.

During the '80s and early '90s, Dr. Wolfe would take his life-saving, massive, inexpensive book onto the *Donahue Show*. There, in a gripping interaction with Phil and patients in the audience, he would communicate to millions how to use the information. He showed how to avoid drugs with bad side effects on select drugs with few side effects, though all were approved by the Food and Drug Administration for dozens of ailments such as high blood pressure, chronic pain, colds, allergies, diabetes, infec-

tions, osteoporosis, vitamin deficiencies, depression, heart conditions and eye disorders.

This show produced great ratings and the largest number of audience inquiries and orders in the history of the *Donahue Show*. Dr. Wolfe recently came out with his latest edition of *Worst Pills, Best Pills*. None of the daily afternoon shows would have him on, even though more people are taking more drugs than ever before and adverse side-effects are growing in lethality.

Exclusion is the experience of many other prominent authors and advocates. Food and health writer, Jean Carper, who has had numerous best sellers to her credit, in part from appearing in major television shows, scarcely appears today. Authors of great contemporary research and substance, including William Grieder, Jim Hightower and Robert Kuttner, used to introduce their books on the national morning talk shows. No more. They're lucky to even get on the *Charlie Rose Show*—perhaps the only frequently serious over-the-air daily national television talk show left in the United States—population nearly 300 million! These morning network shows are heavily into entertainment, celebrities, when not reporting some important news.

Why, even humorist Art Buchwald, whose many books used to be staples of the afternoon entertainment shows, has been unable for years to sneak by the congealed silliness that swarms onto their stages. The audiences have become so hyped with the weird and sexual that the funny Buchwald is not seen as being able "to hold the audience."

Last week, Ted Koppel signed off a quarter century of anchoring ABC's *Nightline*. In his place, where for some twenty-two minutes an important contemporary situation or conflict was analyzed, will be a show with a lighter mix of segments. Who knows how long this experiment in reduced attention span will last?

"Dumbing down the audience" is the infelicitous phrase used by some media critics. You expect less and less of your audience and that is the audience you'll get. This also holds true for the evening television news which blots out civic actions in the home city in favor of ample sports, lengthy weather times, street crime, light news, a health story, an animal story and up to a minute of contrived, spontaneous chitchat between the anchors.

All this junk television is transmitted, without the stations paying rent, to us for the public airwaves that we the people own.

The examples abound. The point is clear. Overweening commercialism, a docile Federal Communications Commission, an unenforced Communications Act of 1934, and an unorganized viewer-listenership are leaving diverse thinkers and doers without a national or even a local audience.

We, the most powerful, technologically-equipped nation on Earth are left with C-SPAN and the suggestion that we can always start our own blog. Folks, they're laughing at us and taking their hilarity all the way to the bank—at our expense and that of our children's futures.

Passing The Buck
May 14, 2005

An astonishing message came forth on May 12, 2005 from ABC News political unit's *The Note*. I shall quote verbatim from Mark Halperin and his associate editors:

> We say with all the genuine apolitical and nonpartisan human concern that we can muster that the death and carnage in Iraq is truly staggering. But we are sort of resigned to the no-

tion that it simply isn't going to break through to American news organizations, or, for the most part, Americans.

Democrats are so thoroughly spooked by John Kerry's loss—and Republicans so inspired by their stay-the-course Commander in Chief—that what is hands down the biggest story every day in the world will get almost no coverage. No conflict at home = no coverage.

How to respond? There are several ways. First, ABC is right in saying there is no opposition party on the Iraq War, as a party. From the Democratic National Committee to the Democratic leadership in the House and Senate, the party line is "wish Bush success, support the troops to die and destroy in Iraq, and keep voting $80 billion or more a year for that illegal quagmire which is breeding more terrorists and is turning the world against Washington."

That is not exactly the way the Democrats are verbalizing their position, but that is what they are doing and what they are thinking in private conversations, whatever the semantic gloss they are applying.

The Democrats are taking this prolonged dive in spite of a growing majority of Americans wanting out of Iraq, now believing it was a mistake to invade Iraq (since there are no WMDs or al-Qaeda connections), and even larger majorities do not think the war-occupation is worth the price in human casualties and taxpayer dollars needed here at home.

Moreover, most of the retired Generals, Admirals, diplomatic and intelligence officials were against this war of choice from the beginning and believed it was our national security interests.

What more do the Democrats need to take a stand, to demand a responsible exit strategy with a timetable so as to give Iraq back to

the Iraqis and pull the bottom out of the resistance? Well, what about massive corruption and waste by the Halliburtons and other
corporations ripping off Uncle Sam and you
the taxpayers. Maybe the Democratic leadership should pause in their incessant fundraising from corporate interests and read the daily
documentation of this corruption and waste by
their own Cong. Henry Waxman (D-Calif.)
(see   www.democrats.reform.house.gov/in-
vestigations.asp?Issue=Iraq=Reconstruction).
And what about Bush not supporting the
troops—first by putting them in harm's way
with an illegal war, then not providing them
with adequate body armor and vehicle armor
(outraging military families in their grief), then
cutting their health benefits and other services
when they come back home?

And what about the first president in US history deliberately lowballing US casualties so as
not to further arouse public opposition to his
war crimes? American men and women injured,
sickened or severely mentally traumatized in
Iraq, but not in actual combat, are not counted in the casualty toll. Tens of thousands not
counted, disrespecting them and their parents.

What else do the Democrats need to jettison
their chronic cowardliness? Well they can sign
on to the House Congressional Resolution 35,
urging Bush "to develop and implement a plan
to begin the immediate withdrawal of US armed
forces from Iraq. Led by Rep. Lynn Woolsey
and about thirty other Democrats, the party can
at least take this modest step.

Or they can hold Senator John W. Warner
(R-Va.), Senator John McCain (R-Ariz.) and
Senator Lindsey O. Graham (R-S.C.) to their
strong determination last year to hold anyone
culpable for torture at Abu Ghraib and other
prisons accountable, no matter how senior. Tor-

ture policies, lack of proper supervision from the
top of the Bush regime, and ignoring information brought to their attention by human rights
groups have ranged from Guantanamo to Iraq
to Afghanistan, repeated documentation demonstrates. This is a no-fault, out of control Bush
government. Yet the Democratic Party sleeps.

Still, is ABC's excuse wholly understandable?
Can't this and other networks do much more to
investigate what has been going on and then ask
the Democrats when they interview them about
their findings? Can't the networks provide more
coverage to the conflict represented by the dissenting military families, by the coalitions of
labor, religious, civic, veterans and other groups
(see veteransforpeace.org and DemocracyRis-
ing.us).

These same networks certainly did not show
such inhibitions when they went out of their
way day after day to celebrate the coming invasion of Iraq and not question the unsupported
claims for going to war by Bush, Cheney, Rice,
Rumsfeld and Powell. The networks in varying
decrees were either cheerleaders or ditto machines.

Passing the buck can be very costly to the
American people's right to know—in time.

Hear Ye Media!
April 15, 2005

Question, have you ever heard of Maurice Hilleman? If your answer is "no" or "who?," join
about 99 percent of the American people. He
passed away this month in Philadelphia at the
age of eighty-five. Here is what the front page
New York Times article said about his medical
career:

Dr. Maurice R. Hilleman developed vaccines for mumps, measles, chickenpox, pneumonia, meningitis and other diseases, saving tens of millions of lives . . .

Much of modern preventive medicine is based on Dr. Hilleman's work, though he never received the public recognition of Salk, Sabin or Pasteur. He is credited with having developed more human and animal vaccines than any other scientist, helping to extend human life expectancy and improving the economies of many countries.

The *Times* quotes Dr. Anthony Fauci of the National Institutes of Health as saying: "The scientific quality and quantity of what he did was amazing . . . One can say without hyperbole that Maurice changed the world with his extraordinary contributions in so many disciplines: virology, epidemiology, immunology, cancer research and vaccinology."

His associates, whom he regularly credited for their contributions, marveled at his artistry in safely producing large quantities of weakened live or dead micro-organisms. Dr. Hilleman credited his skills wryly to growing up on a farm in Montana where he worked as a boy with chickens. Chicken eggs are the fertilizing sites for many vaccines.

There are many fascinating stories about this scientist. Yet almost no one knew about him, saw him on television, or read about him in newspapers or magazines. His anonymity, in comparison with Madonna, Michael Jackson, Jose Canseco, or an assortment of grade B actors, tells something about our society's and media's concepts of celebrity; much less of the heroic.

This is not a frivolous observation. Bringing the work of individuals who matter to so many people on the important issues of lives and livelihoods is a prime way of educating the citizenry about important matters. Media trumpeting of Madonna's latest escapades alerts and motivates the public quite differently than highlighting the frequent breakthroughs of a scientist like Dr. Hilleman. The former sells records and pulp magazines, the latter keeps the American people more knowledgeable about the critical perils that confront them if recognition and resources are not dedicated to their prevention.

Today, in America, there are tens of billions of dollars being spent and misspent on the struggle against stateless terrorists. Despite being warned repeatedly by the Centers for Disease Control and the World Health Organization, the Bush Administration is reacting feebly to the avian flu risks coming from the Far East. Already having taken nearly one hundred lives, should this avian flu mutate with a human virus, a deadly pandemic could sweep the world with tens of millions of fatalities.

I have written thrice to President Bush about the need to launch a war against this kind of microscopic terrorism by diversifying his speeches and making room for a major national address on this subject. He could put forth a program of greater support for training more infectious diseases specialists and working with other countries for an early alert system so that the requisite quarantines and vaccine development can get underway in time. There have been no responses from the White House.

Such an initiative would cost a fraction of the annual $9 to $10 billion dollars that Bush is spending on the boondoggle missile defense business. (A technology so easily decoyable and dubious that it has been deemed unworkable by the American Physical Society). But missile defense and other massive military weapons programs, conceived for a Soviet Union era of hostility, make big profits for corporations. Vaccines do not make big profits for drug companies the way lifestyle drugs do.

The daily headlines are sounding grave alarms. Rob Stein and Shankar Vedantam of the *Washington Post* report that a strain of the flu virus H2N2 that caused a worldwide pandemic and killed more than one million people worldwide in 1957 and 1958 was mistakenly sent to thousands of laboratories in the United States and around the world. Keith Bradsher's reports from China for the *Times* have been getting ever more somber. The latest dispatch headlines "Some Asian Bankers worry about the Economic Toll from Bird Flu." Maybe if business profits are jeopardized by what a pandemic can do to an economy, officialdom will reorder its twisted priorities.

The deadly Marburg virus (nine of ten people afflicted die) now spreading slowly in Angola is another wake up call for our country to change its priorities from continually adding to the largest major weapons arsenal in world history (nuclear submarines, aircraft carriers, missiles, planes, etc.) and moving to life-saving and health-preserving investments for prevention before vaccines are needed.

It is time to know the names of the scientists already working on this great venture for health and hear them out. Hear ye, media!

Citizens' Debate Commission

January 17, 2004

You have heard, no doubt, about Michael Jackson's troubles, but have you heard about a new Presidential Citizens' Debate Commission that could give Americans more choices and voices when they watch these debates later this autumn?

Probably not. This is the trouble with the media's sense of what is news and what is important to their readers and audiences. But is it an accurate sense? One story deals with allegations against an entertainer. The other deals with the major way that voters get to see, hear and evaluate candidates vying for the top political position in our country with immense power to affect their lives.

I know a little about the present Commission on Presidential Debates (CPD). It is a private corporation created in 1987 by the Republican and Democratic Parties to replace the League of Women Voters as debate sponsor and seize complete control over the presidential debate process. Its principal objectives are to exclude competitors from third parties or independent candidacies, control the number of debates, and control their format and questioner(s).

Since 1980 only Ross Perot has gotten in on these debates (actually they are parallel interviews). After gaining 19 million votes in 1992, he was kept off the debates in 1996 by his two major competitors.

Unless you are like Perot—a billionaire—you can campaign in all the states and before large arena audiences and still speak to less than 2 percent of the voters that you would reach by being on just one debate.

These presidential debates, with the involvement of the major TV networks, become the only way to reach tens of millions of Americans for a non-rich candidate. And the gateway is controlled by a private corporation controlled by the two major parties. Pretty neat cabal, aye, and one that is authorized by no law or regulation. It is a private corporate government.

The new Citizens Debate Commission was launched on January 12, 2004 at the national Press Club in Washington by "national civic leaders from the left, right and center of the political spectrum," says the news release. John Anderson, independent presidential candidate in 1980, Angela "Bay" Buchanan, president of the American Cause, Mark Weisbrot, co-Director of the Center for Economic and Policy Research spoke at the news conference about their common concern that debates "put voter education first," in Anderson's words.

The present CPD is grossly partisan for the two major parties. The new Commission is totally non-partisan and is not controlled by any party or candidate. On its board is Chellie Pingree of Common Cause, Alan Keyes, Paul Weyrich, Tony Perkins of the Family Research Council, Veronica de la Garza of the Youth Vote Coalition and the Brennan Center. You can see how broadly representative it is. (For much more information, see OpenDebates.org)

The new Commission has criteria for who can come onto the debates, as well as much more fluid and candidate-interactive procedures. If a presidential candidate is on enough state ballots to gain an electoral college majority and registers at five percent in the polls or registers a majority in national polls asking eligible voters which candidates they would like to see in the debates, then it is a green light no matter what party or independent ticket the candidate hails from.

Walter Cronkite called the CPD's presidential debates an "unconscionable fraud" because the debate format "defies meaningful discourse."

To the *Washington Post*, the *New York Times*, the *Wall Street Journal*, the three networks and cable news shows, news about this "unconscionable fraud" and a prestigious potential replacement was blacked out.

In a few weeks, George Farah, who worked on my last campaign, will publish his expose of the CPD in a book titled *No Debate*. Mr. Farah, now ably assisted by Chris Shaw, is attracting public support nationwide.

Environment & Health

In 2011, there was a citizen initiative to stop the Keystone XL dirty tar sands oil pipeline from being built from Canada down to the US Gulf Coast. Thousands of concerned Americans came together at the White House to protest the proposed pipeline. President Obama delayed the pipeline due to the concerted effort of these thousands of active citizens, but the project is slated to continue through piecemeal development.

Today most people and scientists believe that humans are polluting our environment and atmosphere, leading to increased health problems and global warming. The push to develop new technologies that use renewable energy is a priority for the environmental movement, but there is much work to be done in terms of developing public policy that meaningfully develops clean energy. Unfortunately, American energy policy remains in the grip of the oil, gas, coal, and nuclear industries, as practical renewable energy sources are neglected.

Environmentalism is as much a matter of public health and ethics as it is about aesthetics or nature-loving. Several columns in this section detail the controversies the poorly-regulated nuclear industry develops when its systems fail and pollute our environment and bodies. Some columns also talk about natural disasters and the ripple effect of catastrophic accidents such as the BP oil spill. Other columns delve more specifically into health issues that remain on the backburner despite their prominence in our lives, such as bacterial outbreaks and the obesity epidemic.

Some columns in this section deal with different threats to public health stemming from a failed healthcare system. The elderly and others often find drugs prohibitively expensive, and nearly forty-five million Americans have no health insurance. The Institute of Medicine estimates the loss of 45,000 American lives a year because there was no health insurance to afford diagnosis and treatment. These and other healthcare problems are neither accidental nor inevitable. They result from deliberate economic and political actions by insurers, pharmaceutical companies, and HMOs that obviously care a great deal about their profits and too little about our health. So, while single-payer healthcare (full Medicare for all) has been the subject of a serious debate and popularity in recent years, it was taken off the table by the president and the Congress precluding even a discussion of that more efficient and humane system in the White House and Congressional deliberations.

In sum, those entrusted with protecting our health and environment are part of the problem. As you read accounts of their indifference, remember that the power of these political institutions is entirely delegated by "We the People." Shouldn't we expect and demand better performance?

In sum, those entrusted with protecting our health and environment are part of the problem. As you read accounts of their indifference, remember that the power of these political institutions is entirely delegated by "We the People." Shouldn't we expect and demand better performance?

Obama's Pipeline Quagmire

September 13, 2011

It was the most extraordinary citizen organizing feat in recent White House history. Over 1200 Americans from 50 states came to Washington and were arrested in front of the White House to demonstrate their opposition to a forthcoming Obama approval of the Keystone XL dirty oil pipeline from Alberta, Canada down to the Gulf Coast.

Anyone who has tried to mobilize people in open non-violent civil disobedience knows how hard it is to have that many people pay their way to Washington to join a select group of civic champions. The first round of arrestees—about 100 of them—were brought to a jail and kept on cement floors for 52 hours—presumably, said one guard, on orders from "above" to discourage those who were slated to follow this first wave in the two weeks ending September 3, 2011.

The Keystone XL pipeline project—owned by a consortium of oil companies—is a many faceted abomination. It will, if constructed, take its raw, tar sands carbon down through the agricultural heartland of the United States—through the Missouri and Niobrara Rivers, the great Ogallala aquifer, fragile natural habitats and Native American lands. Major breaks and accidents on pipelines—four of them with loss of human life—have occurred just in the past year from California to Pennsylvania, including a recent, major Exxon/Mobile pipeline rupture which resulted in many gallons of oil spilling into the Yellowstone River.

The Office of Pipeline Safety in the Department of Transportation has been a pitiful rubberstamp patsy for the pipeline industry for 40 years. There are larger objections—a huge contribution to greenhouse gases and further expansion of the destruction of northern Albertan terrain, forests and water—expected to cover an area the size of Florida.

Furthermore, as the Energy Department report on Keystone XL pointed out, decreasing demand for petroleum through advances in fuel efficiency is the major way to reduce reliance on imported oil with or without the pipeline. There is no assurance whatsoever that the refined tar sands oil in Gulf Coast refineries will even get to the motorists here. They can be exported more profitably to Europe and South America.

In ads on Washington, DC's WTOP news station, the industry is claiming that the project will create more than 100,000 jobs. They cannot substantiate this figure. It is vastly exaggerated. TransCanada's permit application for Keystone XL to the US State Department estimated a "peak workforce of approximately 3,500 to 4,200 construction personnel" to build the pipeline.

The Amalgamated Transit Union (ATU) and the Transport Workers Union (TWU) oppose the pipeline. In their August 2011 statement they said: "We need jobs, but not ones based on increasing our reliance on Tar Sands oil. [. . .] Many jobs could be created in energy conservation, upgrading the grid, maintaining and expanding public transportation—jobs that can help us reduce air pollution, greenhouse gas emissions, and improve energy efficiency."

The demonstrators before the White House, led by prominent environmentalist Bill McKibben and other stalwarts, focused on President Obama because he and he alone will make the decision either for or against building what they call "North America's biggest carbon bomb." He does not have to ask Congress.

Already the State Department, in their latest report, is moving to recommend approval. The demonstrators and their supporters, including leaders of the Native American Dene tribe in Canada and the Lakota nation in the US, filled much of the area in front of the White House and Lafayette Square. On September 2, I went down to express my support for their cause. Assistants to Mr. McKibben asked me to speak at the final rally at the square on Saturday. I agreed. At 6:25 p.m. we received an e-mail from Daniel Kessler withdrawing their invitation because of "how packed our schedule already is. We'd love to have Ralph there in any other capacity, including participating in the protest."

The next day, many of the speakers went way over their allotted five to six minute time slots. Observers told me that there were to be no criticisms of Barack Obama. McKibben wore an Obama pin on the stage. Obama t-shirts were seen out in the crowd. McKibben did not want their efforts to be "marginalized" by criticizing the president, which they expected I would do. He said that "he would not do Obama the favor" of criticizing him.

To each one's own strategy. I do not believe McKibben's strategy is up to the brilliance of his tactics involving the mass arrests. (Which by the way received deplorably little mass media coverage).

Obama believes that those demonstrators and their followers around the country are his voters (they were in 2008) and that they have nowhere to go in 2012. So long as environmentalists do not find a way to disabuse him of this impression long before Election Day, they should get ready for an Obama approval of the Keystone XL monstrosity.

Sun and Sanity

August 29, 2011

This is the second week of protests, led by Bill McKibben, in front of the White House demanding that President Barack Obama reject a proposed 1700 mile pipeline transporting the dirtiest oil from Alberta, Canada through fragile ecologies down to the Gulf Coast refineries. One thousand people will be arrested there from all fifty states before their demonstration is over. The vast majority voted for Obama and they are plenty angry with his brittleness on environmental issues in general.

Following the large BP discharge in the Gulf of Mexico, Obama gave the OK to expand drilling over 20 million acres in the Gulf and soon probably in the Arctic Ocean. He delayed clean air rules over at EPA. Following the worsening Fukushima nuclear disaster last March in Japan, he reaffirmed his support for more taxpayer guaranteed nuclear plants in the US adding his Administration's hopes to learn from the mistakes there.

He proposed an average fuel efficiency standard for 2005 at 62 miles per gallon, quickly conceded to industry's objection and brought it down to 54 mpg. The industry's trade journal *Automotive News* calculated the loopholes and brought it down to "real-world industry wide fleet average in the 2025 model year" of about 40 mpg. No wonder the auto companies effusively praised Obama's give-it-up negotiator, Ron Bloom at the Treasury Department of all places.

Were Obama to look out his White House window and see the arrested and handcuffed demonstrators against this $7 billion Keystone XL pipeline, he might think: "This will upset my environmental supporters, but heck, where can they go in November 2012?"

He is right. No matter what Mr. Obama does to surrender environmental health and safety to corporatist demands, they will vote for him. They certainly won't vote for the Republican corporate mascots. They wouldn't vote for a Green Party candidate either. This is not only the environmentalists' dilemma, it is the liberal/progressive/labor union dilemma as well. They have no bargaining power with Obama.

He did not propose a carbon tax when the Democrats controlled Congress in 2009-2010. Even Exxon prefers a carbon tax to the corruption-inducing complex cap and trade bill the House passed only to have the Senate sit on it. So doing nothing on climate change is soon to be followed by approval of the destructive tar sands pipeline which will add significantly to greenhouse gases.

Pipelines have been busting out recently in California, near Yellowstone and in Pennsylvania. People died and water was polluted. Pipeland standards are old, weak and hardly enforced by the tiny pipeline safety office at the Department of Transportation. Obama hasn't been pushing for needed money and stronger standards with tougher enforcement.

Over-riding, in Obama's mind, is being accused of blocking job formation. But had he pushed for a major public-works program in 2009, as many economists still beg him to do, he wouldn't be in the position of being called a job-destroyer. He also is sensitive to rebuttable charges that he would be preferring future oil from unfriendly countries abroad to Canadian oil.

You can see the corner he is in because he didn't come out strongly for major solar, wind power, energy conservation and immediate retrofit programs in 2009. Instead he swallowed the oil industry line that his proposed energy policy should be a mix of fossil fuels, nuclear power, solar and conservation in that order. No, Mr. Obama, some energy sources are too superior in too many ways to be a part of this manipulative greenwashing propaganda displayed in oil company newspaper ads.

Even nature contradicts Mr. Obama. Obama's Nuclear Regulatory Commission (NRC) recently gave a pass to the Indian Point Unit 2 Reactor, a menacingly-troubled reactor 30 miles north of Manhattan, after its inspectors discovered a refueling-cavity liner had been leaking for years at rates up to 10 gallons per minute. Just last week the strongest earthquake in 140 years struck the east coast. Even though the liner's "sole safety function is the prevention of leakage after a seismic event," according to David Lochbaum of the Union of Concerned Scientists, the NRC did not require the plant's owner to repair the design defect.

This is only one of many defects, inspection lapses, close calls, corrosions, and aging problems with many US nuclear plants that Secretary of Energy Stephen Chu and President Obama have not seriously addressed. This is the case even though the news from Fukushima becomes worse every week. More food is found contaminated. Radiation readings at the site reached their highest level in August. Now the Japanese government is about to declare a wide area around the nine destroyed or disabled nuclear plants uninhabitable for decades to come due to radiation.

Nearly fifty years ago, the industry regulator and vigorous promoter, the Atomic Energy Commissions estimated that a class nine nuclear meltdown in the US would contaminate "an area the size of Pennsylvania." That was before we had dozens of even larger aging nuclear plants whose owners are brazenly pressing for license extensions beyond the normal life expectancy of many over-the-hill nuke plants. Please face up to it Mr. President.

At moments of reflection, those 1000 citizens standing tall before the White House must look up at the sun and all the forms of available renewable energy it gave this planet zillions of years ago and wonder how nuts our life-sustaining star must think Earthlings have been all these years.

Open Letter to President Obama from E. coli 0104:H4

June 3, 2011

Dear President Obama:

My name is E. coli 0104:H4. I am being detained in a German Laboratory in Bavaria, charged with being "a highly virulent strain of bacteria." Together with many others like me, the police have accused us of causing about 20 deaths and nearly five hundred cases of kidney failure—so far. Massive publicity and panic all around.

You can't see me, but your scientists can. They are examining me and I know my days are numbered. I hear them calling me a "biological terrorist," an unusual combination of two different E. coli bacteria cells. One even referred to me as a "conspiracy of mutants."

It is not my fault, I want you to know. I cannot help but harm innocent humans, and I am very sad about this. I want to redeem myself, so I am sending this life-saving message straight from my Petri dish to you.

This outbreak in Germany has been traced to food—location unknown. What is known to you is that invisible terrorism from bacterium and viruses take massively greater lives than the terrorism you are spending billions of dollars and armaments to stop in Iraq, Afghanistan and Pakistan.

Malaria, caused by infection with one of four species of Plasmodium, a parasite transmitted by *Anopheles* mosquitoes destroys a million lives a year. Many of the victims are children and pregnant women. Mycobacterium tuberculosis takes nearly three million lives. The human immuno-deficiency virus (HIV) causes over a million deaths. Many other microorganisms in the water, soil, air, and food are daily weapons of mass destruction. Very little in your defense budget goes for operational armed forces against this kind of violence. Your agencies, such as the Center for Disease Control, conduct some research but again nothing compared to the research for your missiles, drones, aircraft and satellites.

Your associates are obsessed with possible bacteriological warfare by your human enemies. Yet you are hardly doing anything on the ongoing silent violence of my indiscriminate brethren.

You and your predecessor George W. Bush made many speeches about fighting terrorism by humans. Have you made a major speech about us?

You speak regularly about crushing the resistance of your enemies. But you splash around so many antibiotics (obviously I don't like this word and consider it genocidal) in cows, bulls, chickens, pigs and fish that your species is creating massive *antibiotic* resistance, provoking our mutations, so that we can breed even stronger progeny. You are regarded as the smartest beings on Earth, yet you seem to have too many neurons backfiring.

In the past two days of detention, scientists have subjected me to "enhanced interrogation," as if I have any will to give up my secrets. It doesn't work. What they will find out will be from their insights about me under their microscopes. I am lethal, I guess, but I'm not very complicated.

The United States, together with other countries, needs more laboratories where scientists can detain samples of us and subject us to extraordinary rendition to infectious disease research centers. Many infectious disease scientists need to be trained, especially in the southern hemispheres, to staff these labs.

You are hung up on certain kinds of preventable violence without any risk/benefit analysis. This, you should agree, is utterly irrational. You should not care where the preventable violence comes from except to focus on its range of devastation and its susceptibility to prevention or cure!

Well, here they come to my Petri dish for some more waterboarding. One last item: You may wonder *how* tiny bacterial me, probably not even harboring a virus, can send you such a letter. My oozing sense is that I'm just a carrier, being used by oodles of scientists taking advantage of a high profile infectious outbreak in Europe to catch your attention.

Whatever the *how* does it really matter to the need to act now?

E-cologically yours,

E. coli 0104:H4 (for the time being)

Obama's March Madness
March 28, 2011

President Obama's pick of Kansas to win the "March Madness" collegiate basketball tournament ended with their defeat by Virginia Commonwealth University this past Saturday. He must know how the Jay Hawks are feeling because he is entangled in his own March Madness that will continue after this month ends.

The expanding nuclear meltdown disaster from Japan's cluster of nuclear plants gets worse by the day, yet President Obama continues to reassure the nuclear industry that he supports more plants guaranteed by the US taxpayers because Wall Street otherwise will not risk loaning billions of dollars per plant.

Mr. Obama, Secretary of Energy Steven Chu, and their atomic power allies say that they'll learn from the Japanese failures and make the US plants safer. That puts off the urgency to act for an indefinite period.

What Mr. Obama should realize is that Japan's human and economic catastrophe was a gigantic wakeup call to stop playing Russian roulette with the lives of millions of Americans and swing into action. First, he should shut down any plants near large population centers where untested evacuation plans are tragic farces. That means plants in San Onofre and Diablo Canyon in California and the troubled Indian Point plant 26 miles from Manhattan that are near active seismic faults. That means closing all aging nukes as recommended by Russian scientist Alexey Yablokov (a member of the prestigious Russian Academy of Sciences), who had a news conference in Washington last Thursday (ignored by the major newspapers and network television but covered by CNN and C-SPAN) regarding 5000 scientific papers in Slavic languages on the consequences of the 1986 meltdown at Chernobyl. (See his report at: http://books.google.com/books?id=g34tNlYOB3AC&lpg=PP1&ots=O15UeQYVf5&dq=alexey%20yablokov%20chernobyl&pg=PP1#v=onepage&q&f=false) He estimated at least one million lives have been lost since.

Third, there should be an immediate analysis of electric generating capacity substitutes and the many ways to reduce energy waste so as to close out the uneconomic, unnecessary and unsafe nuclear industry forever. (See: RMI.org)

Corporations must not be allowed to jeopardize the habitability of American land and the lives of the American people with a technology that's only purpose is to boil water to produce steam. An area half the size of New Jersey around Chernobyl is uninhabitable with abandoned towns and villages. The Japanese, with reactors manufactured by General Electric (whose $14.2 billion in profits escaped taxation last year and got $3.2 billion in tax benefits) are in the early stages of figuring out how many square kilometers will have to be abandoned by families and workers.

Yesterday, the *New York Times* reporter George Johnson wrote: "With radiation, the terror lies in the abstraction. It kills incrementally—slowly, diffusely, invisibly. 'Afterheat,' Robert Socolow, a Princeton University professor, called it in an essay for the *Bulletin of the Atomic Scientists*, 'the fire that you can't put out.'"

Professor Socolow works on energy conservation and renewable energy. He and hundreds of other experts know that efficient renewable technologies and conservation can substitute more safely and more efficiently far more megawatts than 104 nukes are producing now from their deadly hot radioactive nuclear cores.

It is way past time to end this government guaranteed, corporate Mutational Madness once and for all.

On Capitol Hill, President Obama is still surrendering to House Republican extortions in return for them agreeing to extend the budget resolution every three weeks the budget resolution so as to avoid a government shutdown. The

president simply doesn't know how to throw the Republican know-nothings on the defensive by discrediting their craven inebriating ideology of fact-starved abstractions. He prefers to do his fighting overseas.

While on the other side of the world, the wars of Obama have added Libya, notwithstanding his Secretary of Defense Robert Gates expressed disinclination to start this latest attack, before it started. Again, without an end strategy and or the candor to tell the American people and their Congress that the no-fly zone is moving into a full-fledged attack, under NATO cover, with ground forces aided by US Special Forces already in Libya. So much for our Constitution's allocation of authority.

Long ago, humanitarian interventions should have been initiated by an independent United Nations standing military capability pursuant to the appropriate UN resolutions. After all, over 190 countries—just about all the countries of the world—are members of the UN and adhere to the UN Charter, which has the force of international law upon signatory countries. You would think that King Clinton, King Bush and King Obama would have advanced this concept to relieve the American Empire of some of its burdens. Then our government could pay more attention here to saving lives and advancing health by reducing the millions of preventable deaths, injuries and diseases from toxic pollution, occupation perils, hospital malpractice and infections, product defects and poverty. Imagine real healthcare for all!

Nuclear Nightmare
March 18, 2011

The unfolding multiple nuclear reactor catastrophe in Japan is prompting overdue attention to the 104 nuclear plants in the United States—many of them aging, many of them near earthquake faults, some on the West Coast exposed to potential tsunamis.

Nuclear power plants boil water to produce steam to turn turbines that generate electricity. Nuclear power's overly complex fuel cycle begins with uranium mines and ends with deadly radioactive wastes for which there still are no permanent storage facilities to contain them for tens of thousands of years.

Atomic power plants generate 20 percent of the nation's electricity. Over forty years ago, the industry's promoter and regulator, the Atomic Energy Commission estimated that a full nuclear meltdown could contaminate an area "the size of Pennsylvania" and cause massive casualties. You, the taxpayers, have heavily subsidized nuclear power research, development, and promotion from day one with tens of billions of dollars.

Because of many costs, perils, close calls at various reactors, and the partial meltdown at the Three Mile Island plant in Pennsylvania in 1979, there has not been a nuclear power plant built in the United States since 1974.

Now the industry is coming back "on your back" claiming it will help reduce global warming from fossil fuel emitted greenhouse gases.

Pushed aggressively by President Obama and Energy Secretary Chu, who refuses to meet with longtime nuclear industry critics, here is what "on your back" means:

1. Wall Street will not finance new nuclear plants without a 100 percent taxpayer loan guarantee. Too risky. That's a lot of guarantee given that new nukes cost $12 billion each, assuming no mishaps. Obama and the Congress are OK with that arrangement.

2. Nuclear power is uninsurable in the private insurance market—too risky. Under the Price-Anderson Act, taxpayers pay the greatest cost of a meltdown's devastation.

3. Nuclear power plants and transports of radioactive wastes are a national security nightmare for the Department of Homeland Security. Imagine the target that thousands of vulnerable spent fuel rods present for sabotage.

4. Guess who pays for whatever final waste repositories are licensed? You the taxpayer and your descendants as far as your gene line persists. Huge decommissioning costs, at the end of a nuclear plant's existence come from the ratepayers' pockets.

5. Nuclear plant disasters present impossible evacuation burdens for those living anywhere near a plant, especially if time is short.

Imagine evacuating the long-troubled Indian Point plant 26 miles north of New York City. Workers in that region have a hard enough time evacuating their places of employment during 5 pm rush hour. That's one reason Secretary of State Clinton (in her time as Senator of New York) and Governor Andrew Cuomo called for the shutdown of Indian Point.

6. Nuclear power is both uneconomical and unnecessary. It can't compete against energy conservation, including cogeneration, windpower and ever more efficient, quicker, safer, renewable forms of providing electricity. Amory Lovins argues this point convincingly (see RMI. org). Physicist Lovins asserts that nuclear power "will reduce and retard climate protection." His reasoning: shifting the tens of billions invested in nuclear power to efficiency and renewables reduce far more carbon per dollar (http://www.nirs.org/factsheets/whynewnukesareriskyfcts.pdf). The country should move deliberately to shutdown nuclear plants, starting with the aging and seismically threatened reactors. Peter

Bradford, a former Nuclear Regulatory Commission (NRC) commissioner has also made a compelling case against nuclear power on economic and safety grounds (http://www.nirs.org/factsheets/whynewnukesareriskyfcts.pdf).

There is far more for ratepayers, taxpayers and families near nuclear plants to find out. Here's how you can start:

1. Demand public hearings in your communities where there is a nuke, sponsored either by your member of Congress or the NRC, to put the facts, risks and evacuation plans on the table. Insist that the critics as well as the proponents testify and cross-examine each other in front of you and the media.

2. If you call yourself conservative, ask why nuclear power requires such huge amounts of your tax dollars and guarantees and can't buy adequate private insurance. If you have a small business that can't buy insurance because what you do is too risky, you don't stay in business.

3. If you are an environmentalist, ask why nuclear power isn't required to meet a cost-efficient market test against investments in energy conservation and renewables.

4. If you understand traffic congestion, ask for an actual real life evacuation drill for those living and working 10 miles around the plant (some scientists think it should be at least 25 miles) and watch the hemming and hawing from proponents of nuclear power.

The people in northern Japan may lose their land, homes, relatives, and friends as a result of a dangerous technology designed simply to boil water. There are better ways to generate steam.

Like the troubled Japanese nuclear plants, the Indian Point plant and the four plants at San Onofre and Diablo Canyon in southern California rest near earthquake faults. The seismologists concur that there is a 94 percent chance of a big earthquake in California within the next thirty years. Obama, Chu and the powerful nuke industry must not be allowed to force the American people to play Russian Roulette!

Overuse of Antibiotics
January 24, 2011

Reading a recent issue of Public Citizen's excellent *Health Letter* titled "Know When Antibiotics Work," I recalled the recent tragic loss of a healthy history professor who was rushed to a fine urban hospital, with a leading infectious disease specialist by his side. No antibiotics could treat his mysterious "superbug." He died in 36 hours.

Wrongful or overuse of antibiotics has a perverse effect—causing the kinds of bacteria that these drugs can no longer destroy. The World Health Organization has cited antibiotic resistance as one of the three most serious public health threats of the twenty-first century.

The Centers for Disease Control and Prevention (CDC) notes that just in hospitals, where between 5 and 10 percent of all patients develop an infection, about 90,000 of these patients die each year as a result of their infection. This toll is up from 13,300 patient deaths in 1992. Some percentage of these people have problems because of antibiotic resistance.

No matter how many national and global public health organizations warn about this silent, deadly epidemic, no matter how many official recognitions and definition of the problems and demands for local and international action, the fatality toll and the economic costs keep growing.

As Dr. Sidney Wolfe, editor of the *Health Letter* says: "We've known about this problem and the needed solutions for well over 30 years but almost nothing is being done about it!" The drug companies keep pushing these drugs while investing too little in truly new antibiotics that can overtake resistant bacteria. Too many doctors still prescribe antibiotics for viral infections that should not be treated with antibiotics. They don't work on viruses. These include, says Dr. Wolfe, "colds, flu—in the absence of bacterial complications, most coughs and bronchitis, sore throats (except those resulting from strep throat) and some ear infections.

Doctors say that patients demand antibiotics—its part of the culture. But doctors should be there to inform patients in those instances when antibiotics are inappropriate.

The CDC states that "many infectious diseases are increasingly difficult to treat because of antimicrobial-resistant organisms, including HIV infection, staphylococcal infection, tuberculosis, influenza, gonorrhea, candida infection and malaria."

Dr. Wolfe writes that "drug resistant infections also spread in the community at large. Examples include drug-resistant pneumonias, sexually transmitted diseases (STDs) and skin and soft tissue infections."

Let us pause for a puzzling question. How many elected representatives, whose chore they say is America's safety, spend any time on this devastating taking of lives because of preventable antibiotic resistant infections, compared to the daily focus on terrorism and the trillions of dollars spent on arms, surveillance, searching of tens of millions of Americans (at airports, for example) and sending soldiers all over the world to kill and be killed?

"Smart use of antibiotics," says Dr. Wolfe, "is the key to controlling the spread of resistance. Too many types of bacteria have become stronger and less responsive to antibiotic treatment when it is really needed. These antibiotic resistant bacteria can quickly spread to family members, schoolmates and co-workers—threatening the community with a new strain of infectious diseases that is more difficult to cure and more expensive to treat."

The veterinary medical community as well is showing a growing concern of too many antibiotics in domesticated animals which enter the human food supply.

"Repeated and improper uses of antibiotics are primary causes of the increase in drug-resistant bacteria," says the Public Citizen *Health Letter*, adding that bacteria that survive an antibiotic change so as to "neutralize or escape the effect of the antibiotic" then multiply rapidly.

There are lots to be done by many participants in the production, prescription, sale and use of these drugs. You can start by questioning your doctor and not buying soaps, handwipes and cleaning agents whose vendors lure you with the label "antibacterial."

For more about what you can do, visit citizen. org/hrg.

Planning for Disaster
June 4, 2010

When the Executive Branch does not have worst case scenario planning for each kind of energy source—oil, gas, coal, nuclear, wind, solar and efficiency—the people are not protected.

Enter the 24/7 oil gusher-leak by BP and Transocean—the rig operator—and the impotence of the federal government to do anything but wait and see if BP can find ways to close off the biggest and still growing oil leak in American history. Where is the emergency planning or industry knowhow?

Of course, we all saw Barack Obama's first full press conference in ten months where he said, "In case you were wondering who's responsible? I take responsibility. It is my job to make sure everything is done to shut this down.... The federal government is fully engaged, and I'm fully engaged. Personally, I'm briefed every day. And I probably had more meetings on this issue than just about any issue since we did our Afghan review."

Sure, so he's being kept informed. Those are not the words of leadership five weeks after the preventable blowout on the Deepwater Horizon 40 miles off the Louisiana coast. His problem is how long it took for the White House to see this as a national disaster and not just a corporate disaster for BP to contain.

That default was not just failing to determine the size of the spill (more than ten times greater than BP originally estimated) or the farcical non-regulation, under Republicans and Democrats, by the Minerals Management Service of the Interior Department. It was a failure to realize that our government has no capability, no technology to take control of such disasters or even to find out whether solutions exist elsewhere in the oil and geologic industries. It's like a spreading fire where the perpetrator of the fire has the primary responsibility to put the fire out because there is no properly equipped public fire department.

James Carville, an Obama loyalist and defender, called out his champion from new Orleans, where he now lives, and told him: "Man, you got to get down here and take control of this!" With what? Obama has a 16-month long record of turning his back on advice, from the Cajuns of Louisiana to environmental groups in Washington, DC. He shook off warnings about the pathetic, so-called federal regulators cushy with the oil industry. During his campaigns, he allowed McCain's "drill, baby, drill" to turn him more overtly toward favoring offshore drilling, instead of turning onto offshore windpower.

As the multi-directional and multi-depth oil swarm keeps encircling the Gulf of Mexico, strangling the livelihood of its people, the life of its flora and fauna, with its implacably deadly effect, Obama and his supposedly street-smart advisors, led by Rahm Emanuel, started out with a political blunder. Presidential specialist, Professor Paul Light at New York University put his finger on it when he said: "The White House made a deliberate political calculation to stand off . . . to sort of distance themselves from BP, and they've been hammered on that."

Early on, Defense Secretary Robert Gates told him that the federal government does not possess superior technology to BP. And BP CEO Tony Hayward admitted that BP was not prepared for such a blowout. He said "What is undoubtedly true is that we did not have the tools you would want in your tool kit." Gates really meant that Uncle Sam, was completely out to lunch with the chronic deregulators who still infect our national government.

Obama's cool is turning cold. He is not reacting fast enough to the public rage that is building up and over-riding his vacuous statements about taking responsibility and being briefed daily. Much of this public rage, incidentally, is coming from the southern Gulf rim, whose elected politicians consistently opposed any regulation of their campaign contributing oil companies in order to avert just these kinds of disasters. Only Florida's Congressional delegation said stay out of Florida's waters.

Politico reported that "Obama skipped the memorial service for the 11 workers killed on the rig earlier this week, instead flying to California, where he collected $1.7 million for

Democrats and toured a solar panel plant. On the day that the significant clots of oil started appearing on the Louisiana coast, Obama was sitting down for an interview to talk hoops with TNT's Marv Albert."

He must move to properly sequester all the assets of BP and Transocean to fully pay for their damage, thus assuring Americans that BP will not be able to concoct another Exxon/Valdez escape strategy. He must scour the world of knowledge and experience regarding capping underseas oil blowouts, and not just wait week after week for BP to come up with something.

Nobody says that being president is an easy job, even in the best of times. But a president, who can go all out spending hundreds of billions of dollars in Iraq and Afghanistan in ways that bleed the taxpayers and breed more anti-American fighters, in part to protect Big Oil in the Middle East, better come back home and stop Big Oil's war here in the Gulf of Mexico. *That's how he'd better start defining "homeland security."* (See Citizen.org for more on BP.)

King Obesity's Realm

February 17, 2010

King Obesity sat grandly on a huge hassock atop a throne composed of solidified animal fat surveying his domain. The last thirty years have been bullish for Obesity, during which the number of seriously overweight children in America tripled. Eating fat, sugary and salty food while sitting for hours daily looking at video screens, being bused to and from school, and not having to bother with physical education, millions of lads and lassies were following orders.

An agitated messenger arrived in the throne room, breathing heavily from his travels. "Oh, my liege, Obesity, I have disturbing news. Michelle Obama, the First Lady, is launching a nationwide project she calls 'Let's Move' to combat childhood obesity and shed billions of pounds of your stuff. She claims that success would reduce all types of diseases now and later, save on medical costs, as well as raise the energy level and self-esteem of millions of children. Here, Your Eminence, are the complete details of her plan."

Obesity was a hard person to agitate. He had heard of these campaigns before. They went nowhere. He shook his heavy jowls and rubbed his many-layered belly, which was his way of saying "ho, hum, here we go again."

His fleshy fingers clutched the plan by those people he always called the "lean and meaners," and saw that improvement in the school lunch program's menu, exercise at school, farmers' markets and community gardens were at the top of the action list. Obesity chortled at his adversaries' naivete and reticence.

For some reason, they avoided the real causes of his success in pouring massive amounts of empty calories into the mouths and down the throats of these children who cry out for more and more of them.

It is all about who owns the tongues of these youngsters, not who reaches their brains, mused Obesity. Ownership, Obesity knew, belonged to his most faithful allies—the vast fast food and food processing industry and their clever advertisers. For decades these companies have transformed millions of young tongues into fast food first responders.

The tongue has been turned against the brain for so long that the kids' parents and even some grandparents accept this conditioned response. Look what they head for in the movies, what they choose in the supermarkets, what they order in the chain restaurants and takeouts. It's all about the pipeline full of enlarged amounts of sugar, fat and salt, dude! Hour after hour, day after day, these pipelines are flowing to the delight of their video-addicted young customers.

Obesity has been defeating his principal opponents—Knowledge, Nutrition, and Health—for so long, he sleeps most of the day when he is not eating. So, Michelle Obama is going to concentrate on the schools. Hah, not a chance unless she wants a rebellion of the kids, whose habit is to cast aside much of the cooked and raw vegetables even when they're hungry. The school vending machines are stocked with the perfect junk food and nearby stores can make up for any lack of ready supply.

So, though knowing better, school lunch managers, to quell any unrest, load up on sugar-glazed cookies called Crunchmania Cinnamon Buns and sugar-laden cereals for breakfast. At lunch there are dollops of modified cornstarch, lipolyzed butter oil, high-fructose corn syrup, sugar-flavored milk.

It wasn't accidental that McDonald's most successful words to get children to nag their parents were "It's a Child's World." So, if sincere schools can't get the children to eat their fruits and vegetables, what about the burdened, commuting parents? Can they overcome the daily barrage of junk food and drink that shapes their children into Pavlovian specimens—mere conditioned responders? Don't be silly. They eat from the same menu.

Obesity continues to bet on the children's tongues as wards of the irresistible junk food companies. After all, his ranks keep swelling and the Fat Pride movement is picking up steam.

The messenger, standing with military erectness, deferentially asked: "Oh master, what are you thinking?" Obesity looked down on him

and rendered his conclusion: "So long as the lean and meaners do not focus on the battle for the tongues and their captors and instead concentrate on presenting nutritious foods to children while explaining why and how they are good for them, I say to you and all messengers of these tidings, do not worry, Obesity is and will continue to be king."

"Why," he continued, "just a few days before Michelle Obama's multimedia White House event announcing 'Let's Move' with former NFL runner, Tiki Barber, Barack Obama was with a group of schoolchildren. As if being at the White House was not enough excitement for the students, what did Mr. Obama do? He presented each of them with a box of red, white and blue M&Ms imprinted with the presidential seal and his signature, no less."

With that pontification, a smiling Obesity picked up a dozen triple deck cheeseburgers, a gallon of thick ice cream milk shakes, 100 Hostess Twinkies, topped off with a bucket of sweetened lard to start his third meal of the day.

No Nukes
February 12, 2010

A generation of Americans has grown up without a single nuclear power plant being brought on line since before the near meltdown of the Three Mile Island structure in 1979. They have not been exposed to the enormous costs, risks and national security dangers associated with their operations and the large amount of radioactive wastes still without a safe, permanent storage place for tens of thousands of years.

All Americans better get informed soon, for a resurgent atomic power lobby wants the taxpayers to pick up the tab for re-launching this industry. Unless you get Congress to stop this insanely dirty and complex way to boil water to generate steam for electricity, you'll be paying for the industry's research, the industry's loan guarantees and the estimated trillion dollars (inflation-adjusted) cost of just one meltdown, according to the Nuclear Regulatory Commission, plus vast immediate and long-range casualties.

The Russian roulette-playing nuclear industry claims a class nine meltdown will never happen. That none of the thousands of rail cars, trucks and barges with radioactive wastes will ever have a catastrophic accident. That terrorists will forgo striking a nuclear plant or hijacking deadly materials, and go for far less consequential disasters.

The worst nuclear reactor accident occurred in 1986 at Chernobyl in what is now Ukraine. Although of a different design than most US reactors, the resultant breach of containment released a radioactive cloud that spread around the globe but concentrated most intensively in Belarus, Ukraine and European Russia and secondarily over 40 percent of Europe.

For different reasons, both governmental and commercial interests were intent on downplaying both the immediate radioactively-caused deaths and diseases and the longer term devastations from this silent, invisible form of violence. They also were not eager to fund follow up monitoring and research.

Now comes the English translation of the most comprehensive, scientific report to date titled "Chernobyl: Consequences of the Catastrophe for People and the Environment" whose senior author is biologist Alexey V. Yablokov, a member of the prestigious Russian Academy of Sciences.

Available for purchase from the New York Academy of Sciences (visit nyas.org/annals), this densely referenced analysis covers the acute radiation inflicted on both the first-responders (called "liquidators") and on residents nearby, who suffer chronic radioactive sicknesses. "Today," asserts the report, "more than 6 million people live on land with dangerous levels of contamination—land that will continue to be contaminated for decades to centuries."

Back to the US where, deplorably, President Obama has called for more so-called "safe, clean nuclear power plants." He just sent a budget request for another $54 billion in taxpayer loan guarantees on top of a previous $18 billion passed under Bush. You see, Wall Street financiers will not loan electric companies money to build new nuclear plants which cost $12 billion and up, unless Uncle Sam guarantees one hundred percent of the loan.

Strange, if these nuclear power plants are so efficient and safe, why can't they be built with unguaranteed private risk capital? The answer to this question came from testimony by Amory B. Lovins, chief scientist of the Rocky Mountain Institute, in March 2008 before the (House of Representatives of the US) Select Committee on Energy Independence (rmi.org). His thesis: "expanding nuclear power would reduce and retard climate protection and energy security . . . but can't survive free-market capitalism."

Making his case with brilliant concision, Lovins, a consultant to business and the Defense Department, demonstrated with numbers and other data that nuclear power "is being dramatically outcompeted in the global marketplace by no and low-carbon power resources that deliver far more climate solution per dollar, far faster."

Lovins doesn't even include the accident or sabotage risks. He testified that "because it's [nuclear power] uneconomic and unnecessary, we needn't inquire into its other attributes." Renewable energy (eg. wind power), cogeneration and energy efficiencies (megawatts) are now far easier to maintain.

I challenge anybody in the nuclear industry or academia to debate Lovins at the National Press Club in Washington, DC, with a neutral moderator, or before a Congressional Committee.

However, the swarm of nuclear power lobbyists is gaining headway in Congress, spreading their money everywhere and falsely exploiting the concern with global warming fed by fossil fuels.

The powerful nuclear power critics in Congress want the House energy bill to focus on climate change. To diminish the opposition, they entered into a bargain that gave nuclear reactors status with loan guarantees and other subsidies in the same legislation which has passed in the House and, as is usual, languishing in the Senate.

Long-time, staunch opponents of atomic power who are leaders in countering climate change, such as Rep. Ed Markey (D-Mass.), have quieted themselves for the time being, while the Republicans (loving the taxpayer subsidies) and some Democrats are hollering for the nukes. All of this undermines the valiant efforts of the Union of Concerned Scientists, Nuclear Information and Resource Service (NIRS), Friends of the Earth, and other established citizen groups who favor a far safer, more efficient, faster and more secure energy future for our country and the world.

Just recently, a well-designed and documented pamphlet from the group Beyond Nuclear summarized the case against nuclear power as "Expensive, Dangerous and Dirty." The clear, precise detail and docu-

mentation makes for expeditious education of your friends, neighbors and co-workers. You can download it for free and reprint it for wider distribution from www.BeyondNuclear. org. It is very well worth the 10 to 15 minutes it takes to absorb the truth about this troubled technology—replete with delays and large cost-overruns—that has been on government welfare since the 1950s.

Healthcare Hypocrisy

July 24, 2009

About the only lesson Barack Obama has learned from the Hillary and Bill health insurance debacle of 1993–1994 is to leave Michelle Obama out of his current drive to get something—anything—through the Congress labeled "reform."

Otherwise, he is making the same mistakes of blurring his proposal, catering to right-wing Democrats and corporatist Republicans, who want an even mushier "reform" scam, and cutting deals with the drug, hospital, and health insurance industries.

His political opponents become bolder each day as they see his party base in Congress weakening, his polls dropping, and a confused public being saturated with unrebutted propaganda by the insatiable profiteering, subsidized healthcare giants.

Their campaign-money-greased minions on Capitol Hill and the corporatist Think Tanks and columnists are seizing on President Obama's aversion to conflict and repeated willingness to water down what he will fight for.

The loud and cruel baying pack comes in the form of William Kristol ("This is not time to pull punches. Go for the kill."), Senator Jim De-

Mint (R-S.C.) ("If we're able to stop Obama on this, it will be his Waterloo. It will break him."), and Charles Krauthammer yammering wildly about medical malpractice and tort law. Krauthammer does not substantiate his claims or mention the many victims of malpractice as he gleefully predicts "Obamacare sinking."

All these critics have gold-plated health insurance, of course.

Hillary tried to appease the drug and hospital companies. Obama invited them to the White House, where they presumably pledged to give up nearly $300 billion over ten years without any specifics about how this complex assurance can be policed.

No matter, in return Obama and his aides agreed not to press Congress to authorize the federal government to negotiate drug prices with the drug industry. Don't worry: the taxpayers will pay the bill.

At a meeting on July 7 at the White House between drug company executives, Obama's chief of staff, Rahm Emanuel, and Senate Finance Chairman Max Baucus (D-Mont.), the industry, according to the *New York Times*, was promised that the final legislative package would not allow the reimportation of cheaper medicines from Canada or other countries even if they meet our drug safety standards.

Since these industry meetings at the White House are private, no one knows how many other concessions were made. What is known is that Barack Obama knows better. A former supporter of single-payer health insurance (often described as full Medicare for all with free choice of physician and hospital and the elimination of hundreds of billions of dollars of corporate administrative costs and billing fraud), then-Illinois state senator Barack Obama predicted, in 2003, that it would be enacted once

Congress and the White House were controlled by Democrats. Well, that is now the situation, but, as president, he believes single-payer is not "practical."

Single-payer health insurance is supported by a majority of the American people, majority of physicians and nurses, and nearly ninety members of the House of Representatives. (See H.R. 676 and singlepayeraction.org.)

A clear replacement of the private health insurance companies with federal insurance allows for clear language, as Medicare for the elderly did in 1965. Twenty thousand people die in America each year because they cannot afford health insurance, according to the Institute of Medicine. Hundreds of thousands more suffer because they have no insurance to treat their diseases or injuries.

Single payer means everyone is covered from birth, as is the case now in every western nation. Imagine no lives lost or suffering due to no health insurance.

Fuzzy proposals, regularly altered and overcomplicated due to the hordes of avaricious corporate lobbyists, make politicians like Obama very susceptible to lurid descriptions and lies by his vocal, well-insured opponents. Finally, the Obama people are using "health insurance reform", rather than the misnomer "healthcare reform" which opened them up to charges that government would take over healthcare. All proposals, including single-payer, are based on private delivery of healthcare.

Now enters the well-insured libertarian Cato Institute with full-page ads in the *Washington Post* and the *New York Times* charging Obama with pursuing government-run healthcare. Included is a picture of Uncle Sam pointing under the headline "Your New Doctor." Nonsense. The well-insured people at Cato should know better than to declare that this "government takeover" would "reduce healthcare quality."

About 100,000 lives are lost from medical-hospital negligence per year, according to the Harvard School of Public Health. This vast tragedy is hardly going to get worse under universal government health insurance that assembles data patterns to reduce waste, enhances quality, and transparency. By contrast, the secretive big health insurers who make more money the more they deny claims, ignore their loss prevention duties.

In 1950, when President Truman sent a universal health insurance bill to Congress, the American Medical Association (AMA) launched what was then a massive counterattack. The AMA claimed that government health insurance would lead to rationing of healthcare, higher prices, diminished choices and more bureaucracy. The AMA beat both Truman and the unions that were backing the legislation, using the phrase "socialized medicine" to scare the people.

Fifty-nine years later, "corporatized medicine" has produced all these consequences, along with stripping away the medical profession's independence. Today, the irony is that the corporate supremacists are accusing reformers in Washington of what they themselves have produced throughout the country. Rationing, higher prices, less choice, and mounds of paperwork and corporate red tape. Plus, fifty million people without any health insurance at all.

On Thursday, July 30, 2009, there will be a mass rally for a single-payer system in Washington, DC. It is time to put what most Americans want on the table. (See www.Healthcare-Now.org for more information.)

Practicality On the Table
July 10, 2009

A few days ago, a citizen asked the progressive legislator from California, Congressman Henry Waxman, why he took his name off the list of about eighty House sponsors of single-payer health insurance? Mr. Waxman replied: "it [H.R. 676] isn't going to happen."

In early January and in 2008, Americans who believe in presidential accountability for constitutional, statutory and treaty violations asked Democrats in Congress—"If not impeachment, why not at least a resolution of censure of George W. Bush and Dick Cheney?" The uniform reply was "It's not practical."

These lawmakers—all Democrats, who are the majority in Congress and who agree with these questioners—keep saying "It's not going to happen" or "It's not practical."

"It's just not practical" to provide a federal minimum wage equal to that in 1968, adjusted for inflation—$10 an hour.

"It's not going to happen" to get comprehensive corporate reform at a time when a corporate crime wave and the Wall Street multi-trillion dollar collapse on Washington, on taxpayers and on the economy is tearing this country apart. A little regulatory tinkering is all citizens are told to expect.

"It's just not practical" to give workers, consumers and taxpayers simple facilities for banding together in associations with their own voluntary dues to defend these interests in the corporate occupied territory known as Washington, DC.

Last year, the excuse was a Bush veto. So the Democrats didn't even try to advance reforms they believe in, knowing Bush and his Republican Party would stonewall them. What's the excuse this year with Obama in the White House?

After all, it was only a year and a half ago when nominating and then electing an African-American president was "not going to happen," or "was not practical."

But since it did happen, why aren't these and many other long overdue beneficial redirections and efficiencies happening for the American people? Why aren't there rollbacks, at least, of the Bush-driven inequities and injustices that have so damaged the well-being of working people?

Why isn't a simpler and more efficient carbon tax more "practical" than the complex corruption-prone, corporatized cap and trade deal driven by Goldman Sachs and favored by most Democrats? The avaricious tax cuts for the super-wealthy are still there.

The statutory ban on Uncle Sam negotiating volume discounts on medicines purchased by the federal government are still there. Taking the huge budgets for the Bush wars in Iraq and Afghanistan off their annual fast track, and putting them before a meaningful House and Senate Appropriations Committee hearing process has not happened.

Face it, America. You are a corporate-controlled country with the symbols of democracy in the Constitution and statutes just that—symbols of what the founding fathers believed or hoped would be reality.

Even when the global corporate giants come to Washington dripping with crime, greed, speculation and cover-ups, and demand gigantic bailouts on the backs of taxpayers and their children, neither the Republicans nor the now majority Democrats are willing to face them down.

The best of America started with our forebears who faced down those who told them "it's not going to happen," or "it's not practical" to abolish slavery, give women the right to vote,

elevate the conditions of workers and farmers, provide Social Security and Medicare, make the air and water less polluted and so on. These pioneers, with grit and persistence, told their members of Congress and presidents—"It *is* going to happen."

To paraphrase the words of a great man, the late Reverend William Sloan Coffin, it is as if those legendary stalwarts from our past, knowing how much more there is to achieve a practical, just society, are calling out to us, the people today, and saying "get it done, get it done!"

Stop the Single-payer Shut-out!

May 8, 2009

Among the giant taboos afflicting Congress these days is the proposal to create a single-payer health insurance system (often called full Medicare for everyone).

How can this be? Don't the elected politicians represent the people? Don't they always have their finger to the wind?

Well, single-payer is only supported by a majority of the American people, physicians and nurses. They like the idea of public funding and private delivery. They like the free choice of doctors and hospitals that many are now denied by the HMOs.

There are also great administrative efficiencies when single-payer displaces the health insurance industry and its claims-denying, benefit-restricting, bureaucratically-heavy profiteering. According to leading researchers in this area, Dr. David Himmelstein and Dr. Stephanie Woolhandler, single-payer will save $350 billion annually.

Yet, on Capitol Hill and at the White House

there are no meetings, briefings, hearings, or consultations about healthcare reforms that reform the basic price inflation, indifference to prevention, and discrimination by health insurers.

There is no place at the table for single-payer advocates in the view of the Congressional leaders who set the agenda and muzzle dissenters.

Last month at a breakfast meeting with reporters, House Speaker Nancy Pelosi (D-Calif.) responded to a question about healthcare with these revealing and exasperating words: "Over and over again, we hear single-payer, single-payer, single-payer. Well, it's not going to be a single-payer."

Thus spoke Speaker Pelosi, the Representative from Aetna. Never mind that 75 members of her party have signed onto H.R. 676—Rep. John Conyers's single-payer legislation. Never mind that in her San Francisco district, probably three out of four people want single-payer. And never mind that more than 20,000 people die every year, according to the Institute of Medicine, because they cannot afford health insurance.

What is more remarkable is that many more than the 75 members of the House privately believe single-payer is the best option. Hillary Clinton, Barack Obama, Ted Kennedy, and Nancy Pelosi are among them. But they all say, single-payer "is not practical" so it's off the table.

What gives here? The Democrats have the numbers and procedures to pass any kind of health reform this year, including single-payer. President Obama could sign it into law.

But "it's not practical" because these politicians fear the insurance and pharmaceutical industries—and seek their campaign contributions—more than they fear the American people. It comes down to the corporations, who have no votes but are organized to the teeth and the people are not.

When Senator Baucus, chairman of the Senate Finance Committee and a large recipient of health insurance and drug company donations, held a public roundtable discussion on May 5, fifteen witnesses were preparing to deliver their statements. Not one of them was championing single-payer.

As Senator Baucus started his introductory remarks, something happened. One by one, eight people in the audience, most of them physicians and lawyers, stood up to politely but insistently protest the absence of a single-payer presentation.

One by one, the police came, took them out of the hearing room, arrested and handcuffed them. The charge was "disruption of Congress"—a misdemeanor.

They call themselves the "Baucus Eight." Immediately, over the internet and on C-SPAN, public radio, and the Associated Press, the news spread around the country. You can see the video on singlepayeraction.org.

To the many groups and individuals who have labored for single-payer for decades, the Baucus Eight's protest seemed like an epiphany.

Dr. Quentin Young, a veteran leader for single-payer and a founder of Physicians for a National Health Program (PNHP) emailed his reaction: "For our part, when the history of this period is written, we believe your action may well be noted as the turning point from a painful, defensive position to a more appropriate offensive position vis-à-vis Senator Baucus and his health industry co-conspirators."

Webster's dictionary defines "taboo" as "a prohibition against touching, saying, or doing something for fear of a mysterious superhuman force." For both Democrats and Republicans in Congress it is a fear of a very omnipresent supercorporate force.

However, moral and evidential courage is coming. On May 12, 2009, Senator Baucus is having another roundtable discussion with thirteen more witnesses, including those from the business lobbies and their consultants. Word has it that the Senator is about to invite a leading single-payer advocate to sit at the table.

Here come the people! Join this historic drive to have our country join the community of western, and some third-world, nations by adopting a state of the art single-payer system.

Visit singlepayeraction.org and break the taboo in your Congressional District.

The Lethargy Virus

May 1, 2009

The Swine Flu (or H1N1 virus) is in the air. The public health authorities are acting "in excess of caution" to curb its spread from Mexico into this country. Already, however, this virus and the publicity around it is providing another occasion to question our nation's priorities.

Let's put it this way—the gravest terrorists in the world today are viruses and bacterium with their astonishing ability to mutate, hitchhike and devastate human beings. Yet despite small outbreaks—such as the SARS virus from China—we collectively seem to be waiting until the "big pandemic" before we come to our senses and redefine national security and national defense.

It is not that we are unaware of the massive toll that tuberculosis, malaria, AIDS and many other infectious diseases exact year after year. Just those three diseases take over 5 million lives a year. It is not that we fail to realize how international trade, tourism and other travels—together with environmental disruptions—accelerate the spread and range of these silent forms of violence.

Our lethargy stems from the fact that the causes of such casualties are seen as impersonal, unlike 9/11 terrorists or state inflicted terrorism which is viewed as anthropomorphic. That is, they are attributed to proper names of specific people, gangs, armies and nations.

In 2004, when I was on the Bill Maher show, Bill asked me why I was running for president outside the two major parties. I replied that one reason was to call public attention to such issues as our nation's approach to infectious diseases. Maher gave me that look of his and blurted "aw come on!"

For years before that campaign, the inattention given to these invisible marauders was irrational. First came complacency. In the 1950s, professors at Harvard University advised students not to specialize in infectious diseases because the new rush of antibiotics had placed them under control. Myopic indeed. Our country now has a serious shortage of MDs, public health experts and other scientists to confront, prevent and treat these diseases here and abroad.

About 130 countries have signed the International Covenant on Economic, Social and Cultural Rights (ICESCR) which, in Article 12, provides that everyone should enjoy the "highest attainable standard" of well-being, to be attained by the "prevention, treatment, and control of epidemic, endemic, occupational, and other diseases." The US signed this treaty in 1979, but it has never been ratified by the US Senate.

The appearance of drug-resistant tuberculosis in the US during the early 1990s helped prompt the Tuberculosis Initiative, organized in 1997, by my Princeton Class of 1955, to press public and elected officials in Washington to increase funds and activities regarding this scourge. The Soros and Gates Foundations have put resources into a global assault on TB, working with the World Health Organization (WHO).

WHO's total budget last year was $4.2 billion—a pittance given its urgent responsibilities. The United States government's contribution—22 percent—has been in chronic arrears. By comparison, our government has granted trillions of dollars since September to the financial perpetrators of the epidemic of Wall Street speculation, fraud and costly criminal greed.

While for state and local health departments, budget cuts have reduced hundreds of millions of dollars and thousands of workers on what the *New York Times* calls "the front line in the country's defense against a possible swine flu pandemic."

Meanwhile, before the recent swine flu news, Senators, including Republicans Susan Collins and Arlen Specter (before his conversion to the Democratic Party) cut $780 million from Barack Obama's stimulus package for pandemic flu preparation.

To be sure, in recent years, both the Bush Administration and Democrats, such as Senator Patrick Leahy, have moved the needle toward spending more on vaccine research, medical technology and contingency planning. This is a response, in part, to post 9/11 fears and the continuing reluctance of the drug industry CEOs to apply their profits to discovering vaccines, which by their infrequent usage, they deem not profitable enough.

Maybe the giant steps forward will come after some members of Congress themselves come down with these ailments during their travels. As one House legislative aide said, "that'll get their attention," adding wryly "but only if it's broadly bi-partisan."

Almost seventy years ago, Wendell Willkie, the Republican nominee challenging Franklin Delano Roosevelt in the 1940 elections, wrote a prescient book titled *One World*. When it comes to contagious micro-organisms, there are no boundaries without internationally sustained human efforts.

The Sorry State of Healthcare in America
May 5, 2008

This is the grim story of a cancer patient, Lisa Kelly, and the famous, well endowed, non-profit M.D. Anderson Cancer Center of the University of Texas.

Barbara Martinez, a reporter for the *Wall Street Journal*, related the billing hurdles that Mrs. Kelly has been confronting since late 2006 in a shocking front-page story on April 28, 2008.

This is a tale of pay or die that recurs again and again all over our country and nowhere else in the entire western world.

Advised by her physician to go to M.D. Anderson for urgent treatment of her leukemia, Mrs. Kelly was told she had to pay $105,000 up front before being admitted. The hospital declared her limited insurance unacceptable.

Sitting in the business office with seriously advanced cancer, she asked herself—"Are they going to send me home?" "Am I going to die?"

Time out from her torment for a moment. M.D. Anderson started this upfront payment demand in 2005 because of a spike in its bad debt load.

The *Journal* explains—"The bad debt is driven by a larger number of Americans who are uninsured or who don't have enough insurance to cover costs if catastrophe strikes. Even among those with adequate insurance, deductibles and co-payments are growing so big that insured patients also have trouble paying hospitals."

It isn't as if non-profit hospitals like M.D. Anderson are hurting. Look at this finding in an Ohio State University study: net income per bed at non-profit hospitals tripled to $146,273 in 2005 from $50,669 in 2000. And you also may have noticed the huge pay packages awarded to hospital executives.

M.D. Anderson, exempt from taxation, recipient of funds from large government programs and research grants has cash, investments and endowment totaling $1.9 billion, with a net income of $310 million last year, the *Journal* reports.

Back to the fifty-two-year-old, Lisa Kelly. She and her husband returned with a check for $45,000. After a blood test and biopsy, the hospital oncologist urged admittance quickly. Then the hospital demanded an additional $60,000-$45,000 just for the lab tests and $15,000 for part of the cost of the treatment.

To shorten the story, she received chemotherapy for over a year. Often her appointment was "blocked" until she made another payment.

In a particularly grotesque incident, she was hooked up to a chemotherapy pump, but the nurses were not allowed to change the chemo bag until Mr. Kelly made another payment.

She endured other indignities and overcharges. Reporter Martinez cites $360 for blood tests that insurers pay $20 or less for and up to $120 for saline pouches that cost less than $2 retail.

Imagine anything like Mrs. Kelly's predicament and pressures occurring in Canada, Belgium, Germany, Italy, France, Switzerland, Holland, England or any other Western country. It would never happen.

These countries have universal single-payer health insurance. No one dies because they cannot afford healthcare. In America, 18,000 Americans die each year because they cannot afford healthcare, according to the Institute of Medicine of the National Academy of Sciences. Many more get sick or become sicker.

None of these countries spend more than 11 percent of their GDP on healthcare. The US spends over 16 percent of its GDP on healthcare and does not cover 47 million people and tens of millions are under covered

In the US the drug companies charge their highest prices in the world, even though we, the taxpayers, subsidized them in large ways. In other countries like Mexico and Canada, they cannot get away with such drug price gouging, with a pay or die ultimatum.

In the US, computerized billing fraud and abuse cost over $200 billion last year, according to the GAO arm of Congress. In other counties, single-payer systems prevent such looting.

In other countries, administrative expenses of their single-payer system are about a third of what the Aetnas and other insurers rack up.

In other Western countries, medical outcomes for children and adults and paid family leave are far superior to that of the US. The World Health Organization ranks the US healthcare system 37th in the world.

When apologists in Washington hear these statistics, they say "but we have the best medical research centers in the world, like M.D. Anderson."

Clearly much is wrong with the nature of pricing healthcare.

Like other hospitals, M.D. Anderson is caught in a macabre spider's web of cost allocations mixing treatment costs with research budgets, cash reserves, and just plain accounting gimmicks that burden patients. (Documents from Mrs. Kelly's case are available at online .wsj.com today.)

When a friend showed the *Journal*'s article to a Dutch visitor, the latter blurted in anger—"you are a nation of sheep." Not a very flattering description of "the land of the free, home of the brave."

Someday, soon maybe, Americans will finally band together and say "enough already," we're going for full Medicare for all—without loopholes for corporate profiteers and purveyors of waste and fraud.

Last month after being in remission, Lisa Kelly's leukemia has come back.

Fueling Food Shortages

April 25, 2008

Where is Harry Chapin when you need him? The popular folk singer ("Cat's in the Cradle"), who lost his life in an auto crash 27 years ago, was an indefatigable force of nature against hunger—in this country and around the world.

To hear Harry speak out against the scourge of hunger in a world of plenty was to hear relentless informed passion whether on Capitol Hill, at poverty conferences or at his concerts.

Now the specter of world hunger is looming, with sharply rising basic food prices and unnecessary food shortages sparking food riots in places like Haiti and Egypt. Officials with the UN's World Food Programme (WFP) are alarmed. The WFP has put out an emergency appeal for more funds, saying another 100 million humans have been thrown into the desperate hunger pits.

Harry would have been all over the politicians in Congress and the White House who, with their bellies full, could not muster the empathy to do something.

Directly under Bush and the Congress is the authority to reduce the biggest single factor boosting food prices—reversing the tax-subsidized policy of growing ever more corn to turn into fuel at the expense of huge acreages that are used to produce wheat, soy, rice and other edibles.

Corn ethanol is a multifaceted monstrosity—radiating damage in all directions of the compass. Reducing acreage for edible crops has sparked a surge in the price of bread and other foodstuffs. Congress and Bush continue to mandate larger amounts of subsidized corn ethanol.

Republican Representative Robert W. Goodlatte says: "The mandate basically says [corn] ethanol comes ahead of food on your table, comes ahead of feed for livestock, comes ahead of grains available for export."

Corn growing farmers are happy with a bushel coming in at $5 to $6—a record.

A subsidy-laden, once-every-five-years farm bill is winding its way through Congress. The bill keeps the "good-to-fuel" mandates that are expanding corn acreage and contributing to a rise of global food prices.

Of course, more meat diets in China, futures market speculation, higher prices for oil and some bad weather and poor food reserve planning have also contributed to shortages and higher prices.

But subsidized corn ethanol gets the first prize for policy madness. It not only damages the environment, soaks up the water from Midwest aquifers, scuttles set asides for soil conservation, but its net energy equation qualifies for collective insanity on Capitol Hill. To produce a gallon of ethanol from corn requires almost as much energy (mostly coal burning) as it produces.

Designed to alleviate oil imports, hold down gasoline prices and diminish greenhouse gases, corn ethanol has flopped on all three scores.

Princeton scholar Lester Brown, an early sounder of the alarm of global food shortages and higher prices, writes in *Science Magazine* "that the net impact of the food-to-fuel push will be an increase in global carbon emissions—and thus a catalyst for climate change."

Can Congress change course and drop its farm subsidy of corn ethanol this year? Observers say, despite the growing calamities and the real risk of severe malnutrition, even starvation in Africa, Congress will do nothing.

Farm subsidies, once installed, are carved in stone—unless there is enough outcry from food consumers, taxpayers and environmentalists. They are paying from the pocketbook, from their taxes and health. That should be enough motivation, unless they need to see the distended stomachs of African and Asian children on the forthcoming television news.

Unless we wake up, we will continue to be a country stuck in traffic—in more ways than one.

Don't rely on the election year political debates to pay attention to destructive corn ethanol programs. For years I have been speaking out against this boondoggle, while championing the small farmer in America, but no one in positions of Congressional leadership has been listening.

They must be waiting for the situation to get worse before they absorb a fraction of Harry Chapin's empathy and care.

Stop Importing Dangerous Drugs

February 22, 2008

Like other families, the Bush family eats, uses medicines, and relies on the Food and Drug Administration (FDA) to assure the safety of vast amounts of both products.

Like other families, more and more of the food and medicine you consume is coming from other countries where the FDA has very little inspection authority. Nearly 80 percent of active pharmaceutical ingredients are imported from foreign countries.

Hardly a day goes by without a news story recounting or disclosing casualties or serious perils from contaminated food and medicines. Many of these and other medicines have seriously harmful side-effects or lack of efficacy.

President Bush is the leading factor in the country on whether or not the FDA can be an adequately funded, staffed, and empowered agency to urgently fulfill what he says repeatedly is his top priority—to protect the safety of the American people.

So how is the FDA doing under his watch? A troubled agency for decades, politically undermined and deficient in budgets, the FDA is now more burdened and besieged than ever. Its budget last year was $2 billion—the price ten years ago of one B-2 bomber. Here are the FDA's own words:

> More than 250 different foodborne illnesses are food safety threats. Based on Centers for Disease Control estimates, 76 million Americans become sick, more than 300,000 are hospitalized and 5,000 die each year from foodborne illnesses. Recent outbreaks highlight the need for increased resources to strengthen food safety. . . .

The FDA's other major responsibility is to "approve safe and effective drugs and medical products in a timely way and ensure that medical products remain safe."

In recent months, there have been many drugs implicated in preventable heart attacks (Vioxx); one thousand lives lost each month (Trasylol); increased risk of heart attacks (Avandia); hundreds of adverse effects, 4 fatalities so far (heparin from a Chinese factory that the FDA did not inspect. It confused its name with another factory.)

The flood of essentially unregulated, uninspected products from China keeps making headlines. Polluted seafood from fish farms, defective tires, lead-painted toys, poisoned pet food, ingredients in products that appear to be, but are not, made or raised in the USA. Country of origin labels are often not required.

What is called "free trade" with China is really corporate managed trade that ships factories and jobs to China, or contracts with Chinese firms that operated in a Wild West atmosphere. The products are then exported to the United States along with all the hazards and defects allowed by this communist dictatorship.

President Bush is not only doing nothing about a huge trade imbalance with China resulting in huge borrowings from China; he is also allowing the products of corrupt corporatism in China to send products that flow into the bodies of American consumers, American patients and American children.

As the *New York Times* wrote: "Instead of strengthening the government's regulatory systems, the Bush administration has spent years cutting budgets and filling top jobs with industry favorites. The evidence of their failures keeps mounting ..."

Similarly over at the Department of Agriculture, meat and poultry inspectors, authorized by laws we helped pass starting in the late 1960s, are, by and large, not backed up by their superiors. Instead, they are reprimanded or reassigned when they stand firm to protect the food supply against politically-connected companies.

The FDA still, decades after its founding, does not have subpoena power. Its food inspection system, especially for imports, is pathetic. Both the FDA and the Department of Agriculture need stronger law enforcement and mandatory recall power with full White House backing.

In his eighth year of office, President Bush has not been a leader of fighting for comprehensive legislation that would no longer leave Americans defenseless in the markets of food and drugs. When just one drug takes 1000 American lives a month (see CBS *60 Minutes*, February 17, 2008), you better believe this is a national security matter that President Bush should pay focused attention to, even if no suspected terrorists are involved.

However, his ideology is one of no-law-and-order, no regulation, that is, of these corporate outlaws and their profiteering, reckless practices. President Bush and his party's campaign chests are filled by these very corporate interests.

As a result, the FDA shakes from one crisis after another, from one blunder after another, from one missed opportunity for prevention after another.

Yet, he still says that his top priority is "maintaining a culture of life," and that "my number one priority is to protect you."

President Bush owes the American people, in a major national address, an explanation and very soon.

Clean Up the Cruise Industry
August 6, 2007

The multi-billion dollar cruise line business, plying international waters alongside different national jurisdictions, has been playing a hide and seek game for years. Hiding the dumping of harmful wastes and chemicals into marine environments and seeking all kinds of concessions and non-regulation by lobbying and federal regulators.

The media takes them over the coals from time to time when they are caught illegally dumping or in the rare instances when they are prosecuted for felonious behavior. Public exposés, viral or bacterial epidemics causing these companies severe embarrassment and lawsuits, and occasional harrowing stories from mistreated crew members mostly from developing countries, have pressed the industry to adopt improved waste treatment technologies and voluntary industry codes of more acceptable practices.

The rule of American law has still not caught up with them. Until, that is, the companies lost a fierce battle in Alaska last year over a Cruise Ship Ballot Initiative (CSBI) which Alaskans passed in August 2006.

No other state has embraced the cruise companies with an enforceable regime of accountability. Florida and Washington State, for example, have Memorandums of Understanding (MOUs) which have no enforcement mechanism, despite recent findings by Washington state that the discharge point impact on shrimp and other marine life left zero survivors instead of the expected 80 percent (the so-called "wet tests").

So, Alaska is leading the way. Gershon Cohen, who with labor union lawyer, Joseph Geldhof, led the victorious mobilization of voters, described the rationale this way: "We want waste discharges from the cruise industry to meet all Alaska Water Quality Standards as required of every other discharger into Alaskan waters.

"We believe the cruise industry should pay corporate income taxes, from which they were exempted by the Legislature in 1998. We think the cruise industry should pay a percentage of their gambling profits to Alaska like every other gaming operator in the State.

"We need to have an independent marine engineer [the Ocean Ranger Program] aboard every ship to make sure they don't dump untreated wastes into our waters or falsify logbooks—actions that have repeatedly brought them felony convictions in the last decade."

The taxes are now being collected. And the Alaskan Department of Environmental Conservations, together with other agencies, are in the process of issuing the rules to implement the initiative after a public notice and comment period.

The Ocean Ranger Program is about to start to generate the deterrence and inspection programs that will be very useful to other lagging states considering similar legislation to "protect passengers, crew and residents at ports from improper sanitation, health and safety practices," to quote the words from the CSBI.

Given the many thousands of passengers who have gotten sick from contaminated food or from noroviruses, other states need to end their endless indulgence of the cruise industry lobbyists. As for workers, some of the crew are unionized. But most of the laborers have few or no rights and have no organized representatives. Being offshore, US labor laws do not apply to protect them.

With Alaska and Alaskan Native Organizations leading the way, can the other states and the US Environmental Protection Agency (EPA) be that far behind? That depends on the passengers, the more outspoken workers especially when they have quit, the detailed ship and cruise line-specific information coming from Alaska and a more inquiring media.

On March 17, 2000, Clinton's EPA Administrator, Carol Browner, received a petition with detailed recommendations for regulatory action signed by leading Democratic members of the House and Senate, environmental groups, officials from the EPA itself, the Department of Justice and the US Coast Guard.

Result: Nothing has been done under Clinton or under the Bush Government to address this remarkably detailed and documented petition.

The major interaction with the Bush government has been a huge rip-off by Carnival Cruise Lines which received, under a no-bid contract with FEMA, a $236 million contract for three of its ships to house homeless people, post-Katrina. For details see the website for Rep. Henry Waxman (D-Calif.) (http://www.house.gov/waxman/) for letters and testimony regarding this debacle.

When reminded of its felony convictions for deliberate dumping, installing "magic pipes" to facilitate a total bypass of treatment, bypassing the oil bilgewater separators, giving false information to the Coast Guard, the industry's standard reply is "that was then and now conditions are better."

Enforcement of the Alaskan law covering a million passengers plus crew every summer, together with a citizen's lawsuit provision awarding portions of penalties to whistleblowers who provide information leading to convictions, will test that claim.

For more information and ways you can become involved in challenging this industry, see www.cruisejunkie.com and Ross Klein's two books—*Cruise Ship Blue* and *Cruise Ship Squeeze*. Another useful website is www.internationalcruisevictims.org.

Michael Moore and Healthcare Reform
June 25, 2007

He sat there dejected and indignant—twenty years ago—in our office. His position as editor of the monthly muckraking magazine, *Mother Jones*, had broken up. He was looking for a job that would allow him to bring his conscience to work.

We gave him a place and support to start *Moore's Weekly*—a media critique.

Michael Moore has gone a long way since that short-lived publication. He went on to do documentary films, starting with *Roger and Me*.

Rich, famous and Hollywood chic, Moore will open his latest film, *Sicko*, in theatres around the country on June 29, 2007. To many of those who have already seen this indictment and conviction of the corporations that sell healthcare under an array of tricky conditions, it is his best move yet.

He was in Washington, DC last week, for a preview at the large Uptown Theatre and for testimony before a House Committee. The media followed him with a frenzy hitherto reserved for Paris Hilton.

But Michael Moore is no Paris Hilton from any dimension you wish to choose. He is a heavyweight reformer, pitching his film toward full Medicare for everyone. This also means displacing the health insurance industry the way Medicare partially did in the mid-Sixties for the elderly.

"I think one movie can make a difference; . . . I believe it will be a catalyst for the type of real change people want," Moore told the *New York Times.*

Great movies and documentaries raise people's latent indignation levels—for a short time.

Norma Rae, *The China Syndrome*, and *The Grapes of Wrath* had this effect. But films do not usually move either people or legislators to action. Their effect does not reach enough people. Their urgent two-hour impact tends to diminish quickly, as compared with the omnipresent and powerful corporate or commercial interests determined to preserve the status quo.

Will *Sicko* be any different? Certainly the giant HMOs, hospital chains and drug companies are firmly entrenched with all the sinews of power that have left this country, alone among Western nations, without healthcare for all. They have endured easily many mainstream print and television exposés (see the *New York Times*, AP, *60 Minutes* and the nightly evening news, for example) year after year.

Authoritative reports documenting over $200 billion a year in computerized billing fraud and abuse or the loss of 18,000 American lives yearly due to the unaffordability of healthcare (The Institute of Medicine) bounce off this two trillion dollar industry like marshmallows.

Learning the ropes as a community organizer in Michigan, (see the new book, *Citizen Moore* by Roger Rapaport) Moore has prepared with all this in mind. He allied himself with the great California Nurses Association and their nationwide colleagues to demonstrate in favor of the film, contact legislators and organize with other large unions.

The anticipatory media for the movie have been generous; citing the US government's move against Moore for what it claims was an unauthorized trip to Cuba. Right-wing think tanks, funded by this hyper-profitable, subsidized industry, pour out inane rebuttals and offer quotes against Moore for reporters.

Unlike other social justice movies, there is even a bill in Congress, H.R. 676 with 74 co-sponsoring legislators, led by Cong. John Conyers (D-Mich.), to establish full Medicare for all.

That is a number of lawmakers considerably less than those who signed on to a similar bill in 1993.

There are 17 million more Americans uninsured today than in that year, totaling nearly 48 million without coverage in 2006. So you see where that trend is heading.

If Moore is serious about getting "real change," as he phrases his goal, he will have to make at least two more contributions. First, he will need to make a comprehensive effort to get many of the 6 million or more people, who will see the film, to sign up as they enter or leave the theatres so that they can be given a chance to connect with each other for a cohesive change constituency.

Secondly, some of the millions he will make from this movie should be put into a full-time lobbying organization in Washington and back in the Congressional districts to press for enactment of H.R. 676.

With all his super-rich Hollywood contacts and admirers, Moore should be able to multiply this proposed group's budget several fold. Michael can even call it "Moore's Miracle!"

Earth Day at 37
April 23, 2007

The first Earth Day—launched in April 1970 with 1,500 events held mostly on college campuses by enormous student groups—led the television network news and made the covers of the national news magazines.

The thirty-seventh Earth Day—in April 2007—was broader based than the first Earth Day but in many ways more debased by corporate greenwashing, and political posturing marinated in corporate campaign cash.

A comparison of the two periods, both characterized by a surge in ecological recognitions of perils and possibilities, is instructive.

In 1970, the environmental arousal focused on pesticides, air and water pollution, with attention to workplace toxics contributing to occupational diseases. Widely publicized were the inversions in the Los Angeles area, chocking with vehicles, and the Cuyahoga River near Cleveland where seeping petroleum slicks were sometimes set on fire—on the river!

The action goals were legislative authority directing the federal executive agencies to regulate and reduce permissible pollution. Compared with today, legislation passed through Congress at a torrid pace. Objecting corporate lobbyists were swept aside.

Among the bills enacted into law were the water pollution and air pollution statutes, the drinking water safety act, the establishment of the Environmental Protection Agency (EPA) and the Occupational Safety and Health Administration (OSHA).

So prevalent and visible were millions of Americans calling for action that Presidents Richard M. Nixon and Gerald Ford signed them into law with strong statements of support for their promised purposes. Ford rode the wave rolling across the country to Washington, DC.

Some results were measurable. The ouster of lead in gasoline and paint reduced the level of lead in peoples' bodies. Levels of vinyl chloride in the bodies of industrial workers disappeared. Asbestos was close to being banned for most commercial purposes. The first mandatory fuel efficiency standards for motor vehicles were issued in 1975 to be met by 1985 at the average fleet mark of 27.5 miles per gallon.

Then came the corporate counterattack replete with money, muscle and daily propaganda. Regulation was blamed for everything save spots on the sun. Deregulation became the mantra that rewarded more and more elected politicians who performed the requisite courtesies and bows. By 1980 the Democrats had joined the race for business campaign cash with the Republicans. The Reagan era began, led by an ex-actor who said that most air pollution came from trees.

Corporate apologists started writing reams of materials about public-private partnerships and marketplace trading of pollution credits. They compromised government's arms length responsibilities with joint ventures where taxpayer monies were used by Washington, DC to subsidize collusive auto industry research, for example, under the Clinton Administration. These projects went nowhere, wasting billions of dollars and shielding in the process auto company exposure to regulation and to the antitrust laws.

The massive environmental stall had begun. Less technology-forcing regulation, less enforcement and less overdue lawmaking to provide ethical-legal frameworks for new risks coming from genetic engineering, nano-technology and the relentless use of many invasive new chemicals in the human environment.

Today, there are reports of many more global Earth Day events, including the global warming networking of Al Gore. Awareness of both the sustaining role of oceans, rivers, air quality, forests, prairies and the enormous costs of their damage or displacement is understood by many more people than in 1970. Consider the remarkable roll-back of the tobacco industry's deliberate addiction of their customers at an early age.

Companies are rushing to give themselves a clearer environmental image with chain stores taking on more organic food and spreading their environmental labeling of products. More so-called green buildings are under construction. Companies like General Electric are talking a good game, but they are working to bring back nuclear power with all its costs, risks and tax-payer subsidies.

So for all the greenwashing, the auto industries are still on Capitol Hill blocking improved fuel efficiencies for motor vehicles which presently are the lowest since 1980. Electric generating plants—often burning coal—have not significantly changed their gross design inefficiencies of bygone years.

The coal barons are still blowing off the mountaintops and widening the land areas they are strip-mining. Asthma rates among children are climbing. Land erosion continues unabated.

One can gauge the lack of progress three ways.

Is the country moving expeditiously to make existing "best practices" the overall practice throughout the economy?

Are we applying the insight of Professor Barry Commoner that prevention is better than tepid often evaded controls of specific, harmful pollutants, as we did when we took the lead out of paint and gasoline?

Do we have a massive conversion agenda, led by leading politicians for solar energy in all its efficient forms, including wind power, and for the dramatic improvements in energy efficiency now readily available for application?

For the most part, the answer to these questions is NO!

Hold the Smoke
February 20, 2007

Among the greatest unsung public health advances of recent times is progress made against the global cigarette industry.

In the United States, cigarette smoking is finally on the decline. The courts have ruled the tobacco industry to be "racketeers." Smokefree spaces, including not just workplaces but restaurants and bars, are proliferating, reducing the harms of second-hand smoke and encouraging millions to quit. States are raising cigarette taxes, reducing smoking and raising funds for important public health programs.

Internationally, progress is speeding even faster. A global treaty, the Framework Convention on Tobacco Control, is encouraging countries to adopt far-reaching anti-smoking measures, including bans on all cigarette advertisements. Countries are emulating and surpassing the smokefree initiatives in the United States—even Irish pubs are now smokefree!

But despite all the public health gains, Big Tobacco is still on the move, addicting millions more smokers. And the industry has some unfortunate allies.

One important cultural ally of Big Tobacco is Hollywood. Smoking in youth-rated movies in on the rise, and it has demonstrable effects on smoking rates.

According to researchers at the University of California San Francisco Center for Tobacco Control Research and Education, smoking appears even more in Hollywood movies released with G/PG/PG-13 than in R-rated films. Altogether, 75 percent of all US releases have smoking scenes. One cartoon film now on DVD, "The Ant Bully," includes 41 tobacco scenes.

Researchers have found that viewing smoking in movies makes it far more likely that children will take up the habit—controlling for all other relevant factors (such as whether parents and peers smoke).

Think about it—the movies are glamorous, and they portray smoking as glamorous, whether or not it is a good guy or bad guy lighting a cigarette.

The public health advances against Big Tobacco are due in significant part to effective efforts to vilify the industry. When children especially appreciate how the companies are manipulating them, they resist. Hollywood's glorification of smoking works directly against this.

US films bring in 30 percent of movie box office sales globally, and Hollywood's contribution to smoking is significant overseas, where the tobacco epidemic is worst. Ten million people are expected to die every year from smoking-related disease by 2025, 70 percent of them in developing countries. Hollywood movies have gigantic appeal overseas, often with even greater cultural influence than in the United States. They appeal exactly to the demographic most likely to take up smoking—urbanized, middle-class youth who aspire to live Western lifestyles.

This is an easy problem to cure. Leading US health groups and the United Nation's World Health Organization have urged Hollywood to adopt R-ratings for movies with tobacco scenes (with exceptions where the presentation of tobacco clearly and unambiguously reflects the dangers and consequences of tobacco use or is necessary to represent the smoking of a real historical figure), to air anti-tobacco spots before films with tobacco imagery, to certify that movies with tobacco received no tobacco industry pay-offs, and to stop identifying tobacco brands in movies. None of these measures involves any "censorship."

The industry has resisted.

This week, leading up to the 79th Annual Academy Awards, public health groups and agencies from New York and Los Angeles, from Liverpool and Sydney have mobilized to demand that Hollywood end its complicity with Big Tobacco.

In Washington, DC, representatives of the Smokefree Movies Action Network, dressed in biohazard suits, called on the Motion Picture Association of America to remove "toxic" tobacco content from youth-rated films. They presented the MPAA with a "golden coffin."

The trade association's representatives declined to accept the award.

The celebration of film at the Oscars reminds us of Hollywood's reach. That's exactly why it is so important to get smoking out of kid-rated films.

For more information about tobacco in Hollywood, the evidence of harm, and the widely endorsed policy solutions, visit www.smokefreemovies.ucsf.edu.

On ABC's Primetime Special Edition "Out of Control: AIDS in Black America"

George W. Bush—the master of fabricated distractions—as with the false pretense invasion of Iraq—has turned the national television news media away from the United States.

So it was a sobering reversal of direction to watch ABC's August 24 *Primetime* Special Edition "Out of Control: AIDS in Black America." It marked the 25th anniversary of the first reported cases of AIDS and the last documentary that the late Peter Jennings worked to put on the air.

With 13 percent of the US population, black Americans constitute over 50 percent of all new cases of HIV. This infection rate is eight times the rate of whites. It gets worse. Almost 70 percent of new female cases of HIV-positive women are black women who are a stunning 13 times more likely to be diagnosed with AIDS than white women. Black women get AIDS overwhelmingly through heterosexual contact, the documentary reported.

Terry Moran, who did a fine job as anchor, candidly interviewed black leaders working on AIDS and infectious disease specialists to find out why.

In summary: (1) infection comes more heavily to the black community due to high rates of HIV-positive men coming out of prison, (2) drug addiction and the widespread use of dirty needles, (3) the taboo against talking about the problem of homosexual-related AIDS transmission in many black religious circles and (4) the absence of any comprehensive AIDS prevention and treatment programs that reach the netherworld of community-wide poverty, despair and lack of information.

Still, the attentive viewer would want to know more. Moran obliged. He asked Jesse Jackson and others why prominent black leaders do not highlight this disaster more than they do, or as they do for the AIDS epidemic in Africa. One reply was that there are so many disasters afflicting black America that attention to one takes away from the other.

Moran then showed a clip of a sermon by well-known Rev. Calvin Butts of the Abyssinian Baptist Church in New York City. "You can't sleep with everyone you want to sleep with," bewailed a tormented Rev. Butts.

It is not as if whites are much less drug-addicted. But there is a disproportionate percentage of black men in jail where homosexual contact is the HIV transmitter. Moran pointed to

studies from the Universities of Chicago and North Carolina which conclude that black men are more than twice as likely as white men to have multiple female partners.

Still, the disproportions noted in *Out of Control* are so vast between blacks and whites that a deeper condition must be at work here. Call it another vast disproportion. A sub-society of deep poverty, unemployment, despair, street drugs, documented discriminatory law enforcement and prison incarceration rates, the absence of neighborhood public health facilities skilled in addressing the triple needs of testing, prevention and treatment are all incubators without portfolios. A vicious cycle of infection is out of control in these environments.

The social services, such as health coverage, that have restrained the AIDS epidemic among whites are not proportionately there among black communities.

The ABC documentary may be crying out in the wilderness or it may be a wake-up call with its own multiplier effect. Don't count on the Bush regime, bogged down in the Iraq quagmire and looking for other wars, to take notice. The lead burden will be on black community leaders and an aroused public health profession to turn around our country's priorities in Congress, the White House, state and local governments, and prod more media attention. On the local and national television news, there is certainly enough trivia to replace.

You may wonder what the fatality count among blacks is each year. More than ten thousand black Americans died from AIDS last year. The family agonies and deprivations are not compiled in these statistics.

New Approaches To End Malaria

November 5, 2005

Suppose every day for the past umpteen years, four fully loaded Boeing 747 Jumbo Jets crashed full of African children. Suppose further that no one doubted that similar children-filled jumbo jets would crash at this level every day into the indefinite future. Don't you think that at some point something big would be done about this slaughter of the innocents? Well, every day about 2,000 African children die from malaria as their predecessors have died for centuries. Only now the mortality levels are as high or higher than they have ever been in this modern, technology-driven 21st century. What goes here?

For starters, children are not dying from malaria in Western countries that have the wealth, know-how and discovery-potential to do something. Second, these massive fatalities, which often include their mothers, are not caused by terrorists. Unless, that is the malarial mosquito and its deadly parasite can be called "terrorists" of real weapons of mass destruction. Third, death from malaria has been going on since time immemorial; its part of the developing countries' landscape of banal inevitability. It doesn't have the novelty of a new disease such as AIDS or a looming avian influenza pandemic.

Malaria has not had any single-minded lobbyists who are either fortified by big money or have Hollywood celebrity status. I know this because for the last 13 years, some of us have been grappling with this puzzling disinterest regarding both malaria and tuberculosis, which between them take about four million lives a year.

Even the Bill and Melinda Gates Foundation's grants for malaria research in recent years have not sparked that "fire in the belly" feeling either among the health powers-that-be in governments or among the general public.

Just last month, the Gates Foundation pledged $258 million for research toward a malaria vaccine, new drugs and improved ways of mosquito control. That's big by malaria budget standards. The Gates announcement did not even make page one on most newspapers. It was an inside story for the *Washington Post,* the *New York Times* and the *Wall Street Journal* and not a very large one at that.

Enter Lance Laifer, a Hedge Fund manager, commuting between Connecticut and New Jersey. One evening last June he was watching a television interview program, which reported that malaria was taking well over a million lives a year and the world was not doing much about it. He was, in his words, "amazed since I thought Malaria was eradicated hundreds of years ago." Possessed by a sense of urgency, he started researching. His conclusion: "what I found was that this disease is the worse positioned and marketed disease on the planet."

In searching the internet, he called me after coming across my column urging Hedge Fund zillionaires to establish a revolving $100 million fund for immediate response to famines erupting in places like Niger. It was during our conversation and after his first conference of malarial experts in New York City on September 20 that I sensed Mr. Laifer knew what it was going to take to put the chronic malarial epidemic on the front burner of public health action.

He started "Hedge Funds Against Malaria"—an eyebrow raiser to be sure—because "there are no business people involved in fighting this disease day in and day out. . . . There are no fundraisers. There are no Malaria Political Action Committees. It is not thought about creatively."

Mr. Laifer takes off on the "good news," that "malaria is fundamentally a preventable disease transmitted by mosquitoes. If the children and adults—malaria is the largest killer of mothers on the planet—are provided with bed nets, sprays, and medicines, they can be protected. . . ." he says.

It is time for relentless repetition of the message, drama in its delivery and a firestorm of emergency. So this Hedge Fund man is organizing action conferences in Atlanta with follow up conferences around the nation to build a broad-based anti-malaria coalition among business people, students, and alumni while all along working with All Africa Global Media.

He is in the process of establishing Malaria Free Zones in three villages in Africa (Ghana, Kenya and Nigeria) that will be supplied with bed nets, medication and sprays—as pilot projects.

More flamboyantly, he has started Dunk Malaria I—a grassroots initiative to recruit millions of people worldwide to shoot a basketball through a basketball net (the tie-in to bed nets) next March 19, as a participatory charity activity. NBA star Dikembe Mutombo has agreed to a high visibility role here. (Contact atvs.malaria@gmail.com).

In early December, 2005, Lance Laifer will swim in the ocean to help a benefit he calls "the World Swim for Malaria." It will be chilling he says, but nothing like malaria chills and the chills associated with mothers and fathers burying a young child stricken with this disease. Proceeds will go to benefit the Global Fund Bednet purchase program. (See worldswim4malaria.com/en/.)

I suppose Mr. Laifer believes that if you try for the impossible, you'll be more likely to achieve the possible.

For more information, contact allafrica.com

Solar Power
June 3, 2005

One of my favorite publications—one that you may never have heard about—is the *Co-op America Quarterly: Economic Actions for a Just Planet*. The current issue is devoted to "The Promise of the Solar Future." Co-op America brings together buyers and sellers who want products and services that are environmentally benign and made by companies and co-ops that are sensitive to their workers' health and safety. Co-op America (Green America now) attracts tens of thousands of members who peruse its National Green Pages to purchase what they need and to invest in responsible ways and support sustainable economic activities. (See greenamerica.org and www.greenpages.org.)

Obviously, solar energy is high on its priority list. But has there ever been a longer, more proven, more diverse source of energy so continually neglected, ignored, distorted, suppressed or given lip service than the best, most permanent, most decentralized flow of energy on Earth?

Why, the ancient Greeks, Persians and East Africans used passive solar energy in the architecture of their homes and other structures they built. Remember our school books picturing the many windmills of Holland from centuries ago. Whether its wind power, solar thermal, solar photovoltaic or biomass, the many faces of the sun have been giving us a free lunch of energy, awaiting our transmitting of this energy into appropriate technologies that deliver the electricity and fuel.

Still the resistance. Why? Well, put yourself in the shoes of the coal, oil, gas and nuclear companies. Do you want to be diminished or displaced by the sun—a gigantic energy source you cannot own nor control? These companies, ever larger and more global in size, know how to say NO to governments that do anything other than give fossil fuel and uranium companies subsidies which tilt heavily the playing field against the fledging solar energy firms.

The decades-long eclipse of solar energy development by the Exxon/Mobil moguls persists in periods of increasing imports of oil, military conflicts rooted in oil, and ongoing environmental contamination. We have witnessed spiraling gasoline and heating oil prices, staggering oil and gas industry profits and gross distortions of solar power's potential, meanwhile the petroleum industry uses acquisitions to bottle up small solar companies, and the unceasing shrinkage of domestic refinery capacity, continues.

Having marinated the Bush regime with former oil executives, the fossils fuel and nuclear companies have secured House passage of the worst federal energy legislation in American history. Not only does it raid your tax dollars to further subsidize these greedy companies in ways that would cause a near riot if announced at the NASCAR race, but the bill also destroys the states' historical regulatory authority, for example, to establish safety standards for the location of liquefied natural gas facilities that could blow up a city in an accident or from sabotage.

Overturned also would be state and local government authority regarding the location of electrical transmission and distribution lines.

Gone would be the successful Public Utility Holding Company Act of 1935 that has prevented Exxon/Mobil or Wall Street firms from buying up electric companies. Dirtier air, toxic drinking water, liability immunity from the courts, and the weakening of controls over radioactive wastes will be your future, if your senators go along with Bush's nightmare (to him, dream) legislation.

What of solar? Ninety-five percent of the tax dollars and subsidies in current energy legislation are slated for the polluters while only five percent goes to energy efficiency and renewable technologies like geothermal and solar power. Big Business plunders while the people sleep.

Co-op America's solar magazine whets your appetite for solar. the *Quarterly* has a useful list of what you can do solarwise from old knowledge known as thrift. Hang your clothes out to dry instead of firing up the energy wasteful clothes dryer, for example. It shows you how to visit existing solar homes (www.ases.org), tap state programs that give you a break if you install solar devices or systems. It takes you around the country and world where solar is being used for a wide variety of purposes efficiently.

Ten years ago Japan's solar electricity output was less than half that of the USA. Now Japan is looking to bigger export markets for solar and is 50 percent of their domestic electricity from solar power by 2030, giving new meaning to the "land of the rising sun."

Germany has sped ahead of the United States as well, creating last year alone 5000 new jobs and generating nearly $3 billion in revenue by expanding more solar power facilities than any other nation.

The American people and our country are being held back from solar power because we let the oil/gas barons set energy policy and limit our choices.

Sure, places like San Francisco and Chicago are showing activity, but until a couple of million Americans bear down on their senators in the next month, Bush will sign this legislation with oil dripping from his pen and oil dollars spilling lustily into Republican campaign coffers. Do your part, the way Co-op America does.

Ralf Hotchkiss

December 23, 2004

Nearly forty years ago, a young high school motorcycle rider in Rockford, Illinois went over a grate, flipped over into the air and landed with a broken body. He became paraplegic. Because of the remarkable way Ralf Hotchkiss responded to his disability, thousands of people with disabilities here and in developing countries are now riding in durable, affordable wheelchairs.

After his accident, Hotchkiss attended Oberlin College and graduated with an engineering degree. After interning with one of our groups as an undergraduate, he started the Center for Concerned Engineering where he began taking on a British corporation which monopolized wheelchair production and charged unaffordable prices for an inferior product. Hotchkiss began inventing improvements using inexpensive materials and then making them available publicly. He took no patents out on his inventions.

Not content with both helping start competitors to this British monopoly and perfecting wheelchair engineering design, Hotchkiss widened his area of advocacy to help make possible the great breakthroughs in access to buildings, airplanes, buses and trains for physically disabled people. You can witness the results everyday where wheelchair riders (as he prefers to call them) can participate in so many occupations, community and athletic activities formerly denied them.

Handing out wheelchairs to people—the charity model—did not appeal to this determined, problem-solving young man. First, the wheelchairs were not that good. Wheelchairs currently being imported from China are designed for hospital floors, not outdoors where

paths and terrain are quite uneven. Such chairs can be dangerous to their occupants by breaking and tipping over riders. And, it is often difficult to obtain spare parts.

Hotchkiss started Whirwind Wheelchair International (WWI) to teach people in South America, Africa and Asia how to manufacture their own wheelchairs in small shop facilities.

The need is vast and growing. As WWI says: "Mobility is as basic as food and shelter, but 98 percent of the 20 million people who need wheelchairs in developing countries don't yet have one." Western models are prohibitively expensive. Locally produced designs can be not only much cheaper, more rugged and more drawing on locally available materials that simplify repairs, but they also elicit the pride and care that goes along with locally producing what you own.

Many of these shops are owned and operated by women with disabilities. More and more of the inventive ideas to improve a wheelchair's responses to the stresses, pressures and bumps are coming from riders and mechanics. One such invention was the Zimbabwe front caster wheel. It was adapted from a pushcart that was observed in Harare, Zimbabwe and is now used for negotiating rugged paths.

Based at San Francisco State University's School of Engineering, with key participation of Professor Peter Pfaelzer, Whirlwind Wheelchair International brims with new ideas. Hotchkiss is driven by a technical and moral imagination. He says, "Imagine not being able to go where you want, when you want. Imagine being stranded the last place someone set you down. Imagine the waiting, the frustration, the loneliness. Imagine it is lifelong." He aims to break what he calls "the imprisonment of immobility" by expanding his coalition to be beyond the nearly 50 workshops in 25 countries from Nicaragua to Uganda to Afghanistan.

Current initiatives include a new toddler's wheelchair for children one to six, built low enough to the ground to allow interactions with other small children. His valiant crew is pioneering new distribution and marketing strategies to get "wheeled mobility into the lives of people with fewer resources." Jobs are produced for people with disabilities along with greatly enhanced mobility.

Next year Hotchkiss will travel, in his easy riding wheelchair, to Columbia, Uganda, Eritrea, Vietnam and Thailand to launch or expand these production workshops. His energy is irrepressible; all obstacles and difficult circumstances, regarding his life's mission, are only problems to be methodically analyzed and dealt solutions.

Now, wouldn't you think his Center would be besieged with public and private donors? If you did you would be rational. But Hotchkiss's group is battling for funds constantly. Foundations too often favor long-winded studies about what needs to be achieved like the endless large grants for groups to produce the redundant report on energy policies or ways of learning in schools. His group's non-profit budget, which was around $400,000 three years ago, is now down by half, to about $200,000!

The more he produces with fewer resources, the fewer resources he can raise. He is now down to four staff, including himself, to help turn around, with his sustainable and multiple trim tabs, the lives of 20 million people.

The US government, which plows tens of billions of dollars into unneeded weapons systems from the wasteful Lockheed-Martin et al, which blows tens of millions of dollars regularly on foreign aid and consultants' projects which do not work, can't seem to lend Whirlwind Wheelchair International a hand. Imagine the goodwill for America's best instincts that some modest assistance will facilitate.

Hotchkiss has received the prestigious MacArthur "genius" fellowship and been given many engineering design and other major awards. It isn't as if he has trouble filling out a one page vitae. It is just our society's messed-up, cruel priorities that prevent making possible thousands of more locally produced wheelchairs of rugged, affordable design, from rolling into their grateful riders' arms.

If you want to help or suggest sources of help, call Ralf Hotchkiss at (415) 338-1290, e-mail him at whirlwind@sfsu.edu or log into his website at whirlwindwheelchair.org. Contributions are deductible.

Resolution 202

June 4, 2004

Unless cooler heads prevail, the American Medical Association is teetering on the brink of public ridicule, mockery and indignation. Resolution 202 has been introduced by Dr. J. Chris Hawk III from South Carolina to the AMA's Committee B. It is aimed directly at trial lawyers as patients.

This resolution sets a new record for loss of sensitivity toward the tens of thousands of patients who die every year due to the gross negligence or incompetence called medical malpractice. This proposed resolution reflects the AMA's disappointment that the doctor's lobby has not adequately torpedoed the legal rights of these innocent plaintiffs in court. So it recommends major legal "surgery" that should turn the stomachs of more conscientious ethical and competent physicians than just gastroenterologists.

Here are the chilling words: "RESOLVED, that our American Medical Association notify physicians that, except in emergencies and except as otherwise required by law or other professional regulation, it is not unethical to refuse care to plaintiffs' attorneys and their spouses."

Well at least Hawk, a third-generation doctor, left out the children. The chilling explanation by Dr. Hawk for this proposed resolution is that lawsuits against medical-practice mayhem raise malpractice insurance premiums "forcing physicians to reduce their scope of practice, relocate, and retire early." Therefore, he concludes, trial attorneys should be given "the opportunity to experience the access problems caused by the professional liability crisis," [and] then "perhaps they would be willing to help change the system."

The main problem with this sadistic sequence of illogic is that it is false. The insurance companies are gouging the physicians by creating a phony crisis and playing off the natural desire of physicians never to be sued. Take all the premiums paid by doctors to insurance companies for malpractice coverage and divide the sum by all the practicing physicians. The premium would be about $10,000 a year—a third of what they pay an experienced receptionist in their offices.

Regulating insurance premiums to prevent over-classification of specialists (which jack-up rates), promoting experience loss rating (so that the fewer bad doctors pay more than the competent doctors) and stiffening regulation by state licensing boards to focus on the chronically harmful physicians would help reduce the damage to innocent patients.

Five percent of physicians account for about fifty percent of filed medical malpractice lawsuits. The total amount paid out in verdicts and settlements in all malpractice lawsuits is between $5 and $6 billion—less than the amount spent just on dog food in this country. Only ten percent of medical malpractice victims even file a claim.

Yet according to the Harvard School of Public Health Physicians, 80,000 Americans die every year from medical negligence or worse, just in hospitals alone. Hundreds of thousands are significantly injured. By comparison with the insurance premiums paid, one of the Harvard physicians estimated the cost of medical malpractice casualties to be over $60 billion a year.

Dr. Hawk III's narrow frame of reference must have precluded him from reading the data and studies that contradict his precipitous attempt to embrace the AMA with a sordid display of unethical recommendations. He should log onto the websites Citizen.org and Centerjd.org for his enlightenment (the web sites include data countering the allegation that doctors are abandoning their practice).

It would be nice to refer him to an AMA website on medical malpractice and what his organization is doing about this preventable violence. But there is none. The AMA is oblivious, showing no interest in this nationwide tragedy.

Dr. Hawk III's proposed resolution goes to Committee B and, if approved, will go to the American Medical Association's House of Delegates for deliberation. Let Americans see how out of touch the AMA is with reality and how subservient to the insurance industry they continue to be.

Editor's note: Though the AMA did not accept Resolution 202, the frustration and anger underlying it remained with some malpractice lawyers after this debacle http://www.upstate.edu/bioethics/bio_brief_fall_04.pdf.

Infectious Disease

January 31, 2004

Each day the news becomes more ominous regarding the spread of a "bird flu" or avian influenza through nine East Asian countries. Millions of chickens have died from this disease and millions more have been slaughtered to stop the spread to humans. For now, humans can contract this flu by direct contact with the fowl's faces but health experts fear the virus could mutate with a human influenza virus that would then be transmissible from human to human and produce an epidemic spreading around the world.

Over 30,000 Americans die from influenza or flu every year. Ever wonder why so many of the annual flu strains have Chinese names? Because ducks get infected on Chinese farms, give the virus to pigs that then transmit it to farm families who live in very close proximities to their animals. Then the virus takes off across the pacific and over the past century has taken millions of American lives.

This is not, however, the weapon of mass destruction that concerns President George W. Bush. He has spent over $400 million taxpayer dollars since March looking and not finding weapons of mass destruction in Iraq. He has his government deeply involved in this futile quest which even his chief weapons inspector, David Kay, finds an exercise without results. The media covers this subject almost daily.

Have you heard much about Mr. Bush turning his attention and skilled health personnel in a major way toward China's deadliest annual export to the US? He certainly has condoned and facilitated the export of American factories and industries to the Chinese communist regime. This exodus has left hollowed communities and

unemployment lines behind—all in the name of "free trade" which is really corporate-managed trade with a dictatorial government.

Meanwhile, infectious disease experts at the US Centers for Disease Control in Atlanta fear the onset of a massive pandemic, like the one in 1919 that took more than one million American lives and some 20 million worldwide.

The level of response and resources amount the world's nations is nowhere near the needs for prevention, early surveillance, testing, diagnosis, treatment and the application of modern epidemiological sciences.

President Bush would do well to intensively brief himself about the dire necessity of international health cooperation in this area. Health treaties against infectious diseases epidemics are a top priority, ahead of Mr. Bush's concentration on industry-exporting trade treaties with authoritarian regimes.

What would these health treaties provide for? For starters, technical expert assistance, quicker and better laboratory testing, the placement of US infectious disease specialists in China beyond the handful who are already there. There are far more American salesmen in China representing US shaving firms than these life-saving experts.

In addition, since the US imports over $150 billion worth of Chinese goods a year (producing a massive trade imbalance), the US should be able to persuade Chinese officials to stop denying there is a problem—as with the SARS epidemic—until it is late in the transmission stage. China should establish a timely, precise, accurate, open disclosure system. It did not in the SARS case. The results were hundreds of fatalities and tens of billions of dollars of lost production and sales to the Chinese economy.

Most fundamentally, animal health specialists

and agronomists are needed in both countries to cooperate over ways to separate the close proximities between these animals and their caretakers and to provide adequate equipment (like goggles, gloves and face masks) when massive flocks of afflicted chickens have to be destroyed.

The chain of infections from domesticated Chinese ducks to pigs to humans can explode into a world war of mutant viruses taking millions of casualties before vaccines can be developed and deployed. Mr. Bush must pay serious attention to this form of biological warfare and listen to his scientists and physicians before they are too far down his chain of command and control.

Civil Rights/Civil Liberties/Civil Justice

"Civil rights" has a powerful resonance and privileged place in our country. But we shouldn't use the term too narrowly to refer only to the fights for equality for historically disadvantaged groups like African-Americans, Latinos, and women (not to mention LGBTQ, the disabled, and others who have suffered pervasive legal and social discrimination).

The victories achieved by and on behalf of these groups deserve celebration. Nonetheless, these groups' quest for equality is far from over. African Americans and Arab Americans still endure racial profiling and other indignities at the hands of the justice system. Women remain second-class citizens in various places, ranging from professional suites to the amateur sports field. Some of the columns in this section deal with these and other instances of unequal treatment of groups not fully empowered within the political process.

But "civil rights," and the concomitant "civil liberties," mean much more. They entail the terms of association between a citizenry and its government, as well as the relationship among different parts of the citizenry.

The columns in this section cover a variety of topics. One topic is the problem of fine-print contracts that hide stipulations and hidden clauses amongst the verbose terms and conditions you hurriedly sign when buying new things. Some columns deal with the corporate assault of the civic justice system and our rights to fair trials by juries of our peers. Others range to broader issues of privacy violations—such as those associated with TSA full-body airport scanners and oppressive anti-terrorism laws. Columns talk about the war crimes of Presidents Bush and Obama, as well as the whole war on terror effort.

Columns in this section address miscellaneous abuses of our rights and liberties. Several concern the predatory lending practices of financial institutions, and other economic crimes against the poor, one of the most underrated and neglected civil rights abuses today.

Still others deal with a pre-condition for a just society: open and equal political participation. Deprived of statehood, the residents of the District of Columbia are not afforded the voting rights provided to other US citizens. Those officials and other interests obstruct millions of Americans from voting, depriving citizens of their democratic birthright, and weakening our democracy. And a political system that equates wealth with influence mocks the very notion of responsive and accountable government and predictably produces the injustice of concentrated unaccountable power.

It is no accident that the section of the book dealing most directly with civil rights and civil liberties should range far and wide, for the threats to our civil rights and liberties are multiple and far-reaching. Eternal vigilance by "We the People" remains the only reliable safeguard.

Contract Peonage
May 31, 2011

It is time to shine the light on the big, afflu-ent corporate lawyers who anonymously create those non-competitive fine print contracts we all have to sign to purchase goods and services.

It's time for an open letter to these Darth Vaders of business law who have destroyed our freedom of contract and built a new road to serf-dom made of corporate cement.

Dear Attorneys for Contract Incarceration:

Remember when you were at law school studying contracts? Your professor pressed you socratically to understand *Hadley vs. Baxendale et al.* You spent just one or two classes on what are called "contracts of adhesion"—those fine print one-sided contracts that only make up 99 percent of all the contracts we'll ever sign.

There they are—page after page exuding the silent message of "take it or leave it." If you "leave it," then you must cross the street to a competitor—an insurance company, credit card firm, bank, auto dealer, hospital, realtor, airline, student loan company or cell phone company, awaiting you is the same fine-print contract de-signed to nail you to the mast. Then there are the shrink-wrap software contracts you can't even see before you buy.

If your contracts professor bothered to explain why so little course time is spent on these standard form contracts involving tril-lions of dollars in annual sales, he/she might have used the French phrase—"fait accompli." After all, the consumer signed or acquiesced in some way. That met the basic principle of a binding contract, say the courts (with a rare exception now and then) which is a meeting of the minds between the willing seller and the willing buyer.

Discussion over! As a shopper, prepare for the daily coercive harmony.

Imagine all the times you've "met the minds" of Bank of America, Metropolitan, Aetna, General Motors, Walmart, American Express, AT&T, Sallie Mae, US Airways and your favor-ite time-sharing company for that vacation trip to Antigua. What a myth!

In this legal fiction land, the law presumes that you've read the fine print and understood it. Inscrutability is no defense. It doesn't mat-ter that law professors, Supreme Court Chief Justice Roberts and your partners admit to not reading the dense legalese when they shop. Why waste their time? They can't get out of con-tractual prison any more than you can. But you make zillions figuring out how to lock millions of Americans into one-side anti-consumer con-tracts.

You misuse your intellect to create a modern contract straitjacket that gets tighter year by year. Your innovations are enforced by status-quo judges, credit ratings, credit scores and the absence of any competition over contracts be-tween companies in the same industry.

The straitjacket is made of figurative steel fibers composed of enforceable words. Here is a partial list of your inventions which Harvard Law Professor Elizabeth Warren aptly calls "mice type" the equivalent of "shrubbery for muggers!"

They include (1) seller's power to unilaterally change terms or assign the contract, (2) waiver provisions of the seller's liability and payment of seller's attorney fees, (3) acceleration and de-linquency clauses, (4) binding arbitration and blocking the consumer's resort to the courts and right to jury trials, (5) liquidated damage claus-es. On and on go the layers of incarceration.

Pretty clever maybe, but, you aren't being fair

to the powerless consumers. Remember, you've got a professional code of ethics that informs you of the obligation sometimes to say no—enough already—to your demanding corporate clients even if they can always go to another law firm that they can pay handsomely to say yes. It can be, for you, a dilemma.

Listen, I've got an exit plan for those of you pondering quitting or retiring because you can no longer stand destroying peoples' freedom of contract—one of the main pillars of our democracy—with their consequential losses of money, time, health and safety.

Come to the other side. A movement for consumer contract justice is heading your way. Don't laugh as General Motors once did in the 1960s. Don't think that the complexity of these fine prints cannot be communicated to the buying public. ABC's Peter Jennings showed the opposite with a crisp five-part TV series a few years ago. This fall, a sure best-seller by David Cay Johnston titled *The Fine Print* is coming out. He has prior best sellers on tax laws that clarify the abstruse to arouse readers.

There is a huge compression of repression and resentment ready to be unleashed and converted into a widely perceived injustice. Ridding themselves of the feeling that "that's the way it is," this consumer uprising will be holding you and your companies responsible by name.

Quit and join the right side of the coming historical change breaking the chains of contract bondage. Bring your knowhow and stored archives (names redacted) of "mice type" to fair-contracts.org, directed by the relentless lawyer, Theresa Amato. Soon!

Your brother in law,
Ralph Nader, Esq.

From Charity to Justice

May 3, 2011

On the evening of May 4, a day before he was to join dozens of billionaires convened by Warren Buffett and Bill Gates in Phoenix, Arizona to discuss how they might spend over half their wealth for "good works," media entrepreneur, peace advocate and environmentalist, Ted Turner joined another billionaire, Peter B. Lewis (chairman of Progressive Insurance) and me at the New York Public Library to discuss a similar topic. C-SPAN covered the event.

The event was titled "Billionaires Against Bull, Going from Charity to Justice." It was a far-ranging exchange before an audience as civically committed as some of the notables who were there, including Lewis Lapham of *Lapham's Quarterly*, Amy Goodman of Democracy Now, Victor Navasky (Columbia Journalism School), Patti Smith (singer, poet and author), Mark Green (author of *Losing Our Democracy*), and Eugene Jarecki, (documentary film maker "Why We Fight and author of *The American Way of War*).

The launching point for our discourse was my work of political fiction *Only the Super-Rich Can Save Us!* Turner and Lewis were two of 17 real, very rich persons, led by Warren Buffett, who in fictional roles decided to put their money, contacts and facilities behind a mass mobilization of the people to effect long-overdue redirections.

What are the chances of a small number of many mega-rich putting ample resources behind basic changes that benefit people but upset vested interests? Issues such as a living wage, Medicare for all, and cracking down on corporate crime were part of the agenda for the Meliorists featured in my book. The difference between justice and charity is taking on power to benefit people.

Billionaires don't work together, they're used to people under them working together, said Lewis. Moreover, he added, so often no one knows how to get such things done.

Lewis spent $20 million to increase voter turnout. The results were disappointing. Lewis said: "If I had spent another $200 million, I might have gotten another seven or eight more people to vote."

He had a point. But what if major money was used to make voting a legal duty, like jury duty, only with the full choice of voting for the candidates on the ballot, writing in a candidate or voting for binding none-of-the-above. That would remove the civil liberties problem and make obstructing people from voting a crime. Both Lewis and Turner seemed interested in that idea.

Turner, a big solar and wind energy advocate, liked the idea of a carbon tax. Lewis advanced the idea that wealthy people like to see proposals with clear objectives and detailed action plans. Too often that does not happen, which is why he funded a new group named The Management Center to help groups work more effectively.

I put forth several "projects" such as closing down the troubled Indian Point nuclear plants 26 miles from New York City, pressing for a Wall Street speculation tax, creating watchdog groups on nanotechnology, biotechnology, investor and consumer rights, diminishing the bloated military budget, breaking the grip of the two-party controlled Commission on Presidential Debates by organizing broad coalitions in numerous cities to sponsor candidate debates in 2012.

Only a few of the increasing numbers of mega-billionaires are needed to show the way to shift power from the few to the many, to take fundamental solutions to serious problems off the shelf, to give people access to justice and voice. In short, to strengthen democracy at its people base.

There is a broad consensus in our country around certain redirections, but the people need more civic infrastructure to organize and end the oligarchic gridlocks that have entrenched greed and myopia. As the best moments of our past show, institution building works. Expansion of our civil liberties and civil rights are almost synonymous with the ACLU and the NAACP, for instance.

We need to develop a new matrix for philanthropy, building new constituencies to make government honest and reflective of public sentiments. This also involves new experiments such as new approaches to permanent organizing, to motivating citizens, to opening up new strategies and new areas.

Presently, most philanthropy goes to needed charities. Some billions of dollars should go to preventing pain and deprivation in the first place. A society that has more justice is a society that needs less charity. This approach has been proven again and again in the areas of public health and safety. Think seat belts and safe vaccines.

Vast frontiers of opportunities await for our political economy to serve the many and not just the few (think the CEO of Walmart making $11,000 an hour while his workers make $9 or $10 an hour). Justice needs resources to spread. Give our citizens some lift, some help, some organization and media attention and let them show the way in communities around the country. Looking back, they may have stopped unconstitutional wars of aggression.

The conversation with Turner and Lewis could be the beginning of further exchanges between older billionaires, with a larger perspective on life, who respect posterity and the civic culture, which needs many smarter, systemic approaches to improve our democracy in expeditious ways.

Naked Insecurity

Jne 24, 2010

If you are planning to fly during the 4th of July holiday, be aware of your rights at airport security checkpoints.

The Transportation Security Administration (TSA) has mandated that passengers can opt out of going through a whole body scanning machine in favor of a physical pat down. Unfortunately, opting for the pat down requires passengers to be assertive since TSA screeners do not tell travelers about their right to refuse a scan. Harried passengers must spot the TSA signs posted at hectic security checkpoints to inform themselves of their rights before they move to a body scanning security line

Since the failed Christmas Day bombing of a Northwest Airlines flight by a passenger hiding explosives in his underwear, TSA has accelerated its program of deploying whole body scanning machines, including x-ray scanners, at airport security checkpoints throughout the United States. Scanning machines peek beneath passengers' clothing looking for concealed weapons and explosives that can elude airport metal detectors. So far, TSA has placed 111 scanners at 32 airports. They expect to have 450 scanners deployed by the end of the year at an estimated cost of $170,000 each.

Privacy, civil rights and religious groups object to whole body scanning machines as uniquely intrusive. Naked images of passengers'

bodies are captured by these machines that can reveal very personal medical conditions such as prosthetics, colostomy bags and mastectomy scars. The TSA responded by setting the scanners to blur the facial features of travelers, placing TSA employees who view the images in a separate room and assuring the public that the images are deleted after initial viewing.

Yet, a successful Freedom of Information Act lawsuit by the Electronic Privacy Information Center against the Department of Homeland Security (DHS) uncovered documents showing that the scanning machines' procurement specifications include the ability to store, record and transfer revealing digital images of passengers. The specifications allow TSA to disable any privacy filters permitting the exporting of raw images, contrary to TSA assurances.

It begs logic that the TSA would not retain their ability to store images particularly in the event of a terrorist getting through the scan and later attacking an aircraft. One of the first searches by the TSA would be to review images taken by the scanners to identify the attacker.

The Amsterdam airport is using a less intrusive security device called "auto detection" scanning which generates stick figures instead of the real image of the person and avoids exposing passengers to radiation. Three United States Senators recently wrote to DHS Secretary Janet Napolitano urging her to consider these devices. (http://bit.ly/bJFn5K)

More pointedly, security experts, such as Edward Luttwak from the Center for Strategic and International Studies, have come forward questioning the effectiveness of whole body scanners since they can be defeated by hiding explosives in body cavities. The General Accounting Office, an investigative arm of Congress, has stated that it is unclear whether scanners would have spotted the kind of explosives carried by the "Christmas Day" bomber.

About one-half of these body scanning machines use low dose x-rays to scan passengers. Last May, a group of esteemed scientists from the University of California, San Francisco wrote to John Holdren, President Obama's science adviser, voicing their concerns about the rapid roll out of scanners without a rigorous safety review by an impartial panel of experts. The scientists caution that the TSA has miscalculated the radiation dose to the skin from scanners and that there is "good reason to believe that these scanners will increase the risk of cancer to children and other vulnerable populations." (http://n.pr/bKGCKx).

David Brenner, director of Columbia University's Center for Radiological Research, has also voiced caution about x-raying millions of air travelers. He was a member of the government committee that set the safety guidelines for the x-ray scanners, and he now says he would not have signed onto the report had he known that TSA wanted to scan almost every air traveler. (http://www.columbia.edu/~djb3/)

Passenger complaints to TSA and newspaper accounts of passenger experiences with scanners contradict TSA assurances that checkpoint signs provide adequate notice to travelers about the scanning procedure and the pat-down option. Travelers, who reported that they were not fully aware what the scanning procedure involved, said they were not made aware of alternative search options. (http://nyti.ms/9hGtU0)

Many travelers complained about their privacy, and their families' privacy, being invaded. Some were concerned about the radiation risk, particularly to pregnant women and children. Some travelers felt bullied by rude TSA screeners. The *Wall Street Journal* reported that one woman who refused to go through the body scanner was called "unpatriotic" by the TSA screener.

Expensive state-of-the-art security technology that poses potentially serious health risks to vulnerable passengers, invades privacy, and provides questionable security is neither smart nor safe. For the White House it is a political embarrassment waiting to happen.

President Obama should suspend the body scanning program and appoint an independent panel of experts to review the issues of privacy, health and effectiveness. After such a review, should the DHS and TSA still want to deploy body scanners at airports, they should initiate a public rulemaking, which they have refused thus far, so that the public can have their say in the matter.

If you experience any push-back from TSA screeners when you assert your right to refuse to go through a whole body scanner and request a pat down security search instead, please write to info@csrl.org.

Open Letter to President-Elect Obama

January 9, 2009

Dear President-Elect Obama:

You have been receiving a great deal of advice since November 4, 2008 from people and groups who either want you to advance policies not covered in your campaign or who want you to be more specific about initiatives you emphasized.

There are two suggestions which may not be among your store of recommendations that need to be considered before you take office on January 20, 2009.

First, the public would benefit from a concise recounting of the State of the Union and where the Bush Administration has left our country. As is your style, you can render such a bright line of serious problems inside and outside the government in a matter-of-fact manner. Otherwise, a blurring of who was responsible for what can taint your presidency.

Second, you need to make a clean break from the Bush regime's *law of rule* to our declared commitment to the *rule of law* as in the firm adherence to constitutional requirements and statutory and treaty compliance. There is a Bush-Cheney stream of criminal and unconstitutional actions which are on auto-pilot day after day. You have pointed out some of these abominations such as a policy and practice of torture and violations of due process and probable cause. The task before you is to break these daily patterns just as soon as you ascend to the presidency or be held increasingly responsible for them. This can be significantly accomplished by executive orders, agency or departmental directives, whistleblower protections, enforcement actions and explicit legislative proposals.

With Americans wishing you well in this most portentous of times, the last thing they want to see is you tarnished by the preceding rogue regime and its ruthless monarchical forays. To avoid this contagion of power over law and its contiguous accountabilities at a time when you are striving for a "clean slate" administration, you must be decisive and eschew any excessive harmony ideology which has seemed to be your nature vis-à-vis those who are powerful but are opposed to your views.

One possible impediment to your making a comprehensive clean break for restoring the rule of law is that you have too easy an act to follow. There are a long list of violated civil liberties that need to be restored (the American Civil Liberties Union has compiled a list of immediate actions for you to take), and resolute commitments must be made so that it is clear the United States, for example, will not engage in, or countenance, torture. Only a few restorations, however, would produce a sense of relief and flurry of accolades –but they are hardly sufficient.

There are also regulations and interpretations of statutes that scholars believe to have been erroneous as a matter of law. As one guide for your new era of overdue regulation or reregulation— given the corporate wrongdoing these days— you may wish to refer to the Center for Progressive Reform's report "By the Stroke of the Pen."

The Bush lawlessness and state terrorism are like a contagious disease. If you do not remove their sprawling incidence, you will become their carrier. This means you must move fast to eject the mantle of war criminality and repeated unconstitutional outrages committed in the name of the American people here and abroad.

Sincerely,

Ralph Nader

Restoring the Constitution
November 12, 2008

Barack Obama is receiving lots of advice from many people these days about the collapse of Wall Street, the sinking economy and the quagmire wars he will inherit from the Bush regime. However, there is one important matter that he alone can address with his legal training and the sworn oath he will take on January 20 to uphold the Constitution. That phenomenon is the systemic, chronic lawlessness and criminality of the Bush/Cheney regime which he must unravel and stop.

To handle this immense responsibility as president, he needs to bring together a volunteer task force of very knowledgeable persons plus wise, retired civil servants to inventory the outlaw workings of this rogue regime.

Much is already known and documented officially and by academic studies and media reporting. In the category of "high crimes and misdemeanors," are (1) the criminal war-occupation of Iraq, (2) systemic torture as a White House policy, (3) arrests of thousands of Americans without charges or habeas corpus rights, (4) spying on large numbers of Americans without judicial warrants and (5) hundreds of signing statements by George W. Bush declaring that, he of the unitary presidency, will decide whether to obey the enacted bills or not.

To its everlasting credit, the conservative American Bar Association sent three reports to President Bush in 2005-2006 concluding that he has been engaged in continuing serious violations of the Constitution. This is no one-time Watergate obstruction of justice episode ala Nixon that led to his resignation just before his impeachment in the House of Representatives.

Nearly two years ago Senator Obama, contrary to what he knows and believes, vigorously came out against the House commencing impeachment proceedings. It would be too divisive, he said. As one of one hundred senators who might have had to try the president and vice president in the Senate were the House to impeach, he should have kept impartial and remained silent on the subject.

As president, he cannot remain silent and do nothing, otherwise he will inherit the war crimes of Mr. Bush and Mr. Cheney and become soon thereafter a war criminal himself. Inaction cannot be an option.

Violating the Constitution and federal laws is now routine. What is routine after a while becomes institutionalized lawlessness by official outlaws.

Domestic policy abuses are also rampant. Just what are the limits of the statutory authority of the US Treasury Department or the government within a government funded by bank assessments known as the Federal Reserve?

Don't read the $750 billion bailout law for any answers! The Speaker of the House, Nancy Pelosi and the Majority Leader of the Senate Harry Reid just sent a letter to Bush asking whether the White House believes the bailout law could be interpreted to save not just the reckless banks, but also the grossly mismanaged Big Three auto companies in Michigan.

Didn't Congress know what they were or were not authorizing? Or did the stampede started by the demanding Bush result in blanket or panicked ambiguity by a cowardly Congress?

This week, the *Washington Post* front paged an article that the Treasury Department unilaterally gave the banks a tax break that was estimated to be worth a staggering $140 billion. Just like that! Fiat! The *Post* reported that impartial legal experts flatly declared such a decision to be without statutory authority which means the Bush regime usurped the constitutional authority of Congress in matters of taxation and basically took out a 22-year-old law enacted by Congress. Not to be outdone, on the same day, the lead article in the *New York Times* reported a four-year-old Bush doctrine allowing Special Forces and other armed force to pursue terrorists in any country in the world. The *Times* specified incursions at will into Syria, Iran, Somalia, Pakistan and other countries.

Such violations of national sovereignty without formal declarations of war or through formal interventions by the United Nations are violations of international law. The Bush government answers this assertion by its open-ended, totally self-defined, right of "self-defense" under the UN Charter. The same self-determining argument can be made by covert terrorists or covert actions by adversarial governments. This is an example of make-up-your-own international law to suit your own covert operations.

As a country that has the most to lose from the shredding of international law and order, the United States under Bush is giving many IOUs to revenge-minded suicidal adversaries. They can simply say to their mass audiences, "if the US can do anything it wants, why shouldn't we?"

It has been widely reported that the Justice Department under Mr. Ashcroft and Mr. Gonzalez epitomized contempt for compliance with the laws regarding civil liberties, due process and politically interference with US Attorneys.

Less publicized was its refusal to enforce the laws routinely transgressed by the corporate patrons of the White House—such as environmental crimes, consumer fraud, and anti-trust violations.

Obama has tools to restore law and order by the government itself: The bully pulpit. Ordering departmental directives. Issuing executive orders. Requesting legislation. Highlighting the integrity of the subdued and buffeted federal civil service which, with its oath of office, deserves far more effective whistleblowing protection laws.

The ACLU has just released: "Actions For Restoring America: How to Begin Repairing the Damage to Freedom in America After Bush." Mr. Obama would do well to use this important report as blueprint for restoring faith in the US Government's commitment to the Constitution (see http://www.aclu.org/transi-tion/). A second report titled: "Protecting Public Health and the Environment by the Stroke of a Presidential Pen by the Center for Progressive Reform suggests several Executive Orders that Mr. Obama could sign to advance important health, safety and the environment goals (see http://www.progressivereform.org/).

Barack Obama taught constitutional law at the University of Chicago. Let's have it operate out of the Obama White House. And the time to start laying the groundwork is now!

Rosa Parks, Hail to Thee!

July 30, 2008

Montgomery, Alabama—The Troy University Rosa Parks Museum is located on the side of the old Empire Theatre where this courageous African-American woman declined to "move to the back of the bus" in 1955.

A visit to the museum honoring her and other civil rights champions is a sobering reminder of just how courageous such a refusal was in that very segregated South. With Mrs. Parks's arrest the historic Montgomery Bus Boycott launched shortly thereafter, which is credited with igniting the Civil Rights Movement of the 1950s.

What most people do not know about Rosa Parks is that she was a trained civil rights worker who knew the significance of staying in her front seat and not giving it up to a white man. But she could not have predicted what happened after the police took her away.

Four days after she was arrested, the bus boycott started on December 5, 1955. A flyer distributed on that date by the Women's Political Council of Montgomery noted the arrest of Mrs. Parks and two teenage "Negro" women—Claudette Colvin and Mary Louise Smith—

who earlier that year were arrested and fined for refusing to give up their seats.

The flyer went on to urge "every Negro to stay off the buses Monday in protest of the arrest and trial. Don't ride the buses to work, to town, to school, or anywhere on Monday." They stayed off in the thousands.

Since three-fourths of the Montgomery bus riders were "Negroes," the growing boycott grew to become a serious economic drain on the bus company. As it grew, and as the accompanying street marches and demonstrations started, the national news media began to cover it and a young charismatic minister by the name of Martin Luther King, Jr. came forth to be the voice of the movement.

Sam Cook was at the museum during our visit. He had a scrapbook of old newspaper clippings and photographs from those heady days when he occasionally was a driver for Rev. King.

In addition to the museum's timelines of history, artifacts, documents and memorabilia—there is a replica of the public bus on which Mrs. Parks was sitting—there are classrooms and a library to enhance the serious educational purposes for today that the museum's staff espouses.

As the museum's website states, the new Children's Wing conveys to youngsters that "things just don't happen—people make things happen. Visitors come to realize that they, too, can make a difference just as Rosa Parks, E.D. Nixon, Jo Anne Robinson, Fred Gray, Claudette Colvin, and many others made a difference following in the footsteps of Dred Scott, Harriet Tubman, Homer Plessy and others who had gone on before."

Students today in Montgomery and other southern cities might wonder what all the fuss was about from white folk. The races mix easily in this city on buses, in stores, restaurants, cinemas, schools, hospitals and ballparks. Race, like class, still matters a great deal throughout the United States; but there has been undeniable progress.

The contemporary struggles for justice can learn from the ways the civil rights movement overcame a media boycott and moved hitherto immovable forces.

To be sure, it used the courts and the streets with non-violent demonstrations. But never underestimate the personal story of an individual who heroically and selflessly takes on the Machine to spark the requisite rage and empathy that leads to larger and larger numbers of similarly situated people who swell the ranks of those demanding change or reform.

So powerful a model is this civil rights approach that when Mubarak Awad, a Palestinian-American youth counselor in Palestine's West Bank tried to organize nonviolent civil disobedience against the Israeli occupation and repression, the Israeli government deported him in 1988 back to the United States. He proceeded to establish the group, Non-Violence International, but he is still banned from Israel.

Commercial or labor strikes as a form of political protest received the ire of the Israelis. They would routinely break up strikes by cutting the locks on closed shops or welding doors shut and fining the shop owners.

In our country, we need the Rosa Parks of rebellion against gas and drug prices, home foreclosures, cruel prison conditions, huge upfront payments before entering hospitals, junk, obesity-illness-producing food, and breakdowns in municipal services.

Each historic, citizen-fueled movement has its own style and personality. Granted, the mass media can be very picky indeed, as it has been with the soldiers who have refused to return to the unconstitutional, illegal war-occupation in Iraq. The heartfelt stories of these soldiers told at a recent "Winter Soldiers" gathering were not even covered by the *New York Times* or the evening news programs. (But Amy Goodman did on *Democracy Now!*)

One must believe there is always a way to produce the human spark for a broader public morality and a deeper commitment to a more just society.

Rosa Parks, hail to thee!

Youth Voting Rights

June 3, 2008

You are sixteen. You can legally work, drive a motor vehicle, and with parental consent, get married in most states. Why can't you legally vote?

Good question, and one that supporters for dropping the voting age from eighteen to sixteen will be asking politicians more and more. Much has been made of the youth vote this year amid evidence that more young people are turning out to vote in the primaries than ever before. Let's take it to the next step.

I argued for the voting age drop from 21 to 18 back in the 1960s before it finally happened in 1971 with the ratification of the 26th Amendment to our Constitution. The absence of a vibrant civic culture inside and outside our schools drained away much of the potential of this electoral liberation for youngsters. Their turnout was lower than older adults.

Sixteen-year-olds are likely to be more excited. They are studying and learning about the country and the world in high school. They're still at home and can bring their discussions to their parents, who may turnout at the polls more as a result.

Fifteen-year-old Danielle Charette, writing last January in the *Hartford Courant* says: "Consumed in the distraction of their first semester at college, many eligible voters fail to arrange for absentee ballots. Of course, if annual voting became more habitual starting in high school, reading up on the candidates and voting while away from home wouldn't seem out of the ordinary."

Moreover, social studies teachers in high school would be keener on non-partisan class analyses of candidates if their students were able to vote.

Ms. Charette made another telling point. Sixteen-year-olds who also work pay taxes but they have no vote. This is "taxation without representation," she exclaimed.

Austria lowered its voting age to 16 last year, prompting similar proposals by New Zealand legislators. One Swiss Canton (Glarus) lowered the voting age to participate in local and cantonal elections to 16 in 2007. British Member of Parliament, Sarah McCarthy-Fry expects a debate on the 16-year-old vote issue soon in the House of Commons.

Austrian Social Democrat Chancellor Alfred Gusenbauer said that lowering the voting age was a "challenge to Austria's school system" in the field of political education. While New Zealand MP, Sue Bradford ties this voting reform in her proposed legislation with making civics education compulsory in high school to enhance students' understanding of the political system.

Bills in Minnesota and Michigan have been introduced to lower the voting age. Their rationale is to give a "real opportunity for young people to vote on something that affects their daily lives," according to Sen. Sandy Pappas of St. Paul.

Now it's time to hear from these young Americans. They can exchange and spread words faster and cheaper than any generation in history—what with YouTube, MySpace and Facebook communications.

Here is some advice to them: First don't just make it a matter of your voting right as "citizens now," not citizens in waiting. Recognize your responsibilities and duties of engaged citizenship.

Second, raise some compelling changes and redirections that will improve life in America especially for you and generally for all Americans. You know lots of them. Just ask yourself, as you shop, study, work, play, breathe the air and drink the water, and watch the TV news, what kind of country do you want to see in the coming months and years?

To jumpstart the 16-year-old voting movement, youngsters need to start jumping. Needed are rallies, marches, and personal group visits to your members of Congress and state legislatures at their local offices, especially when the lawmakers are not in session and are back in their home communities.

Don't over rely on the internet. The impact from showing up in person is far greater.

I'll be talking up the sixteen-year-old vote. But it will only become a reality if a teenage political revolution makes it happen.

Where are the Lawyers of America?

October 5, 2007

The rogue regime of George W. Bush and Dick Cheney—so widely condemned for its unconstitutional, criminal Iraq War, its spying on Americans illegally, its repeated illegal torture practices, its arrests and imprisonment of thou-

sands in this country without charges and its pathological secrecy and corporate corruption—still has not felt the heat of the 800,000 practicing lawyers and their many bar organizations.

Lawyer jokes aside, the first defense outside of government against the rejection of due process, probable cause and habeas corpus should come from the officers of the courts—the attorneys of America. With few exceptions, they have flunked, asleep at the wheel or loaded with excuses.

The exceptions include dozens of pro-bono attorneys representing defendants and a number of law professors such as David Cole (Georgetown University) and Jonathan Turley (George Washington University) and the magnificent one-year presidency of Michael Greco at the conservative American Bar Association.

Mr. Greco, appalled at the outlaw nature of the Bush White House, now wallowing in the pits of the public opinion polls, organized former counsel to the CIA, the National Security Agency and the FBI, among others, to produce detailed reports and resolutions assailing the Bush government for repeatedly violating the constitution in numerous ways. (http://www.abanet.org/)

Reports were sent to Mr. Bush personally. He did not even bother to acknowledge receipt. The ABA has over 400,000 members and is the largest bar association in the world. Not even a courtesy reply from George Bush, the American Caesar.

Unfortunately, the courage of Greco and his colleagues has not been contagious with hundreds of thousands of lawyers throughout America or the 50 state bar associations who might have taken some action or position to stand after the ABA stood tall in 2005-2006.

Mind you, the climate for lawyers defending

the rule of law is quite enabling. Seventy percent of the American people want out of Iraq and nearly as many would like to see this presidency end. A poll of soldiers in Iraq back in January 2006 registered 72 percent of them wanting the US out of Iraq within six to twelve months.

In addition, scores of former generals and high military officers, retired intelligence officials and diplomats have openly criticized the intransigence, incompetence and harm to the US national security. These leaders include the national security advisers to Bush's father, Brent Snowcroft, the anti-terrorism advisor to George W. Bush, Richard Clark, and many others who served in high government office.

With all this in mind, I have been asking lawyers why they do not become directly active in challenging what they themselves believe is a reckless above-the-law presidency and its enormous concentration of unlawful power. Here are some examples of their replies.

- real estate attorney with a sterling civil liberties background says "I am just too busy."
- numerous retired lawyers of considerable accomplishment simply say they are retired.
- mid-career business attorneys say they have too many clients who might object (too much wheeling and dealing to uphold the rule of law in Washington, DC).
- public interest lawyers say it is not within their declared mission—eg. environmental, consumer, poverty or law reform work.
- "Too controversial," and "I'm not up to it," announced a prominent trial lawyer.
- "I wouldn't know where to start and I just need my leisure time," replied a highly specialized estate and trusts attorney.

And so it goes. Too preoccupied, too many deals in the works, too controversial, too retired . . .

The Democratic leadership in the Congress has given Bush/Cheney a giant nod by taking a pass on holding them accountable through impeachment, through conditions in budget bills, through making them answer subpoenas by playing hardball on Bush's nominees, such as his new choice for Attorney General.

It is up to the lawyers to rally for the Republic. This is deep patriotism, for without upholding our Constitution, and the laws of the land, what will become of our country?

What will our children and their grandchildren inherit—a bankrupt government that contracts out more and more of its core functions to staggeringly expensive giant corporations seeking limitless profits, while they finance and corrupt politicians to turn their back on the peoples' needs?

Lawyers are supposed to know how to apply law to raw power. They know how to use the courts and lobby (there are hundreds or thousands of attorneys in each of most congressional districts). They can cut through the arcane camouflage of legalese. They know when the laws are being violated and what the remedies are for the violators. They know how to draft legislation. They have contacts and money and are not supposed to be frightened of conflict. The super-lawyers invariably get their calls returned.

Where are the lawyers of America?

Two major terrorist strikes, with a messianic, compulsively-obsessed president, can do to America what nine months of nightly bombing by the Nazis could not do to England—move us much closer to a police state.

Where are the stand-up lawyers of America?

Eroding Americans' Last Defense: The Civil Justice System

February 4, 2005

Our lawless president and his Congressional cohorts are pushing legislation that would significantly erode the American people's last defense against corporate crimes and frauds; the civil justice system. With a bill scheduled to reach the Senate floor next week, our freedom to redress harms in courts of law is in danger. S.5, a proxy for last year's misnamed "Class Action Fairness Act," emerged from the Senate Judiciary Committee this week with little discussion and no public hearings. No public hearings! It will be rushed to the Senate floor next week, as befits this increasingly dictatorial Congress.

While the class action remedy has successfully provided many of those harmed by negligent actions an efficient means of redress for wrongful injuries and violations of civil and consumer rights since the 1960s, S.5 would send most class actions to procedural purgatory. It would shift class action suits—where any member of the class is from a different state than the defendant—from state court to federal court. This coup encompasses class actions of any significance, according to respected legal scholar and Harvard professor Arthur Miller.

Before enacting such legislation, the burden of proof is on the Congress to demonstrate that state judges and jurors are unwilling, incompetent or unable to dispense justice based on the common law and state statutes. If proponents of this legislation were to talk to their home state judges, they would not support this federal usurpation of state judicial responsibilities. S.5's backers also ignore the dire warnings of federal judges who are already presiding over congested courts and who admit that this bill will result in most cases being summarily dismissed on procedural grounds as being "unmanageable."

On what basis could such a fundamental right be taken from us?

In his State of the Union address this week, President Bush said that, "our economy is held back by irresponsible class-actions and frivolous asbestos claims." The president is ignorant. He provides no data for his repeated corporate bellowing.

There simply is no causal link between taking judicial rights away from Americans and making our economy stronger or more competitive. Just the opposite. Justice enhances economic development and worker productivity. Many countries overseas do not have these judicial rights, and their GDP per capita shows it. The "tort costs" that proponents of judicial limitations often cite are actually costs of the entire tort-insurance system in America. This includes costs that have absolutely nothing to do with lawsuits.

This bill will take away crucial consumer safeguards and allow businesses to avoid corporate responsibility to innocent workers, consumers, patients and community residents. But that's the point: this bill is not designed to make America more competitive, its manifest purpose is to erase the accountability that limits deadly harms from the likes of Vioxx, flammable children's pajamas, or asbestos.

The president's callous remark about "frivolous asbestos claims" in his speech speaks volumes for the monetized backers of this bill. Those who struggle to breathe because of exposure to asbestos have suffered real and lasting harm, if they survived.

When it comes to protecting his business cronies, notice how President Bush dramatically deviates from his usual "freedom for all" rhetoric. He is essentially telling the American people that there is a finite amount of freedom and liberty left in America; and he's taking away our individual freedoms and replacing them with the corporate license to avoid responsibility and repeat their reckless ways into the future.

Make no mistake, the Bush administration is asking that we give up our freedom to fully use the courts. And while the Republican Party routinely calls for personal responsibility on the part of the people, it seems to have little interest in corporate responsibility. Corporate interests have wrested control of the legislature from an under-engaged populace. This bill is an archetype of Washington's unchecked pay-to-play politics.

The civil justice system is a noble pillar of our democracy. It needs to be improved, not weakened to favor further criminality, negligence and irresponsibility. The media reporting of hazardous drugs, defective medical, automotive and other equipment, unsafe medical and hospital practices, toxics in the environment and workplace, the fleecing of investors, and the manipulation of energy and electricity markets should serve as a reminder that prevention of human casualties, suffering and economic loss should be the top concern of Congress, not the incremental closing of the courtroom doors to favor corporate donors.

For years, when constituents could not count on their elected officials to protect their interests through protective legislation, the courts have offered a last refuge for justice. Members of Congress should do the right thing and reject this weakening of contemporary civil justice freedoms accorded wrongfully injured and defrauded men, women and children. You should demand no less when you contact your Senators before next week's vote.

Call (202) 224-3121 to speak with your Senator's office.

Court Funding

August 22, 2004

You won't find the *Judges' Journal* on any newsstands, but the Summer 2004 issue headlined "Justice in Jeopardy: The State Court Funding Crisis" will affect you more than most of the magazines that are so posted. State court budgets all over the country are being cut, which means reduced services and longer delays for trials for injured or violated people and small businesses that cannot wait.

The reductions are so severe that courts are increasing fees to users and thinking of other ways to pass the tin cup for contributions. Higher court fees obstruct access to the courts by lower income citizens.

New Hampshire suspended civil jury trials for a few months while Oregon went to the extreme of closing its courts to the public on Fridays.

The *Journal* writes: "Cuts to crisis centers in Minnesota mean that victims of domestic violence get less help navigating the sometimes confusing legal system." For four months Oregon was unable to prosecute property crimes such as arson and car theft.

In Rochester, New York, cuts in the budget of the Public Interest Law Office led to 200 low-income residents being denied help to resolve legal problems such as securing "supplemental security income benefits for people with disabilities and preserving the homes of low-income debtors victimized by predatory lenders."

A majority of state courts are funded from state income and sales taxes while the rest draw on property taxes. The *Journal* contained warnings that the very independence of the judiciary can be compromised when the other two branches—legislative and executive—gang up on the courts' budget. Judges are hampered by judicial ethics and tradition from slugging it out with their budget cutters, leaving them mostly defenseless. And courts are not known to have powerful citizen lobbies to support the services they provide.

Considered against the background of how your tax dollars are spent, misspent, wasted and used against you at the local state and national governmental levels, the plight of the courts demonstrates the neglect and deterioration of our democratic institutions.

Our founding fathers and the colonial patriots before them fought to defend their right to use the courts, to have a trial by a jury of their peers. This complaint against King George III was a number two on the list after "no taxation without representation."

In the very cities where the courts are located, there are billions of taxpayer dollars poured into gleaming stadiums, arenas, ballparks and galleries. But the courts are required to ration justice—the antithesis of democracy as Judge Learned Hand wrote years ago—for lack of tax dollars.

Courts are supposed to meet standards of accessibility, timeliness, equality, fairness and integrity. This requires in the *Journal's* words "sound administration of justice." This in turn requires good people running and judging in the courts. But it also requires money.

When courts have to shorten hours, reduce juror pay and funding for interpreters, cut back on security, and cut back on office staff, justice is impaired. Suspension of jury trials, less funding for public defense counsel results in what happened in Oregon. The *Journal* writes that in that state "nonviolent criminal cases were not heard for nearly a year if the defendant required counsel at public expense. In Virginia, the prosecution of domestic violence cases was delayed."

The authors of these articles noted one upside to tighter budgets, greater emphasis on "efficiency, accountability and revenue enhancement." By the latter words "revenue enhancement," they meant, I gather, keeping more of the fines and other revenue they collect.

The authors of this collection could have strengthened their case by a chart showing what percentage of the overall state budget goes to the courts in the fifty states and the District of Columbia. Pause and see if you can guess.

The Empire State—loaded with wealthy corporate executives, lawyers and power brokers—provides just 1.5 percent of the overall state budget for its courts. The chief administrative judge of New York's court system, Judge Jonathan Lippman, drives his point home in another way: "Consider the post-September 11 security measures in New York now costing the judiciary about $300 million annually, roughly 20 percent of all spending."

Forty years ago, court budgets were larger than prison budgets. Now in almost all the states, the prison budgets are much larger than the court budgets. Maybe the courts should stop sending non-violent drug addicts to jail and assign them to rehabilitation as one judge is doing in upstate New York.

A rational society will want to fill the courts with justice seekers instead of filling the prisons with drug addicts who need help at far less expensive levels than their being maintained in jail cells.

To obtain a copy of the "Justice in Jeopardy" report visit: www.abanet.org/judind/home.html.

Carving Out Your Vote

August 13, 2004

Anchorage, Alaska, His eyes were darting and his voice was urgent with a compelling message. Peter Gruenstein, an Alaskan trial attorney and co-author of a book on Alaska, was speaking against the greatest blow to our political democracy since big money started buying the two major parties. He calls gerrymandering, often known as redistricting, "the civil rights issue of the decade."

On the federal level, about 95 percent of the House of Representatives' districts are carved up in ways that are dominated by either the Republican or Democratic Parties. Leaders of both parties acknowledge their handiwork. There is no dispute over their belief that only about 25 House districts are competitive; the rest are slam dunks for one or the other party's candidate.

Does this sound boring to you? Consider further. When politicians and their computers start choosing their voters, you lose your choice. You go to the polls and there is the incumbent's name for you to coronate. Because there is no real choice offered by any other candidate. Your electoral district has been conceded.

Instead of you picking the candidates with your vote on a ballot line with more choices, the incumbent and his/her party are picking which voters to put in which district. This is the end of the very meaning of elections which imply that there are selections. No selections, no real elections. Down to one.

In 2002, only four members of the House of Representatives out of 435 were defeated. Four members! Never before in American history has there been anywhere near such an absence of two-party competition. In the 19th century, sometimes a third of the House would be re-

jected by the voters. But politicians have learned how to turn a two-party duopoly into a single-party monopoly facing most voters.

Two years ago in California, Congressman Gary Condit lost his seat only due to the widely publicized uproar over his behavior. All the other 52 members of the California Delegation in Congress, both Republican and Democrats, seeking to retain their positions, won re-election. The closest race was an incumbent representative who won "only" 59 percent of the votes against his challenger's 41 percent.

The same incumbent monopoly is spreading at the state legislative level. Forty percent of all state legislators are not even facing an opponent from the other major party in November. In Massachusetts, the figure rises to about 60 percent! Not even a nominal opponent.

Redistricting used to occur every ten years after the census. Now the politicians think they can do it every two or four years.

Gruenstein says that "the loss of equal voting rights caused by gerrymandering, taken to new depths of precision through computer programs and immunized by jelly-kneed courts, has disenfranchised the vast majority of Americans just as effectively as King George did, and more insidiously. What would Thomas Jefferson say?"

"Gerrymandering fundamentally undermines the democratic process itself, and there is essentially no rational basis for opposing reform," Gruenstein adds.

So see if your fellow citizens give a damn. Describe the situation to them and watch their eyes glaze over, as if to say, what can you expect from the politicians and what has this got to do with my daily struggle?

It has a lot to do with your daily life. Want a few examples? How about the gouging of prices of medicines, crumbling schools while stadiums take your tax dollars, the air you breath, the water you drink, the jobs you lose, the cutbacks in wages and benefits, the outsourcing, the healthcare you cannot afford, the looting of your pension plan or savings by corporate crooks, the suction of your tax dollars for corporate subsidies and giveaways and the overall failure of governments to defend your interests.

Why should elected officials care about you when they can raise money from your commercial opponents and get elected automatically?

Redistricting can be done by non-partisan commissions, as in western Europe, and it can be done rationally with minimal partisan bias in the voter makeup. Iowa comes closer to this approach and guess what, they have more competitive elections.

Remember today's redistricting via computers takes away the voices and choices that would listen and respond to your concerns, your desires for a better future for your children.

Also remember, the replacement of democracy with autocracy in our country comes not with heavy boots and smashed doors. It is coming, to use the words of the poet Robert Frost, "on little cat feet."

For more on electoral reform, contact the Center for Voting and Democracy, 6930 Carroll Avenue, Suite 610, Takoma Park, Maryland 20912; by phone: 301-270-4616, fax: 301-270-4133 and at www.fairvote.org.

Tort Deform Bill

July 10, 2004

Another tort deform bill—just one in a seemingly endless string of attacks on our civil justice system—has failed in the Senate this week. American consumers should be thankful that

the so-called "Class Action Fairness Act" was mired in election year posturing by both parties. Some, mainly Republicans and corporations, would have you believe that this is a "victory for trial lawyers." It is not. Sadly, this is not even that much of a victory for the aggrieved consumers who, as a result of the failed legislation, will retain access to their state judges and courts. No, maintaining the status quo by defeating this bill is just a makeshift buttress to slow the constant erosion of our civil justice system at the hands of corporate America's loyal soldiers who occupy the House of Representatives, the Senate, and the White House.

In the year running up to an election, Congress rarely passes contentious legislation. In fact, the Senate will now abandon class action legislation to pursue other hot election-year issues that stand no chance of bicameral passage. Our Senators will spend the rest of the year (and your tax dollars) taking staunch positions that will shore up their party base, but accomplish little else. Republicans will no doubt decry Democrats as "obstructionists" for blocking a class action bill.

But they should be careful about making this issue a central one in the upcoming election lest the truth regarding tort deform actually emerge in the debate.

But with the presumptive Democratic presidential candidate's choice of John Edwards for the vice president slot, Republican tort deformers and their corporate taskmasters have already ratcheted up their rhetoric.

Even usually neutral business lobbies like the Chamber of Commerce have broken with tradition to condemn the choice of Senator Edwards due to his career as a trial lawyer. While Republicans and business interests attack the character of John Edwards by branding him "a friend to trial lawyers," let us hope that the senator from North Carolina will not shy away from the opportunity to make tort deform a substantive, national, election-year issue. The facts are on his side, and the public deserves to hear them.

Tort deform is little more than a legislated escape from accountability; a free pass to abuse consumers so that business can march on unfettered by those nasty little attempts to hold it responsible in a court of law for negligent actions. When it comes to molding our judicial system, the corporations know few limits to their contempt for Americans' right to trial by jury. They do demand that corporations remain free to sue anyone without restrictions.

Class action lawsuits were initially created as a vehicle to offer a degree of fairness and efficiency to citizens collectively when pitted against the comparatively limitless resources of a predatory corporation. Multiple plaintiffs are allowed a more level playing field by pooling together their grievances because each taken alone may not warrant the expense of an individual lawsuit. A collective injury and established pattern of fraudulent or harmful behavior by a corporation as a whole is more substantial and often merits significant damages.

This helps to deter future infliction of injury or fraud while properly compensating affected individuals as determined by state judges and juries—the only people who hear, see and evaluate the evidence and law for such cases. No case has been made that state judges are unwilling or unable to control their courtrooms to a degree warranting this radical federal preemption of state jurisdiction. Under the proposed legislation, innocent victims of fraud, labor law violations, civil rights abuses, unsafe products and environmental harm would be left with limited remedies toward the corporation's defendant.

So it should surprise Americans that without the slightest trace of shame, Stanton D. Anderson, executive vice president for the Chamber of Commerce said of the bill's defeat in the Senate, "This was a vote against America's workers, employers, and consumers that continue to be victimized by a legal system run amok." It is with these skewed distortions, one that reduces individual workers and consumers to pitiless abstractions who, when harmed, threaten profitability—that we must interpret corporate cries of victimization by the tort system.

Not even the high-powered propaganda of the Chamber of Commerce can conceal the absurdity of Mr. Anderson's words.

Another popular tort deform effort in the Senate has revolved around medical malpractice. Its popularity is a direct result of the relentless push made by the insurance industry to gut the civil justice system as we know it. But before any American willingly accepts the insurance industry's propaganda claiming that doctors' insurance premiums are rising solely because of our legal system, we should demand full disclosure from the insurance companies. It is a known fact that lawsuits, lawsuit filings, and jury verdicts have all been trending downward in recent years. The insurance industry is driving the tort deform effort to make up for lost investment income in the bond market when rates were unfavorable. If the insurers want to claim otherwise, let them open their books to public scrutiny.

Since it was founded, our nation's legislature has never attempted to federally tie the hands of judges and juries in the manner advocated by business interests today. The reason we are seeing tort deformers push the myriad pieces of legislation that would immunize doctors from malpractice responsibility; that would protect oil companies from cleaning up polluting components of gasoline from our drinking water sources; or that would make more onerous the ability of class actions to succeed against wealthy cigarette manufacturers, asbestos manufacturers and other corporations, is because they need only establish a few federal legislative precedents to open the tort deform floodgates.

The resulting slippery slope would have lobbyists from every conceivable industry clamoring for their own set of legislated escapes from the law. Take the time to familiarize yourself with the tort deform debate, don't let Congress brush aside the most fundamental tenets of the judicial system, in case you are wrongfully injured or defrauded, to satisfy corporate avarice and greed.

For more information on this topic, please visit: www.centerjd.org, www.citizen.org, and www.consumerwatchdog.org

Government: Imagination & Stagnation

Congress is beyond dysfunctional. The in-fighting, constant arguing, and focusing on partisan political advantages politics rather than what the country needs, shows Congress has forgotten that they have been chosen by "We the People" to make our democracy function for the people. The founding period of our country produced many visionary statesmen. The group included George Washington, Benjamin Franklin, John Adams, Thomas Jefferson, James Madison and Patrick Henry. It is interesting to compare this collection of talent to our current "leaders" from a country over a hundred times more populated than the early years of the Republic.

We are sorely in need of leaders with vision as well as the courage to take action in service of that vision. More often than not, we get the opposite: politicians who respond to narrow, abstract polls or sell out to their biggest campaign contributors.

The columns in this section describe numerous instances when political gridlocks within Congress and between the White House and Congress block progress. The battles rage over raising or lowering taxes, instating single-payer healthcare, cutting defense spending, increasing funding to social programs and saving desiccated agencies or the United States Postal Service (USPS). Much of it involves substantive policies, including corporate welfare and assorted government boondoggles. Your taxpayer dollars are spent without regard, efficiency or efficacy.

An equally important concern is government process or procedures. The "corporate" Supreme Court cares too little about protecting the Constitution and rights of the American people, and instead cares too much about monetary interests.

As you read all this, you may get indignant. This is our government, and the officials, who commit various acts of commission and omission, as my father once said, work for us. We should be angry at them, but also upset with ourselves for letting them get away with rampant abuses using the power we give them. These columns should encourage citizens to organize Congress Watch Locals to help keep Congress on track.

Congress Needs to Get to Work

January 18, 2012

The editor of *The Hill*, a newspaper exclusively covering Congress, said that Congress was not going to do very much in 2012, except for "the big bill" which is extending the payroll tax cut and unemployment compensation, both of which expire in late February. That two-month extension will likely reignite the fight between Democrats and Republicans that flared last month.

In 2012, Congress, the editor implied, would be busy electioneering. That is, the Senators and Representatives will be busy raising money from commercial interests so they can keep their jobs. There won't be much time to change anything about misallocated public budgets, unfair tax rules, undeclared costly wars, and job-depleting trade policies that, if fixed, would increase employment and public investment.

So this year, Congress will spend well over $3 billion on its own expenses to do nothing of significance other than shift more debt to individual taxpayers by depleting the Social Security payroll tax by over $100 billion so both parties can say they enacted a tax cut! That is what the Democrats in Congress and the president call a significant accomplishment.

Will someone call a psychiatrist? This is a Congress that is beyond dysfunctional. It is an obstacle to progress in America, a graveyard for both democracy and justice. No wonder a new *Washington Post*-ABC news poll found an all-time high of 84 percent of Americans disapprove of the job Congress is doing.

Both Republicans and Democrats say they want to reduce the deficit. But they are avoiding, in varying degrees, doing this in any way that would discomfort the rich and powerful. One would think that, especially in an election year, the following legislative agenda would be very popular with the voters.

First, restore the taxes on the rich that George W. Bush cut ten years ago which expanded the deficit. So clueless are the Democrats that they have not learned to use the word "restore" instead of the Republican word "increase" when talking about taxes that were previously cut for the millionaires and billionaires.

Second, collect unpaid taxes. The IRS estimates that $385 billion of tax revenues are not collected yearly. If the IRS budget increased and more people were hired, every dollar it spent would return $200 from tax evaders, including corporations and the wealthy. When taxes are not collected, the large majority of honest taxpayers are left with the unfair consequences. Imagine that money being applied to jobs that repair our crumbling public works.

Third, end the outrageous corporate loopholes that allow profitable large corporations to pay just half of the statutory tax rate of thirty-five percent. More than a few pay less than five percent and many pay zero on major profits. During a recent three-year period, according to the Citizens for Tax Justice, a dozen major corporations such as Verizon and Honeywell paid no taxes on many billions of profits, and the legendary tax escapee, General Electric, managed to pay zero and even receive billions in benefits from the US Treasury.

Fourth, do what most US soldiers in the field have believed should have been done years ago—get out of Afghanistan and Iraq and nearby countries like Kuwait where thousands of US soldiers based in Iraq have moved.

Fifth, to increase consumer demand, which creates jobs, raise the federal minimum wage from the present level of $7.25—which is $2.75

less than it was way back in 1968, adjusted for inflation—to $10 per hour. Businesses who keep raising prices and executive salaries (eg. Walmart and McDonalds) since 1968 should be reminded of their windfall in that period.

In addition, President Obama can urge mutual and pension funds and individual shareholders to demand higher dividends from companies like EMC, Google, Apple, Cisco, Oracle and others firms hoarding two trillion dollars in cash as if this money was the corporate bosses', not the owner-shareholders. More dividends, more consumer demand, more jobs.

Want to know why Congress doesn't make such popular and prudent decisions for the American people? Because the people are not objecting to all the power that their Congressional representatives and their corporate allies have sucked away from them. Because the people are not putting teeth and time into the "sovereignty of the people" expressed in the preamble to our Constitution which begins with "We the people," not "We the corporation."

So citizens, it's your choice. If you don't demand a say day after day, you'll continue to pay day after day.

By the way, the Congressional switchboard number is 202-224-3121.

Congressional Tyranny, White House Surrender

December 14, 2011

Paraphrasing Shakespeare, something is rotten in the state of Capitol Hill. A majority of Congress is just about to put the finishing touches on an amendment to the military budget authorization legislation that will finish off some critical American rights under our Constitution.

Here is how in the *New York Times* two retired four-star Marine Generals Charles C. Krulak and Joseph P. Hoar described the strip-mining of your freedom to resist tyranny in urging a veto by President Obama:

> One provision would authorize the military to indefinitely detain without charge people suspected of involvement with terrorism, including United States citizens apprehended on American soil. Due process would be a thing of the past. . . .
>
> A second provision would mandate military custody for most terrorism suspects. It would force on the military responsibilities it hasn't sought . . . for domestic law enforcement. . . .
>
> A third provision would further extend a ban on transfers from Guantanamo, ensuring that this morally and financially expensive symbol of detainee abuse will remain open well into the future.

All of Obama's leading military and security officials oppose this codification of the ultimate Big Brother power. Imagine allowing the government to deny people accused of involvement with terrorism (undefined), including US citizens arrested within the United States, the right to a trial by jury. Imagine allowing indefinite imprisonment for those accused without even proffering charges against them. Goodbye 5th and 6th Amendments.

On some government agency's unbridled order: just pick them up, arrest them without charges and throw them into the military brig indefinitely. This atrocity deserves to be repeatedly condemned loudly throughout the land by Americans who believe in the rights of due process, habeas corpus, right to confront your accusers, right to a jury trial—in short, liberty and the just rule of law.

Some stalwart lawyers are speaking out

soundly: They include Georgetown Law Professor David Cole, George Washington University Law Professor Jonathan Turley, Republican lawyer Bruce Fein, former American Bar Association (2005-2006) president Michael Greco, and the always alert lawyers at the civil liberties groups. Their well-grounded outcries are not awakening the citizenry.

Where are the one million lawyers? Where are the thousands of law professors? Where are the scores of law school deans? Are they not supposed to be our first constitutional responders?

Where is the Tea Party and its haughty rhetoric about the sanctity of constitutional liberty? Most of the Tea Party caucus voted for tyranny. Presidential candidate Rep. Ron Paul has been an outspoken critic of this attack on our civil liberties.

The majority also voted to ratify a dictatorial procedure in the Congress, as well. This indefinite, arbitrary, open-ended dictatorial White House mandate was never subjected to even a House or Senate Committee hearing, and was not explained with any rationale known as legislative "findings." It was rammed through by the House and Senate Armed Services Committees without the Judiciary and Intelligence Committees invoking their concurrent jurisdiction for public hearings.

So extreme are these majority Congressional extremists, composed of both Republicans and renegade Democrats, the latter led by Senator Carl Levin, that the Obama Administration has to lecture them about the fundamental American principle that "our military does not patrol our streets."

It is not as if the imperial presidencies of Bush and Obama need any more encouragement and legitimization to continue on their lawless paths to criminal wars of aggression, unlawful surveillance, arbitrary slayings of innocents, wrongful imprisonments, and unauthorized spending. Instead of Congress using its constitutional authority regarding the war, appropriations and investigative powers, it formalizes its impotence by handing the "go for it" power to the Executive Branch with the vaguest of language boundaries.

Usually there are a few senators whose upfront defense of our Constitution would lead them to stand tall against the "Senate Club" and put a "hold" on this pernicious amendment. Civil libertarians hope that, before the final Senate vote in the rush to get home for the holidays, Senators Rand Paul, Tom Harkin, Al Franken, Richard Blumenthal, Ron Wyden, Bernie Sanders, Jeff Merkley, Tom Coburn or Mike Lee would step forth. A "hold" could spark the demand for public hearings and floor debate to give the American people the time and information to react and ask themselves "how dare Congress take away our most fundamental rights?"

President Obama initially threatened to veto the entire bill and make Congress drop these pernicious dictates that so insult the memory and vision of our founding fathers. He is already signaling that he doesn't have the backbone to reject the false choice "between our safety and our ideals," that he asserted in his inaugural address.

Time to Save the Post Office
December 7, 2011

The battered national consensus behind a national universal postal service—conceived by Benjamin Franklin—is heading for a free fall due to bad management, corporate barracudas and a bevy of editors and reporters enamored with the supremacy of the internet which makes up their world.

Postmaster General Patrick Donahoe is pursuing a strategy of cutting or delaying services while increasing prices. Usually that is a sure prescription for continuing decline. For Mr. Donahoe, the drop in first class mail has left the Post Office with an over-capacity problem. So he is closing over 200 processing centers, and shuttering hundreds of post offices, including Philadelphia's original Ben Franklin post offices. He mistakenly thinks closing additional USPS facilities' will not result in revenue reductions and service abandonment.

Never mind the intangibles of convenience, safety (eg. receiving medicines) and collegiality that characterizes many rural, small town and suburban post offices.

Mr. Donahoe tells reporters that he is acting the way any beleaguered business executive would, even though he knows that the Postal Service is not just another big business feeding off corporate welfare. The USPS has not taken any taxpayer money since 1971.

By contrast the federal government has taken money from the USPS and owes our Postal Service between $50 and $70 billion dollars in excess retirement benefits payments. The other overpayments to the federal government are for the unprecedented advanced payment of health benefits of future retirees of the next 75 years by 2016, amounting to $5 billion a year (Congress is considering a bill to rectify this problem). Without corrective legislation, the Postal Service says it would have lost $8.5 billion this year. (By comparison, in addition to lost lives and destruction, the Afghan War quagmire costs the US taxpayer over $2 billion a week.)

If all this sounds bizarre to you, it is. No other public department is a defacto creditor of the federal government. The USPS is a hybrid public corporation, created in 1970, from the old Post Office Department. It has been run into the ground on the installment plan by commercial competitors aggressively taking advantage of a weak-willed, unimaginative succession of postmaster generals ruled by a corporate Board of Governors ideologically rooting for corporate privatizers.

In his media interviews of woe, Mr. Donahoe talks precious little either about revenue increases or about long-overdue expansions of service. Abolished because of banking industry pressure in 1966, the Postal Savings System for simple savings accounts needed by tens of millions of "unbanked" Americans could be reactivated. Mr. Donahoe has been telling people that he's thinking about it, but this self-styled salesman has proposed nothing to date. (See the letter urging this expansion by the Appleseed Foundation, dated October 14, 2011, at: savethepostoffice.com/sites/default/files/appleseed_11.11.11%20copy.pdf)

Each time I ask Mr. Donahoe to tell us how he is increasing revenue through this remarkable local network of 32,000 post offices, there is no response. Postal Regulatory Commission Chairperson Ruth Goldway has proposed about two dozen ways to increase revenue. Why not explore new ways to use the internet to produce new revenue?

My conversations with postal workers and letter carriers are filled with revenue-increasing ideas from them. These workers are frustrated because the suggestion forms they are asked to regularly fill out are sent to headquarters with nary a feedback. One simple idea, establish a more vigorous staff culture of selling existing and new services. Poor morale loses sales. Are there too many "supervisors" lording it over their underlings? Why can't Express Mail or parcel post shipments rise from their abysmal level of under 10 percent of the current marketplace.

The USPS is aggressive in selling new stamps, but it falls down when confronted by FedEx, UPS and others in the lucrative overnight express delivery and package business. The truck bays in Congress itself are full of these company vehicles. Let's recognize that Congress often has tied the Post Office's hands on what it can sell. But that cannot excuse post office problems such as long lines, long phone delays, other mismatches between staff and levels of fluctuating business, including a USPS proposal to reduce their time of delivery standards.

Recessions take their toll, more from many large companies (take the auto companies) than from the Postal Service on a percentage of sales basis. So there is no need to panic and stripmine the Postal Service. This could create a decline in usage and a fatal downward revenue spiral.

Sometimes the problem is illustrated by simple experiences. A month ago I wanted to send an Express Mail package from Washington, DC to Darien, Connecticut. The branch manager told my associate that the USPS could not guarantee next day delivery for Express Mail! The postal worker said the computer told her to tell patrons about this risk. So my colleague went to FedEx to ensure overnight delivery. On her way back home she stopped at another postal branch and was told "why of course your Express Mail will get there tomorrow. That's what Express Mail is about." Multiply that first response thousands of times and you get thousands of lost sales.

Postal staff know about "lost sales" to individuals and businesses. They use the phrase "lost sales" all the time when they bewail management. This is a management that spends too much of its time cutting, abandoning, closing,

delaying and outsourcing postal services to K-Mart and Walmart locations.

Want to do something about a great American institution that is perfectly capable of adapting and benefiting from new times? Visit save-thepostoffice.com. If you want to help us build a strong residential postal user group, send an email to info@csrl.org.

Ideological Inebriation on Capitol Hill
July 26, 2011

Legislating while under the influence of ideological inebriation is not yet a statutory offense. It is only a multi-directional menace to much of what anxious Americans hold dear for themselves and their children.

The dominant Republicans in Congress—both the new and many of the longer-term incumbents—are in heat. It is as if a mob psychology has seized them, starved them of facts, and deprived them of reality. Their chief mad dog is Eric Cantor—he of the sneering soundbites so memorably described in a recent *Washington Post* column by Dana Milbank.

Cantor is the big burr under Speaker John Boehner's saddle; Boehner himself is terrified of the young fanatic from Virginia and the even younger fanatics elected in 2010 on the Tea Party wave. The Republicans have suckered President Obama into a game of chicken, but fanatic Republicans don't blink. Why not raise the nation's debt limit to pay for debts already incurred by Congressional appropriations, as has been routinely done nearly 60 times since the 1930s? "No way!" say the self-styled Tea Partiers.

Polls show that 70 percent of Republicans believe that, along with spending cuts, there need to be some tax increases for more revenue. Nearly half of people polled back home who called themselves Tea Party people even agree.

So what gives with these hard core Tea Partiers behind Cantor? First, it seems they're having fun just hypocritically shaking up Washington on spending while pushing for funding their own pet projects back home, like Republican Steve Fincher's (R-Tenn.) Port of Cates Landing project. The Republicans are having fun with a spineless President Obama who already has given them 80 percent of what they want and seems ready to slip further into their budgetary abyss. Bill Curry, former special assistant to President Clinton, says it isn't that Obama is spineless; it is that he is closer to his opponents in his real beliefs than his liberal/progressive supporters like to think.

They're having fun because many of the House Republican freshmen class don't care about being re-elected if the price is to adopt the old ways of despised Washington. Yet, they are raising campaign money vigorously in the old Washington ways.

Still, most of the newly-elected Republicans are upper-middle-class, come from successful small businesses or professional firms and don't empathize with tens of millions of impoverished or heavily indebted Americans.

It's fun being the center of attention, holding hostage small health and safety budgets such as food safety, auto/truck safety, air and water safety, and needy children's programs, while giving a pass to massively bloated military spending and very profitable corporations like General Electric that pay no federal income taxes.

It's fun going back to the country clubs where the wealthy undertaxed slap them on the back and exclaim, "Way to go, Congressman." After all, the wealthy are paying the lowest rates

of taxation, especially on their capital gains and dividends, in modern American history.

Conservative columnist, David Brooks, is not amused with them. He thinks the Republican Party has gotten far more than they envisioned at the beginning of the negotiations with Obama and should take this "mother of all no brainers." That they do not, says Brooks, is because the "Republican Party may no longer be a normal party," but is "infected by a faction that is more psychological protest than a practical governing alternative." He sees this dominant faction as having "no sense of moral decency," having "no economic theory worthy of the name."

The latter is certainly true. For if they are really against Big Government, why aren't they cutting hundreds of billions of dollars in corporate welfare, subsidies, handouts and giveaways or gigantic Pentagon over-spending and waste, or enabling federal law enforcement to crack down on corporate crime that is looting Medicare, Medicaid, royalty collections and violating pro-competition laws?

Arrogant fanatics tend to outsmart themselves. Already, 470 business leaders have written Congress urging it to raise the debt ceiling to avoid a financial crisis, along with spending restraints. More than a few of these leaders, Republicans or not, think the Tea Party faction on Capitol Hill is nuts and playing Russian roulette with the American economy. The Senate rules don't help, allowing a minority party to control the Senate.

These fanatical Republicans are playing another game of Russian roulette with their own Party's electoral future. The polls are starting to turn ominously against them. Wait until October when the cuts hit Main Street and Elm Street. Back home, most Republican voters want tax increases, probably on the wealthy and corporations, as part of negotiating a deal. The critical independent vote is starting to turn away from this extremism on Capitol Hill.

The Republican faction that David Brooks is so appalled by may well destroy the Republican Party's chances for electoral victory through and well beyond 2012.

Who said the Tea Party takeover has no redeeming value?

For more information on budget news, check out the Project on Government Oversight (POGO), Citizens for Tax Justice (CTJ), and Taxpayers for Common Sense (TCS).

The Corporate Supreme Court

July 18, 2011

Five Supreme Court Justices—Scalia, Thomas, Roberts, Alito and Kennedy—are entrenching, in a whirlwind of judicial dictates, judicial legislating and sheer ideological judgments, a mega-corporate supremacy over the rights and remedies of individuals.

The artificial entity called "the corporation" has no mention in our Constitution whose preamble starts with "We the People," not "We the Corporation."

Taken together the decisions are brazenly overriding sensible precedents, tearing apart the state common law of torts and blocking class actions, shoving aside jury verdicts, limiting people's "standing to sue", pre-empting state jurisdictions—anything that serves to centralize power and hand it over to the corporate conquistadores.

Here are some examples. (For more see: thecorporatecourt.com). Remember the disastrous Exxon Valdez oil spill in Alaska's Prince William Sound twenty two years ago? It destroyed marine life and the livelihoods of many landowners, fishermen and native Alaskans. Its toxic effects continue to this day.

Well, after years of litigation by Alaskan fishermen, the Supreme Court took the case to review a $5 billion award the trial court had assessed in punitive damages. A 5-to-3 decision lowered the sum to $507.5 million which is less than what Exxon made in interest by delaying the case for twenty years. Moreover, the drunken Exxon captain's oil tanker calamity raised the price of gasoline at the pump for a while. Exxon actually made a profit despite its discharge of 50 million gallons.

The unelected, life-tenured corporate court was just getting started and every year they tighten the noose of corporatism around the American people.

In *Bush v. Gore* (5-4 decision), the Court picked the more corporate president of the United States in 2000, leaving constitutional scholars thunderstruck at this breathtaking seizure of the electoral process, stopping the Florida Supreme Court's ongoing state-wide recount. The five Republican Justices behaved as political hacks conducting a judicial coup d'etat.

But then what do you expect from justices like Thomas and Scalia who participate in a Koch brothers' political retreat or engage in extrajudicial activities that shake the public confidence in the highest court of the land.

Last year came the *Citizens United v. FEC* case where the Republican majority went out of its way to decide a question that the parties to the appeal never asked. In a predatory "frolic and detour," the five justices declared that corporations (including foreign companies) no longer have to obey the prohibitory federal law and their own court's precedents.

Corporations like Pfizer, Aetna, Chevron, GM, Citigroup, Monsanto can spend unlimited funds (without asking their shareholders) in independent expenditures to oppose or support candidates for public office from a local city council election to federal Congressional and presidential elections.

Once again our judicial dictatorship has spoken for corporate privilege and power overriding the rights of individual voters.

Eighty percent of the American people, reported a the *Washington Post* poll, reject the Court's view that a business corporation is entitled to the same free speech rights as citizens.

Chances are very high that in cases between workers and companies, consumers and companies, communities and corporations, taxpayers and military contractors—big business wins.

Inanimate corporations created by state government charters have risen as Frankensteins to control the people through one judicial activist decision after another. It was the Supreme Court in 1886 that started treating a corporation as a "person" for purposes of the equal protection right in the Fourteenth Amendment. Actually the scribe manufactured that conclusion in the headnotes even though the Court's opinion did not go that far. But then it was off to the races. These inanimate giants, astride the globe, have privileges and immunities that "We the People" can only dream about, yet they have equal constitutional rights with us (except for the right against self-incrimination with the Fifth Amendment and more limited privacy rights.)

What is behind these five corporate justices' decisions is a commercial philosophy that big business knows best for you and your children. These justices intend to drive this political jurisprudence to further extremes, so long as they are in command, to twist our founders clear writings that the Constitution was for the supremacy of human beings.

To see how extreme the five corporate justices are, consider the strong contrary view of one of their conservative heroes, the late Chief Justice William Rehnquist in a case where a plurality of justices threw out a California regulation requiring an insert in utility bills inviting residential ratepayers to band together to advance their interests against Pacific Gas and Electric. The prevailing justices said—get this—that it violated the electric company monopoly's First Amendment right to remain silent and not respond to the insert's message.

Conservative Justice Rehnquist's dissent contained these words—so totally rejected by the present-day usurpers: "Extension of the individual freedom of conscience decisions to business corporations strains the rationale of those cases beyond the breaking point. To ascribe to such artificial entities an "intellect" or "mind" for freedom of conscience purposes is to confuse metaphor with reality."

It was left to another conservative jurist, the late Justice Byron White, dissenting in the corporatist decision *First Nat'l Bank v. Bellotti (1978)* to recognize the essential principle.

Corporations, Justice White wrote, are "in a position to control vast amounts of economic power which may, if not regulated, dominate not only the economy but also the very heart of our democracy, the electoral process." The state, he continued, has a compelling interest in "preventing institutions which have been permitted to amass wealth as a result of special advantages extended by the state for certain economic purposes from using that wealth to acquire an unfair advantage in the political process. . . . *The state need not permit its own creation to consume it.*" (emphasis added)

Never have I urged impeachment of Supreme Court justices. I do so now, for the sake of ending the Supreme Court's corporate-judicial dictatorship that is not accountable under our system of checks and balance in any other way.

Fighting for FOIA

June 14, 2011

The 45th anniversary of the Freedom of Information Act (FOIA) next month should remind all who have used this wonderful citizen tool against government secrecy and cover-ups of FOIA's towering champion Congressman John Moss (D-Calif.).

As a legislator, John Moss was a wonder of integrity, diligence, strategic and populist follow-through. Although Moss was not a lawyer, he read more bills cover to cover than most lawyers who were members of Congress.

As a freshmen legislator in Sacramento, he took on the powerful speaker of the state's House of Representatives for having too much concentrated power. You can count on the fingers of both hands the number of new lawmakers who have done that anywhere in the 50-state legislatures over the past century. It usually means, at the least, the end of the upstart's political career. Talk about courage.

Moss came to Congress in 1952 and by 1955, his twelve years of relentless drive for the public's right to know was underway. He had to take on the corporate lobbies and their cushy relationship with the secrecy-loving bureaucrats, including their president, Lyndon B. Johnson. Moss successfully built support in Congress and nationwide.

Later in 1974, I worked with Chairman Moss to advance the strengthening amendments that allowed judicial review of agency denials of information requests. Toughening the best freedom of information law in the world prompted each of the states to pass their own state freedom of information laws.

Before Moss and FOIA, the Navy Department refused to divulge to environmentalists the amount of sewage dumped into bays from naval bases. Seems that the Navy brass thought the Russians or Chinese, with such data, could figure out how many sailors were stationed at a particular base.

The Postmaster General kept secret public employee salaries. Americans could not access their FBI files. Meat and poultry inspection reports were often held in closed government files. In the foreign policy/military area, the national security state behaved as if secrecy was their birthright.

Each time you see a great segment on "60 Minutes," or read exposés in the newspapers and magazines, chances are that they were made possible in part, if not in whole, by reporters using the FOIA. Americans learned about how far up the George W. Bush chain of command the torture policy in Iraq reached from an ACLU request under FOIA.

To be sure, federal agencies are known to delay or redact far more than they should. These agencies take more advantage of the specific exemptions in the FOIA than they should. But compared to the pre-FOIA laws, our ability to find out what the government is or is not doing is almost like night and day.

Our Freedom of Information Clearing House (http://www.citizen.org/litigation/free_info/) has filed dozens of lawsuits against government agencies for unlawful secrecy. We have won most of them and in the process, improved agency procedures. Our cases provided the evidence showing the need for the 1974 amendments to FOIA as well.

Coming from a humble background—his mother died when he was 12 years old—John Moss is an American hero. His 25 years in the House of Representatives was marked by leadership in the areas of consumer protection and a level of Congressional oversight of federal agencies, almost unknown by today's abdicatory Congress.

His life should be a model for high school and college students. They should want to see how his singular character and personality put reality into the saying "information is the currency of democracy," rather than just following the latest peccadilloes of tawdry entertainment and sports celebrities.

Now the young and adults alike have the new book that does Chairman Moss overdue justice. From Michael R. Lemov, chief of the counsel to the Congressman's two major subcommittees, comes *People's Warrior: John Moss and the Fight for Freedom of Information and Consumer Rights*. This 237-page book covers the personal and professional life of Moss who believed in the political accountability of politicians. More than anyone else in Congress, he gave us a unique law that is invoked only by the desire of people or institutions in the US, and sometimes from outside the country. We are the ones who apply this law by using it and improving it.

Of all the legislators I have worked with, John Moss was the most no-nonsense craftsman of them all. Sitting in his office, one did not have to worry about his caving to commercial interests. He took on the auto industry lobbyists in shepherding the Magnuson-Moss Warranty bill through the House (for example, if you bought a lemon car, you can remedy your situation thanks to Moss and his formidable drive for justice).

In so doing, I recommend *People's Warrior* especially for young people today, beset with cynicism about Congress or simply "turned off" from politics. The book is an awakening antidote that shows, not so long ago, that there were key members of Congress who made regular, significant decisions on behalf of the people. They were not "cash and carry" politicians as is the norm today at both ends of Pennsylvania Avenue.

Open Letter to President Obama on the Nomination of Elizabeth Warren

April 1, 2011

Dear President Obama:

An interesting contrast is playing out at the White House these days—between your expressed praise of General Electric's CEO, Jeffrey R. Immelt and the silence regarding the widely-desired nomination of Elizabeth Warren to head the new Consumer Financial Regulatory Bureau within the Federal Reserve.

On one hand, you promptly appointed Mr. Immelt to be the chairman of the President's Council on Jobs and Competitiveness, while letting him keep his full-time lucrative position as CEO of General Electric (The Corporate State Expands). At the announcement, you said that Mr. Immelt "understands what it takes for America to compete in the global economy."

Did you mean that he understands how to avoid all federal income taxes for his company's $14.2 billion in profits last year, while corralling a $3.2 billion benefit? Or did you mean that he understands how to get a federal bailout for GE Capital and its reckless exposure to risky debt? Or could you have meant that GE knows how to block unionization of its far-flung workers here and abroad? Perhaps Mr. Immelt can share with you GE's historical experience with lucrative campaign contributions, price-fixing, pollution and those nuclear reactors that are giving people fits in Japan and worrying millions of Americans here living or working near similar reactors.

Compare, if you will, the record of Elizabeth Warren and her acutely informed knowledge about delivering justice to those innocents harmed by injustice in the financial services industry. A stand-up law professor at your alma mater, author of highly regarded articles and books connecting knowledge to action, the probing Chair of the Congressional Oversight Panel (COP), now working intensively in the Treasury Department to get the CFRB underway by the statutory deadline this July with competent, public-oriented staff.

There were many good reasons why Senate leader Harry Reid (D-Nev.) called Professor Warren and asked her to be his choice for Chair of COP. Hailing from an Oklahoman blue-collar family, Professor Warren is just the "working class hero" needed to make the new Bureau a sober, law and order enforcer, deterrer and empowerer of consumers vis-à-vis the companies whose enormous greed, recklessness and crimes tanked our economy into a deep recession. The consequences produced 8 million unemployed workers and shattered trillions of dollars in pensions and other savings along with the dreams which they embodied for American workers.

Much more than you perhaps realize, millions of people, who have heard and seen Elizabeth Warren, rejoice in her brainy, heartfelt knowledge and concern over their plight. They see her as just the kind of regulator (federal cop on the beat) for their legitimate interests in a more competitive marketplace who you should be overjoyed in nominating.

Yet there are corporate forces from Wall Street to Washington determined to derail her nomination—forces with their avaricious hooks into the Republicans on Capitol Hill and the corporatists in the Treasury and White House.

You have obliged these forces again and again over the last two years, most recently with the appointment of William M. Daley, recently of Wall Street, as your chief of staff.

How about one nomination for the People? The accolades on hearing the news of Elizabeth Warren's nomination may actually exceed the enduring indignation were she not to be nominated. Just feed the Senate Republicans to the mass media that would cover the nomination hearings, all that calm, solid, wisdom and humanity that she communicates without peer. See who prevails.

Selecting Elizabeth Warren and backing her fully though the nomination process will always be remembered by Americans across the land. Not doing so will not be forgotten by those same persons. This is another way of saying she has the enthusiastic constituency of "hope and change"—that is "change you can believe in!"*

I look forward with many others to your response.

Sincerely yours,
Ralph Nader
PO Box 19312
Washington, DC 20036

---

*If you doubt this observation and would like to see one million Americans on a petition favoring her selection, ask us and see how long that would take.

Open Letter to President Obama

January 10, 2011

Dear President Obama:

The sentiments expressed in this letter may have more meaning more for you now that the results of the mid-term elections are clear. You have seen what can happen when a number of your supporters lose their enthusiasm and stay home or do not actively participate as volunteers.

In your first two years, you have developed a wide asymmetry between your association with Big Business executives and the leaders of national civic and labor groups whose members are in the tens of millions. You have met repeatedly at the White House and other locales with corporate officials, spoken to their gatherings and even traveled abroad with them to promote their exports.

Recently on your trip to India with a covey of business leaders, you vigorously touted their products, some by brand name (Boeing and Harley-Davidson's expensive motorcycles). Your traveling companions could not have been more gratified as you legitimized their view that WTO trade rules were a net plus for employment in the United States as well as India. Imagine—the president as a business agent.

Contrast this close relationship with profit-making firms, many subsidized by the taxpayers in various ways, and probed for health, safety or economic violations by regulatory agencies, with your refusal to openly and regularly address the large non-profit civic groups. Before your inauguration, I wrote requesting that you do what Jimmy Carter did just after his election when he addressed and interacted with nearly one thousand civic leaders at a Washington hotel. They addressed a broad array of issues: environment, food, labor, energy, consumer, equality for women, civil rights-civil liberties and other endeavors for a better society. It was a grand and productive occasion.

You know that the civic groups—often called the Independent Sector—employ many thousands of people around the country often on shoestring budgets with no profits in mind. They work for health, safety, economic and environmental well-being, for living wages and access to justice, for peace and the rule of law in domestic and foreign policy. Yet you as president do not adequately attach your cachet in their favor and give them the visibility that you give commercial businesses. Strange! For profits and jobs, yes I'm coming says the president. For justice and jobs, no I'm not coming says the president.

It is time to associate yourself with civil society, name some with approbation as you have done with companies, express your support for the expansion of their budgets and activities, in short, identify with them.

Please note that when you invite the CEOs of Aetna and Pfizer numerous times to the White House and cut deals not exactly in the patients' best interest, while you decline to invite old friends and mentors on these health insurance and healthcare subjects like Dr. Quentin Young in Chicago, people are perplexed and communicate their displeasure via their networks.

Last Friday, the *Wall Street Journal* reported that on February 7, you "will cross Lafayette Park from the White House to the headquarters of the US Chamber of Commerce, his longtime political nemesis…" What about walking up the street and visiting your political friends at the headquarters of the AFL-CIO whose member unions represent millions of working Americans?

You can discuss your campaign promises in 2008 with Richard Trumka, a former coal miner and the new president of the AFL-CIO. Repeatedly you said to the American people that you supported the "card check" and a "federal minimum wage of $9.50 in 2011." The 1968 minimum wage, adjusted for inflation would be about $10 today. (The federal minimum wage is now $7.25.)

Moving up the minimum wage to nearly what it was back in 1968, in purchasing power, would increase consumer demand by over $200 billion a year. Isn't that what this economy needs right now, not to mention the boon it would be to long deprived, underpaid workers and their families? After all, businesses of all sizes have received a variety of substantial tax breaks during this windfall period of a stagnant federal minimum wage. Isn't it time for some equity for the people?

On a related note, over a year ago, Mr. Mike Kelleher, the man in charge of letters written to you, said he would get back to me about your policy on replying to letters that deal with substantive matters, whether under your signature or the signature of your assistants and department heads. I have not heard from Mr. Kelleher.

Let me give you an example. Months ago I wrote to inform you that several prominent environmental and energy groups, such as Friends of the Earth, Greenpeace, and the Union of Concerned Scientists, were at their wit's end trying to arrange a joint meeting with Secretary Steven Chu. He repeatedly declined to meet, though he has often met with nuclear energy business executives and has gone so far as to tout nuclear energy's desirability in an op-ed. The environmental groups wanted a serious exchange with him on your administration's energy policies, including your request to Congress for very large loan guarantees by taxpayers for utilities that want to build more nuclear plants.

My letter asked you to intercede and urge Secretary Chu that it is only fair and constructive to hear what these groups have to say. There never was an answer from the White House or the Department of Energy. You know that for years many citizen advocates have worked hard to improve the federal government and they have rarely experienced such discourtesies of no replies.

Perhaps you do not care. But you should know that there are people who do. What is your response?

Sincerely,

Ralph Nader

Majority of One

December 14, 2010

On Friday, December 10, 2010, Senator Bernie Sanders, Independent Socialist, of Vermont, came of age. At last. With just about the best progressive voting record, Senator Sanders has nonetheless been an underachiever in the minds of those Americans who marveled at his tenure as mayor of Burlington, Vt. before he became a representative and now a senator.

Last Friday, Sanders tore the covers off an oligarchic driven Congress and a concessionary president with eight-and-a-half hours of nonstop presentations of facts and figures and a plea for fairness and justice. His goal was not heated rhetoric, though he showed deep moral indignation, but to attempt to rally the American people "to voice their feelings" to their members of Congress via phone calls, letters and e-mails. C-SPAN carried him live, since he was the only activity on the Senate floor that day.

He asked the overriding question of "who is winning and who is losing?" The winners were the giant, bailed-out corporations and other companies so coddled with tax breaks and subsidies that they pay no federal income tax at all.

He named some of these company bosses who make sky-high salaries and bonuses and take advantage of tax havens. ExxonMobil, Sanders noted, made $19 billion in profits last year, paid no federal income taxes and even received a $156 million refund from the US Treasury!

Senator Sanders filled the Congressional Record with statements about a variety of inequities and contradictions regarding President Obama's capitulation. Highlights follow:

- A Government Accountability Office report states that two-thirds of corporations making $2.5 trillion in sales over several years paid no federal income taxes.

- During the giant Wall Street bailout of 2008-2009, the Federal Reserve also bailed out with huge credit draws foreign banks from Bavaria to Japan. Such disclosures will be more common as a result of a successful Sanders amendment to the financial reform law earlier this year.

- The Obama-Republican deal would increase the deficit by $900 billion dollars over ten years but devote "not one nickel" to any infrastructure projects in local communities.

- He cited Warren Buffet and 90 other very rich Americans who wrote a letter to Congress opposing a tax cut for rich people like themselves.

- He cited the top one percent of the richest Americans who have wealth equal to the bottom 90 percent and receive 24 percent of all income. "When is enough, enough,

do you want it all?" cried Sanders to an empty Senate chamber. (His colleagues had gone home Friday morning except for Senators Sherrod Brown and Mary Landrieu who conducted brief colloquies with Sanders while he rested his voice or went to the men's room.)

- The top 25 hedge fund managers each made an average of a billion dollars last year with much of that income taxed only at a 15 percent rate. The richest 400 families paid a 16.6 percent effective tax rate on average. The Obama deal would extend their tax cuts for another two years.

- There has been zero net job creation since 1999 leading to a decline in average household income. Inequality of wealth in the US is the worst in the industrialized world.

- The US has the highest rate of child poverty in the western world, in some cases five to six times that of Scandinavia.

- The Obama Republican deal would divert for the first time $120 billion from the payroll tax, leading Sanders to say this is the beginning of the unraveling of Social Security, "eating our own seed," he added.

- "Let us be very clear: This [estate] tax applies only—only—to the top three-tenths of 1 percent of American families; 99.7 percent of American families will not pay one nickel in an estate tax. This is not a tax on the rich, this is a tax on the very, very, very rich." (The estate tax is reduced, while the exemption is increased, leading to $30-52 billion retained by the very wealthiest of estates over two years.)

- And of course over $120 billion over two years are left with the highest income rich, worsening the deficit in the coming years.

"We can do better" repeated Sanders, noting that Obama challenged his liberal base in Congress by asking "where are the votes?" To which, Sanders replied: "Our job is to mobilize the people of America," noting a rising flood of support for a fairer deal.

Of course, Obama has a healthy majority in Congress until January 2011. It is the threat of a Senate Republican filibuster—which Majority Leader Senator Harry Reid et al have never made the Republicans use during the first two years of the Obama Administration—that has neutralized that majority. Moreover, the Senate Democrats could have changed these obstructive rules by a simple majority vote back in January 2009. But they chose not to allow their own working majority of well over 50 votes to prevail.

Obama came to the White House swearing that he would not live in "a bubble" and that he would keep his promises, which explicitly included no further extensions of tax cuts for the rich and a $9.50 federal minimum wage (still lower in purchasing power than the federal minimum wage in 1968!) by 2011.

So what do we see from the president? Well, he boasted about being a community organizer in Chicago years ago. Yet for months, knowing what was coming, he failed to arouse the citizenry against the Republican tax cuts for the wealthy which Obama swallowed last week. He is known to be an expert poker player, but he displayed none of that skill with the Republican

corporacrats, Rep. John Boehner and Senator Mitch McConnell. Where are Obama's touted oratorical skills? How smart can he be—undercutting his own Democrats and presenting them with the results of a closed-door sweetheart deal with their Republican adversaries?

Obama has frittered away his comfortable majority in Congress on many accounts for two years. And millions of people and their children will be paying the bill for his failure to fight for them.

Time for OTA

May 28, 2010

When the Republican Gingrich devolution took over Congress in 1995, it stripped the Congressional Office of Technology Assessment (OTA) of all its funding and left it a shell with no experts to advise committees and members of Congress.

Whereupon Congress was plunged into a dark age regarding decisions about trillions of national security, offshore oil drilling, transportation, energy, health, computer, biotech, nanotechnology and many other executive branch programs in science and technology.

Confronted with partisan vested interests by federal departments and their corporate lobbies, Congress could not get objective, unbiased reports and testimony from the OTA. For a budget of $20 million a year, OTA ground out over 700 peer reviewed sound reports and many more Congressional testimonies by its staff between 1972 and 1995. Last year Congress had an overall budget for itself of $3.2 billion.

Representative Amo Houghton (R-N.Y.) commented at the time of OTA's demise that "we are cutting off one of the most important arms of Congress when we cut off unbiased knowledge about science and technology."

Now, Rush Holt (D-N.J.) backed by leading scientists and about 100 citizen, technical and academic groups, organized by the Union of Concerned Scientists (UCS), is urging Speaker Nancy Pelosi to permit a modest restart of the OTA. As noted above, OTA was never abolished, just defunded.

Speaker Pelosi has been resisting, even though this tiny office can provide members of Congress with the technical assessments that could easily save billions of dollars a year. Apparently, she believes that the Republicans will accuse her of empire building, though the OTA is run by an evenly appointed Democratic-Republican Board of Congressional Overseers.

Without the OTA, commercially driven or otherwise wild claims are made for and against Congressionally funded programs.

The UCS (www.ucsusa.org) gives many examples of where OTA saved huge amounts of taxpayer money and improved the health, safety and economic well-being of the American people as well. OTA reports, by responding to requests by members of Congress, analyzed what technologies worked or did not work.

After OTA was defunded, the UCS asserts, "the Department of Homeland Security (DHS) spent three years pushing for a costly radiation detection system for smuggled nuclear material that did not work as promised, while neglecting to upgrade existing equipment that could have improved security." Billions of dollars were wasted.

Were it operating today, OTA reports and testimony might question DHS's installation of whole body back scatter x-ray airport security scanners. Scientific experts are urging independent testing for effectiveness <u>and</u> safety for exposed passengers (see csrl.org).

On other fronts, Congress is buckling to corporate lobbies and requiring taxpayer guarantees for nuclear power plants that are not nearly as cost effective as energy efficiency and renewables without the perils of atomic power and its unstored radioactive wastes.

The $9 billion a year missile defense project has been condemned as unworkable by the mainstream American Physical Society but the military corporations that receive these boondoggle contracts get it funded year after year.

The risks of nanotechnology, biotechnology and numerous medical devices continue to not be assessed, thereby allowing congressional advocates to tout benefits and ignore costs.

Congress spends billions of dollars a year on technologies driven by commercial partisan interests, whether from government departments, corporate interests or campaign cash. Congress also ignores promising technologies. Decades of little or no solar energy research and development funding, and billions of dollars into atomic, coal and other fossil fuels, directly or indirectly through tax breaks, have cost Americans in their pocketbooks and in the air and water they breath and drink.

In 1985, OTA issued a report cautioning about the lack of preparedness and knowledge regarding potentially "catastrophic oil spills from offshore operations." OTA could not follow up on this report, as the oil companies went into deeper seas, because it was silenced in 1995. Clearly, the Minerals Management Service of the Interior Department—a sleazy, wholly-owned subsidiary of Big Oil—was not going to advise Congress truthfully.

Through its impartial assessment capability, OTA could have alerted Congress to defective body armor that unscrupulous companies sold to the Army.

Congress needs an independent, impartial, no-axe-to-grind technical adviser under its own roof and responsive to the unique and timely needs of members of Congress and Congressional committees. Imagine, for example, the computer procurement waste that could have been prevented.

Speaker Pelosi, don't you want to make this overwhelming case for a revived OTA? Why are you silent when you should be outspoken on behalf of taxpayers and appropriate, safe technology? Be assured that having championed OTA since the days of Director John H. Gibbons many other groups and I will be working to secure your backing sooner rather than later.

Getting to Know Elena Kagan

May 14, 2010

Given the Niagara of commentary on the nomination of Elena Kagan to become an Associate Justice of the Supreme Court of the United States, we know very little about the nominee. For friend and critic alike, the predominant view of Ms. Kagan is that she has publically uttered or written remarkably little of her own views on any subject that directly or remotely relates to her forthcoming position.

As a law school graduate, brief stint as a practitioner, special assistant on domestic policy to President Clinton, professor of law and Dean of Harvard Law School, Elena Kagan has been unusually circumspect, despite her lively tenure as editor of the *Daily Princetonian* while an undergraduate in Tigertown.

Here is how a colleague of equal rank in the Clinton White House describes many group meetings there on important matters: "She nev-

er said much, was very pleasant, smiled a lot, the type of person who rises by not giving offense. She almost never engaged in give or take at the often spirited meetings. Her opinions weren't known. But she is what she is which is exactly what President Obama wants."

The problem for Ms. Kagan is that there was one occasion where she was wonderfully outspoken—her long review of Professor Stephan L. Carter's book *The Confirmation Mess* in the *University of Chicago Law Review* during the Spring of 1995. Taking Professor Carter sharply to task she comes out as a full-throated champion of confirmation hearings that deal with "substantive issues," adding that the "Senate ought to view the hearings as an opportunity to gain knowledge and promote public understanding of what the nominee believes the Court should do and how she would affect its conduct."

Continuing, Ms. Kagan asserts that "[O]pen exploration of the nominee's substantive views . . . enables senators and their constituents to engage in a focused discussion of constitutional values, to ascertain the values held by the nominee, and to evaluate whether the nominee possesses the values that the Supreme Court most urgently requires. These are the issues of greatest consequence surrounding any Supreme Court nomination (not the objective qualifications or personal morality of the nominee . . .)."

Those are strong words in today's flabby pretense of Senate confirmation hearings of judicial nominees—hearings which Ms. Kagan described later in her review as presenting to the public "a vapid and hollow charade, in which repetition of platitudes has replaced discussion of viewpoints and personal anecdotes have supplanted legal analysis."

So, should you look forward to a spectacular demonstration of fire and brain power between the Senators and Elena Kagan? Not likely. The word is that now she has backed away from such authenticity and so has her boss, Barack Obama.

No one can attribute her earlier stands to being naive about Capitol Hill. To the contrary, her strong stand for robust, serious confirmation hearings on "legal issues," draws on her experience as Special Counsel to the Senate Judiciary Committee "in connection with the nomination of Justice Ruth Bader Ginsburg to the Supreme Court."

So, it looks like the first casualty of her nomination will be the authenticity (one of her favorite words) she craved for such nominees as Justices Kennedy, Souter, Thomas, Ginsburg and Breyer, having been quoted years ago as how to evasively behave in order to finesse any controversies during the hearing process.

So since it takes at least two to make a charade game, it is left to the senators to fulfill the vision of the earlier Elena Kagan when she sits in that chair facing her inquisitors. Some senators will use the pretext that deep questions on issues and philosophy would compromise the independence of the judiciary—a view Ms. Kagan explicitly rejected in her book review.

Others, being partisan Democrats, want to get the hearing over at super speed, which means a few pro forma questions. A few will take their constitutional responsibilities or their partisan roles seriously and probe into her qualifications—such as not coming from a judgeship background—or her imputed ideological biases.

In any event, this state of affairs is not the worst of the confirmation process. The deterioration reaches the exclusion of witnesses that reflect just the wide range of questions and judgments that Ms. Kagan championed.

I know this from my own request to testify, for example, on the Roberts nomination re-garding an ignored area of his experience. I was turned down by the Democrats on the Judiciary Committee.

During the Stephen Breyer nomination, Dr. Sidney Wolfe and I presented detailed testimony regarding Mr. Breyer's de-regulatory philosophy and the raw empirical reality of human casualties and tortious products that rebut it. That participation would not likely be repeated today. Instead, there are a few carefully choreographed panels of constitutional law specialists, each given five minutes, and all presented as window dressing after, not before or between, the testimony and questioning of the nominee.

So, short of a cumulative public protest before the hearings begin in July, expect the words of assistant professor of law, Elena Kagan, to be relegated to an everlasting limbo as an expression of youthful exuberance replaced by the political realism of autocratic minds.

Empower The People
April 26, 2010

Dear President Obama, Senator Dodd, Senator Schumer and Senator Shelby:
On the eve of the portentous Senate debate over the extent to which the financial industry is to be held accountable so as to avert future megacollapses on the backs of taxpayers, workers and consumers, a great gap has been left unattended.

That gap pertains to the continued powerlessness of the investors and consumers—the people who bear the ultimate brunt of Wall Street's recklessness, avarice and crimes and who have the greatest interest in strong regulatory enforcement.

Among all the amendments filed for the upcoming Senate debate, only amendment number 29, introduced by Senator Schumer, provides a facility to establish an independent non-governmental non-profit Financial Consumers' Association (FCA).

Amendment 29 includes the following for funding this unique institution:

". . . the financial industry has enjoyed virtually unlimited access to represent its interest before Congress, the courts, and State and Federal regulators, while financial services consumers have had limited representation before Congress and financial regulatory entities;" and

". . . the Federal Government has a substantial interest in the creation of a public purpose, democratically-controlled, self-funded, nationwide membership association of financial services consumers to enhance their representation and to effectively combat unsound financial practices."

Anyone modestly familiar with the history of regulatory failures knows that the gross disparity of power and organized advocacy between big business and consumers outside of government leads to an absence of fair standards and law enforcement.

It also leads, as everyone knows, to massive taxpayer bailouts, subsidies and guarantees when these giant banks and other financial firms immolate themselves, after enriching their bosses, while engulfing tens of millions of innocent people in the subsequent economic conflagration.

Given all the privileges and costly rescues for culpable corporations that flow regularly from Washington, DC, adopting ever so mildly the principle of reciprocity makes a powerful case for facilitating a nationwide Financial Consumers' Association—one that would be composed of voluntary memberships by consumers who,

through their annual dues, will sustain the FCA for an expert place at the table.

Senator Schumer, when he was a Congressman during the savings and loan bailout in the 1980s, introduced such a proposal. But the bankers took the $150 billion bailout and blocked this reciprocal respect for depositors in the House Banking Committee.

Then Representative Schumer and his supporting colleagues on that Committee understood that without the supposed beneficiaries of regulatory authority being organized to make regulation and deterrence work, the Savings and Loan collapse could happen again. And so they became prophetic beyond their wildest nightmares.

Before he died in a plane crash in 2002, Senator Paul Wellstone recognized the need for such a facility, when he introduced the Consumer and Shareholder Protection Association Act.

A key enhancing feature in amendment 29 is a requirement that invitations to membership in the FCA be included in the billing envelopes or electronic communications of financial institutions with their customers. At no expense to these vendors, these notices would ensure that the maximum number of consumers are invited to join and fund such a democratically run, educational and advocacy organization.

In early 2009 I met with Chairman Christopher Dodd and explained the nature and importance of the FCA and Senator Schumer's earlier role in advancing this civic innovation. He seemed receptive to the idea and urged us to have his colleague Senator Schumer take the lead, which he has done with amendment 29 just a few weeks ago. Senator Shelby and I have also discussed the FCA proposal.

The major valiant but overwhelmed consumer groups, who experience daily this enormous imbalance of power between corporations and consumers, presently stacked by unprecedented amounts of federal funds and bailout facilities for the misbehaving companies, support the creation of a self-funded FCA.

The Federal Government has long paid for facilities in the US Department of Agriculture for agricultural businesses to band together and assess themselves to promote beef, corn, cotton and other commodities to increase their profits. By contrast the FCA, once launched, would be composed of consumers paying their own way to preserve their hard-earned savings from predatory financial speculators.

Allow one prediction. Even if the ultimate legislation comes out stronger than expected on such matters as derivatives, rating agencies, too big to fail, using depositor funds for speculation, and the consumer financial regulatory bureau, unless the consumer-investor is afforded modest facilities to band together with their experts and advocates, the laws will hardly be enforced with sufficient budgets, personnel and regulatory willpower.

Give the consumer a modest round in this prolonged deliberation following the destructive events of 2008.

Sincerely,

Ralph Nader

For more information, see:

The Financial Consumers' Association-Amendment

Financial Consumers' Association Q&A

Consumer Groups Support Financial Consumers' Association

Empire, Oligarchy and Democracy

March 1, 2010

The twin swelling heads of Empire and Oligarchy are driving our country into an ever-deepening corporate state, wholly incompatible with democracy and the rule of law.

Once again the *New York Times* offers its readers the evidence. In its February 25, 2010 issue, two page-one stories confirm this relentless deterioration at the expense of so many innocent people.

The lead story illustrates that the type of massive speculation—casino capitalism, *BusinessWeek* once called it—in complex derivatives is still going strong and exploiting the weak and powerless who pay the ultimate bill.

Titled "Banks Bet Greece Defaults on Debt They Helped Hide," the article shocks even readers hardened to tales of greed and abuse of power. Here are the opening paragraphs:

> Bets by some of the same banks that helped Greece shroud its mounting debts may actually now be pushing the nation closer to the brink of financial ruin.
>
> Echoing the kind of trades that nearly toppled the American International Group (AIG), the increasingly popular insurance against the risk of a Greek default is making it harder for Athens to raise the money it needs to pay its bills, according to traders and money managers.
>
> These contracts, known as credit-default swaps, effectively let banks and hedge funds wager on the financial equivalent of a four-alarm fire: a default by a company, or in the case of Greece, an entire country. If Greece reneges on its debts, traders who own these swaps stand to profit.
>
> "It's like buying fire insurance on your

neighbor's house—you create an incentive to burn down the house," said Philip Gisdakis, head of credit strategy at UniCredit in Munich.

These credit-default swaps increase the dreaded "systemic risk" that proliferates until it lands on the backs of taxpayers, workers and savers who pay the price. And if Greece goes, Spain or Portugal or Italy may be next and globalization will eventually bring the rapacious effects of mindless speculation to our shores.

Greece got into financial trouble for a variety of reasons, but it was widely reported that Goldman Sachs and other big banks showed them, for generous fees, how to hide the country's true financial condition. Avarice at work.

Note two points. These derivatives are contracts involving hundreds of billions of dollars and are essentially unregulated. These transactions are also essentially untaxed, unlike Europe's value added tax on manufacturing, wholesale and retail purchases. The absence of government restraints produces unlimited predation.

As astute investors in the real economy have said, when money for speculation replaces money for investment, the real economy suffers and so do real people. Remember the Wall Street collapse of 2008 and who is paying for the huge Washington bailout.

The other story shows that the presidency has become a self-driven empire outside the law and unaccountable to its citizens. The *Times* reports "how far the C.I.A. has extended its extraordinary secret war beyond the mountainous tribal belt and deep into Pakistan's sprawling cities." Working with Pakistan's counterpart agency, the C.I.A. has had some cover to do what it wants in carrying out "dozens of raids throughout Pakistan over the past year," according to the *Times*.

"Secret War" has been a phrase applied numerous times throughout the C.I.A's history, even though the agency was initially created by Congress right after World War II to gather intelligence, not engage in lethal operations worldwide.

Unrestrained by either Congress or the federal courts, presidents say they can and do order their subordinates to go anywhere in the world, penetrate into any country, if they alone say it is necessary to seize and destroy for what they believe is the national security. American citizens abroad are not excluded. Above and beyond the law spells the kind of lawlessness that the framers of our Constitution abhorred in King George and limited in our country's separation of powers.

Because our founders would not tolerate the president being prosecutor, judge, jury and executioner, they placed the war-declaration and appropriations authorities in the Congress.

Both Presidents George W. Bush and Barack Obama believe they have unbridled discretion to engage in almost any overt or covert acts. That is a definition of empire that flouts international law and more than one treaty which the United States helped shape and sign.

Equipped with remote and deadly technologies like drones flying over Pakistan and Afghanistan by operators in Nevada, many civilians have been slain, including those in wedding parties and homes. Still, it is taking 15,000 soldiers (US and Afghan) with the most modern armaments to deal with three hundred Taliban fighters in Marja who with many other Afghans, for various motivations, want us out of their country. Former Marine Combat Captain Matthew Hoh described these reasons in his detailed resignation letter last fall.

Mr. Obama's national security advisor, Ret.

General James Jones estimated that there are about 100 al-Qaeda in Afghanistan with the rest migrating to other countries. And one might add, those whose migrate are increasing their numbers because they cast themselves as fighting to expel the foreign invaders.

So many capable observers have made this point: occupation by our military fuels insurgencies and creates the conditions for more recruits and more mayhem. Even Bush's military and national security people have made this point.

The American people must realize that their reckless government and corporate contractors are banking lots of revenge among the occupied regions that may come back to haunt. We have much more to lose by flouting international law than the suicidal terrorists reacting to what they believe is the West's state terrorism against their people and the West's historical backing of dictatorships which oppress their own population.

America was not designed for Kings and their runaway military pursuits. How tragic it is that we have now come to this entrenched imperium so loathed by the founding fathers and so forewarned by George Washington's enduring farewell address.

Where are "We the People"?

Dodd and Dorgan Depart
January 8, 2010

The retiring of veteran Democratic Senators, Christopher Dodd, age 65, of Connecticut and Byron Dorgan, age 67, of North Dakota, have some short-term and long-term consequences for the Democratic Party and its members.

Senator Dodd's announcement that he was finished did not surprise me. He was going through difficult times with his health, the loss of his closest sibling, and his closest friend in the Senate, Ted Kennedy, and was not inclined to battle through an uphill fight for re-election. 2010 is, arguably, the most important legislative year of his career for financial and health insurance reforms.

Mr. Dodd should be comforted because it is very likely he will be succeeded by Connecticut Attorney General Richard Blumenthal, who leads the polls and is expected to win handily. Mr. Blumenthal will find a great opportunity to use his enforcement experience as a leading consumer advocate in the Senate against corporate wrongdoing.

Senator Joseph Lieberman—the political hermaphrodite of national politics—is probably elated. Blumenthal detests Lieberman's politics and unctuous self-righteousness and was ready to unseat him in 2012. Once again, Lieberman finds four-leaf clovers—first when he was the 50th Democratic vote in the Senate, then the 60th vote in the Senate—in order to push the Democratic Party to the right, and now having lost a formidable contender in 2012.

For Senator Dodd, the question is whether, now freed from his Wall Street fundraising, he can blossom as a tough legislative advocate for consumers and investors in the major bill to regulate Wall Street that is now in the Senate Banking Committee where he is the Chairman and the most powerful force.

As a lame duck, all his expertise and determination will have to be used to avoid his colleagues taking advantage of his announced retirement.

The prairie populist from North Dakota, Senator Byron Dorgan leaves after 30 years in the House and Senate. He will leave a big hole that will be all the larger with his replacement expected to be the incumbent Republican Governor John

Hoeven. Dorgan was an authentic American populist. As a child, his parents would take him to the rallies of the tough anti-corporate farmers who remembered the Non-Partisan League tradition of fundamental landed populism.

As North Dakota's tax commissioner, he blazed the way to challenge multinational corporations that were using evasive tactics to escape state taxation.

In the Senate 11 years ago, he led a handful of prophetic Senators in a losing battle to preserve the successful Glass-Steagall Act, which kept commercial banking separate from investment banking. Clinton, the big bankers and Treasury Secretary Robert Rubin got their way and the economy proceeded to lose its way in an orgy of disastrous speculation fueled with other peoples' money.

With his feet always on the ground, with the working people, Dorgan never bought into the empirically starved theory of "free trade" used to export jobs and industries to countries run by fascist and Communist dictators who know how to keep their workers in their place. His criticism of the Federal Reserve was informed and relentless, as were his warnings of the growing media monopoly in fewer and fewer hands.

So needed, why did he decide to quit? In his words, he wanted to write a couple of books, teach a little and do some work in the energy field "in the private sector." The latter raises some worries among his closest friends.

As one who has known Senator Dorgan for years, I suspect there was another reason in the mix. He wants to get changes made, which he believes are supported by most Americans. He has waited a long time for the Democrats to take control of the Congress and the White House. That has happened and little has changed.

Late last year, during the Senate debate on health insurance, Dorgan proposed and eloquently explained an amendment to reduce drug prices—the highest in the world—by allowing so-call drug re-importation from countries such as Canada under regulatory safeguards.

He expected Obama's active support since Mr. Obama promised to press for this needed competition in his presidential campaign. He figured wrong. The White House used none of its capital to get the few extra votes needed. For Mr. Obama had already cut a deal privately with the drug company chieftains.

That may have been the last straw for Senator Dorgan. He is not the only progressive Democrat in the Congress who is saying, "What does President Obama really stand for?"

I would like to see a petition signed by dozens of national civic, labor and farm groups urging Senator Dorgan to reconsider his decision and go for one more six-year term.

Otherwise another lifeline for the people in Congress is snapped. That inside voice of justice has got to be worth saving, even if two books and a little teaching are deferred.

Agent of Change
December 29, 2009

The ancient Greek philosopher, Heraclitus (535-475 BC) said that "character is destiny." He might have added that "personality is decisive." Where is Barack Obama in this framework?

The venerable historian, James MacGregor Burns, in his book *Transforming Leadership* drew an important distinction between "transforming and transactional leadership," and calling Franklin Delano Roosevelt a reflection of the former genre.

Given all the burgeoning crises in the United States and the world, the only global military and economic superpower (albeit in serious deficit straits) needs a transforming leader, when, at best, it has a transactional leader in the White House.

I say "at best," because President Obama displays an uncanny inability to deal. He is not even anywhere near Lyndon Baines Johnson in that regard. This lack is due more to his personality than to his character.

His is a concessionary demeanor, an aversion to conflict and to taking on entrenched power, a devotee of harmony ideology not because he doesn't believe in necessary re-directions, but because he does not project the strength of his beliefs and willingness to draw the line—here and no further—as did Ronald Reagan or FDR.

In the shark tank known as the federal Washington, DC, Obama's personality projects weakness as someone who does not take a stand and fight, as someone inclined to rely on his rhetoric to explain his withdrawals, retreats and reversals. Some examples follow.

First, the president has been openly for single-payer health insurance (full Medicare for all with free choice of physician and hospital) since before he became a politician. His friends included single-payer leaders such as the stalwart Dr. Quentin Young in Chicago.

So, instead of starting with "single-payer," he descends to vague policy declarations, asks Congress to come up with a specific bill, while cutting private deals in meetings in the White House with drug industry and health insurance executives.

Now months later, with Blue Dog Democrats emboldened, with his progressive wing angry and starting to rebel, a hocked up insurance bill is having many provisions eviscerated. Once

the Republicans smelled his lack of resolve, his wavering on one amendment after another, they became ravenous in their demands and obstructions.

Second, Barack Obama, before he came to Washington, was also a supporter of Palestinian rights. Between election and inauguration, he proceeded to categorically back the illegal blockade and invasion of Gaza by Israel and did not object to the slaughter of 1400 Palestinians, mostly civilians, young and old. Apparently, the impoverished, pummeled people of a half-destroyed Gaza, whose many newly elected members of the Palestinian parliament were kidnapped and jailed by the Israelis two years earlier, had no right to feebly defend themselves against constant border raids and missiles by the fifth most powerful army in the world.

Third, Mr. Obama's tough talk about a reckless and greedy Wall Street is not paralleled with tough regulatory proposals. He allowed, without working his will, the banks and Banking Committee Chairman, Barney Frank to produce a weakened regulatory bill that passed the House of Representatives.

For example, regulatory provisions on the rating agencies (such as Standard and Poor's and Moody's) and derivatives were mere taps on the wrists, ridiculed by former Chairs of the Securities and Exchange Commission from both parties.

Fourth, on labor and NAFTA, his campaign speeches were about the need for reform. He has started nothing there and says nothing about this promise to revisit the US participation in NAFTA. He believes in the card check version of labor law reform but has not used his political capital to advance this modest reform at all.

Fifth, on climate change, where so much of the world looks for him to be a transforming leader, Mr. Obama has bought into the cap and trade morass instead of a simpler, more enforceable carbon tax. His words on this subject are often well-spoken but his rhetoric is undermined by his inaction. His opponents in Congress and the corporate sector are strengthened as a consequence.

Mr. Obama leaves Copenhagen without a deal after outlining three steps—mitigation of greenhouse gases, openness of each country's progress or lack thereof, and a very modest financial commitment from the world's biggest polluter to help the more beleaguered countries with climate change (poor countries that are recipients of the Western countries' emissions.) He hardly set an example for a government whose ownership and control of GM and Chrysler could transform automotive technology.

He cannot transform his hope and change slogan into meaningful policies if he signals that he can be had on one issue after another by being desperate to get any legislation so long as he can give it the right public relations label.

Most importantly, the president cannot be a transforming leader if he turns his back on the liberal and progressive constituency that elected him because he thinks they have nowhere to go.

He must give visibility to their expectations of him, including access to many cabinet secretaries and regulatory agency heads who have been reluctant even to meet with civic leaders, unlike the open doors regularly available to the corporatists and their lobbyists.

"Personality," "character," pretty soon they become indistinguishable and very resistant to both "hope and change."

Between the Rhetoric and the Reality
August 24, 2009

The Obama White House—full of supposedly smart political advisors led by the president of the "Change You Can Believe In" campaign movement of 2008—is in disarray. Worse, multiple, confusing varieties of disarray provoking public confusion, internal Democratic Party strife, and the slow withdrawal of belief in Mr. Obama by his strongest supporters around the country.

Two of his most steadfast supporters in the media—columnists Paul Krugman and Bob Herbert of the *New York Times* are wondering about Mr. Obama's plans. Krugman repeated his fellow *Sunday Times* essayist Frank Rich's observation who wrote about Obama "punking" his supporters with his waffling, reversals and frequent astonishing adoption of Bush's worst corporatist and military policies.

While Bob Herbert, taking to task his political hero for waffling and vagueness regarding healthcare, issued this reluctant appraisal:

> I hear almost daily from men and women who voted enthusiastically for Mr. Obama but are feeling disappointed. They feel that the banks made out like bandits in the bailouts, and that the healthcare initiative could become a boondoggle. Their biggest worry is that Mr. Obama is soft, that he is unwilling or incapable of fighting hard enough to counter the forces responsible for the sorry state the country is in.

There has rarely been a more auspicious time for a transforming presidential leadership. Disgraced corporate capitalism has shattered the economy. The living conditions of millions of workers and pensioners whose taxes were taken to bail out these Wall Street crooks and gamblers are dismal.

Rather than expressing remorse, the arrogant corporate lobbyists are working over Congress with ferocious demands, fueled by cash-register politics and paid Astroturf rallies back in the Congressional districts.

The giant corporations and their trade lobbies want no real health insurance reform that will reduce their monopolies and profiteering. They want no renewable and energy efficient standards interfering with their massive waste, pollution and inefficiency. They want no reductions in the bloated military budget surrounded by the waste, fraud and abuse of what President Eisenhower called the "military-industrial complex" in his farewell warning to the American people.

The corporate supremacists want no changes in the deliberately complex and obscure tax laws favoring the corporate evaders and avoiders and the tax havens for the super-wealthy.

In short, the global corporations want Washington, DC; to continue being their massive deregulator and cash cow perpetuating the abandoning of American workers, the pillaging of the American taxpayer and the defrauding of the American consumer.

Forget about corporate law and order to restrain the corporate crime wave. The harmony, bipartisan President Obama and his chief of staff, Rahm Emanuel, have outsmarted themselves. What worked to defeat Hillary Clinton last year has succeeded in splitting the Congressional Democrats into progressives, corporate liberals and Blue Dog Conservatives. Republicans can scarcely believe their luck and are busy exploiting these schisms.

Rep. Steny Hoyer, the number two House Democrat, undermines his Speaker Nancy Pelosi's "public option" plan for health insurance.

Senator Max Baucus—a closet Republican masquerading as the Democratic Chair of the Senate Finance Committee, is working hand-in-glove with right-wing Republicans and the White House to craft a weak "bi-partisan" bill that keeps getting weaker as the corporatist Republicans sniff increasing weakness in the White House.

Meanwhile, in the House of Representatives, the more progressive legislators are accusing their former colleague, Committee Chair, Henry Waxman of selling out to the defiant Blue Dog Democrats on his Committee. While Mr. Waxman himself has to be worried that even his compromised "public option" (which Democrats should be calling "public choice") will be derailed by the bill that the Baucus/Grassley/Obama axis will soon reveal in the Senate.

The Obama voters do not know what they are supposed to support. Obama never did identify with a clear health insurance proposal—not to mention the single-payer approach (full Medicare for all) he says he would favor if he was "starting from scratch." There has been nothing upstanding for his supporters around the country to rally around.

It is sad to say that all this could have been predicted by Obama's political record as an Illinois and US Senator. He rarely has taken a stand and fought against his adversaries. Even after he cuts a deal with them, they continue to undermine his agenda.

Once again, Bob Herbert senses the disturbing trend: "More and more the president is being seen by his own supporters as someone who would like to please everybody, who is naïve about the prospects for bipartisanship, who believes that his strongest supporters will stay with him because they have nowhere else to go, and who will retreat whenever the Republicans and the corporate crowd come after him."

Mr. Herbert can speak from authority. He has written many columns over the past 18 months reflecting that "nowhere else to go" attitude. If he is going off the bandwagon, more will follow. Mr. Obama better wake up and pay attention to his base before they either have somewhere else to go or simply stay home. It happened to Clinton in 1994.

Six Avoidance Indicators

March 13, 2009

Indicators of avoidance are what come to mind while absorbing the various rescue, recovery, stimulus and guarantee programs coming out of the Obama Administration to slow and reverse a splintering and shattering economy. If the Obamites do not act now when the political time is ripest, to put into motion forces of deterrence and prevention, the casino capitalists of tomorrow will again be able to de-stabilize our economy.

The other day I saw Alan Greenspan, former chairman of the Federal Reserve, just about predicting another round of recklessness in fifteen years. But he called it "human nature" not casino capitalism.

Here are seven avoidance indicators which outline what Washington is not doing to prevent another round of greed and misdeeds by the Wall Street few against the innocent many throughout the country.

1. Where are the resources for comprehensive law enforcement against the Wall Street crooks, swindlers and purveyors of costly deceptive practices? Isn't there a need to add $200-300 million for more FBI agents, prosecutors and corporate crime attorneys under the Justice Department to obtain the fines and disgorgements

which will far exceed in dollars what is spent by the forces of law and order?

Americans want justice. They want jailtime not bailtime for these crooks. Look how many of the swindled just turned out in a New York City winter to let Bernard Madoff have a piece of their mind as he entered the courtroom and immediate imprisonment.

There has been very little movement so far in Congress or the White House toward this necessary action.

2. Where are the anti-trusters to revive the moribund divisions in the Justice Department and Federal Trade Commission? Failed banks, brokerage firms, and now insurance companies are being taken over by shaky acquirers, often with the encouragement of the federal government. Other industries are experiencing similar mergers and acquisitions in an already over-concentrated economy.

Our government needs to be on top of this accelerating creation of more companies deemed to be "too big to fail." A variety of antitrust policies are needed to prevent, restructure or, at least, require spinoffs to minimize the anti-competitive effects of the "urge to merge."

3. What about Congress and Obama shifting some power to the investors and shareholders who are paying for all these losses? The corporate bosses have made sure for many years that shareholders, who own their companies, have little or no right to control them. Had there been less of a gap between ownership and control, the bosses could never have engaged in such reckless speculation, looting and draining of the trillions of dollars with which they were entrusted. These include mutual funds, pension funds and various trusts. Power to the owners seems to be off the table.

4. The federal officials are talking up stron-

ger regulation and re-regulation proposals but we have not yet been informed of their specific plans. There is not much talk of regulatory prohibition. That is, flat-out prohibition of banks, insurance companies, and other fiduciary institutions from speculating in derivatives or, to be more specific, bets on debts and the even more hyped creations of bets on bets on debts on debts.

5. By now, Washington should be devising ways to pay for these gigantic deficits and bailouts. A fraction of one percent sales tax on the hundreds of trillions of dollars in derivative transactions annually would produce hundreds of billions of dollars in revenue and tamp down some of this Wall Street gambling with other peoples' money.

Such a tax on speculative trades in these abstract instruments can make the Wall Streeters pay for their own bailouts and reduce some of the taxes on human labor.

6. Our government doesn't highlight not-for-profit institutions like the 8000 credit unions that are increasing their loans and continue to serve over 80 million Americans without a single insolvency. One would think that with the financial goliaths in a free fall, despite ever-larger bailouts from the federal government, that the cooperative model of credit unions would become a useful teaching instrument.

In his new paperback book, *Agenda for a New Economy*, David Korten makes an important distinction between the "phantom wealth" of Wall Street and the "real wealth" of Main Street.

His twelve-point agenda raises the fundamental question of why Wall Street is needed and how the functions of a just and progressive economy can be fulfilled with a sensible transition to a "real wealth" economy engaged by and accountable to real people striving for the necessities and wants

of life through environmentally-friendly, more efficient institutions.

Lest any remaining doubters out there are thinking about our country returning to business as usual Wall Street style, please read the confidential powerpoint presentation "AIG: Is the Risk Systemic?" by the AIG financial giant grasping $180 billion, so far, in federal aid and guarantees

In 21 pages of very large type, you will see why the AIG bosses believe that failure of their gigantic corporation would only "trigger a cascading set of further failures which cannot be stopped except by extraordinary means." In other words, AIG says to Uncle Sam and you the taxpayer save it or be prepared for a global collapse through a domino effect of unknown catastrophic sequences. For the full astonishing AIG text, see: http://www.aig.com/Related-Resources_385_136430.html. Right from the horse's mouth!

The Bottomless Bailout

March 6, 2009

Does anybody in the federal government know or could know "who, what, where and when" of the massive, complex, vertical, horizontal, global collapse of Wall Street and its planetary tentacles in over 100 countries abroad? Step forward if you exist! Uncle Sam needs you!

Is the multi-million dollar bailout of this financial mess and house of cards, this phantom wealth mummy hitting air beyond the federal governments' salvage capability?

It is relatively easy to announce hundreds of billions of dollars of corporate rescue programs *here* and hundreds of billions of dollars of guarantees of corporate recklessness *there* and trillions of dollars of assorted stimulus, loan availabilities and foreclosure prevention initiatives in all directions. Now comes the rubber hitting the road.

Where are the skilled people to be hired by the federal agencies—the administrators, field implementers, auditors, financial whizzes able to understand the complexity of greed and overreach, the inspectors, prosecutors and contract negotiators to name a few?

In other words, how is a hurried President Obama and his deputies going to rapidly build up the *infrastructure* of the federal government itself to advance all these "public works" efficiently and to avoid expenditure disasters amidst a potential orgy of waste, fraud and abuse by the coast to coast recipients?

So many of the federal government's functions have been contracted out to corporations and consulting firms under Clinton and the Bushes that there is a serious dearth of skilled civil servants. Moreover, Obama has indicated he wants this work done by an accountable government and not by Halliburton-type outside contractors at greater expense to taxpayers.

Knowing and *doing* have to go hand in hand. Some Congressional committees have finally gotten around to asking the basic questions about what is actually going on inside companies like the giant financial conglomerate AIG. Since the Goliath's near collapse in September, the federal government has committed $160 billion to keep it from splattering its reckless red ink over small businesses, municipalities, 401(k) plans, policyholders and of course the Fortune 500 big companies led by the omnipresent Goldman Sachs bank.

At a Senate hearing on March 5, 2009 to review yet another $30 billion in rescue funds, Senators from both parties demanded that the Federal Reserve make public the names of the parties benefiting from all this taxpayer largesse. These include the derivatives trading partners (eg. credit default swappers) who have received tens of billions of these dollars passing from Washington through AIG to them.

Senators Chris Dodd, Richard Shelby and Jim Bunning went after Donald L. Kohn, the vice-chairman of the Fed board of governors who finally promised he would ask the other governors to reconsider their corporate privacy policy under these megabailouts. Don't hold your breath!

Surprisingly, the *Wall Street Journal* editorial writers weighed in three days earlier about this fourth ever-sweeter rescue of AIG in six months. In an editorial titled "AIG's Black Box" the *Journal* thundered: "Perhaps someday the feds will even explain to taxpayers which AIG creditors had to be rescued and why . . . try figuring out exactly who benefits when taxpayer money arrives at the insurance giant."

Besides rebuilding the federal workforce and finding out what is going on inside casino capitalism begging for bailouts, the Obama Administration is wading into an administrative nightmare that could run through trillions of mis-directed dollars and not turn around a deep Recession plunging toward Depression.

When dealing with esoteric gambling chips called "derivatives" that are bets on bets on debts on debts, more than astute regulations and prosecutions are needed to punish, disgorge and deter present and future self-paid corporate crooks looting and draining other people's pensions and savings. What is essential is that the federal surgeons have to know just where to apply their scalpel on the continuum spanning the big predators to the millions of direct and indirect victims.

So, during the next Congressional hearings featuring government witnesses from the Federal Reserve, the Treasury Department and the securities, insurance and banking regulatory agencies, the Senators should start with four direct questions:

1. Just what is it that you do NOT understand about what is going on inside this widening Wall Street mess?

2. Why don't you understand what you need to know?

3. How are you going to use your powers to achieve such understanding?

4. Finally, if these corporations like AIG are too big to fail, too secret to fail and overwhelmingly global in structure and operations, why aren't you asking other governments to pitch in with their own rescue packages and tell you what they know?

As one solid small town banker in Indiana put it recently: "If these big companies are too big to fail, then they're too big."

Wither Wall Street
January 30, 2009

Soon after the passage in 1999 of the Clinton-Rubin-Summers-Gramm deregulation of the financial industry, I boarded a US Airways flight to Boston and discovered none other than then-Secretary of the Treasury Lawrence Summers a few seats away. He was speaking loudly and constantly on his cell phone. When the plane took off he invited me to sit by him and talk.

After reviewing the contents of this Citibank-friendly new law called the *Financial Modernization Act*—I asked him: "Do you think the big banks have too much power?"

He paused for a few seconds and replied: "not

yet." Intrigued by his two-word answer, I noted the rejection of modest pro-consumer provisions, adding that now that the banks had had their round, wasn't it time for the consumers to have their own round soon?

Mr. Summer allowed that such an expectation was not unreasonable and that he was willing to meet with some seasoned consumer advocates and go over such an agenda. We sent him an agenda and met with him and his staff. Unfortunately, neither his boss, Bill Clinton, nor the Congress were in any mood to revisit this heavily lobbied federal deregulation law and reconsider the blocked consumer rights.

The rest is unfolding, tragic history. The law abolished the *Glass-Steagall Act* which separated commercial banking from investment banking. This opened the floodgates for unwise mergers, acquisitions and other unregulated risky financial instruments. Laced with limitless greed, casino capitalism ran wild, tanking economies here and abroad.

One champion of this market fundamentalism was Alan Greenspan, then chairman of the Federal Reserve. Last October before a House Committee, Greenspan admitted he was mistaken and expressed astonishment at how corporations could not even safeguard their own self-interest from going over steep speculative cliffs.

Greenspan and Summers were deemed "brilliant" by the press and most of Congress. Summers' predecessor at Treasury—Robert Rubin—was also a charter member of the Oracles—those larger-than-life men who just knew that the unfettered market and giant financial conglomerates would be the one-stop shopping mart consumers were assumed to be craving.

Now the world knows that these men belong to the "oops oligarchy" that bails itself out while it lets the companies collapse into the hand-cuffed arms of Uncle Sam and bridled taxpayers who have to pay for unconditional megabail-outs. Instead of the Wall Street crooks being convicted and imprisoned, they have fled the jurisdiction with their self-determined compensation. Corporate crime pays, while pensions and mutual fund savings evaporate.

Now comes the next stage of the Washington rescue effort in a variety of stimulus packages which every vendor group imaginable wants a piece of these days. When trillions are offered, many come running.

As the public focus is on how much, when and where all this money should be spent, there are very serious consequences to be foreseen and forestalled. First, consider how much more concentrated corporate power is occurring. Forced or willing mergers, acquisitions and panic takeovers of big banks by bigger banks along with bankruptcies of companies further reduce what is left of quality competition for consumer benefit.

Remember the anti-trust laws. Obama needs to be their champion. The fallout from the Wall Street binge is likely to lead to a country run by an even smaller handful of monopolistic global goliaths.

In the stampede for stimulus legislation, there is a foreboding feeling on Capitol Hill that there is no proposal on the table to pay for it other than by the children and grandchildren. Just the opposite is raining down on them. Everybody including the private equity gamblers, Las Vegas casinos and Hollywood studios along with the banks and auto companies are looking for tax breaks.

So with the economy deteriorating and taxes being cut, where is the enormous money coming from? From borrowing and from printing money. So look out for big time inflation and decline in the dollar's value vis-à-vis other currencies.

In all the hundreds of pages of stimulus bills, there is nothing that would facilitate the banding together of consumers and investors into strong advocacy groups. We have long proposed Financial Consumer Associations, privately and voluntarily funded through inserts in the monthly statements of financial firms.

If this bailout—stimulus—Wall Street funny money waste, fraud and abuse sounds confusing, that is because it is. A brand new paperback *Why Wall Street Can't Be Fixed and How to Replace It: Agenda For a New Economy* by long-time corporate critic, David C. Korten will explain some of the wheeling and dealing.

You don't have to agree with all or many of Korten's nostrums. Just read Part II—The Case For Eliminating Wall Street. He considers three central questions:

First, do Wall Street Institutions do anything so vital for the national interest that they justify trillions of dollars to save them from the consequences of their own excess?

Second, is it possible that the whole Wall Street edifice is built on an illusion of phantom wealth that carries deadly economic, social, and environmental consequences for the larger society?

Third, are there other ways to provide needed financial services with greater results and at lesser cost?

Government Without Law
December 26, 2008

Over three decades ago, a book came out titled *How the Government Breaks the Law*, by Jethro K. Lieberman. Even then it was old news and the examples cited seemed small compared to today's chronic law-breakers in the White House and at many federal departments and agencies. Many recent books have been written on the expansive outlaw behavior of George W. Bush and Dick Cheney.

Less attention has been devoted to the explosion of unauthorized actions by the executive in recent years. What should be the most frequent question by reporters to government officials— namely, "By what authority are you acting?"—is the rarest of inquiries.

A two-part series on Treasury Secretary Henry M. Paulson, Jr. in the *Washington Post* by David Cho in late November brought this point out in a stunningly frank admission by the corporate bailout czar himself.

Speaking of the takeover of Fannie Mae and Freddie Mac, as well as other megaseizures of failing Wall Street firms, Mr. Paulson expressed these anarchic words: "Even if you don't have the authorities—and frankly I didn't have the authorities for anything—if you take charge, people will follow."

Whew! There you have it! He becomes the law and the law is what he says it is because no one—neither a rubber-stamping president, nor a supine Congress, nor any citizen, deprived of any standing to sue, is going or can do anything about it.

Reporter Cho goes on to write: "Senior government officials said Paulson helped craft rescue programs for financial firms, though he was not sure he had an unquestionable legal basis for the initiatives including the bailouts of the failing investment bank Bear Stearns in March and the wounded insurance giant American International Group (AIG) in September."

Mr. Paulson went further. Playing Congress, he backed the Federal Reserve—already a government within a government funded by banks– to unprecedented unilateral expansion of its powers and its self-made assets. The Post

reported that officials from the Treasury and the Fed "never knew whether they had the legal authority to interfere with the market for such derivatives but did so anyway because the opaque trading threatened the wider financial system."

Unauthorized Executive Branch actions tend to be contagious. Noticing that the crisis left Wall Street on its knees and willing to unilaterally assume over $8 trillion in a variety of loan, subsidy and capital obligations, the Bush regime kept making more of its powers all by itself. Why not, they may have been thinking? Look what they've gotten away with in the areas of military and foreign policy actions.

Weekend gigantic corporate bailouts—a more recent one being the $300 billion plus assumption of Citigroup's financial risks—engineered by Citigroup co-boss, Robert Rubin— were very secret affairs.

The more public grab of power was the $700 billion goliath to rescue the casino capitalists on Wall Street which was submitted in only 3 ½ pages of proposed legislation to Congress by Paulson and Ben Bernake, the Fed's chairman in September.

This was too much for the ideologies of House Republicans who beat it on the first round. Even the spineless Democrats thought the requested authority was too much of a blank check. So what happened? Bush told Paulson to give various members of Congress "sweeteners" such as pork and tax breaks for favored lobbyists to get the required votes. Consequently, Paulson was granted staggering discretion to spend the $700 billion when, where and to whom he wanted under whatever conditions or no conditions at all. All in the name of socialism saving capitalism from massive collapse. Ironic.

Mr. Paulson came away from Capitol Hill with Congress in his back pocket—not exactly what the framers of our Constitution had in mind in 1787.

Thus emboldened Paulson initiated a unilateral, administrative repeal of a Congressional enactment in the tax code—section 382—to give the banks a huge windfall of about $140 billion. George K. Yin, former chief of staff of the Congressional Joint Committee on Taxation, rejected the legality of the Treasury Department's decision. He told the *Post*: "I think almost every tax expert would agree that the answer is no. They basically repealed a 22-year-old law that Congress passed [and Reagan signed] as a backdoor way of providing aid to banks."

Section 382 of the US tax code "sharply restricts a company from using the tax losses of a company it acquires to reduce its own tax liability," according to the respected Citizens for Tax Justice. The Treasury's two-page notice generated a brief specialized display of outrage from members of the tax writing committees in Congress and a hundred national, state and local organizations signed a joint letter to Congress demanding the legislators reverse the Treasury' unauthorized edict.

So what did the House of Representatives do? It passed a provision in the auto bailout bill, later rejected by the Senate, that would have extended the unauthorized Treasury ruling to the automobile industry!

What is going on here is a revolutionary coup d'etat of our legal system by executive branch diktats.

Is the organized legal profession through their bar associations in challenge mode? Are law professors churning over this mockery of the legislature and Executive Branch administrative law? Are conservative groups—always upset about judicial activism—going into high gear against the new monarchy in and around the White House in downtown Washington, DC? Are all those futurists worried enough about the trillions of debt dollars being piled on our children and grandchildren to protest and act? Not really.

Obviously, all this is a developing story. Stay tuned, unless you are willing to be turned out.

Crisis and Opportunity
December 3, 2008

In ancient Chinese, the character for "crisis" was associated with "opportunity." This month Congress will be faced with both challenges from General Motors, Ford and Chrysler, whose CEOs are begging for a very rapid $34 billion in emergency government loans.

The three auto giants have few cards to play other than the domino effect on the economy, should they collapse into bankruptcy and liquidation. Once Congress signals that, on behalf of its sullen taxpayers, going into this abyss will not happen, our national legislature will hold all the cards.

So if Congress and George W. Bush agree to have Uncle Sam bail out the auto bosses and their tanking companies, important reforms and models can emerge from this multi-faceted mega rescue.

Let it be called the coming of a vigorous government capitalism, based on rigorous conventional reciprocity. First, since the government is contributing tax dollars, taxpayers should receive taxpayer warrants and preferred shares held by the Treasury Department, for stock in the companies. Second, since the government would be a senior creditor, it should exercise restructuring powers to remove the top executives and the boards of directors along with other functional re-alignments.

Third, since the government is essentially performing as an insurer, basic standards of loss prevention should be applied. In this context, this means stronger fuel efficiency, emission-control and safety standards to enhance sales and increase the pressure on foreign auto companies. This insurance-driven requirement would further long-existing federal statutory missions in three areas of engineering performance.

In the past ten weeks, "government capitalism" has been a patsy, absorbing huge taxpayer dollars and liabilities to save an assortment of Wall Street financial corporations. Washington is guaranteeing a clutch of securitized mortgages and consumer loans and even guaranteeing, for the first time, $4 trillion of money market funds.

The bailout of Citigroup illustrates the paucity of reciprocity. It is a sweetheart deal. With Citigroup's co-executive Robert Rubin rushing to Washington to structure the deal to save his bank and his own stock portfolio, the Bush regime took on $20 billion in preferred shares and put taxpayers at risk for over $300 billion in the big bank's loan portfolio. Earlier in October, taxpayers were compelled to buy $25 billion in Citi preferred shares.

Whereas the Feds earlier took a potential 79 percent ownership of Freddie Mac and Fannie Mae to save those companies, for Citi the government only took 7.8 percent stake and left the management and board of directors intact.

Since these enormous bailouts and revisions of bailouts largely occur over weekends in frantic secret huddles between government officials formerly from Wall Street and their former colleagues from Wall Street, the actual agreements are not disclosed. They are considered official secrets, assuming they even have been finalized beyond mere memoranda of understanding.

Since all these deals, and more seem to be coming from other commercial and industrial pleaders, are general and appear to be open-ended, resourceful government capitalism can advance shareholder rights across the board and compel a variety of corporate reforms and accountabilities long-desired by progressives and conservatives alike.

At least the auto companies are being subjected to public Congressional hearings for this latest bailout round. In contrast, the CEOs of the financial goliaths got private roundtable treatment at the Treasury Department and the Federal Reserve for far greater rescue packages, revealed in brief statements on Monday morning.

Let's have a level playing field here and treat all corporate welfare demanders under equal procedural rules shaped on Capitol Hill. Remember the Constitution. It says all spending bills start with the House of Representatives and then go to the Senate and then to the president. Secret taxpayer bailouts by executive branch press releases are not what the framers had in mind when they wrote the Constitution.

With the installation of a new president and a new Congress next month, the process must be reversed and these White House-corporate "understandings" have to be reconsidered and, if maintained, revised.

This is a rare moment in American economic history. Just as the multinational corporations were about to complete the entrenchment of the corporate state in Washington, DC—what President Franklin Delano Roosevelt described in 1939 as a condition of fascism—their speculative greed, recklessness, mismanagement and de-regulatory license turned them into massive supplicants at the taxpayers' trough.

In early October, Washington has Wall Street

over a Congressional barrel. Still, Wall Street rolled Washington into a $700 billion bailout barrel and rolled it back to New York City.

With a supposedly reformist Democratically-dominated Congress and Obama in the White House, the balance of power for the people of our country can turn. But it will take prompt new exertions by the people, citizen groups, organized investors, taxpayers and workers. Seize the moment.

Congressional Backbone Needed

September 24, 2008

Congress needs to show some backbone before the federal government pours more money on the financial bonfire started by the arsonists on Wall Street.

1. Congress should hold a series of hearings and invite broad public comment on any proposed bailout. Congress is supposed to be a co-equal branch of our federal government. It needs to stop the stampede to give Bush a $700 billion check. Public hearings should be held to determine what alternatives might exist to the four-page proposal advanced by Treasury Secretary Henry M. Paulson.

2. Whatever is ultimately done, the bailout plan should not be insulated from judicial review. Remember there is a third co-equal branch of government—the judiciary. The judiciary does not need to review each buy-and-sell decision by the Treasury Department, but there should be some boundaries established to the Treasury Department's discretion, and judicial review is needed to ensure that unbridled discretion is not abused.

3. Sunlight is a good disinfectant. The bailout that is ultimately approved must provide for full and timely disclosure of all bailout details. This will discourage conflicts of interest and limit the potential of sweetheart deals.

4. Firms that accept government bailout monies must agree to disclose their transactions and be more honest in their accounting. They should agree to end off-the-books accounting maneuvers, for example.

5. Taxpayers must be protected by having a stake in any recovery. The bailout plan should provide opportunities for taxpayers to recoup funds that are made available to problem financial institutions or to benefit from the financial institutions' rising stock price and increased profitability after being bailed out.

6. The current so-called "regulators" cannot be trusted. The US Government Accountability Office (GAO), "the investigative arm of Congress" and "the congressional watchdog," must regularly review the bailout. We cannot trust the financial "regulators," who allowed the slide into financial disaster, to manage the bailout without outside monitoring.

7. It is time to put the federal cop back on the financial services beat. Strong financial regulations and independent regulators are necessary to rebuild trust in our financial institutions and to prevent further squandering of our tax dollars. The Justice Department and the SEC also need to scrutinize the expanding mess with an eye to uncovering corporate crime and misdeeds. Major news outlets are reporting that the FBI is investigating American International Group, Fannie Mae, Freddie Mac, and Lehman Brothers.

8. Cap executive compensation and stop giving the Wall Street gamblers golden parachutes. The CEOs who have created the financial disaster should not be allowed to leave with mil-

lions in hand when so many pensioners and small shareholders are seeing their investments evaporate. The taxpayers are bailing out Wall Street so that the financial system continues to function, not to further enrich the CEOs and executives who created this mess.

9. Congress should pass the *Financial Consumers' Information and Representation Act*, to permit citizens to form a federally-chartered nonprofit membership organization to strengthen consumer representation in government proceedings that concern the financial services industry. As the savings and loan disasters of the 1980s and the Wall Street debacles of the last few years have demonstrated, there is an overriding need for consumers and taxpayers to have the organized means to enhance their influence on financial issues.

10. The repeal of the *Glass–Steagall Act*, separating traditional banks from investment banks, helped pave the way for the current disaster. It is time to re-regulate the financial sector. The current crisis is also leading to even further conglomeration and concentration in the financial sector. We must revive and apply antitrust principles, so that banking consumers can benefit from competition and taxpayers are less vulnerable to too-big-to-fail institutions, merging with each other to further concentration.

11. Congress should impose a securities and derivatives speculation tax. A tax on financial trading would slow down the churning of stocks and financial instruments, and could raise substantial monies to pay for the bailout.

12. Regulators should impose greater margin requirements, making speculators use more of their own money and diminishing reckless casino capitalism.

Ask your representative a few questions: "What should be done to limit banking insti-

tutions from investing in high-risk activities? What should be done to ensure banks are meeting proper capital standards given the financial quicksand that has spread as a result of the former Senator Phil Gramm's deregulation efforts? And, "What is being done to protect small investors?"

P.S. Shareholders also have some work to do. They should have listened when Warren Buffett called securities derivatives a "time bomb" and "financial weapons of mass destruction." The Wall Street crooks and unscrupulous speculators use and draining of "other people's money" out of pension funds and mutual funds should motivate painfully passive shareholders to organize to gain greater authority to control the companies they own. Where is the shareholder uprising?

Banking on Congress
August 20, 2008

This week, the *Wall Street Journal* reported that Federal Deposit Insurance Corporation (FDIC) officials are pushing various agencies charged with regulating banks, such as the Treasury's Office of Thrift Supervision to more aggressively give problem banks lower ratings than they may now be receiving from regulators. Regulators give banks a rank between 1 and 5. Well-managed banks get a 1, problem banks receive a 4 or 5. The FDIC wants to see more banks getting 4s or 5s.

In late July, I wrote to US Senate Committee on Banking, Housing and Urban Affairs Chairman Christopher Dodd (D-Conn.) and House Financial Services Committee Chairman Barney Frank, (D-Mass.) to suggest that they jointly hold hearings on the FDIC's ability to deal with potential bank failures in the next several years. In the letter, I noted that in a March 10, 2008 memorandum on insurance assessment rates, Arthur J. Murton, Director of the Division of Insurance and Research for the FDIC stated:

While 99 percent of insured institutions meet the "well capitalized" criteria, the possibility remains that the fund could suffer insurance losses that are significantly higher than anticipated. The US economy and the banking sector currently face a significant amount of uncertainty from ongoing housing sector problems, financial market turbulence and potentially weak prospects for consumer spending. These problems could lead to significantly higher loan losses and weaker earnings for insured institutions.

FDIC Chairman Sheila C. Bair, however, has been singing a more upbeat tune. She recently said, "The banking system in this country remains on a solid footing through the guarantees provided by FDIC insurance. The overwhelming majority of banks in this country are safe and sound and the chances that your own bank could fail are remote. However, if that does happen, the FDIC will be there—as always—to protect your insured deposits."

Despite these reassuring words, the recent failure of IndyMac highlights the need for tough Congressional oversight. Banking experts have indicated that the cost of the collapse of IndyMac alone will be between $4 billion and $8 billion. The FDIC has approximately $53 billion on hand to deal with bank failures. This amount may not be adequate, given the cost of IndyMac and given the approximately $4 trillion in deposits the FDIC insures.

Congressional oversight of the financial services industry and its regulators should be a topic priority for Congress. I even suggested several questions that should be put to FDIC officials such as:

1. Was IndyMac on the list of "Problem Institutions" before it failed?

2. Were the other banks that failed this year on the FDIC list of "Problem Institutions"?

3. What is the anticipated cost of dealing with the failures of the other four banks that failed this year?

4. As of March 31, 2008 the FDIC reported 90 "Problem Institutions" with assets of $26 billion. What is the current number of "Problem Institutions" and what are the assets of these "Problem Institutions"?

5. How many banks are likely to fail in 2008 and 2009 respectively?

6. What is the estimated range of costs of dealing with the projected failures?

7. What will the effect of higher losses than those projected be on the FDIC's estimate of the proper reserve ratio?

8. What are the FDIC's projections for reserves needed and potential bank failures beyond 2009?

9. Is the FDIC resisting raising the current rates of assessments on FDIC insured banks so that the cost of any significant bailouts will have to be shifted to the taxpayers?

10. Does the Government Accountability Office (GAO) believe that the existing rate schedule for banks to pay into the Deposit Insurance Fund (DIF) is set at the proper level?

It would also make sense for Congress to revisit the FDIC's current approach to setting reserve ratios for banks.

The FDIC is not likely to address its own inability to clearly assess the current risks posed to depositors and taxpayers by the high-rolling, bailout-prone banking industry.

When Congress reconvenes after Labor Day it would be prudent for Senator Dodd and Congressman Frank to focus on the FDIC and our nation's troubled banks through some tough no-holds-barred hearings. These two lawmakers are going to have to hear from the people back home soon.

Neither Senator Dodd nor Congressman Frank have responded to my letter of July 23, 2008.

Socialism for Speculators

July 16, 2008

Here they go again! Financial capitalism is crashing. So the lights are on late in Washington's Federal Reserve, SEC and Treasury Department trying to figure out how socialism (your tax dollars and credits) can once again bail out these big time gamblers with our money.

Every cycle of casino capitalism that heads for, or goes over, the bankruptcy cliffs gets larger and larger. This year's collapse towers over the bailout of the Savings and Loan banks in the 1980s.

This unfolding cycle of the Washington-to-Wall Street gravy train is not based on a huge spike in interest rates that tanked so many thrift institutions nearly twenty years ago. It is based on unbridled greed by the bosses of these big commercial banks, investment banks, brokerage giants and those two goliaths—Fannie Mae and Freddie Mac.

"Unbridled" because the financial institutions got themselves unregulated during the reign of Bill Clinton and his Treasury Secretary Robert Rubin. Rubin skipped out of town to become a wildly overpaid official with Citigroup—the leading lobbyist for his disastrous, so-called Financial Services Modernization Act of 1999.

Fannie and Freddie have been deeply unregulated for decades which allowed their capital ratios to be lower—far lower—than even

investment banks like Morgan Stanley. With that long-time implicit guarantee by the federal government, these two secondary marketers for home mortgages became more and more reckless so as to raise the corporate profits that their top executives need to skyrocket their personal compensation packages!

In 1991, lawyer Tom Stanton warned about the risks and non-regulation of Fannie and Freddie in his prophetic book—*A State of Risk* (Harper Business).

A decade ago, our banking specialists warned about the Federal Deposit Insurance Corporation (FDIC) under assessing its member banks thus leaving its reserves at the risk of being perilously low when needed. Today, these reserves are very much needed and perilously low.

Combined with the limitless greed, unbridled corporate power can wreak havoc with our entire economy. As it is doing now. The domino effect is underway.

So the Bush boys and the Congressional leaders, so to speak, are busy reassuring the investors that they will in some way make things stable. This time, however, they seem to be offering too little too late and the investors aren't buying.

The stocks of the banks keep plunging down anywhere from seventy to ninety percent from their last year's high.

The nation's largest savings bank—Washington Mutual—closed at under $4.00 per share down from over $40 last year.

Again and again, year after year, the CEOs and the patsy federal agency heads have lied to the people about the financial status of these corporations. There is no credibility left and therefore no confidence. Over three trillion dollars is sitting in disbelief on the sidelines. Trillions of dollars have been looted or lost in the meantime, draining worker pension funds, mutual funds and the savings of small investors.

None of this had to happen. Regulation against conflicts of interest and hyper risk-taking could have stopped it, including preventing the housing mortgage crisis. Empowering investor-owners could have headed it off. But Washington-based right wing corporate funded think tanks and the banking lobbies battered down the regulatory guards and the federal cops.

So now only the American taxpayers and their creditworthiness inside a deficit-ridden government and a debt-loaded Federal Reserve stand in the way of a far bigger financial collapse than the stock market crash of 1929. Will it be done smartly this time around?

Reckless, self-enriching capitalists get on your knees and thank the rescuing Washington socialists, for without them, you would surely be in chains.

Riding the Rails

June 24, 2008

With the rapid expansion of federal spending responding to the perceived national security requirements after 9/11, passenger railroad supporters looked forward to a tripleheader.

First passenger railroad service would have to be upgraded and expanded to facilitate mass population evacuations from cities during attack emergencies.

Second, by embarking on a "national defense" passenger rail program, there would be less consumption of gasoline and less gridlock on congested highways.

Third, the energy efficiency of transporting people by intercity rail and commuter rail would diminish some of the buildup of greenhouse gases.

Right after 9/11, the airlines descended on Washington, DC and got a package of loans, guarantees and other federal assistance amounting to $15 billion.

Amtrak got just about nothing. But then for this vast nation with large pockets of consistently clogged highways, Amtrak has been getting very little federal aid since its creation in 1971 as a public service corporation. President Bush wants to cut what little (just over $1 billion a year) Amtrak receives.

Consider this: according to the Government Accountability Office, Amtrak has received a total of $30 billion during the last thirty six years in federal aid for its intercity train service over the entire country. A few weeks ago, the Federal Reserve bailed out Bear Stearns, a large, reckless investment banking firm on Wall Street for just under $30 billion.

Japan and Western European countries have modern, fast rail services, with modern equipment and solid rail beds coursing throughout their territories with governmental assistance. They are a public service, not meant to make a profit, any more than public libraries or public schools, although the rail passengers do pay for their tickets.

In our country, Amtrak has been starved by the federal government which lavishes taxpayer money on the airlines in a variety of ways.

As a result, Amtrak has aging equipment, has to use the freight railroad beds and has very little money for rolling stock and track capacity, especially at critical "chokepoints" where delays occur with freight trains.

With soaring gasoline and airfare prices, more Americans are taking mass transit and Amtrak to get to their destinations. Amtrak is on the way to a record year, transporting over 27 million passengers in 2008, with ridership up over 12 percent from last year.

Amtrak and its equipment suppliers, constrained by money, have been shrinking. Routes have been abandoned. Manufacturers of rail cars and locomotives have also diminished. So, expansion to meet the growing demand will be difficult and take some time. This passenger railroad carries less than 5 percent of the domestic passengers carried by the airlines.

Losing about $1 billion a year, Amtrak's financial needs are trivial compared to large for-profit corporations who feed from the public trough in Washington, DC. Some Congressional help is finally on the way.

The House and the Senate have passed the *Passenger Rail Investment and Improvement Act* with veto-proof margins to over-ride a threatened veto by George W. Bush.

Assuming no major changes in the House-Senate conference on the bill, Amtrak will receive annual appropriations closer to $2 billion a year, compared to the current level of $1.2 billion. This includes money for capital investment, for reducing debt and expanding operating budgets for more passengers. There is also a matching-grant program for the states to expand service, similar to the program long in place for highway construction.

The large freight railroads are pressing Congress for public money and tax credits to upgrade railroad beds and pay for track expansion, which could redound to the benefit of passenger rail service as well.

The American people have to ask themselves how robust and convenient a modern passenger rail system they want. As good as the one in Canada? As good as the systems in France and Germany?

Given the way the federal government wastes money, there are many ways to justify a first-class, high-speed passenger rail system that will save more than it costs—especially in a security emergency, a national disaster like Katrina and the delays, fuel and pollution avoided.

All in all, a worthy topic for public debate during this political year.

Stadiums, Libraries and Taxpayers
April 2, 2008

There used to be a time when baseball parks were built by private investors—usually a wealthy local family—and the stands were full of what used to be called the "masses."

There used to be a time when libraries were maintained and stocked as an integral part of the neighborhood and community. Not a single library closed in America due to the great economic depression of the 1930s.

As illustrated so elaborately in Washington, DC last week, the "gleaming new baseball stadium" temporarily named "Nationals Park" for the local major league baseball team, opened with $611 million dollars—mostly taxpayers money—going into its constructions. A *Washington Post* editorial crowed that the stadium was built "on time and within budget." Why not? The cost came in at twice the estimate five years ago and its frantic construction pace reflected the priorities of the nation's capital.

Consider one aspect of this "tale of two cities"—the depleted and disrepaired condition of the main Martin Luther King, Jr. Memorial Library and its 26 neighborhood branches. The annual budget last year was only $33 million. Four of the branches were shut down for remodeling or rebuilding three and a half years ago. The money has been appropriated. But with the sites being eyed by avaricious developers for "multi-use" complexes, among other reasons, the residents still do not have operating libraries. "On time and within budget" is not even on the radar.

Now I ask you—what is the most appropriate, profound, and respectful use of tax dollars? A ballpark built for mega-millionaire owners who could have raised their own capital? Or "gleaming new libraries" which edify a metropolis and play a critical role in educational, civic and urban renewal?

The question would answer itself were the decision made by local referendum. Polls continually showed that the disenfranchised people of the District of Columbia opposed a taxpayer-funded professional ballpark. The new mayor Adrian Fenty made this opposition a major issue in his improbable run for that office in 2006.

There is little doubt that the people would have preferred to use that $611 million (and other estimates are higher) for library renovations and acquisitions as well as neighborhood recreational facilities for participatory sports by all ages. Studies have shown that afterschool programs at libraries help children learn better and participatory sports—indoor and outdoor—keep physically exercised youngsters from getting into street trouble.

Nationals Park opened to great fanfare this past weekend, hailed by page after page of coverage in excruciating detail by the *Washington Post*. Would that this major newspaper devote such attention to the details of 27 library buildings, many of them crumbling and dysfunctional, in its home town.

When *Post* opinion writer Marc Fisher did devote two columns to the library's plight in

2002, it helped spark our DC Library Renaissance Project, headed by Robin Diener. With library-minded citizens, the DCLRP has brought more public attention, an increased budget and some improvement in the DC Library system, long considered to be in the bottom tier of library systems in major American cities.

When power is concentrated in the hands of the few, it's small wonder that priorities are inverted to the level of the grotesque. Our national capital has been undergoing one of the biggest commercial building booms in its history. Cranes are busy everywhere, except for building the schools, libraries, clinics and neighborhood parks. Real estate developers and their customary allies—banks, mortgage firms, corporate law firms and trade associations—dominate. Not the people, who cannot even have the right to vote for two Senators and a Representative having full voting power in the Congress.

In its March 28, 2008 special, ten-page section on Nationals Park, the *Washington Post* printed a full page "Letter to Nats Fans" by the team's owners, the Lerner family. They profusely thanked the Mayor, the DC City Council, the corporate-welfare promoter called the DC Sports and Entertainment Commission, along with the construction firms, consultants, and workers.

Remarkably absent from their list of gratitude were the DC taxpayers who paid for the building that will make the Lerners and their partners even more wealthy. (These owners are in arbitration over their demand that the taxpayers even pay for the uniforms of the multi-millionaire ball players!)

The Lerners, in all decency, should name the stadium "Taxpayers Stadium." Instead, they are shopping around the corporate groves for a company to pay to put its name on the building instead of its present "Nationals Park" designation.

Once again the boosteristic *Washington Post* headlined "Millions Ride on Nats' Naming Rights." It is the Lerners who get the millions, but Mark Lerner shared a worry, during an interview with the *Post* reporter while looking around the Park.

"It's going to be a huge and expensive task between the signs on the roadways, and all the signs in here—all these neon signs. It's going to cost a fortune—when the time comes," he declared.

DC taxpayers are left to wonder who will pay for replacing these Nationals Park signs? They better check the fine print.

Let the Sun Shine on Government Contracts
February 11, 2008

It is dull but so very important.

It is sub-visible but in your pocket and on your back.

I speak of the hundreds of billions each year of federal government contracts, grants, leaseholds and licenses given to corporations to run our government, exploit our taxpayer assets and lay waste to efficient, responsive public services.

Before he left Washington in 2003 to run for Governor of Indiana, the hyper-conservative Director of Bush's Office of Management and Budget (OMB), Mitch Daniels, endorsed the policy of having all federal departments and agencies place the full text of their contracts, leases of natural resources and other agreements on the internet.

He placed a notice in the Federal Register inviting comments. Obviously, the large corporate contractors and lessees of minerals and other public resources did not like the idea. After all,

information is the currency of democracy. Big businesses, like Dick Cheney's Halliburton, love oligarchies and corporate socialism featuring subsidies, handouts, bailouts and contracted out governmental functions.

Big bureaucracies in Washington, DC were not exactly enthusiastic about applying Supreme Court Justice Louis Brandeis' comment that "sunlight is the best disinfectant."

Unfortunately, Daniels' successor at OMB, Bush loyalist and now his chief of staff, Josh Bolten, was totally cold to the proposal. Activity grinded to a halt.

There is new activity on other fronts, however. Congress, in 2006, passed legislation to shed light on the contracting process. Starting in January of 2008, the government website: usaspending.gov started providing the public with the following information:

1. the name of the entity receiving the award;

2. the amount of the award;

3. information on the award including transaction type, funding agency, etc;

4. the location of the entity receiving the award; and

5. a unique identifier of the entity receiving the award.

But the essential requirement—placing the entire text of these contracts on the web is the unfinished business of Congress which some Democrats and Republicans are turning their attention to in the coming months. In a meeting, Senator Chuck Grassley (R-Iowa) declared his support. Democrat and chairman of the House Judiciary Committee, John Conyers, has also assented. Others from both parties are on board.

The next step will either be placing the requisite amendment in must-pass legislation or having public hearings to show the American people the advantages as a taxpayer and citizen of expanding their "right to know."

Consider the groups who will benefit from such open government:

1. Small business competitors who are often aced out of no-bid contracts and over-ridden by major prime contractors' influence on federal agencies. The quality of competitive bidding and performance should go up.

2. Taxpayers and taxpayer groups have opportunities to review, challenge or oppose where their money is going.

3. The media will be able to report to the public about the doings of contracting and leasing and licensing government in faster and much greater detail.

4. Scholars and students at universities, business schools and law schools will be able to provide analyses, improvements on both the substantive content and proper procedures for making these agreements. Sweetheart giveaways, for example, of minerals on public land and easy avoidance of responsibilities should be reduced. Archives of these contracts will be created for historical reference.

5. Local and state governments and legislatures will find themselves equipped to participate where their interests are at stake and may be encouraged to emulate such openness with their own texts of contracts, leases and so forth.

Already, some states like Texas and Indiana are placing notices of state contracts on their websites.

Last week, Michigan Attorney General Mike Cox, took the initiative by placing on his department's website. "Track Your Taxes,"(http://www.michigan.gov/ag/0,1607,7-164-34391-184786--,00.html) details on his office's spending, "including every single contract that our department has entered into, including legal ser-

vices, such as Special Assistant Attorneys General, and expert witnesses." Mr. Cox added that all vendor contracts, "the type of service being provided, the term of the contract, the amount of the contract, how much has been spent, and how much is left," will be online.

Good step forward. But much more at all levels of government is needed, including the full texts and any performance information about delays, incomplete or incompetent work and other qualitative information such as cost overruns. You may wish to contact your legislators and solicit their support.

Is it "mission accomplished" when all such outsourcing information is online for everyone to see? Of course not. Information has to be used. This requires that new habits be established.

Reporters, scholars, taxpayer groups and other are not used to this "beat." They have to expand their time and resources to get on it. Otherwise, the bureaucrats and the business lobbies will continue with business as usual.

Contracts Online Now!
August 24, 2007

Several weeks ago, I joined with Grover Norquist, president of Americans for Tax Reform in urging state governors to emulate and go beyond the advances in bringing more openness to governmental expenditures put forth by Indiana Governor Mitch Daniels.

Early in 2005, Governor Daniels issued an executive order which enables Hoosiers to find on the internet the total number of state contracts entered into each year, the total amount of dollars awarded under state contracts each year, and the number and percentage of Indiana businesses and out-of-state businesses to whom state contracts are awarded each year. In addition the entire text of most contracts covered by the executive order is available online.

Mr. Norquist and I disagree on many other issues, but we strongly share the belief that taxpayers should be able to easily access clear and concise information on how their tax dollars are being spent by governments at all levels.

At the federal level, the Federal Funding Accountability and Transparency Act will create a free, publicly searchable website for all federal contracts and grants. Senator Tom Coburn (R., Okla.) and Senator Barack Obama (D. Ill.) introduced this bill requiring the dollar amounts and recipients of all grants and earmarked contracts be placed in a publicly accessible database.

This important step toward transparency was signed into law by President Bush on September 26, 2006, the law states that the Office of Management and Budget (OMB) has to ensure the existence of a searchable website is available no later than January 1, 2008. Lawmakers from both sides of the aisle came together and joined forces to move in the right direction. But this is only a first step, since the actual contract language will not be made available.

When he was director of the OMB in the federal government, Mitch Daniels expressed his support for putting all federal contracts and grants online above a minimum amount and invited public comment. Included in his proposal were defense contracts, prudently redacted, which, of course, means a large area of governmental spending historically off limits to public scrutiny.

Recently Iowa's Republican Senator Chuck Grassley enthusiastically supported the idea of amending the *Federal Funding Accountability and Transparency Act*, to include the full text of contracts. Senator Grassley, a champion of the taxpayer and government whistleblowers knows that greater transparency will benefit taxpayers.

There is momentum to require the full text of government contracts be put online. But, don't underestimate the power of lethargy. I first wrote to President Bill Clinton and asked him to issue an executive order setting procedures for every agency of the federal government to place its contracts online back in January of 2000. On February 8, 2000, President Clinton wrote back saying he had forwarded this request to the OMB's Office of Information and Regulatory Affairs for review. On September 10, 2001, I wrote to Mitchell E. Daniels, Jr., then the Director of the Office of Management and Budget, urging him to give taxpayers access to the full text of government contracts. On June 6, 2003, as a result of Mr. Daniels drive on this issue, a Federal Register Notice was issued asking for public comments on a pilot project to put contracts online. His successors at the OMB have not followed up.

We are moving in the right direction with the Federal Funding Accountability and Transparency Act, but as we all know the "devil is in the details." Requiring federal agencies and departments to post online the full text of all federal contracts would be a wonderful next step. The computer age should make it possible to efficiently allow for certain redactions related to legitimate concerns about business confidentiality and national security in contracts before they are posted online in a publicly-available database.

A large coalition from across the political spectrum has been pushing for increased transparency in government, which is good for a more competitive procurement process, the taxpayer and our democracy.

Contracting out what the state and federal

government do and contracting to obtain what governments need is a large part of our economy. The former includes letting corporations perform government functions and the latter includes buying supplies like fuel, paper, food, medicines and vehicles. Taken together, they amount to spending trillions of dollars over the past decade—our tax dollars.

Putting the full text of these contracts online could give taxpayers both savings and better value; let the media focus more incisively on this vast area of government disbursements to inform the wider public; encourage constructive comments and alarms from the citizenry; and stimulate legal and economic research by scholars interested in structural topics related to government procurement, transfers, subsidies and giveaways.

Congress should amend the *Federal Funding Accountability and Transparency Act.*

And, governors should work expeditiously to make the full text of all state contracts, ranging from procurement of goods and services to grants, leaseholds and labor contracts, available to the public on the internet in a clear and searchable format.

Transparency is one of the core principles of representative democracy. Another way of putting it is that "information is the currency of democracy."

Nader Urges Congress Watchdog Effort

December 29, 2006

SAN FRANCISCO—It was a packed house at the historic old Roxie Theatre in this city's Mission District. A diverse group of citizens gathered here between Christmas and the New Year to listen and discuss the prospects of progressive politics following the Democrats' victory in Congress and the election of a Green Party candidate as mayor of the troubled nearby city of Richmond (population 102,000).

Gayle McLaughlin—the mayor-elect—demonstrated why she defeated Chevron (which operates a refinery in Richmond) and other corporate interests, winning decisive votes from the African-American and Hispanic communities that make up a majority of the city's population.

Going door-to-door since March, she and her volunteers conveyed specific improvements through a mobilized citizenry that hit home with the residents.

Matt Gonzalez, who narrowly missed winning the mayoralty of San Francisco in 2003 as a Green Party candidate, spoke of his decision to vote only for the candidates whose record and agenda he believes in, regardless of Party affiliation. Since leaving the Democratic Party in 2000, he would no longer be trapped into voting for the "least worst" major Party candidate. Mr. Gonzalez has a bright state-wide political future in California.

As an elected member of San Francisco's Board of Supervisors, Ross Mirkarimi—a long time Green Party leader—spoke of what it will take to create a new politics of sustaining vision with its feet in the neighborhoods and communities.

Introduced by Peter Gabel—former president of New College and a veteran leader in public interest law—I commented on the roles of citizens in the home district of the next Speaker of the US House of Representatives—Nancy Pelosi.

I urged the audience to constitute themselves as a non-partisan Congress Watchdog organization to leverage, through their newly empowered Speaker Pelosi, the start of important changes for our country, led by an end to the US war-quagmire in Iraq and fundamental corporate reforms.

Clipboards were passed through the aisles for people to sign up and many did. It was an enthusiastic, uplifting gathering with more than a few seasoned citizen activists in attendance, as the discussion period showed.

One of them, Medea Benjamin, quickly took responsibility to get this watchdog effort off the ground. Known nationally as a demonstrative peace activist against the Iraq War, Ms. Benjamin is a cunning counterweight to the warmongering and corporate pressures sure to come down on Speaker Pelosi.

If Medea Benjamin were to have a middle name, it would be Medea "here, there and everywhere" Benjamin. In 2004, she submarined the head of the California Green Party, Peter Camejo, splitting his delegation and providing the critical votes at the Green Party Convention to a nominee she supported precisely because he would receive only a few votes, while she urged Greens to vote for John Kerry in the close states.

She then played a shadowy role with the Democrats in this close state strategy, while still protesting inside the Democrats' Nominating Convention in Boston against the war.

Speakers of the House almost never experience their districts' organized in any way to watch their performance, much less to press them toward more progressive agendas. Speakers get the expected free ride and very easy re-elections.

This tradition will be up-ended if Medea Benjamin and her associates become responsible for a growing progressive "Pelosi Watchdog" group in her backyard.

Speaker Pelosi should welcome such pressure because starting in January, 2007 all kinds of

grasping commercial lobbyists will be knocking on her door looking to retain or enlarge their unconscionable privileges and immunities.

She would be advised not to turn her back on Medea Benjamin who is "here, there and everywhere" in more ways than one.

Hurricane Horrors
October 7, 2005

Amidst the wailing and grieving by those many victims of Hurricanes Katrina and Rita come the growls of greed from those corporations getting huge contracts from the US government to supply emergency relief, reconstruction services and materials.

From everywhere—the press, citizen groups, lawmakers, federal inspectors general—come the howls and charges of profiteering, gouging the taxpayers, political favoritism, Halliburton again and so forth. Clark Kent Ervin, formerly the inspector general at the Department of Homeland Security, says "when they issue rapid-fire, no-bid contracts, they're basically asking companies to gouge them."

Some of the early disclosures seem to confirm Mr. Ervin's experience. According to Senators Tom Coburn (R-Okla.) and Barack Obama (D-Ill.), FEMA has entered a no-bid contract with Carnival Cruise Lines for $192 million to house hurricane evacuees on three cruise ships. Senators Coburn and Obama note the price the taxpayers are paying a company that has polluted offshore waters for years: "$2,550 per guest, per week, which is four times the cost of a $599 per tourist 7-Day Western Caribbean Cruise from Galveston, Texas."

Halliburton—flush with so many Iraq War contracts that one cannot keep up with all the

Pentagon and Congressional charges of waste, fraud and abuse—has got it hands on $60 million in Katrina contracts. This is the company that charges the Pentagon $100 for 15 pounds of laundry, gouges the Army on fuel and has charged the Defense Department for undelivered meals for soldiers. (The Army decided it cannot feed itself anymore in the field.)

Hundreds of companies are rushing for the gold. During a Katrina reconstruction summit at the Senate Office Building, *US News and World Report* describes the scene: "Edward Badolato, a retired Marine colonel who is now an executive with the Shaw Group, reportedly reassured attendees. 'Trust me', he said, 'there's going to be enough for everybody down there.'"

Indeed there will be plenty of money—taxpayer money heading toward $100 billion, charitable money in the billions and uncountable donations in kind. Will the million displaced Americans receive the bulk of the benefits?

If you ask the Bush administration, the answer of assurance comes from all the teams of inspectors and auditors it is sending to the Gulf states. There will be an Office of Hurricane Katrina Oversight. Auditing offices are operating in Baton Rouge, Montgomery, AL and Jackson, MS. Pentagon auditors will help those from the Department of Homeland Security.

And of course the Government Accountability Office (GAO), the investigative arm of Congress, will have its sleuths prowling around the region and looking at the Bush regime's books.

What is an average taxpayer to think of the likelihood of success here? Let's ask some questions. How many people have been fired or demoted following the gross boondoggles revealed in the federal and state governments after Hurricane Katrina passed through? Count your fingers and you have more of them.

What has been the result of scores of Pentagon audits of private contracting abuses in Iraq? Very few debarments, very few prosecutions and the enormous fraud and abuse continue. The big companies over there just ride out the bad publicity and rake in the money. Apparently they are too big to fire.

Will the trustworthy, professional GAO reports produce any changes? Not if the GAO's mountains of critical reports of Pentagon contracting are any basis for prediction. Over ten years ago the GAO threw its hands in the air and pronounced the Pentagon's $300 billion budget "unauditable."

This is, to say the least, a serious charge. Especially when subsequent reports futilely repeat the same findings as the Pentagon budget nears $500 billion a year.

In its latest report to Congressional committees last month, the GAO wearily referred to its repeated findings about "the long-standing weaknesses in the Department of Defense's (DOD) financial management and related business processes and systems." These deficiencies, the GAO concludes, have "(1) resulted in a lack of reliable information needed to make sound decisions and report on the status of DOD activities, including the accountability of assets, . . . (2) hindered its operational efficiency; (3) adversely affected mission performance; and (4) left the department vulnerable to fraud, waste and abuse."

The Bush administration could not account for the first $9 billion spent in Iraq, according to these auditors.

Fundamentally, the federal budgets in the Department of Homeland Security and the Department of Defense are out of control, by the Office of Management and Budget (OMB), which is an arm of the White House. The draconian imposition of cost-benefit rigor that John Graham,

OMB's regulatory czar, imposes on the little federal health and safety agencies, dealing with auto safety and food and drug safety and efficacy, does not extend to the gargantuan Departments of Defense or Homeland Security.

More than two years ago, we thought that the OMB was going to require both the cost-benefit yardstick for the Homeland Security Department and the placement online of all major government contracts with corporations. Then Mitch Daniels, head of OMB, left to run for governor of Indiana. His successor, Josh Bolton, has displayed no interest thus far in the reforms we had suggested to Mr. Daniels.

So taxpayers, ask yourself: how long you are going to remain inactive while this no-fault government headed by a no-fault president who is spreading fault in every direction but his own as he presides over the accelerating deficit and debasement of the USA's budget?

How Safe Are We?

February 25, 2005

George W. Bush often says that the safety of all Americans is his highest priority. He doesn't mean advancing vigorously the implementation of laws he has sworn to enforce against occupational disease and trauma, traffic injuries, air pollution, medical malpractice and other unsafe conditions that are taking the lives of many tens of thousands of Americans annually. What he means is commanding the "war on terrorism."

So let's evaluate him at his narrowest definition of safety. First, it is clear that the budget of the Department of Homeland Security, a huge amalgam of government agencies proud to defend their turf even after their consolidation, is out of control.

There are no cost-benefit criteria in operation about how to spend the burgeoning monies Congress and Bush are throwing at this department. One of its arms is the Transportation Security Agency. You know, the agency that makes you take your shoes off or pats you down at airports. Its money is flying around as well.

Back in 2002, the Office of Management and Budget's chief, Mitch Daniels, told us that his office essentially has no control over the ways Homeland Security spends its budget. He agreed, in a series of meetings with me and our economist, James Love, to file a notice in the Federal Register inviting public comments about the best ways to place the Department under a cost-benefit regime.

The comments were duly received and analyzed by OMB staff and the General Services Administration. But in June 2003, Mr. Daniels resigned his post to run for the Governorship of Indiana. He won. His successor, Josh Bolten, a White House political appointee, has shown no interest, thus far, in continuing his successor's mission.

Just calling any expenditure "homeland security" defers most members of Congress from exercising any real oversight. So dollars are easy to waste because the symbol is nearly untouchable. But Mr. Bolten, who does not return our calls or respond to letters requesting a meeting, is the man who is supposed to be in charge of a tough OMB seeking prudent uses of tax dollars (with the help of several little-noticed Government Accountability Office reports).

On January 20th, the *New York Times* published a masterful editorial titled "Our Unnecessary Insecurity." It pointed out "troubling vulnerabilities that have yet to be seriously addressed by Bush and his Department of Homeland Security. Among these risks are chemical plants, nuclear materials, nuclear power plants, port security, hazardous waste transport and bioterrorism (eg. anthrax).

While the *Times* properly acknowledges that a complex industrial society can never be super-safe, especially given suicidal attacks, it does take to task the chemical industry whose lobbyists continue to block reasonable safety rules proposed by the Department and EPA.

In fact, many industries have opposed such regulations in their backyards, and where they accede, they demand government subsidies even for normal security precautions, as for guarding nuclear power plants.

It gets worse. Every day, toxic chemicals and lethal wastes are transported by rail and truck through many populated areas. Within a few blocks of the Congress, about 8500 rail cars pass every year, loaded with chlorine, sulfuric acid, hydrochloric acid and other toxic vapors that could destroy the lives of tens of thousands of people in an hour.

The District of Columbia recently adopted a temporary ban on such shipments, but the railroad company CSX objected. Resolution of this conflict is still pending.

Now either Bush is severely negligent, while using the "war on terrorism" to help him get re-elected, or he knows that he and his cabinet members are exaggerating the terrorist threat here. For if, as Bush often says, there are al-Qaeda cells in this country that are suicidal, funded, hate this country and know they are being hunted, why have they not struck back at any one of a million targets since 9/11? One answer could be that they are simply not here. Out of 5,000 arrests by Attorney General John Ashcroft of suspected terrorists, he has convicted two, and these convictions were overturned by a court in Michigan. He is zero for 5,000, according to

Professor David Cole of Georgetown University, author of *Enemy Aliens*.

What does Bush think about these issues and questions? He is almost never asked by the press, when they can reach him, which is not often. Besides, Bush is too busy being the conqueror of Iraq with a worsening war-occupation that his own CIA Director Porter Goss described, at a Senate hearing, as providing the occasion for the recruitment and training of many new terrorists.

Fighting stateless terrorism in ways that create more terrorists is what is keeping many an active and retired military, diplomatic and intelligence person awake at night. But not George Bush, who assures us that he loses no sleep over his decisions or their consequences. See www.democracyrising.us for more information.

The People's Business
November 20, 2004

The massive corporate wave of crime, fraud and abuse rolls on, is undeterred by regular exposés in the business media itself. My favorite corporate crime journal (aka the *Wall Street Journal*) is a daily newspaper that never runs out of material.

Daily *Journal* headlines recently alerted readers to: (1) "Lucent Faces Bribery Allegations," (2) "Companies Sue Union Retirees to Cut Promised Health Benefits," (3) "How Drug's Rebirth as Treatment for Cancer Fueled Price Rises," reporting one capsule for $29 compared to a price of seven cents in Brazil, (4) "A Retired Maid's Questions About her ATM Card Led Lawyer to Georgia Scandal," (5) "At Cigna, Some Patients Found Conflict of Interest in System," (6) "As Corporate Fines Grow, SEC

Debates How Much Good They do." (7) From the Associated Press, "Calif. Insurance Chief Sues Four Insurance Giants in Kickback Probe."

Also in the headlines are the pharmaceutical companies led by Merck's deadly fiasco with Vioxx.

In the midst of the daily revelations, most of which produce no corrective behavior, the federal and state legislatures are paid to sleep through it all. Aside from a modest new law called Sarbanes/Oxley designed to deter some of the big accounting firm scandals, there is no corporate reform drive on Capitol Hill, and no demands for larger prosecution budgets for the Justice Department. During the recent political campaigns by the two major parties, there was no focus on a continuing pattern of corporate outlaws damaging the health and safety of the people and draining trillions of dollars from investors, worker pensions and 401ks.

There is, however, activity among business lobbies, like the US Chamber of Commerce, to water down law enforcement, weaken the Sarbanes law, block the Securities and Exchange Commission's efforts to protect investors, and make it harder for the defrauded to have their full day in court.

The political and legal systems are not just crumbling before these business lobbies; they are even failing to articulate a comprehensive "law and order" philosophy toward large multinational corporations playing one national jurisdiction off of another one across the globe.

To demonstrate the untapped potential for prosecution, note that New York state Attorney General Eliot Spitzer is accomplishing his moves against Wall Street with fewer than 85 attorneys in his corporate crime division. There are corporate law firms defending these culprits that each have over 1000 attorneys in their offices.

Inside the government's law enforcement agencies are officials and commissioners who can barely serve out their few years before accepting lucrative offers to join the other side. Even in office they concoct excuses for voting against significant corporate fines on the grounds that such penalties would punish shareholders and diminish the value of corporate shares. (SEC Commissioners Paul Atkins and Cynthia Glassman tried this absurdity recently.)

All this, along with the corporate domination of our government, argues for a more comprehensive approach to "controlling corporations and restoring democracy." These words comprise the subtitle of a new book called *The People's Business*, the report of the Citizen Works Corporate Reform Commission.

Having founded Citizen Works, I am pleased to trumpet this endeavor written by Lee Drutman and Charlie Cray as a long overdue, timely and fundamental challenge to the judicial usurpation of our Constitution which have given these companies, that are artificial entities and not human beings or voters, almost all the rights possessed by real people.

There can be no equal justice under the law between you and Pfizer or General Motors under such equivalence.

The steady and accelerating erosion of democracy by the corporate supremacists was not envisioned by the framers of our Constitution.

There is no mention of the "Corporation" in that founding document ratified well before the emergence of the modern corporation in the 19th century. The framers were far more worried about too much governmental power and could not foresee the many uses of that very power by corporations against the interests of "we the people."

Even the owners of the large corporation, the

shareholders, do not control their company. It is a highly autocratic structure controlled by the officers and their rubber stamp boards of directors. Making corporations into the servants of people, not their masters, is the challenge of *The People's Business.*

The many-splendored ways that this work meets this challenge can open up a major public debate. An exciting public inquiry is needed by the workers, consumers, taxpayers, voters and various communities of citizens who are now being driven backwards despite the overall conventional economic growth that has enriched the few against the well-being of these people.

Leave No Calories Behind

September 17, 2004

For years, many school administrators, hard-pressed to find extra funds to finance student activities and supplement needed classroom supplies, have allowed the installation of vending machines which dispense soft drinks, candy and a variety of junk foods. The machines may well be significant money makers, but it is a sad and ill thought out bargain which gambles recklessly with the health of young students. For the corporations which produce and distribute the sugar-laden soft drinks and snacks saturated with fat, it is a profitable market which also gives them an early opportunity to hook young students on junk food. For these junk food pushers it is a case of leaving "no calories behind."

The folly and danger of putting the health of students on the line to finance school activities, however, is beginning to attract some long over-due attention. The Education Committee of the New Jersey Assembly has approved legislation which would ban junk food vending machines from all public elementary and middle schools in the state. Schools would be allowed only to have machines which dispense whole grain foods, juice, milk and water and similar products. In addition, the legislation would eliminate from school cafeterias any product that is made up of 35 percent sugar or contains more than 8 grams of fat.

A co-sponsor of the legislation, Assemblyman Craig Stanley, said, "public schools need to be a place where both healthy minds and bodies are created. Sugary fat-laden foods have no place in our schools." The bill now heads to the floor for a vote of the New Jersey Assembly, and it's a safe bet that soft drink manufacturers, the candy companies and the junk food merchants will have their lobbyists out in full force to block the legislation.

Hopefully, the medical community and health groups will counter the junk food pushers. Certainly there is abundant evidence that obesity, fueled by unhealthy diets and excessive consumption of soft drinks and fatty foods, is a major national health problem.

The Centers for Disease Control and Prevention (CDC) estimates that the obesity rate for children and adolescents has more than doubled in the last 30 years. In 1999, an estimated 61 percent of adults in the United States were overweight. The report by the Surgeon General found that at least 13 percent of young children and adolescents were seriously overweight.

Studies by the CDC and other health research organizations suggest that obesity in the United States occurs at higher rates among African Americans and Hispanic Americans than among white Americans, while Asian Americans have relatively low levels of obesity. Some of the highest rates were among the American Indian population. In Arizona, for example, 80 percent of females and 67 percent of the males were found to be overweight among the Native American population.

The American Obesity Association says that factors influencing the disparities in levels of obesity among racial and ethnic groups include cultural differences involving dietary choices, physical activity and the acceptance of excess weight among some groups. Sedentary life-styles, particularly among middle-age and older citizens, contribute significantly to overweight and obesity.

Whatever the causes and the distribution of obesity among different population groupings, according to a 2001 report by the US Surgeon General David Satcher, the cost of obesity, both in terms of lives and healthcare costs, are staggering. "Overweight and obesity may soon cause as much preventable disease and death as cigarette smoking," Satcher predicted.

The U. S. Department of Health and Human Services (HHS) estimates conservatively that 300,000 US deaths annually are associated with obesity and being overweight. This means that obesity is catching up rapidly with the 400,000 annual deaths associated with cigarette smoking. The total direct and indirect costs attributed to obesity amounted to $117 billion in 2000, HHS says.

There is a long list of obesity-related diseases including diabetes, cancer, heart disease and hypertension. The Surgeon General has warned that overweight and obesity have the potential to "wipe out the gains the nation has made in areas such as heart disease, cancer and other chronic health problems."

The New Jersey Assembly's Education Committee has taken a gutsy position in sounding the alarm about the dangers of junk food and its close link to obesity. More importantly, they have been willing to step forward with specific legislation which would ban the junk from the schools. The New Jersey legislators recognize that the effort to reduce obesity is a community responsibility.

As former Surgeon General Satcher said in his "Call to Action To Prevent Overweight and Obesity" three years ago:

> Communities can help when it comes to health promotion and disease prevention. When there are no safe places for children to play, or for adults to walk, jog or ride a bike, that's a community responsibility. When school lunchrooms or workplace cafeterias don't offer healthy or appealing food choices, that is a community responsibility. When new or expectant parents are not educated about the benefits of breast-feeding, that's a community responsibility. And when we don't require daily physical education in our schools that's a community responsibility.

The Buddy-to-Buddy Regulatory System
September 10, 2004

Banks and their regulators have always enjoyed a cozy relationship. Regulators are notorious for going slow in clamping down hard on practices that might be unsafe and unsound. Cease and desist orders, a weapon available to all the regulators, are used sparingly and usually only in the most egregious cases. The hundreds of billions of dollars of deposit insurance and taxpayer money lost in the savings and loan debacle of the 1980s stand as a monument to regulatory laxness and delay.

One of the prime reasons for this buddy-to-buddy regulatory system is the fact that both the financial institutions and the regulators find it comfortable and mutually beneficial. Under the disjointed federal financial regulatory system each niche of banking has its own separate regulator, and when regulators appear before Congressional Committees they are always protective of their own group of institutions.

The Office of the Comptroller of the Currency (OCC) has a particular concern about keeping its flock of national banks in a happy mood. OCC derives all its operating funds from assessments on national banks under its jurisdiction. When a large national bank decides to switch to a state charter, it can leave a gaping hole in the budget of the Comptroller. So it is not surprising to see the Comptroller vigorously protect his flock of national banks through lawsuits preempting the application of state and local consumer protection laws to national banks. The unspoken and quite effective message is clear-"stick with the national charter and thumb your nose at state consumer laws."

Now other federal financial regulators are finding some new ways to stroke the institutions under their jurisdiction. This time, the Community Reinvestment Act, so important in moving credit into low and moderate income and minority neighborhoods, is endangered by a new effort to mollify banks and thrift institutions.

The Office of Thrift Supervision (OTS) kicked off the new war on CRA by proposing a regulation which would limit full examinations of CRA performance to only those thrift institutions with assets of $1 billion or more. Institutions below that threshold would only be subject to limited "streamlined" and "simplified exams."

It is not surprising that OTS is anxious to keep its own constituency happy. For several years, plans have been floated to eliminate the agency and let its functions be absorbed by the Office of the Comptroller of the Currency. In addition, some institutions have abandoned their thrift charters to convert to bank charters. So, OTS figures that easier CRA exams just might keep their wandering institutions home.

OTS's new easy CRA exam rule takes effect on October 1. And surprise of surprises, the other financial agencies are now eyeing the same thought of easing the burdens for their member institutions. No one wants to be left out when it is time to pass out new gifts to the banks.

The Federal Deposit Insurance Corporation (FDIC), which examines state banks, has issued a proposed rule similar to the handiwork of OTS. The rule is now out for comment. The Comptroller of the Currency, Jerry Hawke, already under fire for his scorched earth attacks on consumer protections, is urging his fellow regulators to adopt a uniform streamlined CRA exam rule, undoubtedly thinking that he would have protection behind a solid regulatory front. But the reports coming out of OCC suggest that on substance, OCC will be in agreement on CRA-light exams for all institutions of less than $1 billion in assets. Earlier, the Federal Reserve was behind a move to a $500 million threshold for full exams, but the Fed seems certain to join the others at the billion dollar mark.

The adoption of weaker CRA exam rules will signal to the banking industry a de-emphasis of efforts to push bank credit into low and moderate income and minority communities. It will mean a sharp reduction in data and analysis needed to judge how well financial institutions are helping to meet the credit needs of all areas of their communities.

Much of the effective enforcement of CRA as a prod to push banks to serve all their communities comes to the forefront when banks file merger applications. Community activists have been effective in pointing to data generated in

CRA examinations to challenge the proposed mergers. In many cases, the protests constructed from the data have led to significant concessions that have assured critically needed credit for many communities. Even when the regulatory agencies want to make an informed decision on the community lending of the merging banks, the cupboard will be bare under the CRA-light approach to examinations.

The proposals for barebones exams are on top of an already absurd rating system applied for CRA performance by each institution. Almost all the financial institutions—98 percent—receive either a "satisfactory" or an "outstanding" rating for their performance as community lenders. Nothing is so rare as a regulator applying a "need to improve" or a substantial non-compliance rating to a bank. If there were any validity to the ratings and credit was actually flowing at a "satisfactory" level to all neighborhoods, our inner cities would, indeed, be shining cities on the hill. The conditions don't match the glowing CRA ratings awarded by the regulators.

Until OTS leaped out with its billion-dollar rule, the only banks that were eligible for limited streamlined CRA examinations were small institutions under $250 million. But, the billion dollar threshold lets the vast majority of the nation's commercial banks off the hook.

There are 7,691 commercial banks nationwide, with only 428 of them having more than $1 billion in assets. If the OTS-generated rule becomes standard, this means that 7,263 banks will be on the regulators' CRA-light list.

CRA has been a valuable economic tool for people who have few tools with which to build their communities. CRA has generated at least $1.75 trillion in credit to inner city and depressed rural areas since its adoption in 1977. It should not be weakened by regulators shame-lessly attempting to please their banker-constituency. People need to speak to their members of Congress about this matter.

Corporatizing the Pentagon
May 7, 2004

Remarkable what digital cameras can do. The photos of low-level prisoners being abused and humiliated by both US troops and private contractors in an Iraqi prison are the beginning of what Senator Lindsay Graham (R-S.C.) called "the worst is yet to come." The Senator warned Defense Secretary, Donald Rumsfeld, at a Senate Hearing on May 7, 2004, that he doesn't want to see just sergeants and privates punished with the higher-ups getting away.

The higher-ups are not just military brass; they include private corporate contractors who are so embedded in the military operations in Iraq that it is increasingly difficult to tell the difference. Contractors were involved in the interrogation of the prisoners in that notorious Saddam-era jail near Baghdad.

About 20,000 employees of the Halliburtons and hundreds of other companies are feeding the troops, guarding installations, managing logistics, and in some cases even doing the fighting. Blackwater Security Consulting, for example, was engaged in full-scale battle in Najaf, with its helicopters involved in a firefight while resupplying its own commandos.

These growing military theatre contractors are now forming their own lobby to represent their interests before Congress. Their interests are clearly not peace. The profits are in war and the more war, the more profits.

What's wrong with corporatizing more and more of the Pentagon's functions? Don't the corporate members of the military-industrial complex, as President Eisenhower called them in his famous farewell warning to Americans, already have plenty of power? Yes, they do, as illustrated in half of our federal government's operating budget going for military expenditures in a world where we no longer have a major state enemy. But this encroachment (another Eisenhower description) moves deeply into an operational dimension without adequate laws or disclosure for accountability. Nobody elected these mercenaries to perform governmental missions.

Franklin Delano Roosevelt in 1939 called the control of government by private power "fascism." He probably never envisioned such control would be so embedded as to constitute a virtual merger of corporate power over government power.

Here is what is happening. Without letting the American people know what is going on in recent years, the corporatists, who fund both major parties, have been turning more and more essential governmental functions into business deals. More and more, the corporations are not just controlling our government, they literally are running it. Years ago, it was disclosed that even the speeches for the Secretary of Energy were being written by private consulting firms.

In addition to secrecy and lack of accountability, these corporate contractors are costing taxpayers a bundle, while some of these companies move to tax havens like Bermuda. Pentagon contractors have told me that it cost you $120,000 for a corporate cook to do a six-month tour of duty in Iraq to feed the Army troops. Some of you old Army hands know how much less Army cooks used to make to give you the nutrition.

How about one corporate dog handler and a team of dogs to sniff out road mines—a dangerous mission to be sure? Well, that goes for $666,000 for a six-month tour of duty with the trained dog handler making $200,000 of that sum.

We read about these tens of millions and billion dollar corporate contracts being announced in the press. We almost never read about how these contracts break down. Why the secrecy? Well the disclosure in the 1980s of the $435 claw hammer sparked public outrage about the waste when such a hammer cost $10 or $12 in a hardware store. (For obvious reasons, the Pentagon contractor felt the need to describe this simple claw hammer as a "uni-directional impact generator.") That's why the secrecy. These companies and their Washington buddies don't want the people to know.

There is another consequence to contracting out Pentagon operators to private corporations. It is causing a brain drain and a skills drain from the Department of Defense. Why stay in the Army, Navy, Air Force and Marines when you can double, triple or quadruple your pay by moving over to these companies and do the same job.

It is way overdue for a major Congressional hearing on what Peter Singer called his new book "Corporate Warriors." It is time for the media to become specifically interested in the details of these deals and these policy implications, and demand more disclosure of these government contracts.

Even George W. Bush's first director of the Office of Management and Budget, Mitchell Daniels, favored suitably redacted placement of all government contracts on the government's internet. The Pentagon developed the internet. It is time they used it for the taxpayers who are funding this increasingly outsourced department.

The Ultimate Oligarch

February 27, 2004

Federal Reserve Chairman Alan Greenspan strayed away from his charter once again to warn about the people's entitlement programs-Social Security and Medicare- becoming unaffordable. He suggested cuts in benefits to reduce deficits.

In the same breath, Mr. Greenspan urged that Mr. Bush's tax cuts for the wealthy-a huge cause of the growing federal deficits-be made permanent.

His priorities should come as no surprise, for Mr. Greenspan is the ultimate oligarch.

The hundreds of billions of dollars in corporate welfare giveaways annually, from local to state to federal governments, are not his concern. He is comfortable with this kind of direct and indirect corporate socialism where profits are less taxed and costs are socialized on the backs of individual taxpayers.

Instead, what bothers Mr. Greenspan are the social insurance programs for tens of millions of Americans-most of them the coming elderly. He raises the specter of Social Security insolvency because fewer workers will be supporting retirees. He testified that "It is important that we tell people who are about to retire what it is they will have."

If so, why didn't the Chairman recall the projections by the Social Security trustees who tell us that the retirement fund is solid until 2042 without any changes or benefit cuts, based on an average GDP growth rate of 1.7 percent annually? The latter figure is very conservative.

For the past 50 years the average GDP growth rate has been well over three percent.

At 1.7 percent, after 2042 without any changes, the decline in benefits would be gradual. At over three percent growth rates, benefitswould continue beyond that date. Curious, isn't it, that the Chairman would ignore the corporate lob-bying causes of the federal deficits, such as corporate tax shelters, loopholes, subsidies, handouts, giveaways and so forth. Why, if corporations and the wealthy were taxed at the rates prevailing in the prosperous 1960s, the deficits would be no more, quite soon.

Medicare is another matter. Its precarious future state is hostage to staggering annual price increases by the healthcare and drug industries which could be addressed by an efficient single-payer health insurance system.

Mr. Greenspan chose not to mention the budget busting corporate bonanzas embedded in the $540 billion ten-year prescription drug deal. The massive drug industry lobbying battalions raised their champagne glasses when they got a ban on Uncle Sam negotiating drug price discounts for medicines paid for by the government. There was no mention of that lurking Niagara of red ink, corporate profiteering by the Chairman.

Mr. Greenspan needs to be more introspective about why he focuses on benefits for the people that stimulate economic demand and ignores budgets and handouts for the corporations. It is not enough for him to pronounce the tautology that the latter stimulate economic growth. For whom? The increasing number of unemployed uninsured and undefended workers, whose white collar and blue collar jobs are being exported to very low wage authoritarian countries? The Chairman has serious trouble criticizing the corporate state, including doing anything about the consumer credit abuses that the Federal Reserve directly is supposed to stop, like predatory lending.

Reaction by the Democrats-John Kerry and John Edwards-was one of proper outrage to Mr. Greenspan's remarks. In their mind they may have been regretting why President Bill Clinton re-nominated the Republican Greenspan to another four-year term in 2000.

Global & Labor Concerns

The columns in this section focus on broader issues of globalization—ending undeclared and unjust wars, stopping the spread of labor outsourcing and the erosion of labor rights, and revitalizing the US economy. Organized labor has played a key role in promoting safe working conditions and fair wages. But the forces of globalization have cost millions of American jobs as corporations find cheap labor overseas. Labor has faced the failure of the minimum wage to keep pace with the cost of living; the decline or elimination of traditional pension contributions; and the weakening of the Occupational Safety and Health Administration (OSHA) and consequent evisceration of regulations promoting workplace safety.

The globalization trend has not only hurt the American worker, but workers in other nations where our corporations shift operations. Workers in those countries are paid minimal wages and suffer horrific conditions. Sweatshop conditions and child labor are part and parcel of globalization. Globalization also contributes to environmental degradation and deteriorating health around the world. Just ask the fast-food and tobacco industries, which are delighted to find vast new markets for their health-damaging products.

Our government's shortsighted policies have too many devastating effects all around the globe. The problems go far beyond any one administration. Assorted international bodies, including the International Monetary Fund, World Bank, and even the United Nations, have adopted corporate-first policies that wreak havoc on the developing world.

The columns in this section explain the many ways in which resourcing our economy back in the US on our soil with a revitalized minimum wage and labor representation will promote a stronger US economy. We need a renaissance of organized labor. And we need to stop instigating and perpetuating wars overseas. The US should be a model of fair labor practices and sustainable development. The following columns offer a glimpse of the problems associated with globalization and more than a few remedies.

Iran: The Neocons Are At It Again

January 11, 2012

The same neocons who persuaded George W. Bush and crew to, in Ron Paul's inimitable words, "lie their way into invading Iraq" in 2003, are beating the drums of war more loudly these days to attack Iran. It is remarkable how many of these warmongers are former draft dodgers who wanted other Americans to fight the war in Vietnam.

With the exception of Ron Paul, who actually knows the history of US-Iranian relations, the Republican presidential contenders have declared their belligerency toward Iranian officials who they accuse of moving toward nuclear weapons.

The Iranian regime disputes that charge, claiming they are developing the technology for nuclear power and nuclear medicine.

The inspection teams of the International Atomic Energy Authority (IAEA) that monitor compliance with the Nuclear Non-Proliferation Treaty, to which Iran belongs, have entered Iran numerous times and, while remaining suspicious, have not been able to find that country on the direct road to the bomb.

While many Western and some Arab countries in the Gulf region have condemned Iran's alleged nuclear arms quest, Israel maintains some 200 ready nuclear weapons and has refused to sign the non-proliferation treaty, thereby avoiding the IAEA inspectors.

Israelis in the know have much to say. Defense minister, Ehud Barak, responded to PBS's Charlie Rose's question "If you were Iran wouldn't you want a nuclear weapon?" with these words:

"Probably, probably. I don't delude myself that they are doing it just because of Israel. They have their history of 4,000 years. They look around and they see the Indians are nuclear. The Chinese are nuclear, Pakistan is nuclear as well as North Korea, not to mention the Russians."

The Iranian regime, with a national GDP smaller than Massachusetts, is terrified. It is surrounded by powerful adversaries, including the US military on three of its borders. President George W. Bush labeled Iran, along with Iraq and North Korea, one of the three "axis of evil," and Teheran knows what happened to Iraq after that White House assertion. They also know that North Korea inoculated itself from invasion by testing nuclear bombs. And all Iranians remember that the US overthrew their popular-

elected Prime Minister Mohammad Mossadegh in 1953 and installed the dictatorial shah who ruled tyrannically for the next 27 years.

Recently, Iran has experienced mysterious cyber sabotage, drone violations of its air space, the slaying of its nuclear scientists and the blowing up of its military sites, including a major missile installation. Israeli and American officials are not trying too hard to conceal this low-level warfare.

Israeli military historian-strategist Martin van Creveld said in 2004, that Iranians "would be crazy not to build nuclear weapons considering the security threats they face." Three years later he stated that "the world must now learn to live with a nuclear Iran the way we learned to live with a nuclear Soviet Union and a nuclear China. . . . We Israelis have what it takes to deter an Iranian attack. We are in no danger at all of having an Iranian nuclear weapon dropped on us . . . thanks to the Iranian threat, we are getting weapons from the US and Germany."

US General John Abizaid is one of numerous military people who say that the world can tolerate a nuclear Iran—which, like other countries, does not wish to commit suicide.

Using the "Iranian threat," served Israeli Prime Minister Netanyahu, who on his first tour of duty back in 1996, speaking to a joint session of Congress, made a big point of the forthcoming Iranian bomb.

Somehow the Iranians, who were invaded in 1980 by a US-backed Saddam Hussein, resulting in a million casualties, and who have not invaded anybody for 250 years, are taking a very long time to build a capability for atomic bomb production, much less the actual weapons.

In mid-2011, Meir Dagan, recently retired head of Israel's "CIA," repeated his opposition to a military attack on Iran's nuclear facilities, adding it would engulf the region in a conventional war.

He further took the Israeli government to task for failing "to put forth a vision," noting that "Israel must present an initiative to the Palestinians and adopt the 2002 Saudi Arabia peace proposal, reiterated since, that would open full diplomatic relations with some two dozen Arab and Islamic countries in return for an Israeli pullback to the 1967 borders and recognition of a Palestinian state."

The warmongers against Iran have often distorted Iranian statements to suit their purpose and kept in the shadows several friendly Iranian initiatives offered to the George W. Bush administration.

Flynt L. Leverett, now with the Brookings Institution and before a State Department and CIA official, listed three initiatives that were rejected. Right after the September 11 attacks, Iran offered to help Washington overthrow the Taliban. The US declined the offer. Second, in the spring of 2003, top Iranian officials sent the White House a detailed proposal for comprehensive negotiations to resolve questions regarding its weapons programs, relations with Hezbollah and Hamas and a Palestinian peace agreement with Israel. This proposal was rebuffed and ignored.

Third, in October 2003, European officials secured an agreement from Iran to suspend Iranian uranium enrichment and to pursue talks that Mr. Leverett said "might lead to an economic, nuclear deal." The Bush administration "rebuffed the European initiative, ensuring [that it] failed," he added.

A few days ago, US Defense Secretary Leon Panetta said Iran was developing a capability to produce nuclear weapons someday but was not building a bomb. So why is the Obama administration talking about a Western boycott of Iran's oil exports, so crucial to its faltering, sanctions-ridden economy? Is this latest sanction designed to squeeze Iranian civilians and lead to the overthrow of the regime? Arguably it may backfire and produce more support for the government.

Backing the Iranian regime into such a fateful corner risks countermeasures that may disrupt the gigantic flow of oil through the Strait of Hormuz. Should that occur, watch the prices of your gasoline, heating, and other related products go through the roof—among other consequences.

Isn't it about time for the abdicatory Congress to reassert its constitutional responsibilities? It owes the American people comprehensive, public House and Senate hearings that produce knowledgeable testimony about these issues and all relevant history for wide media coverage.

The drums of war should not move our country into a propagandized media frenzy that preceded and helped cause the Iraq invasion with all the sociocide in that country and all the costly blowbacks against US national interests.

It is past time for the American citizenry to wake up and declare: Iran will not be an Iraq redux!

Not Made in America
November 30, 2011

"Here, look at this handsome L.L. Bean catalog and tell me what you want for Christmas," said a relative over Thanksgiving weekend. I started leafing through the 88-page cornucopia with hundreds of clothing and household products, garnished by free gift cards and guaranteed free shipping. I wasn't perusing it for any suggested gifts; instead, I was going through every offering to see whether they were made in the USA or in other countries.

This is what I found: over 97 percent of all the items pictured and priced were noted "imported" by L.L. Bean. The only ones manufactured in the US were fireplace gloves, an L.L. Bean jean belt, a dress chino belt, quilted faux-shearling-lined L.L. Bean boots (made in Maine), a personalized web collar and leash (for your pet), and symbolically enough, the "made in Maine using American-made cotton canvas are the Original Boat and Tote Bags" to carry all those goodies coming in from China and elsewhere.

That was it for the products that were "Made in America." The former fountainhead of global manufacturing has been largely deflated by the flight of US companies to fascist or communist regimes noted for holding down their repressed workers.

But there is much more to this story and the plight of millions of American workers and hundreds of their hollowed-out communities that are the visible results of corporate free trade propaganda.

How many times have the politicians and their corporate paymasters told us that "free trade" with other nations is a "win-win" proposition? They win and we win. After all, isn't that what happened two hundred years ago when Portugal sold its wine to England in return for British textiles? Economists have won many prizes elaborating this theory of comparative advantage.

That is what Nobel laureate super-economist Paul Samuelson believed in the many years he wrote and updated his standard *Economics 101* textbook, studied by millions of college students for nearly 50 years. For many of his colleagues,

the theory of "free trade" had become an ideology bordering on a secular religion. Don't bother them with the facts.

Some of their students became reporters, such as Thomas Friedman of the *New York Times*, taking this prejudgment of reality into their uncritical coverage of the very flawed NAFTA and World Trade Organization agreements under President Clinton in the 1990s.

But Samuelson increasingly became an empiricist, along with his academic contributions in mathematical economics. Before one of his book revisions in the '70s, he wrote me asking for whatever materials I thought would be useful regarding consumer protection and consumer fraud. He presaged the relatively new field of behavioral economics and their obvious findings that consumers do not always maximize their best interests, and can act "irrationally" in a fast-paced marketplace of clever or unscrupulous sellers.

Gradually, Professor Samuelson saw trade between nations move from "comparative advantage" to more and more "absolute advantage." That is, companies were using the swift mobility of capital, modern factory machinery and transport to locate all elements of production—labor, capital, raw materials, and advanced know-how—in one place, now most notably in China.

Absolute advantages have been aided by the corporate-managed trade agreements of WTO and NAFTA. These treaties are also conveniently violated to facilitate large subsidies that are not supposed to be used to lure companies to move. This trade in giveaways has China winning over the US, most recently in pulling American solar factories to China.

If corporate "free trade" is a win-win proposition, adhered to by one president after another, including Barack Obama, how come our country has piled up bigger trade deficits every year since 1976? Big is really big. Over the past decade our country has bought from abroad more than it has sold—an average of well over half a trillion dollars each year.

In 1980 the US was the world leading creditor—they owed us—while now, the US is by far the world's leading debtor—we owe them!

At what point do the "free traders" cry "uncle" and rethink their commercial catechism? So long as multinational corporations control our politicians, it will not happen. For these companies are looking for the most worker-controlled, environmentally-pollutable and bribable countries to locate their manufacturing bases. Global companies are just that, bereft of any allegiance or grateful patriotism to their country of birth, profit and bailout salvation.

Here are three questions you may wish to ask any self-styled "free traders":

What amount of evidence do you require to get rid of your dogma and, at minimum, start thinking like Paul Samuelson?

How much of the savings from lower costs abroad are going for large profits and not being passed on to the consumer, who also has to endure the reported hazards of unregulated imports?

And at what point do you look at L.L. Bean-type catalogs and ask whether you are getting a price break that is worth the debilitating dependency on other nations that use exploitation, repression, violations and outright counterfeiting as unfair methods of competition against our stateside companies and workers?

Let Our Farmers Grow
October 16, 2011

Congressman Ron Paul introduced H.R. 1831, the "Industrial Hemp Farming Act of 2011" on May 11th of this year. It is a simple bill at two pages in length, and it would legalize the growing of industrial hemp in the United States.

Currently farmers can grow industrial hemp only if they have received a permit from the Drug Enforcement Agency (DEA)—a prospect that the agency has made all but impossible for decades. Otherwise, it is illegal to grow.

Although Rep. Paul has introduced several bills like this one in the past, there are several reasons that this bill should be passed now. Hemp has an amazing number of uses. Its fiber can be used in carpeting, home furnishings, construction materials, auto parts, textiles, and paper. Its seeds can be used in food, industrial oils, cosmetics, and pharmaceuticals. There are assertions, reported by the *Guardian* and *Biodiesel Magazine*, that using industrial hemp in biofuels instead of crops like corn and other feedstock provides greater environmental benefits. The expansion of industrial hemp as a feedstock for biofuels could also help to reduce oil imports.

Not only does hemp have a wide range of uses, but its cultivation in the United States could help to spur our lagging economy. Since the cultivation of hemp is outlawed in the United States, the US market for hemp and hemp-based products is entirely dependent upon imports. A 2010 Congressional Research Service report cited an estimate that the US market for hemp-based products may exceed $350 million annually.

A ban on the agricultural production of hemp simply doesn't make sense. Farmers in places like Iowa could benefit greatly from the production of industrial hemp. In a crippling recession, unemployed Americans could receive a boost from such an emerging industry, from farms to value-added businesses. And many firms here in the United States that sell hemp-based products would reap the benefits.

Currently they import their hemp from places like Canada, China, or France, which can increase their costs from 10 to 15 percent or more. As the only remaining developed nation in which the production of industrial hemp is not permitted, the United States is not only missing out on a large—and growing—global market, but limiting the livelihoods of farmers, processors and fabricators.

Industrial hemp could benefit our environment greatly. A range of studies have shown the benefits: hemp can thrive with minimal—or even without—herbicides, it reinvigorates the soil, and it requires less water than crops like cotton. Furthermore, it could prevent the deforestation of large portions of the US landscape and presents significant benefits compared with wood in the production of paper. Industrial hemp matures in three to four months. It takes years for trees to grow. It can also yield four times as much paper per acre as trees.

Critics of industrial hemp may point to its relation to marijuana in order to claim that if one smokes industrial hemp, they can become high. Although industrial hemp and marijuana share the same species, cannabis sativa, industrial hemp is genetically and chemically different. Industrial hemp, at most, contains one third of 1 percent THC, the drug that produces a psychoactive effect in marijuana. However, marijuana is often between 10 and 30 percent THC. Smoking industrial hemp will not make an individual high.

The DEA will claim that growing industrial hemp next to marijuana may serve to impede law enforcement against the latter. However, countries that have legal cultivation of industrial hemp do not have similar problems. Furthermore, since industrial hemp has such little THC, growing it next to marijuana would only serve to dilute by cross pollinations the illegal marijuana plants—something no marijuana grower wants.

Industrial hemp has a distinguished history in this country, dating before the revolution and its founding. The Declaration of Independence was drafted on hemp paper, and George Washington and Thomas Jefferson grew industrial hemp on their farms. During World War II, hemp was used to make very strong rope, and the Department of Agriculture made a film *Hemp for Victory* to encourage its cultivation.

Despite the importance of this issue, we rarely see it discussed in the headlines or by political candidates. Farmers in Iowa could benefit greatly from the cultivation of industrial hemp. Citizens in Iowa, who have the ear of presidential hopefuls, have an opportunity to move this issue back into the spotlight during the December 10th Republican Presidential Primary debate.

Let's hope Congressman Paul and his fellow candidates agree that it is time to allow farmers in Iowa and other states to once again start growing industrial hemp.

Jeff Musto of CSRL contributed to this article.

As The Drone Flies . . .

September 26, 2011

The fast developing predator drone technology, officially called unmanned aerial vehicles or UAVs, is becoming so dominant and so beyond any restraining framework of law or ethics, that its use by the US government around the world may invite a horrific blowback.

First some background. The Pentagon has about 7,000 aerial drones. Ten years ago there were less than 50. According to the website longwarjournal.com, they have destroyed about 1900 insurgents in Pakistan's tribal regions. How these fighters are so clearly distinguished from civilians in those mountain areas is not clear.

Nor is it clear how or from whom the government gets such "precise" information about the guerilla leaders' whereabouts night and day. The drones are beyond any counterattack—flying often at 50,000 feet. But the Air Force has recognized that a third of the Predators have crashed by themselves.

Compared to mass transit, housing, energy technology, infection control, food and drug safety, the innovation in the world of drones is incredible. Coming soon are hummingbird-sized drones, submersible drones and software-driven autonomous UAVs. The *Washington Post* described these inventions as "aircraft [that] would hunt, identify and fire at [the] enemy—all on its own." It is called "lethal autonomy" in the trade.

Military ethicists and legal experts inside and outside the government are debating how far UAVs can go and still stay within what one imaginative booster, Ronald C. Arkin, called international humanitarian law and the rules of engagement. Concerns over restraint can already be considered academic. Drones are going anywhere their governors want them to go already—Iraq, Yemen, Somalia, Libya, and countries in North Africa, to name a few known jurisdictions.

Last year a worried group of robotic special-ists, philosophers and human rights activists formed the International Committee for Robot Arms Control (ICRAC) (http://www.icrac.co.uk/). They fear that such instruments may make wars more likely by the strong against the weak because there will be fewer human casualties by those waging robotic war. But proliferation is now a fact. Forty countries are reported to be working on drone technology or acquiring it. Some experts at the founding conference of ICRAC forshadowed hostile states or terrorist organizations hacking into robotic systems to redirect them.

ICRAC wants an international treaty against machines of lethal autonomy along the lines of the ones banning land mines and cluster bombs. The trouble is that the United States, unlike over one hundred signatory nations, does not belong to either the land mines treaty or the more recent anti-cluster bomb treaty. Historically, the US has been a major manufacturer and deployer of both. Don't count on the Obama White House to take the lead anytime soon.

Columnist David Ignatius wrote that "A world where drones are constantly buzzing overhead—waiting to zap those deemed threats under a cloaked and controversial process—risks being, even more, a world of lawlessness and chaos."

Consider how terrifying it must be to the populations, especially the children, living under the threat of drones that can attack through clouds and dark skies. UAVs are hardly visible but sometimes audible through their frightful whining sound. Polls show Pakistanis overwhelmingly believe most of the drone-driven fatalities are civilians.

US Air Force Colonel Matt Martin has written a book titled *Predator*. He was a remote operator sitting in the control room in Nellis

Air Force Base in Nevada watching "suspects" transversing a mountain ridge in Afghanistan 8,000 miles away. In a review of Martin's book, Christian Cary writes, "The eerie acuity of vision afforded by the Predator's multiple high-powered video cameras enables him to watch as the objects of his interest light up cigarettes, go to the bathroom, or engage in amorous adventures with animals on the other side of the world, never suspecting that they are under observation as they do."

For most of a decade the asymmetrical warfare between the most modern, military force in world history and Iraqi and Afghani fighters has left the latter with little conventional aerial or land-based weaponry other than rifles, rocket propelled grenades, roadside IEDs and suicide-belted youths.

People who see invaders occupying their land with military domination that is beyond reach will resort to ever more desperate counterattacks, however primitive in nature. When the time comes that robotic weapons of physics cannot be counteracted at all with these simple handmade weapons because the occupier's arsenals are remote, deadly and without the need for soldiers, what will be the blowback?

Already, people like retired Admiral Dennis Blair, former director of National Intelligence under President Obama, are saying, according to POLITICO, that the administration should curtail US-led drone strikes on suspected terrorists in Pakistan, Yemen and Somalia because the missiles fired from unmanned aircraft are fueling anti-American sentiment and undercutting reform efforts in those countries.

While scores of physicists and engineers are working on refining further advances in UAVs, thousands of others are staying silent. In prior years, their counterparts spoke out against the nuclear arms race or exposed the unworkability of long-range missile defense. They need to re-engage. Because the next blowback may soon move into chemical and biological resistance against invaders. Suicide belts may contain pathogens—bacterial and viral—and chemical agents deposited in food and water supplies.

Professions are supposed to operate within an ethical code and exercise independent judgment. Doctors have a duty to prevent harm. Biologists and chemists should urge their colleagues in physics to take a greater role as to where their knowhow is leading this tormented world of ours before the blowback spills over into even more lethally indefensible chemical and biological attacks.

Obama's Laborious Labor Day
September 2, 2011

Dear President Obama:

Happy Labor Day! This is your third opportunity as president to go beyond your past tepid Labor Day proclamations.

You could convey to 150 million workers that you can add that a $9.50 minimum is still less than what workers made under the minimum wage in 1968, adjusted for inflation, when worker productivity was half of what it is today. Besides, businesses like Walmart have received windfalls year after year due to the minimum wage lagging behind inflation for decades.

Your second promise in 2008 was pushing for card-check legislation—a top priority for the AFL-CIO whose member unions helped elect you. "Give me the cardcheck," Rich Trumka, now AFL-CIO president, told me in 2004, "and millions of workers will organize into unions."

I may have missed something but when was the last time you championed card check after you took your oath of office? Did you bring labor together, the way you brought big business together for their demands, and launch a public drive to overcome many of the obstructions workers now have to confront under the present corporate-driven union-busting climate?

I met with Mr. Trumka recently. It seemed he's given up on you for the card check or minimum wage. With such low expectations, you probably can make organized labor a little more enthusiastic for you if you simply mentioned these two measures in your next State of the Union address. You could even break an old taboo and say that the notoriously anti-worker Taft-Hartley Act of 1947 needs to be changed. Just talking about those issues will "keep hope alive" for "change you can believe in."

Even better, mention these with a paragraph on the spreading poverty—yes, finally use that word "poverty," which is decidedly not "middle-class." Last January, your State of the Union address ignored poverty—accelerating child poverty, hunger, homelessness, mass unemployment and underemployment do add up to that phenomenon. If not deeds or action, at least just give them some words.

As big business abandons American workers and takes jobs and industries to communist and fascist regimes abroad—regimes that know how to keep workers in their place at 50 or 80 cents an hour—reactionary Republican governors are stripping public employees of their collective bargaining rights. These Republicans are laying off their teachers and other workers so they do not have to repeal the corporate welfare drains on their state treasuries. Dozens of corporate welfare tax abatements, subsidies, giveaways, bailouts and other freebies are embedded in their state laws.

When the Wisconsin workers protested and filled the square in Madison, Wisconsin, they were expressing your "fierce urgency of now." But you would not go and address just one of their rallies to support their jobs and rights.

Just before the last big rally of some 100,000 people from all over Wisconsin, the state federation of labor invited the vice president to speak to them in Madison. The White House said no. Isn't Joe Biden known for saying "I'm a union guy"?

Can you imagine a national Republican presidential candidate refusing an invitation to speak to 100,000 Tea Partiers by comparison?

But then these Democratic workers, you may believe, have nowhere to go in November 2012. That's right, they don't have to go anywhere; they can stay right at home along with their volunteer hours and Get-Out-The-Vote calls. Political withdrawal is real easy to do. Remember 2010. Remember the sharp drop in the youth vote. You may be met with less enthusiasm than Congressional Democrats encountered in 2010.

Sincerely,
Ralph Nader

Waging Another Unconstitutional War

JUne 17, 2011

The meticulous *Harvard Law Review* editors should be rolling over in their footnotes. The recidivist violations of constitutional and statutory requirements by their celebrated predecessor at that journal—Barack Obama—has reached Orwellian dimensions in the war against Libya.

You see, the widespread daily bombing of Libya, the strict naval blockade of Muammar Gadhafi-controlled Libya, the destruction of Gadhafi's family compound and tent encampment in the desert—killing his son and three grandchildren—and the deployment of Special Forces inside Libya is not a "war." It is, in the Obama White House's evasive nomenclature, just a "time-limited, scope-limited military action." Can you find that phrase in the Constitution?

If Obama used the word "war," he would have a more difficult time explaining to Congress and the American people (three out of four oppose this war) why he did not (1) seek a declaration of war under Article I, section 8, clause 11 of the Constitution, or (2) seek Congressional authorization for appropriated funds to further the war with our NATO co-warriors, or (3) comply with the deadlines of the War Powers Resolution. He threw all three lawful restraints on his presidential unilateralism overboard.

So, in the invidious tradition of George W. Bush and his indentured confessor, Justice Department lawyer, John Yoo, now comfortably ensconced on the law faculty of the University of California Berkeley, Mr. Obama is blithely claiming as authority for taking our country into another war "the inherent powers of the president under Article II of the Constitution." This wouldn't pass the laugh test by Jefferson, Madison, Franklin, Mason, or even Hamilton. James Madison believed placing the war-declaring power in the exclusive hands of Congress was the most significant achievement during the convention in Philadelphia that summer of 1787. No more King George substitutes for America's future, they demanded.

Note that Libya did not attack the US or its appendages, and did not attack a member of NATO. Obama admits these points. Libya's trusting government sovereign fund even left $37 billion in the US, which Obama promptly froze. Lacking even the prevaricatory pretens-

es for Bush's illegal invasion of Iraq in 2003, Obama and Hillary Clinton now say the US is militarily involved "to protect our interests and advance our values" in the region and, of course, to protect the "universal rights" of the Libyan people. (Opportunities abound for this Obama doctrine around the world from the Congo to Syria, to Burma, to occupied Palestine and many other areas.)

Desperately seeking legitimacy, Mr. Obama cites the UN resolution, NATO, and the Arab League instead of seeking it from Congress. For all treaties with foreign countries, including the UN Charter, are trumped by the US Constitution (*Reid v. Covert*, 354 US 1 (1957)). As a former teacher of constitutional law, the president knows this basic principle but then, as Lord Acton declared: "Power corrupts and absolute power corrupts absolutely."

Congress, rendered a rubber stamp by President George W. Bush, is bestirring itself. On June 3, 2011, the House of Representatives passed H.R. Res. 292, declaring that the president shall not deploy, establish, or maintain the presence of units and members of the United States Armed Forces on the ground in Libya. On this matter, Obama pleads state secrets.

On June 16, 2011, ten members of the House—five conservative Republicans (including Walter B. Jones (R-N.C.) and Ron Paul (R-Texas) and five Democrats (including Dennis Kucinich (D-Ohio) and John Conyers (D-Mich.) filed suit against President Obama in federal district court for an order declaring the US war in Libya "without a declaration of Congress with the use of funds never approved for such a war" to be unconstitutional. Given past judicial decisions declaring members of Congress to have "no standing to sue" on what they call "political matters," this suit is facing an uphill barrier.

Congress has appropriated no money for this war, already costing nearly a billion dollars, nor has the lawless Obama asked for it because he knows there will be strong bi-partisan resistance.

So where is the Congress to go but to the courts to decide this internal, domestic issue affecting the separation of powers provoked by a clearly lawless president? The degraded, politicized, formerly professional, Office of Legal Counsel has been a sleazy apologist for presidential overreaching for over two decades.

The expanding immunities of the Executive Branch, now increasingly embracing the military contractors of the corporate state, is destroying the remaining pretensions that we are a nation under law. When he was inaugurated as president in January 2009, President Obama said he wanted his administration to be known as one of "transparency and the rule of law." You'll recall during his 2008 campaign he trumpeted that he would obey the Constitution, inferring the Republican regime was trampling the rule of law.

Indeed in 2007, then-Senator Barack Obama stated that "the president does not have any power under the Constitution to unilaterally authorize a military attack in a situation that does not involve stopping an actual or imminent threat to the nation." Vice President Biden was even more vehement on this issue. And Secretary of Defense Robert Gates originally opposed the attack on Libya before falling in line.

Gadhafi's dictatorship is a brutal one. Civil wars are brutal. People are dying and suffering. The country is being torn apart. Obama and NATO are not adequately testing offers for a truce and supervised elections. Top level officials are defecting from Gadhafi and hoping to help lead any successor government.

Regimes brutalize their people whether as dictatorships, authoritarian rulers, connected with dominant oligarchies, or through racial, religious or other sectarian repressions. Is the US, mired in deep recession, debt and its own kleptocracy, going to continue to police the world with bases, interventions, subversions or occupation?

The cause of human rights everywhere needs a permanent, well-equipped, professional United Nations peace-keeping force and effective international courts to prevent mass massacres and mass brutalities. That time is not near, but it should be at the top of the agenda of civilized nations.

The US, as the number one military superpower, provoking antagonisms by its penchant for control throughout the world, should not imperially advance the empire. It is that belief which is bringing Right and Left together, not just in Congress, but around the country.

(See: ComeHomeAmerica.us, edited by George D. O'Neill, Jr. Paul Buhle; Bill Kauffman and Kevin Zeese, Titan Publishing Company [2010].)

Revitalizing the AFL-CIO

May 23, 2011

When Harry Kelber, the relentless 96-year-old labor advocate and editor of the *Labor Educator* speaks, the leadership of the AFL-CIO should listen. A vigorous champion for the rights of rank-and-file workers vis-a-vis their corporate employers and their labor union leaders, Kelber has recently completed a series of five articles titled "The reaction: Silence from union leaders, their union publications and at union gatherings."

Kelber, operating out of a tiny New York City office, knows more firsthand about unions, their historical triumphs, their contemporary deficiencies and their potential for tens of millions of working families than almost anyone in the country. Over the decades, no one has written more widely distributed pamphlets that cogently and concisely explain unions, the labor movement, and anti-worker restrictive laws like the Taft-Hartley Act of 1947, than this honest, sensitive worker campaigner.

At a perilous period for both working and unemployed Americans, facing deep recession, corporate abandonment to China and other repressive regimes, and the Republicans' virulent assault on livelihoods and labor rights, Kelber believes that the AFL-CIO should be on the ramparts. Instead, he sees it as moribund, hunkering down, with control of the power and purse concentrated in the hands of the silent and Sphinx-like Federation officers and the tiny clique of bureaucrats who run the show.

"In the AFL-CIO, the rank-and-file have no voice in electing their officials, because only the candidates of the Old Guard can be on the ballot," he writes.

Certainly, the AFL-CIO is not reflecting the old adage that when "the going gets tough, the tough get going." They recoil from any public criticism of Barack Obama, who disregards and humiliates them by his actions.

Mr. Obama promised labor in 2008 to press for a $9.50 federal minimum wage by 2011, and the "Employee Free Choice Act," especially "card check," and then forgot about both commitments. He has not spoken out or vigorously fought for an adequate OSHA inspection and enforcement budget to diminish the tens of thousands of workplace-related fatalities every year. He's been too busy managing drones, Kandahar and outlying regions of the quagmire of our undeclared wars.

Nothing Obama does seems to publically rile the AFL-CIO. In February, he crossed Lafayette Square from the White House with great fanfare to visit his pro-Republican opponents at the US Chamber of Commerce yet declined to go around the corner and visit the AFL-CIO headquarters. Where was the public objection from the House of Labor?

He prevents his vice-president from responding to the Wisconsin State Federation of Labor's invitation to address the biggest rally in Madison, Wisconsin, protesting labor's arch enemy, Republican Governor Scott Walker. Biden, a self-styled "union guy," wanted to go but the political operatives in the White House said NO. Still no public objection from Labor's leaders.

Kelber describes the lack of a strong, funded national and international strategy to deal with the growing gap between rich and poor and the expanding shipment of both blue- and white-collar jobs abroad. He laments AFL-CIO's failure to develop a "working relation with the new global unions that are challenging transnational corporations and winning some agreements." He also notes that the AFL's top leaders "have minimal influence at world labor conferences. They rarely attend them, even when they are invited."

Pushing for higher wages and workers' rights in the poorer developing countries, including the adoption of International Labor Organization (ILO) standards, has great merit and is also a constructive way to protect American workers.

Kelber believes it is obvious "that US cooperation with labor unions from other countries with the same employer is the best way to organize giant multinationals, but the AFL-CIO has spent little time, money, or resources in building close working relations with unions from abroad."

What is restraining AFL-CIO president Richard Trumka? A former coal miner, then a coal miners' lawyer and president of the United

Mine Workers, Mr. Trumka has been at the Federation for over a decade. He knows the politics of the AFL-CIO, makes great speeches about callous corporatism around the country, and has a useful website detailing corporate greed.

Unfortunately, words aside, he is not putting real, bold muscle behind the needs of America's desperate workers.

He can start by shaking up his bureaucracy and putting forth an emancipation manifesto of democratic reforms, internal to the unions themselves and external to the government and the corporate giants. They all go together.

When I asked Harry Kelber whether there were any unions he admires, he named the fast-growing California Nurses Association (CNA) and the United Electrical Workers.

CNA's executive director Rose Ann DeMoro is on the AFL-CIO Board, and has urged Mr. Trumka to be more aggressive. She has secured his stepped-up support for a Wall Street financial speculation tax that could bring in over $300 billion a year. He may even join her and the nurses in a symbolic picketing of the US Chamber of Commerce headquarters next month.

The ever fundamental Kelber, however, sees a plan B if the AFL-CIO does not change. "Union members should be thinking about creating a new bottom-up labor federation," he urges, reminding them that in the 1930s, the Committee of Industrial Organizations (CIO) seceded from the American Federation of Labor (AFL) and went on "to organize millions of workers in such major corporations as General Motors, General Electric, US Steel, Westinghouse, Hormel, and others."

The new labor federation he envisions for today's times would be controlled by the membership and led by local unions and central labor councils that are impatient with the sluggish leadership of their international union presidents.

Harry Kelber, you epitomize the saying that "the only true aging is the erosion of one's ideals."

(Visit Harry Kelber's website laboreducator.org for more of his insights.)

End the Land Mine Plague
May 16, 2011

Every day around the world, innocent people, many of them children, are killed or injured by millions of unexploded land mines and cluster bombs. Some of the cluster bomblets look like candy or a toy, which attracts a child in a field, orchard, schoolyard, or by the roadside.

Powerful aggressor nations are responsible for most of these anti-personnel weapons being laid from land or by air. Most recently, Libya's rulers laid mines on the outskirts of Ajdabiya as part of its battle against the resistance.

In 2006, Israel laid huge numbers of cluster bombs in southern Lebanon, each of which contains lethal bomblets. For many months after the ceasefire, the United Nations could not get Israel to provide its cluster bomb algorithms to UN experts so they could safely neutralize these heinous weapons. In that period many Lebanese, adults and children, became cluster bomb casualties. (Visit atfl.org and see the Cluster Bomb Victims photo gallery.)

Two broad-based international treaties address the humanitarian necessity to ban both weapons, just as many horrific chemical and biological weapons have been banned for years. For both treaties, one on land mines, and one more recently on cluster bombs, the United States has been the egregious odd man out under both Republican and Democratic administrations.

The 1997 Mine Ban Treaty has been signed by 133 countries, including many US allies. Not the United States, Russia, Israel, and China, all of whom are major producers, users, or sellers of these lethal weapons. As reported by Human Rights Watch, sixty-eight US senators, enough votes to ratify the land mine treaty, have urged President Obama to move on this urgent matter. Sixteen Nobel Peace laureates have urged their fellow laureate, Barack Obama, to live up to the spirit of this award and lead the US in embracing this treaty.

But the permanent government persists, especially when its current president is so preoccupied with all his wars, attacks, incursions, and intrigues with foreign leaders, tribes, clans, and spies.

Presently, the US has a stockpile of ten million land mines. Washington claims it has not used any since the 1991 Gulf War, has not exported any since 1992, and has not produced them since 1997, according to a Reuters report. The federal government also says it spent $1.5 billion since 1993 to help clear landmines and treat accident victims.

The State Department and the Pentagon stall and year after year say they are reviewing US land mine policy. Years pass. Still no decision. One reason is that the US wants flexibility to maintain mines in areas like the demilitarized zone between North and South Korea.

When it comes to the more grisly cluster bombs, the Convention on Cluster Munitions, a treaty banning the use, stockpiling, production, and transfer of cluster munitions and requiring the disassembling and clearing of the remaining stockpiles within ten years, has been signed by 108 nations. It went into effect August 2010 without the signature of the United States.

From Laos to Kosovo and from Chechnya to Iraq, these savage weapons continue their daily devastation. Pictures of the survivors with lost limbs provide evidence of what havoc weapons profiteering and unaccountable bureaucrats can wreak. Some of this unexploded ordnance in Iraq and Afghanistan-Pakistan can be reworked into the dreaded IEDs against US soldiers. Maybe that's a wake-up call for the White House.

Still Obama fiddles and perplexes our allies with his indecision. He displays no such hesitancy about ordering more and more drones to fire on homes, buildings, and vehicles with the imprecision of suspicion that has blown up wedding parties, gatherings of innocent noncombatants, and recently, nine boys collecting firewood for their families.

More and more international civic organizations, often backed by their governments, are working together for a mine-free world. However, sluggishness in Washington can be compared with the speedy innovation by defense firms in the demonic configuration of evermore deadly cluster bombs. Wait and see what nanotechnology can do when basic research moves to application in this violent area.

There is all too much secrecy and too little open discussion in the political and electoral arenas. Obama's annual weapons destruction report does not tell Americans why he refuses to sign either treaty.

Mr. Obama has been to many ceremonies and photo opportunities lately. Perhaps he can reserve some space on his calendar to take a photo with some children seriously maimed by cluster bombs and land mines coupled with an announcement that he will take this next long-overdue step toward disarmament and lessen man's inhumanity to man.

In the meantime, go to Human Rights

Watch's website (http://hrw.org) and sign their anti–land mine letter to President Barack Obama. Then call the White House comment hotline (202-456-1111) and voice your resolve to end this scattered and often invisible scourge plaguing war-torn areas of the world.

"Mad as Hell" in Madison

February 25, 2011

The large demonstrations at the state capitol in Madison, Wisconsin are driven by a middle class awakening to the spectre of its destruction by the corporate reactionaries and their toady, Governor Scott Walker.

For years, the middle class has watched plutocrats stomp on the poor while listening to the two parties exalt the great middle class, but never mentioning the tens of millions of poor Americans. And for years, the middle class was shrinking due significantly to corporate globalization shipping good-paying jobs overseas to repressive dictatorships like China. It took Governor Walker's legislative proposal to do away with most collective bargaining rights for most public employee unions to jolt people to hit the streets.

Republicans take rigged elections awash in corporatist campaign cash seriously. When they win, they aggressively advance their corporate agenda, unlike the wishy-washy Democrats who flutter weakly after a victory. Republicans mean business. A ramrod wins against a straw every time.

Governor Walker won his election, along with other Republicans in Wisconsin, on mass-media driven Tea Party rhetoric. His platform was deceitful enough to get the endorsement of the police and firefighters' unions, which the latter have now indignantly withdrawn.

These unions should have known better. The Walker Republicans were following the Reagan playbook. The air traffic controllers' union endorsed Reagan in 1980. The next year he fired 12,000 of them during a labor dispute. (This made flying unnecessarily dangerous.)

Then Reagan pushed for tax cuts—primarily for the wealthy—which led to larger deficits to turn the screws on programs benefiting the people. Reagan, though opposed to corporate welfare years earlier, not only maintained these taxpayer subsidies but created a government deficit, over eight years, that was twice that of all the accumulated deficits from George Washington to Jimmy Carter.

Maybe the unions that endorsed Walker will soon realize that not even being a "Reagan Democrat" will save them from being losers under the boot of the corporate supremacists.

The rumble of the people in Madison illustrates the following:

1. There is an ideological plan driving these corporatists. They create "useful crises" and then hammer the unorganized people to benefit the wealthy classes. Governor Walker last year gave $140 million in tax breaks to corporations. This fiscal year's deficit is $137 million. Note this oft-repeated dynamic. President Obama caved to the minority party Republicans in Congress last December by going along with the deficit-deepening extension of the huge dollar volume tax cuts for the rich. Now the Republicans want drastic cuts in programs that help the poor.

2. Whatever non-union or private union workers, who are giving ground or losing jobs, think of the sometimes better pay and benefits of unionized public employees, they need to close ranks without giving up their opposition to government waste. Corporate lobbyists and their corporate governments are going after all

collective bargaining rights for every worker and they want to further weaken the National Labor Relations Board.

3. Whenever corporations and government want to cut workers' incomes, the corporate tax abatements, bloated contracts, handouts, and bailouts should be pulled into the public debate. What should go first?

4. The public university students in these rallies might ponder their own tuition bills and high interest loans, compared to students in Western Europe, and question why they have to bear the burden of massive corporate welfare payouts—foodstamps for the rich. What should go first?

5. The bigger picture should be part of the more localized dispute. Governor Walker also wants weaker safety and environmental regulations, as well as bargain-basement sell-outs of state public power plants and other taxpayer assets.

6. The mega-billionaire Koch brothers are in the news. They are bankrolling politicians and rump advocacy groups, and funding media campaigns in Wisconsin and all over the country. Koch Industries designs and builds facilities for the natural gas industry. Neither the company nor the brothers like the publicity they deserve to get every time their role is exposed. Always put the spotlight on the backroom boys.

7. Focusing on the larger struggle between the people and the plutocracy should be part and parcel of every march, demonstration, or any other kind of mass mobilization. The signs at the Madison rallies make the point, to wit—"2/3 of Wisconsin Corporations Pay No Taxes," "Why Should Public Workers Pay For Wall Street's Mess?", "Corporate Greed Did the Deed."

8. Look how little energy it took for these tens of thousands of people to sound the national alarm for hard-pressed Americans. Just showing up is democracy's barn raiser. This should persuade people that a big start for a better America can begin with a little effort and a well-attended rally. Imagine what even more civic energy could produce!

Showing up lets people feel their potential power to subordinate corporatism to the sovereignty of the people. After all, the Constitution's preamble begins with "We the People," not "We the Corporations." In fact, the founders never put the word "corporation" or "company" in our constitution, which was designed for real people.

As for Governor Walker's projected two-year $3.6 billion deficit, read what Jon Peacock of the respected nonprofit Wisconsin Budget Project writes at wisconsinbudgetproject.org about how to handle the state budget *without* adopting the draconian measures now before the legislature.

Civic Institutions Essential for Egypt's Democracy
February 14, 2011

Colman McCarthy, a former *Washington Post* writer and founder of the Center for Teaching Peace, must be very happy with the news from Egypt. For twenty-five years, McCarthy has been persuading high schools and colleges to adopt peace studies into their curriculum. Now he has another example of a largely nonviolent revolution—led by young people of all backgrounds—successfully ousting a dictatorial regime.

The moral power of nonviolence against tyrants is ridiculed by the militaristic mind. Tell that to Gandhi and Mandela and to US civil rights leaders. Those who say these are exceptions due to the relative lower brutality of what they were up against should read the history. Those entrenched regimes were plenty brutal over the years. But when nonviolent protests became organized and disciplined enough to reach critical mass, brutality only strengthened and enlarged the uprisings.

Hosni Mubarak's inadvertent gift to the January 25 Revolution was that he united the protestors beyond class, religious, and ideological lines. His regular oppression over the years led to the April 6, 2008 youth movement and organized labor strikes at textile mills. An auspicious spark came with the Tunisian upheaval of December.

The shaming jolt of immolations in Egypt to overcome widespread fear and reticence to join with others in those frightening early rallies in Cairo's Tahrir Square can scarcely be exaggerated.

The 18 days that shook Egypt will make for fascinating study. The self-discipline and power of mutual self-respect with others locked arm-in-arm tested the regime and the protestors.

First came the security police with tear gas, rubber bullets, concussion grenades and water cannons. The resisters held. Three days later, the police were pulled back and replaced by the respected and familiar army (Egypt has a draft). The soldiers mostly kept a kind of neutral order, but some soldiers showed their support for the demonstrators by allowing them to decorate the tanks with flowers and freedom signs.

February 2 and 3 brought the ominous pro-Mubarak plain-clothesmen into the Square. That drew new resolve among the crowds that vastly outnumbered what they saw as the government's thugs. The protestors held. From then on, bolstered by demonstrations in Alexandria—Egypt's second largest city—Suez and other metropolitan centers, the momentum swung decisively in favor of the rebels whose ranks swelled with each day.

Certainly, Al-Jazeera countered the state-run television to inform the people, almost by the minute, about what was transpiring in the streets. Certainly, the internet kept the protestors in touch with one another, though the government briefly shut it down along with the mobile phone networks.

But far from most cameras, residents organized Cairo's vast neighborhoods to defend and supply themselves. They were the real glue, the real depth that convinced the regime that it was all over.

The fall of Mubarak led to the assumption of power by the Supreme Council of the Armed Forces, which suspended the disliked constitution, dissolved the rubber-stamp Parliament, and announced "free and fair" elections with multi-party candidates in six months. They pledged to remove the despised "emergency law," allowing arrests without charges or trial, and promised immunity for the protestors whom they described as "honest people who refused the corruption and demanded reforms."

Now comes the hard part. Three "cultures" are presently the best organized—the military, commercial and religious groups. Least established is the civic culture that is now, in its revelry and formative stage, the toast of the nation.

But it is the civic-political culture at the urban neighborhood and village levels that will shape the future democratic processes and structures to avert falling back into a military-oligarchic concentration of power—one backed by the same old US support for authoritarian stability over democracy. "Much of the old regime remains," wrote David Porter, author of "On Leaderless Revolutions."

As the *New York Times* columnist Nicholas D. Kristof wrote from Cairo, where he once was a university student: "We tie ourselves in knots when we act as if democracy is good for the United States and Israel but not for the Arab world. For far too long, we've treated the Arab world as just an oil field."

The peril for the protestors in the critical next six months is how to keep the momentum of unity going behind a broad universal agenda that would lead to the election without opening up rending sectarian divisions.

In 1990, I was in Moscow as a guest of the Soviet Union's US and Canada Institute just before Boris Yeltsin replaced Mikhail Gorbachev. The audiences were overjoyed at the looming prospect of democracy replacing Soviet dictatorship. I cautioned that there would be a large vacuum, should this occur, and joy and relief should not supplant the creation of civic institutions, independent judiciaries and prosecutors, and the broadest possible civic participation by the people. Otherwise, the vacuum would be filled with forces not to their liking.

Sure enough, authoritarian practices and the corrupt giveaway of Russia's massive natural resources to a dozen oligarchs filled the vacuum.

The Egyptian resistance—politically savvy from dealing with years of repression—is anything but naïve. They know what they have to do and by when, taking nothing for granted. This wariness, they have made clear, includes not taking for granted Washington's sudden praise of their unfolding quest for what President Obama called a "genuine democracy."

Wouldn't it be a surprising change if the Obama administration were to stand resolutely with the workers and peasants in this ancient land of 80 million people?

King's Gamble
January 17, 2011

Bob King, the new president of the United Auto Workers, whose membership is down under 400,000 from a peak of 1.5 million in 1979, is rolling out an initiative to organize foreign auto plants in the US, expand the union's reach overseas, and forge alliances with social justice organizations.

Ordinarily, the response to these ambitions would be "with what?" Few unions have been beaten down as much as the UAW, whose workers are enduring the bankruptcy of General Motors and Chrysler in 2009 and a debt-burdened Ford Motor company. During this period the UAW gave up billions of dollars in wages and benefits. Thousands of workers were laid off to save these companies.

Well, for starters, Bob King starts with the union's strike fund. It contains over $800 million. "We have really unlimited resources to devote to this. It's unlike anything that's been seen in the UAW in many, many years," King told the *Wall Street Journal*.

King would agree with Labor Professor Harley Shaiken of the University of California, Berkeley, that this "unprecedented effort. . . . is pivotal to its survival." I interpret his remarks to mean that a long declining union has to push forward, or its spirit and ranks will shrink further as automation and the taxpayer-rescued auto makers seize the initiative for more concessions.

The UAW's problems start with those earlier concessions that included the astounding two-tier wage system. New workers start at $14 an hour, less than half of what senior workers are paid. If Bob King cannot offer a better deal for non-unionized workers (108,000 of them) at US factories run by Toyota, Honda, Nissan (where the union failed in an earlier organizing drive), Volkswagen, Hyundai, BMW, Mercedes, and Kia, what is going to be the appeal? To make matters more difficult, most of these plants are in so-called "right-to-work" southern states.

First, King is offering 11 principles of cooperation with the auto companies, eschewing confrontation or disruption on both sides, so long as the elections are free and fair. Second, he is touting the relationships with domestic companies, saying that "the winning team today is the UAW and American employers; with GM, Chrysler and Ford, we are building the best vehicles and have the most productive workplaces."

Soon, however, the UAW begins contract renewal negotiations with these companies, which are recovering both their sales, profits, and stock values. No doubt the members will expect their union to fight for a share of this rebound. It may become acrimonious.

Toyota is not worried at all about the UAW's organizing drive announcement. Company spokesman Mike Goss said that of Toyota's 20,000 US manufacturing plant workers, no hourly employees have ever been laid off, despite the economic downturn. The Big Three US manufacturers have laid off workers in droves, many permanently.

So again, what is Bob King's appeal to an auto worker employed by a foreign manufacturer? It is nice that he wants to enlist the support of various national citizen groups, including Jesse Jackson's PUSH and chapters of the NAACP. That may be good for publicizing equity, but the Toyota, et al. pay packages are fairly equivalent with those of the US manufacturers.

Mr. King may see leverage in his global strategy to connect with overseas unions and agitate for independent unions in Mexico and Brazil to raise auto worker wages there. King is no stranger to social justice movements and protests, having participated personally in marches here and with delegations to El Salvador, Mexico, and other developing countries.

Still, it is difficult to see what he expects to get out of what seems on the surface at least to be an enormous gamble. Of course, there may be much more between the lines here.

My suggestion is that Mr. King and his colleagues spend a weekend at their union retreat in northern Michigan with some other seasoned thinkers and organizers to ponder how most effectively to spend the union's allotted money.

One needed priority is to set up a small ten-person advocacy group in Washington, DC to prod OSHA on worker health and safety. That would increase the AFL-CIO's personnel commitment *tenfold* for advancing OSHA's responsibility to reduce the loss of nearly 60,000 Americans a year due to workplace trauma and disease, including autoworkers.

Out of Afghanistan
July 30, 2010

The war in Afghanistan is nearly nine years old—the longest in American history. After the US quickly toppled the Taliban regime in October 2001, the Taliban, by all accounts, came back stronger and harsher enough to control now at least 30 percent of the country. During this time, US casualties, armaments, and expenditures are at record levels.

America's overseas wars have different outcomes when they have no constitutional authority, no war tax, no draft, no regular on-the-ground press coverage, no Congressional oversight, no spending accountability and, importantly, no affirmative consent of the governed who are, apart from the military families, hardly noticing.

This is an asymmetrical, multi-matrix war. It is a war defined by complex intrigue, shifting alliances, mutating motivations, chronic bribery, remotely-generated civilian deaths, insuperable barriers of language, and ethnic and subtribal conflicts. It is fought by warlords, militias, criminal gangs, and Special Forces discretionary death squads. Millions of civilians are impoverished and terrified, living with violent disruptions. There is no central government to speak of. The White House uses illusions of strategies and tactics to bid for time. In Afghanistan, the historic graveyard of invaders, hope springs infernal.

Neatly dressed generals—who probably would never have gotten into this mess if they, not the civilian neocon draft dodgers in the Bush regime, had made the call—regularly trudge up to Congress to testify. There they caveat their status reports, keeping expectations alive, while cowardly politicians praise their bravery. General David Petraeus could receive an Oscar in Hollywood next year, as long as he doesn't say what he really thinks, obedient soldier that he is. Listen to General Stanley A. McChrystal, not known for his squeamishness. Speaking of civilian deaths and injuries at military checkpoints, he said: "We have shot an amazing number of people, but to my knowledge, none have ever proven to be a threat."

On the ground are 100,000 US soldiers with another 100,000 corporate contractors. The human and economic costs are huge. According to the CIA, James Jones—Obama's national security adviser—and other officials, there are only fifty to one hundred al-Qaeda operatives in Afghanistan and 300 to 400 members of the group in Pakistan. The rest have scattered to other nations or just melded back into the population. Affiliates of al-Qaeda have emerged in the southern Arabian peninsula, Somalia, North Africa, Indonesia, and other locales. There is something awry about this asymmetry.

The Taliban number no more than 30,000 irregular fighters of decidedly mixed motivations who are entirely focused over there, not toward the US mainland. President Obama describes the Taliban as "a blend of hard-core ideologues, tribal leaders, kids that basically sign up because it's the best job available to them. Not all of them are going to be thinking the same way about the Afghan government, about the future of Afghanistan. And so we're going to have to sort through how these talks take place."

Helping Obama "sort through" are drones blowing up civilian gatherings—by mistake, of course—to destroy suspected militants often casually chosen by other natives because of grudges or the transfer of money. Helicopter gunships and fighter planes spread havoc and terror through the populace. "Special forces" go deeper into Pakistan with their secret missions of mayhem. Local resentment and anger continues to boomerang against the US occupiers.

US Army truckloads of hundred-dollar bills are paying off various personages of uncertain reliability. At the same time, Obama's representatives regularly accuse President Karzai of rampant corruption. In between, civilian Americans and USAID try to dig wells and construct clinics and schools that might not be there very long in the anarchic, violent, nightfall world of the Afghan tribal areas.

More military force is expected to clear the way for the assumption of Afghan-run duties and security in 2014 by a central government that is neither central nor governmental. The locals loathe the government's attempt to collect taxes, and continue to survive by growing poppies (opium).

In early 2001, George W. Bush awarded the Taliban $40 million for stamping out the poppy trade; Afghanistan is now the number one narco grower in the world. US soldiers walk right past the poppy fields so as not to turn the locals against them.

US dollars pay warlords and the Taliban in order for them not to blow up US convoys going through mountain passes, some carrying fuel that costs taxpayers $400 per delivered gallon. The Taliban receive half the electricity from a US-built power plant and collect the monthly electric bills in their controlled areas. The more electricity, the more money for the Taliban to fight the American and British soldiers.

Last year, over three billion dollars in cash moved *out* of Kabul's airport unaccounted for, while billions of US dollars flow *into* Kabul for undocumented purposes.

Despite fighting against "insurgents" possessing rifles, rocket-propelled grenades, and suicide vests, the Obama administration—with an arsenal of massive super-modern weaponry at hand—keeps saying there is no military solution and that only a political settlement will end the conflict.

Tell that to the Afghan people, who suffer from brutal sectarian struggles fueled by American and coalition occupiers and invaders. To them, there's a disconnect between what Obama does and what he says he wants.

Meanwhile, the war spills ever more into Pakistan, and its turbulent politics generates more hatred against Americans. These people had nothing to do with 9/11, so why, they ask, are the Americans blowing up their neighborhood?

President Obama says the soldiers should start coming home in July 2011, depending on conditions on the ground. He wants the Taliban commanders, whom he is destroying one by one, to agree to negotiations with Kabul that require their subservience. His formula is peace through more war. But the Taliban are not known to surrender. They know the terrain where they live and they believe they can wear Obama down, notwithstanding US Special Forces and drones expected to stay there for years.

Congress—an inkblot so far—needs to assert its constitutional authority over budgets and policy toward the war. Members are regular rubberstamps of White House recklessness under Bush and Obama.

Furthermore, nothing will happen without a few million Americans back home stomping, marching, and bellowing to end the boomeranging, costly invasions of Iraq and Afghanistan and concentrate on America's needs at home.

The Miserable State of Mine Safety
April 9, 2010

The tragedy at the Massey Energy Company's very profitable Upper Big Branch coal mine at Montcoal, West Virginia, which so far has cost 25 miners' lives, is another reminder of the immense human and environmental cost of this fuel.

More coal miners have lost their lives from cave-ins, explosions, and lung disease since 1900 than all the Americans who died in World War II. The devastation extends to chronic sickness from breathing coal dust and to maimed coal miners, often seen walking on crutches in the hollows of Appalachia.

During our struggle in the late sixties and seventies to get Congress to authorize the federal government to regulate these pugnacious corporations, and protect some of the most defenseless workers in our country (try working 700 to 1800 feet underground six days a week), coal company executives perpetuated a culture tolerant of safety violations. Coal companies are known for greasing their way with political campaign contributions, gross underpayments of property taxes, and intimidation of people in poor coal mining country who had few alternative employment opportunities.

Safety and health improvements finally came from the forces of the law (especially the Coal Mine Health and Safety Act of 1969) and from an awakened United Mine Workers union. The safety efforts have had to overcome industry lawyers, lobbyists, corporate cover-ups, refusals to pay fines, and other misbehavior stemming from unaccountable corporate bosses sitting in fancy offices far from the coal fields.

Half of the nation's coal companies were fined a modest total of $7 million under the first Bush administration for faking coal dust samples in 847 underground mines. This is just a cost of doing business instead of a serious deterrent to an epidemic of coal miners' deadly pneumoconiosis.

Until new leadership came under Joseph Main in 2009 to run the Mine Safety and Health Administration (MSHA), Richard L. Trumka, former coal miner and head of the United Mine Workers (UMW) union and now president of the AFL-CIO, said that George W. Bush converted "MSHA from an enforcement agency to a business consulting group" to King Coal.

With the sharp decline of UMW workers, as non-union strip-mining expands, studies have shown a consistently better safety record of unionized coal mines. The devastated Massey mine was non-union.

The media, which rushes to the scene of mining disasters while ignoring interim warning reports such as ours in 2008, knew who to interview. He was Massey's defiant, outspoken, arrogant CEO Don Blankenship, whose Montcoal mine was cited by MSHA over 500 times in 2009-2010 for safety violations, including the kinds of violations suspected in the explosion on April 5th. Two citations came on the very day of the calamity. The paltry $1 million in fines covered more than fifty "unwarrantable failure" violations. Among the most serious were citations for problems with escape routes and air quality ventilation.

In 2006, another Massey mine, Aracoma Alma No. 1, was recommended for shutdown by a government inspector, who was overruled. The subsequent fire killed two miners and led to a guilty plea for 10 criminal mine safety violations, a $2.5 million fine. Massey also paid the federal government $20 million to settle charges of violating water pollution controls in 2008.

J. Davitt McAteer, the former MSHA administrator, called the Massey conglomerate "certainly one of the worst in the industry" from a safety standpoint. CEO Blankenship, of course, denies McAteer's and other workers' and inspectors' assessments. "Violations are unfortunately a normal part of the mining process. There are violations at every coal mine in America."

Tell that to the grieving families, some of whom yelled at Blankenship while twelve protective police officers were whisking him away from the mine site.

People in West Virginia fear Blankenship not just because of his verbal belligerence, his intimidation of critics and workers, and his sway with campaign financed politicians and judges, but also because they believe he can get away with abuses of power, that he is beyond the reach of the law.

This time, however, the combative, anti-regulatory Blankenship is in a tight spot, what with Massey's stock dropping and his carefully cultivated image of tough-guy sometime-philanthropist increasingly tarnished under a national media spotlight he cannot control or bully.

West Virginia law defines "involuntary manslaughter" as "the accidental causing of death of another person, although unintended, whose death is the proximate result of negligence so gross, wanton, and culpable as to show a reckless disregard for human life."

In the last month, MSHA has filed a dozen citations specifically alleging the mines' failure to properly ventilate the lethal, highly volatile methane gas. That is why affected people are wondering whether any district attorneys will have the will and an adequate budget to charge Massey officials with "involuntary manslaughter," should the findings of the completed investigation meet the statutory definition. For if Blankenship, who really should resign, has anything, he has a battalion of lawyers and accommodating judges with whom to fight back. Time will tell.

Israel & Aid

March 23, 2010

On July 10, 1996, at a Joint Session of the United States Congress, Israeli Prime Minister Benjamin Netanyahu received a standing ovation for these words: "With America's help, Israel has grown to be a powerful, modern state. . . . But I believe there can be no greater tribute to America's long-standing economic aid to Israel than for us to be able to say: we are going to achieve economic independence. We are going to do it. In the next four years, we will begin the long-term process of gradually reducing the level of your generous economic assistance to Israel."

Since 1996, the American taxpayers are still sending Israel $3 billion a year and providing assorted loan guarantees, waivers, rich technology transfers, and other indirect assistance. Before George W. Bush left office, a memorandum of understanding between the US and Israel stipulated an assistance package of $30 billion over the next ten years to be transferred in a lump sum at the beginning of every fiscal year. Israel's wars and unlawful colonies still receive US taxpayer monies.

What happened to Mr. Netanyahu's solemn pledge to Congress? The short answer is that Congress never called in the pledge.

In the intervening years, Israel has become an economic, technological, and military juggernaut. Its GDP is larger than Egypt's, even though Israel's population is less than one tenth that of the Arab world's most populous nation. The second-largest number of listings on America's NASDAQ Exchange, after US companies, are from Israel, exceeding listings of Japan, Korea, China, and India combined. Its venture capital investments exceed those in the US, Europe and China on a per capita basis.

Israel is arguably the fifth most powerful military force in the world, and Israel's claims on the US's latest weapon systems and research/development breakthroughs are unsurpassed. This combination has helped to make Israel a major arms exporter.

The Israeli "economic miracle" and technological innovations have spawned articles and a best-selling book in recent months. The country's average GDP growth rate has exceeded the average rate of most Western countries over the past five years. Israel provides universal health insurance, unlike the US, which raises the question: who should be aiding whom?

Keep in mind, the US economy is mired in a recession, with large rates of growing poverty, unemployment, consumer debt, and state and federal deficits. In some states, public schools are closing, public health services are being slashed, and universities are increasing tuition while also cutting programs. Even state government buildings are being sold off.

Under specific US law, military sales to Israel cannot be used for offensive purposes, only for "legitimate self-defense." Nonetheless, there have been numerous violations of the Arms Export Control Act by Israel. Even the indifferent State Department has found, from time to time, that munitions such as cluster bombs were "likely violations."

Violations would lead to a cut-off in aid, but with the completely pro-Israel climate in Washington, the White House has never allowed such findings to be definitive.

The same indifference applies to violations of the US Foreign Assistance Act that prohibits aid to countries engaging in consistent international human rights violations. These include the occupation, colonization, blockades, and military assaults on civilians in the Palestinian West Bank and Gaza, regularly documented by the highly regarded Israeli human rights group B'Tselem, as well as by Amnesty International and Human Rights Watch.

This week, Prime Minister Netanyahu visits President Barack Obama after the recent Israeli announcement of 1,600 new housing units in East Jerusalem, made while Vice President Joe Biden was visiting that country.

The affront infuriated the *New York Times* columnist Tom Friedman, who wrote that Mr. Biden should have packed his bags and flown away leaving behind a scribbled note saying "You think you can embarrass your only true ally in the world, to satisfy some domestic political need, with no consequences? You have lost total contact with reality."

Friedman, a former *Times* Middle East correspondent, concluded his rebuke by writing: "Palestinian leaders Mahmoud Abbas and Salam Fayyad are as genuine and serious about working toward a solution as any Israel can hope to find."

But until a few days ago, the US government had no levers over the Israeli government. Cutting off aid isn't even whispered in the halls of Congress. Raising the issue would further galvanize Israel's allies, including AIPAC.

The only lever left for the US suddenly erupted into the public media a few days ago. General David Petraeus told the Senate that resolving the Israeli-Palestinian conflict has foreign policy and national security ramifications for the United States.

He said that "the conflict foments anti-American sentiment, due to a perception of US favoritism for Israel. Arab anger over the Palestinian question limits the strength and depth of US partnerships with governments and peoples in the area of responsibility (. . .) meanwhile, al-Qaeda and other military groups exploit that anger to mobilize support."

A few days earlier, Vice President Joe Biden told Prime Minister Netanyahu in Israel that "what you're doing here undermines the security of our troops who are fighting in Iraq, Afghanistan, and Pakistan."

What Obama's people are publically starting to say is that regional peace is about US vital interests in that large part of the Middle East and, ultimately, the safety of American soldiers and personnel.

As one retired diplomat commented, "This could be a game-changer."

Privatization Profiteering
January 15, 2010

Whenever Frank Anderson speaks the way he did at a recent public forum in Washington, DC about "essential state functions performed by businesses," people better listen. Anderson is the president of the Middle East Policy Council, but previously he was the chief of the Near East and South Asia Division of the CIA.

A discussion—relayed over C-SPAN—featuring Mr. Anderson was among established scholars and policy wonks focused on national security in that tumultuous area of the world. Mr. Anderson was asked about Blackwater, the controversial corporation whose profits come from Pentagon and State Department contracts to provide security to US government personnel in West and Central Asia and to perform such secret operations that it could have an identity crisis with the CIA.

Blackwater has gotten in trouble for shooting up Iraqi civilians in unprovoked situations. The corporation's operatives are involved in sensitive missions, such as the recent double-agent suicide explosion in Afghanistan. Again and again, the line between corporate and governmental functions is not only blurred, it has ceased to exist.

Rep. Jan Schakowsky (D-Ill.) called Blackwater a "repeat offender endangering our mission repeatedly, endangering the lives of our military, and costing the lives of innocent civil-

ians." She asked why Blackwater is employed anywhere by the US government.

Outsourcing national security activities, right down to interviewing job applicants for intelligence agencies, is troubling many retired and active members of the national defense and security agencies. Yet corporate contracting, launched big-time by Ronald Reagan, seems unstoppable. There are more contractors in Iraq and Afghanistan than there are US soldiers. Over 200,000 of them and counting.

The rationale for these contracts is that they provide (1) greater efficiency, (2) greater talent, and (3) more flexible personnel in and out whenever they are needed.

First, throw out the tax dollar savings argument. Mr. Anderson estimates that the costs are two to three times more when corporations do the work. Other estimates are higher, even when non-deliveries, contaminated food and drinking water, and embezzlements and fraud that keep Pentagon auditors awake at night, are not included.

Government acquisition specialists accuse politicians of creating layers and layers of contractors with their massive, convoluted contracts dissipating accountability. It is a Kafkaesque nightmare of corporate statism. Of course, all this has led to a government brain and skill drain over to the corporate sector, which pays so much more than the government. A vicious cycle of incapacity and hollowing-out sets in and allows the governmental departments to rationalize more outsourcing.

"No way that we should have allowed businessmen to perform essential state functions," said Mr. Anderson, especially, he added, in the areas of "intelligence and the application of violence."

At the same forum, Bruce Riedel, senior fellow in foreign policy at the Brookings Institution and former CIA officer and specialist in

Middle East Affairs, agreed with Mr. Anderson, bemoaning more and more layers of reviews and contracts.

Messrs. Anderson and Riedel are not loners. Their views often reflect a larger circle of governmental professionals who have seen the wholesale stampede of contracting out government from DOD, CIA, USAID, and NASA. The Congress is sort of looking into this mindlessness that is swelling deficits and escaping standards of public service and ethics. The prospects for change? Mr. Anderson said "fixing this would require revolutionary changes." That objective can only come from the proverbial people—aroused and determined. If that does not happen, what Franklin Delano Roosevelt called fascism in 1938—that is, corporate control of government—will tighten its very costly grip.

The corporate government mentality is not restricted to Washington, DC. State governments are also outsourcing with similar—though lesser—waste, fraud, and escape from accountability.

Just last week, Virginia's incoming governor, Robert F. McDonnell, announced that he will let his Cabinet secretaries have dual allegiances by serving on commercial corporate boards of directors. Virginia is one of the states that permits this in built conflict of interest between duty to the citizens and loyalty to specific corporate profit.

So his new Secretary of Commerce and Trade, Robert Sledd, will continue to sit on three corporate boards. In his day job, Sledd is responsible for thirteen agencies that regulate business policy, according to the *Washington Post*. On the side, he sits on the board of a tobacco company and a medical supplies business.

Down in Arizona, a new slide toward the pits is about to occur. Beset with a large state deficit, the state officials and their governor re-fuse to end corporate welfare and corporate tax abatements and subsidies. Instead—get this—they have put "for sale" signs on Arizona's state buildings, hoping to realize $735 million and then start paying the buyers rent! (Breaking news—they've got a sale!)

Also up for sale, among other structures, go the legislative buildings, the Department of Public Safety, the prisons, and the state Coliseum. Organizational psychiatrists and efficiency economists, please help us understand.

Wouldn't it have been better for the state legislators to just sell the back of their jackets to corporate advertisers? Then, at least, there would be truth in advertising!

For a regular stream of news about privatization, visit privatizationwatch.org

"Just War" Is Just Words
December 11, 2009

President Obama, the Afghan war escalator, received the Nobel Peace Prize in Oslo, Norway, and proceeded to deliver his acceptance speech outlining the three criteria for a "just war" which he himself is violating.

The criteria are, in his words: "If it is waged as a last resort or in self-defense; if the force used is proportional; and if, whenever possible, civilians are spared from violence."

After 9/11, warmonger George W. Bush could have used the international law doctrine of hot pursuit with a multilateral force of commandoes, linguists, and bribers to pursue the backers of the attackers. Instead, he blew the country of Afghanistan apart and started occupying it, joined forces with a rump regime, and launched a divide-and-rule tribal strategy that set the stage for a low-tiered civil war.

Eight years later, Obama is expanding the war within a graft-ridden government in Kabul, fraudulent elections, an Afghan army of northern tribesmen loathed by the southern and southeastern tribes of 40 million Pashtuns, an impoverished economy whose largest crop by far is a narcotic, and a devastated population embittered by foreign occupiers and nonexistent government services.

President Obama's national security adviser, former Marine General James Jones, said two months ago: "The al-Qaeda presence is very diminished. The maximum estimate is less than one hundred operating in the country, no bases, no ability to launch attacks on either us or our allies."

Since Mr. Obama repeats George W. Bush's reason for going into Afghanistan—to destroy al-Qaeda—why is he sending 30,000 more soldiers plus an even greater number of corporate contractors there in the near future at a cost stated by the White House of $1 million per solider per year? Is this "proportional force"?

Always small in number, al-Qaeda has moved over the border into Pakistan and anywhere its supporters can in the world—East Africa, North Africa, Indonesia. The gang is a migrant traveler.

Is Obama pouring soldiers into Afghanistan so that they and our inaccurate, civilian-destroying drones can expand the fighting across the border in Pakistan, as indicated by the *New York Times*? Beyond the violations of international law and absence of constitutional authorization involved, this could so roil Pakistanis as to make the US experience next door look like a modest struggle.

Obama has emphasized weakening the Taliban as the other objective of our military buildup with its horrible consequence in casualties and other costs. Who are the Taliban? They include people with different causes, such as protecting their valleys, drug trafficking to live on, fighting against foreign occupiers or, being mostly Pashtuns, protecting their tribal turf against the northern Tajiks and Uzbeks.

How many Taliban fighters are there? The Pentagon estimates around 25,000. Their methods make them unpopular with the villagers. They have no air force, navy, artillery, tanks, missiles, no bases, no central command. They have rifles, grenade launchers, bombs and suiciders. Unlike al-Qaeda, they have only domestic ambitions, counteracted by their adversarial tribesmen who make up most of the Afghan army.

Robert Baer, a former CIA officer with experience in that part of Asia, asserted: "The people that want their country liberated from the West have nothing to do with al-Qaeda. They simply want us gone because we're foreigners, and they're rallying behind the Taliban because the Taliban are experienced, effective fighters."

To say, as Obama inferred in his Oslo speech, that the greater plunge into Afghanistan is self-defense with proportional force and sparing civilians from violence, is a scale of self-delusion or political cowardliness that is dejecting his liberal base.

For, as President Eisenhower stated so eloquently in his 1953 "Cross of Iron" speech, every dollar spent on munitions and saber-rattling takes away from building schools, clinics, roads and other necessities for the American people.

The Afghan War and the Iraq War-occupation—already directly costing a trillion dollars—are costing the American people every time Washington says there is not enough money for neonatal care, occupational disease prevention, cleaner drinking water systems, safer hospitals, prosecution of corporate criminals, cleaner air, or upgrading and repairing key public facilities.

Even the hardiest and earliest supporters of Obama's presidential campaign in 2008 are speaking out. Senior members of the Congressional Black Caucus, such as John Conyers (D-Mich.) and Maxine Waters (D-Calif.), have recently criticized the president for not doing enough to help African Americans weather the hard times.

In a stinging, ironic rebuke to the first African-American president, Rep. Waters declared, "We can no longer afford for our public policy to be defined by the worldview of Wall Street."

According to Congressman Conyers, an upset Barack Obama called to ask why the Michigan lawmaker was "demeaning" him. Conyers has been increasingly turned off by the president's policies—among them healthcare reform, the war in Afghanistan, slippage on Guantanamo and the extension of the Patriot Act's invasive provisions.

The 80-year old Congressman spent most weekends in 2007 and 2008 on the campaign trail tirelessly trying to get Obama elected.

White House aides are not troubled by the rumblings from the moderate left. They said they have all of 2010 to bring them back into the fold by the November Congressional elections. Besides, where else are they going to go?

Well, they could stay home. Remember 1994 and the Gingrich takeover.

Challenging China

November 24, 2009

There was something both sad and strange about President Obama's weak presence in China last week.

Sad, because he arrived with no seeming goals and left empty-handed just after visiting the ancient Great Wall, which he said gave him a perspective on time.

Strange, because he allowed the Chinese rulers to quarantine his stops from the Chinese people—whether in person or on television. His main public meeting was with young Communist League students who came with scripted questions.

All the outward signs were that Mr. Obama had no cards to play. The US is by far the world's biggest debtor. It was hard to challenge his Chinese hosts, who made crisp mention of our government's deep deficits and deficit spending. They did not have to describe our weakened economy, its declining dollar, and the huge indebtedness that the US has with its Chinese creditors. Everybody knows how rickety America's global financial situation is.

Of course, we do not know what went on in the private discussions between Mr. Obama and his Chinese counterparts. Suffice it to say that the president could not have gotten very far on the undervaluation of the yuan, the gross inequities in the trading rules, and hazardous practices from China's exports to its biggest customer on the other side of the Pacific.

Had Obama raised the major trade, investment, military and security issues of conflict with China depicted in the just-released 2009 Report to Congress of the US-China Economic and Security Review Commission, the chilly reception that China's leaders accorded him in public would have turned decidedly frosty. (For the full report, visit www.uscc.gov.)

David Shambaugh, director of the China Policy Program at George Washington University, praised the US-China joint statement as being "filled with multiple tangible areas of cooperation." The statement, however, is mere words without any binding details.

On the minus side, Mr. Shambaugh was unsparing. He said: "The failures lay in how the president spent his time in China. Not interacting with Chinese people, not giving an uncensored nationally televised speech, not visiting any civic organizations or businesses, not visiting a wind farm or clean-energy firm, not meeting human rights lawyers or activists, and not meeting with the American business or scholarly community must all be counted as failures. He did not send positive signals in these areas—but the Chinese government did not permit it and the American side did not insist on it."

This first trip to China by Mr. Obama was a lost opportunity in three ways that cannot be excused, no matter the absence of proactive status and power.

First, the US is China's biggest consumer, and it has not been treated well. Contaminated fish, dangerous ingredients in medicines, defective tires, and lead-contaminated products are some of the continuing problems that have cost American lives and health.

Mr. Obama should have concluded a pending consumer protection treaty with China requiring access to their laboratories, factories, and exporters for product inspection and certification. Such a treaty should include safeguards against importation of counterfeit goods and subject Chinese companies who want to do business in our country to our laws of tort and contract in our courts.

Second, there should be a bilateral agreement focused on the enormous rush of air pollution coming from China over the Pacific carried by the prevailing winds. China is opening two large electricity-generating coal plants every week, and Korea, Japan, and North America are suf-

fering the effects, along with the effects of emissions from huge belching factories. This agreement would be helpful, now that the Copenhagen Conference has been consigned to rhetoric and exhortation, in paving the way for greater cooperation on acid rain, acidification of the ocean and, of course, climate change.

China is worried about our deficits. We should be worrying about their emissions.

Third, a long-overdue pact regarding infectious diseases is needed. Many Americans over the decades have lost their lives from influenza sourced out of China. The virus is passed in China from pigs to farmers, who live in very close proximity, over to the rest of the world.

China learned from the SARS epidemic of 2003 how economically damaging secrecy can be. But it still needs to be more cooperative with international early alert systems. The government needs to allow more American infectious disease specialists to work with their Chinese counterparts full-time in China.

A major expansion of cooperative facilities, detection and data analysis, tests, and other anti-epidemic initiatives that together can save millions of lives in the future, both in China and the US, is an urgent priority.

Maybe Mr. Obama spoke privately about these matters. But that is a sign of weakness. He owed the American people some public energy and leadership in Beijing to protect them—as consumers—from these fallouts of corporate globalization, since he clearly did not move to protect them as workers.

Why and to What End in Afghanistan

November 3, 2009

Matthew P. Hoh, a former US combat Marine captain, Department of Defense civilian in Iraq starting in 2004 and, until September, a political officer in the Foreign Service stationed in Afghanistan, is giving some consternation to President Obama's advisors as the commander in chief considers sending more soldiers to that war-torn country next to Pakistan.

Mr. Hoh wrote a letter of resignation to the State Department in September. His four-page letter frames his doubts about what he said is the "why and to what end" behind "the strategic purposes of the United States' presence in Afghanistan." He notes that like the Soviets' nine year occupation, "we continue to secure and bolster a failing state, while encouraging an ideology and system of government unknown and unwanted by its people."

Mr. Hoh focuses on the giant Pashtun society composed of 42 million people and moves to his conclusions. Read his words:

"The Pashtun insurgency, which is composed of multiple, seemingly infinite, local groups, is fed by what is perceived by the Pashtun people as a continued and sustained assault, going back centuries, on Pashtun land, culture, traditions, and religion by internal and external enemies. The US and NATO presence and operations in Pashtun valleys and villages, as well as Afghan army and police units that are led and composed of non-Pashtun soldiers and police, provide an occupation force against which the insurgency is justified. In both RC East and South, I have observed that the bulk of the insurgency fights not for the white banner of the Taliban, but rather against the presence of foreign soldiers and taxes imposed by an unrepresentative government in Kabul.

"The United States military presence in Afghanistan greatly contributes to the legitimacy and strategic message of the Pashtun insurgency. In a like manner, our backing of the Afghan government in its current form continues to distance the government from the people. The Afghan government's failings, particularly when weighed against the sacrifice of American lives and dollars, appear legion and metastatic:

- Glaring corruption and unabashed graft;

- A president whose confidants and chief advisers comprise drug lords and war crimes villains, who mock our own rule of law and counternarcotics efforts;

- A system of provincial and district leaders constituted of local power brokers, opportunists, and strongmen allied to the United States solely for, and limited by, the value of our USAID and CERP contracts and whose own political and economic interests stand nothing to gain from any positive or genuine attempts at reconciliation; and

- The recent election process, dominated by fraud and discredited by low voter turnout, which has created an enormous victory for our enemy who now claims a popular boycott and will call into question worldwide our government's military, economic and diplomatic support for an invalid and illegitimate Afghan government.

"Our support for this kind of government,

coupled with a misunderstanding of the insurgency's true nature, reminds me horribly of our involvement with South Vietnam; an unpopular and corrupt government we backed at the expense of our Nation's own internal peace, against an insurgency whose nationalism we arrogantly and ignorantly mistook as a rival to our own Cold War ideology.

"I find specious the reasons we ask for bloodshed and sacrifice from our young men and women in Afghanistan. If honest, our stated strategy of securing Afghanistan to prevent al-Qaeda resurgence or regrouping would require us to additionally invade and occupy western Pakistan, Somalia, Sudan, Yemen, etc. Our presence in Afghanistan has only increased destabilization and insurgency in Pakistan where we rightly fear a toppled or weakened Pakistani government may lose control of its nuclear weapons. However, again, to follow the logic of our stated goals, we should garrison Pakistan, not Afghanistan. More so, the September 11th attacks, as well as the Madrid and London bombings, were primarily planned and organized in Western Europe; a point that highlights the threat is not one tied to traditional geographic or political boundaries. Finally, if our concern is for a failed state crippled by corruption and poverty and under assault from criminal and drug lords, then if we bear our military and financial contributions to Afghanistan, we must reevaluate and increase our commitment to and involvement in Mexico.

"Eight years into war, no nation has ever known a more dedicated, well trained, experienced and disciplined military as the US Armed Forces. I do not believe any military force has ever been tasked with such a complex, opaque and Sisyphean mission as the US military has received in Afghanistan . . .

'We are spending ourselves into oblivion' a very talented and intelligent commander, one of America's best, briefs every visitor, staff delegation and senior officer. We are mortgaging our nation's economy on a war, which, even with increased commitment, will remain a draw for years to come. Success and victory, whatever they may be, will be realized not in years, after billions more spent, but in decades and generations. The United States does not enjoy a national treasury for such success and victory . . .

"Thousands of our men and women have returned home with physical and mental wounds, some that will never heal or will only worsen with time. The dead return only in bodily form to be received by families who must be reassured their dead have sacrificed for a purpose worthy of futures lost, love vanished, and promised dreams unkept. I have lost confidence such assurances can anymore be made. As such, I submit my resignation." (See: http://www.washingtonpost. com/wp srv/hp/ssi/wpc/ResignationLetter.pdf)

Will Mr. Hoh's highly-regarded experience, sensitivity and judgment reach the attention of millions of Americans? That will depend on whether President Obama meets with him, whether Congressional committees will provide a hearing for him and others of similar persuasion, and whether the mass media will suspend their dittoheading and trivia long enough to report these views, so that we the people can deliberate better about avoiding a devastating, worsening quagmire replete with serial tragedies over there and boomerangs back here.

Back in the USA
July 17, 2009

On July 30th, an American manufacturer in China and Korea will officially announce the move of its tool manufacturing facilities to Houston, Texas. Farouk Systems will open a factory with the goal of creating 1277 jobs at a new 189,000 square foot facility in the South's largest metropolis.

Farouk Shami, founder and executive chairman, says the new plant will manufacture "three of its top-selling flat irons and two top-selling hair dryers, of which the company sells over three million a year."

How can this be? Thousands of American companies—electronic, machinery, auto supply, and many other sectors—have rushed to the communist dictatorship of China in the past two decades to take advantage of repressed labor and the relative freedom to pollute and get away with activities banned in the USA. Millions of American jobs and hundreds of communities have suffered due to this exodus.

Why are Mr. Shami and his colleagues returning to the USA?

Company officials gave several economic reasons. First, new super-automation in the US increases worker productivity far beyond productivity in China. Second, the company was experiencing levels of product defects in China that were costly. Third, the increased costs of transportation—bottlenecks to Chinese ports and the burden of crossing the Pacific—helped to level the cost playing-field.

Farouk Systems' lowest wages will be $10.00 per hour, or $2.75 higher than the new federal minimum wage effective this month.

The firm expects to have 1,277 employees by the end of this year and intends to expand further into the production of small home appliance such as blenders, toasters, coffee makers, vacuum cleaners and clothing irons.

Mr. Shami—a Palestinian immigrant of considerable entrepreneurial exuberance—says that this move from China "will enable us to assure the best quality, safest, and lead-free products, and also will help reverse the outsourcing trend by bringing manufacturing back to the USA in order to stimulate the American economy."

Is this a harbinger of a trend against industrial flight from our country? That remains to be seen. What is more certain is that trade relations between China and the US challenge the ideology of "win-win" free trade.

The US trade deficit with China has deepened over the last quarter-century. In 1985, the trade deficit was $6 billion. In 1995, China sold us over $33 billion more than we sold to China. In 2005, the trade deficit ballooned to over $202 billion dollars. Last year, it zoomed to $268 billion.

Imagine exporting so many jobs to a country which has sold us contaminated fish, defective tires, hazardous materials for medicines and housing, and lead-tainted products—to name a few of the hazardous products shipped past the porous portals of the USDA, the Food and Drug Administration, and the Customs Service.

In addition, as detailed regularly in the reports of the US-China Economic and Security Review Commission (www.uscc.gov) there are the manipulated undervaluing of China's currency, import barriers, violations of the World Trade Organization's rules, and other trade-distorting measures that tilt the balance heavily in China's favor.

What is the US getting out of this continually deteriorating imbalance of trade and its accompanying technology transfer to a nation that admits it has not had much success in curbing the large volume of counterfeit goods that are exported? Huge indebtedness. China does loan us money, to finance our huge deficits.

Established "free trade" economists like retired MIT professor Paul Samuelson are re-thinking the classical principles of free trade and comparative advantage. When the advantages of capital, labor and technology are heavily with one trading partner, "absolute advantage" replaces "comparative advantage." With such conditions, the 19th century metaphor of trading Portuguese wine for British textiles is not operative.

So anemic is the US government that it cannot even enforce a 15-year-old memorandum of cooperation that relates to detecting any Chinese prison labor exports to the United States, which would be WTO-illegal. China has repeatedly violated the bilateral agreement to grant permission for US authorities to visit suspect prison labor sites.

Any demand or request that Congress and the White House re-evaluate this kind of systemically unfair trade with dictatorial regimes is met with the chorus of "free trade, free trade" and the riposte of "protectionism." Dogmatic proponents of corporate-managed trade masquerading as free trade reject "options for revision," no matter what the evidence.

Punishing the Palestinians

January 16, 2009

In the tortured sixty-year history of the Palestinian expulsion from their lands, Congress has maintained that it is always the Palestinians, the Palestinian Authority, and now Hamas who are to blame for all hostilities and their consequences with the Israeli government.

The latest illustration of this Washington puppet show, backed by the most modern weapons and billions of taxpayer dollars annually sent to Israel, was the grotesquely one-sided resolution whisked through the Senate and the House of Representatives.

While a massive bombing and invasion of Gaza was underway, the resolution blaming Hamas for all the civilian casualties and devastation—99 percent inflicted on Palestinians—zoomed through the Senate by voice vote and through the House by a vote of 390 to 5, with 22 legislators voting present.

There is more dissent against this destruction of Gaza among the Israeli people, in the Knesset, the Israeli media, and Jewish-Americans than among the dittoheads on Capitol Hill.

The reasons for such near-unanimous support for Israeli actions—no matter how often they are condemned by peace advocates such as Bishop Desmond Tutu, United Nations resolutions, the World Court, and leading human rights groups inside and outside of Israel—are numerous. The pro-Israeli government lobby and the right-wing Christian evangelicals, lubricated by campaign money of many Political Action Committees (PACs), certainly are key.

There is also more than a little bigotry in Congress against Arabs and Muslims, reinforced by the mass media yahoos who set new records for biased reporting each time this conflict erupts.

The bias is clear. It is always the occupied Palestinians' fault. Right-wingers who would never view the US government as perfect see the Israeli government as never doing anything wrong. Liberals who do not hesitate to criticize the US military somehow view all Israeli military attacks, invasions and civilian devastation as heroic manifestations of Israeli defense.

The inversion of history and the scope of amnesia know no limits. What about the fact that the Israeli government drove Palestinians from their lands in 1947-48, with tens of thousands pushed into the Gaza strip? No problem to Congress.

Then, the fact that the Israeli government cruelly occupied, in violation of UN resolutions, the West Bank and Gaza in 1967 and only removed its soldiers and colonists from Gaza (1.5 million people in a tiny area twice the size of the District of Columbia) in 2005. To Congress, the Palestinians deserved it.

Then when Hamas was freely elected to run Gaza, the Israeli authorities cut off the tax revenues on imports that belonged to the Gaza government. This threw the Gazans into a fiscal crisis—they were unable to pay their civil servants and police.

In 2006, the Israelis added to their unrelieved control of air, water and land around the open-air prison by establishing a blockade. The natives became restless. Under international law, a blockade is an act of war. Primitive rockets, called by "wildly inaccurate" reporters were fired into Israel. During this same period, Israeli soldiers, artillery, and missiles would go into Gaza at will and take far more lives and cause far more injuries than those incurred by those rockets. Civilians—especially children, the infirm, and elderly—died or suffered week after week for lack of medicines, medical equipment, food, electricity, fuel, and water, which were embargoed by the Israelis.

Then the Israeli bombing, followed by the invasion during the past three weeks with what prominent Israeli writer Gideon Levy called "a brutal and violent operation . . . far beyond what was needed for protecting the people in its south." Mr. Levy observed what the president of the United Nations General Assembly, Miguel d'Escoto Brockmann, called a war against "a helpless and defenseless imprisoned population."

The horror of being trapped from fleeing the torrent of the most modern weapons of war from the land, air, and seas is reflected in this passage from Amira Hass, writing in the leading Israeli newspaper Haaretz:

"The earth shaking under your feet, clouds of choking smoke, explosions like a fireworks display, bombs bursting into all-consuming flames that cannot be extinguished with water, mushroom clouds of pinkish-red smoke, suffocating gas, harsh burns on the skin, extraordinary maimed live and dead bodies."

Ms. Hass is pointing to the use of new anti-civilian weapons used on the Gazan people. So far there have been over 1,100 fatalities, many thousands of injuries, and the destruction of homes, schools, mosques, hospitals, pharmacies, granaries, farmers' fields, and many critical public facilities. The clearly marked UN headquarters and UN school were smashed, along with stored medicines and food supplies.

Why? The Congressional response: "Hamas terrorists" everywhere. Sure, defending their Palestinian families is called terrorism. The truth is there is no Hamas army, airforce, and navy up against the fourth most powerful military in the world. As one Israeli gunner on an armored personnel carrier frankly said to the New York Times: "They are villagers with guns. They don't even aim when they shoot."

Injured Gazans are dying in damaged hospital corridors, bleeding to death because rescuers were not permitted to reach them or are endangered themselves. Thousands of units of blood donated by Jordanians are stopped by the Israeli blockade. Israel has kept the international press out of the Gazan killing fields.

What is going on in Gaza is what Bill Moyers called it earlier this month—"state terrorism." Already about 400 children are known to have died. More will be added who are under the rubble.

Since 2002, more than 20 Arab and Muslim nations have had a standing offer, repeated often, that if Israel obeys several UN resolutions and withdraws to the 1967 borders, leaving 22 percent of the original Palestine for an independent Palestinian state, they will open full diplomatic relations and there will be peace. Israel has declined to accept or even consider this offer.

None of these and many other aspects of this conflict matter to Congress. Its members do not want to hear even from the Israeli peace movement, composed of retired generals, security chiefs, mayors, former government ministers, and members of the Knesset. In 60 years these savvy peace advocates have not been able to give one hour of testimony before a Congressional committee.

Members of Congress may wish to weigh the words of the founder of Israel, David Ben-Gurion, years ago, when he said:

"There has been anti-Semitism, the Nazis, Hitler, Auschwitz, but was that their [the Palestinian's] fault? They only see one thing: We have come here and stolen their country."

Doesn't that observation invite some compassion for the Palestinian people and their right to be free of Israeli occupation, containing illegal land and water grabs and blockades in the 22 percent left of Palestine?

Letter to Bush on Gaza Crisis

December 31, 2008

Dear George W. Bush,

Congressman Barney Frank said recently that Barack Obama's declaration that "there is only one president at a time" over-estimated the number. He was referring to the economic crisis. But where are you on the Gaza crisis where the civilian population of Gaza, its civil servants, and its public facilities are being massacred and destroyed respectively by U.S built F-16s and US built helicopter gunships?

The deliberate suspension of your power to stop this terrorizing of 1.5 million people, mostly refugees, blockaded for months by air, sea, and land in their tiny slice of land, is cowardly contrasting the position taken by President Dwight Eisenhower in 1956. That year, he single-handedly stopped the British, French, and Israeli aircraft attack against Egypt during the Suez Canal dispute.

Fatalities in Gaza are already over 400 and injuries close to 2000, so far as is known. Total Palestinian civilian casualties are 400 times greater then the casualties incurred by Israelis. But why should anyone be surprised at your blanket support for Israel's attack, given what you have done to a far greater number of civilians in Iraq and now in Afghanistan?

Confirmed visual reports show that Israeli warplanes and warships have destroyed or severely damaged police stations, homes, hospitals, pharmacies, mosques, fishing boats, and a range of public facilities providing electricity and other necessities.

Why should this trouble you at all? It violates international law, including the Geneva Conventions and the UN Charter. You, too, have repeatedly violated international law and committed serious constitutional transgressions.

Then there is the matter of the Israeli government blocking imports of critical medicines, equipment such as dialysis machines, fuel, food, water, spare parts and electricity at varying intensities for almost two years. The depleted UN aid mission there has called this illegal blockade a humanitarian crisis especially devastating to children, the aged, and the infirm. Chronic malnutrition among children is rising rapidly. UN rations support eighty percent of this impoverished population.

How do these incontrovertible facts affect you? Do you have any empathy or what you have called Christian charity? What would Texas do up against the fourth most powerful military in the world if it were the size of Gaza? Would these embattled Texans be spending their time chopping wood?

Gideon Levy, the veteran Israeli columnist for Haaretz.com, called the Israeli attack a "brutal and violent operation" far beyond what was needed for protecting the people in its south. He added: "The diplomatic efforts were just in the beginning, and I believe we could have got to a new truce without this bloodshed . . . to send dozens of jets to bomb a totally helpless civilian society with hundreds of bombs—just today, they were burying five sisters. I mean, this is unheard of. This cannot go on like this. And this has nothing to do with self-defense or with retaliation even. It went out of proportion, exactly like two-and-a-half years ago in Lebanon."

Apparently, thousands of Israelis, including some army reservists who have demonstrated against this destruction of Gaza, agree with Mr. Levy. However, their courageous stands have not reached the mass media in the US, whose own reporters cannot even get into Gaza due to Israeli prohibitions on the international press.

Your spokespeople are making much ado about the breaking of the six-month truce. Who is the occupier? Who is the most powerful military force? Who controls and blocks the necessities of life? Who has sent raiding missions across the border most often? Who has sent artillery shells and missiles at close range into populated areas? Who has refused the repeated comprehensive peace offerings of the Arab countries issued in 2002 if Israel would agree to return to the 1967 borders and agree to the creation of a small independent Palestinian state possessing just twenty-two percent of the original Palestine?

The "wildly inaccurate rockets," as reporters describe them, coming from Hamas and other groups cannot compare with the modern precision armaments and human damage generated from the Israeli side.

There are no rockets coming from the West Bank into Israel. Yet the Israeli government is still sending raiders into that essentially occupied territory, still further entrenching its colonial outposts, still taking water and land and increasing the checkpoints. This is going on despite a most amenable West Bank leader, Mahmoud Abbas, whom you have met with at the White House and praised repeatedly. Is it all vague words and no real initiatives with you and your emissary Condoleezza Rice?

Peace was possible, but you provided no leadership, preferring instead to comply with all wishes and demands by the Israeli government—even resupplying it with the still-active cluster bombs in south Lebanon during the invasion of that country in 2006.

The arguments about who started the latest hostilities go on and on with Israel always blaming the Palestinians to justify all kinds of violence and harsh treatment against innocent civilians.

From the Palestinian standpoint, you would do well to remember the origin of this conflict, which was the dispossession of their lands. To afford you some empathy, recall the oft-quoted comment by the founder of Israel, David Ben-

Gurion, who told the Zionist leader, Nahum Goldmann:

"There has been anti-Semitism, the Nazis, Hitler, Auschwitz, but was that their [the Palestinians'] fault? They only see one thing: We have come here and stolen their country. Why should they accept that?"

Alfred North Whitehead once said: "Duty arises out of the power to alter the course of events." By that standard, you have shirked mightily your duty over the past eight years to bring peace to both Palestinians and Israelis and more security to a good part of the world.

The least you can do in your remaining days at the White House is adopt a modest profile in courage, and vigorously demand and secure a ceasefire and a solidly based truce. Then your successor, President-elect Obama, can inherit something more than the usual self-censoring Washington puppet show that eschews a proper focus on the national interests of the United States.

Fight For Workers' Rights

September 2, 2008

Labor Day just isn't what it used to be. The parades are smaller, the unionized workforce is smaller, the share of the economic pie available for working people in the United States is smaller, and the demands by organized labor on Congress and the presidential candidates are embarrassingly smaller than the times demand.

Last year I issued a Labor Day statement noting that the Taft-Hartley Act, one of the great blows to American democracy, had been in effect for sixty years. Well, another year has come and gone, and this law is still in place. Taft-Hartley continues to impede employees'

right to join together in labor unions; undermine the power of unions to represent workers' interests effectively; and authorize an array of anti-union activities by employers. (See: Statement On Taft-Hartley for a more detailed description of the anti-worker provisions of this anti-worker law.)

Union officials should speak out for abolition of Taft-Hartley, and not concede this monumental employer usurpation of worker rights. Against the backdrop of the assault on labor that has included aggressive employer demands for concessions, the downward pull of international low-wage workers, weak and barely enforced labor and workplace safety laws, most workers have seen wage rates almost stagnate over the past several decades—even as CEO salaries have skyrocketed.

Major union leaders in the United States do vocally support the Employee Free Choice Act (H.R. 800, S. 1041) which, according to the AFL-CIO, will: "Establish stronger penalties for violation of employee rights when workers seek to form a union and during first-contract negotiations. Provide mediation and arbitration for first-contract disputes. [And,] [a]llow employees to form unions by signing cards authorizing union representation." On March 1, 2007 H.R. 800, which was introduced by Congressman George Miller, D-Calif., and which has 233 co-sponsors, passed on a roll call vote with 241 votes in favor of the bill and 185 opposed. On June 26, 2007 the Senate tried to pass the Employee Free Choice Act, but the Republicans, with the exception of Republican Senator Arlen Specter of Pennsylvania, filibustered the bill. The Employee Free Choice Act should, however, be but one battle in the fight to restore workers' rights in the United States.

Remember, the "fat cats" continue to accumulate and concentrate wealth. And George W. Bush's recession has only exacerbated the plight of working men and women.

Employers have slashed benefits for those workers lucky enough to retain a job. And many workplaces remain far more hazardous than necessary.

Most people struggle to get by and they are working more and more—either working longer hours or picking up a second or third job—to pay the bills and meet rent or mortgage payments. In two-parent families, increasingly both parents are in the workforce. Just to meet everyday expenses, they're borrowing more and more from credit cards, home equity loans or second mortgages, or from legal loan sharks at check-cashing operations. If someone in the family gets sick and lacks health insurance—45 million Americans are in that boat—the economic pressures on the family can be overwhelming. Even if a family has insurance, the exorbitant price of medicine may not be covered, or covered entirely, and paying for the pills can drive a family into despair.

The Economic Policy Institute reports that "the inflation-adjusted value of the minimum wage is 19 percent lower in 2008 than it was in 1979. Since September 1997, the cost of living has risen 32 percent, while the minimum wage, even after the increase to $6.55, has fallen in real value."

In recent times, the gap between haves and have-nots is more severe, and the demands for workers' rights have never been more powerless since World War 2.

Consider the following:

- S&P 500 CEOs now make about 344 times more than the average worker at their firms.

- The top fifth of households own more than 84.7 percent of the nation's wealth; the middle fifth less than 3.8 percent of the nation's wealth.

- The percent of wealth owned and controlled by the wealthiest 1 percent of households now equals that of the bottom 92 percent.

- Women and minority males earn 69 percent to 80 percent of what white men make. In addition, more than a third of single mothers with children live in poverty.

Repealing Taft-Hartley would certainly help workers to organize for better wages and working conditions. The fight would be monumental, but so would the gains.

Healthcare Politics
August 13, 2008

One of my favorite monthly publications is *Registered Nurse*—the journal of the fast growing, progressive California Nurses Association (CNA), a union that stands up for patients' rights and well-being.

The June 2008 issue contains stories that illustrate how this nurses' group takes stands. On June 19, the CNA sponsored street rallies for its Medicare for all (single-payer with free choice of doctor and hospital) in San Francisco and a dozen other major cities around the nation.

For over a decade, these nurses have made full Medicare for all their major goal. They have run voter initiatives, lobbied legislatures, and have opposed sweetheart labor-management deals like those embraced by the Service Employees International Union—SEIU. (SEIU also opposes single-payer health insurance, which is supported by a majority of physicians and the American people.)

The June magazine describes the autocratic nature of SEIU toward its members and how its leader, Andy Stern, cuts labor deals with large corporate employers that shockingly deprive workers of normal union rights.

Here is an example of what CNA says:

"In exchange for access to more dues units, SEIU gave California nursing home operators the 'exclusive right' to set all pay rates and working conditions, speed up and reassign work, eliminate jobs at will, and outsource union work.

"SEIU also agreed to support legislation limiting patients' right to sue over care abuses, to oppose reforms to require better staffing for patients' safety, and to never report healthcare code violations."

Stern rejected single-payer health insurance at his recent union convention. Senator Barack Obama has declined to propose single-payer as well. SEIU is pouring tens of millions of dollars to elect Senator Obama president. CNA works to eliminate "the insurance nightmare through establishing a high-quality, single-payer healthcare system." (See: guaranteedhealthcare.org/blog)

The current healthcare industry is a wasteful, redundant, defrauding mess, costing Americans over $2.2 trillion this year and hundreds of thousands of avoidable injuries, fatalities, and serious infections a year. The honest, competent caregivers are on the edge of despair, unable to do their best work due to the domination and control of commercial-profit priorities which include denial of care by these corporations.

People sometimes die or get sicker when they are denied healthcare. People die when they can-

not afford health insurance—18,000 Americans a year, according to the Institute of Medicine.

Corporate billing fraud and abuse costs over $200 billion a year. Ask Malcolm Sparrow of the Kennedy School at Harvard University, or read his book *License to Steal*.

Do you ever hear John McCain or Barack Obama focus public attention on these tragedies and rip-offs of consumers and taxpayers?

The employers of health insurance companies, hospital chains, and the drug industry are pouring money into the coffers of these two men and their parties.

Strange as it many seem, on June 26, 2008 even the principled, independent California Nurses Association fell in line with the AFL-CIO. The CNA endorsed Senator Barack Obama.

Well, Senator Obama doesn't have to worry a minute about CNA's nurses putting up one of their famous critical demonstrations at his events. He can continue dialing for corporate dollars.

Gaza Under Siege
March 7, 2008

The world's largest prison—Gaza prison with 1.5 million inmates, many of them starving, sick and penniless—is receiving more sympathy and protest by Israeli citizens, of widely impressive backgrounds, than is reported in the US press.

In contrast, the humanitarian crisis brought about by Israeli government blockades that prevent food, medicine, fuel, and other necessities from coming into this tiny enclave through international relief organizations is received with predictable silence or callousness by members of Congress, including John McCain, Hillary Clinton, and Barack Obama.

The contrast invites more public attention and discussion.

Israel has militarily occupied Gaza for forty years. It pulled out its colonials in 2005, but maintained an iron grip on the area—controlling all access, including its airspace and territorial waters. Its F-16s and helicopter gunships regularly shred more and more of the areas' public works and neighborhoods, and inflict collective punishment on civilians in violation of Article 55 of the Fourth Geneva Convention.

As the International Red Cross declares, citing treaties establishing international humanitarian law, "Neither the civilian population as a whole nor individual civilians may be attacked."

According to the *Nation* magazine, the great Israeli human rights organization B'Tselem reports that the primitive rockets from Gaza have taken thirteen Israeli lives in the past four years, while Israeli forces have killed more than 1,000 Palestinians in the occupied territories in the past two years alone. *Almost half of them were civilians*, including some 200 children.

The Israeli government is barring most of the trucks from entering Gaza to feed the nearly one million Palestinians depending on international relief, from groups such as the United Nations Relief and Works Agency (UNRWA). The loss of life from crumbling healthcare facilities, disastrous electricity cutoffs, gross malnutrition, and contaminated drinking water from broken public water systems does not get totaled. These are the children and their civilian adult relatives who expire in a silent violence of suffering that 98 percent of Congress avoids mentioning while extending billions of taxpayer dollars to Israel annually.

UNRWA says "We are seeing evidence of the stunting of children, their growth is slowing . . ." Cancer patients are deprived of their chemo-therapy, kidney patients are cut off from dialysis treatments, and premature babies cannot receive blood-clotting medications, reports Professor Saree Makdisi in the February 2, 2008 issue of the *Nation*.

The misery, mortality and morbidity worsens day by day. Here is how the commissioner-general of UNRWA sums it up: "Gaza is on the threshold of becoming the first territory to be intentionally reduced to a state of abject destitution, with the knowledge, acquiescence, and—some would say—encouragement of the international community."

Amidst the swirl of hard-liners on both sides and in both Democratic and Republican parties, consider the latest poll (February 27, 2008) of Israelis in the highly respected newspaper Haaretz: "Sixty-four percent of Israelis say the government must hold direct talks with the Hamas government in Gaza toward a cease-fire and the release of captive soldier Gilad Shalit. Less than one-third (28 percent) still opposes such talks. An increasing number of public figures, including senior officers in the Israeli Defense Forces' reserves have expressed similar positions on talks with Hamas."

Hamas, which was created with the support of Israel and the US government years ago to counter the Palestine Liberation Organization (PLO), has repeatedly offered cease-fire proposals.

The Israeli prime minister rejected them, notwithstanding "a growing number of politicians and security officials who are calling for Israel to accept a cease-fire," according to Middle East specialist Professor Steve Niva.

There is a similar contrast between the hardline Bush regime, the comparably hardline Democrats in Congress, and a recent survey by the American Jewish Committee (itself often hawkish on Israeli actions toward the Palestinians) of Jewish-Americans.

As reported by Eric Alterman in the January 7, 2008 issue of the *Nation*, "a majority of Jews in this country oppose virtually every aspect of the Bush Admistration/neocon agenda," including his war in Iraq and his belligerence toward Iran.

By a 46-to-43 percent plurality, American Jews continue to support the creation of a Palestinian state, notes Alterman. Other polls show even higher support among Jews in America for a two-state solution.

Then Alterman comes to his conclusion, writing: "These views, however, have been obscured in our political discourse by an unholy alliance between conservative-dominated professional Jewish organizations and neoconservative Jewish pundits, aided by pliant and frequently clueless mainstream media that empower these right-wingers to speak for a people [Jewish-Americans] with values diametrically opposed to theirs."

Makes for a healthy, constructive political debate, doesn't it?

If Democrats and Republicans were serious about peace in the Middle East, they would showcase the broad joint Israeli and Palestinian peace movements. These efforts now include the over 500 courageous Israeli and Palestinian families who have lost a loved one to the conflict and who have joined forces to form the *Parents Circle—Bereaved Families Forum*.

Together, these families are expanding a nonviolent initiative to push for a peaceful resolution to the conflict. Even though some of the families have visited the United States, their efforts are almost unknown even to US observers of that area's turmoil.

A new DVD documentary titled *Encounter Point* (see www.justvision.org/encounterpoint)

recounts the activities and passion of these Palestinian and Israeli families steeped in the peace philosophies of Mahatma Gandhi and Nelson Mandela.

Do you think members of Congress will give them a public hearing? A meeting? It would be worth asking your members of Congress to do so.

The Imperial Presidency
October 22, 2007

Mired in the disastrous Iraq quagmire, opposed by a majority of Americans, George W. Bush has reached new depths of reckless, belligerent bellowing. At a recent news conference, he volunteered that he told our allies that if they're "interested in avoiding World War III," Iran must be prevented from both developing a nuclear weapon or having "the knowledge necessary to make a nuclear weapon."

To what level of political insanity has this Washington Caesar descended? Only two countries can start World War III—Russia and the United States. Is Bush saying that if Russia, presently opposed to military action against Iran, persists with its position, Bush may risk World War III? If not, why is this law-breaking warmonger looking for another war for American GIs to fight, while his military-age daughters bask in the celebrity limelight?

Why is he using such catastrophic language? Surely he does not think Iran could start World War III. His own intelligence agencies say that, even assuming that the international inspectors are wrong and Iran is moving toward developing the "knowledge" of such weapons, it can't build its first such weapon before three to five years at the earliest.

Why would a regime ruling an impoverished country risk suicide, surrounded as it is by countries armed to the nuclear teeth, such as Israel and the United States? This nation of nearly 80 million people hardly needs to be reminded that the US overthrew its popular premier in 1953, installing for the next twenty-seven years the brutal regime of the Shah.

They recall that President Reagan and his vice president, George Herbert Walker Bush, urged, funded, and equipped Saddam Hussein in his invasion of Iran—a nation that has not invaded any country in over 250 years—which took around 700,000 Iranian lives.

Moreover, the undeniable historical record shows that US companies received licenses from the Department of Commerce, under Reagan, to ship Saddam the raw materials necessary to make chemical and biological weapons. Saddam used such lethal chemical weapons, with the tolerance of Reagan and Rumsfeld, on Iranians to devastating effect in terms of lives lost.

Then George W. Bush labels Iran a member of the "axis of evil" along with Iraq, ignoring a serious proposal by Iran in 2003 for negotiations, and shows what his language means by invading Iraq.

The authoritarian Iranian government is frightened enough to hurl some defiant rhetoric back at Washington and widen its perimeter defense. Seymour Hersh, the topflight investigative reporter for the *New Yorker* magazine, has written numerous articles on how the crowding of Iran, including infiltrating its interior, has become an obsession of the messianic militarist in the White House.

The Pentagon is more cautious, worrying about our already drained army and the absence of any military strategy and readiness for many consequences that would follow Bush's "bombs away" mentality.

Then there is the matter of the Democrats in Congress. After their costly fumble on Iraq, the opposition party should make it very constitutionally clear, as recommended by former New York governor Mario Cuomo in a recent op-ed, that there can be no funded attacks on any country without a Congressional declaration of war, as explicitly required by the framers of our Constitution.

But the Democrats are too busy surrendering to other Bush demands, whether unconstitutional, above the law, or just plain marinated in corporate greed. Some of this obeisance was all too clear in the Democrats' questioning of Bush's nominee for Attorney General, Michael B. Mukasey.

After the two days of hearings, no Democrat has yet announced a vote against Mukasey, even after he evaded questions on torture and argued for the inherent power of the president to act contrary to the laws of the land if he unilaterally believes he has the inherent constitutional authority to do so.

This position aligns Mukasey with the imperial views of Bush, Cheney, Ashcroft, and Gonzales on the "unitary executive." In short, reminiscent of the divine right of kings, the forthcoming Attorney General believes Bush can say that "he is the law," regardless of Congress and the judiciary.

After two recent lead editorials demonstrating its specific exasperation over the Democrats' kowtowing to the White House, the *New York Times* added a third on October 20, 2007 titled "With Democrats Like These . . ." The editorial recounted the ways Democrats, especially in the Senate, have caved on critical constitutional and statutory safeguards regarding the Bush-Cheney policies and practices of spying on Americans without judicial approval and accountability.

Accusing the Democrats of "the politics of fear," the *Times* concluded: "It was bad enough having a one-party government when the Republicans controlled the White House and both houses of Congress. But the Democrats took over, and still the one-party system continues."

There is more grist coming for the *Times'* editorial mill. Last week, the first African-American chair of the powerful House Ways and Means Committee, Charles Rangel (D-N.Y.), declared that Treasury Secretary Henry Paulson, Jr., fresh from Wall Street, had persuaded him, during a decade of increasing record profits, to lower the porous corporate income tax rate from 35 percent to 25 percent.

"We can live with that," Chairman Rangel declared.

Would the working families in his district, who would be paying a higher tax rate on their modest income, agree?

Bush-Cheney Making Things Worse Day by Day

July 13, 2007

Thursday, July 12, 2007's *Washington Post* was another day of well-supported headlines chronicling the lawless, incompetent, wasteful, negligent, bumbling, and multiple perils to our nation's security and safety caused by the Bush-Cheney regime.

One headline reads: "US Warns of Stronger al-Qaeda." The report by the Bush Administration's National Counterterrorism Center was titled "al-Qaeda Better Positioned to Strike the West." Safe havens are being established in remote tribal areas of western Pakistan.

In recent days, George W. Bush has told audiences of the growing menace of al-Qaeda inside Iraq.

There was no al-Qaeda in Iraq before Bush's invasion.

Five hundred billion dollars (and vast bloodshed) later, and we are left with the Bush government's own assessment of al-Qaeda's resurgence and spread!

Officials inside and retired generals, diplomats, and intelligence specialists outside the Bush government have warned before and after the Iraq invasion of the disastrous consequences of this maneuver. Inside the Pentagon, the US Army personnel, up to four-star generals, have warned against the invasion but have been muzzled.

Bush's own CIA director Porter J. Goss, General William Casey, and others declared that the US military presence was fueling the insurgency in Iraq. Goss added that our presence in Iraq is a magnet attracting more people from other countries to learn the skills of sabotage and terror.

Bush's own counter-terrorism advisor in the White House, Richard Clarke, wrote in his book *Against All Enemies* that Osama bin Laden must be beseeching Bush to invade Iraq to inflame the Muslim world and generate new recruits.

Nothing—not facts, judgment, the destruction of Iraq, the US casualties, the massive drain on the taxpayers, or the distraction from the needs of the American people—affect this obsessively-compulsed duo in the White House.

Another headline in the *Post* that day was an assessment by Bush's CIA chief, Michael V. Hayden, that the US-installed Iraqi government was unable to govern and that the situation seems irreversible. He added that he could not "point to any milestone or checkpoint where we can turn this thing around." Those words were conveyed to the Iraq study group on the same day (November 13, 2006) that the group heard Mr. Bush give an upbeat assessment of that same government. Bush has been chronically detached from the reality of his own advisors.

Also on page one was this stunner of a sting: "Undercover congressional investigators posing as West Virginia businessmen obtained a license with almost no scrutiny from the Nuclear Regulatory Commission that enabled them to buy enough radioactive material from US suppliers to build a 'dirty bomb,' a new government [GAO] report says."

How about that for Bush's agency, which is supposed to keep the atom in safe hands!

Inside on the Business page is "Armored Vehicles Chronically Late." This latest chapter in Bush's management is characterized by criminal negligence, leaving soldiers without adequate body armor for many, many months of preventable fatalities.

The reporter, Renae Merle, writes: "The Pentagon inspector general's office has found that a program to deliver special armored vehicles to protect military personnel in Iraq from roadside bombs has been marred by delays and questionable contracting practices that may have endangered troops." May have? When such vehicles are not shipped out, soldiers lose their lives and limbs.

If George W. Bush's daughters, Jenna and Barbara, were on those Iraqi roads, wanna bet how fast Laura Bush would get George to focus?

Day after day in the papers and on the television news, the endemic mismanagement of corrupt corporate contracts, flouting of civil liberties and due process of law, and inability to get anything done, even in widespread post-Katrina emergencies, produces no accountability, no compelling changes from the Congress, no impeachment proceedings.

Poll after poll shows Bush-Cheney approval ratings below 30 percent. About 70 percent of the people want out of Iraq. And many polls show the public wants the Bush regime to end, believes that Bush does not care for people like themselves, and that corporations have too much control over their lives.

And not only conservatives are appalled by the gigantic deficits Bush is piling up for future generations of Americans.

This government leaves Americans defenseless when it comes to occupational diseases, medical malpractice, and air and water pollution. Bush can't even police defective or contaminated products pouring into this country from communist China.

Because it has no quorum, his Consumer Product Safety Commission (CPSC) is just about powerless to impose civil penalties or otherwise regulate or recall defective products, domestic or imported.

As reported in the useful *Loyola Consumer Law Review* (luc.edu/law/activities/publications/consumer.html), Bush has not filled the third commissioner's position for over a year, which prevents the CPSC from exercising its authority over dangerous products. The agency is in limbo, while injuries mount.

Ban the Cluster Bomb
March 16, 2007

The global movement to ban cluster munitions received a big lift last month when forty-six nations at the Oslo Conference agreed on an action plan for "developing a new international treaty on cluster munitions by the end of 2008." Neither the United States, China, Russia, nor Israel—manufacturers of cluster bombs—were participants in Oslo.

"We have given ourselves a strict deadline for concluding our efforts. This is ambitious, but we have to respond to the urgency of this humanitarian problem," declared Norway's Minister of Foreign Affairs, Jonas Gahr Store.

The proposed international treaty would:

(i) prohibit the use, production, transfer and stockpiling of cluster munitions that cause unacceptable harm to civilians, and:

(ii) establish a framework for cooperation and assistance that ensures adequate provision of care and rehabilitation to survivors and their communities, clearance of contaminated areas, risk education and destruction of stockpiles of prohibited cluster munitions.

The Oslo Participants planned to continue their work in Lima, Peru, in May/June and Vienna in November/December 2007, and in Dublin in early 2008. On March 1, Belgium became the first country to criminalize investment in companies that manufacture cluster bombs and prohibit Belgian banks from owning shares in these companies or offering them credit.

Last summer's conflict between Israel and Hezbollah lent more urgency to the "ban the bomblets drive." Israel dropped an estimated four million cluster "bomblets" on Lebanon from rockets, artillery, and airplanes. The United Nations Mine Action Coordination Center of South Lebanon (MACC SL) estimates that Israel fired 90 percent of these munitions during the last seventy-two hours of the conflict, when Israel knew that a UN Security Council ceasefire was imminent. Most of these bomblets were produced in the United States. Since the ceasefire in August, the UN has documented thirty fatalities and 191 injuries so far from unexploded bomblets in orchards, fields, school locales, paths and residential areas of South Lebanon.

Left hidden on the ground, according to the American Task Force for Lebanon (ATFL), "a slight disturbance may cause bomblets to explode. Worse, many bomblets are brightly colored, with others attached to small parachutes, making them look like toys and enticing kids to pick them up."

The cluster bombs unleashed during the pre-truce hours on South Lebanon sparked press criticism inside Israel and reviews inside the government. The leading Israeli newspaper, *Haaretz*, reported the following on November 20, 2006:

Israel Defense Forces Chief of Staff Dan Halutz plans to appoint a major general to investigate the use of cluster bombs—some of which were fired against his order—during the Lebanon war.

Still, the Israeli government will not give the United Nations' field teams, searching for these deadly weapons, the coordinates which identify the cluster bomb strikes in South Lebanon.

Much credit for keeping the issue of cluster munitions before the attention of the State Department and the Congress goes to the American Task Force on Lebanon (ATFL) and its energetic executive director Dr. George Cody. He spent 10 days in Lebanon after the conflict ended to observe the damage and what he called the continuing very high price that Israel imposed on Lebanon and its civilians, many of them children, who continue to be killed and maimed by unexploded Israeli cluster bomblets.

Dr. Cody met with UN Battle Area Clearance teams. Chris Clark, the UN's programme manager for the Mine Action Coordination Centre, informed him that the cluster bomb contamination in Lebanon is the worst ever seen, worse than the contamination in Kosovo,

Afghanistan and Iraq, given the density of these munitions in the afflicted territory.

ATFL's "Ban the Cluster Bomb" campaign is supporting the Feinstein-Leahy Senate bill 594 which restricts the US use, sale, or transfer of cluster bombs where 1 percent or more of the munitions fail to detonate on contact.

ATFL has pressed the State Department to find the Israeli government to be in violation of federal law prohibiting sales to countries for offensive purposes. The State Department's review has been sent to Congress with the conclusion that Israel "may" have violated such prohibitions.

Along with Amnesty International, Human Rights Watch wants a ban because cluster bombs "cannot be directed in a way that distinguishes between military targets and civilians," thereby violating international humanitarian law prohibiting indiscriminate attacks.

HRW says that 98 pecent of all those killed by cluster bombs are civilians. Its report estimates worldwide approximately 100,000 civilians, many of them children, have been killed or injured since cluster bombs began to be used.

Dr. George T. Cody and ATFL would like you to sign their petition to Congress, President Bush, and the State Department to "Ban the Cluster Bomb," at their website www.atfl.org.

Sacrifice in Iraq

March 9, 2007

On many occasions, President George W. Bush has lectured the American people that "amidst all this violence and bloodshed" in Iraq, "is the sacrifice worth it? It is worth it, and it is vital to the security of our country."

Well then, why don't his daughters, twenty-five-year-old Barbara and Jenna, join the armed services and share in the sacrifice? Or is the sacrifice only to be borne overwhelmingly by lower-income whites, Hispanics and African-Americans who comprise the bulk of the casualties?

Mr. Bush is constantly speechifying to the American people, and increasingly failing to secure their support. Nearly 70 percent of Americans want out of Iraq and believe it was not worth the price. Americans may be wondering why neither Bush, nor Cheney, nor the neocons, who fabricated the causes for invading Iraq, nor the corporate bosses raking in war profits—why neither they nor their families are showing any signs of sacrifice?

By contrast, across the Atlantic Ocean in England, the British Defense Ministry announced last month that "His Royal Highness Prince Harry will deploy to Iraq later this year." Harry, age twenty-two, is a second lieutenant who insists on going to Iraq with the soldiers under his command.

"There's no way I'm going to put myself through Sandhurst (the military academy), and then sit on my arse back home while my boys are out fighting for their country," he told a television interviewer.

It is not as if Prince Harry is a stern, militant young fellow. The *New York Times* called him "something of a playboy prince," who frequents "London's more exclusive nightclubs."

Jenna and Barbara like to go out on the town as well. The *Washington Post* reported in early January that the twins went out "with a well-heeled entourage—crushed velvet sport coats for the men, trendy leggings, silk dresses and platform heels for the women," before Barbara heads back "to New York and her job at the

Cooper-Hewitt museum" and Jenna returns "to her UNICEF gig in Central America."

The old 1960s phrase, "if you're not part of the risk, you won't be part of the solution" applies to the Bush family. It's even worse. Some of Bush's relatives are involved in the war business, making money from their participation in companies and firms thriving off Defense Department contracts. (See Democracyrising.us)

Himself an adroit avoider of the Vietnam era draft, using his connections to enlist in the Texas Air National Guard that was not slated to embark for southeast Asia, George W. Bush finds solace in saying that he is "in awe of the men and women who sacrifice for the freedom of the United States of America, who volunteer to confront our adversaries abroad so we do not have to face them here at home."

With such an awe-inspiring mission in Iraq to which he and Cheney have tied our country, its soldiers and its strained budget of billions of dollars, one might imagine George and Laura having a fireside chat in the White House with their able and spirited daughters in uniform talking about joining this noble Iraq mission.

Imagine further what privates Jenna and Barbara would have to tell a president known for his traits of not listening and not admitting any mistakes (note the bungling Iraq occupation, the post-Katrina debacles and the recent Walter Reed deprivations which are never the fault of this no-fault commander in chief).

Let's envision the twins back on leave as medics from their first deployment to Baghdad sitting with father in the family quarters upstairs in the White House.

Jenna: "Daddy, you must listen to us and not ignore what we want to say, as you have disregarded our emails. Most of our soldiers in Iraq have lost faith and want the US out of there. If you don't believe me, look at this year old Zogby poll reporting 72 percent of the soldiers want the US out in six months to a year. And things are much worse now."

Barbara: "Daddy, you're spending $12 million an hour in Iraq and the soldiers are still short of body armor, armored vehicles and communications equipment. Still! Four years after the war started. Much of their equipment needs repair or replacement and there is no money. One of your Congressional critics reacting to the Department of Defense's Inspector General report of January 2007 said, 'If our troops aren't the priority, who is? Halliburton, Blackwater, other corporate chums of the president?'"

The president: "Reports, polls, what nonsense; what are your soldier friends fighting courageously over there against those hit and run cowards telling you?"

Barbara: "Some were too ripped up in the hospitals to tell us, but we knew they were torn apart by IEDs in their unprotected vehicles. We can tell you other horrible eye-witness stories about undertrained and underequipped national guardsmen and reservists. It won't inspire you, but we can tell you, if you wish. We're on the receiving end of the battered men and women who come to us on stretchers."

The president: "Don't bother, Barbara, Jenna, it all keeps me and Laura up at night, worrying so about you. I hear you. I hear you."

If you agree that having Jenna and Barbara join the armed forces will help bring George W. Bush closer to bringing the soldiers home and ending this boomeranging war-occupation, express your support at democracyrising.us:

The Minimum Wage

June 23, 2006

Whatever led to the metastasis of corporate demons inside the brain of the Democratic Party over the last thirty years, it has paid off the business establishment. The cost of freezing the minimum wage has deprived millions of working Americans of trillions of dollars for their necessities of life.

A few Democrats, most prominently Senator Edward M. Kennedy, have championed keeping the minimum wage up with inflation for years. But the Republicans and the somnolent Democratic Party have combined to defeat Kennedy's bills over and over again.

Last year the federal minimum wage at $5.15 per hour was $3.50 below in purchasing power of what it was in 1968. Today's minimum wage has the lowest purchasing power since 1949 when economic productivity per worker was a fraction of what it is today, when the super-rich corporate bosses had not become hyper-rich averaging over $8,000 an hour.

Add no health insurance for the working poor and there are added pressures on livelihoods for parents and children.

The last increase to $5.15 per hour was in 1997. Except for one year of restraint, members of Congress have zipped their annual pay grab through the House and Senate every year. Just the increases in that period amount to about three times the annual minimum wage income for millions of American laborers. No wonder poverty has been on the increase.

The abdication of the congressional Democrats, even when they were the majority and Clinton was president, on the living wage matter has cost them as well. More than any other single issue, save possibly health insurance for all, their reluctance to boldly and visibly champion the living wage has cost them the presidential and congressional elections.

People want politicians to STAND FOR THE PEOPLE, not grovel beneath the corporations.

Mindful of the political appeal of the living wage issue in our country since the onset of the industrial age, I sent an open letter in May 2004 to the Democratic leadership—Rep. Nancy Pelosi and Senator Tom Daschle—urging them to pledge that members of their party would resist all future raises for the lawmakers until the federal minimum wage was restored to its 1968 purchasing power. Hardly revolutionary.

But for Pelosi and Daschle and their leadership circle, that was too much alienation of the Walmarts, the McDonalds, other fast food and retail chains and their allies. They never responded to my letter, and, along with John Kerry, plunged headlong to defeat in November. Meanwhile, though opposed by Governor Jeb Bush and the fast food chains with big television gadgets, a Florida referendum raising the minimum wage by a dollar won with a 72 percent majority in November.

Twenty-one states have lately raised their minimum wage above the federal minimum. None have reached the 1968 purchasing power level yet.

The Democrats finally sense the minimum wage issue to be a bright line position with the retrograde Republicans whose ideological heads are in the sands. But look how long the Democrats took to wake up their earlier political history.

At last, led by Senator Kennedy, they are attaching amendments to legislation and last week got fifty-two senators to back raising the wage to $7.25 in three stages. At that level, minimum wage workers would earn an additional $4,370 a year to support their families.

However, the Republican filibuster opposition can only be overcome by getting sixty votes, so Kennedy has a ways to go. But the issue is getting hotter, though it's far from being visible to most Americans, including poor families.

The best thing going for the Democrats' November prospects is bonehead John Boehner, Republican Majority Leader of the House who has dug in his heels. His spokesman, Kevin Madden, said Congressman Boehner "remains convinced that a minimum wage hike will destroy jobs." Rep. Ray LaHood (R-Ill.) is trying to convince his leader, John Boehner, that raising the minimum wage "is a no-brainer. It's just something that we should do."

The loss of jobs argument is the Republicans' stalwart justification for keeping down the minimum wage while their coffers grow with campaign contributions. As one wag put it, by that reasoning, the Republicans should push down the minimum wage to add more jobs.

Princeton economists blew that "job loss" claim out of the water after the 1997 increase. In the four years after the last minimum wage increase, 11 million new jobs were added including 600,000 restaurants jobs.

More to the point is the public philosophy that working full-time should provide enough income for your family's necessities. There is also the matter of simple fairness. Walmart's CEO made $12,000 an hour, plus perks, in a recent year, while hundreds of thousands of his workers were making between $6 and $9 per hour, with very few if any benefits.

Rest assured, neither the Democratic nor the Republican leadership will stop their annual pay raise. The House already has passed their pay grab. Shame is a rare commodity when it comes to the moral authority to govern.

Why do we let them get away with such Marie Antoinette values?

Take Back Your Time
January 7, 2006

A small conference was held on January 6th in Washington, DC about a big concern for tens of millions of American workers—the loss of free time due to the omnivorous demands of their workplace obligations.

The gathering, which met to press for public policies which will give workers a better work/life balance, was organized by John de Graaf and Gretchen Burger. They direct a group called Take Back Your Time.

De Graaf has just edited an action book called *Take Back Your Time: Fighting Overwork and Time Poverty in America*. Thirty national leaders in this little publicized movement contributed chapters describing the many harmful results to families, health, safety, civic and community life, environment and just plain yearnings for living a higher quality of life.

Where did the time go? I just don't have the time. When will I ever be able to relax? How many times have you heard these exclamations or their variations? In this superage of labor-saving technology, pushbutton communications, and all those things that are supposed to save you time, just the opposite is happening to most people—they're desperate for working to live rather than living to work through ever longer congested commutes.

This "Time to Care" conference got down to business with workshops on a series of ways our society can start to tackle what de Graaf calls "time poverty." They've come up with a list of measures that they want to become labor laws, which have been in the statute books for a long time in other Western countries.

Their recommendations embarrass our corporate dominated economy when it is compared with the economies of far smaller and less wealthy nations. First up is paid family leave "when workers have a child or other family member" in need.

Currently, there is a federal law that allows up to twelve weeks of unpaid family leave. All other industrial nations except Australia presently have a national paid family leave policy for all workers. Not the United States.

Second proposal is paid sick leave. About half of American workers receive no paid sick leave, unlike workers in every other industrial country.

Third proposal is paid vacation time. Every other industrial country mandates at least ten days a year for all workers. No federal or state law in the US requires any paid vacations.

Senator Edward Kennedy (D-Mass.) is the lead legislator in Congress championing these and other measures by the "Time to Care" movement.

Of course a living wage will reduce the pressure to hold one and a half or two jobs to stave off bankruptcy or debt slavery. A living wage allows time for a living family with time for children and community activities.

A few weeks ago, members of Congress once again gave themselves their automatic annual salary increase while sitting on the long frozen federal minimum wage of $5.15 an hour. Even the CEO of Walmart urges a minimum wage increase. Yet the Democratic Party still resists making this issue a front and center national initiative in Congress.

It is remarkable how modest is the awareness of millions of American workers that companies like Walmart and other giant multinationals have to treat their workers much better in western Europe and Japan than they do for workers in the land of their corporate birth and profitable success. Why? Because that is the labor law in those countries.

The labor unions need to make these comparisons much more prominent in their publicity and organizing drives.

163 countries offer some form of paid family leave, including paid childbirth or maternity leave. There is no national law in the US to provide for such priorities.

The polls show all kinds of stress, anxiety, pain and mental breakdowns that come from these workplace pressures. Imagine the world's richest country allowing this collision between facing family crises and earning a modest living to avert some other future family crises.

Standing in the way of minimum justice for workers are the big corporate lobbies, their trade associations in Washington, DC and their political slush funds for the politicians. Changes have to begin with the indignation of the millions of deprived workers who have contributed to the doubling of labor productivity since 1969 but are receiving less by way of inflation-adjusted returns.

Start with researching Congress for a few minutes a week. That will certainly be time well spent. It's already happening—visit www.timeday.org for starting a Take Back Your Time committee in your town.

Mass Starvation in a World of Plenty
August 12, 2005

Babies are dying of starvation in Niger—a large country in dry northern Africa with 12 million people. Their emaciated mothers and fathers are eating rats except lately the rats themselves are starving. A massive attack of locusts in the midst of a prolonged drought led to a harvest failure and the spreading fatal famine.

The government, a nominal democracy and very poor, has exhausted its grain stores, having sounded the international alarm in November. The United Nations–connected World Food Program, beset with similar demands in parts of Zimbabwe, Ethiopia and Darfur, is now distributing sacks of grain. The United Nations estimates 800,000 little children to be in mortal peril and overall 2.5 million humans on the edge of survival.

There is no drought nor are there any locusts in Greenwich, Connecticut. The lawns of the hyper-rich's mansions are green, immaculately manicured. Their pets are groomed, wardrobed and housed in grand style.

Greenwich is the hedge fund capital of the United States. Over 100 hedge funds solicit the vast liquid wealth of the wealthy and package it through investment strategies resting on tiers of speculative instruments (e.g. convertible arbitrage, long/short, event driven). Making money from money. Not making money from producing any goods or services. Not even providing anything discernibly useful. The hedge fund managers will mumble about their contributions to risk management (of their risky, speculative, investment instruments). Very abstract, are these mega-speculators.

Back in Niger, the vast areas of parched, sun-baked earth fissure. The carcasses of cattle rot and some are eaten by their desperate owners, before the vultures descend to dine. Families trek six hours over the arid savannas looking for help or anything edible, while their trip makes them weaker and further from their homes.

Even in normal times, one in four children die before they reach their fifth birthday. Now the call is out to foreign charities. As of August, the UN has now requested $30 million, but only $7 million has been donated since November.

In late July, the BBC, as it did in the 1980s, in Ethiopia, came through with the wrenching visuals—little babies with toothpick wrists and sticks for legs, crying their last cries. Dehydration and infectious diseases close in on the children and their parents.

One haunting segment showed a father, losing his extended family day by day, looking to the sky. "Forgive me, God, for weeping," he exclaimed. "I can't feed my family. I have nothing."

The BBC program showed once again that a "picture is worth a thousand words." Quickly, ABC's *Nightline* took portions of the report and played them with other commentary on July 26th. The *New York Times* followed with two features.

Still, the Niger calamity has not reached more than a fraction of the audience watching one reality show.

Back in Greenwich, the dreams of riches by Edward Lampert, Phil Tudor Jones and Steven Cohen have long since been exceeded by surrealistic paydays. According to the *Wall Street Journal*, these hedge fund billionaires made respectively last year $1.02 billion, $300 million and $450 million. Just in one year. Broken down into fifty weeks, five days a week, a full eight-hour day, Mr. Lampert's rewards come to $20 million a week, or $4 million a day or $1/2 million an hour! Every hour, on the average.

Ted Koppel asked Mark Malloch Brown of the UN Development Program about a stand-by fund. Each famine should not require taking out the giant tin cup before the family of nations, after the BBC alerts the public. Mr. Brown said, "there's talk of a revolving fund of something like $1 billion, which would fund all of this up front . . . Even 100 million would make a huge difference."

The Greenwich hedge fund people have

started their equivalent of charity balls and dinners for poverty organizations in our country. The Manhattan super-rich have been doing this for many years. It is a successful way to receive both approbation and subservience by the receiving non-profit poverty service organizations.

Now suppose Messrs Lampert, Jones and Cohen, along with their comparably enriched colleagues sat down in a Greenwich country club to a private viewing of the most devastating African famines. Suppose they were informed by development experts that, of course, the true solution to the "poverty trap" in these societies are aid programs to assist farmers in growing and storing safely more food, having safe drinking water (preventing many diseases) together with effective assaults against TB, malaria and AIDS. All within a framework of advancing political democracy.

But right now and for the foreseeable future, what is needed is a revolving fund well within the means of the dozen speculation kings in the room. That such a fund would enable quick response teams, transportation, food and provide basic medicines directly to the mouths of the needy. That they can put together just such a standby monetary fund and even find ways to establish an income revenue stream to keep it going. A little highly nutritious food goes a long way when people are starving.

Play the searing videos again for these gentlemen. Give them a frame of reference for their humanity. After the accolades pour in, should they act, they'll realize that what they did was not just for eradicating the crime of avoidable mass starvation in a world of plenty. They'll realize they did it for themselves as well.

The Future of Organized Labor

May 8, 2005

With US union membership down to only 8 percent of the workers in the corporate sector—the lowest in ninety years—a clash of unions is underway within the AFL-CIO over the future direction of organized labor. The unions challenging the leadership of President John J. Sweeney—the Service Employees International Union (SEIU), Teamsters UNITE and the Laborers—want more of member unions dues to the AFL-CIO returned for expanded organizing and want more mergers among the seventy-six existing national unions.

Beyond what they call "restructuring," it is remarkable what they are not demanding, other than new leadership this year from their own ranks. They are not focusing on the fundamental corporate attack on unions, workers and, via corporate globalization, the American economy itself. To be sure, these "rebel" unions do not see themselves as affected by WTO, NAFTA and the shipment of whole industries and jobs to authoritarian or dictatorial countries such as Mexico and China. SEIU represents service workers, retail, hospital and other jobs not easily shifted abroad.

But as long-time United Autoworkers' reformer, Jerry Tucker declared, the insurgents' declaration of principles makes "only passing reference" to "the sustained destruction of decent jobs, the systematic forced reduction in wages, benefits and working conditions. And, little attention is paid to labor's inability, or unwillingness, to collectively marshal its forces to confront management's concerted aggression at the center of the crisis facing US unions today."

Indeed in a long profile-interview of SEIU's

president, Andrew Stern, in the *New York Times* magazine, there was no mention of the critical need for labor law reform to jettison the many obstacles to and opportunities for corporations and their union-busting law firms to smash any incipient organizing drive in factories or other large low-pay corporate workplaces like Walmart.

In no other Western country do such facile obstructions exist in law. In no other Western country do the top executives of the largest corporations have compensation so massively larger than their workers.

In 2002, the CEOs were averaging $7400 per hour (apart from perks and benefits), while their workers were making anywhere from $6 to $26 per hour.

Tucker drives his point home this way: "Fifty years of business unionism, abetted by an evolving legal framework, have all but eliminated the most democratic of worker expressions, direct action . . . What's also missing in today's debate among the union heads is anger, a deep and resolute class-anger . . . Ours is a crisis with millions of victims. Those victims are being attacked by enemies—corporate and governmental—with a shared ideology. Labor should not shrink from condemning that ideology."

The AFL-CIO has pressed their Democratic allies in Congress to sponsor the Employee Free Choice Act, designed to remove some of the unconscionable obstacles to collective bargaining drives. By April 2004, the bill had 179 sponsors in the House of Representatives and thirty-one in the Senate. Not bad. But did you ever hear Kerry (a sponsor) or Edwards give this bill any punctuation marks in their many speeches and debates? Have you heard any of those sponsors, other than Senator Ted Kennedy, go out of their way to highlight this legislation?

The Chamber of Commerce building in Washington is full of energetic anti-union officials. They are even plotting to further weaken an already anemic OSHA which is supposed to do something about the more than one thousand Americans who die from workplace diseases and trauma weekly. The AFL-CIO headquarters is almost next door. I have never heard of the AFL picketing the Commerce's building, where its arrogant arch-adversaries are so immersed in their war on workers.

The bureaucratization of the labor movement has drained away the steam, the spirit, the grass roots militancy that characterized organized labor in the 1930s and 1940s. The late Tony Mazzocchi, who founded the Labor Party (visit thelaborparty.org) was keenly aware of this basic lethargy—a lassitude extended to organized labor's automatic support, without heightened and insistent demands, of the Democratic Party.

A showdown may be coming between the insurgents and the Sweeney administration at the AFL-CIO Convention in late July. Already four of these dissident union presidents are demanding that the names of their members be deleted from the AFL-CIO's grand computerized list of 13 million union men and women. These unions represent about a third of the total AFL-CIO 13 million plus households.

According to a union insider, the rebel unions do not have the votes to topple Sweeney. He estimates there are 4,578,867 per capita votes against Sweeney and 6,566,605 per capita votes for another term for the AFL-CIO leader.

If this is so, SEIU and other allied unions may bolt the labor Federation, further weakening the AFL-CIO in an age of corporate gigantism, corporate globalization and corporate government.

Tearing Down Democracy

April 24, 2005

You would think that Bush-Cheney would be sensitive to avoiding the weakening of democracy in our country while going around the world with Secretary of State, Condoleezza Rice, hectoring other countries about their anti-democratic practices.

After all, the moral authority to admonish comes from the power of example. Instead brazen hypocrisy prevails. Bush and Cheney inherited past democratic institutions and practices, which they are tearing down in many directions.

On the way to Russia recently, Secretary Rice told accompanying reporters of her and the president's concerns over the centralization of power by President Vladimir Putin (who was overwhelmingly elected) at the expense of the states, as well as his prosecution of giant oligarchs. The crimes of these oligarchs were obvious to everyone during and after the great giveaways by then President Yeltsin of so much of Russia's natural resources.

Of course, Rice has a point. Putin is cracking down on the media and some political rivals. But rankling Washington, he also prefers Russian companies in the bidding for oil and gas fields. Furthermore, he opposed demands by US companies to be exempted from liability in Russia for negligent damage. Rice softens her stance by saying that today's Russia is not the Soviet Union.

But let's look at what Bush-Cheney is doing to democracy in the USA. First, these two authoritarians have centralized more power in the White House-Executive Branch at the expense of Congress, the courts and the states than previous Republican leaders would ever have done. From the PATRIOT Act to pursuing tort reform, from federalizing many class actions in federal courts (usurping the role of state courts) to the pre-emptive banking laws and regulations to the "No Child Left Behind" takeover, these two pro-Vietnam war draft dodgers have generated a cascade of powers into the Oval Office.

Second, the two-party Electoral College duopoly with its "wealth elections," exclusive control of debates, and ballot access barriers, have effectively stifled competition by third party or independent candidates. Our country is dominated by a two-party elected dictatorship that carves up most districts into one-party monopolies, re-districted either by Republicans or Democrats who control the state governments.

About 95 percent of House of Representatives' Districts are monopolized by one party and where elections are really coronations. Bush-Cheney and Representative Tom DeLay have worsened this downward trend.

No other country in the Western world is down to a two-party duopoly. Many countries have four, six, eight, ten viable parties, instant runoff voting and often proportional representation so that more votes matter.

Bush-Cheney have set records for secret arrests and jailings without charges and without allowing defendants to have attorneys. Dragnet roundups have proved to be wasteful and harmful to thousands of innocent prisoners who were never tried, including people suspected just of being material witnesses. Bush and John Ashcroft have yet to catch and convict a terrorist, though they have arrested over 5,000 people suspected of terrorism. The two convictions they secured were overturned by courts in Michigan.

The violation of due process, probable cause and the rule of law has damaged America's standing in the world where billions of people believe, given the illegal invasion of Iraq under false pretenses, that the Bush's government stands for "might is right."

Former General Wesley Clark has called the Bush Administration "a threat to domestic liberty." While the respected columnist and editor, Michael Kinsley, writing in the *Washington Post*, said "in terms of the power he now claims, George W. Bush is now the closest thing in a long time to dictator of the world."

In Cicero's words, "freedom is participation in power." Bush-Cheney have made sure fewer people are participating, while poverty, hunger, consumer debt, non-living wages, the uninsured, environmental damage, electoral shenanigans, tax cuts for large corporations and the wealthy, militarization of both foreign policy and federal budgets keep worsening.

Recently, spokesmen for foreign countries, including Russia and China, have begun to mock Bush-Cheney, urging them to look at their own backyards. It is easy to dismiss such charges from more authoritarian nations, including the communist dictatorship in China. But remember, these officials, coming off the iron rule of Stalin and Mao and their predecessors, think they are making progress by comparison.

What are the excuses of Bush-Cheney? They are coming off the traditions of Jefferson, Madison, Lincoln, Teddy Roosevelt and Franklin Delano Roosevelt. Bush-Cheney, instead of standing on their and others' shoulders, are driving America backwards into the future.

Keep that in mind, Secretary Rice, during your foreign travels. Fig leafs of hubris do not make an exemplary foreign policy.

Corporate Cyborg

March 13, 2005

Corporate cyborg Arnold Schwarzenegger must be thinking these days that it was not like this in his movies. On the screen, Arnold was the pursuer, the hunter, and the attacker. On the hustings now, it is the nurses, along with the teachers, and the firefighters, who are dogging him everywhere with their protests against his policies and actions.

When he ignored the law stipulating one nurse for every five hospital patients the opposition from the militant California Nurses Association intensified. Then Arnold made the mistake that keeps on giving. Before an audience of 10,000 women, he was challenged by a group of nurses.

"Pay no attention to those voices over there. They are the special interests, and you know what I mean. The special interests don't like me in Sacramento because I am always kicking their butts."

"Kicking their butts," roars the famous grouper and fondler from Hollywood? Ever full of himself, basking in high poll numbers, Arnold couldn't get away with that remark. Nurses have just about the best image around. They are there by the bedside when the doctors have left for home. They are the people who watch lives ebbing away, who hear the cries of pain and the spasms of sorrow day after day. "Kicking their butts"? Whoa! The nurses were off to the Arnold races.

Arnold moves fast: limousines, police escorts, helicopters, and airplanes. He has many fundraisers to attend, just about every covey of corporate interests willing to shell out thousands to hear him, see him, touch him, be pictured with him, buy him. Among those interests are the hospital industry, the insurance industry, and just about every wealthy clique that is enjoying the corporate welfare, lower taxes hayride in the rich state of California. Oh, how the expensive wines in delicate glasses click in unison when he is rubbing shoulders with his class in splendid hotel ballrooms or ornate private clubs.

But Arnold now has company and it is not the corporate type. Real human beings, who work with their hands, hearts and minds, often in uniforms, are greeting him as he disembarks for his political auctions. Arnold is on his way to raising $100 million, a portion of which he wants to use to qualify referenda in November to privatize public pensions, restrict spending and other proposals he calls "reforms."

Trouble with Arnold's ideas is that they all come from the hide of people who cannot attend his fund-raisers and are designed to allow the affluent classes to continue escaping their fair share of the fiscal burden.

As Green Party candidate for California governor Peter M. Camejo said during the candidates' televised debate with Arnold in 2003, merely restoring the earlier tax level on the wealthiest 5 percent would produce revenues to close the deficit. Instead, Arnold keeps borrowing money for the state, which is another way of raising taxes on babies who will be paying the interest on that gigantic debt when they grow up.

From California to New Orleans to Ohio, New York to Washington, DC, the nurses and their labor allies are there to greet him, sometimes with coffins, bands, blimps, toting banners and other media magnets. And they are getting media, in part, because their issues are common to many workers' worries about concessions or regresses around the country. They have the perfect foil. Arnold digs in his heels,

throws out pugnacious words that fuel the eager media's fires, and does not reach out to meet with them or indicate that his proposals would get a thorough airing in the legislature with a Democratic Party which he treats as a sideshow. He describes the nurse's protest derisively as extras in a movie.

Political observers and pollsters are reporting that Arnold is starting to lose his entertainment grip on the population. His polls have slipped from 65 percent approval in September to 55 percent in February. More and more people are concluding that the showboating and sugarcoating are overdone. The hammers are falling harder on the people so that the rich and corporations can continue their profitable tenure in the golden state without contributing.

Arnold is clever, to be sure. He has supported an environmental move or two, and has urged needed reform of the notoriously gerrymandered electoral districts by having redistricting decided through a panel of retired judges.

But make no mistake about it, Arnold is true to his movie roles. Life imitates art. Politics is a juggernaut. And if you have to go to the people on waves of corporate cash and deceptive television ads, then perfect the practice of flatter, fooling and faking to win the vote. The trouble with this situation is that there is no prominent, well-known political figure on the other side to rebut him daily. So, except for the nurses protests, he dominates each day.

On their part, the nurses and their union, the patient-sensitive California Nurses Association, are showing other unions and the AFL-CIO what they need to do fast in the labor-bashing Bush-era politics. Go back to the old days, go to the streets, show up, give your rank and file a chance to have a collectible voice and confront power with justice.

CNA has almost tripled its membership, to over 60,000 members, in the last twelve years. Funny isn't it? Workers like unions who really fight for them and the people they serve.

Walmart
November 27, 2004

Law-breaker, union-buster, tax-escapee, and shifter of costs to others, the world's largest retailer, Walmart, announced last week that it would respect the wishes of its Chinese workers to form a union. As is usual with Walmart announcements, a substantial overstatement is working here.

In China, unions are not independent; they are government-controlled with the Chinese Communist Party turning them into what would be called "company unions" in the US. With forty stores in China already, Walmart understands that these essentially Communist Party-controlled unions serve as a controlling mechanism over workers, a one-stop system which often have an in-company manager in charge.

China is seen by Walmart as the future. With the US market approaching saturation (Walmart has 3,600 big and bigger stores here), the company with the biggest gross revenues in the world—$258.7 billion last year, is importing more from Chinese factories then is the entire country of Germany.

Its message to US suppliers is that if they cannot meet the "China price," they should close down in America and open up in the world's largest communist dictatorship. Astonishing, isn't it, that this giant capitalist corporation is using this Communist regime as its labor enforcement arm to drive down wages and benefits in the US.

In Western Europe, Walmart has to treat its workers better than it treats its American workers. European labor laws are much tougher than those in the US. Walmart has to give its workers paid vacations (from four to eight weeks depending on the country), better benefits and working conditions. There is no "off the clock" work or wages not fully paid for long periods of time. Walmart has even agreed to collectively bargain with a large German union.

In the country of its birth, Walmart is wrecking havoc with worker standards of living. It forces other large grocery chains to demand lower wages and benefits from their unionized employees to be able to compete with Wall-Mart's race to the bottom. This direction is a historically tragic reverse for the US economy that before World War II featured rising wages that increased consumer demand and improved livelihoods. Increasingly, Walmart's immense arc of influence here is pushing wages and benefits downward. With hundreds of thousands of its nearly 1.4 million workers making under $7.50 an hour, before payroll deductions, (the average wage is between $7.50 and $8.50 an hour), the average-on-the-clock workweek is only thirty-two hours. Since Wal-Mart defines anyone working fewer than thirty-four hours per week as part-time, they have to wait for two years before qualifying for health insurance whose co-payment takes one-fifth of the average paycheck. Get the idea of what is meant by the Walmart way.

Waiting periods are key to Walmart's flimsy health insurance boasting in their television ads. Impoverished employees don't stay, with turnover rates for these hourly employees at 50 percent to 100 percent at many stores.

Wal-Mart is devilishly ingenious in thinking up ways to have taxpayers fill in its wage gap.

Put them on partial welfare, says the very well-paid company bosses who make millions of dollars each per year. These workers are given advice on how to apply so that taxpayers subsidize Walmart's profits.

For example, in Georgia, over 10,261 children of Walmart employees are enrolled in the state's Peachcare program for health insurance in families meeting federal poverty criteria.

According to the report *Everyday Low Wages*, one 200-person Walmart store could cost federal taxpayers over $420,000 per year. These costs include subsidized lunches, health insurance and housing assistance, federal tax credits and deductions for low-income families, among other examples of Walmart's freeloading.

Enough is never enough for this corporation. It often demands substantial local tax breaks from municipalities as a condition for locating there. Although successful local opposition is blocking dozens of Walmart location plans, this corporate welfare King still manages to escape its fair share of taxes, while local home owner and small businesses ante up for local public services and assume Walmart's share. That is, small businesses that manages to remain in the hollowed out Main Streets that are the aftermath of a Walmart opening. Minimal thinking by consumers say Walmart is a bargain; maximum thinking starts adding up the local, national and global costs of this Goliath depressor of purchasing power by workers.

For more information on these cost burdens, see the website WalMartWatch.com which also shows how communities have stopped the Walmart invasion.

The Plight of Labor
September 5, 2004

Labor Day comes and goes, but Congress does little to improve the plight of workers in our country. In the last three decades our elected officials have too often chosen to side with big corporations rather than the working people in the United States.

In the face of aggressive employer demands for concessions, the downward pull of international competition, weak and barely enforced labor and workplace safety laws, relatively high unemployment rates, and a struggling labor movement, most workers have seen wage rates stay practically flat over the past several decades even as CEO salaries and profitability have skyrocketed.

The executive class has captured almost all of the gains in wealth from the growth in gross domestic product (GDP) in recent decades. And George W. Bush's recession and jobless recovery has only worsened the problem.

A Wall Street analyst said in March 2004, "We'd thought that the labor share of national income was in the process of bottoming out, but whether we're talking outsourcing or just old-style downsizing, the effort by US business to pare costs (and extract productivity gains in services) continues apace." Meanwhile, employers have slashed benefits for those workers lucky enough to retain a job. And workplaces remain far more hazardous than necessary.

There are glimmers of hope that the situation can be improved. Some unions and communities have won important victories that have made a difference in workers' lives, but they remain a rarity.

Most people earn no more an hour than they did three decades ago (adjusting for inflation), but those at the top have enjoyed substantial increases in salary and those at the very top of the CEOs and top company executives have seen their compensation go through the roof.

Most people struggle to get by with rock-bottom net worth. They're working more and more either working longer hours or picking up a second or third job to pay the bills and meet rent or mortgage payments. (Americans worked on average two hundred hours a year more from 1973 to 2000—the equivalent of five full-time weeks.) In two-parent families, increasingly both parents are in the workforce. Just to meet everyday expenses, they're borrowing more and more from credit cards, home equity loans, or second mortgages, or from legal loan sharks at check-cashing operations. If someone in the family gets sick and lacks health insurance—45 million Americans are in that boat—the family is in a jam. Even if they have insurance, the extravagant price of medicine may not be covered, or covered entirely, and paying for the pills can drive a family into despair.

Meanwhile, the executive class rakes in more money than ever before, and indulges new forms of conspicuous consumption. We have competition among CEOs over who has the bigger yacht. If an executive has to go to the hospital, they can check into platinum class luxury suites offered by leading medical institutions for $10,000 a night. The *New York Times* recently reported on a new convenience for rich New Yorkers: private indoor pools, with start-up costs of $500,000.

Any way you slice the numbers, you get the same result: a deeply divided America with a struggling majority and a super-rich clique. It's a story of a gap between haves and have-nots more severe than anything this country has witnessed for a century, since the start of the Manufacturing Age:

- *For the private production and non-supervisory workers who make up 80 percent of the workforce, it took until the late 1990s to return to thereal earnings levels of 1979.* CEOs at large corporations now make about three hundred times more than the average worker at their firms. In 1982, they made just forty-two times more; in 1965, twenty-six times more.

- *The top fifth of households own more than 83 percent of the nation's wealth, the bottom 80 percent less than 17 percent.* The top 1 percent owns over 38 percent of the nation's wealth, more than double the amount of wealth controlled by the bottom 80 percent. The top 1 percent's financial wealth is equal to that of the bottom 95 percent.

- *In 1979, the top 5 percent had eleven times the average income of the bottom 20 percent. By 2000, the top 5 percent had nineteen times the income of the bottom 20 percent.* Whatever the data examined, it's worse for women and people of color, who receive lower wages and have much less accumulated wealth than white men. Women and minority males earn 70 percent to 80 percent of what white men make. More than a third of single mothers with children live in poverty.

Thanks to low levels of unemployment in the late 1990s, worker wages started rising, eventually catching up to the levels of twenty years earlier. But the recession and high rates of unemployment that have persisted into the new millennium have almost surely ended that trend. The effective stagnation in worker wages for three decades occurred even though productivity rose steadily. Productivity is the amount of output per person hour worked. In other words, workers were making and producing more, but not receiving any share of the increased wealth.

Virtually all of it was captured by increased corporate profit-taking. CEO pay grew at a much faster rate than even corporate profitability. From 1990 to 2003, inflation rose 41 percent. Average worker pay rose 49 percent. Corporate profits jumped 128 percent. CEO compensation rose 313 percent.

If the federal minimum wage had increased as quickly as CEO pay since 1990, it would today be $15.71 per hour, more than three times the actual minimum wage of $5.15 an hour, as calculated by Boston-based United for a Fair Economy.

It is time for Congress to show some courage and some compassion and side with the workers who struggle to make ends meet.

Iraq Labor

June 25, 2004

What is going on among Iraq's working classes? We do not hear about those workers except for the high number of unemployed.

Thanks to the Labor Party Press (www.thelaborparty.org) we learn that George W. Bush's top representative in Iraq, Paul Bremer, continues to enforce Saddam Hussein's decree banning unions using military force where necessary.

Bush's coalition authority also would interpret "illegal" unions, demonstrations and strikes as inciting civil disorder which can result in the workers being arrested and treated as prisoners of war.

Labor Party Press reports that Bremer has lowered Saddam Hussein's minimum wage and has cutoff the dictator's welfare benefits of housing and food. Ironic! All this is depriving and embittering millions of Iraqi families and increasing their sympathy for the insurgency.

The Federation of Workers' Councils and Unions in Iraq (FWCUI) has been working to keep both the occupying soldiers and the insurgents from remaining inside the cities and residential areas.

All kinds of political movements, secular and religious, are churning in Iraq. The secular populist associations, labor, women, self-help, civic, believe the US occupation has attracted fundamentalist mobilizations from outside and inside the country.

There is now a Union of the Unemployed (UUI) that in the past year has enrolled 300,000 members. Their desire is to get some of the 300,000 reconstruction jobs under the US occupation. Apparently Labor Party Press reports UUI spokesman describing then meeting with the US Coalition authority as follows.

"We went in with out [membership] records in our hands, and they said 'Who are you? Who do you represent? You are nobody. We are the power here.'"

Well, at least, that is the impression by the UUI of the reception they received. So they demonstrated in front of the Coalition's Palace, followed by a sit-in. Fifty of the demonstrators were arrested.

Daily life is what concerns most Iraqis, not the politics of various religions and ethnic groups. The US occupation still has not meet the people's needs for adequate water, food, cooking, oil and often electricity.

Before Saddam came to power, with US help in 1979, there used to be a strong labor movement. Now two union federations are emerging. American labor journalist David Bacon is reporting on the struggles of Iraqi workers to restore their jobs in the oil industry that US companies like Halliburton were replacing with foreign workers. Teachers and women workers are also engaging in labor activity, he says.

For more information, see www.laboragainst-war.org.

Victor Reuther

June 11, 2004

Two very different men in their early 90s passed away last week. Both were active in their unions, Ronald Reagan in the Actors Guild, Victor Reuther in the United Auto Workers (UAW). Then, needless to say, their paths diverged markedly.

Ronald Reagan became the conservative politician with the dulcet speaking voice. Victor Reuther became the labor leader with the deeply resonating voice of a stump orator.

As governor and president, Ronald Reagan demonstrated, as columnist Richard Reeves observed, "that words are more important than deeds." As a major organizer of workers at General Motors and Ford Motor Company factories, Victor Reuther was a courageous man of action, a reader, thinker and compelling speaker who improved the lives of millions of American workers and their families.

Ronald Reagan who spoke often of "morning in America" never awoke to the necessities of working families, the poor, and the environment. He spoke more than any politician against government deficits and big government, but left office after eight years of piling larger government debt than all previous presidents from George Washington to Jimmy Carter combined. He flew back to California leaving a corporate government bigger than ever.

Victor Reuther and his brothers, Walter and Roy, built the United Auto Workers into a powerful, exemplary union while at the same time the auto companies grew and made more and more money. The Reuthers showed that making big corporations responsive to their workers helped lift all boats.

Ronald Reagan, a man from a humble working class background, became the champion of big business and the opponent of regulatory law and order.

He was hostile, in his friendly way, to defending consumers from fraud and harm by business practices and defective products. The "Gipper" was almost contemptuous of labor rights, freezing the minimum wage and the work of the Occupational Health and Safety Administration (OSHA) relating to fatalities, injuries and diseases in the workplace.

His firing of the striking Air Traffic Controllers could have backfired with a single two plane collision. But Reagan always had four leaf clovers in his pocket. He got away with this airline safety gamble and delivered a severe setback to an already weakened labor movement.

Victor Reuther always opposed the UAW and other unions becoming too chummy with companies and their executives. He viewed the role of the union movement as more than cutting ever more "realistic" deals. He saw the UAW as a mover for women's rights and started a Women's Bureau at the UAW in the 1950s. He also got the Union to work toward improved housing for working people.

In his later active years, Reuther ranged broadly over the field of international labor issues, objecting to the UAW receiving funds from a CIA-front organization and opposing the Vietnam War. A self-educated man, he believed strongly in the continuing education of workers, spearheading the creation of labor institutes, media production units and the UAW's own drama schools and summer camps.

While Ronald Reagan went on to fame in the White House, Victor Reuther was supporting a worker reform group challenging the UAW's conservative policies and solarizing his home in Washington, DC. I recall over ten years ago how proud he was showing visitors his personal demonstration of the energy path he wanted the world to pursue.

In 1976, he published his memoir about the tumultuous times of the labor movement in the 1930s and 1940s titled *The Brothers Reuther and the Story of the UAW*. In 2004, he was in his assisted living home dismayed by the deterioration of the standards of living for tens of millions of American workers.

The struggle for justice continues, as it has over the centuries, illuminated by the beacons of fortitude and rectitude such as the likes of Victor Reuther.

Consumers & the Economy

The relentless expansion of corporate control over our political economy has proven nearly immune to daily reporting by the mainstream media. Corporate crime, fraud and abuse have become like the weather; everyone is talking about the storm but no one seems to do anything about it. Corporate capitalism has not succeeded even on its own theoretical terms. In the United States, government subsidies, and government bailouts keep capitalism working.

When reckless corporations fail, the debt falls on the shoulders of taxpayers and they suffer the financial strain not only of an economic recession but also of wrongheaded blank-check bailouts.

President Clinton and Republicans in Congress both pushed for deregulation of the banks and the derivative markets. Wall Street's bets went sour, and the entire financial system was thrown into chaos. Coupled with the now notorious sub-prime mortgage scandals speculation in reckless derivatives, and mega-losses, the financial industry has demonstrated that its devotion to greed knows few bounds.

America's brand of corporate capitalism has produced unprecedented concentration of wealth, and unprecedented gambling by Wall Street. The columns in this section reject such a pessimistic view, and offer a vision of more just economic arrangements that help make business more humane, more equitable, and more accountable to its investor-owners, and to the taxpayers who have been forced to pick up the tab for wild casino capitalism.

The columns in this section deal with:

- *Battles between consumers and big corporations such as Exxon, GM*
- *Wall Street corruption*
- *Alternative Economic Enterprises*

"Corporate socialism"—the privatization of profit and the socialization of risks and misconduct—is displacing capitalist canons. This condition prevents an adaptable capitalism, served by equal justice under law, from delivering higher standards of living and enlarging its absorptive capacity for broader community and environmental values. Civic and political movements must call for a decent separation of corporation and state. The columns in this section address the many facets of the corporate control in the US.

Stop the Public University Tuition Spiral

December 28, 2011

Students of California, arise. You have nothing to lose but a crushing debt!

The corporate state of California, ever ready to seize its ideological and commercial hour during a recession, has a chokehold on California's public universities. With its tax-coddled plutocracy and a nod to further corporatization, the state government has taken the lid off tuition increases big time.

Students of the University of California at Berkeley may pay a proposed $23,000 in tuition by the 2015–16 school year, up from $11,160 this year (2011) that in turn is up from $2,716 in the academic year 2001–02. In short, tuition for resident undergraduates has more than quadrupled in ten years.

Before and right after World War II the idea of a public university included a then-called "educational fee" close to zero, from City College of New York to UC Berkeley. Old timers now look back at those days as economic life-savers toward a degree and a productive life for them and the American economy.

No more. Those gates of opportunity are crumbling at an accelerating pace. More street protests by students are focusing on relentless tuition hikes and years of repaying student debt loans while the rich get richer and the tax cuts for the rich are extended. As Mike Konzcal writes, "One of the Occupy movements' major objectives is combating the privatization of public higher education and its replacement with a debt-fueled economy of indenture."

So far the students have gotten nowhere in the Golden State. The Board of Regents rules with an iron hand. Their chancellors are enforc-ing the state government's unprecedented cutbacks of facilities, faculty, courses and maintenance-repairs.

Berkeley Professor Nancy Scheper-Hughes called the "current crisis" as being "fundamentally about privatization and the dismantling of a national public treasure."

But the students have a very powerful unused tool of direct democracy—thanks to Governor Hiram Johnson's enactment of the voters' initiative process nearly a hundred years ago. They can qualify an initiative on the ballot that would set tuition at affordable levels or even become like some leading European countries where free schooling extends through the university years.

Planning and implementing this people's legislation would be a rigorous course in law, political science and communications.

The effort invites the best minds from the faculty. The language of the initiative must be clear, persuasive and as devoid of ambiguity and openings for circumvention as possible.

Depending on whether the initiative amends the California Constitution or has statutory status, the students will have to collect as many as 810,000 or as few as 505,000 valid signatures on petitions to get on the November 2012 ballot. Ordinarily, without lots of money for paid petitioners, this can be a formidable challenge. But with millions of community college and university students reachable on campus, combined with their families, this should be a fast piece of cake.

According to the eminent University of San Diego Law Professor Robert Fellmeth, there is no legal obstacle to a statutory initiative tied to the funding power of the legislature. It would stipulate, as a condition precedent to state general fund monies, specified tuition limits (perhaps at least a freeze), to provide equitable access to higher education opportunity.

Of course an initiative that is a constitutional amendment can be more supremely declarative.

There are other states where students can establish a legal protection for publically accessible universities by enacting statewide initiatives. All these tools of democracy should be obvious to any high school student were functional civics and democratic practices taught with the same fervor devoted to computer training.

So let's see if California's deteriorating public university systems can be rescued by their undergraduate and graduate students who place the priority of accessible, adequate public higher education where it belongs for the longer run.

Missing the Mark on Deficits

November 29, 2010

The recent reports by the two deficit commissions—one appointed by President Obama (fiscalcommission.gov) and the other from the private Bipartisan Policy Center (bipartisanpolicy.org)–do not lack specifics. In fact, they are so specific that they obscure the need for a more explicit public philosophy that reveals both their value biases and their establishment thinking.

The compositions of the two task forces clearly are designed to achieve a legislative consensus on Capitol Hill. There are self-styled centrists, moderates, conservatives and liberals. There are no paradigm-busters, few challengers of assumptions, no backgrounds from unorganized labor, elderly or youth activists. Even trade unions advocates are rare. About the only eyebrow raisers are provided by the relentlessly wise-cracking co-chair of Obama's Commission—former Wyoming Republican Senator, Alan K. Simpson.

It is true that both panels do include very modest cuts in the vast bloated military bud-

get whose empire takes half of the entire federal government's discretionary spending (not including the insurance programs Medicare and Social Security). Already a tentative suggestion by the Commission's co-chairs to "save" $100 billion in the Pentagon budget by 2015 was called "catastrophic" by Secretary of Defense Robert M. Gates. The two reports make no mention of ending the Iraq and Afghanistan wars, or stopping contractor lobbies from bleeding the Pentagon dry, which would be a solid rejoinder to Gates.

That's the problem throughout these reports. They do not come to grips with the need for fundamental changes to expand the economy as if people matter first, to locate new revenues, launch long-overdue public works programs with their jobs throughout communities in America, and reduce the kind of deficits which are empty calories that create no real wealth, such as corporate welfare bailouts and giveaways.

For example, there is much reference to tax reform that rearranges tax rates. The private task force—chaired by Alice Rivlin and former Senator Pete Domenici (R-N.M.)—would eliminate special tax rates for capital gains and dividends. Fine. But why not also shift the incidence of some taxes from workers to a Wall Street tax or what may be called tiny sales taxes on purchases of speculative derivatives, as well as stocks and bonds that economists Dean Baker and Robert Pollin say would raise several hundred billion dollars a year?

The Rivlin-Domenici report noted but did not recommend a carbon tax—another major revenue-raiser that would reduce pollution, greenhouse gases and advance solar energy and energy conservation. An added humane and economic benefit is that less coal burning would also save thousands of lives a year from air pollution, according to the EPA. Instead the Task Force proposed a sizable regressive national sales tax.

Under healthcare, both reports go for what they call medical malpractice reform. What they mean is *not* doing anything about the 100,000 Americans who die and many more sickened every year from hospital malpractice, not to mention adverse affects from drugs and hospital-clinic infections. No, by reform they mean cutting back on judicially-decided damages now being awarded to far less than the one-out-of-ten victims who even file a claim. Grotesque! A *Business Week* editorial years ago said the medical malpractice crisis *is malpractice*. Prevention is the way to save lives *and* money—a policy entirety ignored by the two commissions.

There is no mention in either report about ending notorious foreign corporate tax havens for US companies that would bring in nearly $100 billion a year. And, remarkably, though some mention is made of tax compliance, they ignore the regular estimate by the Treasury Department of $300 billion a year in uncollected taxes.

Not surprisingly, the two establishment reports did not consider the enormous economic savings from adopting a single-payer—*full Medicare for all*—health insurance system. (See: pnhp.org/news/2009/april/testimony_of_david_u.php).

Three other large areas were ignored. First is cracking down on corporate crime, including at least $250 billion dollars in annual healthcare billing fraud and abuse. (See: http://www.corporatecrimereporter.com/sparrow091409.htm). Both the fines, the disgorgement back to the defrauded and the deterrence to corporate crime amount to large sums of money.

Second, the commission-co-chairs and the task force avoided recommending the proper pricing of our commonwealth assets that are regularly given away free (eg. the public airwaves and hard rock minerals, such as gold and silver, on federal land) or at bargain basement fees (the national forest timber and other minerals).

Third, although both reports emphasize the need for economic growth (which produces more tax revenues to reduce red ink), there was no reference to revising global trade agreements that have left our country's huge trade deficits and its workers in dire straits. Keeping industries and jobs from moving to repressive regimes like China for reexport to the US should not have been ignored. But then, look at the composition of these Task Forces and you'll see why.

Since Unsafe At Any Speed
September 20, 2010

Let's celebrate some good news, before some qualifications are considered. Traffic fatalities in the USA have dropped to a 60 year low. There were 33,808 deaths in 2009—a 9.7 percent decline from the previous year, according to the National Highway Traffic Safety Administration (NHTSA). The reduction was across the board from passenger vehicles, light trucks, large trucks, motorcycles and pedestrians.

Since 1966 when the motor vehicle and highway safety laws were passed by Congress—led by Democrats but with significant Republican support—the fatality rate dropped from 5.49 percent (50,894 lives lost) to 1.13 percent in 2009 (33,808 lives lost). This large live-saving reduction occurred while absolute vehicle miles traveled increased more than threefold in those intervening decades.

These sharp reductions in "accidents" did not

happen by chance. They came about because the national highway safety mission was enacted into law.

The national policy to address a major public safety epidemic—started with the Congressional outrage following General Motors and its clumsy attempt to have private detectives try to "dig up dirt" on me before and after publication of my book *Unsafe at Any Speed* in November 1965.

Extensive Congressional hearings in the Senate and the House pulled together the overwhelming evidence that the auto companies were suppressing the use of long-available safety devices and selling style and horsepower over safety and fuel efficiency. Forty-four years ago in September 1966, President Lyndon Baines Johnson signed the legislation and presented me with one of the pens at the White House ceremony.

The deliberate legislative process worked as it was supposed to work. The press and TV in Washington and Detroit covered the auto safety developments week after week in 1966 as a regular reporting beat instead of just an occasional feature. This kept the heat on any recalcitrance by members of Congress. The auto company executives had their say at hearings and proved unpersuasive.

NHTSA was established as an agency in the Department of Transportation with Dr. William Haddon, a very knowledgeable scholar and specialist in trauma prevention on the highway. NHTSA was given regulatory authority to establish mandatory safety standards, require vehicle defect recalls and research advanced prototype safety vehicles suitable for mass production.

Intelligent, experienced people went to work for NHTSA to tackle this fourth leading cause of death in the US integrating vehicle, highway and driver inputs. Useful research and testing expanded rapidly along with motorist expectation levels for safer vehicles.

Far fewer people were losing their lives and incurring serious injuries due to greater seat-belt usage, better air bags, brakes and tires, stronger enforcement of drunk-driving laws, improvements in highway design right down to "hot spot" corrections at high-casualty locations.

More recently, the wider adoption of electronic stability controls and better collision avoidance capabilities augur even better safety on the roads.

Along the way since 1966, however, there were many missed opportunities, delays, suppression of needed upgrades of existing vehicle and tire standards, and avoidance of necessary recalls. Many lives have been lost and injuries inflicted as a result of such callousness.

Pressure came from the auto company lobbying operation and their friends in the White House and Congress, especially their powerful perennial defender, Democrat John Dingell from Michigan, who almost never saw a safety standard or fuel efficiency upgrade he liked. On the consumer side have been long-time advocates Joan Claybrook and Clarence Ditlow.

In the past decade, distracted drivers using cell phones and other electronic gadgets are involved in the loss of over 1000 lives a year. Secretary of Transportation, Ray LaHood has made this growing peril a major cause.

With the rise in the number of motorcycles to 11 million, there has been a steady rise in motorcycle fatalities over the years. This is due in no small part to 30 states not having a mandatory helmet law. "Along with taxes and weather, there is the certainty that no mandatory helmet laws leave more motorcyclists dead on the highway," says Jackie Gillan, vice president of Advocates for Highway and Auto Safety. "It's like having a cure for AIDS over twenty years and not applying it in certain states," she added.

Safety laws have to be updated and strengthened from time to time. Currently a bill is moving through Congress, largely opposed by industry, to toughen the weak penalty provisions, strengthen some safeguards against newly discovered defects and increase the pitifully small budget in NHTSA for motor vehicle safety standards, recalls and research.

The current annual budget is about $150 million, which is less than three months worth of your tax dollars paying corporate contractors to guard the US Embassy and its personnel in Baghdad, Iraq.

While the decline in highway casualties in 2009 can be attributed to a considerable degree to the recession, the record of highway safety regulation, bumps and all, certainly compares favorably with the anemic safety frameworks set up for other widespread technologies such as offshore drilling and spilling.

Of Big Banks and ShoreBank

August 13, 2010

The Obama administration's treatment of its current majority ownership of bailed-out General Motors and its standoffishness toward the pioneering but troubled ShoreBank, a community bank based in Chicago, are lessons in how the big/bad fare in Washington, DC, as compared with the small/good.

Having shed its bad assets and abandoned its common shareholders, the new GM emerged from bankruptcy in 2009 with a clean balance sheet and lots of taxpayer cash. For the first two quarters of 2010, it has signaled a comeback by reporting over $2 billion in profits.

In return for a federal infusion of well over $50 billion, the government took a 61 percent ownership stake. The Canadian government received 10 percent ownership for its financial assistance, and the United Auto Workers received 17.5 percent ownership in return for major concessions and a two-tier salary scale starting at $14 an hour.

The Obama Administration exercises its trust duties on behalf of the taxpayers by repeatedly saying it would not use any powers of majority ownership at all. The Obama Administration is urging GM to issue stock sooner than later so that the government can sell its stock and get out of the company completely.

GM's CEO Edward E. Whitacre Jr., former CEO of AT&T, agrees. In recent weeks, he has been telling the press that GM is losing sales because of its moniker "Government Motors." Not known for his graciousness, he did not add that without the government a bankrupt General Motors would not have any sales at all.

There are serious consequences for Obama's absentee management style. First, he did not prohibit GM from lobbying, as was required for the bailouts of Fannie Mae and Freddie Mac. As a major member of the Alliance of Automobile Manufacturers, GM has been part of a lobbying force that seeks to weaken auto safety legislation now moving through the House and the Senate. Historically, GM has been the most strident in its opposition to mandatory pollution control, fuel efficiency and safety standards. The company's strategy for decades has been to defeat, delay or weaken efforts to clean your air, safeguard your motor vehicle and get you more miles per gallon of gasoline.

Now, when the government, as a majority

owner, can at last tell GM to support long established national policies in these three areas, Obama is hands off. The new GM is free to return to its old obstructive ways.

Moreover, GM's recovery is just beginning. It has cut its costs very significantly so that its breakeven mark is at a low production volume by historical standards. Starting from nearly rock-bottom sales volume, GM is making money in the US and booming in China. So why would Obama want to sell the government's share so early when waiting a couple of years will make a nice profit for the taxpayers and, in the meantime, restrain GM's opposition to innovation-driven regulations for the health, safety and economic well-being of consumers?

Now, consider ShoreBank's predicament. This bank broke ground since its founding in 1973 by providing loans for lower-income homebuyers, apartment building owners and small businesses. Year after year, this community bank proved it could make money by opening up markets that the big banks chose to red-line in Chicago and later in Detroit and Cleveland. Hundreds of articles and news reports heralded its success.

Then the Wall Street–produced recession struck the country. Through little fault of its own, many of its hard-pressed lower-income debtors began to miss or default on their loans. ShoreBank started to register losses—$119 million in 2009. Unlike the big banks, ShoreBank did not deal in risky speculative derivatives—like credit default swaps, collaterized debt obligations or subprime mortgage lending.

Washington is drawn irresistibly to bail out the big banks' wildly speculative, toxic paper investments with no redeeming social value. George W. Bush took the taxpayers to levels of corporate welfare beyond the dreams of corporate avarice.

Neil M. Barofsky, the valiant special inspector general for the Treasury Department's Troubled Asset Relief Program (TARP) reported that the giant AIG bailout ($182 billion) gave its trading partners—bonus-rich Goldman Sachs, Merrill Lynch, Societe Generale and other banks—100 cents on the dollar for their notorious credit default swaps. Had AIG defaulted, it would have been a fraction of that sum.

Barofsky's report denounced the Federal Reserve for not negotiating strongly with the banks. Incredibly, the Fed gave the banks $27 billion in taxpayer cash and let them keep $35 billion more in collateral already posted by AIG. Barofsky declared that these vastly overpaid sums were way "above [these contracts'] market value at the time."

Compare these amounts to what ShoreBank needs in additional investment to provide liquidity and adequate capital reserves to ride out the recession. It projects losses of about $200 million before returning to black ink and another $300 million or so to support future operations.

The community bank has raised $150 million in pledges from several Wall Street firms—a little P.R. redemption here—and it needs $75 million in TARP funds from the Obama Administration.

At this writing, Washington is balking and the Bank, willing to shink down further, finds its hopes dimming.

The *Chicago Tribune* editorial "Still Worth Saving" put it well: "ShoreBank, for many years, showed that operating honorably in low-income neighborhoods could pay off for everybody. One way or another, we can't let its shining example disappear."

No Time For Consumer Power

May 21, 2010

In the end, late on Thursday's Senate passage of the financial regulation bill, the Senate had no time for independent, non-government consumer power. In the end, after listening to swarms of corporate bank, brokerage, hedge fund, private equity, and insurance lobbyists, the Senate had no time for Senator Chuck Schumer's amendment to create a non-profit Financial Consumers Association (FCA, SA 3772).

In the end, this massive 1500 page bill shifted very little power directly to shareholders and consumers of financial services (meaning just about everyone) either to better use the courts and to organize nationwide to counteract the lobbying muscle of the financial goliaths ready to turn the new regulators into procrastinatory putty.

The FCA proposal (see www.csrl.org/model-laws/introduction-the-public-empowerment-act-of-1997/), which Senator Schumer had backed in 1985 when he was dealing with the savings and loan scandal, did not receive the time of day. It would have required the companies to place an invitation to their customers in their mailing and electronic communications (bank statements, bills, etc.) inviting consumers to voluntarily join and pay dues to build a powerful consumer lobby to countervail what Thomas Jefferson once called the "monied interests."

After all, the criminal, reckless, self-enriching collapse of the economy by the Wall Streeters—the millions of lost jobs, the trillions of dollars in lost pensions and savings—Main Streeters deserved some reciprocal gesture for all the Americans who were forced, as taxpayers, savers

and workers to bailout the crooks and ultimately pay the costs of this financial disaster.

In the end, the Senate, like the House of Representatives, told their consumers—their voters—to get lost. There was no room for a Financial Consumers Association in the 1500 pages.

The FCA is crucial to assure that many of the other parts of this bill are enforced. For very little in this legislation includes outright prohibitions. Rather the Senate, like the House, delegates the authority, within a broad range of discretion, to a variety of existing agencies, and a new consumer financial protection agency nesting allegedly independently inside the big bankers' Federal Reserve.

There are so many complex reviews and procedural obstacles for these agencies that the corporate lawyers will collect enough fees to spoil their great-grandchildren. "Paralysis by analysis" is what consumer groups call such legislation. I call them no-law laws—mired in pits of quicksand that mock everything but eternity.

Without an FCA, with millions of members, and hundreds of investigators, organizers, lawyers, economists, accountants and publicists, the good people inside government will lack powerful, knowledgeable public champions to counter industry abuses.

The bill that passed both Houses does not explicitly ban totally speculative derivatives, does not ban banks and other firms above a certain size (where they again become too big to fail), does not declare that the shareholder-owners must have the authority to control their own companies, does not ban companies that mix trading for their own account with other people's money backed by federal insurance. It does not circumscribe the enormous power of the Federal Reserve, short of a one-time Congressional audit, even after all the Congressional bellowing about the Fed's derelictions and looking the other way while Wall Street robbed the American people.

Many of the major consumer groups supported the creation of a Financial Consumer Association. Their guarded support of the Senate-passed S.3217 came with the caution that this is an important first step and one that at least recognizes many frauds and rip-offs that still must be curbed.

Yet whether their hopes are even modestly realized will be determined more by how the corporate lawyers wired the bill with many ways to tie up the regulatory processes *ad infinitum* than anything an unorganized public can demand.

In one major respect, the big bank lobby lost one. They could not stop the creation of a consumer financial protection bureau. But without an FCA, the Bureau will too often find itself with one hand clapping.

However, if that one hand is that of Harvard Law Professor Elizabeth Warren, the odds on favorite to run the Bureau, there will be instances when the big boys on Wall Street will have to face the music.

The Cash or Credit Conundrum

October 5, 2009

Consumers rejoice. Floyd Norris has just penned a piece for the *New York Times* titled: "Rich and Poor Should Pay Same Price."

Mr. Norris said, it seems "absurd to have a system that requires people who do not use credit to subsidize those who do. You know there is something wrong when a middle-class person can get a part of his purchases refunded by the bank, or can collect miles good for free airline tickets, while paying the same price as a poor person who can get none of those benefits."

Mr. Norris is on to something important. He reminded me of an article I wrote in December 1985. I asked readers of my weekly column to consider some of the pitfalls of credit card purchasing. I noted that the big banks relentlessly promote credit card usage without adequately presenting the downside of credit card debt. I asked readers to imagine seeing a television presentation by an organization known as the "Cash Payment Fans of America." The made-for-television production sponsored by this imaginary organization would ask viewers to consider some counter-marketing advice with the following declaration: "Credit Cards: Maybe You DO Want to Leave Home Without Them."

Law Professor Adam J. Levitin, in a 2008 article in the Harvard Journal on Legislation reports, "On average, credit card transactions cost merchants six times as much as cash transactions and twice as much as checks or PIN-based debit card transactions." Professor Levitin also notes that in 2006, "US merchants paid nearly $57 billion to accept payment card transactions, which makes this component of the payments industry larger than the entire biotech industry, the music industry, the microprocessor industry, the electronic game industry, Hollywood box office sales, and worldwide venture capital investments." These are stunning observations.

Alas, our collective imagination may not yet have evolved to the point where we can consider a day without VISA and MasterCard. The buy now, pay later credit card cabal knows few bounds. The credit card vendors want you to forget that using a credit card means you are borrowing money and that you must repay what you borrowed with interest. And, the interest rates can be staggering. Until recently credit card companies could charge annual percentage rates (APR) of up to 36 percent. And the fine print in your credit card agreement might allow the "merchants of credit" to charge membership fees—described as "participation fees," "maintenance fees," or "activation fees"—on top of the interest fees. And don't forget the "transaction fees," for getting cash with your card, the fees for exceeding your credit limit or for making a late payment.

Ed Mierzwinski of USPIRG, a consumer watchdog organization, monitors the credit card racket and the slippery practices of banks that gouge consumers with a variety of fees. USPIRG notes that credit card issuers have tricked consumers by:

1. suddenly advancing long-standing regular due dates by five days or more to trick consumers into paying late;

2. arranging for due dates to fall on weekends and then claiming that bills received after 12 noon or 1 pm were late;

3. imposing late fees not only when bills were 30 days late, but as little as one minute or one day late; and,

4. raising the interest rate if your credit score declines.

Fortunately, some of the most egregious credit card abuses will be eliminated by legislation signed into law on May 22, 2009. The Credit Card Accountability, Responsibility and Disclosure (CARD) Act of 2009, while not perfect, will generally require forty-five days advance notice of any rate increase or any other significant changes in account terms, up from fifteen days, and card issuers will have to inform consumers of their right to cancel their card before rate increases or account changes take effect.

Credit card statements must also be mailed out twenty-one days before they are due. The new law also limits some interest rate hikes for late payments.

Unfortunately, the problems associated with getting on the credit card treadmill are still overwhelming. Despite some modest legislative reforms, too many credit card issuers are still predators waiting to pounce. Representative Peter Welch (VT) and thirteen House co-sponsors have introduced the Credit Card Interchange Fees Act of 2009. This piece of legislation is designed to limit some of the fees credit card companies charge retailers and shed some light on the costs of credit card transactions to consumers and merchants.

Consumers can make some additional waves themselves by pretending they have joined Cash Payment Fans of America and for one week paying with cash for goods and services. The results could be illuminating.

Rolling the Dice Again
September 11, 2009

The Wall Street gang is at it again! It's been one year since Wall Street's collapse and bailout took trillions from taxpayers and the sinking economy. The speculative instruments that pulled down the economy were those super-risky subprime mortgages, credit default swaps, collaterized debt obligations—you know—Las Vegas East, using other peoples' savings.

As if to elaborate their gigantic con job, the investment banks, guaranteed by you the taxpayers, are now packaging life insurances policies in what sane, on the ground businesses would consider deranged exotic money plays.

Here is how the *New York Times* described

the new securitization packages emerging from such corporate welfare goliaths as Goldman Sachs, Credit Suisse and their eager rating agency, DBRS.

"The bankers plan to buy 'life settlements,' life insurance policies that ill and elderly people sell for cash . . . depending on the life expectancy of the insured person. Then they plan to 'securitize' these policies . . . by packaging hundred or thousands together into bonds. They will then resell these bonds to investors, like big pension funds, who will receive the payouts when people with the insurance die.

"The earlier the policy holder dies, the bigger the return—though if people live longer than expected, investors could get poor returns or even lose money."

Continuing its lead front-page story last Sunday, the *Times* describes Wall Street as "racing ahead for a simple reason: with $26 trillion of life insurance policies in force in the United States, the market could be huge."

The Insurance Information Institute's chief economist was not impressed. Speaking for the life insurance business, he said: "It's not an investment product, [it's] a gambling product."

The wild and crazy derivative spree is about to inject a new and recklessly ghoulish game of chance into the financial industry. The Wall Street casino boys are already drooling over the huge fees they expect to collect. Whatever wreckage occurs down the road will soak the investors. Washington, standby for another bailout!

If this sounds alarming, consider the fact that Congress has not even reported out of any House or Senate Committee any regulatory authority for the giant derivatives businesses that places bets on bets on bets in very complex financial instruments.

Trillions of lost dollars, destabilization of the economy, depletion of pension funds and college endowments—to name some affects—and Washington is still in stasis, sitting on its cushions of corporate campaign cash and consorting with industry lobbyists who want nothing done.

Still, you the taxpayers are on the hook for another round with these corporate delinquents and gamblers!

The only difference is that this time the insurance industry seems ready to fight. It does not want to be tarred with what one executive called "the brush of subprime life insurance settlements."

If so, my advice to insurance companies is to nip this in the bud by going to Capitol Hill. This madness will not be stopped by scattered state insurance commissioners.

With all the unmet needs for productive capital, the masters of the financial universe prefer making money from money through high velocity paper speculation, instead of financing real capital structures strengthening communities around the country.

To be sure, abstract derivatives are where the huge commissions and gigantic executive pay packages flourish. It is the arena where investment banks play blackjack. Heads they win, tails you lose.

But why do people have to pay 5, 6, 7 percent sales taxes in stores, but the derivative dealers on Wall Street pay no sales tax on hundreds of trillions of transactions every year? Seems like a hefty double standard, which is why Cong. Peter DeFazio (D-Ore.) has introduced legislation to tax such speculation (HR 1068).

In addition, Congress needs to get going and regulate these derivatives and finally repeal Clinton-era and Bush-era laws that gave them a free ride.

Finally, there needs to be a prohibition on investments in such risky instruments by fiduciary institutions. And, standards of prudence have to be reinstated. Old time bankers and pensions managers would understand such reforms. Investor rights to sue these investment firms and rating agencies for deception and fraud are weak and require strengthening.

Someday, our society needs to decide how to increase peoples' control over their own money and establish incentives that can attract capital flows to where they can be productive. At present, perverse incentives are reflecting sheer speculative power and are promoting grotesque uses of money.

Let these casinos and their gamblers on Wall Street do what they want with their own money, but don't let them gamble with other peoples' money.

Faulty Forecasting
August 7, 2009

Companies that specialize in stock market forecasting and trading—such as Goldman Sachs, Citigroup, Morgan Stanley, and JPMorgan Chase—pay very high salaries to their employee-vendors. New York Attorney General Andrew Cuomo just released data showing that these and other large banks are giving each of their 5,000 trader-forecasters bonuses of at least one million dollars.

In return, these fat cats are very frequently wrong in their recommendations and decidedly unprofessional in their fiduciary relationships with the clueless, trusting clients who rely on them. Win or lose, they get their fees.

These firms and brokers are making money largely from other people's money—pensions,

savings and investments. Overall many produce little more than gambling tips. When these moneyboys try to justify their doings as providing liquidity, hedging against risk, assembling capital for productive investment, listeners are permitted to robustly laugh. This is especially so now during Wall Street's massive, self-inflicted financial collapse. The economy, and taxpayers, are paying for this reckless speculation.

Meanwhile, outside this paper economy, people are producing for the real economy—manufacturing, repairing and maintaining products and structures, offering needed services for consumers. These people are far lower on the income ladder. Unlike their speculating counterparts, if the workers in the real economy stayed home, the economy would stop cold.

I was rummaging recently through some old publications and randomly came across the March 24, 2008 issue of *Barron's*, a leading financial weekly. Its contributors and interviewees are supposed to be among the savviest around. Here are some samples of their perspicacity.

The cover story asserts that "the financial sector's strongest players probably don't have further to sink, even with the ongoing pressure of negative news. Stocks of the industry's strongest players could climb by 10 percent to 20 percent over the next year as panic recedes, earnings improve and price-to-earnings multiples expand."

The author, Jacqueline Doherty, got specific. She cited Merrill Lynch, Citigroup, Bank of America, Washington Mutual, among others, for the predicted upswing. At the time (March 24, 2008), Merrill stock was selling for $46.85. Before the year's end, the stock was worthless and Merrill was swallowed by Bank of America. Washington Mutual, the nation's largest savings bank, saw its stock, selling at $11.70, go to zero as it was absorbed by JPMorgan Chase in September 2008. Citigroup was selling at $22.50 per share. Now, it has climbed just above $3 per share, and Citigroup narrowly avoided bankruptcy due to a huge federal bailout.

Leafing through *Barron's* pages of that week of March 24, 2008, I read a prediction by James Finucane—who is described as a "talented strategist"—that the Dow would reach 20,000 within a year. A year later in late March 2009, the Dow was below 8,000. Even James Glassman, who loudly predicted in 1999 that the Dow would go to 36,000 by 2005, has been mercifully quiet.

Unlike sloppy plumbers and carpenters who pay a price for their mistakes, Wall Street forecasters seem to be paid very well despite being chronically wrong.

A few *Barron's* pages later, columnist Eric J. Savitz was writing that worries about NVIDIA were overblown. The computer chip company stock having peaked in October 2007 at just under $40 a share, was selling for $18.52 when Mr. Savitz was touting its prospects. On August 4, 2009, NVIDIA closed at $13.37 per share.

And so it goes week after week in the financial world of pundits. Do you know of any other profession that can be so wrong so often and be rewarded so well again and again? On their behalf, they say that they cannot guarantee against risk and that they rely on cues from the watchdogs.

The first defense is unrebuttable because it shifts all risk away from the purportedly knowledgeable minds and onto market imponderables. Then why be so cocksure of what you urge investors to buy?

Second, they know that the watchdogs are paid to look the other way and let avarice and deception prevail. These "watchdogs" include the boards of directors, the large law firms, the

major accounting firms, and the ratings companies like Moody's and Standard and Poor's.

Looking the other way also pays for most state and federal legislators and the regulators. The former solicit campaign contributions and the latter are looking forward to cushy positions in the industries they failed to regulate as government servants.

The forecasters' excuse is that the watchdogs weren't barking to alert them. Come on! These forecasters weren't born yesterday.

Barron's veteran columnist Alan Abelson is a sharp pen hedger who calls his weekly commentary "Up and Down Wall Street." Abelson is a wry, irreverent free-thinker on the conservative side, but he sometimes offers useful insights. Maybe he can break his remaining taboo and apply his mordant, satirical style to review a year of *Barron's* recommendations and see whether short sellers made more money than investors did who bought on the suspect advice.

It could be that the fog at Barron's is lifting; it just recently offered a year's subscription for $52, a sharp discount from its $260 yearly newsstand cost of $5 per copy. Now that's a realistic price worth paying at least if you like comedic doses of illusion and the fullest stock tables on paper east of the Pecos.

CPAs MIA
April 10, 2009

Where were the giant accounting firms, the CPAs, and the rest of the accounting profession while the Wall Street towers of fraud, deception and cover-ups were fracturing our economy, looting and draining trillions of dollars of other peoples' money?

This is the licensed profession that is paid

to exercise independent judgment with independent standards to give investors, pension funds, mutual funds, and the rest of the financial world accurate descriptions of corporate financial realities.

It is now obvious that the accountants collapsed their own skill, integrity and self-respect faster and earlier than the collapse of Wall Street and the corporate barons. The accountants—both external and internal—could have blown the whistle on what Teddy Roosevelt called the "malefactors of great wealth."

The Big Four auditors knew what was going on with these complex, abstractly structured finance instruments, these collateralized debt obligations (CDOs) and other financial products too abstruse to label. They were on high alert after early warning scandals involving Long Term Capital Management, Enron, and others a decade or so ago.

These corporate casino capitalists used the latest tricks to cook the books with many of the on-balance sheet or off-balance sheet structured investment vehicles that metastasized big time in the first decade of this new century. These big firms can't excuse themselves for relying on conflicted rating companies, like Moody's or Standard & Poor, that gave triple-A ratings to CDO tranches in return for big fees. Imagine the conflict. After all, "prestigious" outside auditors were supposed to be on the inside incisively examining the books and their footnotes, on which the rating firms excessively relied.

Let's be specific with names. Carl Olson, chairman of the Fund for Stockowners Rights wrote in the letters column of the *New York Times Magazine* (January 28, 2009) that "PricewaterhouseCoopers O.K.'d AIG and Freddie Mac. Deloitte & Touche certified Merrill Lynch and Bear Stearns. Ernst & Young vouched for

Lehman Brothers and IndyMac Bank. KPMG assured over Countrywide and Wachovia. These 'Big Four' CPA firms apparently felt they could act with impunity."

"Undoubtedly they knew that the state boards of accountancy," continued Mr. Olson, "which granted them their licenses to audit, would not consider these transgressions seriously. And they were right . . . not one of them has taken up any serious investigation of the misbehaving auditors of the recent debacle companies."

"Misbehaving" is too kind a word. The "Big Four" destroyed their very reason for being by their involvement in these and other boondoggles that have made headlines and dragooned our federal government into bailing them out with disbursements, loans and guarantees totaling trillions of dollars. "Criminally negligent" is a better phrase for what these big accounting firms got rich doing—which is to look the other way.

Holding accounting firms like these accountable is very difficult. It got more difficult in 1995 when Congress passed a bill shielding them from investor lawsuits charging that they "aided and abetted" fraudulent or deceptive schemes by their corporate clients. Clinton vetoed the legislation, but Senator Chris Dodd (D-Conn.) led the fight to over-ride the veto.

Moreover, the under-funded and understaffed state boards of accountancy are dominated by accountants and are beyond inaction. What can you expect?

As for the Securities and Exchange Commission (SEC), "asleep at the switch for years" would be a charitable description of that now embarrassed agency whose mission is to supposedly protect savers and shareholders. This agency even missed the massive Madoff Ponzi scheme.

The question of accounting probity will not

go away. In the past couple of weeks, the non-profit Financial Accounting Standards Board (FASB)—assigned to be the professional conscience of accountancy—buckled under overt pressure from Congress and the banks. It loosened the mark-to-market requirement to value assets at fair market value or what buyers are willing to pay.

This decision by the FASB is enforceable by the SEC and immediately "cheered Wall Street" and pushed big bank stocks upward. Robert Willens, an accounting analyst, estimated this change could boost earnings at some banks by up to 20 percent. Voilà, just like that. Magic!

Overpricing depressed assets may make bank bosses happy, but not investors or a former SEC Chairman, Arthur Levitt, who was "very disappointed" and called the FASB decision "a step toward the kind of opaqueness that created the economic problems that we're enduring today."

To show the deterioration in standards, banks tried to get the FASB and the SEC in the 1980s to water down fair-value accounting during the savings and loan failures. Then-SEC Chairman Richard Breeden refused outright. Not today.

Former SEC chief accountant, Lynn Turner—presently a reformer of his own profession—supports mark-to-market or fair value accounting as part of bringing all assets and liabilities, including credit derivatives, back on the balance sheets of the financial firms. He wants regulation of the credit rating agencies, mortgage originators and the perverse incentives that lead to making bad loans. He even wants the SEC to review these new financial products before they come to market, eliminating "hidden financing." Now comes the life insurance industry, buying up some small banks to qualify for their own large federal bailouts for making bad, risky speculations.

The brilliant Joseph M. Belth, writing in his astute newsletter, the Insurance Forum (May 2009), noted that life insurers are lobbying state insurance departments to weaken statutory accounting rules so as to "increase assets and/or decrease liabilities." Some states have already caved. Again, voilà, suddenly there is an increase in capital. Magic. Here we go again.

Who among the brainy, head-up accountants, in practice or in academia, will join with Lynn Turner and rescue this demeaned, chronically rubber-stamping "profession," especially the "Big Four," from its pathetic pretension for which tens of millions of people are paying dearly?

Banking on Credit Unions
February 20, 2009

While the reckless giant banks are shattering like an over-heated glacier day by day, the nation's credit unions are a relative island of calm largely apart from the vortex of casino capitalism.

Eighty five million Americans belong to credit unions which are not-for-profit cooperatives owned by their members who are depositors and borrowers. Your neighborhood or workplace credit union did not invest in these notorious speculative derivatives nor did they offer people "teaser rates" to sign on for a home mortgage they could not afford.

Ninety-one percent of the 8,000 credit unions are reporting greater overall growth in mortgage lending than any other kinds of consumer loans they are extending. They are federally insured by the National Credit Union Administration (NCUA) for up to $250,000 per account, such as the FDIC does for depositors in commercial banks.

They are well-capitalized because of regulation and because they do not have an incentive to go for high-risk, highly leveraged speculation to increase stock values and the value of the bosses' stock options as do the commercial banks.

Credit Unions have no shareholders nor stock nor stock options; they are responsible to their owner-members who are their customers.

There are even some special low-income credit unions—thought not nearly enough—to stimulate economic activities in these communities and to provide "banking" services in areas where poor people can't afford or are not provided services by commercial banks.

According to Mike Schenk, an economist with the Credit Union National Association, there is another reason why credit unions avoided the mortgage debacle that is consuming the big banks.

Credit Unions, he says, are "portfolio lenders. That means they hold in their portfolios most of the loans they originate instead of selling them to investors. . . . so they care about the financial performance of those loans."

Mr. Schenk allowed that with the deepening recession, credit unions are not making as much surplus and "their asset quality has deteriorated a bit. But that's the beauty of the credit union model. Credit unions can live with those conditions without suffering dire consequences," he asserted.

His use of the word "model" is instructive. In recent decades, credit unions sometimes leaned toward commercial bank practices instead of strict cooperative principles. They developed a penchant for mergers into larger and larger credit unions. Some even toyed with converting out of the cooperative model into the shareholder model the way insurance and bank mutuals have done. The cooperative model—whether in finance, food, housing or any other sector of the economy—does best when the owner-cooperators are active in the general operations and directions of their co-op. Passive owners allow managers to stray or contemplate straying from cooperative practices.

The one area that is now spelling some trouble for retail cooperatives comes from the so-called "corporate credit unions"—a terrible nomenclature—which were established to provide liquidity for the retail credit unions. These large wholesale credit unions are not exactly infused with the cooperative philosophy. Some of them gravitate toward the corporate banking model. They invested in those risky mortgage securities with the money from the retail credit unions. These "toxic assets" have fallen $14 billion among the twenty-eight corporate credit unions involved.

So the National Credit Union Administration is expanding its lending programs to these corporate credit unions to a maximum capacity of $41.5 billion. NCUA also wants to have retail credit unions qualified for the TARP rescue program just to provide a level playing field with the commercial banks.

Becoming more like investment banks, the wholesale credit unions wanted to attract more of the retail credit union deposits with ever higher riskier yields. This set the stage for the one major blemish of imprudence on the credit union subeconomy.

There are very contemporary lessons to be learned from the successes of the credit union model such as being responsive to consumer loan needs and down to earth with their portfolios. Yet in all the massive media coverage of the Wall Street barons and their lethal financial escapades, crimes and frauds, little is being written about how the regulation, philosophy and behavior of the credit unions largely escaped this catastrophe.

There is, moreover, a lesson for retail credit unions. Beware and avoid the seepage or supremacy of the corporate financial model which, in its present degraded overly complex and abstract form, has become what one prosecutor called "lying, cheating, and stealing" in fancy clothing.

Open Letter to President Obama on Consumer Protection

January 23, 2009

Dear President Obama:

Underneath many of our country's economic problems is the thirty-year collapse of consumer protection—both of the regulatory kind and of the self-help kind known as proper access to justice.

Last month major consumer groups sent you a letter proposing action to rein in exploitation of consumers as debtors, as buyers of oil, gas and electricity, as patients needing health insurance and as eaters wanting safe goods.

Under the Bush regime, the words "consumer protection" were rarely uttered and the Bush administration almost never initiated any pro-consumer efforts, even with massive evidence before it, such as predatory lending and credit card abuses.

You need to recognize and elevate the GDP significance of fair consumer policies along with their moral and just attributes at a time of worsening recession.

I suggest you focus on the state of the poorest consumers in the urban and rural ghettos. As you know from your days with the New York Public Interest Group (NYPIRG) and as a community organizer in Chicago, the consumers in these areas are the most gouged and least protected. That the "poor pay more" has been extensively documented by civic, official and academic studies, and numerous local newspaper and television news reports.

Unfortunately, neither Congress nor the Executive Branch have paid adequate attention to the tens of millions of people who lose at least 25 percent of their consumer dollars to multiple frauds and shoddy merchandise. You should establish special task forces in the Justice Department and the Federal Trade Commission on their plight and on the many proven but unused remedies to assure a fair marketplace with effective enforcement and grievance procedures.

Working with and galvanizing local and state agencies to enlarge their capacity and staff—with stimulus monies—can produce a triple-header—making the federal effort more effective, providing valuable jobs and freeing up billions of consumer dollars from the financial sink-hole of commercial crimes.

It requires the visibility and eloquence of your personal leadership to launch this long-overdue defense of poor people.

A second area of action is simply to update major areas of regulatory health and safety that have been frozen for thirty years. These include modernizing standards for auto and tire safety, food safety, aviation and railroad safety and occupational health and trauma protection.

New knowledge, new marketing forays, and new technologies have accumulated during this period without application. It is the obsolescence of so many safety standards hailing from the '50s, '60s, and '70s that permits the tricky, corporate advertising claims that products "exceed federal safety standards."

Note for example that the SEC has never come close to regulating the recent explosion of myriad collateralized debt obligations (CDOs). The massive speculation in this area is destabilizing the national and world economies.

Third, you need to articulate and provide a high profile to what western Europeans have long called "social consumerism." Citizens are consumers of government services for which they pay as taxpayers. In return they are entitled to prompt, accurate and courteous responses to their inquiries and to their perceived needs as embraced by the authorizing statutes.

To begin with, Americans need to be able to get through to their government agencies and departments. Being put on hold interminably with automated messages to nowhere, not receiving replies of any kind to their letters, and generally getting the brush-off even with the deadlines explicated in the Freedom of Information Act have been a bi-partisan failure.

However, under the Bush regime, not answering serious letters from dedicated individuals and groups on time-sensitive matters of policy and action—as with the Iraq War and occupation—became standard operating procedure—starting with President Bush himself.

This stonewalling has turned people off so much that they do not even bother to "ask their government" for assistance and that includes an astonishingly unresponsive Congress (other than for ministerial requests such as locating lost VA or Social Security checks).

As you shape the Obama White House, bear in mind that the "change you can believe in" is one of kind, not just degree.

Sincerely yours,
Ralph Nader

Closing the Courthouse Door

October 16, 2008

"Real change comes from the bottom up, not the top down. The genius of the American system has been to let that change flow upward, from neighborhoods to cities to states and then to the federal government." George W. Bush, February 26, 2001.

Unfortunately, the difference between words and deeds in Washington is often shocking even to those who think they have seen it all. Alicia Mundy in the October 15, 2008 edition of the *Wall Street Journal* reports, "Bush administration officials, in their last weeks in office, are pushing to rewrite a wide array of federal rules with changes or additions that could block product-safety lawsuits by consumers and states."

What President George W. Bush should have said is that he believes in states rights when they are in the interest of Big Business and their lobbyists in Washington. Mr. Bush and his cronies would like to forget about those harmed by dangerous products or reckless conduct. Indeed, Bush & Company seem to regard the civil justice system as a nuisance that threatens to destroy our economy and way of life.

In reality, America's civil justice system plays an indispensable role in our democracy. When the rights of injured consumers are vindicated in court, our society benefits in countless ways: compensating victims and their families for shattering losses (with the cost borne by the wrongdoers rather than taxpayers); preventing future injuries by deterring dangerous products and practices and spurring safety innovation; stimulating enforceable safety standards; educating the public to risks associated with certain products and services; and providing society with its moral and ethical fiber by defining appropriate norms of conduct.

The Center for Progressive Reform has in painstaking detail chronicled the attack on the civil justice system by the Bush Administration. In "The Truth about Torts: Using Agency Preemption to Undercut Consumer Health and Safety," legal scholars William Funk, Sidney Shapiro, David Vladeck and Karen Sokol write: "In recent years, the Bush administration has launched an unprecedented aggressive campaign to persuade the courts to preempt state tort actions . . . Widespread preemption of state tort law would significantly undermine, if not eliminate, the rights of individuals to seek redress for injuries caused by irresponsible and dangerous business practices and to hold manufacturers and others accountable for such socially unreasonable conduct." (See: progressiveregulation.org).

And, Les Weisbrod, the president of the American Association for Justice (formerly known as the Association of Trial Lawyers of America), hit the nail on the head when he said, "In effect the Bush administration made the safety of Americans secondary to corporate profits." Weisbrod added, "Big business lobbyists have been on a crusade to destroy state consumer protection laws, and further stack the deck against American consumers." The American Association for Justice has just published a report titled, "Get Out of Jail Free: A Historical Perspective of How the Bush Administration Helps Corporations Escape Accountability." This report is available at: justice.org/getoutofjailfree.

Tort deform comes in many shapes and sizes—but the common theme is that tort deform severely damages Americans' cherished constitutional right to trial by jury. It ties the hands of jurors, preventing them from doing justice as the case before them requires. Only the judges and juries see, hear, and evaluate the evidence in these cases. But it is the politicians, absent from the courtrooms, who push bills greased by campaign cash that send a perverse order to judge and jury.

Tort law has produced decades of slow but steady progress in state after state respecting the physical integrity of human beings against harm and recognition that even the weak and defenseless deserve justice. Instead of seeing this evolution as a source of national and global pride, a coalition of insurance companies, corporate defendants' lobbies, and craven politicians, led by George W. Bush, want to destroy our civil justice system.

When Georgetown Law School Professor David Vladeck testified before the Senate Judiciary Committee on September 12, 2007, he noted that the Bush Administration has "seized on regulatory preemption as a way to cut back dramatically on State law remedies for those injured by products and services Americans depend on every day for their health and well-being—medicines, medical devices, motor vehicles, the mattress on which we and our children sleep, and the commuter trains millions of us take to work every day."

Let us hope that Congress and the Supreme Court stop Mr. Bush from once again trampling the Constitutional rights of citizens throughout the land and preventing victims of corporate violence from obtaining justice in a court of law.

Rolling the Dice on Derivatives

October 10, 2008

The derivatives markets of today have become a high stakes casino of unimaginable magnitude. Wall Street's bets have gone bad, and now the whole financial system is in peril. In a best-case scenario, it appears, the taxpayers will be required to rescue the system from itself. This is why Warren Buffett labeled derivatives "weapons of financial mass destruction."

Amazingly, there seems to be some lingering sense that current-day derivatives properly perform an insurance function.

Case in point: Alan Greenspan, the former Federal Reserve Chairman. Greenspan says the world is facing "the type of wrenching financial crisis that comes along only once in a century," but, reports the New York Times, "his faith in derivatives remains unshaken." Greenspan believes that the problem is not with derivatives, but that the people using them got greedy, according to the Times.

This is quite a view. Is it a surprise to Alan Greenspan that the people on Wall Street—said to be ruled only by the opposing instincts of greed and fear—"got greedy?"

This might be taken as just a bizarre comment, except that, of course, Alan Greenspan had some considerable influence in driving us to the current financial meltdown through his opposition to regulation of derivatives.

A series of deregulatory moves, blessed by Alan Greenspan, helped immunize Wall Street derivatives traders from proper oversight.

In 1995, Congress enacted the Private Securities Litigation Reform Act (PSLRA) which imposed onerous restrictions on plaintiffs suing wrongdoers in the stock market. The law was enacted in the wake of Orange County, California's government bankruptcy caused by abuses in derivatives trading. An amendment offered by Rep. Ed Markey would have exempted derivatives trading abuse lawsuits from the PSLRA restrictions. In defeating the amendment, then-Representative and now-SEC Chairman Chris Cox quoted Alan Greenspan, saying, "It would be a grave error to demonize derivatives;" and, "It would be a serious mistake to respond to these developments [in Orange County, California] by singling out derivative instruments for special regulatory treatment."

The New York Times reports how the Commodity Futures Trading Commission aimed for some modest regulatory authority over derivatives in the late 1990s. Strident opposition from Treasury Secretary Robert Rubin and Alan Greenspan spelled doom for that effort.

Senator Phil Gramm helped drive the process along with the Commodities Futures Modernization Act of 2000, which deregulated the derivatives market.

Defenders of deregulation argued that sophisticated players were involved in the derivatives markets, and they could handle themselves.

It's now apparent that not only could these sophisticated players not handle themselves, but that their reckless gambling has placed the entire world's financial system at risk.

It seems to be, then, a remarkably modest proposal for derivatives to be brought under regulatory control.

Warren Buffett cut to the heart of the problem in 2003: "Another problem about derivatives is that they can exacerbate trouble that a corporation has run into for completely unrelated reasons," he wrote in his annual letter to shareholders. "This pile-on effect occurs because many derivatives contracts require that a company suffering a credit downgrade immediately supply collateral to counterparties. Imagine, then, that a company is downgraded because of general adversity and that its derivatives instantly kick in with their requirement, imposing an unexpected and enormous demand for cash collateral on the company. The need to meet this demand can then throw the company into a liquidity crisis that may, in some cases, trigger still more downgrades. It all becomes a spiral that can lead to a corporate meltdown."

That is to say, our current problems were foreseeable, and foreseen. There is no excuse for those who suggest that present circumstances—what many are calling a once-in-a-hundred-years event—were unimaginable during earlier debates about regulation.

Some ideologues continue to defend derivatives from very strict government control. As Congress moves to adopt new financial regulations next year, hopefully the proponents of casino capitalism will be given no more credence than those insisting that the sun revolves around the earth.

Statement on Auto Industry Bailouts

September 17, 2008

The Big Three are in big trouble, and they have themselves to thank for it.

Ford and General Motors have reported substantial losses in the second quarter amounting to $15.5 billion, and $8.7 billion, respectively, while Chrysler, which was bought off last year by a private equity firm, Cerberus, refuses to reveal its financial standing.

It is no wonder why their lobbyists were spotted schmoozing with members of Congress at the Democratic and Republican National Conventions, liquoring up in their plush suites and private parties while they made their case for direct government loans which, if approved, would likely add to our federal deficit.

Last December, Congress approved a $25 billion loan to automakers and their suppliers under the Energy Independence and Security Act, though it has yet to be funded. That bill includes a modest requirement for automakers to increase their average vehicle fuel efficiency to 35 mpg—a benchmark we should have set decades ago, and would allow the companies to have their way with virtually no oversight or accountability.

This corporate Congress cannot be expected to issue serious demands, set tough conditions, or impose strict rules on the auto companies to ensure their workers receive fair pay and benefits, and prevent their fat-cat executives from making off big while leaving their companies in shambles.

Such blatant giveaways have become the norm in Washington since the corporate stranglehold of Congress and the White House have smothered the forces seeking worker, consumer and environmental justice.

But this recent example should not discount our long history of dealing with corporate failures in more public and effective ways than just ponying up billions on demand at any big corporation's whim.

In 1979 when Chrysler was on the verge of bankruptcy, the automaker came crying to Congress for a bailout, which they eventually got, but Congress wasn't as much of a pushover.

Back then, at least the corporate chieftains were grilled by Congress and had to agree to give something back for Uncle Sam bailing them out—good jobs and pensions for their workers, and more efficient cars to reduce reliance on foreign oil and reduce prices at the pump.

Now the CEOs don't even have to leave Detroit and they get much more money for almost no return commitment to America, while they outsource jobs and pollute our environment.

During discussion on a proposed loan bill to bailout Chrysler in October 1979, Senator William Proxmire (D-Wis.) who chaired the Senate Banking Committee, issued his opposition to Chrysler's request and noted, "We let 7,000 companies fail last year—we didn't bail them out. Now we are being told that if a company is big enough . . . we can't let it go under." He went on to call the proposed deal "a terrible precedent."

Raising the government's demand for performance standards, President Carter's Treasury Secretary William Miller told Chrysler officials, "It's going to be so awful, you'll wish you never brought the whole thing up."

Today, we rarely hear such candid opposition to corporate orders shouted at their congressional servants who lack the fortitude to put serious restraints and conditions on mismanaged, reckless big business and their overpaid CEOs seeking tax-payer salvation.

As a part of the Chrysler deal in the late 1970s, the government took out preferred stock warrants and after the company turned itself around and repaid its loan seven years early, the government ended up cashing out, receiving $400 million in the appreciated stock.

And Congress made it clear to Chrysler that it had specific conditions the company had to meet before receiving the loan guarantee. It forced the company to contribute $162,500,000 into an employee stock ownership trust fund geared to benefit at least 90 percent of its employees, design more fuel efficient autos to help reduce consumption of foreign oil, and prohibit wages and benefits from falling below a level set three months before the legislation was passed.

Today, congressional actions to grant multi-billion dollar loans to the corporations lack the reciprocity some in Congress demanded thirty years ago. Before Congress irresponsibly dips into the public piggy bank, this time it would be wise to look back at how the government once dealt with Chrysler's dilemma, require clear benchmarks to deliver on the next generation of green collar jobs, improved fuel efficiency and gain a substantial return on its investment, not just in monetary value, but in the longterm viability of the domestic motor vehicle fleet.

Congress needs to call on the auto industry to innovate their way out of this morass into which they've engineered themselves into. A sensible strategy would be to issue stock warrants to the government, like in the '70s, which would create an incentive for Congress to keep pressure on the auto industry to improve. Public Congressional hearings are a must.

Will Congress echo its actions of thirty years ago when it scrutinized corporate demands, grilled company executives, and imposed conditions to ensure fair compensation and safety for workers? Or will Congress continue down the road of corporate servitude, refusing to stand up for workers, consumers, taxpayers and the environment in its session-ending stampede and flight away from auto industry accountabilities?

Bailing Out Fannie and Freddie
September 9, 2008

When Members of Congress or the Administration or the corporate CEOs or the empirically starved right-wing ideologues start whining about regulation, the right-wing echo chamber goes wild. When the absence of adequate regulation lets an industry wreak havoc, Congress and the Administration meekly admit a bit of regulation might have averted disaster. The corporate CEOs, expelled with their lucrative golden parachutes, have "no comment."

The taxpayers, who are too often the guarantors of last resort and who are stuck with the tab, are asking each other why their public watchdogs were asleep at the switch. The Washington merry-go-round is something to behold.

As the recent headlines note, the Federal Government has taken over the giant companies Fannie Mae and Freddie Mac. The Federal Housing Finance Agency (FHFA) is using the legal process of a "conservatorship" to "stabilize" Fannie Mae and Freddie Mac. Talk about regulation!

On Sunday, September 7, 2008, US Treasury Secretary Henry Paulson said, "Since this difficult period for the GSEs began, I have clearly stated three critical objectives: providing stability to financial markets, supporting the availability of mortgage finance, and protecting taxpayers—both by minimizing the near term costs to the taxpayer and by setting policymakers on a course to resolve the systemic risk created by the inherent conflict in the GSE structure."

Nice words—but they will provide little comfort to the many common shareholders who have seen the value of their Fannie Mae and Freddie Mac stock collapse to pennies per share. And more than a few taxpayers are wondering what the Fannie/Freddie debacle will end up costing them.

We and others have been telling members of Congress, government regulators and members of the media about the structural and operational problems of Fannie and Freddie for years. I have written many columns about the lack of proper regulation of Fannie and Freddie. I testified before Congress about the need to focus Fannie and Freddie, and my long-time associates Jonathan Brown and Jake Lewis have spent countless hours advocating that federal regulators push Fannie and Freddie to meet housing goals that would benefit under-served populations.

In 1991, lawyer Tom Stanton, a former colleague, warned about the risks and non-regulation of Fannie and Freddie in his prophetic book—*A State of Risk* (Harper Business).

In May of 1998, we even held a conference dedicated to Fannie and Freddie. In my welcoming statement to the conference participants, I noted that we would be discussing the adequacy of capital required of Fannie and Freddie and the efficacy of regulation of the two GSEs. I noted that both corporations had been enjoying good times. And, I cautioned that one of the unintended consequences of fat profits over a long period is the tendency of governments and private corporations to start believing in fantasies about living happily ever after in the glory of ever-rising profits.

My statement asserted that, "Taxpayers have learned that contingent liabilities such as those inherent in the GSE structure do, at times, become quite costly. It wasn't long ago—in the high interest rate period in the late 1970s and early 1980s—that Fannie Mae was having serious financial troubles. And the Farm Credit System, another GSE, required a bail out of approximately $5 billion in the 1980s when the agricultural industry had a severe downturn."

In July of this year I lamented the fact that Fannie and Freddie have been deeply unregulated for decades which allowed their capital ratios to be lower—far lower—than they should have been.

Over at the multi-trillion dollar companies Fannie Mae and Freddie Mac, the shareholders have lost about 75 percent of their stock value in one year. Farcically regulated by the Department of Housing and Urban Affairs, Fannie and Freddie were run into the ground by taking on very shaky mortgages under the command of CEOs and their top executives who paid themselves enormous sums.

These two institutions were set up many years ago to provide liquidity in the housing and loan markets and thereby expand home ownership especially among lower income families. Instead, they turned themselves into casinos, taking advantage of an implied US government guarantee.

The Fannie and Freddie bosses created another guarantee. They hired top appointees from both Republican and Democratic administrations (such as Deputy Attorney General Jamie Gorelick) and lathered them with tens of millions of dollars in executive compensation. In this way, they kept federal supervision at a minimum and held off efforts in Congress to toughen regulation.

So here we are. On Monday September 8, 2008, the value of common Fannie and Freddie stock dropped to under one dollar—just one day after the Secretary of the Treasury, Henry Paulson, announced the government takeover. White House Press Secretary Dana Perino said, "[F]or years we have encouraged Congress to put in place a strong, independent regulator to oversee the institutions. We believe the actions will help to improve conditions in the housing market."

Senate Banking Committee Chairman Christopher J. Dodd (D-Conn.) has questions for the administration, so there is more to be revealed. And, reporters are spilling buckets of ink talking about the takeover of Fannie and Freddie and the lack of proper oversight by regulators and Congress which brought us to this day of appreciation for regulation. Too bad it is all a little late for the small shareholders, and pensioners and taxpayers who pay the bill for speculators and executives, many of whom seem to escape with lots of money.

Bad Mouthing De-regulation
January 18, 2008

It was at a large wedding reception in New York City that I saw Chairman of the Federal Reserve, Alan Greenspan, sitting down to dinner one spring evening in 2000. Having heard through grapevine that the Federal Reserve was finally going to do something about predatory lending—an area of enforcement under their jurisdiction—I went over to his table and asked him this question:

> "Mr. Chairman, I hear that you are going to crack down on predatory lending practices." He nodded and said quite firmly, "Yes, enough is enough."

Since it was, after all, a social occasion, those words were enough for me and I returned to my table with the good news. For years, my associates, Jon Brown and Jake Lewis, had been working to document the prevalence of predatory lending and communicate our concern to the federal banking agencies and members of Congress.

Jon Brown developed detailed computerized maps of bank redlining in low-income areas, city by city, which were geographic guides to places where there were plenty of predatory lending practices.

As it turned out, Chairman Greenspan's Federal Reserve did nothing about either traditional predatory lending or the rise of the latest version of that abusive pattern—the now notorious sub-prime mortgage scandals and mega-losses that are shaking the financial industry to its foundations.

Actually, Mr. Greenspan often praised leveraged, collateralized sub-prime lending as helping lower-income people to get home mortgages. He did not give much weight to the deception and imprudence and gouging of the lenders lurking in the fine print and flowing from the silver tongues of the salespeople.

The Federal Reserve touts itself as the agency where lots of smart people work—economists, statisticians, forecasters—and, of course, the often-described very smart Chairman. Yet as the speculative greed that developed, sold and resold ever more abstract and risky financial instruments comprised of bundled home mortgages went toward its final orbit of collapse, these "best and the brightest," failed to act. They failed to regulate.

The business assault on regulation and its drumbeat demands for de-regulation over the past quarter century have now caused a burgeoning sub-prime mortgage collapse that is producing hundreds of thousands of home foreclosures. The housing market is plummeting. Giant banks are desperate for infusions of capital from abroad to save them from insolvency. Huge mortgage lenders are teetering on bankruptcy, looking desperately to be taken over by other financial companies.

Foreign banks and municipalities around the world that assumed these risks are marking down big losses.

All this has been caused by a combination of speculative greed, taking on huge risks for higher returns and the refusal to apply financial law and order—i.e., regulation—by the Bush regime. All this was preventable by institutional prudence and a vigilant Federal Reserve.

So what are all these giant financial corporations on their knees begging for these grim days? They are begging the Federal Reserve to use every bit of its authority to save them through lower interest rates and by using a variety of other more abstruse tools the Fed has to rescue the very banks that help fund its budget and dominate the regional Boards of the Federal Reserve.

It is true that corporate heads have rolled—most notably the CEOs of Citigroup and Merrill Lynch. By and large, however, the remaining top culprits who got their banks and mortgage lending firms into such deep losses for investor-share holders are staying put with their enormous compensation packages.

When the big boys get into trouble, they expect Uncle Sam to bail them out. Who pays the ultimate bill? You guessed it. The small taxpayer and the consumer.

So next time your hear the words—deregulation or over-regulation—by the thoughtless think tanks, heavily funded by business money, remind yourself that you believe in tough law and order for big business and your demand that politicians weigh in with a strong enforcement crackdown on corporate crime and fraud.

Big Oils Profit and Plunder
December 21, 2007

While many impoverished American families are shivering in the winter cold for lack of money to pay the oil baron their exorbitant price for home heating oil, ex-oil man, George W. Bush sleeps in a warm White House and relishes his defeat of the Congressional attempt to get rid of $15 billion in unconscionable tax breaks given those same profit-glutted oil companies like ExxonMobil when crude oil was half the price it is today.

This is the same George W. Bush who, calling himself a "compassionate conservative" in October 2000 made this promise to the American people: "First and foremost, we've got to make sure we fully fund the Low Income Home Energy Assistance Program (LIHEAP), which is a way to help low-income folks, particularly here in the East, pay for their high, high fuel bills."

So what did this serial promise-breaker propose this year? Mr. Bush wanted to cut the fuel aid program by $379 million! This entire assistance program is funded at about half of the $5 billion that state governors and lawmakers believe is essential to meet the needs of the six million people eligible to apply for such help this year.

Everyone in Washington knows that the big, coddled, subsidized oil industry has many politicians over a barrel. When it comes to oily Bush and Cheney though, the global melting industry has these two indentured servants marinated in oil.

Look at what ending regulation of natural gas prices has produced: prices up 50 percent since last year. Home heating oil prices are up 30 percent. Bush's own Energy Department estimates the rise of heating oil costs will impose an average increase of $375 for customers this winter. No way that supply and demand explains this gouge.

If a home dweller is too poor to order more than 100 gallons at a time, they get smacked with an extra surcharge of 60 to 70 cents per gallon for delivery.

Some states set aside some money. New York State will spend $25 million. Joe Kennedy and Citgo sell discounted heating oil, but that Venezuelan program is undergoing a reduction.

Efforts in Congress to impose a windfall-profits tax on the King Kong, record-profit-setting oil companies got nowhere.

Two years ago, efforts by Senator Charles Grassley (Rep-Iowa), then chairman of the Senate Finance Committee, begging the major oil giants to slice off a tiny portion of their profits for charitable contributions toward energy assistance for the poor did not receive even the courtesy of a response.

I've asked members of Congress, including the Black Caucus and the Hispanic Caucus in the House of Representatives to take up this cause vigorously and prominently on behalf of their constituents back home. Have you heard any high-visibility demand from these veteran lawmakers? I haven't.

Even Senator Grassley seems to have despaired.

Please note that ExxonMobil alone made $36 billion in profits last year. That's one company profiting over seven times the amount of dollars needed for energy assistance. Greed, arrogance, callousness and far too much unaccountable power exists in Big Oil and in its White House.

Enforcing the antitrust laws and prohibiting organized speculators at the Mercantile Exchange from determining the price of an essential product like petroleum will bring prices down. But there is no action in the White House. No demand from the Congress.

Veteran freelance reporter, Lance Tapley has been reporting for the *Portland Phoenix* newspaper on the price bilking of recipients of energy assistance programs. For thirty years, he writes, the oil dealers have been charging the Maine state housing authority, which administers the LIHEAP program, higher prices than they set for their payment-plan customers, despite the large bulk purchasing by this housing authority.

Tapley severely criticizes the failure of Governor John Baldacci for not standing up for poor Maine people at the same time he promotes large subsidies for business and sells off state-owned assets at bargain-basement prices to corporations.

Mr. Tapley writes, "The heating oil crisis could be a big test in 2008 for Baldacci and the State House Democrats. The picture will not be pretty if elderly poor people freeze in their trailers while rich Republicans and professional-class Democrats snuggle up in their McMansions or old Colonials . . . but, with our Democrats, who needs Republicans?"

Some day, the tens of millions of poor people in America, most of them working poor, will be heard from. Until now, they have been exhausted, powerless, despairing, fearful and grasping for whatever crumbs fall off the table. History teaches us that such a subdued human condition does not continue indefinitely.

Call the White House switchboard (202-456-1414) and your member of Congress (Senate Information: 202-224-3121; House Information: 202-225-3121). Tell them not all of these low-income Americans have been sent to oil-rich Iraq. Many are here mourning their losses of and injuries to loved ones while they shiver in the cold.

Tell them to make those big oil CEOs making as much as $50,000 an hour to ante up.

How to Stiff Your Customers and Still Stay in Business

August 31, 2007

You are a shopper. Let me ask you this question: is there such a thing as advertising reaching such a saturation level that would cause you to rebel and reject buying from companies that are the worst abusers?

In other words, do you have an annoyance break point? Do you have a strong sense that there should be "advertising-free zones" in public life?

There is advertising now in public rest rooms, on the floors of supermarkets, in elevators, even on the walls of schools and the sides of school buses.

Advertisers are relentlessly searching and probing for new locations. Years ago, we helped beat back corporate attempts to "rent" a corner of US Postage stamps for corporate logos. These firms still dream of putting their labels on the uniforms of major league baseball players. Most players said, unequivocally, no, leaving money on the table.

A decent sense of limits escapes many in the commercial advertising industry. In the past few days, there was a report in the *New York Times* about companies paying thousands of motorists for the opportunity to wrap their automobiles and trucks with their company logos and slogans.

A Brian Katz was paid $500 a month for the use of space on his Ford Expedition. Onlookers can see Jamba Juice and Verizon Wireless publicized on his vehicle. The "wrapped car" craze has a million car owners who are ready to have their cars wrapped for a fee.

Wrapping is getting more intrusive for the driver. He or she is expected not to smoke, curse or litter. In some cases, they are supposed to hand out samples.

Up in the air, the advertisers are pushing to sign up airlines for commercials on the overhead baggage compartments, the backs of closed tray tables and on whatever paper products they bring with their drinks. Headway on this latest intrusion is occurring among European low-cost carriers like Ryanair and Germanwings.

Customer passivity invites more advertisements in more and more places long considered off-limits. Want to fight back? For starters, just grumble out loud, complain to service people closest to you.

Second, check out commercialalert.org to see what other people, like yourself, are doing to confront and rollback the rampaging commercialization of society in hitherto taboo regions.

Third, someone please start a website that signs up consumers who won't buy the products or services of corporate advertisers run amok. The website can describe or depict the ad and its location by company name and let consumers choose where and what their outrage will boycott.

Companies are sensitive to such fight back methods. Even the tiniest loss of sales margins makes them rethink their indiscretion. But if they don't hear from you, they'll be pushing the envelope further, such as renting the cheeks, earlobes, arms and legs of humans. They've already got millions of people sporting their designer labels prominently on their clothing and their cars.

Sometime ago, one alert man in Maryland marched back to his auto dealer and demanded that it take out the embedded company name or pay him for carrying it along the highways.

Companies sure want *you* to notice *them*. But many make it very difficult for *you* to make *them*

notice *you*. United Airlines service, in contrast to its safety record, would make a fertile case study by a business school entitled "How to Stiff Your Customers and Still Stay in Business."

Once one of my favorite airlines for service, United Airlines, whether in or out of bankruptcy, seems to keep thinking up ways to irritate its passengers. From making you wait and wait on its automated phone lines to answer a question they have not programmed for, to the outrageous fees for changing a reservation ($100) or an additional checked suitcase ($100), to making it super-difficult just to contact their customer relations office for more sweeping suggestions, United keeps on adding new ways to drain your budget, your time and your patience. The wondrous Southwest Airlines, it is not!

Recently, I asked my associate Barry Williams, to get the uniquely titled "vice president of customer experience" on the phone. Just to course his way through the barriers of rejection and then the transfer experience to get her name and number took him over thirty minutes. Finally, he succeeded! You can call too. She is Ms. Barbara Higgins, P.O. 66100, 14th Floor, Chicago, Illinois, 60666. Tel: 312-997-8120.

Coincidentally, the August 28, 2007 issue of the *Wall Street Journal* featured on its front page the remarkable, amazing passenger service provided by United Airlines Capt. Denny Flanagan. So astonishing is his care and anticipation that he has been discussed often on FlyerTalk.com.

United Airlines is proud of Capt. Flanagan. Too bad it doesn't find him contagious!

Imports Cause Consumer Safety Concern

July 9, 2007

It has been a long time coming, but now the mass media and even the "look-the-other-way" Food and Drug Administration (FDA) are focusing on a stream of Chinese imports that are contaminated or defective.

After years of warnings about farm-raised seafood imports from the Chinese mainland, the FDA's Dr. David Acheson, in charge of food protection, said, "There's been a continued pattern of violations with no signs of abatement." So, finally, the FDA in late June blocked the sale of shrimp, frozen eel, catfish, basa and dace. The reasons included carcinogens and too many antibiotic residues.

Crowded into ponds, farmed Chinese fish are breeding grounds for disease, lice and contaminated water. So heavy doses of antibiotics and other food additives—many illegal in the US—are applied. China is a major exporter of seafood to the US. We import 80 percent of all our seafood.

In recent weeks, disclosures of hundreds of thousands of defective tires (tread separation problems), lead-coated toys, contaminated toothpaste and pet food (which *destroyed* about 6,000 pets) have raised the profile of a situation which is likely to get worse.

China produces products in a horrifically polluted environment—of the water, air and soil. Industrial chemicals, farm run-offs, and mountains of toxic waste are alarming Beijing for both domestic consumption as well as foreign trade reasons. Despite loud proclamations of forthcoming action, the Chinese government has waited too long, allowed too much corruption and lax enforcement, and condoned a huge industry in exported counterfeit goods where anything goes.

Although country-of-origin legislation passed Congress in 2002, Mr. Bush—obsessed by the costly Iraq War and indentured to large corporate importers—did not push his Republicans in Congress to provide funds for enforcement. Instead, the president has signed into law delays in the labeling rule. Therefore, except for the required labeling of seafood from foreign countries (consumers take note), all other food in your supermarket is not required to have a label of the country that exported it. It is the majority Democrats' job now to compel mandatory labeling of all imported foods.

China is the largest apple juice exporter in the world. Apple juice from China is pouring into the United States. Is there anything left that cannot be imported into what was once the greatest food exporter the world has ever seen?

It gets worse. The US is on the verge of becoming a net food importer!

China has allies in the US—the giant food processors that love to rely on profit-maximizing Chinese foodstuffs, additives and other ingredients. The large wholesalers and retail chains, like WalMart, buffer the Chinese export machine from long overdue inspections and enforcement actions.

The inadequate budget of the FDA, and its fractured role with other federal agencies such as the US Department of Agriculture, contributes to the failure of consumer protection. The FDA 2007 budget is only $1.5 billion, or one eighth of the price of just one aircraft carrier. That is not enough to defend the health and safety of the 300 million Americans from hazardous drugs and foodstuffs.

Especially since the FDA has weak or non-existent enforcement powers to obtain information, keep records, demand recalls or impose effective fines.

Presently, the FDA is able to inspect about one percent of food shipments into the US. What can consumers do? Start yelling at your Senators and Representatives. This is one issue they are afraid to duck if the heat is on them. Second, buy from farmers and other producers near you, so you can skip the long chain of middlemen from China to your area who could have caught the problem but just pass the buck, so to speak.

Farmers markets from nearby farms are one way you can avoid contaminated imports.

Eighty percent of all children's toys in America come from China. They come with too many hazards—burning, choking risks for small children, toxics in or on the toys. Some are recalled by the Consumer Product Safety Commission (CPSC). You can be automatically notified of all CPSC recalls by registering with http://www.cpsc.gov/cpsclist.asp.

But, really, the fundamental responsibility here is with Beijing and Washington when careless or criminal companies fail their responsibilities. There needs to be a consumer safety treaty between the two countries where consumer needs are supreme.

Consumer groups and advocates in China need encouragement from their US counterparts.

As far as those half a million or more replacement tires on the US highways—already linked to two fatalities, the US distributor in New Jersey says it doesn't have enough money to recall them all. What about the Chinese exporter?

What is the US Department of Transportation going to do about what will become more such defect-caused tragedies from a flood of auto parts and tires imported from China and other countries?

Phone Tax Refund

April 6, 2007

The IRS has a $10 billion tax credit for 140 million American taxpayers. But the deadline is April 17th—unless you file for an automatic extension.

On May 25, 2006 the US Treasury Department decided to stop fighting successful litigation over a federal excise tax on long-distance service first imposed on wealthy people owning telephones to help pay for the Spanish-American war in 1898. Then the IRS announced a refund of these taxes paid over the past three years.

You have to fill in a clearly marked line on your 1040 income tax return (line 71) to receive between $30 and $60 depending on the number of dependents. If you have long-distance service but your income is so low that you do not have to file any federal income tax return (estimated to be 15 million households by the Center on Budget and Policy Priorities), there is a special Form 1040EZ-T.

Depending on your taxable income situation, by simply filling in the line next to the description "credit for federal telephone excise tax paid," will either reduce the taxes you owe or increase the refund due you.

Sounds simple, right? Not for about one third of the taxpayers who filed, but neglected to fill in the line, as of February 16th, according to the IRS. That meant over 10 million taxpayers did not request the telephone refund. Even more remarkable, the Maryland IRS office reported on March 27th that only one in three of those from Maryland filing federal tax returns to that date claimed a refund.

Even though the IRS initiated a media campaign to get the word out about the refund program, and even though nearly half of all tax returns are prepared by commercial preparers like H&R Block, it looks like billions of dollars will not be refunded by the coming deadlines.

Presumably the additional $10 billion slated to be refunded to businesses and non-profits will have a higher percentage filling in the special line on their returns.

The IRS announcement has been conveyed through numerous large and small newspaper, magazine and radio-television outlets. But in today's multi-media fractured environment, it takes a lot more trumpeting and a lot more repetition to get through daily information blizzards.

Then there is the bad news syndrome. A few days ago I called up ABC television's "It's Your Money" office. The researcher told me that those in charge of selecting topics turned down the telephone excise tax story. As you may recall, "It's Your Money" has been on ABC television news for years both exposing government and corporate waste of your money without finding a way to get you involved in stopping these takeaways.

Well, now with the perfect example of "It's Your Money" and a simple way for you to get some of your money back, this segment apparently felt that such yawning good news would not sufficiently grab or retain audience share against the other networks.

Nonetheless, one would think that fast word of mouth over the past months would have reached most people. That assumes people talking with one another—not a sure assumption during these days of watching screens and listening to your choice of non-stop music.

It is still not too late for numerous blitzes. For example, churches in low income districts, members of Congress and state legislatures, na-tional television comedians (Jay Leno and David Letterman) and talk shows making light but still reaching people with the message can all help spread the word.

There are many highways to many people. Trade associations notifying their company members to notify their employees; labor unions have ready contact with millions of customers. So do bookkeepers and accountants. Strange that there is even a problem.

After April 17, what can be done with the leftover unclaimed billions of dollars? As of now, they're probably going back into the general budget. What about taking this money and creating a perpetual taxpayers' watchdog endowment trust whose income will expose and help stop government waste as well as businesses and others ripping off the government, such as the healthcare industry cheating Medicare and Medicaid? Something for Congress to consider.

For now, you can get information about the refund by calling IRS toll-free at 1-800-829-1040. Or just remember to fill in one of the following—Line 71 of Form 1040, Line 42 on the 1040A, Line 9 on the 1040-EZ, Line 69 on the 1040NR, or Line 21 on the 1040NR-EZ.

Enjoy!

For More Information:

http://www.irs.gov/newsroom/
    article/0,,id=164032,00.html

http://www.irstelephonetaxrefund.info/Home.cfm

http://www.RefundsforGood.org

IRS—Telephone Excise Tax Refund: 1-800-
    829-4477, Topic #611

Real Estate Investment Trusts

November 24, 2006

The torrid pace of risks and valuations reached a new level in the business known as Real Estate Investment Trusts (REITs). Required by federal law to pass on most of their earnings to their shareholders, REIT shares have been going up and up for eight straight years, with this year clocking an unexpected 30 percent rise all by itself for commercial real estate.

Judging by the absence of warnings from financial writers and columnists about soaring REIT stocks and the recent record prices paid by debt-loaded private-equity firms to buy publicly held REITs listed on the stock exchanges, the tempo is still bullish—full speed ahead!

That's when you know that trouble with this bubble lies on the horizon. When it's all bulls and no bears.

Twenty years ago, Felix Rohatyn, leading partner of Lazard Frères & Company, a major investment bank, told me he worries a lot about speculative excess on Wall Street. "The thing that strikes me in a lot of this is how little real professionals," he said, "understand risk. . . . The leveraged buyout is a risk evaluation. People take a pedestrian company with 20 percent debt and 80 percent equity and they turn it into 80 percent debt and 20 percent equity, all of a sudden you have a terrific business. It doesn't make any sense."

It may not have made sense then, but for the first acquirers it usually made them a lot of dollars. Mr. Rohatyn saw "a massive and deeply institutionalized gap between those who risk and those who pay."

I wonder what he thinks about gaps, risks and valuations now as he looks out of his Manhattan suite at New York's real estate spiral. He could envision the following prudent behavior. That these commercial apartment and office buildings would be valued at about ten times their net annual earnings. Or he could observe what is really going on when these structures—individually or in clusters—change hands.

In recent days, private-equity companies are reported to be interested in buying public REITs that are trading between thirty and fifty-five times earnings. When the Blackstone Group paid about a ten percent premium to acquire Equity Office REIT—already selling at its high for the year—Equity Office's largest shareholder, Cohen & Steers, thought the sales price at $48 was too low. C & S's Jim Corl explained his appraisal by declaring the cost of buying all the properties in Equity Office's portfolio would have been in the $60 range.

One New York City-based REIT saw its stock double in the past twelve months to $138 a share from a then record high. It is presently selling at fifty-five times earnings and yielding 1.7 percent. Like many other REITs, this one experienced a sharp share increase the day of the Blackstone acquisition news announcement that was seen by Wall Street as possibly signaling a takeover binge by these cash-loaded private-equity firms.

Now, to repeat, apartment and other commercial buildings are bought to make profit. Why would a buyer pay not ten times the net annual income, but thirty, forty, fifty or more times? The answers to that question would probe deeply into the ways complicated financial deals hand off that risk to other investors, tier the risk through instruments such as "toggle" bonds, and take advantage of accommodating tax breaks and low interest rates in a period of bulging capital surpluses looking for appreciating investments.

The *Wall Street Journal*'s Jennifer S. Forsyth was intrigued enough to interview Sam Zell, called the legendary Chicago-based real estate mogul who sold Equity Office to the Blackstone Group. Zell quickly told her that "this is the greatest period of monetization in the history of the world. That huge amount of liquidity that's floating around is not something that would be absorbed in weeks. I think it will take more like six years."

Ms. Forsyth asked why are so many REITs being taken private? Ever the booster, Mr. Zell replied that private investors are willing to work at higher risk-levels than the public markets which have fiduciary obligations to their shareholders and therefore have adopted "a philosophy of very conservative leverage." Most public REITs pay between 3 and 7 percent dividends. These private investors are really seeking quick capital gains for the risk—a more risky adventure.

Now comes the key question. She asked, "You've said that the public markets undervalued your company. Why?"

Mr. Zell's response: "Basically over the last few years, the analytical community was continually behind in their evaluations of office assets." Whew!

The absence of any concern about excessive risk, any reference to the slowdown in the economy, any mention that the amount of space companies leased during the third quarter was significantly lower than the first half of 2006, as was any reference to continuing construction of new buildings, or most remarkable, the huge debt loads that are being incurred.

Mr. Zell has been around since the 1960s and has seen busts followed by booms in real estate. Yet he seems to see nothing scary on the horizon.

Tiers of debt always are scary, especially when Uncle Sam does not actively bail out real estate and its financiers. Millions of younger, middle-age and older adults find it scary because they are being driven out of cities due to unaffordable rents and condo prices. Small businesses also find it scary having to close their stores when their leases expire because they can't come close to paying the new rents.

Maybe the major question of them all is: Who is real estate for first? Real people or speculating financiers. Real people or corporations playing with bricks-and-mortars as if they were just a numbers game in a fast turnover bazaar.

Speak out, Mr. Rohatyn.

Student Loan Shenanigans
May 12, 2006

Al Lord is thinking about building his own private golf course. Not bad for an ex-corporate socialist. The former CEO of Sallie Mae is worth about a quarter of a billion dollars, running a company for which Uncle Sam virtually guarantees against any losses while it makes enormous profits in the college student loan business.

In 2003, Mr. Lord told a public audience that "it would be very hard for me to tell you that what I make is not a lot of money." But the company he ran has been making it very hard for hundreds of thousands of students and blocking any reforms in Congress that would make his company less hard on American taxpayers.

Last year, citing George W. Bush's own budget office, Senator Ted Kennedy (D-Mass.) declared, "We waste billions of dollars in corporate welfare every year on student loans, and we cannot afford it any longer."

Sallie Mae lobbyists have heard this before from Democrats and some Republicans, such as Representative Thomas Petri (R-Wis.). They are not worried. Sallie Mae executives own the majority leader in the House of Representatives, John Boehner (R-Ind.). He has been wined and dined with over $200,000 in campaign contributions to his PAC from individuals affiliated with the private student-loan industry in the 2003–4 election cycle.

In December 2005, Mr. Boehner reassured a group of Sallie Mae types who wanted reassurance that their cushy deals would continue. "Know that I have all of you in my two trusted hands."

And what a cushy deal it is. Your federal government guarantees returns for these companies on student loans of at least 2.34 percent higher than the rates paid on commercial loans. At least. If the student borrower defaults, you the taxpayer pick up the tab for Sallie Mae and the banks.

If the student falls on very hard times after graduation and goes bankrupt, federal law says bankruptcy does not affect collection of student loans. Even the powerful credit card industry can't get past bankruptcy to garnish what's left of the graduate's assets. The student lending industry can even get to a debtor's disability insurance payments under Social Security.

In February Congress did act on student loans in another way—backward. It cut $12 billion out of the student loan programs, mostly from students and parents. In a report just out, the California Public Interest Research Group (CALPIRG) found that in California, 17.9 percent of public college students and 28.8 percent of private college graduates have unmanageable student loan debt were they to take jobs as teachers or social workers. Yet these critical careers desperately need college graduates to replenish their ranks. (To download the full report, go to http://www.calpirg.org. See also http://www.studentloanjustice.org.)

Last Sunday, May 7th, I turned on CBS to *60 Minutes* which unloaded on Sallie Mae in a devastating segment about its power, greed and profits.

Originally a government-sponsored enterprise like Fannie Mae, Sallie Mae was privatized in 1997 and is now the largest private lender to students. But not entirely private. The federal government is its guarantor. Michael Dannenberg of the New America Foundation told Leslie Stahl, "It may be called 'private' . . . but it's not private at all. Frankly it's a socialist-like system. It's not as if this private entity is assuming any risks. No, no, no. The law makes sure that this so-called private entity has virtually no risk."

It gets worse. Let's say a graduated student defaults. The government pays Sallie Mae both the principal and the interest compounded. But the loan is still subject to collection. Guess who owns some of the largest collection agencies—you guessed it, Sallie Mae. When its collection agency collects, it gets 25 percent of the recovery. The profits go to Sallie Mae.

The corporate lawyers who conceived this self-enriching system ought to get the nation's top prize for shameless perversity.

Corporate socialism—an Uncle Sam (meaning you) guarantee—has been very good for Sallie Mae's stock, which has gone up twenty-fold since 1995, when it was already a mature, profitable company.

Ms. Stahl interviewed one graduate, Lynnae Brown, who borrowed $60,000 starting in college in 1985. She has been ill since her sophomore year. She keeps paying to avoid default, but by the time she is finished, she will have paid Sallie Mae $262,383. Now one can sense why Al Lord can build his private golf course.

The bright and compassionate Harvard Law

School professor, Elizabeth Warren, told Ms. Stahl, "Sallie Mae makes money if you pay back on time. And Sallie Mae makes money if you don't pay back on time. It shouldn't be the case that Sallie Mae gets to play every hand at the poker table while the government is the one that keeps anteing up the money."

But the solution is plain. The government's Department of Education offers student loans directly, bypassing the middleman. It gives the loan money to Ohio State University, for example, which then loans it to students. Direct lending by Uncle Sam is far cheaper. It will cost taxpayers less than one cent on the dollar, while Sallie Mae guaranteed loans will cost taxpayers twelve cents on the dollar. Who made these projections? Mr. Bush's own budget analysts.

I have observed previously that our weakened, disorganized democracy is increasingly both exposé-proof and solution-proof. Nonetheless, the solution is for the government to stop allowing companies special advantages like Sallie Mae kickbacks to universities in order to get the student business, as *60 Minutes* pointed out. Then more direct Department of Education lending can save taxpayers money and provide more loans for hardpressed students and parents.

Was there any uproar after the "60 Minutes" criticism? If so, I didn't hear it either from Congress or anywhere else. Well, at least Sallie Mae was affected; its stock *went up* the next day on Monday $1.70, to $53.85!

The Price of Oil

April 28, 2006

What a week it has been for the giant oil companies! Billions in record quarterly profits rushing into their coffers. An even bigger round of quarterly profits coming up. Gargantuan executive pay bonanzas. And a pile of "forces beyond our control" excuses to publicize in response to the empty outrage of Washington politicians and the real squeeze on consumers and small businesses.

Oil man Bush, atop his administration marinated with ex-oil executives in high positions, keeps saying there is little he can do. It is the market of supply and demand. Only fuel cells and hydrogen sometime down the 21st-century road can save the country from dependency on foreign oil, he says repeatedly. Plus more drilling in the Arctic Wildlife Refuge.

The public heat about energy prices prodded Mr. Bush this week, however, to at least make a little change in rhetoric. He repeated his warning that his government will not tolerate any gouging. Yet the supine reporters did not ask him whether he has ever caught a gouger. But he did mumble something about higher fuel economy standards so that your car guzzles a little less gasoline. He said he will be meeting with the domestic auto company executives in the White House in mid-May. He praised ethanol again. He visited a gas station in Mississippi to feel the pain of the motorists.

Will Hollywood ever leave Washington, DC?

On Capitol Hill—aka Withering Heights—the Republicans are starting to talk tough, mumbling about larger taxes on oil industry profits—an idea Bush said he would veto last year. The Democrats cannot even agree on an excess profits tax, preferring the greasy band-aid of lifting the 18.4 cent gasoline tax for sixty days. This new detour is pathetic since it takes the heat off the industry's skyrocketing gasoline price which are well into the $3 to $4/gallon range in many places.

A few, very few members of Congress, like Senator Byron Dorgan (D-N.D.) know what has to be done to this industry and its long-time grip over the federal government. First, the gouging profits must be recaptured and returned now to the consumer. The government must also invest in advanced public transit systems.

Big oil has been on a marriage binge and the mergers, including the wedding of Exxon (number one) and Mobil (number two), have further tightened the corporate cartel of oil as it feeds off the government producers' cartel of oil abroad. Antitrust break up action is necessary.

The claim by the oil barons that they're just responding to the marketplace of supply and demand is laughable. Why are they making double and triple profits? Why are their top executives tripling their own pay? Hard-pressed sellers of oil would not have such a luxurious profit and pay spiral. Hard-pressed sellers of oil would not have paid $144,000 every day to Exxon CEO, Lee Raymond since 1993 and then send him off with a $398 million retirement deal!

A competitive domestic oil industry would not be so able to close down scores of refineries and then turn "refinery shortages" into higher gas prices at the pump. Nor would competitive companies get away with a return on capital of 46 percent for upstream drilling and production operations, plus a 32 percent for refining and marketing. *Washington Post* business reporter, Steven Pearlstein, call these returns "hedge fund returns." Except with hedge funds there is a risk of losing from time to time. Not so with the corporate government of Big Oil.

A president, preoccupied with his criminal, fabricated war in Iraq, would not leave Americans defenseless as oil prices eat into their family budgets. A standup president would order an all-fronts investigation of the oil industry's pric-

ing practices from the oil well to the gasoline station.

There would be full use of subpoenas and public testimony from the oil bosses under oath by his regulatory agencies. He would organize with his Republican majority in Congress a repeal of past and recent unconscionable tax breaks and stop giving away your oil on federal property in the Gulf of Mexico to the oil companies without adequate royalties. He would press for an excess-profits tax and legislation raising by statute the fuel efficiency performance for new motor vehicles, including SUVs, Minivans and light trucks.

A standup president would raise margin requirements to tone down the speculation in oil futures that are swelling the New York Mercantile Exchange and contributing to higher gasoline and heating oil prices. He would support tariffs on imported refinery products to push the companies to expand and build new cleaner refineries in the US. Where? In some of the exact locations where the oil industry shut down these refineries over the past thirty years to diminish overall output and move operations to cheap labor locations abroad.

A standup president would give an address to the nation that mobilizes small and larger businesses which use oil to join with consumers in a common cause against the looming inflationary jolts that will raise prices for many regular products and lead to higher interest rates by the Federal Reserve.

Bush can never proactively do this for the American people who already, by more than a two to one margin, believe he cares more about the interests of Big Business than the interests of regular people.

But, mobilized small business can get him to relent and let some of these changes happen.

The small business revolt can start with several hundred economically squeezed truckers bringing their eighteen wheelers to Washington in a protest that encircles in a wide arc the Congress and the White House and the federal buildings in between. Now that would be more than a message. It would be an irresistible visual image for the television cameras day after day.

Auto Industry: Innovation and Stagnation
February 28, 2006

It is time for the American people to send a wake-up call to the domestic auto industry (General Motors, Ford Motor Company and DaimlerChrysler). Backlogged engineering advances well suited for commercial application and widespread diffusion are ready for use. Unfortunately, today, as was the case forty years ago, auto company management stands in the way of benign and efficient automotive technology.

With few exceptions, a vast wasteland of technological stagnation and junk engineering from domestic automakers has destroyed over three decades of opportunities for increasing the health, safety and economic efficiency of the motoring public. This "dark age" of the domestic motor vehicle industry was not the result of a series of omissions. It was the product of a deliberate expansion of the auto giants' power to block innovation.

During this period, the Big Three, with all their autocratic hierarchical bureaucracies, managed to continue losing market share to foreign manufacturers. General Motors and Ford are experiencing massive annual losses, which would be even more immense absent their profitable financing arms. Their bonds have been downgraded to junk status—something unthinkable a decade or two ago.

One might think that such a state of affairs would itself constitute an internal wake-up call to change directions and provide annual value improvements in their products. No way. Notwithstanding the "talk" in their advertising campaigns, it is still business as usual.

Unwilling over the years to regenerate themselves from within their ranks, despite substantial investment, marketing and engineering/scientific resources, top executives managed to mismanage and waste these estimable assets, reserving their energies to blockade external pressures that would have saved them from their own ineptitude.

Instead, the auto manufacturers, together with their dealers and sometimes the United Auto Workers, used political muscle to freeze regulatory activity in both NHTSA and the EPA into obsolescence and even on occasion rolled back simple standards (such as bumper protections requirements).

The formidable auto industry and auto dealer lobby in Washington stopped any effort in Congress to recharge the General Services Administration into upgrading its safety, fuel and emissions specifications for its fleet purchases over the past twenty years. This occurred even though the GSA, under the leadership of Administrator Gerald Carmen, advanced air bag installations through fleet purchases in the mid-'80s under Reagan.

Having nullified both the internal and external pressures that would have pressed forward toward engineering excellence, the domestic Big Three reverted to their age-old profit formula. They jerry-built junk, profitable junk, called SUVs. They sold a mirage of safety, the status of size and huge horsepower and less cramped interiors. They invested tens of billions of dollars into more powerful and wasteful engines. They made up for declining market share with higher profit margins on vehicles sold. SUVs were the opiate of the auto executives, making them more complacent and sluggish during a lengthy period of stable gasoline prices.

Now the price of oil and gasoline is rising and the motorists may be awakening. So too should motorists raise their expectations for the kinds of vehicles they should be able to purchase in their own multiple interests. Imagine political candidates making the state of motor vehicle engineering a major political issue, extending to health, safety, efficiency and beyond to global warming, and the lack of modern mass transit.

My associate Rob Cirincione, Princeton-trained engineer, has just completed a report titled "Innovation and Stagnation in Automotive Safety and Fuel Efficiency." This report makes the case for raising public expectations and demands upon the auto industry. It demonstrates how automotive suppliers and solid inventors and university-based researchers have indeed innovated while the auto makers have obstructed widespread commercial application of their innovations. Important, feasible engineering innovations are ready to diminish serious national transportation problems.

Our government has the authority and the tools to move their applications into the assembly lines and the dealer showrooms. The engineers and scientists inside the auto companies are ready to work at higher levels of significance. There are serious roadway, environmental, economic and global urgencies at stake. We all have a role in confronting the executive mastodons of the auto industry who are stuck in their own traffic. It is time to put the federal cop back on the auto companies' beat. Get rid of the backlog.

Put the benefits in the hands of the motorists. And, save the domestic auto companies from their own witless masochism.

Over thirty years of stagnation are quite enough. An entire new corps of the top executives is needed to provide a leadership of receptivity, if not of outright initiation toward a new generation of motor vehicles.

To obtain a copy of the report please send a $30.00 check or money order to CSRL, to: CSRL, P.O. Box 19367, Washington, DC 20036.

Cooperatives
October 13, 2005

New Orleans, the largest city devastated by two hurricanes, lies in ruins. The reconstruction plans are forming and the usual commercial interests are in the forefront to receive large subsidies, federal overpayments and special immunities from having to meet labor, environmental and other normal legal safeguards for the people.

The corporate looting of New Orleans is underway. The charges of corruption, political favoritism and poor delivery of services by corporate contractors for government projects are already being leveled by the media and some alert officials. After all, over $100 billion of taxpayer monies will be flowing to New Orleans and the Gulf area communities in the next several months.

Plans for the new New Orleans by the large corporate developers are not including many poor or low income families. These developers see a smaller ritzier New Orleans with gentrified neighborhoods and acres of entertainment, gambling and tourist industries. In a phrase, the corporatization of New Orleans' renewal.

A different more cooperative scenario needs

attention. Here is a flattened major city in America where a cooperative economy can take hold that puts people first, that allows the return of low-income families back home with dignity, self-determination and opportunity.

Cooperatives are businesses owned by their consumers. They operate as non-profits. They are all over the United States and are often taken for granted by their customer-owners. There are housing cooperatives. There are health cooperatives like the successful Puget Sound Health Coop in Seattle. There are banking cooperatives called credit unions with 50 million members. There are food store cooperatives and even energy cooperatives in farm country from refineries to pipelines to gas stations. These are electric cooperatives providing electricity to millions of rural Americans. There are student coops in universities all over the country.

All these different cooperatives have their national and sometimes their state associations. They know how to spread their numbers, though I often wish they would do so more aggressively and more distinctly from the dominant corporate commercial model.

New Orleans provides possibly the finest opportunity in many years for the cooperative movement to make itself known and to save New Orleans from being looted by corporate predators of various stripes who are presently designing the new New Orleans. Cooperatives demand grass roots organization and customer responsibility or they cannot exist. Cooperators, as customers are called, started these cooperatives in the early days—both consumer and producer cooperatives—throughout farm country USA.

Cooperative principles and member participation have been undermined by the hectic pace of a commuting workforce in a corporate economy that requires two breadwinners or more per

family to have a chance at a middle class standard of living. Cooperatives provide many tangible and intangible community values but they need the time of their members to truly flower.

New Orleans and other Hurricane-stricken communities can give new life to the cooperative movement, and it can give new life to the shattered lives of these residents as they try to rebuild their livelihoods.

I called up James R. Jones, the executive director of the National Association of Student Organizations (NASCO) in Ann Arbor, Michigan and tendered these suggestions. He was quite receptive. What is needed is for all the various category cooperatives mentioned above, and others too, to convene a planning session about how to introduce cooperatives to the neighborhoods and commercial districts of New Orleans.

There is a little known bank in Washington, DC, originally established by Congress in 1978, but now private, whose sole purpose is to provide loans and technical assistance to existing and startup cooperatives. It has provided substantial credit for housing cooperatives and has a development division whose mission is to help cooperatives in low income areas. The National Cooperative Bank is an asset to be invigorated.

Along with other national associations of different kinds of cooperatives, many in Washington, DC, there is the National Cooperative Business Association—an umbrella organization of the cooperative subeconomy. The National Rural Electric Association represents many rural electric systems. Co-op America promotes the sales of small producer cooperatives selling a variety of useful products from clothing to food to sporting goods to arts and crafts.

It will not be easy for cooperatives, large and

small, to pull together for the renaissance of New Orleans and other neighboring towns in Louisiana, Mississippi and Alabama. But, oh, how important a contribution it could become for our entire economy, so gouged, so controlled by absentee multinationals, so inimical to community economics and control, to succeed in the wake of these hurricanes.

People interested in this cooperative mission or cooperatives generally can contact the following websites:

http://www.ncba.coop/
http://www.coopamerica.org/
http://www.nreca.org/
http://www.nasco.coop/
http://www.chsinc.com/

To send your reactions, write me at PO Box 19312, Washington, DC 20036.

The True Cost Of Undergraduate Education

August 26, 2005

Soon millions of parents will be writing tuition checks for their children at public universities, believing that they are paying much less than the actual cost of an undergraduate education.

Tuition at these public institutions has been going up quickly in the past decade, reversing the long-held public policy that tax monies should pay for most of the tuition and the rest of the expenses of public higher education. Quietly year by year, privatization of a public good has been growing.

Public undergraduate tuition at schools such as the University of California has almost reached a level beyond which parents may be starting to subsidize teacher research and related graduate education. This is the argument made

by a retired professor of Physics at UC Berkeley, Charles Schwartz.

First a word about the remarkable Charles Schwartz. For over a decade this scientist has volunteered thousands of hours pouring over the gigantic multi-billion-dollar budgets of the University of California. Most recently he alleged secret, poor management of pension and endowment funds.

University budgets have few faculty, student or alumni overseers. For one thing they are very complex to understand; for another, the critical breakdown details are either not there or are considered confidential.

Professor Schwartz, knowing and caring more than anyone else outside of officialdom, has become the learned hair shirt of the university administration. He has pointed out many deficiencies in the annual budget at public meetings with University officials and on his extraordinary website (http://ist-socrates.berkeley.edu/~schwrtz/).

The University reaction, with few exceptions, has been to ignore his protestations or to dismiss his figures as attempting to disaggregate the cost of education in a way that will be of little value.

Dr. Schwartz disagrees, in his usual meticulous manner, with a 16 page paper (posted at http://socrates.berkeley.edu/%7Eschwrtz/Undergrad-Cost.html). He calculates the actual expenditure for undergraduate education at the University of California as averaging $6,648 per student with the parents-students paying 95 percent of that cost. By contrast, the University officials say the average cost of such an education is $15,810 per student.

He explains the discrepancy due to his disaggregating undergraduate education from the whole bundle of academic functions, which includes other levels of education plus faculty research. Unlike for graduate education, he says there is very little connection between faculty research and undergraduate education.

So why should anyone care about this, asks Professor Schwartz? Because the state subsidy for UC undergraduate education is almost entirely replaced by what students or their families are paying for tuition. And if student fees continue to rise, as is widely expected, then tuition checks will start subsidizing faculty research and related graduate programs. In short, public university student tuition may start becoming like private universities where cross-subsidies have been long standing.

After establishing his methodology, Dr. Schwartz lists several anticipated objections and methodically responds to them. He then argues that student tuition should not be permitted to rise above the actual cost of their undergraduate education. Otherwise the undergraduate subsidy begins. "Such a forced subsidization," he asserts, "is something that deserves a most serious debate as a matter of public policy." He believes his research methodology "should be applicable to any major [public] research university."

Dr. Schwartz worries about an emerging vicious circle. As undergraduate student tuition charges continue their annual increase, qualified lower-income students may not be able to afford them. With the shift to admitting more students from more affluent families, the state legislatures may reduce their state funding, which in turn will accelerate the increase in student tuition. He calls this "a transition—the privatization of undergraduate education at the public universities," leading to greater class stratification and reduced class mobility.

University administrators at Berkeley and elsewhere are not about to change the bundled accounting system used by their financial managers. But Professor Schwartz says there should be an open and honest debate about these choices. "Our duty," he adds, "is to not allow it to remain hidden."

Industrial Hemp
June 24, 2005

Congressman Ron Paul, a libertarian from Texas and an obstetrician who has delivered over 6,000 babies, is trying to deliver our farmers from a bureaucratic medievalism in Washington that keeps saying "No" to growing industrial hemp.

Many farmers want to grow this 5,000-year-old fiber plant that has been turned into thousands of products since being domesticated by the ancient Chinese. That is their heresy. The enforcer is the Drug Enforcement Agency (DEA) in Washington, DC, which has placed industrial hemp on its proscribed list next to marijuana.

Detailed petitions signed by agricultural groups, agricultural commissioners, International Paper Co. and others were presented to both Clinton and Bush to take industrial hemp off the DEA list and let the states allow farmers to grow it. The DEA turned the petitions down cold.

The arguments for this great, sturdy and environmentally benign plant are legion. In over thirty countries where it is commercially grown, including Canada, France, China and Romania, industrial hemp has been used to produce hemp food, hemp fuel, hemp paper, hemp cloth, hemp cosmetics, hemp carpet and even hemp door frames (Ford and Mercedes).

Factories, food stores and paper manufacturers are free to import raw hemp or finished hemp materials from foreign countries. Last year, about $250 million worth of hemp products were purchased from abroad. But federal law in the US prohibits farmers or anyone else from growing it on US soil.

Why? The DEA says that industrial hemp grown next to marijuana can camouflage and impede law enforcement against the latter. Strange. This problem doesn't bother Canadian police authorities or similar officials in other nations. Besides, since industrial hemp is only one-third of one percent THC, growing it next to marijuana would cross-pollinate and dilute the illegal marijuana plants. No marijuana grower wants industrial hemp anywhere near his or her pot plots.

You can smoke a bushel of industrial hemp and not get high. Far too little THC. Like poppy seeds on bread. You may, however, get a headache, if you try.

George Washington and Thomas Jefferson grew industrial hemp on their farms. Drafts of the Declaration of Independence were written on hemp paper. Imagine the billions of trees and tons of bleach chemicals which would have been saved were hemp a big source of paper. A multibillion dollar a year farm crop blocked.

During World War II, the US Navy used hemp for very strong rope during the war effort. The Department of Agriculture made a film "Hemp for Victory" to encourage more cultivation.

Enter Ron Paul, the courageous. Numerous colleagues of Rep. Paul, in both the House and Senate, believe as he does regarding the legalization of industrial hemp farming, but they are afraid to go public lest they be accused of being "soft on drugs." This is true, for example, of the North Dakota Congressional delegation, in spite of overwhelming private and public support for farmers being allowed to plant it in their spacious state.

On June 23, 2005, Congressman Paul introduced HR 3037, the Industrial Hemp Farming Act. The bill requires the federal government to respect state laws (already five of them) allowing the growing of industrial hemp. Immediately, Congressmen Peter Stark (D-Calif.) and Jim McDermott (D-Wash.) co-sponsored the legislation.

Rep. Paul's announcement was made during lunchtime in the Rayburn Office Building at the House of Representatives. Denis Cicero, owner of the Galaxy Global Eatery in New York City, served up a delicious and nutritious luncheon featuring industrial hemp. Speaking were two leading North Dakota farmers, David Monson, also a state legislator, and Roger Johnson, the North Dakota Agriculture Commissioner. Their remarks were so compelling that in my remarks, I asked whether there were any DEA representatives in the audience who wished to reply. Nobody responded.

Last summer I shared a podium with Rep. Paul at a large gathering of organic farm and food enthusiasts in New England. It was a debate of sorts. At one point, I challenged the Congressman to apply his libertarian philosophy by introducing legislation to let farmers have the freedom to grow industrial hemp and sell it to manufacturers, wholesalers and retailers. He immediately said he would. And he has done it.

There are those like former CIA chief, James Woolsey, who support growing hemp to reduce our reliance on imported oil. More broadly, industrial hemp advances the growth of a carbohydrate-based economy instead of a hydrocarbon-based economy.

Thomas Alva Edison, Henry Ford, and the presidents of MIT and Harvard dreamed of this transition during the nineteen-twenties. Unfortunately, the synthetic chemical industry of DuPont, Dow Chemical and others pushed this dream aside. The rest is the history of environmental damage, pollution-disease, geopolitical crises and many other external costs.

Please urge your members of Congress to support HR 3037. Free our farmers and you, the consumers, to move toward a more sustainable economy.

Visit woodconsumption.org, votehemp.org and NAIHC.org for more information.

Sign on the Dotted Line . . .

December 6, 2004

Michael Sommer, a technology consultant, found out the hard way about one-way fine print contracts as he checked in recently for a flight to Buenos Aires. A United Arlines supervisor at the gate handed him a letter that decreed the confiscation of his 2 million frequent flier miles, dozens of flight coupons and his elite status. United Airlines had audited his account, discovering violations of passenger program rules, which he denied so doing.

Now, regardless of the violations alleged, such as misusing denied boarding certificates, is this unilateral wipeout the way to treat a loyal customer racking up over 2 million frequent miles? Especially when United Airlines is in bankruptcy and presumably wanting to make friends and influence people to use its services!

Mr. Sommer's case led the *New York Times* to further inquiries which resulted in finding that some other airlines are conducting these tougher "audits" of their most loyal customers and making decisions from special software that looks for suspicious patterns. These include, the *Times* reports, "claiming miles for a nonrevenue

ticket or using the wrong frequent-flier number when requesting mileage credit."

The procedures are autocratic. Paul Dingham, an economic consultant, found out about his audit only after US Airways slammed down the gavel on him. "The airline didn't inform me in advance of the audit, nor did they offer me an opportunity to appeal," he complained.

What these seasoned travelers discover is the fine print on most of these frequent flier programs declare the miles to be owned by the airline and they can be diluted, deadlined or removed by the unbridled judgment of the carrier.

Mr. Sommer may contest this assertion by United Airlines in court. Thus far, the courts have not been congenial to passengers when the airlines dilute the frequent flier program by requiring, for example, more miles, already earned, for a round trip.

American consumers are fast losing their contractual rights in the service area of the economy. Fine print contracts, such as credit card agreements, brokerage agreements and insurance policy contracts, are very one-sided and getting worse each year. Have you ever read the shrink-wrap license agreement after you buy software?

More and more of these standard/form take-it-or-leave-it contracts contain binding arbitration clauses that prevent you from suing vendors to resolve a dispute. They even contain the ultimate mockery of the meaning of the word "contract" as a mutually binding agreement. The large companies increasingly stipulate in microscopic print that they reserve the unilateral right to change the terms of their sales agreement.

Well, you may say, you don't have to sign on the dotted line and can look for another competitor to patronize. Sure, but the competitor has the same fine print contract, whether General Motors or Ford, State Farm or Allstate, Citigroup or Bank of America.

These big company standardized contracts regulate your relationship with the company. That fine print is enforceable in most courts. Judges rarely invalidate these provisions anymore under the historic doctrine of unconscionability. Giant corporations have become their own private legislatures. Perhaps someday, antitrust doctrine can be invoked if there is evidence of collusion by sellers to suppress competition in pre-printed contractual offerings.

Meanwhile, the dotted line moves on to fiat after fiat, as in the recent proliferation of wholly unregulated stored value cards offered to millions of desperate "unbanked" consumers. The control of peoples' money by the financial industry not only gouges with sky-high interest rates and penalties. It also ranks your credit rating, and credit score in ways that deter your ability to complain and assigns you a number that determines where, how, when and even whether you can or cannot buy.

Congress and the state legislatures are way behind the curve in protecting consumers here. It is time for citizens to start giving these lawmakers a scorecard for being absent without leave of the voters, thereby leaving them defenseless before these modern day Mammons.

Pay Day Loans
July 23, 2004

Consumer and community organizations have waged a lengthy and intense campaign to warn the public about the high cost of payday loans and the dangers of being entrapped in spiraling unaffordable debt.

Despite these efforts the pay day lenders and their profits are multiplying. The yellow pages in telephone directories are filled with advertisements for "easy and quick" pay day loans. The internet is becoming a favorite venue for these lenders to peddle their credit products. The landscape in low and moderate income neighborhoods is dotted with "check cashing" stores which specialize in these quick cash schemes.

A spokesman for the Consumer Financial Services Association which represents payday lenders boasts that "our business has been growing and growing and growing." The numbers support the claim. The association's members have 22,000 locations up from 12,000 in 2000. Last year, the association's members made $40 billion of loans, generating $6 billion of revenue.

The payoff may be big, but the scheme is simple. The borrower provides the lender with a post-dated check and receives an amount less than the face value of the check, the deduction representing the lender's fee. The check is then held until the borrower's next payday, a week or two or a month later. But the scheme becomes even more lucrative for the lender when the borrower asks for an extension, a rollover until a later pay day. The charges mount with successive rollovers, ultimately leaving borrowers under a mountain of debt carrying what amounts to an effective interest rate of 390 percent on average. And consumer groups cite numerous transactions with rates as high as 600 percent based on an annual percentage rate (APR).

Why would anyone become involved in such one-sided transactions? Most of them are born of desperation: A sick child needing costly prescriptions in a family without medical insurance; major repairs for an automobile needed by a worker who must travel to a construction job in the distant suburbs; and a family attempting to forestall aggressive collection efforts and legal action on overdue bills or to pay back rent to avoid eviction.

We have a far flung "recently modernized" financial system much ballyhooed as the envy of the world, subsidized and coddled by a friendly regulatory system and rendered essentially fail-safe by taxpayer-backed insurance. Why can't borrowers turn to the insured government-chartered banks instead of to payday loan operators operating on the fringe?

The hard truth is that banks with few exceptions don't make small consumer loans, of the $200 or $500 or even the $1,000 and $2,000 variety. That always has been the case and to-day banks substitute fee-ridden credit cards for small consumer loans. Most of the payday borrowers lack the credit standing to obtain credit cards and if they did they would face the tricky world of annual membership fees, the late charges when the monthly payment misses the post date by a few hours and ultimately the "over the limit" fees when charges exceed some previously ordained limit imposed by the card issuer. And interest charges on credit cards can and are arbitrarily raised and many of these hikes look like first cousins to the rate schedules for the payday merchants.

Banks are quite happy to leave the consumer loans for the low and moderate income population, the working poor, to payday merchants. Of course, many "respectable" banks quietly furnish the capital for the payday operations, getting a cut of the lucrative payday business without getting their hands dirty or taking any risks.

The growing role of payday lending and its big brother, predatory lending, in the lives of low and moderate income and minority citizens is discouraging, but there are solutions, solutions already on the books that can reign in the payday lenders. The answer lies in an underused provision of the National Credit Union Act which authorizes the formation of Community Development Credit Unions in low-income neighborhoods.

A few of the Community Development Credit Unions (CDCUs) were formed fifty years ago as a weapon in combating loan discrimination in inner city neighborhoods. The effort got a second wind when big banks launched a massive closing of branches in low income and minority neighborhoods.

But, the biggest boost for the low-income credit unions came in 1994 when the new Chairman of the National Credit Unions Administration, former New Hampshire Congressman Norm D'Amours, announced the formation of the Office of Community Development Credit Unions.

D'Amours followed up this initiative in speeches to credit union audiences urging their support for low-income credit unions.

Under the leadership of Cliff Rosenthal, the National Federation of Community Development Credit Unions was formed and today there are about 400-member credit unions operating under low-income charters around the nation. The charters allow low-income credit unions to obtain technical assistance from the National Credit Union Administration (NCUA) as well as low-interest loans (one to three percent) from a revolving fund at NCUA and to accept a limited amount of deposits from non members.

Credit Unions are cooperatives, consumer owned, non-profit institutions with no outside stockholders. There is no incentive to exploit their "customers" who are the member-owners and there are no outside investors to demand a share of "profits."

What is needed to end the plague of predatory lending and paydayscams is a crash effort on the part of the National Credit Union Administration to establish a network of low income citizen-owned development credit unions throughout the inner cities. Rest assured, the pay day lenders won't try to compete on the credit union terms.

But, this can't be a passive effort on the part of NCUA. The agency needs to beef up its staff by hiring organizers who will go into communities, set up meetings to explain how the credit cooperatives can be established and help move the applications forward.

There is precedent for this kind of outreach. That's how electricity was brought to rural areas for the first time in the 1930s after investor-owned power companies had stiffed rural communities for decades. Staff members of the new Rural Electrification Administration (REA) drove their Model T's down dirt roads, posted signs on school house doors announcing meetings and then worked into the night to help organize cooperatives and to process applications for 2 percent loans to finance the systems. The effort revolutionized farm and rural life.

Credit cooperatives can do same for low- and moderate-income families, particularly in our inner cities. It's a sure way to end the destructive reign of the payday lenders.

"Meet the 'China Price'"
June 20, 2004

"Meet the 'China Price' or else." Remember that phrase—"meet the China Price," because you'll be reading much more about what it means to this country, its working families and its communities.

US chartered corporations are telling their suppliers that if they do not meet the "China Price," they can either lose business, cut their employees' wages and benefits further, or close down and open up their production facilities in China.

WalMart is a gigantic pressure cooker in the "meet the China Price" rat race. With a relentlessness similar to its own low-wage, union-busting practices, WalMart tells its suppliers to find ways to meet the "China Price" or pick up and move to China with its hardworking, non-union, 30 or 40 cents per hour workers.

The *Wall Street Journal* reported that the Big Three auto makers are outsourcing through their parts suppliers. A leading aluminum wheel manufacturer in Van Nuys, California—Superior Industries International, Inc.—was told bluntly by General Motors and Ford Motor Co. to match the prices they were getting from Chinese wheel suppliers.

The message was clear—if Superior did not comply, the two companies could buy from China or some company that did. So Superior is opening a joint-venture plant near Shanghai.

Superior's president, Steve Borick, was quite open about the situation: "We have to take the posture that we are going to continue to work with our major customers . . . who keep pressing us to be in China."

"All of this," the *Journal* declares, "is contributing to the disappearance of US jobs in the parts industry."

"The China Price" is emptying out many factories even in Mexico that were set up by US corporations a few years ago. Apparently, one dollar an hour is too much to pay for Mexican labor.

In the US from 2000 to 2010 there will be a loss of 260,000 jobs from the auto parts industry alone, according to a Roland Berger study.

Both the furniture industry and the textile industry have been losing large numbers of jobs as the "China Price" manufacturers have been collapsing companies in such states as North and South Carolina.

Consider the irony. Here are US corporations—pampered for years with lower taxes, de-regulation, and taxpayer subsidies of various kinds—aggressively turning their backs on America and American workers in favor of production facilities inside a communist dictatorship. A self-described conservative, President George W. Bush is not only silent but is presiding over policies that favor such flight to China and other low-wage, authoritarian regimes.

By bringing these regimes into the World Trade Organization (backed by Clinton and Bush) and by Congress providing China with most-favored nation status, Uncle Sam's hands are quite tied. There is no more tying trade to human rights standards by the United States.

A few days ago, however, a US government panel found that some Chinese furniture makers were "dumping" products into the US at below cost. If upheld, this will presumably lead to tariff sanctions.

Generally, the accelerating impact of the "China Price" will hold wages down in this country or hollow out communities reliant on manufacturers and suppliers that have pulled up stakes and gone to China. The number of lost jobs will grow faster in the next decade.

Our government and both parties (with few exceptions) are leaving our workers defenseless. You cannot have free trade with a dictatorship that controls labor and other prices. So we the people better start focusing fast on this exodus.

Retrospective Commissions
May 2, 2004

Big time middlemen merchants have a hard time avoiding conflicts of interests where they say they represent your interests as buyers while they are receiving kickbacks or, more politely, "retrospective commissions" from the sellers. Such situations undermine making deals on your behalf that are on the merits of the product or service instead of on the money secretly passing from the sellers to the agent, broker or any other Mr. In-Between.

Tens of billions of dollars are at stake here every year. It has been going on for decades before an investigative reporter or law enforcement agency stumbles on the practice whether through a whistleblower or simply random discovery. Such are the features of the growing epidemic of corporate crime, fraud and abuse—it goes on and on, known to thousands of people in the industry, but years go by before it is publically detected.

But now a veritable Niagara has been unleashed. As Steven Pearlstein writes in the *Washington Post*: "In truth, the drug industry now is built on a foundation of kickbacks masquerading as marketing expenses." He and others noted that last month Medco—the large pharmacy benefits manager (PBM) that allegedly negotiates lower prices for health plans and their patients, settled charges that it received over $400 million from just one drug company (Merck) in just one year 2001 to favor drugs by that company even if they were more expensive or another drug was prescribed. For this bonanza, Medco settled for a mere $29 million with twenty states' Attorneys General. Criminogenic behavior pays indeed. And what about all the other years?

The kickback tsunami comes in waves. First

were the disclosed conflicts involving security analysts who touted stocks for you to buy while their colleagues or even themselves were dumping them. Of course, they just needed cash for their son's wedding or they thought it prudent to diversify their firm's portfolio. Ah, yes.

Then, as Professor John C. Coffee Jr. of Columbia Law School, pointed out, there were the mutual funds favoring wealthy clients with "timing" purchases after hours and in other ways over the regular Joes and Janes they had as trusting clients. Then, he adds, there were the securities brokers marketing products from the mutual funds.

Most recently, it turns out those giant commercial insurance brokers like Marsh Inc., Willis Group Holdings, Aon and others were taking payments from the insurance companies to promote their business. Big money is involved here—a total of $656 million in insurance company payments in 2003 just to the top eight brokers.

Who can you trust in the marketplace of deceit, coverup and breach of fiduciary duties? Well let's see. Can we trust the boards of directors of these companies, the outside accounting firms, the outside law firms, the state and federal regulators, the state and federal legislative committees? To ask the question of these supposed sentinels is to answer it. They, year after year, look the other way. They are paid to look the other way or they are receiving campaign contributions to look the other way. Still they cannot be excused. There is something rotten in the state of Wall Street, in the state of brokerdom or agentdom. Yet the carrier of the rot never seems to go to jail to have time to think things over. The thefts never seem to be paid back fully plus interest and penalties.

I listened to a recent House hearing on CSPAN radio a few weeks ago watching a minuet between the Subcommittee Chairman, who used to be in the real estate industry, lather witnesses from his former occupation whoever denouncing one of the very few pro- consumer moves by the Bush Administration. This proposed rule would require mortgage brokers to disclose how much they are paid (wholesale markups are the euphemism) so that consumers can compare costs and up-front fees. The corporate witnesses were trying to explain that the Department of Housing and Urban Affairs proposal would cost consumers more and produce no benefit. That's what they think about the consumer's right to know and be able to deconstruct the gobbledygook called "yield spread premium."

The remarkable resistance of corporate crime and fraud to being uprooted through the years suggests that they are above and beyond the law, when they do not produce the enabling laws in the first place that gives them de facto immunity and cover. Examples are their lobbying to repeal the usury laws in the seventies in most states, or making sure that the laws do not have criminal penalties for criminal practices.

Caveat emptor (let the buyer beware) is our governments' consumer protection policies these days. Some day, consumers will band together and do the uprooting themselves.

Surviving on Today's Family Income
March 19, 2004

A book came out last year which should have gotten more attention had the nation's news media not fallen in the obsessive trap of the Iraq-obsessive president. It is called *The Two-Income Trap: Why Middle-Class Mothers and Fathers Are Going Broke* (Basic Books).

Written by Harvard Law Professor Elizabeth Warren, an expert on consumer bankruptcy, and her Wharton MBA daughter, Amelia Warren Tyagi, this volume provides insights not normally revealed by aggregate economic data. It is about real earnest people in financial trouble.

The Warrens stimulated my recollection of growing up in a New England mill town in the late 1940s, where one breadwinner could provide a family with a middle-class living standard as then defined. Even in the seventies, the authors report that most families could do fairly well on one income. An average family paid 56 percent of its single breadwinner's wages for housing, health insurance and other fixed costs.

Today that family, notwithstanding the availability of two incomes, pays 75 percent for these necessities and has 25 percent left over for discretionary purchases. It gets worse of course for single parents who have only 4 percent of income after fixed costs.

Compared with the 1950s, the share of family income going to housing now is much higher. You think interest rates on mortgages are low today, between 5.5 and 6 percent? Fifty years ago, the interest rates on fixed mortgages were under 3 percent and better yet with a VA housing loan.

There were millions of veterans then.

With the decline of the extended family and the shattering of the nuclear family for many, the ever-longer commutes, costs of getting to work and placing the children in daycare all take a sizable chunk of the paycheck. Less time for comparison shopping increases the consumer dollars spent on items. Then come the charges, fees and penalties associated with an overextended credit card economy. Credit has a million pushers—subprime predatory lending rates, pay day loans, rent-to-own rackets.

The lending industry has been all over Congress in recent years to pass legislation making it even more difficult to go into bankruptcy. To gain more influence on Capitol Hill beyond their buying and renting of lawmakers, these lobbyists spread the myth of immoral borrowers exorbitantly dining out and buying too many fancy clothes. An intensive study of 2,000 families who fell into dire financial straits, if not bankruptcy shows a different real picture. Warren says, "It's about homes in safe neighborhoods (which raises prices)." She gives many more examples of the "two income trap."

A major study is needed on the costs associated with two spouses going to work, in addition to daycare which now can cost $500 a month or more. For instance, another used car, another auto insurance policy, repair and maintenance expenses, and parking fees add up to real money.

Consumers ought to spend some time netting out what is left after these and other expenses. Of course, there are expenses from the consequences of children being without their parents for hours during the day—delinquency, guilt-based expensive gifts to the children (Nintendo games instead of quality playful time), and the credentialed counselors who now take the place of aunt, grandma or uncle.

Much of economic growth in recent years has come from the commercializing of family functions once provided free. The time pressures on working parents leads to this need to pay for what the family formerly provided cheaper or free.

The Warrens recommend re-instating the usury laws which protected consumers from staggering interest rates that amount to a debtors' prison without walls. Learning how to control some of these traps through consumer financial knowhow also helps.

The basic problem is that with the inflation-adjusted twenty to twenty-five fold increase in productivity per capita since 1900, why don't we have an economy where one working person per family can sustain a middle-class standard of living? Why indeed are there any working poor families in our country? Where is this massive increase in per capita productivity going? It's going to the top 5 percent to sharpen disparities of wealth between the few at the top and the rest of America?

Those questions may become the next stage of research by the Warrens and other scholars sensitive to economic injustice.

Pension Rights

March 4, 2004

Over thirty years ago, I started the Pension Rights Center which concerned itself with such issues as shortening the time of corporate pensions vesting or improving their portability for job-changing employees. No one nightmared that companies would dramatically cut their contributions to these defined benefit plans during years of economic growth and record company profits. That is not the least of a trail of broken promises by these vastly overpaid corporate executives (with their gigantic special pensions) to their loyal workers.

Recently, employees from some major corporations highlighted some of the tricky ways these bosses are betraying the people who made their companies perform and profit. Under the name of the "Ad Hoc Coalition to Restore Retirement Security," five broken promises were described.

First, companies broke promises to older employees by unfairly changing plan rules. AT&T, for example, was one of several large firms, to switch to a "cash balance" pension plan costing long-service salaried employees as much as half of their expected pensions. The employees want a federal law change to give them a "choice at retirement between receiving their promised pensions and those offered under any new rules."

Second, Dresser-Rand was a division of Halliburton until the parent company sold it. Seemed pretty routine. Later, the Dresser employees learned that a loophole in the law allowed Halliburton to shift the pension funds into a plan for its own employees. This maneuver left the spun-off employees without their full early retirement pensions. They want to end the loophole where pensions can be devastated merely by selling a subsidiary to another owner.

Third, companies break pension promises to older employees by reclassifying them as independent contractors. Allstate did this to their insurance agents, who were on staff. The agents fought back, filing a law suit claiming that Allstate unlawfully deprived them of much of their pensions.

Fourth, GM resorted to the "fine print" to cutback or even cancel lifetime health insurance for its retirees if they accepted early retirement packages. Changing the rules after people have retired should be prohibited, say these workers.

Fifth, MCI/WorldCom employees trusted their executives when told that the company stock was a sound investment for their 401(k) plans. Actually, these executives knew the company was inflating its books while these bosses were selling their own company stock at the same time. Once again, gaps in the law need to be filled to allow for full remedies against such self-enriching deception at the top.

Obviously, these are devastating times for millions of workers who retired believing and then found out that their company leaders were lying. One wonders why Congress is taking so long to amend the federal pension laws to prevent such sabotage of loyal workers. But then, the bosses are more likely to get their calls returned by many members of Congress than these employees.

But these veteran employees have organized. They need to expand their organizations to other companies where workers face similar trapdoors. For further information, go to pensions-r-us.org.

Deeper and Deeper in Debt

January 9, 2004

Rising consumer debt—much of it fueled by deceptive credit card operations, predatory lending and other "easy credit" schemes—is casting a dark cloud across the national economy. The numbers paint a sad picture of low, moderate and middle income citizens caught in impossible burdens of debt plus mounting fees and late charges.

Consumer debt has more than doubled in the past ten years to a record level of $1.98 trillion according to data compiled by the Federal Reserve. This staggering amount—averaging $18,700 per household—represents primarily credit card debt and car loans and does not include home mortgages. By itself, credit card debt—nearly all of accruing interest at double digit rates—stands at $735 billion despite the fact that many families have refinanced their homes in recent years in an attempt to deal with mounting credit card debts and fees.

With payments on debt taking such huge chunks of family income, it is not surprising that savings rates are dropping. Savings were at just 2 percent of after-tax income during the first six months of last year. This means there is

very little cushion for consumers to fallback on to meet the rising demands of the credit card merchants.

While most bankruptcies are the result of sickness, loss of jobs and divorce, the rapid rise in costly forms of fee-laden high interest consumer debt, particularly skyrocketing credit card balances, is a significant factor in the increasing number of bankruptcies. Consumer bankruptcies have exceeded one million a year since 1996, reaching 1.54 million in 2002 and topping 1.25 million in the first nine months of 2003.

The financial industry, led by an assortment of credit card operators, automobile dealers and big banks, instead of reforming unfair, deceptive and often predatory credit practices, are demanding that the Congress shut the door on bankruptcy protections for families facing ruin in impossible debt servitude situations.

Under legislation pushed by the merchants of debt, hard-pressed consumers in bankruptcy will face a draconian means test that will leave them in virtual debtors prisons for years. Gone will be the concept—long central to our bankruptcy system—of a second chance for Americans, an opportunity to pick up their lives again as productive citizens. The legislation would take away the discretion of the experts—bankruptcy judges—to make reasoned judgments on the ability of consumers to pay. Left would be a rigid system which would crush debt-ridden families and leave them with no hope for recovery.

The legislation, which has been before the last three Congresses in various forms, passed the House of Representatives in the first session of the 108th Congress and is pending in the Judiciary Committee in the Senate.

Efforts by consumer groups, women's and civil rights organizations and advocates for low and moderate income families to preserve the bankruptcy code are up against a heavily financed lobbying coalition of the most powerful in the financial industry-lobbyists tightly connected with the Bush Administration and the Republican leadership of the House and Senate as well as to important members of the Democratic Party. It is a classic case of money and more money outweighing the interests of consumers.

Finance and credit card companies contributed $6.1 million in individual, PAC soft money donations to candidates during the 2002 election cycle, 63 percent of it going to Republicans, according to the Center for Responsive Politics. But even greater muscle is being funneled into Congress by a thirty-member lobbying coalition which includes MasterCard, MBNA Corporation, Daimler-Chrysler and the American Bankers Association.

The coalition donated nearly $20 million to candidates in the last election, 64 percent of it to the Republican Party which controls both Houses of Congress and the chairmanships of the House and Senate Judiciary Committees where the legislation to wipe out consumer bankruptcy protections originates.

And members of the financial industry are not neglecting President Bush as it hands out "forget-me-nots" this presidential campaign year. A study by the Center for Public Integrity this week revealed that six of President Bush's top ten career contributors were employees and political action committees from the financial sector including banks and credit companies.

Employees and political committees of MBNA Corporation, the biggest credit card issuer, alone, has contributed $493,291 to the president, according to the study.

"This money is not coming from backyard bake sales and barbecues," Charles Lewis, the Center's executive director, said. "It's coming from powerful special interests who want something." (This is what is meant by cash-register politics.)

And among the financial community's desired something clearly is a punitive rewrite of the bankruptcy laws for the credit merchants and a wipe out of rights of consumers who face impossible debt situations. By the way, their cruel legislation just happens to exempt corporations that are in deep debt.

Observations & Inspirations

Chroniclers of current events focus attention on those at or near the seat of power. But a healthy society also depends on the daily public-spirited actions of citizens whose names we rarely learn.

Many of the columns in this section celebrate seemingly ordinary Americans with an extraordinary devotion to the public good. We will remember the life of World War II veteran Howard Zinn, teacher-writer-activist whose legacy reminds us to celebrate him in the most appropriate way possible, through organizing. We will meet Reverend William Sloane Coffin, an outspoken activist and proponent of non-violent civil disobedience who rallied against Jim Crow, the draft, poverty, wars, and the atomic arms race. The lives of the public citizens in this section inspire us to live a life of purpose and remind us that unsung heroes are still, indeed, heroes.

We will take time to acknowledge those who have the moral courage to write the truth, even when it is not politically popular. Among other brave authors and reporters, we remember David Halberstam, a journalist and author, whose courage in speaking truth to power spanned the Vietnam, Korean and Iraq Wars.

Other columns revolve around inspiring, public-spirited citizens with a somewhat higher profile such as Warren Buffett and other super-rich Americans who have shown that those with money have a responsibility to give back to America and contribute their fair share. As the divide between the wealthy and all other Americans has grown into a chasm, they have helped to be a moral compass for the one percent. Similarly, we will remember the activist CEO Anita Roddick, founder of the Body Shop, who championed human rights, especially of indigenous people, environmental protection and corporate accountability.

Finally, we should all be reminded that it only takes a small spark to set a fire ablaze. The columns in this section recount moments from around the world where the self-sacrifice and courage of a few sparked an avalanche of change. The eclectic observations about some less-than-inspiring developments in our society, including the increasing prevalence of impersonal forms of communication, such as text messages and emails, provide a contrast to these featured heroes. This juxtaposition reflects a pull between the grand and the gross.

The goal in this section is to spur each reader to tap the best in themselves, to draw inspiration from the special people who grace these pages, and in turn find, sustain, or deepen their own commitments to justice and action. Often, you'll see that it's easier than you think to start moving in that direction.

Ray Anderson: Enlightened CEO and Environmentalist

August 12, 2011

He took his position as the founder and CEO of Interface, the world's largest modular carpet manufacturing firm, and made environmental history that is extending into many sustainability commitments for the industrial managers he educated.

The loss of Ray Anderson at age seventy-seven took from our country the greatest CEO, the greatest engineer, the greatest hands-on educator of industry making peace with the planet, of them all.

In 1994, Mr. Anderson had what he called his "epiphanal moment" when he read Paul Hawken's book, *The Ecology of Commerce*. That is when he gathered his colleagues and set his company on a mission to reach zero pollution by 2020 "by focusing on energy efficiency, renewable energy, and closed-loop recycling." Interface is more than halfway there reducing expenses and increasing sales and profits in the process. He liked to call himself a "radical industrialist" or a "recovering plunderer of the Earth."

In 2000 he relinquished the day-to-day running of the company to Dan Hendrix so he could become the synergistic advocate around the country and the world for what he called a "zero footprint." That is, going beyond the sustainable "to restorative" "to put back more than we take and do good to the earth, not just no harm, through the power of example."

Years ago I heard him speak in Washington. He sounded like a very precise and enlightened industrial engineering professor, except he was also meeting a payroll and outcompeting his competitors. In 1998 he agreed to sign on to our widely supported petition to USDA and DEA to remove industrial hemp from the DEA's restrictions and allow our farmers to grow this very versatile plant for energy, food, clothing, paper, and many other uses including carpets. Mr. Anderson promised that his company would buy more hemp for its products—industrial hemp can legally be imported from Canada and China—but is not permitted to be grown in the United States. "We have experimented with hemp in carpets and fabrics," he said, "and it is a very good fiber for both. However, supply is very limited because of laws against hemp growing."

Ray Anderson was authentic. He intensely disliked corporate "greenwashing," which he defined as "letting words get ahead of deeds purely for economic or personal gain." At Interface (located in Atlanta), he significantly advanced John Elkington's concept of the "triple bottom line"—economic, social, and environmental which come together into one bottom line (economic) as a better way to make a bigger profit.

Take note of his approach—he starts with a set of deep ethical values, translates them into industrial processes that do not damage the Earth and then bends the corporate behavior to those two predicates.

Asked two years ago what he wants from the government, he replied "a carbon tax . . . taxing bad things instead of good things, so that an honest market can then work. Today it's a dishonest market, just stumbling around ignoring the externalities."

In his first book *Mid-Course Correction*, he refers people to page 172 to meet "tomorrow's child," as his reply to the question of what motivates him? Posterity, "tomorrow's child," includes his five grandchildren.

Hundreds of thousands of engineers should read his book *Business Lessons from a Radical Industrialist*. As a renaissance engineer with his feet on the ground, Mr. Anderson set the standards for professionalism which starts with prevention of damage and ends with restoration. He motivated those in his company and leaders in other companies with his inspirational imagery. He talked of climbing the seven faces of "Mount Sustainability." "Every foothold gained," he declared, "begins with a self-questioning analysis of our process and materials and the determination to achieve even better results with less, and ultimately, no impact on our environment."

Here are the Seven Fronts on "Mount Sustainability":

Eliminate Waste: Eliminate all forms of waste in every area of business;

Benign Emissions: Eliminate toxic substances from products, vehicles and facilities;

Renewable Energy: Operate facilities with renewable energy sources—solar, wind, landfill gas, biomass and low impact hydroelectric;

Resource-Efficient Transportation: Transport people and products efficiently to reduce waste and emissions;

Sensitize Stakeholders: Create a culture that integrates sustainability principles and improves peoples' lives and livelihoods; and

Redesign Commerce: Create a new business model that demonstrates and supports the value of sustainability-based commerce.

While Anderson spoke from details, he moved to inspiration and philosophy. He would say to hard-bitten industrialists and idealistic students, "You, too, have influence. You have the power of one. Your organization has influence, too—the collective influence of one and one and one. Knowledge, deep (not superficial) knowledge, getting well up that curve, comes first. Doing (taking action) must follow—in your personal lives and at work. Knowledge and ac-

tion are critical. They give credibility and validity to your examples and to your influence, which can spread and grow without limit."

He even got top executives at Walmart to listen and move.

Ray Anderson's greatness came from the expansion of his vision from year to year. He was a learner par excellence—from books, from the people at Interface, from academics, and from advisors like David Suzuki and Amory Lovins. In his last book he wrote, "[we] are all part of the continuum of humanity and the web of life in general. We will have lived our brief span and either helped or hurt that continuum, that web, and the Earth that sustains all life. Which will it be? It's your call."

Ray Anderson's legacy lights the way for the future of the world's productive and living environment.

To his wife Pat, his children and grandchildren go our sorrows and sympathies imbued with a deep appreciation of Ray Anderson's magnificence that touched all who followed and extended his embracing humanity.

The Sports Fan's Manifesto
June 27, 2011

Why do many serious readers of newspapers go first to the Sports section? Maybe because they want to read about teams playing fun games by sports journalists and columnists, who have more freedom to use imaginative words and phrases than others in their craft.

The trouble is that ever-more organized and commercialized sports are squeezing the fun out of the games. I'm not just referring to struggles between multimillionaire players against billionaire owners—as in the current NFL lockout and the looming NBA imbroglio. I am referring to what our League of Fans Sports Policy Director, Ken Reed, calls the "win-at-all-costs (WAAC) and profit-at-all-costs (PAAC) mentalities, policies and decisions that are resulting in a variety of abuses from the pros all the way to Little League." When WAAC and PAAC run amok—and what's best for the players, the fans and the game are shoved aside—"sport begins to lose its soul."

In his first of ten League of Fans reports, Reed makes the case against this "soul sickness" in a twenty-seven-page Sports Manifesto (www.leagueoffans.org). The range of endemic and often worsening problems is startling for how often they have been exposed without anything significantly being done about them.

Here is a list of Reed's choices for civic action:

- Academic corruption in college and high school athletic programs.

- Rampant commercialization from the pros to our little leagues.

- Publicly-financed stadiums for wealthy owners.

- The perversity of forcing loyal fans to purchase personal seat licenses (PSLs) in pro and college football just to have the right to buy season tickets.

- The sports cartel in Division I football known as the Bowl Championship Series (BCS)—which limits revenues and opportunities (e.g., a legitimate chance at a national championship) for the conferences and schools left on the outside.

- Work stoppages in the professional sports leagues in which fans have no voice.

- Exorbitant ticket and concession prices at taxpayer-funded stadiums (where most, if not all, ticket, concession, merchandise, and parking revenues typically go to the franchise owners). In addition, there are also television blackouts from these taxpayer-financed stadiums.

- A focus on elite athletic teams in high schools and middle schools at the expense of diminishing intramural programs and physical education classes for all students.

- The practice of requiring college athletes to pay their own medical bills, even though they were injured while playing for their university.

- Disparities in opportunities for females, disabled individuals, and people of color despite Title IX and other civil rights advances.

- The proliferation of youth club sports organizations that have a financial vs. an educational mission.

- The specialization and professionalization of young athletes at earlier and earlier ages.

- The increasing use of performance-enhancing drugs at all ages, by both males and females.

- The erosion of the core ideals, values and ethics of sports, resulting in escalating incidents of poor sportsmanship.

- An increase in sports injuries, most alarmingly concussions.

- A shocking increase in obesity, accompanied by a decline in physical fitness—especially among our youth.

- Dehumanizing coaches at all levels, most disturbingly, at the youth level.

As a college varsity player, a coach, marketer, teacher and author, Reed is in touch with many worried and upset sports lovers. They include parents, current and retired players, leading analysts, academics, educators, physicians, reporters, and civil rights advocates. League of Fans, which I started, wants to build a strong and growing reform movement not just to curb the "excesses of the monied interests," to use a Jeffersonian phrase, but to open up opportunities for more participatory sports right down to the neighborhood levels. We have too few players and too many spectators—a reality that sports journalism should pay more attention to regularly.

There is a problem afflicting sports journalism and its comparatively immense space and time devoted to professional sports. It goes beyond a largely indifferent attitude toward this imbalance between spectators and participatory sports. Even though the concerns of many sports-lovers are based on the occasional investigatory reports or columns documenting abuses, when people acting as citizens try to do something about them, their efforts receive little, if any media coverage.

So what's the point to these exposés other than to make readers and viewers angry, cynical or frustrated, if when the readers use this information to follow up and sound the alarm to do something, the sports media looks the other way and gives the space to some athlete who is pouting or showing up late for practice?

Sports journalism has to introspect a little about a larger view of newsworthiness. Otherwise they continue to uncritically cover the big league sports business that, with few exceptions, knows few restraints to its greed and insensitivity toward fans whom they are increasingly turning off.

League of Fans wants to hear from you. E-mail comments/questions to ken.reed@league-offans.org or write to League of Fans, PO Box 19367, Washington, DC 20036.

Small Press with Big Ideas
May 3, 2011

Among the vast daily news sources bidding for our readership, I find four little-heralded publications representing major causes worthy of attention.

Spotlighting the dwindling survival of the family farm and ranch is the monthly *OCM News* published by the Organization for Competitive Markets (OCM). OCM is opposed to the concentration of power in a few megacorporate hands such as the four giant meatpackers and the giant seed company, Monsanto. The effect on farmers is to increase their costs of supplies and decrease their right, under neglected federal law, to receive competitive bids for their product, such as beef.

OCM executive director, Fred Stokes, in a recent editorial on the "changing structure of American agriculture," quotes Bill Bishop, an editorial writer, as saying that companies like Cargill and Smithfield "don't own farms, they'll own the farmers."

In another recent issue, Randy Stevenson, OCM's president decries "the merger of government and business" to serve the politically very influential corporate agribusiness giants. In the December 2010 issue, Mr. Stevens calls for any evidence as to the existence of significant competition in the cattle market. He wants to know if there are "specific instances when they have observed two different packers making differing bids on the same lot of cattle." He was speaking of the rarity of more than one giant packer competing against another "through negotiated purchases."

For more information about the unenforced Packers and Stockyards Act—which was passed ninety years ago to assure competitive markets see www.competitivemarkets.com.

The American Conservative (amconmag.com), published monthly, contains more than a few articles that reflect a return to historic conservative principles, so long debauched by corporatists and neocons masquerading as conservatives.

In a cover story in its April 2011 issues, titled "Poisoned Generation: For Iraq's Children the War is Not Over," author Kelley B. Vlahos describes the large increase in infant mortality and birth defects from the massive contamination of air, water, soil, and food from Bush's invasion. His depiction of hospital records from Fallujah warrant an independent study by the World Health Organization (WHO). He writes that "looking at the photographs of babies barely recognizable as human, of toddlers frighteningly tiny, limp from their own deformities, the toll of war and the conditions it creates is evident."

Other articles in the April issue included "Beyond Free Trade," covering the "heterodox economists challenging globalism," and commentaries praising Governor Jerry Brown and decorated Marine General Smedley Butler who

became an anti-war, anti-multinational corporation advocate before World War II, writing the popular book "War is a Racket," that ended with the declaration "To Hell With War!"

For the politically jaded, try *PEEReview*, a sprightly quarterly newsletter published by the Public Employees for Environmental Responsibility. This group started in the early nineties by professional foresters in the US Forest Service to defend their expert judgment against such corporate power moves as mindless clearcutting by large timber companies cutting the public's trees for a pittance in payment. Membership since has come from other employees at federal agencies who work on natural resources and environmental health issues.

PEER is remarkably effective in its litigation, lobbying and exposés. Its specificity is remarkable, as are its sources from Washington down to the state and local level, to stop the rollback of clean water and air protections and the protection of one third of America that comprise "the public lands." All this is being supported by civil servants who want to take their conscience to work (see www.peer.org).

Speaking of civil servants, those much stereotyped and maligned Americans, you may wish to get on the free mailing list for a fascinating monthly publication by the US Department of Health and Human Services. It is called *Research Activities* assembled by the Agency for Healthcare Research and Quality. (Send an email to HRQPubs@ahrq.hhs.gov for an online copy.)

This newsletter has an academic name, but its writing is engrossing, covering as it does improvements or declines in healthcare quality and the nagging health disparities based on race, ethnicity, socioeconomic status, and other factors it deems unacceptable.

Keeping its quality of reporting high, whether under the Bush or Obama Administrations, *Research Activities* testifies to the importance of a prudent degree of political independence for the nation's civil service.

Its April 2011 issue reports that "few disparities in quality of care are getting smaller, and almost no disparities in access to care are getting smaller." One hopeful improvement: "the proportion of heart attack patients who underwent procedures to unblock heart arteries within ninety minutes improved from 42 percent in 2005 to 81 percent in 2008."

Information increases the mind's range to fulfill the citizenry's potential for connecting reality with higher and nobler expectations.

Waiting for the Spark
April 18, 2011

What could start a popular resurgence in this country against the abuses of concentrated, avaricious corporatism? Imagine the arrogance of passing on enormous corporate losses to already cheated working people and the jobless. This is achieved through government bailouts and tax escapes.

History teaches us that the spark usually is smaller than expected and of a nature that is wholly unpredictable or even unimaginable. But if the dry tinder is all around, as many deprivations and polls reveal, the spark, no matter how small, can turn into a raging inferno.

The Boston Tea Party lit up the American Revolution. Storming the hated Bastille (prison) by impoverished Parisians launched the French Revolution. More recently, in December 1997, an Israeli military vehicle rammed a civilian van in the West Bank killing seven occupants and igniting the first intifada.

Last December, a young fruit vendor, abused by thieving police in a small Tunisian town, immolated himself in the local square. Seen by millions on Facebook, this self-sacrifice launched the Tunisian and Egyptian overthrow of their long-time dictators. Later, in Syria, after police arrested thirteen youngsters in a southern border town for anti-government graffiti the place erupted in riots and rallies that are spreading to other cities.

A few weeks ago, many progressives and quite a few pundits believed that the recurrent, ever larger February-March rallies in Madison, Wisconsin by workers, students and others against the governor's and the legislature's attack on public employee unions and social services, following earlier blatant corporate welfare enactments, would be the long-awaited spark.

The Madison eruption spread briefly to Ohio and Indiana where Republican officials were moving in the same direction, punishing workers and families while leaving the corporate and wealthy to count their mounting privileges. There, the crowds were neither as large nor as frequent. In all these states, the Republicans got most of what they wanted, albeit with a possible, future political price to be paid. The rallies have subsided, not even culminating—as some organizers hoped—in a gigantic march on Washington, DC.

Granted, rallying a long repressed people into losing their fear and demanding, as in Cairo's huge Tahrir Square "out with the dictator," is a simple, anthromorphic goal. In our country, the rallies are hardly as clearcut, though use of the citizen right of recall for Republican legislators, and later Governor Walker himself, may produce an interesting accountability election. But sparks are difficult to sustain.

In authoritarian regimes, there are few options for dissent or airing one's grievances. So when the spark does occur, the climate is fertile for an explosion of outrages.

In the United States, there are largely myths such as "anyone can sue," or "anyone can run," or "anyone can directly tell off the president or the mayor," or "anyone can blow the whistle." These combine with a few celebrated successes by rebels or an ordinary David taking on a Goliath for a win here and there, from a corporate-government ruling class that bends a little so that it doesn't break.

Meanwhile, the inequality, gouging, political exclusions and overall gaps between the top one percent and the rest tighten the grip of the oligarchy and its draining, violent militarized empire.

Loss of control over almost everything that matters, including their children to daily direct corporate marketing of junk food and violent programming, is rampant. Over 70 percent of those polled told *Business Week* that they believed corporations had "too much control over their lives"—and that was in 2000 before conditions and controls—viz, the Wall Street collapse, severe recession and taxpayer bailouts—worsened.

The American people don't see much they can do to counter the pressures of greed and power that tracks them daily from debt to debt, from lower standards of living to outright penury, from denial of critical healthcare to the iron collar of the cruel credit score, from inscrutable, computerized bills to fine-print contracts trapping their sense of unfairness into waves of frustrations, from being put on hold by the companies until they're told no, no, no or penalty, penalty, penalty!

How do we break the cycle of despair, exclusion, powerlessness, and endless betrayal by those given the authority to bring down the exploiters and oppressors to lawful accountability?

The Empire rips up the Constitution and takes the reserve army of the young unemployed to kill and die in aggressive wars of the White House's choice, with Congress watching from the sidelines; its only role to funnel trillions of tax dollars into the insatiable war machine's unauditable budgets. President Eisenhower wanted us to control the "military-industrial complex." Instead it grew much more out of control. Eisenhower's grave warning as expressed in his farewell address in 1961 was prescient.

The spark can come from a recurrent sequence of abuses that strike a special chord of deeply felt injustice. Or it could be a unique episode or bullying that tolls the feeling "enough already" throughout the land. Such sparks cannot be manufactured; the power to arouse and break people's routines is spontaneous.

When that moment comes, millions of Americans whose self-respect and keen sense of wrong will remind them precisely why our Constitution begins with "We the People" and not "We the Corporations." They will realize the necessity for a Jeffersonian revolution.

Tweeting Away the Time
January 3, 2011

The start of the New Year is a good time to talk about time. About this, we can all agree—there are only twenty-four hours in a day. Zillions of companies and persons want a piece of that time from us in order to make money. But that supply of time is not expandable. Unlike other supplies in the marketplace, this one has no give beyond twenty-four hours a day.

Note the massive increase in commercial requests for our time in return for our dollars—directly or indirectly—compared to sixty years ago. Instead of three television networks bidding for our time in order to sell advertising, there are over one hundred channels on any cable system. There are ever more radio stations, more online blogs and websites, more video games, more music. In 1950, there were no cell phones, no iPhones, no Blackberries, no e-mails, no text messaging, no apps, no E-books, no faxes. Entertainment fare is now 24/7 and expanding rapidly on the internet.

But there are still only twenty-four hours per day. What are these merchants expecting of the consumers' time? Squeezing more into less time as attention spans shorten, for one. Marketing so irresistible that people buy far more of these videos and other entertainment services than they have time to listen or to view.

Think of the VCRs and the DVDs piled up at home that have never been seen. Same for many books. The big bestseller on the universe: *The Grand Design* by scientist Stephen Hawking became status furniture on sitting room tables except for the one in a hundred who actually read that book.

In short, the gap between what we think we have time for when we buy these products and what we actually expend time on is setting records every day.

However, people of all ages are spending more time on casual gaming (75 million Americans is the estimate) than on solitaire or cards—apart from being addicted to competitive video games. So there is some substitution at play here.

Emails and text messaging are taking a large slice out of the day, in part because they are so cheap and in part because they are so personal. "What gives" here is that less time is being spent on the telephone but by no means in equal measure.

So cheap and easy are modern communications that it is often harder to actually reach most people than during the days of the dial phone.

How much time do we spend trying to get someone to return calls or even to react to emails (which are increasingly passé in favor of text messages) during the day or week? After a while one stops trying to make telephone contact because of the low probability of actually talking to the person you want to reach.

People are so overloaded that just getting them to respond to a friendly letter, call or electronic message requires many repetitions. The banality of abundance is at work here.

On the other hand, where you do get quick replies are from your "friends" with mutual gossip and personal tid-bits drive up the back and forth volume immensely. A sixteen-year-old girl said that she sends 600 text messages a day and "would die without her cell phone."

Still the sellers are more and more vigorously competing for a piece of the buyers' time. Where is all this going? First the sales appeal may ostensibly be for the buyers' time—eg. toys, DVDs—but it really is an appeal to the buyers' hope or belief that he/she has the time sometime. That is what gives what economists call the "elasticity" to the seemingly finite twenty-four hour day. Whether that time is devoted to the program or product is immaterial to the seller once the sale is made. The successful seller is happy.

But what is happening to the buyer? More stuff piles up. More sense of being time burdened when weeks and months pass without getting around to using the purchased goods or services. More susceptibility to buying the newest upgrade or version out of a sense of getting to now what they haven't had time to get to before with the older purchase.

Moreover, as a society of buyers, we become ever more fractured audiences—especially for national television—and it is less likely that we see or react to the events of the day as a community.

I was reminded of this observation recently when Washington's current outrages of endemic wars, waste and corruption rattle the public far less than Nixon's Watergate behavior. In 1974 after Nixon fired his Attorney General and the Special Prosecutor who were investigating his involvement in the Watergate burglary and cover-up, Tennesseans sent 40,000 telegrams to one of their senators over three days. Members of Congress, even with the ease of email and Twitter, do not get that kind of meaningful volume.

When our time feels overwhelmed and the marketers are banging on our doors for more time claims, what time is there left for necessary solitude, for family and other socializing, for kids playing outside instead of being addicted to indoor screens, even at dinner, for, excuse the words, reflection and contemplation?

It comes down to whether we have any time from our absorption into virtual reality to engage reality, including civil and political realities. A society whose people do not show up for public meetings, hearings, protests, and even local folklore events is a society that is cannibalizing its democracy, its critical sense of community purpose.

Take back some of those discretionary hours from the marketers and electronic entertainers. Devote them to shaping the future for you and your children.

Honoring Those Who Toil

September 8, 2010

What does Labor Day mean anymore other than another day off, another store sale and, in some cities, parades ever smaller and more devoid of passion for elevating the well-being of working people?

Philosopher/mechanic Matthew B. Crawford, in his recent, embracing book, *Shop Craft as Soulcraft* has a thoughtful consideration. He deflates the high-prestige workplace and makes the case for millions of Americans who still make and fix things with their hands.

"I want to suggest we can take a broader view of what a good job might consist of, and therefore what kind of education is important. We seem to have developed an educational monoculture, tied to a vision of what kind of work is valuable and important—everyone gets herded into a certain track where they end up working in an office, regardless of their natural bents.

"But some people, including some who are very smart, would rather be learning to build things or fix things. Why not honor that? I think one reason we don't is that we've had this fantasy that we're going to somehow take leave of material reality and glide around in a pure information economy."

Dr. Crawford has a PhD in political philosophy and is a mechanic who runs Shockoe Moto, an independent motorcycle repair shop in Richmond, Virginia. This gives him a deep sense of skill and broader perspective with which to evaluate these ways of satisfying one's value of locally-rooted work. He contrasts these traits with the deadening assembly line and computer focused office work, both of which can be outsourced on the whims of a boss.

The Winsted, Connecticut Deck's Fix-It

Shop, operated joyously by an aunt and her nephew, until they retired last year, would have been exhibit A for Dr. Crawford. They fixed hundreds of different products brought to them by the townspeople. Their small shop was filled horizontally and vertically with items donated, about to be fixed or were unfixable by the manufacturers' design. They could have charged a museum entrance fee for browsing if their shop had more room. Oh, what pride they regularly took in their work.

Electricians, plumbers, carpenters, painters, tailors, car and bike repairers, restorers of stoves, refrigerators, air conditioners, furnaces, locks, windows, sidewalks, and streets enjoy a special kind of personal job gratification that is alien to the pre-designed, robotic labors of their friends who come home every day with clean clothes.

I've often wondered why the knowledge of tradespeople about the best, middling, and worst brands of equipment, products and materials they work with or have to install (such as furnaces) isn't collected by some magazine or consumer group. After all Angie's List is surveying what their customers around the country think about the quality of the service.

Along with the repairers, we should recognize the inspectors—millions of them working for government agencies and companies to assure that health and safety laws are observed and quality controls are maintained. They are the meat and poultry inspectors, OSHA and Customs inspectors, sanitation inspectors of food stores and restaurants, motor vehicle inspectors, nuclear, chemical and aircraft inspectors, inspectors of laboratories, hospitals, clinics, building code inspectors, and the insurance inspectors assigned to loss prevention duties.

The more conscientious of these inspectors are vulnerable to being over-ridden by their less committed superiors (such as meat inspectors for the US Department of Agriculture) or harassed (inspectors for the US Forest Service on corporately exploited federal timber land). Sometimes inspectors so commit their conscience to their work that they become whistle-blowers about safety hazards or hanky panky, which too often invites career-ending retaliation.

How little attention we devote to those inspectors who are sentinels for the well-being of the American people. As a result, the courageous are not honored—if only to motivate the young to choose these careers. Moreover, a culture of corruption, that can erode their alertness or burdens them with weak standards to enforce, escapes exposure.

Then there are the near invisibles—the cleaners who do their thankless but essential jobs in hotels, airports, bus and train stations, office buildings, factories, schools, libraries, museums, streets, restaurants, and homes.

Strange how we don't react to cleaners—rarely thanking them or greeting them with salutations. Notice how airline passengers rush past them on the jetway while they wait to clean up the messes under severe time pressure. People who babble incessantly at airports or bus and train stations, while waiting for their departure, ignore the sweepers and dusters, automatically averting their eyes, and almost never acknowledging their work.

Taxi drivers are often tipped and thanked. How many hotel maids, who clean twelve or more soiled rooms and toilets a day, receive any thanks or tips by the guests? Cleaners are among the lowest paid workers, often handle not the safest of chemicals, and receive very little respect or recognition. Their lowly status has to affect their morale and maybe their performance.

Yet what would we do if these workers went

on a general strike from the nursing homes to the garbage trucks? We'd feel it a lot more than if the overpaid Wall Street traders went on strike.

One day I was at BWI airport and went to the crowded men's room. As I entered, the elderly cleaning man erupted in frustration. "I'm sick of this job," he shouted to no one in particular. "Hour after hour I clean up, come back, see the crap, clean up some more. It never ends," he wailed. The men who were wiping, flushing, washing, drying, and zipping were stunned and silently shuffled out, as if he wasn't there. I thanked him for his work and candor, calmed him down and gave him a gratuity. The others looked at me blankly as if I was dealing with a ghost they never see as a human being.

Cultures can be astonishing. The hands-on workers who harvest our food, clean up after us, repair our property, look out after our health and safety conditions and serve as nannies to our children receive few honors, status or anywhere near the compensation of those who gamble with our money, entertain us or drive us into wars they don't fight themselves.

Shouldn't Labor Day be a time to gather and contemplate such inverted values and celebrate those who toil without proper recognition?

Katsuko Nomura: Consumer Champion

August 27, 2010

Katsuko Nomura—a builder of consumer, labor, cooperative and women's rights groups for over fifty-five years in Japan—passed away this month at the age of ninety-nine. She was one of the most remarkable civic leaders anywhere in the world. With her range of activities, she could be called a world citizen.

To recognize her indomitable spirit and humanity, one has to understand the conditions with which she had to contend. Born in 1910 in Kyoto, she lost her husband and many relatives and friends during World War II. By August 1945, her country was reduced to rubble. Destitution, hunger, homelessness, inflation were daily experiences.

Mrs. Nomura witnessed crises everywhere, but she also saw vast opportunities for building a just and democratic society. This was no small feat in a male-dominated society under US military occupation.

She started her dynamic career building consumer cooperatives—a banding together that was then critical for families facing drastic shortages of life's necessities. She took her experience and legislative success with the Cooperative League of Japan to become a founder of the Japan Housewives' Association whose mass boycotts and marches challenged Japanese companies accustomed to very little government regulation.

During these struggles, she forged a unitary approach to those kept powerless in the economy—organizing consumers, workers and small businesses around their common interests. She became a strong voice, especially for women, in the General Council of Trade Unions of Japan and helped found the Consumers' Union of Japan, which she directed for over a decade.

All these formal associations cannot do credit to watching her in action. Well into her eighties, she aroused audiences of younger Japanese activists and prodded them to raise expectations for themselves as change-agents. She was often the toughest person at any gathering.

A devourer of information, a prodigious translator into Japanese of what US consumer groups were reporting and doing, she fought for economic, health and safety advances in Japan by publicizing better practices she discovered in other countries.

Neither US food exports to Japan of dubious safety nor the injustices inflicted on less developed countries by Japanese multinationals escaped her pointed criticism and agendas for action.

Of course, the mix of political, economic and cultural factors are quire different in Japan as compared with the US, where citizen and labor groups focus heavily on regulatory and judicial tools to achieve their goals. In Japan, more nuanced informal pressures, demands and shame can be used, though the country is moving toward more reliance on agencies and courts.

In 1990, with considerably less than half the population of the US, there were thirty-one national consumer organizations with a combined membership of over eleven million people and 1,267 consumer cooperatives serving roughly 35 million Japanese. Today, with over 300 million people, the comparative US membership figures may not reach that level.

On the occasion of the celebration of Mrs. Nomura's eighty-eighth birthday, I wrote the following words:

> An ancient Greek philosopher said that "character is destiny." Mrs. Nomura's life of dedication to the pursuit of justice, to the building of a deeper democracy reflects her many skills but above all her character.
>
> Her character is a finely textured collection of traits, beyond honesty, which are attentive to the many obstacles, problems and power centers which she and her associates have had to confront. She is always focused on the ultimate objectives while paying close scrutiny to the many paths that must be traveled to reach these objectives. She transcends discouragement and fatigue. She deploys a limitless ability to absorb information, to digest it into many strands for distribution to others. She needs no motivation because she possesses a public philosophy that has given her *the* Motivator's role.

> This public philosophy produces a consistency over the years—so much so that she is still the most concrete, grass roots organizer among citizen activists half her age or less. She sees through politicians or anyone who displays insincerity, deception or superficial rhetoric.

> She was nominated as one of "1000 women" for the 2005 Nobel Peace Prize. But Mrs. Nomura was never interested in honors and resolutions, not to mention endless meetings without action, bureaucratic pomposity, or make-work. She always had her *focus on results*, on helping those in need confront the abuses of the corporate powers.

> In her later years, she wanted to write an autobiography. But in failing health, she used her time fighting for rights instead of writing her own story so that future generations could stand on her shoulders and spirit, moving forward.

> Perhaps, her friends and admirers can produce a biography and a documentary on her life—one that teaches so well the wisdom of the Chinese saying that "to know and not to do is not to know."

As she advanced in years, Mrs. Nomura would call herself "an old woman" followed by a short, wistful laugh. It was as if she regretted not having more time to put more forces into motion.

Such regret was not unfounded. A wise person once said that "the only true aging is the erosion of one's ideals." Mrs. Nomura was always the most curious, creative and youngest of leaders in this respect, making the most out of small budgets.

May her legacy be a source of self-renewing energy for many seekers of justice in this tormented world of ours. For she was the essence of resilient self-renewal.

Cashiering Helen Thomas

June 15, 2010

The termination of Helen Thomas' sixty-two-year long career as a pioneering, no-nonsense newswoman was swift and intriguingly merciless.

The event leading to her termination began when she was sitting on a White House bench under oppressive summer heat. The eighty-nine-year old hero of honest journalism and women's rights, the scourge of dissembling presidents and White House press secretaries, answered a passing visitor's question about Israel with a snappish comment worded in a way she didn't mean; she promptly apologized in writing (see http://www.democracynow.org/2010/6/8/veteran_white_house_reporter_helen_thomas). Recorded without permission on a hand video, the brief exchange, that included a defense of dispossessed Palestinians, went internet viral on Friday, June 7.

By Monday, Helen Thomas was considered finished, even though she embodied a steadfast belief, in the praiseworthy words of *Washington Post* columnist, Dana Milbank, "that anybody standing on that podium [in the White House] should be regarded with skepticism."

Over the weekend, her lecture agent dropped her. Her column syndicator, the Hearst company, pressed her to quit "effective immediately," and, it was believed that the White House Correspondents Association, of which she was the first female president, was about to take away her coveted front row seat in the White House press room.

Then, Helen Thomas announced her retirement on Monday, June 10. No doubt she's had her fill of ethnic, sexist, and ageist epithets hurled her way over the years—the very decades she was broadly challenging racism, sexism and, more recently, ageism.

Although the behind the scenes story has yet to come out, the evisceration was launched by two pro-Israeli war hawks, Ari Fleischer and Lanny Davis. Fleischer was George W. Bush's press secretary who bridled under Helen Thomas' questioning regarding the horrors of the Bush-Cheney war crimes and illegal torture. His job was not to answer this uppity woman but to deflect, avoid and cover up for his bosses.

Davis was the designated defender whenever Clinton got into hot water. As journalist Paul Jay pointed out, he is now a Washington lobbyist whose clients include the cruel corporate junta that overthrew the elected president of Honduras. Both men rustled up the baying pack of Thomas-haters during the weekend and filled the unanswered narrative on Fox and other facilitating media.

Then, belatedly, something remarkable occurred. People reacted against this grossly disproportionate punishment. Ellen Ratner, a Fox News contributor, wrote, "I'm Jewish and a supporter of Israel. Let's face it: we all have said things—or thought things—about 'other' groups of people, things that we wouldn't want to see in print or on video. Anyone who denies it is a liar. Give [Helen] a break."

Apparently, many people agree. In an internet poll by the *Washington Post*, 92 percent of respondents said she should not be removed from the White House press room. As an NPR listener, R. Carey, e-mailed, "DC would be void of journalists if they all were to quit, get fired, or retire after making potentially offensive comments."

Listen to Michael Freedman, former managing editor for United Press International. "After seven decades of setting standards for quality journalism and demolishing barriers for women in the workplace, Helen Thomas has now shown that most dreaded of vulnerabilities—she is human. . . . Who among us does not have strong feelings about the endless warfare in the Middle East? Who among us has said something we have come to regret? . . . Let's not destroy Ms. Thomas now."

Katrina vanden Heuvel, editor and publisher of the *Nation*, wrote, "Thomas was the only accredited White House correspondent with the guts to ask Bush the tough questions that define a free press. . . . Her remarks were offensive, but considering her journalistic moxie and courage over many decades—a sharp contrast to the despicable deeds committed by so many littering the Washington political scene—isn't there room for someone who made a mistake, apologized for it and wants to continue speaking truth to power and asking tough questions?"

Last week, in front of the White House, people calling themselves "Jews for Helen Thomas" gathered in a small demonstration. Medea Benajmin—cofounder of Global Exchange, declared, "We are clear what Helen Thomas meant to say, which is that Israel should cease its occupation of Palestine and we agree with that." While another demonstrator, Zool Zulkowitz, asserted that "by discrediting Helen Thomas, those who believe that Israel can do no wrong shift attention from the public relations debacle of the Gaza Flotilla killings, and intimidate journalists who would ask hard questions about the Israeli occupation of Palestine and American foreign policy."

Helen Thomas, who grew up in Detroit, is an American of Arab descent. She is understandably alert to the one-sided US military and foreign policy in that region. Her questions reflect concerns about US policy in the Middle East by many Americans, including unmuzzled retired military, diplomatic and intelligence officials.

In 2006 when George W. Bush finally called on her, she started her questioning by saying, "Your decision to invade Iraq has caused the deaths of Americans and Iraqis. Every reason given, publicly at least, has turned out not to be true." Or when she challenged President Obama last month, asking, "When are you going to get out of Afghanistan? Why are we continuing to kill and die there? What is the real excuse?"

Asking the "why" questions was a Thomas trademark. Many self-censoring journalists avoid controversial "why" questions, thereby allowing evasion, dissembling and just plain B.S. to dominate the White House press room. She rejected words that sugarcoated or camouflaged the grim deeds. She started with the grim deeds to expose the doubletalk and officialdom's chronic illegalities.

What appalled Thomas most is the way the media rolls over and fails to hold officials accountable. (British reporters believe they are tougher on their Prime Ministers.) This is a subject about which she has written books and articles—not exactly the way to endear herself to those reporters who go AWOL and look the other way, so that they can continue to be called upon or to be promoted by their superiors.

The abysmal record of the *New York Times* and the *Washington Post* in the months preceding the Iraq invasion filled with Bush-Cheney lies, deception, and cover-ups is a case in point. As usual, she was proven right, not the celebrated reporters and columnists deprecating her work, including the *Post*'s press critic, Howard Kurtz.

Thomas practiced her profession with a deep regard for the peoples' right to know. To her, as Aldous Huxley noted long ago, "facts do not cease to exist because they are ignored."

Lastly, there is the double standard. One off-hand "ill-conceived remark," as NPR

Ombudsman Alicia Shepard stated, in praising Ms. Thomas, ended a groundbreaking
career. While enhanced careers and fat lecture fees are the reward for ultra-right wing
radio and cable ranters, and others like columnist Ann Coulter, who regularly urge
wars, mayhem and dragnets based on bigotry,
stereotypes, and falsehoods directed wholesale against Muslims, including a blatant anti-semitism against Arabs. (See http://www
.adc.org/education/educational-resources/ and
Jack Shaheen's book and companion documentary about cultural portrayal of Arab stereotypes, *Reel Bad Arabs*.)

Ms. Thomas' desk at the Hearst office remains unattended a week after her eviction. One
day she will return to pack up her materials. She
can take with her the satisfaction of joining all
those in our history who were cashiered ostensibly for a gaffe, but really for being too right, too
early, too often.

Her many admirers hope that she continues
to write, speak, and motivate a generation of
young journalists in the spirit of Joseph Pulitzer's advice to his reporters a century ago—that
their job was to "comfort the afflicted and afflict
the comfortable."

Wealth for Justice

April 30, 2010

There are signs that some super-rich are revolt-
ing against their "wealth fraternity." Last fall,
mega-billionaire Warren Buffett traveled to
Washington to meet with Democratic senators
and urge them to raise taxes on the wealthy like
him. He pointedly said he pays at a lower rate
than his secretary.

The liberal senators were either bemused, or

moved away from him as if he had a contagious
disease. Buffett is not deterred. Earlier in this
decade, he joined with a thousand other rich
Americans led by lawyer William Gates, Sr. and
Chuck Collins (founder of United For a Fair
Economy) to successfully block the repeal of the
estate tax (applied to 2 percent of wealthier de-
cedents) by a Republican-controlled Congress.

Just last week, Mr. Gates, father of Microsoft's Bill, Jr. launched an initiative campaign
in Washington state to impose a progressive
income tax on the wealthiest citizens (over
$200,000 income) and roll back taxes on prop-
erty and small business revenues. Initiative 1077
would net $1 billion a year for education and
healthcare. Unlike most states, Washington has
no state income tax at present. Any later downward expansion of such a tax would have to be
decided by a vote of the people themselves, stip-
ulates I-1077.

The "yes" on Initiative 1077 organizers have
to collect 241,153 valid signatures by July 2
to get on the November ballot. This is a huge
hurdle for a relatively small state, but when the
super-rich are on board, the money will be there
for the petitioners.

Last week, several megamillionaires held a
conference call with reporters to express their
desire for high taxes on people like them. "I
would with pleasure sacrifice the income," declared Jeffrey Hollander, CEO of Seventh Generation. Eric Schoenberg, possessing investment
banking riches, bewailed his "absurdly low tax
rates."

According to the *Washington Post*, paper-mill
heir Mike Lapham said, "We're calling on other
wealthy taxpayers to join us, send the message to
Congress and President Obama that it's time to
roll back the tax cuts on upper-income taxpayers." He was referring to the Bush-Cheney tax

cuts which saved the then-White House rulers hundreds of thousands of dollars, personally, over the near decade of cuts. At the time, I requested Bush and Cheney have the decency to exempt themselves from their own tax cuts, but they declined.

According to a Quinnipiac University poll in March, a solid majority of Americans favor raising taxes on those earning more than $250,000 a year.

Then there is Dieter Lehmkuhl. Last October, he delivered to German Chancellor Angela Merkel a petition signed by 44 rich Germans urging a 5 percent wealth tax for two years to fund economic and social programs to aid Germany's economic recovery. The petition asserted that "the path out of the crisis must be paved with massive investment in ecology, education and social justice."

Megabillionaires in our country are encountering their peers here and around the world to commit fifty percent of their estates to "good works." They will grapple with the definition of "good works" as to whether that means charity or justice.

The difference is important. For example, soup kitchens are a necessary and human charity. Whereas justice goes to the causes of why rich economies have any hunger at all.

With some super-rich thinking about moving from soft philanthropy to advocacy, or to shifts of power, I hope my recent work of political imagination—*Only the Super-Rich Can Save Us!* will spark their interest. Drawing on seventeen wealthy Americans in fictional roles, led by Warren Buffett and including George Soros, Yoko Ono, Bill Cosby, Ted Turner, Peter Lewis and others of an advanced age and broader perspectives, a massive, fast, well-funded campaign is launched in January 2006 to galvanize millions of Americans to restore their sovereignty over their government and the large corporations that have captured Washington, DC.

One of the inspirations for this book was the history of the abolitionist movement against slavery—ably funded by rich Bostonians and New Yorkers—and the early civil rights movement in the 1950s and 1960s—significantly funded by rich people like the Stern and Currie families.

Justice movements need a lift, a shoehorn, resources to pay for organizers, facilities, transportation, litigation and media.

Today, with corporations able to amass trillions of dollars to advance harmful corporate interests, a small number of enlightened megarich elders putting their money and smarts behind broad redirections in our country supported by majorities can generate very compelling dynamics for a functioning democratic society.

If you want to see what I mean, just read my book (visit onlythesuperrich.org) and see if you agree with Lesley Stahl of CBS' *60 Minutes* who read and found *Only the Super-Rich Can Save Us!* "engrossing, creative, and funny." Lesley, I'll take all three.

Attention Deficit Democracy
March 9, 2010

A society not alert to signs of its own decay, because its ideology is the continuing myth of progress, separates itself from reality and envelops illusion.

One yardstick by which to measure the decay in our country's political, economic, and cultural life, is the answer to this question: Do the forces of power, which have demonstrably failed, become stronger after their widely perceived damage is common knowledge?

Economic decay is all around. Poverty, unemployment, foreclosures, job export, consumer debt, pension attrition, and crumbling infrastructure are well documented. The self-destruction of the Wall Street financial giants, with their looting and draining of trillions of other people's money, have been headlines for two years. Astonishingly, during and after their gigantic taxpayer bailouts from Washington, DC, the banks, et al, are still the most powerful force in determining the nature of proposed corrective legislation.

"The banks own this place," says Senator Richard Durbin (D-Ill.), evoking the opinion of many members of a supine Congress ready to pass weak consumer and investor protection legislation while leaving dominant fewer and larger banks.

Who hasn't felt the ripoffs and one-sided fine print of the credit card industry? A reform bill finally has passed after years of delay, again weak and incomplete. Shameless over their gouges, the companies have their attorneys already at work to design around the law's modest strictures.

The drug and health insurance industry, swarming with thousands of lobbyists, got pretty much what they wanted in the new health law. Insurers got millions of new customers subsidized by hundreds of billions of taxpayer dollars with very little regulation. The drug companies got their dream—no reimportation of cheaper identical drugs, no authority for Uncle Sam to bargain for discount prices, and a very profitable extension of monopoly patent protection for biologic drugs against cheaper, generic drug competition.

For all their gouges, for all their exclusions, their denial of claims and restrictions of benefits, for all their horrendous price increases, the two industries have come out stronger than ever politically and economically. Small wonder their stocks are rising even in a recession.

The junk food processing industry—on the defensive lately due to some excellent documentaries and exposés—are still the most influential of powers on Capitol Hill when it becomes to delaying for years a decent food safety bill, using tax dollars to pump fat, sugar, and salt into the stomachs of our children, and fighting adequate inspections. Over seven thousand lives are lost due to contaminated food yearly in the US and many millions of illnesses.

The oil, gas, coal, and nuclear power companies are fleecing consumers and taxpayers, depleting and imperiling the environment, yet they continue to block rational energy legislation in Congress to replace carbon and uranium with energy efficiency technology and renewables.

Still, even now after years of cost over-runs and lack of permanent storage for radioactive wastes, the nuclear industry has President Obama, and George W. Bush before him, pushing for many tens of billions of dollars in taxpayer loan guarantees for new nukes. Wall Street won't finance such a risky technology without you, the taxpayers, guaranteeing against any accident or default. Some capitalism!

Both Democrats and Republicans are passing on these outrageous financial and safety risks to taxpayers.

Congress, which receives the brunt of this corporate lobbying—the carrot of money and the stick of financing incumbent challengers—is more of an obstacle to change than ever. In the past after major failures of industry and commerce, there was a higher likelihood of congressional action. Recall the Wall Street and banking collapse in the early 1930s. Congress and

Franklin Delano Roosevelt produced legislation that saved the banks, peoples' savings and regulated the stock markets.

From the time of my book *Unsafe at Any Speed*'s publication in late November 1965, it took just nine months to federally regulate the powerful auto industry for safety and fuel efficiency.

Contrast the two-year delay after the Bear Stearns collapse and still no reform legislation, and what is pending is weak.

Yet the entrenched members of Congress, responsible for this astonishing gridlock, are almost impossible to dislodge even though polls have Congress at its lowest repute ever. It is a place where the majority is terrified of the corporations and the minority can block even the most anemic legislative efforts with archaic rules, especially in the Senate.

Culturally, the canaries in the coal mine are the children. Childhood has been commercialized by the giant marketers reaching them hour by hour with junk food, violent programming, video games, and bad medicine. The result—record obesity, child diabetes, and other ailments.

While the companies undermine parental authority, they laugh all the way to the bank, using our public airwaves, among other media, for their lucre. They can be called electronic child molesters.

We published a book in 1996 called *Children First!: A Parent's Guide to Fighting Corporate Predators in the Media*. This book is an understatement of the problem compared to the worsening of child manipulation today.

In a 24/7 entertained society frenetic with sound bites, Blackberries, iPods, text messages, and emails, there is a deep need for reflection and introspection. We have to discuss face to face in living rooms, school auditoriums, village squares, and town meetings what is happening to us and our diminishing democratic processes by the pressures and controls of the insatiable corporate state.

And what needs to be done from the home to the public arenas and marketplaces involves old and new superior models, new accountabilities, and new thinking.

For our history has shown that whenever the people get more engaged and more serious, they live better on all fronts.

Remember Zinn by Organizing

February 5, 2010

There are several memorial services and events being planned for Howard Zinn whom the *New York Times* called a "historian, shipyard worker, civil rights activist, and World War II bombardier, when he passed away at age 87 late last month."

His legion of friends, students, admirers, and colleagues will be out in force reminding the country about his impact as a civic leader, motivational teacher, author of the ever more popular book *A People's History of the United States*, and all around fine, compassionate, and level-headed human being.

Judging by similar gatherings for remembering other progressive activists and writers, the encomiums for Professor Zinn, who taught at Spelman College in the late fifties and early sixties (two of his students were Marian Wright Edelman and Alice Walker) and at Boston University until 1988, will be heartfelt, wide-ranging, and inspiringly anecdotal.

Receptions will follow and those in attendance will return to their homes, hoping that what Howard Zinn spoke and wrote and how he acted will serve as an example for those who follow his public philosophy of being and doing.

Mr. Zinn's legacy, however, needs more than sweet memories that carry forward the spirit of people. His impact needs more than the adult and youth book version (now in a television miniseries via the History Channel) to continue inspiring what the *Times* described as "a generation of high school and college students to rethink American history."

How about drawing on the large, national constituency whose lives he has informed honestly and helped improve to support the establishment of the Howard Zinn Institute for Advancing Peace and Justice? Thought and action in a seamless flow toward returning the definition of "freedom" back to the words of Marcus Cicero as "participation in power."

When Senator Paul Wellstone and his wife, Sheila, died in a plane crash in 2002, his children started "Wellstone Action!" with contributions from all over the country, to train citizen organizers to help empower underrepresented communities to engage in civic life. As a result, Senator Wellstone's progressive work to deepen our democracy continues in action year after year.

The life of Howard Zinn did not follow the usual pathways. His experience as a manual laborer and organizer in New York City gave depth to his college and graduate years. He entered New York University at the age of twenty-seven and completed his PhD at Columbia University in his thirties.

Consider the origins of his views on war summarized in his own words:

War is by definition the indiscriminate killing of huge numbers of people for ends that are uncertain. Think about means and ends, and apply it to war. The means are horrible, certainly. The ends, uncertain. That alone should make you hesitate.... We are smart in so many ways. Surely we should be able to understand that between war and passivity, there are a thousand possibilities.

Back in World War II, Mr. Zinn was a bombardier in planes that dropped napalm including during a raid over a town in France called Royan. After the war, his sensitivities horrified, Zinn returned to Royan on the ground and interviewed survivors, which included French civilians.

For sixty years, this Army veteran spoke out against all wars, from Vietnam to Iraq, and others, from the Soviet invasion of Afghanistan to Indonesian, African, and Chinese assaults.

Howard Zinn did not choose his injustices. No matter where they came from, he was in opposition. In a poignant tribute of "thank yous" to his regular columnist, Matthew Rothschild, editor of the *Progressive* magazine, wrote, "Thank you, Howard Zinn, for being a Jew who dared to criticize Israel's oppression of the Palestinians, early on."

MIT Professor Noam Chomsky, a long-time friend of Zinn, commented on his "amazing contribution to American intellectual and moral culture," noting his "powerful role in helping . . . the civil rights movement and the antiwar movement."

His two friends from Hollywood, Matt Damon and Ben Affleck, took Zinn's history of the downtrodden, the workers, farmers, women, slaves, and other minorities, into popular culture, culminating in a television version of the book, *The People Speak*.

Perhaps, *Boston Globe* columnist James Carroll touched most personally on Zinn's magnetic persona to so many people. "He had a genius," Carroll wrote, "for the practical meaning of love. That is what drew legions of the young to him and what made the wide circle of his friends so constantly amazed and grateful."

Zinn explained himself in his autobiography *You Can't Be Neutral on a Moving Train*. His two greatest disappointments in the past two years were the loss of his wife Roslyn and the performance of Barack Obama. In his last article on the Obama White House, he wrote, "I've been searching hard for a highlight."

Roslyn and Howard Zinn left two children, Myla and Jeff, and five grandchildren. Together with his publisher, Dan Simon of Seven Stories Press; his editor, Matthew Rothschild; his interviewer, Amy Goodman; his associate, Anthony Arnove; and his innumerable writers and fighters for justice, for the principle that the truth is revolutionary, why not a well-funded and staffed Institute, organizing from the neighborhoods on up, as he urged so often, with horizons for all seasons, as befits his vision?

Although the desire to remember is now intense, it is the willpower that implements the thought.

Jean Monnet, the great postwar French civic leader, put the legacy course on track when he asserted that "without people, nothing is possible, but without institutions, nothing is enduring."

For more information, visit zinnedproject.org, peopleshistory.us, the peoplespeak.com, or howardzinn.org.

A Novel Idea

September 22, 2009

At a little noticed meeting with Senate Democrats, Warren Buffett, the famous investors'

guru, told the lawmakers that rich people are not paying enough taxes.

A tax increase for the very wealthy? Many of the Senators backed away from that recommendation, even though it came from the world's second richest man.

That is just one reason why Mr. Buffett plays a central role in my first work of fiction, *Only the Super-Rich Can Save Us!* The title is derived from an exchange between Buffett and a woman from New Orleans. Buffett is leading a convoy of critical supplies right after Katrina to help the fleeing poor stranded on the highways without food, water, medicine, and shelter. At one stop, Buffett was distributing supplies when a grandmother clasped his hands, looked right into his eyes and cried out, "Only the super-rich can save us!"

Her words jolted Buffett to his core. Arriving back at his modest home in Omaha, he knew what he had to do.

The next scene is early January 2006. Buffett and sixteen enlightened super-rich elders gather at a mountaintop hotel in Maui, and devise an elaborate strategy to take on the corporate goliaths and their Washington allies, and to redirect the country toward long overdue changes.

What follows is a top-down, bottom-up mobilization of Americans from all backgrounds in a head-on power struggle to break the grip of the corporate titans on our government.

With four out of five Americans believing that the US is in decline, imagining the super-rich powerful engine revving up an organized citizenry is a precondition to revitalizing democracy.

Tom Peters, the best selling author of *In Search of Excellence* summed up my book's objective by calling it a work of fiction that he would love to see become nonfiction.

Step by step, week by week, Buffett's super-rich, who call themselves "the Meliorists" build their campaigns—first privately and then openly launching their initiatives during the 4th of July weekend with media, fanfare, and parades.

Turning real, well-known people into fictional roles does not mean that their past achievements and beliefs are overlooked. To the contrary, I extend their achievements and beliefs to a much more intense level of what I believe they wish to see our country become.

Over the years, I have spoken to many superrich and found many of them discouraged and saddened about our nation's inability to solve major problems—a society paralyzed because the few have too much political and economic power over the many.

Buffett, in my "political science fiction," to use my colleague Matt Zawisky's phrase, selected people like George Soros, Ted Turner, Ross Perot, Sol Price, Yoko Ono, William Gates Sr., Barry Diller, Bill Cosby, Joe Jamail, Bernard Rapoport, Leonard Riggio, Phil Donahue, and others because each brought unique experience, determination, money, and rolodexes to that secluded Maui hotel where they met every month.

The "Meliorists" address the enormous mismatch of resources between citizen groups and the corporate supremacists. This time the entrenched CEOs are challenged by the retired or elderly billionaires and megamillionaires who know the ways and means of business and political power, and can throw the resources, smarts, and grassroot organizing talent against the corporate behemoths, who are not reluctant to counterattack.

In 1888, a Bostonian by the name of Edward Bellamy published a tremendous bestseller about a utopian US in the year 2000 called *Looking Backward*. The book inspired the then-growing progressive movement.

Obviously, Bellamy's utopian dream was not actualized. In my book, I show not a utopian society but a primer for how the super-rich, as a catalyst, could provide the means for millions of Americans to upgrade their quality of life and their livelihoods while confidently building civic and political institutions to hold and extend their gains.

I mean this book to interest anyone searching for ways to make fundamental, sustainable change. With this book you could see how your favorite big issue could be handled strategically and tactically. If you just want to escape your despair over our national gridlock and peer into the possible, into what could happen now if enough people and the few progressive super-rich come together, this book is for you, too.

Every week, leading reformers in our country produce documentations, diagnoses, denunciations of injustice, and proposals to address it. Little happens. Too many mismatches. We need major catalysts. But first, we need imaginations rooted in fulfilling available potentials—transformations for us and for posterity.

By the way, my fictional "Meliorists" have a task force on posterity as well. For more, see OnlyTheSuperRich.Org. Take it from there.

Words Matter
September 4, 2009

Ever wonder what's happening to words once they fall into the hands of corporate and government propagandists? Too often reporters and editors don't wonder enough. They ditto the words even when the result is deception or doubletalk.

Here are some examples. Day in and day out we read about "detainees" imprisoned for months or years by the federal government in the US, Guantanamo Bay, Iraq, and Afghanistan. Doesn't the media know that the correct word is "prisoners," regardless of what Bush, Cheney, and Rumsfeld disseminated?

The raging debate and controversy over health insurance and the $2.5 trillion spent this year on healthcare involves consumers and "providers." How touching to describe sellers or vendors, often gouging, denying benefits, manipulating fine print contracts, cheating Medicare and Medicaid in the tens of billions as "providers."

I always thought "providers" were persons taking care of their families or engaging in charitable service. Somehow, the dictionary definition does not fit the frequently avaricious profiles of Aetna, United Healthcare, Pfizer, and Merck.

"Privatization" and the "private sector" are widespread euphemisms that the press falls for daily. Moving government owned assets or functions into corporate hands, as with Blackwater, Halliburton, and the conglomerates now controlling public highways, prisons, and drinking water systems is "corporatization," not the soft imagery of going "private" or into the "private sector." It is the corporate sector!

"Medical malpractice reform" is another misnomer. This phrase is used to mean restricting the legal rights of wrongfully injured people by hospitals and doctors, or limiting the liability of these corporate vendors when their negligence harms innocent patients. Well, to anybody interested in straight talk, "medical malpractice reform" or the "medical malpractice crisis" should apply to bad or negligent practices by medical professionals. After all, about 100,000 people die every year from physician/hospital malpractice, according to a Harvard School of Public Health report. Hundreds of thousands are rendered sick or injured, not to mention even larger tolls from hospital-induced infections. Proposed "reforms" are sticking it to the wrong people—the patients—not the sellers.

"Free trade" is a widely used euphemism. It is corporate managed trade as evidenced in hundreds of pages of rules favoring corporations in NAFTA and the World Trade Organization. "Free trade" lowers barriers between countries so that cartels, unjustified patent monopolies, counterfeiting, contraband, and other harmful practices and products can move around the world unhindered by needed consumer, worker, and environmental standards.

What is remarkable about the constant use of these words is that they permeate the language even by those who stand against the policies of those who first coin these euphemisms. You'll read about "detainees" and "providers" and "privatization" and "private sector" and "free trade" in the pages of the *Nation* and *Progressive* magazines, at progressive conferences with progressive leaders, and during media interviews. After people point out these boomeranging words to them, still nothing changes. Their habit is chronic.

A lot of who we are, of what we do and think is expressed through the language we choose. The word tends to become the thing in our mind as Stuart Chase pointed out seventy years ago in his classic work *The Tyranny of Words*. Let us stop disrespecting the dictionary! Let's stop succumbing to the propagandists and the public relations tricksters!

Frank Luntz—the word wizard for the Republicans who invented the term "death tax" to replace "estate tax"—is so contemptuous of the Democratic Party's verbal ineptitude (such as using "public option" instead of "public choice" and regularly using the above-noted misnomers) that he dares them by offering free advice to the Democrats. He suggests they could counteract his "death tax" with their own term "the billionaires' tax." There were no Democratic takers.

Using words that are accurate and at face value is one of the characteristics of a good book. Three new books stand out for their straight talk. In *Grand Illusion: The Myth of Voter Choice in a Two-party Tyranny*, Theresa Amato, my former campaign manager, documents the obstructions that deny voter choice by the two major parties for third party and independent candidates. Just out is *Empire of Illusion: The End of Literacy and the Triumph of Spectacle* by Pulitzer Prize winner, Chris Hedges. Lastly, the boisterous, mischievous short autobiography of that free spirit, Jerry Lee Wilson, *The Soloflex Story: An American Parable*.

Notwithstanding their different styles, these authors exercise semantic discipline. Remember, words matter.

Working With His Hands
June 10, 2009

Although his classic self-designed and hand-built furniture found its way to the White House, the Metropolitan Museum of Art and the Smithsonian, Sam Maloof, who passed away recently at ninety-three, preferred to describe himself simply as a "woodworker."

Completely self-taught, after he served in the Army during World War II, Mr. Maloof became one of the premier woodworkers and designers in the country. His bustling home, workplace and Discovery Garden spread over six acres in Alta Loma, California, draws visiting artisans, high school woodworking classes

and gardeners learning about multiple uses from near and far.

Born in a family of nine children of Lebanese immigrants, Sam Maloof had the character traits of authenticity, elegance, consistency and creativity. He was dedicated to constantly refining his chairs, tables, desks, cabinets and his famous rocking chair. For about twenty years, he made no profit. Now his chairs sell for $20,000 or more each.

As he progressed, his horizons extended into what is now a veritable movement ensconced in the Sam and Alfreda Maloof Foundation for Arts and Crafts. (www.malooffoundation.org).

A measure of the man's spirit is reflected in these words about his work:

Craftsmen in any media know the satisfaction that comes in designing and making an object from raw material. Mine comes from working in wood. Once you have breathed, smelled, and tasted the tanginess of wood and have handled it in the process of giving it form, there is nothing, I believe, that can replace the complete satisfaction granted. Working a rough piece of wood into a complete, useful object is the welding together of man and material.

The exquisite manual workmanship of Mr. Maloof is further stimulating the questioning of the remoteness that modern technology visits on so many people who spend hours in virtual reality, separated from nature and its materials. Our country was built by craftsmen, artisans and other workers who designed and made real things. High schools offered shop class, where students learned skills and the joy of creating. These classes opened doors to a source of livelihood—and pride—for budding artisans.

With the nineteenth century industrial revolution and mass production employing masses of workers, these independent craftsmen tried to remain independent contractors and not become what they called "wage slaves" in giant, often dangerous, factories.

Jeremy Adamson, who organized an exhibition of Mr. Maloof's work in 2001 at the Renwick Gallery of the Smithsonian American Art Museum, remarked that Maloof was a "beacon for woodworkers around the world. That furniture will last forever." The Master used no nails or metal hardware. The designs evolved as he worked. Clearly he possessed stunning visualization capacities. Imagine, he fit the chairs to the human bodies. "You can't help but stroke the darn things," Mr. Adamson added.

Starting in 1952 with a small house in a citrus grove at the foot of the San Gabriel Mountains, Mr. Maloof added sixteen additional rooms branded with his unique use of woods, shapes and function.

In a new book titled *Shop Class as Soulcraft* by Matthew B. Crawford, the author bemoaned the closing at high schools all over the United States of shop classes that taught the mechanical arts like carpentry, woodworking, welding, and other skills. They were closed to allow more funding of computer labs. And also because our throw-away society no longer properly values the fruits of artisan labor.

Crawford goes on to argue and demonstrate what our society loses when we make joining the "paper economy" the chief aspiration of the younger generations or to use Robert Reich's phrase to become "symbolic analysts." Somebody has to keep the real world running maintained, repaired, and replaced—something we realize very quickly when things don't work in our households.

The draining of gratification from work in a techno-computerized environment is a wide-spread condition for millions of people, apart from the automated severance of their judgment and discretion by command and control positions.

Sam Maloof and his wife Beverly prepared his legacy meticulously. His philosophy and nature-related work increasingly steeped in sustainable practices will continue through his many students, trained practitioners and emulators.

He always found a way to wrap his zest in a few personal words. "I hope," he once said, "that my happiness with what I do is reflected in my furniture . . . that it is vibrant, alive, and friendly to the people who use it."

Sam Maloof steadfastly looked ahead. Maybe this is why, in spite of clients waiting years for delivery, he would jump to the head of the line those parents who wanted a cradle for their infants.

An Oscar for Activism

February 26, 2009

As the 2009 Academy Awards swept their way into history, the glitz and the massive global audiences show that across cultures fictional stories, mythologies and money go hand in hand.

As the nominees for the awards were briefly showcased for their artistic imagination in one category after another, it occurred to me that the saying "truth is stranger than fiction" has another meaning. Many people would rather see fiction than the real thing.

What if, permit a flight of fancy, there were the equivalent of the Academy Awards for the civic heroism that goes on every day here and abroad. The powerless valiant ones who challenge the powerful and corrupt in ways that throughout history have broken new ground for more justice, economic well-being, health, safety, and freedom. They are mostly unsung. They are often marginalized or maligned.

The history books make reference to only a very few—anti-slavery abolitionists, women fighting for the vote, workers for the right to organize, farmers for federal regulation of brazen banks and railroads. People take on, for example, corrupt city machines, company towns dominated by a single plant or mine, toxic contamination of drinking water supplies, corporate looters of worker pensions, manufacturers of defective cars and harmful medicines.

Recognition before large audiences keeps a highly nourished concept of the heroic before the people. It gives support to those who take the first step and who speak truth to power. Acclaim is protective and encourages more people to follow in the shoes of these citizen-pioneers. Civic heroism changes the culture and the dreams of youth.

Movies are meant to be dramatic and can take liberties with reality even when they are describing real-life situations and people. But Hollywood can make almost any story dramatic and interesting. Look at *Frost/Nixon*. On the other hand, there have been great flops with pure violent action—consider *Ishtar*.

Anything that is important to people in the course of their daily life can be made interesting. Real life narratives of people taking on power and cruelty can be compelling, without losing authenticity.

How would the Civic Heroism Awards be organized? The process would start at the community level with nominations and take it up to the state, national, and international level. Unlike game shows and beauty contests, the nominees would not be allowed to promote themselves. What they have already done is why they have been nominated. There is no present or future enhancement at ever higher levels of awards for what they had accomplished and striven for in the past.

Consider for a moment the peoples' infrastructure that such a multi-tiered annual award process would stimulate. Local video producers would see an opportunity to profile potential nominees over the internet, cable, and local screenings. The digital era assures the widespread egalitarian prevalence of such productions. Thousands of communities would be involved.

Discussions, debates, and banter would be stimulated over the criteria for nominations which would include awards for "the supporting cast" around the heroes as is done by the Academy Awards.

The teaching of civics in the local schools would become more attached to local activities beyond textbook study. Putting a human face on civic action will stir the minds of youngsters presently saturated with often degrading electronic "virtual realities."

The positive repercussions are many. Just the chance to become civic celebrities through this process of recognition increases media exposure and greater attention to the serious conditions and reforms that the nomination processes highlight.

The formulaic local television evening news—with its nine minutes of ads, four minutes of sports, four minutes of weather, chitchat, animal stories and miscellaneous fluff leaves very little time for civic news to attract the dwindling number of television reporters. Daily civic efforts to improve community life and justice wither on the vine for lack of any media coverage.

Civic heroism awards—done in a professional and exciting manner—can compel news coverage. Even in print form, columnists like Nicholas Kristof of the *New York Times* roams the continents of Asia, Africa, and South America to find the most courageous and besieged people standing up at great risk for human dignity and humane treatment.

The drama is in the people. The search is for the civic dramatists to find their calling. Finally, philanthropy needs to come forward to jumpstart what could become the citizen equivalent of the Academy Awards from the local to the global for these stalwart pillars of just and democratic societies.

Readers: do you know any likely philanthropists? Have them contact Awards Project at PO Box 19367, Washington, DC 20036.

Independence Day

July 7, 2008

One day when I was about eight years old, my mother tossed one of her frequent "out of the blue" questions at me:

"Ralph, do you love your country?"

"Yes, mother," I said, wondering where she was going with this.

"Well, I hope when you grow up, you'll work hard to make it more lovable."

Thus, began my education in the patriotism of deeds, the patriotism of advancing justice. The country was in the middle of World War II and the spirit of patriotism was engulfed by the war effort, by the heroics of our armed forces against the fascists, and, for my parents, by my brother Shaf's impending enlistment into the Navy.

Still, having come as teenage immigrants from Lebanon, during the Ottoman Empire and French mandate periods, my mother and father were very sensitive to any monopolization of patriotic symbols—flags, anthems, the July 4th holiday—to induce public obedience. They were wary of how many politicians would use and misuse these symbols to stifle dissent, hide abuses and manipulate public opinion. They rejected both political and commercial manipulation of patriotic feelings for narrow, often harmful self-serving ends.

Of course, the factory town of Winsted, CT where we grew up had its July 4th parade with marching bands, flags, proud veterans and assorted ceremonies. Its mile long Main Street was perfectly suited for these festivities. Plenty of fireworks in plenty of youthful hands too. We all had a general good time.

During one such parade, it suddenly occurred to me that no one had ever marched holding up a large replica of the Declaration of Independence, which was the reason for the celebration that day. Other than being printed in its entirety by some newspapers, this bold Declaration whose eloquent assertion of human rights was heard around the world for many years, still is not front and center for historical recollection and contemporary contemplations.

My parents prized the freedoms they found in America, and they were alert to anyone who might try to diminish them. At his sprawling restaurant on Main Street opposite the textile factories, my father would always speak his mind. He was a constant critic of power—big business, government, local, and national—and readily offered solutions.

His longtime customers and friends would sometimes say to him, "How do you expect to make a profit if you keep speaking out this way?" He would smile and say, "When I passed the Statue of Liberty, I took it seriously." He cautioned them with this advice: "If you don't use your rights, you will lose your rights."

At the same time, he would challenge attempts to monopolize and debase our country's symbols of flag, pledge and anthem into an unthinking patriotism by politicians to cover their sins. As Dad often reminded anyone who would listen, our flag stands for the principles embodied in the last words of the Pledge of Allegiance—"with liberty and justice for all."

There has always been military patriotism. There is more and more commercialization of the Fourth of July. In our hometown, we were raised to respect and nurture a civic patriotism.

As my brother Shaf said many years later, "A true love for the community of human beings that is our country is expressed when each one of us helps define that patriotism by our deeds and thoughts working together." And, he set a wonderful example when in 1965 he founded the Northwestern Connecticut Community College in town.

Maybe we should start reserving time on the Fourth for assessing the ways forward toward expending those "inalienable rights—life, liberty and the pursuit of happiness."

"To know and not to do is not to know."

May 19, 2008

Mountain View, California—An invitation to visit Google's headquarters and meet some of the people who made this ten-year-old giant that is giving Microsoft the nervies has to start with wonder.

The "campus" keeps spreading with the growth of Google into more and more fields, even though advertising revenue still comprises over 90 percent of its total revenues. The company wants to "change the world," make all information digital and accessible through Google. Its company motto is "Do No Evil," which comes under increasing scrutiny, especially in the firm's business with the national security state in Washington, DC and with the censors of Red China.

Google's two founders out of Stanford graduate school—Sergey Brin and Larry Page—place the highest premium on hiring smart, motivated people who provide their own edge and work their own hours.

We were given "the tour" before entering a large space to be asked and answer questions before an audience of wunderkinds. E-mail traffic was monitored worldwide via a variety of electronic globes with various lights marking which countries were experiencing high or low traffic. Africa was the least lit. One of our photographers started to take a picture but was politely waved away with a few proprietary words. A new breed of trade secrets.

I noticed all the places where food—free and nutritious—was available. The guide said that food is no further than 150 feet from any workplace. "How can they keep their weight down with all these tempting repasts?" I asked. "Wait," he said, leading us toward a large room where an almost eerie silence surrounded dozens of exercising Googlelites going through their solitary motions at 3:45 in the afternoon.

"How many hours do they work?" one of my colleagues asked. "We don't really know. As long as they want to," came the response.

In the amphitheatre, the director of communications and I started a Q & A, followed by more questions from the audience. It was followed by a YouTube interview. You can see both of them on: (Q&A) http://youtube.com/watch?v=KR-

V6bl41zU and (Interview) http://youtube.com/watch?v=zzUrUNhIj4c&feature=related.

Google is a gigantic information means, bedecked with ever complex software, to what end? Information ideally leads to knowledge, then to judgment, then to wisdom and then to some action. As the ancient Chinese proverb succinctly put it, "To know and not to do is not to know."

But what happens when a company is riding an ever-rising crest of digitized information avalanches without being able to catch its breath and ask "information for what?" I commented that we have had more information available in the last twenty-five years, though our country and world seem to be getting worse overall; measured by most indicators of the human condition. With information being the "currency of democracy," conditions instead should be improving across the board.

"Knowledge for what?" I asked. Well, for starters, Google is trying to figure out how to put on its own presidential debates, starting with one in New Orleans in the autumn. Certainly it can deliver an internet audience of considerable size. But will the major candidates balk if there are other candidates meeting polling criteria such as a majority of Americans wanting them to participate?

The present Commission on Presidential Debates is a private nonprofit corporation created and controlled by the Republican and Democratic Parties (see opendebates.org). They do not want other seats on the stage and the television networks follow along with this exclusionary format.

Google, with its own foundation looking for creative applications that produce results for the well-being of people, should hold regular public hearings on the ground around the country for ideas. They may be surprised by what people propose.

In any event, the examples of knowing but not doing are everywhere. More people succumbed to tuberculosis in the world last year than ten years ago. Medical scientists learned how to treat TB nearly fifty years ago. Knowledge alone is not enough.

For years the technology to present the up-to-date voting record of each member of Congress has been available. Yet only about a dozen legislators do so, led by Reps. Frank Wolf (R-Va.) and Chris Shays (R-Conn.). Recalcitrant power blocks what people most want directly from their lawmakers' website. Here Google can make the difference with Capitol Hill, if it wants to connect information technology to informed voters.

When the internet began, some of us thought that it would make it easy and cheap for people to band together for bargaining and lobbying as consumers. At last, the big banks, insurance companies, credit card companies, automobile firms, and so forth would have organized countervailing consumer power with millions of members and ample full time staffs. It has not happened.

Clearly technology and information by themselves do not produce beneficial change. That depends on how decentralized political, economic and social power is exercised in a corporate society where the few decide for the many.

I left Google hoping for a more extensive follow-up conversation, grounded in Marcus Cicero's assertion, over 2000 years ago, that "Freedom is participation in power." That is what connects knowledge to beneficial action, if people have that freedom.

I hope my discussions with the Google staff produced some food for thought that percolates up the organization to Google's leaders.

Country of Laws

March 14, 2008

The Governor of New York, Eliot Spitzer, has resigned for being a longtime customer of a high-priced prostitution ring.

The president of the United States, George W. Bush, remains, disgracing his office for long-time repeated violations of the Constitution, federal laws and several international treaties to which the US is a solemn signatory.

In his forthright resignation statement, Eliot Spitzer—the prominent corporate crime buster—asserted that, "Over the course of my public life, I have insisted, I believe correctly, that people, regardless of their position or power, take responsibility for their conduct. I can and will ask no less of myself."

In a recent speech to a partisan Republican fund-raising audience, George W. Bush fictionalized his Iraq War exploits and other related actions, and said that next January he will leave office "with his head held high."

Eliot Spitzer violated certain laws regarding prostitution and transferring of money through banks—though the latter was disputed by some legal experts—and for such moral turpitude emotionally harmed himself, his family and his friends.

George W. Bush violated federal laws against torture, against spying on Americans without judicial approval, against due process of law and habeas corpus in arresting Americans without charges, imprisoning them and limited their access to attorneys. He committed a massive war of aggression, under false pretenses, violating again and again treaties such as the Geneva Conventions, the UN Charter, federal statutes and the Constitution.

This war and its associated actions have cost the lives of one million Iraqis, over 4000 Americans, caused hundreds of thousands of serious injuries and diseases related to the destruction of Iraq's public health and safety facilities. As the popular button puts it, "He Lied, They Died."

From the moment the news emerged about Spitzer's sexual frolics the calls came for his immediate resignation. They came from the pundits and editorialists, they came from Republicans, and they started coming from his fellow Democrats in the Assembly.

Speaker Sheldon Silver told Spitzer that many Democrats in the Assembly would abandon him in any impeachment vote.

George W. Bush is a recidivist war criminal and chronic violator of so many laws that the Center for Constitutional Rights has clustered them into five major impeachable "High Crimes and Misdemeanors" (under Article II, section 4).

Scores of leaders of the bar, including Michael Greco, former president of the American Bar Association, and legal scholars and former Congressional lawmakers have decried his laceration of the rule of law and his frequent declarations that signify that he believes he is above the law.

Many retired high military officers, diplomats and security officials have openly opposed his costly militaristic disasters.

Only Rep. Dennis Kucinich (D-Ohio) has publicly called for his impeachment.

No other member of Congress has moved toward his impeachment. To the contrary, Speaker Nancy Pelosi (D-Calif.), Rep. Steny Hoyer (D-Md.) and House Judiciary Committee Chairman, John Conyers (D-Mich.) publicly took "impeachment off the table" in 2006.

When Senator Russ Feingold (D-Wisc.) introduced a Resolution to merely *censure* George W. Bush for his clear, repeated violations of the

Foreign Intelligence Surveillance Act—a felony—his fellow Democrats looked the other way and ignored him.

Eliot Spitzer came under the rule of law and paid the price with his governorship and perhaps may face criminal charges.

George W. Bush is effectively immune from federal criminal and civil laws because no American has standing to sue him and the Attorney General, who does, is his handpicked cabinet member.

Moreover, the courts have consistently refused to take cases involving the conduct of foreign and military policy by the president and the vice president regardless of the seriousness of the violation. The courts pronounce such disputes as "political" and say they have to be worked out by the Congress—i.e., mainly the impeachment authority.

Meanwhile, the American people have no authority to challenge these governmental crimes, which are committed in their name, and are rendered defenseless except for elections, which the two party duopoly has rigged, commercialized, and trivialized. Even in this electoral arena, a collective vote of ouster of the incumbents does not bring public officials to justice, just to another position usually in the high paying corporate world.

So, on January 21, 2009, George W. Bush and Dick Cheney will be fugitives from justice without any sheriffs, prosecutors or courts willing to uphold the rule of law.

What are the lessons from the differential treatment of a public official who consorts with prostitutes, without affecting his public policies, and a president who behaves like King George III did in 1776 and commits the exact kinds of multiple violations that Thomas Jefferson, James Madison, and other founders of our Republic envisioned for invoking the impeachment provision of their carefully crafted checks and balances in the Constitution?

Well, let's see.

First, Bush and Cheney are advised not to travel to Brattleboro or Marlboro, Vermont, two New England towns whose voters, in their frustrated outrage, passed non-binding articles instructing town officials to arrest them inside their jurisdictions.

Second, George W. Bush better not go to some men's room at an airport and tap the shoe of the fellow in the next stall. While one lame-duck senator barely survived that charge, for the president it would mean a massive public demand for his resignation.

We certainly can do better as a country of laws, not men.

In Memory of Anita Roddick
September 14, 2007

"This obsession for maximizing profits to shareholders has got to be seen as abusive, as dangerous, and as one of the most appalling situations on this planet. Because it makes for criminal behavior.

"You've got to have solid penalties. Corporate pollution has got to be seen as a criminal act.

"I have a deep sense that to accumulate wealth is obscene. And when the community gives you your wealth, I have a strong belief that you give it back."

The above thoughts were not uttered by some hearty environmental agitator or radical dreamer egged on by a talk show host. They came from the generous, boisterous, daring, humane mind of Anita Roddick—the founder of the global cosmetic company—The Body Shop—with over 2,000 stores.

The world lost Anita Roddick this week from hepatitis C, which she acquired thirty-six years ago while giving birth to her youngest daughter. She was only sixty-four years old.

Anita Lucia Perella, the daughter of immigrants from Italy to England, was raising a family and looking for ways to pay her bills. At age thirty-three, she obtained an $8,000 bank loan and started a little store with her own formula for skin care. The little bottles containing her creations started increasing in number and pretty soon she opened a second store. And a third and fourth store.

From the beginning, she emphasized what today would be called natural ingredients, recycling and sustainability. Her stores were works of art. People felt very comfortable and serene shopping there. She traveled far and wide securing "organic" ingredients to diversify her product.

Anita Roddick was a glorious combination of character and personality who had her priorities high and wide enough to ask the most fundamental questions of big business and answer them by her deeds and her words.

At dozens of conferences on business and the environment, business and globalization, the oil business and developing countries, and gatherings of entrepreneurial companies such as The Body Shop, including Ben and Jerry's, Patagonia and Esprit, Ms. Roddick pushed and pressed, challenged and cajoled to put people and their environment first.

She was a veritable human dynamo, upbeat, funny, inspirational without sonorous oratory. She wrote books such as *Business as Usual* and *Body and Soul* about her business practices and philosophy that astonished readers and angered many of the pompous bosses of big business.

She was hands-on, literally, journeying to Romania after the fall of the communist regime to help the helpless little, institutionalized orphans who were not being cared for in those chaotic times. Or landing in the Amazon, where she insisted with indigenous peoples that they should share in the benefits of the raw materials she purchased for evolving her product line.

Her products were not tested on animals. She searched for the least toxic ingredients. She encouraged workers in her store to take time off periodically to volunteer for community or environmental projects. In fact, it was a requirement for being a Body Shop franchise that workers were given this opportunity.

Her biggest regret in retrospect was agreeing, with her business partner-husband, Gordon, to take The Body Shop public, which soon caused them to lose control of their firm to investors.

Her charities were not just given at the point of immediate need. They were also directed toward strengthening civic institutions and civic education.

She donated $1.8 million to Amnesty International for a "school of activism" in London. She was a supporter of Charles Kernaghan and the National Labor Committee (www.nlcnet.org).

The range of this remarkably empathetic woman's engagements and causes will frame, year after year, the horizons of business leaders who decide, in Alfred North Whitehead's words to "think greatly of their functions."

The legacies of Anita Roddick and her many circles of justice will continue to keep giving and continue to proliferate by the moral authority of her example.

Her husband, Gordon, and her daughters Justine and Samantha, can nourish their memories with these assurances.

In Memory of David Halberstam

June 1, 2007

Anybody who played schoolboy sandlot baseball in Winsted, Connecticut with David Halberstam back in the 1940s would not have been very surprised to observe his spectacular journalistic career that took him to the civil rights struggles in the South, the war torn African and Asian continents, and the writing of some twenty books which required aggressive reporting.

Young David ran and played the bases with a ferocious enthusiasm. Even then I recall noticing that he loved to skewer any boy whose boasting was not up to his playing performance. Over half a century many powerful people learned about that trait of David's firsthand.

After graduating Harvard where he was managing editor of the *Crimson*, the student newspaper, David was a relentlessly truth telling star reporter for the *New York Times* in the Congo and Vietnam. So much so that President John F. Kennedy urged the *Times'* Publisher to reassign him from Vietnam where his reports on official cover-ups and lying regarding the state of the war there were infuriating the generals and their visiting politicians.

The publisher said no way and David won the Pulitzer Prize for his intrepid and accurate reporting in Vietnam.

As impressive as the span covered by his articles and best-selling books were—two volumes on the Vietnam War, books on civil rights, the auto industry, the mass media, sports, and a forthcoming book on the lessons of the Korean War, it was his legwork and moral and physical courage that marked him, in ABC TV's Jim Wooten's words, "as the best reporter in the past 50 years."

Fellow reporter Gay Talese said "there wasn't a lazy bone in his body." Decade after decade, Halberstam was writing from primary sources—his deep interviews, his acute observations, his determination to always go where the action was occurring.

To seek the facts, the truth of murky, tense situations, he took on the Army, the White House, his newspaper, the *New York Times*, or anyone who displayed breaches of trust, secrecy or cover-ups denying the public's right to know.

Jim Wooten put it this way: "There was no one in power that David either respected so much that he would give them a pass, or loathed so much that he would not be fair."

Very few journalists were willing to report truth to power. He broke ground for his profession which had more than its share of lazy, smug, embedded minds who got along by getting along with the influentials they were supposed to cover fearlessly.

Whenever Halberstam spoke at journalism schools the students were spellbound by what he said and what he did in his years on the road.

Jon Meacham wrote in *Newsweek* that through the decades, Halberstam "was always present at the creation, reporting, watching, thinking and writing about the unfolding drama. . . . Halberstam insisted on reporting what he saw happening, not what the government said was happening. The difference was essential, even epochal, and Halberstam achieved something few journalists do. He changed history, for he helped change how America saw not only the war in Vietnam but the ways of Washington."

America needed Halberstam's talents on the Iraq War-quagmire. He called the invasion a massive slam against a giant beehive. I scarcely recall seeing him speak, even on fast-paced television programs, without providing some historical context for his comments.

"Why do things happen? Why do they not happen? What are the forces at play?" Halberstam once asked as his way of explaining why he left daily journalism and wrote historical books packed with fresh "anecdotes and stories and insights."

On Monday, April 23, 2007, this great man, this analytic humanitarian, was in the front passenger seat, belted, of a ten-year-old Toyota driven by a journalism student at the University of California-Berkeley. The intersection was known not to be a safe one. The student took a left turn and another vehicle broadsided the Toyota on David's side, crushing the metal two feet into the passenger space.

The survivor of reporting fifty military missions in Vietnam and scores of other perils around the world lost his life on a highway in Menlo Park, California. Having spoken to the journalism students, he was on his way to another interview for a book he was writing. His legendary work ethic in action.

At 4 p.m. on June 12, 2007, there will be a memorial service at the historic Riverside Church on Riverside Drive in New York City, not far from where he lived with his wife Jean. Present will be his working colleagues, editors, and friends remarking about David's extraordinary, pioneering life.

There will be anecdotes and recollections of light moments. In today's times, memorial services usually veer from presentations which induce weeping. That would suit David fine.

But from this occasion, no doubt attended by many persons of renown, accomplishment, and some considerable wealth, David deserves a legacy that befits his high standards. But how, where, when?

Why not establish a Camp Halberstam, in his beloved Litchfield Hills of northwest Connecticut, devoted to training fifty students each summer who are seriously bent on a career in journalism. David's many friends, colleagues, and admirers could take turns volunteering their time and talent to teach and work with these youngsters in what he called "the craft that keeps learning."

The outdoor life would provide some rugged experience that came naturally to David's physical stamina which was so integral to his mental rigor and persistent travels.

I would like to hear from interested parties, including foundations and people of means, who would like to create this dynamic memorial to the prodigious and robust life of David Halberstam—our early amateur baseball buddy with the mean slide into second base.

Contact Adam Tapley, PO Box 19367, Washington, DC 20036 or info@csrl.org.

Perfecting Protest

May 18, 2007

The current issue of the *UTNE Reader* (May–June '07) carried a short but sensibly provocative article protesting the stagnation and the cul-de-sac nature of street protests that involve nonviolent civil disobedience.

Joseph Hart, the author, asks why the current antiwar movement is so impotent, despite "a staggering 67 percent disapproval of President Bush's handling of the war—a level that matches public sentiment at the tail end of the Vietnam War, when street protests, rallies, and student strikes were daily occurrences."

He believes it is because, quoting Jack DuVall, president of the International Center on

Nonviolent Conflict, "a street demonstration is only one form of protest and protest is only one tactic that can be used in a campaign. If it's not a part of a dedicated strategy to change policy, or to change power, protest is only a form of political exhibitionism."

Both gentlemen are being incomplete. Even without a military draft in place to arouse a larger public, the protestors against the Iraq War have affected the 2006 elections, performed sit-ins in congressional offices, filed lawsuits against Bush's violations of people's civil liberties, brought Iraqi spokespeople to meet with influential Americans, worked with Iraq veterans against the war as well as with numerous former high ranking military, diplomatic and intelligence officials now retired from service in both Republican and Democratic Administrations who openly opposed the invasion at the outset.

Clearly all this has not been enough to move the Democrats to decisive action.

The obstinate, messianic militarist in the White House remains unmoved. With his ignorance of history itself becoming historic, this latter day obsessively compulsed, King George thinks he's a 21st century Winston Churchill.

Through the wide arc of his persistent lawlessness, Mr. Bush has done the country much damage here and abroad. But he has also demonstrated how variously the rule of law can be swept aside with impunity. He is both outside and above the Constitution, federal statutes, international treaties to which the US is solemn signatory, and the restraints of Congress and the federal courts.

A major restructuring of our laws to embrace the outlaw presidency under Mr. Bush, or any like-minded successors, now has a solid empirical basis from which to move forward. Presidential outlawry did not start with Mr. Bush. It has been building up for a long time going from the episodic to institutionalized forms.

For example, it is now routine for the courts to opt out of giving any citizen, group or member of Congress legal standing on matters of foreign and military policy even to plead their cases against the president. Here the courtroom door is closed.

For Mr. Bush, what would be repeated criminal negligence by anyone else, there has been immunity from lawsuits by families of soldiers—and there were hundreds of them—who died because they were not provided with body and Humvee armor over three years or more in Iraq. Immunity even from equitable lawsuits seeking a mandamus for obligated action ignored by the president.

The Bush officials had the funds with which to procure these shields but somehow the corporate Halliburtons got more of their urgent attention.

Clearly, the diverse opposition to Bush's war needs to move to higher levels. More meticulous lobbying in Congressional districts, more pressure to initiate impeachment hearings, more exposure to what the Iraqi people, suffering so terribly, want and need, much more organized focus by the retired, established military and civilian officials whose previous courage and experience give them great credibility today.

The number of active duty soldiers petitioning their member of Congress to end the war now exceeds twelve hundred. Since 72 percent of the soldiers in Iraq wanted the US out within six to twelve months in a Zogby poll released very early in 2006, there is more potential from this source of actual military theatre experience.

The timid, anti-war members of Congress require more than all this opposition. Apparently they are looking for intensity, for more people having the war on their minds, demanding that the huge monies for this overseas destruction be turned into providing necessities for their local communities.

These lawmakers seem to need to be buttonholed whenever they return to their districts. In Washington, they keep saying things like, "Yeah, I know the polls but Americans are more interested in American Idol and their iPods."

So, Americans, start the buttonhole movement—at their Congress members' town meetings, at the clambakes they attend this summer, at the local parades where they strut, over at their local office (see the yellow pages listing under US Government for the addresses and phone numbers) and through letters and telephone calls. You count when you make them count you.

Log onto www.democracyrising.us to keep current with what's going on during this most unpopular war in US history madly driven by arguably the most unpopular president in the last century. *Democracy Rising* director Kevin Zeese has many opportunities for you to get involved back home.

BYU Students Speak Out

April 30, 2007

Could anyone have imagined that the major commencement protest at a University graduation thus far occurred April 26 at Utah's Brigham Young University (BYU)? Probably not.

But then could anyone have imagined that the vice president with the lowest approval rating in modern American history would request and receive an invitation to be the commencement speaker? And no one could have imagined the organized moral courage of seniors like Ashley Sanders, Eric Bybee, Steven Greenstreet, Carl Brinton, and graduate student Joe Vogel.

BYU is owned and run by the Mormon Church. This year it graduated 5,378 students with bachelor's degrees, 717 students with master's degrees and 190 students with doctoral degrees. Ninety-nine percent of the graduates are members of the Church of Jesus Christ of Latter-day Saints (the Mormon Church).

Before wagon-travelling in the mid-1800s to the Great Salt Lake Valley, Mormons were terribly persecuted and brutalized from one escaping migration to another.

The Mormon Church was born from revelation, resistance, and dissent. Its mutual assistance commitment to poor or otherwise needy Mormons remains a marvel of organization and steadfastness. So does its expected regime of no alcohol, tobacco, or drugs—a religious health movement of much success.

The Church today is considered very conservative. Over 80 percent of voting Mormons cast their vote for Republicans. At BYU, obedience, conformity, and not questioning authority are part of the cultural tradition.

So just to read in the newspapers about "dissident BYU graduates" planning an alternative commencement in an alternative auditorium jarred the customary stereotypes.

Supported by some faculty members, alumni, citizens of the local community, and twenty students, in the middle of final exams, no less, they persuaded over 3,000 of their fellow students to sign a petition protesting Cheney and supporting a graduation ceremony with two alternatives.

The core student organizers are devout Mormons—a reality I determined from discussions before and after my giving one of the three alternative commencement addresses. Some had already completed their two-year Mormon "mission" in this country or abroad. They were a little older and more experienced than the usual graduating seniors.

They were not about to remain silent. They believed the standards of their faith and those of the university were being violated by the record of Dick Cheney. Included in their list of criticisms were "Mr. Cheney's involvement in the decision to invade Iraq, his defense of torture as a method of interrogation, his ties to Halliburton, Enron and the Energy Task Force, his extreme conservatism, and the conservative pattern of officials invited to speak at BYU."

The students also wished to "highlight the value of free speech, to give minority students a voice, and to highlight the need for alternatives, dissent, and diversity."

Also invited to speak were Jack Healey, former Amnesty International US Director, and Peter Ashdown, former Democratic US Senate candidate and civic leader.

Raising the money for the event, with help from readers of the *Daily Kos*, was not the most difficult challenge. That was reserved for locating a venue for the large attendance which they expected.

BYU officials promptly turned down their request for a hall. No alternative commencement on campus. The "BYU 25" then went to other educational institutions. A middle school said yes then reversed its decision. The Superintendent for Provo's public schools placed all the auditoriums off-limits.

Finally, several miles from campus, in Orem, Utah, the students secured the large arena at Utah Valley State College. Over 1,200 people showed up, including students and faculty in their caps and gowns. It was a thoughtful and spirited gathering. They knew this was a historic marker for the BYU community.

What most of them did not know was the mettle and wisdom of the student leaders, whose ten days of hectic endeavors, made this unprecedented event a reality. They soon knew why. First, Eric Bybee, who will join Teach for America as a teacher in Harlem this fall, stood up and recounted in detail the hurdles and active obstacles which they overcame. He took three exams in one day.

Then came student organizer, Ashley Sanders, a humanities major. She said, "BYU should have to defend its decision to invite Dick Cheney. Dick Cheney should speak, but we should also be able to respond. When people have to give reasons for their opposition and reasons for their support of something, then we're better people as a civic society."

Cheney did speak—briefly. He spent two thirds of his remarks praising BYU in a variety of ways from their "stone-cold sober" number one rating in the nation to their athletic teams. His comments were designed for applause. Then he offered some homilies about success in life. Then he was off to Air Force Two.

Over at Utah Valley State College, the BYU students were teaching their elders that a critical, humane mind is a difficult thing to silence.

After what they described as a very successful graduation that stressed alternatives, the student organizers held a party at an art gallery. They cooked a delicious and nutritious dinner for all. There was no alcohol imbibed, no tobacco smoked.

They had practiced their faith along with their academic learning and civic responsibilities.

No Thank You!

March 26, 2007

Was Connie Leas, the author *of The Art of Thank You: Crafting Notes of Gratitude* (Beyond Words Publishing, 2002) engaged in a thankless task? For the most part, probably. For conveying "thank yous" these days seems to be a vanishing art.

This impression is nourished with everyday experience by just about everybody who says they are overloaded, don't have time, and spend too much time reading their inboxes. I'm not referring to an occasional oversight, missing sending a thank you by a card, an email or, maybe an entire letter. No, not giving a thank you a second thought has become a chronic cultural abandonment—no matter some touching exceptions to the contrary.

Here are some examples from my experience:

1. My associate sent, via the courtesy of Rep. Chris Shays, Elliot Richardson's book *Reflections of a Radical Moderate* to over thirty-five liberal Republicans in the Congress. Not one note of thanks came back.

2. Two hardback books—one on hunger in America and the other on the wealthy were sent to about thirty salespersons and staff of a friendly lecture bureau. Not one note of thanks. We wondered whether they were delivered. A telephone call confirmed that they did arrive.

3. A book pertinent to civil justice victories was sent to about seventy attorneys for whom the subject was of special interest. Only three of them sent a thank you letter.

4. Two book gifts were sent to twenty outstanding teachers in the Washington, DC area, in recognition of their excellence. We received four nice thank you letters.

5. More recently, like others known to the world of Boy Scouts, I receive regular requests from them, their parents or Scoutmasters to send the boys a letter of commendation on their attainment of Eagle Scout status. These letters are then read or noted at the Eagle Scout award ceremony. Having attended some of them, I am amused to note how blasé were the scouts as they took the news. They knew these were essentially form letters from notables—canned and bland.

So one day we decided to send a handsome facsimile (1 ½ ft. by 2 ft.) of the Declaration of Independence, in a sturdy tube, to twenty five of the requestors whose solicitation letters had just arrived.

We told them they could keep this gift for free if they wished, and hoped that the Scouts would put them on their bedroom walls, along with other more contemporary posters. The Declaration of Independence (1776) after all is the fundamental juridical pre-constitution document of our country.

It's been over eight weeks and still not a word of thanks from any of the Eagle Scouts or their entourage. Presumably the Declarations of Independence will retain their viability with or without the expected courtesies.

To some degree or another most people, including me, miss a thank you here and there. But these gifts were selected to be appropriate to their receivers in one manner or another.

My co-author, Wesley J. Smith, told me that when he was a child his grandparents and parents would say to him, "Now Wesley James, sit you down and write that thank you note." He observes that such civilities do not seem to be required from the young as much anymore.

By the way, thank you for reading this lamentation.

Molly Ivins Remembered

February 5, 2007

If writers, who lasso injustice and give light to justice, lift up our standards of fair play, then on January 31st, the nation suffered a genuine decline. For Molly Ivins lost her seven-year battle with cancer and joined what her friend Bill Moyers called "that great Purgatory of Journalists in the Sky."

Author and columnist syndicated in 400 newspapers, Austin, Texas-based Molly Ivins skewered pompous politicians, raked over corporate criminals and spotlighted the struggles of regular folks against the repressions and maraudings of the Big Boys and their Big Power.

It is a tribute to Molly that the various columns written in her praise each presented a different side of this remarkable Texas maverick and satirist.

New York Times columnist, Paul Krugman, who teaches economics at Princeton, wrote of "her extraordinary prescience on the central political issue of our time"—the invasion and occupation of Iraq. She warned about the risks some five months before Bush took the USA and its soldiers into this deepening quagmire and its boomerang impact. She warned about the dangers of "'the peace' which sure looks like a quagmire," in January, July, and October of 2003.

Krugman continues: "So Molly Ivins—who didn't mingle with the great and famous, didn't have sources high in the administration, and never claimed special expertise on national security or the Middle East—got almost everything right." Meanwhile, he wrote, the specialists got almost everything wrong. The difference? "Was Molly smarter than all the experts? No, she was just braver. The administration's exploitation of 9/11 created a toxic environment in which it took a lot of courage to see and say the obvious."

In an article on CommonDreams.org, people's historian Harvey Wasserman covers Molly as a "doer." It was as if she lived the Chinese proverb—"To know and not act is not to know."

Here is Wasserman: "She puts her heart and soul where her convictions are. She's fought tooth and nail for the *Texas Observer* and whatever other worthwhile publications there are that can muster an audience in the Lone Star State. She's worked with the great Jim Hightower in his climb to elected office. She supports candidates. She goes out of her way. She works hard. She makes her presence felt wherever she thinks it'll do some good, no matter what the personal cost."

John Nichols, who writes for the *Nation* and the Madison, Wisconsin *Capitol Times* had this to say: "The warmest-hearted populist ever to pick up a pen with the purpose of calling the rabble to the battlements, Ivins understood that change came only when some citizen in some off-the-map town passed a petition, called a congressman or cast an angry vote to throw the bums out."

Nichols reminded his readers that it was Molly Ivins who first alerted the country to presidential candidate, George W. Bush with her bestselling book—*Shrub: The Short but Happy Political Life of George W. Bush* (Random House, 2000) and went on a nationwide tour to punctuate her accurate, unauthorized history of the man.

A few months ago, she and Nichols launched a boomlet behind Bill Moyers for president. They received a flood of excited, supportive messages. Wouldn't that be a fine living memorial were Moyers to carry his knowledge, experience and humanity at least through the Democratic primary season?

A longer reach into the future would be to establish summer journalism internships, associated with her *Texas Observer*, for aspiring young journalists and journalism students.

The following words by Molly can inspire and guide the interns:

> So keep fightin' for freedom and justice, beloveds, but don't you forget to have fun doin' it. Lord, let your laughter ring forth. Be outrageous, ridicule the fraidy-cats, rejoice in all the oddities that freedom can produce. And when you get through kickin' ass and celebratin' the sheer joy of a good fight, be sure to tell those who come after you how much fun it was.

I sure hope that your progressive well-to-do friends will do you this honor, Molly, on behalf of the much larger numbers of people who would benefit from those great young journalists carrying your irrepressible spirit forward.

Breaking the BCS
December 22, 2006

As we settle-in to cheer on our favorite college football teams this bowl season, it's important to remember that an undisputed consolidation of power and money—the Bowl Championship Series (BCS)—controls which schools play in the major bowl games and National Championship game.

The BCS operates independently from, and without accountability to, the National Collegiate Athletic Association (NCAA). It is controlled by commissioners from the six major college football "power conferences" (also referred to as "BCS conferences") plus the Athletic Director of the independent Notre Dame. This arrangement is agreed to, reluctantly, by the commissioners of the remaining five "mid-major" conferences (also referred to as "non-BCS conferences" because they do not receive automatic bids to the BCS bowl games as do the others).

The BCS is responsible for concentrating the wealth that comes from the major post-season events (Fiesta, Orange, Rose, and Sugar bowls, and the National Championship game) among the schools in conferences with BCS influence, and leaving the other Division I-A, non-BCS schools at a competitive, financial, and recruiting disadvantage. It's like telling nearly half of your members that they are not welcome at the club and are not eligible for the benefits that membership provides.

According to Brent Schrotenboer of the *San Diego Union-Tribune*, "The six major conference commissioners have gained increasing power in the past ten years and have turned it into television deals worth more than $110 million per year. They broker their power by representing their member school presidents and negotiating with bowls and television networks on their behalf. This year, they will distribute the vast portion of $210 million in bowl payouts to their members."

The biggest area of controversy with the BCS system is unquestionably the disputed method for deciding a national champion. For starters, since the creation of the BCS in 1998, the convoluted mix of polls and computers to decide what schools should be appointed to play in the title game has succeeded only twice without controversy.

But no system could succeed that has to "decide" among schools with equal records and valid claims of inclusion when only two spots are available. And no system could succeed that leaves such a remote chance for a non-BCS school to compete for the championship, even with a perfect record.

Excluding deserving teams and student-athletes from the chance to compete also amounts to consumer fraud for the fans. Such matters should be resolved on the field like every other NCAA sport and every other football division, all of which have tournaments to determine a national champion.

The shrinking number of BCS defenders say the system preserves the tradition of the bowl games. But first, there's no reason why bowl games cannot thrive either outside or within a tournament structure. Secondly, what tradition is left? Traditional match-ups are gone, as is the traditional New Year's Day schedule, and the games have been commercialized to the point of destroying the bowl game experience and tradition for schools, student-athletes and fans.

Finally, bowl games are private businesses that should have no right, in partnership with the BCS, to prevent college football from a fair method of determining a national champion.

Those attempting to preserve the BCS, like the presidents of schools that make up the six BCS conferences and enjoy the BCS payouts, also say a playoff could mean less time for players to concentrate on classes and point to concerns that education would be sacrificed for money. But the BCS is influenced by persons and entities without respect to the interests of student-athletes or educational missions.

Where was the worry from presidents for student-athletes when they recently signed-off on an additional regular season game for every team, or when some conferences added a championship game, or when the presidents agree to allow more and more games every year on weekdays during the academic calendar, all to showcase their conferences and enjoy the television payouts? How do these developments give student-athletes more time for classes and exams?

Scale all these events back for the 119 Div. I-A schools, and add a national tournament for, say, the best sixteen teams (including a few of the very best from traditionally overlooked conferences), and there would be far fewer games played overall. This would leave increased study time for all but the top eight to sixteen teams, depending on whether they currently play a conference championship. (Somehow this issue does not come up during the NCAA Basketball Tournament.)

What has withstood change from outside pressure by excluded schools, alumni, fans, sportswriters, and even from a US House subcommittee, is now experiencing some unrest from within—at least regarding the method of deciding a national champion. Two presidents from schools in conferences with BCS influence, University of Florida president Bernard Machen and Florida State University president T. K. Wetherell, are pushing for a playoff tournament.

"A playoff is inevitable," Machen told Bloomberg News. "The public strongly favors a playoff, but university presidents are in denial about that. They just don't see it. Whatever the format, I believe we need to get ahead of it and create the system rather than responding to external pressures."

Whatever the changes or replacements to the failed BCS, the NCAA needs to take control of Div. I-A college football in the interest of all member institutions, their student-athletes, alumni, and fans. There should never be so much power in the hands of so few without accountability as the BCS demonstrates each year.

(For more information on this and other sports reform issues, visit www.leagueoffans.org).

Galbraith—A Public-Spirited Economist

August 18, 2006

I first came across the name of John Kenneth Galbraith during my student years at Princeton where I picked up his book *American Capitalism*. Wondering why it was not on any reading list for my economics course, I put the question to the professor. He replied, "It's really not about economics. It's about political economy."

Before the discipline of economics broke off from what students used to major in, that is "political economy," early in the 20th century, my professor's comment would not have been a put down. Today, many economists see economics as a branch of mathematics and tend to dismiss economists who bring into their study the variables of politics and power.

The passing at age ninety-seven of Harvard Professor emeritus Ken Galbraith was a loss to the political economy of the United States. His books, articles, letters, testimony and advice to presidents, members of Congress and the general public for over sixty years connected numbers to understanding what was really going on between the powers-that-be: the haves and the powerless, the have-nots. He proposed policies that were designed to lift the livelihoods of regular people and their essential public services.

What would a Galbraithian economy look like in the United States? For starters, major public investments—fueled by corporate tax reforms—in public works—public transit, repaired schools, clinics, upgraded drinking water systems, good parks and libraries, and environmental health projects. These forms of public wealth for everyone, he believed, would also advance the objective of a full-employment economy.

Galbraith believed that uncontrolled capitalism, especially the giant corporations, required prudent regulation to diminish the damage their out-of-control greed and power inflict on society. Always a realist, he was more than aware of the capture of regulatory agencies by the very companies that they were created to regulate.

He saw shame in the pretense that the large defense manufacturers are free market corporations. Since over 90 percent of their business comes from the Department of Defense, he urged that they should be taken over and treated as public corporations shorn of their profiteering, waste and unaccountable lobbying pressure for more and more weapon systems.

It was not for mere rhetorical flourish that he coined the phrase "the conventional wisdom." All his life he was challenging the "vested interest" in one's ideas. He described "economists" as being the "most economical about ideas. They make the ones they learned in graduate school last a lifetime."

Full of sharp wit, humor and irony, Galbraith was a joy to read and a pleasure to correspond with—he responded to letters of all kinds. A man of many causes, he spoke out very early against the Vietnam War, poverty, violations of civil liberties and almost anything that degraded our struggling democratic society. He was one of the founders of Americans for Democratic Action. What impressed me so much about this great political economist was his mostly unfailing good judgment and solid reasoning behind it.

He was quick to see a trend, sense a decay and reprimand both with his fundamental public philosophy. As far back as July 1970, he wrote an article in *Harper's* magazine titled "Who Needs Democrats? And What it Takes to be Needed."

He wrote, "The function of the Democratic

Party, in this century at least, has, in fact, been to embrace its solutions even when . . . it outraged not only Republicans but the Democratic establishment as well. And if the Democratic Party does not render this function, at whatever cost in reputable outrage . . . it has no purpose at all. The play will pass to those who do espouse solutions. . . . The system is not working. . . . The only answer lies in political action to get a system that does work. To this conclusion, if only because there is no alternative conclusion, people will be forced to come."

Ken Galbraith was accurate in observing the decline of the Democratic Party—more accurate than he no doubt wanted to be. What remains is his hope for "political action to get a system that does work."

Maybe Galbraith's thousands of friends, colleagues and admirers could help bring about his desired transformation by establishing the "John Kenneth Galbraith Institute for a Progressive Political Economy." Right wingers do this for their intellectual heroes—to wit the Ludwig von Mises Institute in Alabama. Can progressives do anything less for Canada's gift to America— a man who came from rural Ontario and lived the nexus between knowledge and action as if people mattered?

William Sloane Coffin

April 14, 2006

One of his Yale students, famed cartoonist Garry Trudeau, said of Yale University Chaplain, William Sloane Coffin, during those heady years in the sixties, "Without him, the very air would have lost its charge. With him, we were changed forever."

Who was this former Army Captain, ex-CIA agent, talented musician, linguist, and motorcycle rider? How did he become one of the most influential clergymen of his time by focusing public attention on the essential moral questions so often avoided in times of war, strife over civil rights, and the perilous nuclear arms race between the United States and the Soviet Union? Most clergy do not roam so far from their church.

When challenged to stick with his ministerial duties, this great speaker of sweeping vision and public virtue replied:

> Every minister is given two roles: the priestly and the prophetic. The prophetic role is the disturber of the peace, to bring the minister himself, the congregation and entire social order under some judgment. If one plays a prophetic role, it's going to mitigate against his priestly role. There are going to be those who will hate him.

And with that definition, the Rev. Coffin became the outspoken activist and doer of nonviolent civil disobedience directly from the principles of his Christian faith. He wrote, spoke, organized, marched, protested, was arrested, jailed, and prosecuted. He inspired the struggles against the Vietnam war, Jim Crow laws, the military draft, poverty here and abroad, and the planet-threatening atomic arms race. He did all this with an historical frame of reference, biblical wisdom, and humor which was almost always witty and informative.

There was an arresting moment right after World War II when infantry Captain Coffin was assigned to the French and then the Russian army to compel Soviet refugees, who had been taken prisoner, to return to the Soviet Union. He admits to using deception to lure them onto the trains heading for Russia, leading some to attempt suicide because they knew what awaited them there. Many simply disappeared.

In his memoir *Once to Every Man* (1977), Rev. Coffin said his behavior left him a "burden of guilt I am sure to carry the rest of my life." It led, he wrote, to his spending "three years in the CIA opposing Stalin's regime."

In 1978, he became the head minister at the large, interdenominational Riverside Church in New York City, where he advanced his often affluent congregation toward addressing problems of unemployment and juvenile offenders.

Last October, I arranged a telephone interview about the Iraq War with Rev. Coffin from his Strafford, Vermont home. Though seriously ill, he was typically upbeat. "How are you, Reverend?" "Better than I have any right to feel, the rest is commentary," he replied.

He made a number of cogent points in the interview, to wit:

What the rest of us have to remember is that dissent in a democracy is not unpatriotic, what is unpatriotic is subservience to a bad policy.

Local clergy must brave the accusation of meddling in politics, a charge first made no doubt by the Pharaoh against Moses. When war has a bloodstained face, none of us have the right to avert our gaze. . . .

And the search for peace is biblically mandated. If religious people don't search hard, and only say 'peace is desirable,' then secular authorities are free to decide 'War is necessary.' . . .

I think the absence of a draft has much to do with the present lack of student protest. On the other hand, I think the colossal blunders of the administration will quicken an antiwar movement faster now than during the Vietnam war. . . .

What we shouldn't do is to believe President Bush when he says that to honor those who have died, more Americans must died. That's using examples of his failures to promote still greater failures.

I asked him what he thinks should be done by the peace movement? He was direct, saying, "I am very much in favor of well thought out, nonviolent civil disobedience, of occupying congressional offices, telling lawmakers, 'You have to stop the slaughter, to admit mistakes and to right the wrong.'" (See the entire interview at http://www.DemocracyRising.US.)

Reverend William Sloane Coffin passed away in Strafford on April 12 at the age of eighty-one.

Five weeks earlier, another storied man of conscience who waged peace for sixty-five years died at the age of eighty-eight in Santa Rosa, California. Caleb Foote was such a profound war-resister that he spent eighteen months in federal prison because he did not want to easily fake a religiously-based conscientious objection status, since his opposition was based on humanistic principles.

Foote went on as a law professor to engage decades of championing racial, economic, and criminal justice. Not just by representing aggrieved defendants but by also putting forth studies which addressed systems of reform. He spent his later years active in local conservation initiatives.

Should their relatives and many friends and admirers be contemplating the extension of their legacies, they may wish to consider establishing an institution dedicated to the thought and action which these two men demonstrated.

Around two years ago, Reverend Coffin was honored at a large dinner in New York City. After eloquent encomiums by several noted speakers, he rose to give a few remarks. I paraphrase one of his urgings to carry on: It is as if our long gone, valiant reformers in our country's history were reaching out to us and saying "finish the job, finish the job."

Senator William Proxmire

December 16, 2005

Will this country ever again see the likes of a Senator from Wisconsin—William Proxmire—who passed away this month at age ninety? He came to the Senate, replacing Senator Joseph McCarthy, in 1957 and left in 1989. He was the legislators' legislator. No one worked harder, studied more, listened to more congressional witnesses or cast more consecutive votes in the Senate without being absent.

Except for championing the dairy farmers—whom he considered just about the hardest working farmers in America—he was fiercely independent, unconventional, and fearlessly challenged the entrenched customs of the Senate. Whether taking on the sacred cow of regular Senate pay raises or conducting a lone sixteen and a half hour filibuster or campaigning by literally walking thousands of miles around his state—taking one-day jobs like collecting garbage to get a feel for what ordinary workers go through, he was one of a kind.

Who else could be re-elected with landslides in a politically divided state again and again without spending, raising or taking any campaign money? Zero. He would spend a couple of hundred dollars for postage stamps to send back unsolicited checks for his campaign.

Who else would make 3,000 speeches in the Senate over a period of nineteen years to force

a vote to ratify an anti-genocide treaty? Almost every morning. Three thousand speeches! Don't you think that's determination? As now, in those years there were many Senators with the attention of a humming bird.

He was the go-to Senator against big corporate welfare proposals, such as the federal bailout of Lockheed, the go-to Senator against corporate tax loopholes, the go-to Senator for measures to protect consumers financially like the truth-in-lending law.

As a senior member and then chairman of the Senate Banking Committee, he championed low and middle income housing legislation and supported the creation of the Consumer Cooperative Bank. When he became chairman of the Banking Committee—traditionally a lucrative watering hole for the big bank lobbyists—he refused a delegation of large New York and California bank executives for their traditional orientation of new chairs. No, he would not see them privately, he said. He would be pleased to see them at a public Committee hearing. They could testify on a bill and he would be glad to hear their views.

Residents in northwest Washington, DC became accustomed to Bill Proxmire jogging five miles to work every day, after rising at six a.m. and doing 300 pushups. He popularized physical fitness, by example and his writings, before it became more widely the thing to do.

His greatest regret was supporting the Vietnam War in the early years, unlike his great colleague, Senator Gaylord Nelson. But by 1968 he reversed course and became an opponent.

His greatest triumph, he said, was passage of the anti-genocide treaty.

One day, two young men tried to rob him near the Congress. "Prox," as he was called, held them off until the police came and arrested them. So what did Proxmire do a little later?

Without fanfare, he hired them to do some chores in his Senate office.

Whenever his Senate colleagues were on foreign junkets during Senate recesses, Proxmire would hold significant hearings all by himself. It didn't harm his popularity to be seen as working on the people's necessities while others strayed or played.

Senator Proxmire was good for consumer protection, the environment, worker safety, small farmers, fair taxation, and efficient government. At times he would rebuff labor unions and women's rights groups because of honest disagreements with them. As former Congressman Kastenmeier said the other day, "He was incorruptible."

He could be that because he believed that the folks back home were his "bosses," as he called them while doing all those short-term jobs around the state. Former Wisconsin Governor Tony Earl put it well, when he said, "[Proxmire] made the case that personal contact and keeping in touch with the voters was a lot more important than how much money you had . . . We could sure use a lot more of the frugality today."

The Democratic Party, given its failure to achieve many electoral victories at all levels of government, would do well to study the political stands of Senator William Proxmire and why he was elected in landslides again and again. The Proxmire formula for the Democrats could be a winning one throughout the country, not just Wisconsin.

I have always believed Proxmire could have won in any state. Meetings in the Senator's office were unlike any meetings I have had with other members of Congress. First, he listened intently and then had a conversation with you. No glazed eyes.

He didn't talk like a politician—you know the type with their strained oratorical or practiced phrases. He was a man without guile. He focused on the issues and their relevance to the public interest.

Proxmire fans should move quickly to establish a dynamic memorial so that his style of politics and determination can be taught to a younger generation.

Student Activism: PIRGs Have Led the Way

October 28, 2005

Ask a Washington, DC taxi driver about student activism in the United States and you will likely hear about student involvement in the Civil Rights movement and student opposition to the war in Vietnam. If you push a bit, the driver may mention Earth Day.

Don't blame the driver for providing you with a snapshot of activism that only deals with the '60s. When it comes to students, the media lens is narrow. It focuses on mega events. And it focuses on the zany: swallowing goldfish in the '50s, Nehru jackets in the '60s, streaking in the '70s, toga parties in the '80s, the Macarena in the '90s and so it goes. News of student initiatives after the early '70s barely captures the tip of the iceberg. Just below the surface, however, there is a vibrant and enduring student movement.

One of the shining examples of this student movement are the student Public Interest Research Groups (PIRGs). With the help of our organizers, this campus-based phenomenon that started in 1970 has grown broader and deeper on campuses throughout the country. Students in Oregon and Minnesota launched the first PIRGs. After the initial success in these two pioneering states, attorney and organizer Donald Ross and I wrote a book titled: *Action for a Change: A Students Manual for Public Interest Organizing.*

This 1971 how-to blueprint helped students in other states organize PIRGs. Today they operate in twenty-nine states nationwide—from California to New York, in small states like Vermont and in other states as diverse as New Jersey and Colorado.

Each local PIRG is financed and controlled by students, but guided by a professional staff of attorneys, scientists, organizers and others. Core funding comes from modest annual fees of $5 to $10 automatically billed to all students on campuses who approve a campus PIRG by a majority vote. Once underway, PIRGs work on local, statewide and national issues ranging from improving the quality of subway service in New York City, to making polluters pay for their toxic waste dumps, to reducing fees for banking services, to promoting renewable energy policies. PIRGs are non-partisan, non-ideological, no-nonsense nonprofit groups that make good things happen with creative approaches and hard work.

In 1983, the state PIRGs banded together and created a national lobbying office composed of a full-time staff of advocates working with the state PIRGs on environmental issues such as preserving the Arctic wilderness, protection of forests, and reversing global warming. The PIRG consumer agenda is as broad as the marketplace. It includes challenging both the production of genetically modified food, concentration of media ownership, and safeguarding privacy as well as advocating laws to limit the potential of identity theft. USPIRG also works to prevent fraud and gouging of consumer borrowers and bank depositors.

And, the PIRG democracy initiatives range from campaign finance reform, to ballot access laws that provide equal access to all political parties, to proportional representation, to open access to government information.

Doug Phelps, a student activist in the '60s and a graduate of Harvard Law School, is the overall chair of the state PIRGS. Phelps says for "over three decades in dozens of states on many issues—there is a common thread: research, organizing, and advocacy. In each case, state PIRGs began by investigating the problems at hand, building support for concrete solutions among the public, and then persistently advocating change."

Gene Karpinski, the Executive Director of USPIRG, notes that, "beyond the lobbying, litigation and investigative reports, the PIRGs teach students about the role they can and should have in a democracy." And, the role is indeed significant.

This country has more problems than it should tolerate and more solutions than it uses. Few societies in the course of human history have faced such a situation: most are in the fires without the water to squelch them. Our society has the resources and the skills to keep injustice at bay and to elevate the human condition to a state of enduring compassion and creative fulfillment. How we go about using the resources and skills has consequences which extend beyond our national borders to all the earth's people. These words ring as true today as they did in 1971.

PIRGs have taught students that they can "fight city hall" and that they can win important victories for our society. They have published hundreds of groundbreaking reports and useful guides, helped pass scores of important laws in their state legislatures, called media attention to environmental threats and stopped consumer abuses by corporations. But the work of building and improving our society must continue. The injustices of tomorrow will require the next generation of student activists to rise to the challenge of building a more just and humane society. And just as I said in 1971, "The problems of the present and the risks of the future are deep and plain. But let it not be said that this generation refused to give up so little in order to achieve so much."

For more information on the PIRGs visit: http://uspirg.org/ and http://www.pirg.org/

Alan Dundes—Making Sense of Nonsense

April 8, 2005

On March 30, the world's greatest folklore scholar died, the way he lived, teaching a graduate seminar in anthropology at Giannini Hall on the campus of the University of California-Berkeley.

"To call Alan Dundes a giant in his field is a great understatement," observed George Breslauer, Dean of the Division of Social Sciences, adding that "he virtually constructed the field of modern folklore studies and trained many of its most distinguished scholars."

Yet when I called the obituary departments of three major newspapers, the editors had not heard of Professor Dundes, who probably received more media attention over the years, due to the controversies that arose from his publications and his studied irreverence, than 99 percent of all university teachers.

His students loved the vibrant classes that provocatively opened their imaginations with insight, curiosity, and humor. Heartfelt messages were sent to his family and colleagues from all over the world, Poland, China, Tunisia, Serbia, from

his students and scholars whom he mentored so enthusiastically.

Alan Dundes was given the University's Distinguished Teaching Award in 1994. Addressing students at the Commencement Convocation in 2002, he said, "It may be that your sole purpose in life is simply to serve as a warning to others." That's not something you ordinarily say at graduation. But then that was vintage Dundes, he made you remember what he said because what he said was worthy of being remembered.

He always stayed close to the people. He called Folklore "the autobiography of a people. You're dealing with real people in everyday life." He would ask his students to submit fifty bits of folklore: jokes, proverbs, myths, riddles, games, customs, pranks, limericks, parodies, puns, yells, dances, gestures, graffiti, and more. His archive of more than 500,000 items of folklore is a testimony to prodigious research and publications.

One day he opened a letter from a student he taught in the Sixties, which contained a $1 million personal check. Professor Dundes was astonished and promptly donated the sum to establish a chair in Folklore Studies at Berkeley.

In one of his more concise self-descriptions, Dr. Dundes said, "my professional goals are to make sense of nonsense, find a rationale for the irrational, and seek to make the unconscious conscious."

He rarely lost an opportunity to emphasize the need to explain his specialty. He told the *New York Times* twenty years ago that "folklore is not a matter of running down little wart cures. It is a serious subject that deals with the essence of life."

In a society so increasingly dominated by commercialism that tries to make everything for sale, Professor Dundes was emphatic that folklore continually gets produced year after year and in the most modern technological settings. As his colleague, Laura Nader, pointed out:

> Dundes completely redefined the basic concept of "the folk" which pre-Dundes was defined as "the peasant" and peasant only. His expanded definition included what Dundes called any group of people whatsoever who share at least one common linking factor. That could mean ethnic and religious groups, occupational associations, sports teams, or even individual families.

One of his many books was titled *Never Try to Teach a Pig to Sing,* (co-authored with Carl Pagter). This volume analyzed modern folklore such as the personal exchanges and messages between workers coming out of fax machines, computers, and photocopiers.

Dundes' interpretations and explanations outraged people on just about all sides of any spectrum of belief or loyalty. But his students could not have enough of him. The packed 400-seat classroom for his Introduction to Folklore class had a waiting list.

Certainly, this witty, learned, fast-paced teacher reached thousands of students since he began teaching at Berkeley in 1963. But he could have reached millions with a regular television show or even one interactive television series. Neither commercial nor public television had the vision. Maybe he was too politically incorrect. Or maybe his subject matter was probed too differently in a culture that thinks folklore is like an ancient bedtime story.

Our increasingly monetized, spectator society needs Alan Dundes to help us examine why we do what we do.

In a tormented world so full of daily tragedies and deprivations, it is not hard to recall the words from Joseph Conrad—"the horror of it all." In Alan Dundes' works, the recollection of this man's contributions to the cultures of the world evokes the phrase "the joy of it all."

Professor Seymour Melman
December 20, 2004

In the rarified world of economics and industrial engineering, there was never anyone like Columbia University professor Seymour Melman. I grew up reading and listening to the prophetic, factual and hard-nosed arguments he made for his anti-war and worldwide disarmament causes in the specialized and, occasionally, major media.

There were Seymour Melman's op-eds and letters to the editor in the *New York Times* starting in his twenties. There were his cogent Congressional testimonies about the permanent war economy and its damage to our civilian economy and necessities of the American people. His economic conversion plans and his advocacy for a muscular peace agreement with the Soviet Union illuminated what kind of economy, innovation and prosperity could be ours in the USA.

Melman's work was detailed and he challenged what President Eisenhower critically called the "military-industrial complex" like that of no other academic. He would show how talented scientists and engineers were sucked into this permanent war economy to the detriment of civilian jobs and economic development as if people's well-being mattered. "To eliminate hunger in America = $4-5 billion = C-5A aircraft program," he would say, referring to Lockheed Martin's chronically bungled, defective and costly contract.

Melman's consulting services were in great demand. His numerous books made such sense to people for whom foresight was a valued attitude. He advised citizen groups, unions, legislators and the United Nations. For years he was chairman of the National Commission for Economic Conversion and Disarmament.

Into his eighties, Mr. Melman probed the arcane regions of weapons systems. He meticulously took apart the wrong ways the corporate-dominated Pentagon priced the corporate cost of subs, ships, planes and other modern weaponry, by way of explaining the staggering spiral of weapon budgets.

The titles of his books spoke to his concerns, *Our Depleted Society*, *Pentagon Capitalism* and *Profits Without Production*. As a World War II veteran, he knew the difference between an adequate defense and weaponry "overkill." He calculated that US nuclear weapons had the power to destroy the Soviet Union 1,250 times over. He asked, how much is too much of a drain on our economy and well-being?

With the demise of the Soviet Union and the agreement on dismantling many of those nuclear warheads on both sides, Mr. Melman looked forward to the "peace dividends" and the economic conversion or retooling he so long urged. It was not to happen. The military budget now consumes half of the entire federal government's operating expenditures.

In his later years, Melman promoted the idea of self-management as an alternative to giant corporations. For the last twenty years the media blacked him out. He could scarcely get an article published in the newspapers or even in the progressive magazines. He did not qualify on frenetic radio and television because he spoke in paragraphs and was elderly, an electronic bigotry that is keeping many wise, older Americans from communicating with their younger generations.

It was precisely because he had been right again and again that print media tired of his research even though it was up to date. How many Americans know, for example, that 90 percent of the products sold in the 2002 L.L. Bean catalogue were imported? He counted them, to make his point about the de-industrialization of America.

How many people would want to know that a recent New York City contract for mass transit vehicles received only foreign bidders? Not one American company was there to compete and provide the jobs for the $3 billion dollar project.

Before he passed away this month, Seymour Melman had completed a concise book manuscript titled, *Wars, Ltd.: The Rise and Fall of America's Permanent War Economy*. He was having trouble finding a good publisher, when I spoke with him earlier this summer. But he will leave a legacy of wisdom, insight, humanity, consistency, and diligence. In a society whose rulers and corporatists seal the people off from such magnificent minds and inundate them daily with trivia, distraction, and the hot air artists bellowing their lucrative ignorance, sagacious Americans like Seymour Melman will not receive the attention the citizenry deserves unless we the people, who own the public airwaves, begin to control and use our own media.

Teaching Peace
December 10, 2004

Colman McCarthy believes in "strength through peace." So much so that he left his job as a columnist for the *Washington Post* to expand his Center for Teaching Peace to spread the wisdom of adopting peace studies at high schools and colleges around the country. There are now 300 peace programs in place, offering majors, minors, and concentration (degree programs) at 300 colleges and universities, including Notre Dame, Colgate, and Syracuse.

When Mr. McCarthy started his project to spread peace studies for students, only Manchester College in Indiana had a peace program in its curriculum. He personally teaches courses as eight colleges and schools such as Georgetown, American and Catholic Universities in Washington, DC.

It is truly remarkable how much of the nation's resources goes to preparing for war and the trivial amount devoted to preventing war or settling the conflicts before they erupt into violence. Half of the US government's entire operating budget goes for military expenditures, thirteen years after the demise of the Soviet Union from internal corruption. We have military bases in over 100 countries. Our political rulers want to do something about Islamic madrassahs to make their teaching more peaceful in other lands, yet they rarely speak, spotlight or support peace education in this country.

During the past twenty years, in countries posing no threat to the United States, US troops have been numerous, McCarthy says, with the loss of many innocent civilians. US corporations are the biggest arms exporters in the world, using billions of direct and indirect taxpayer subsidies to inflate their profits.

To anyone who questions the need for peace studies, McCarthy says, "All I ask of these snappy-talking realists is to tune out the blather of militarism and consider the successes of nonviolence. Since 1936, six brutal or corrupt governments have been driven from power not by violence but by organized nonviolent resistance: in Poland, the Philippines, Chile, South Africa, Yugoslavia and Georgia." He may soon add Ukraine to his list.

The necessity to start with the very young,

given today's relentless and violent entertainment games and TV programs beamed into their minds, is a priority for him. His teachings of non-violence "covers a lot of ground: family violence, schoolyard violence and eventually governmental violence." In one of his two books on the subject titled *Solutions to Violence and Strength Through Peace: The Ideas and People of Nonviolence*, he wants to inspire children with stories about Dorothy Day, Martin Luther King, Jane Addams, Albert Einstein, Jeannette Rankin, and Sojourner Truth.

"Unless we teach our children peace," he says, "someone else will teach them violence." Certainly, former West Point professor David Grossman agrees with the latter point. So much that he authored a book about television and video violence, channeled to children around the clock, calling it *Teaching Our Children to Kill*.

The mass media gravitates regularly to stories about violence, except the daily corporate-induced violence like toxics and unsafe products and workplaces. In part, they are reflecting ways to jolt people into watching their programs. But they leave almost no space or time for people like Colman McCarthy who are trying to build a culture of peace through education. Peace is very exciting to people who have known war.

We should try more of the former before getting bogged down more in the latter.

To obtain more information about the Center for Teaching Peace, please write to:

Center for Teaching Peace
4501 Van Ness St. NW
Washington, DC 20016

Project Citizen

April 17, 2004

Byrd Community Academy—notwithstanding its name—is a crumbling elementary school in Chicago next to one of the largest and most perilous public housing projects—Cabrini-Green. It also is the location of one of the more spectacular fifth grade classes in the country.

In Room 405, since December, the entire course curriculum is devoted to one project and one goal—to document the terrible disrepair and lack of facilities of the school and build community, state and national support for a new school!

I asked their teacher, Brian Schultz, how this came to be. He said he asked the nineteen students in this class, all African-Americans from low-income families, what they wanted to work on. They replied "our school." Reading, writing and arithmetic—they learn those and much more through this one single, expanding mission.

The youngsters appear transformed. Their attendance rate is 98 percent and coming from a part of Chicago rife with drugs, street violence, gang activity, physical deterioration, and unemployment, this is testimony to their interest. They design each part of their research and action strategy. They learn how to do surveys, write different letters of support from politicians, community leaders and from their own peers. Nine hundred students from other schools have expressed their support.

I asked their teacher, Mr. Schultz, about the support for such a unique program by his superiors. "My principal and the other teachers are very approving," he said.

Looking over the students' work product so far, I noticed a methodical sequence for their ra-

tionale. First they listed eighty-nine "problems that affect our community and us." They fit their school needs with their community at large in a kind of free association. Then Project Citizen, as they call their initiative, zeroed in on their school—no stage or auditorium, rest rooms dirty and broken, no lunch room—eat in hallway, heat does not work, need to wear coats, no air conditioning, bullet holes/cracks in windows, few books in the library, broken fences outside, no attached gym. They learned how to take photos of what they verbally describe. They each wrote a description of their school.

Together they put together the Comprehensive Action Plan. I looked at it in terms of what the students have to learn in order to implement it and what it takes from the students. It sure does not demand memorization, regurgitation and vegetation as so many school subjects demand. It taps into almost every course taught except laboratory sciences.

The children are doing interviews, a video documentary, expository writing, letters/emails, direct action, surveys, petitions, news releases, photography, fundraising, and research. They're into the costs for the new school, where the money has to come from, the position of the Board of Education (distant), the response from the elected officials (mostly cool up to now) and how to get media for their cause (they have been interviewed by the *Chicago Tribune* and NPR, among several news outlets).

Their self-confidence and maturity are growing. They sense that they have started a process of change. They know that polite recognition for what they are doing is just window-dressing. Vice President Cheney responded to their letter, wishing them luck, for instance.

As a student letter "to whom it may concern" said, "It teaches us about how the government works and how we can affect public policy change even as fifth graders" (age ranges from ten to twelve years). The letter concludes, "We would like to invite you to see our school for yourself. We do not think that you would let your kids come to a school that is falling apart.... The problems are fixable and would not cost too much to fix. Byrd Academy needs a new school building."

The Byrd Academy students, their teacher and principal, Joseph Gartner may have started something. Schools need basic repairs or re-placement all over our country—hundreds of billions of dollars of work projects as well as good jobs that cannot be shipped to China.

Maybe George W. Bush will divert his attention as Mayor of Baghdad and start paying attention to these schools and their needs with some of the money that he is wasting in the massive military budget that now takes half of the federal government's operating expenditures.

Political Games & Shames

In the US we have become accustomed to the dangerous pattern of choosing the "lesser evil" for our elected officials. Throughout the last decade we have seen presidential candidates present platitudes instead of policies. Candidates abstractly talk about "cutting spending," "reducing the deficit," and "creating jobs." Looking at the voting record of most Republicans and Democrats on these issues, it is clear they do not stand for "We the People" but for "We the Corporation." Increasingly, the Democrats and Republicans are fighting for the same corporate campaign dollars. Over the last decade, "We the People" have increasingly lost our voice within our government. The purpose of this section is to shed light on how our elected officials have betrayed the public trust. The following columns should make your blood boil, including:

- *Bush/Cheney and Obama perfecting the "politics of avoidance" on issues of daily importance such as corporate crime, consumer protection, and worker health and safety.*

- *The strengthening of Bush-era policies during the Obama administration with the continuation of the Patriot Act, Iraq-Afghanistan wars and support for the Wall Street bailout. In one column you will read a fictional letter from former President Bush to President Obama in which Bush lauds Obama's continual support for Bush era policies and ideology, especially with regard to the Iraq and Afghanistan quagmires.*

- *Congress, with its allowances for minority rule, permitting the Tea Party, a minority group within the Republican Party, to dominate the House of Representatives.*

- *The truth behind the "Affordable Care Act" which was more a win for the big drug companies and health insurance industries than Americans, a majority of whom support single-payer healthcare—an option that was never even on the table with President Obama.*

- *Yielding control of presidential debates to the Commission on Presidential Debates (CPD), a front for the major parties that is devoted to make sure the American people do not see converging Democrat and Republican candidates forced to respond to thoughtful questions from third-party or independent candidates and outside media.*

- *The multiple impeachable offenses of Bush/Cheney and Obama. These leaders have increasingly expanded unlawful powers of the Executive Branch, while avoiding both punishment and meaningful discussion of their repeated crimes and wrongdoing. This unilateral expansion of aggressive wars, bailouts and other dictates is an offense to our Founding Fathers and their belief in the importance of governmental checks and balances driven by a separation of powers.*

Throughout this section we will see egregious acts on all levels of government and realize that it is up to us to remind our representatives that they represent us, not themselves or the corporations but "We the People."

The Politics of Lowered Expectations

January 3, 2012

Ezra Klein, the bright, young, economic policy columnist for the *Washington Post* believes that Obama came out ahead last year in the "administration's bitter, high-stakes negotiations with the Republicans in Congress."

He cites four major negotiations in 2011 with the Republicans that Obama won. Obama won the game of chicken played in February by the House Speaker John Boehner and Senate Minority Leader Mitch McConnell to avoid a government shutdown. He won the battle to raise the customarily supported debt ceiling on government borrowing. He avoided an embarrassment after he had to concur in the formation of a "Supercommittee" on deficit reduction when Congress couldn't come to an agreement. And he won a two-month extension of the Social Security payroll tax cut and extension of unemployment compensation benefits.

If those were "high stakes," I wonder what microscopic instrument would detect any lower stakes. Obama keeps "winning battles" that he could have avoided. But what about taking the offensive on some really significant matters?

For example, when he caved in December 2010 to the minority Republicans and agreed to extend the deficit-producing Bush tax cuts on the rich, he didn't demand in return a continuation of the regular bi-partisan approval of lifting the debt limit. So over weeks in 2011, unable to focus on other changes, he had to mud-wrestle the Republicans on the debt limit—to the dismay of finance ministers across the world—and won only after conceding the bizarre creation of a Supercommittee to order its own Congress to enact budget cuts. That Supercommittee gridlocked and closed down.

Finally, if he does nothing, the $4 trillion over ten years that are the Bush tax cuts expire automatically on January 1, 2013—after the election. On the same day, the spending trigger automatically kicks in which cuts, over ten years, $500 billion from the bloated Defense budget and another $500 billion from other departments, but not from Social Security and Medicare/Medicaid beneficiaries.

This is an Obama victory? What makes Mr. Klein so sure Obama won't cave again? He has all this year to do so. His own Defense Secretary Leon Panetta has often said that there's no way he would support any further defense cuts. Also, Obama was ready in 2011 to raise the Medicare eligibility age in return for the deal on debt ceiling. He was saved from this folly only by the stubbornness of Boehner and his clenched-teeth sidekick, Virginian Eric Cantor from the arguably most passive Congressional district in the US. Boehner and Cantor wanted more cuts.

Now, look at some high stakes fights where the Republicans defeated the White House and blocked major substantive advances. They stopped the wide-ranging energy bill, and stifled Uncle Sam's authority to bargain for drug discounts that taxpayers are paying to the gouging drug companies for the drug benefit program for the elderly. They kept the coal industry King Coal on Capitol Hill, preserved crass corporate welfare and tax loophole programs, and blocked the able nominee to head the new agency to protect against consumer finance abuses. They also cut budgets for small but crucial safety programs in food, auto safety, and children's hunger.

Republicans also preserved the notorious nuclear power loan guarantee boondoggles, kept a bevy of Soviet-era weapons systems nestled in the arms of the military-industrial complex and mercilessly beat up on the work and budget of the cancer-preventing, illness-reducing Environmental Protection Agency. That's just for starters.

Obama and the majority Democrats in the Senate dug this hole for themselves when they failed to curtail the filibuster in January 2009 and 2011 by majority vote. They doomed themselves with the numerically impossible hurdle of needing sixty votes to pass any measure and avoid filibusters.

Putting themselves on the defensive, while dialing business lobbyists for the same campaign dollars as the Republicans, the Obama crowd, of course, could not advance what they promised the American people. They went silent on raising the federal minimum wage to $9.50, promised by candidate Obama in 2008 for 2011. At $9.50, it would still have been less than the federal minimum wage in 1968, adjusted for inflation. Hardly a radical proposal.

Obama went silent on the union card check, which he promised unorganized American workers in their losing struggle with multinational corporate employers. While bailing out the criminal gamblers on Wall Street, he could have pressed for a stock transaction sales tax that could have raised big revenue and helped dampen speculation with other peoples' money such as pension funds and mutual fund savings.

Before Obama's and his Democrats' self-inflicted loss of the House of Representatives in 2011, he could have pushed seriously for a visible public works program which would produce domestic jobs in thousands of communities for improved public services. He could have directly challenged the Tea Partiers with cuts in corporate welfare, but he did not, except for partly ending an ethanol subsidy. He could have made a big deal of cracking down on corporate fraud on Medicare and Medicaid that totals tens of billions of dollars a year. However, once on the defensive from his own self-inflicted weak hand, he was always on the defensive.

Obama may be in a superior tactical position vis-a-vis the Congressional Republicans, as Mr. Klein posits, but is this all there is left of the touted 2008 movement for hope and change?

President Obama is deemed by his fellow Democrats to have won the financial battles, but the Republicans won the rest. How can the expectation levels of this two party duopoly sink any lower?

Let's face it, if today's Republicans are the most craven, greedy, ignorant, anti-worker, anti-patient, anti-consumer, anti-environment, coddlers of corporate crime in the party's history, why aren't the Democrats landsliding them?

For two answers try reading John F. Kennedy's best-selling *Profiles of Courage*, 1955, or if you favor the ancients, *Plutarch's Lives* (circa 100 A.D.).

Putting the Lie to the Republicans
October 3, 2011

Masters of the repeated lying sound bite, the craven Congressional Republicans are feasting on the health and safety of the American people with gleeful greed while making the corporate and trade association media swoon. "Job-killing regulations" exudes daily from the mouths of Speaker John Boehner, his Wall Street-licking side-kick, Eric Cantor, and Senate minority leader, Mitch McConnell.

Then all the way down the line, the Republicans are on cue bellowing that "job-killing regulations" must be revoked or stopped aborning over at OSHA (protecting workers), EPA (protecting clean air and water), FDA (safer drugs and food), and NHTSA (making your vehicle safer). Imagine how much more civil servants could do to accomplish the statutory missions of their respective agencies if they could get the Republicans and their corporate paymasters off their backs.

These same Republicans get in their cars with their children and put on their seat belts. Out of sight are the air bags ready to deprive them of their freedom to go through the windshield in a crash. Who makes those seat belts and air bags? Workers in the USA.

The jobs these regulations may be "killing" are those that would have swelled the funeral industry, or some jobs in the healthcare and disability-care industry. On the other hand, by not being injured, workers stay on the job and do not drain the workers' compensation funds or hamper the operations of their employer.

About twenty years ago, Professor Nicholas Ashford of MIT came to Washington and testified before Congress in great detail about how and where safety regulations create jobs and make the economy more efficient in avoiding the costs of preventable injuries and disease. He received a respectful hearing from members of the Committee. It is doubtful whether Messers Boehner, Cantor, McConnell and Dr. Coburn (Senator from Oklahoma) are reading Professor Ashford these days, who just co-authored a book with Ralph P. Hall called *Technology, Globalization, and Sustainable Development.*

The corporatist Republicans' minds are made up; don't bother them with the facts. But we must keep trying to dissolve the Big Lie.

In 2009 Professor David Hemenway published a stirring book titled *While You Were Sleeping: Success Stories in Injury and Violence Prevention* which in clear language described the success stories of people, often with the support of

a past, more enlightened Congress, made lives safer and healthier in the US. Yes, life-saving, injury-preventing, disease-stopping regulations resulting in life-sustaining technology produced by American industry and workers.

Wake up Democrats. Learn the political art of truthful repetition to counter the cruelest Republicans who ever crawled up Capitol Hill. You've got massive, documented materials to put the Lie to the Republicans and repeat the words "life-saving regulations."

President Obama should set an example. For instance, on September 2, 2011, President Obama fell for the regulation costs jobs lie. He said, "[I] have continued to underscore the importance of reducing regulatory burdens and regulatory uncertainty, particularly as our economy continues to recover."

Pete Altman, from the Natural Resources Defense Council wrote:

> In reversing his Administration's previously strong support for ozone regulations to protect the health of American children, President Obama (in the words of one observer): "drank the conservative Kool-Aid, and agreed that tightening ozone emission rules would have cost billions and hurt the economy. But clean air is very popular politically, and the EPA's own studies show that a tighter standard could have created $17 billion in economic benefits."

Earlier this month, Public Citizen issued a report about five regulations that spurred innovation and a higher quality of economic growth. As one of the authors, Negah Mouzoon, wrote, "When federal agencies implement rules for efficiency, worker safety, or public health and welfare, companies need to reformulate their products and services to comply. And so begins good ol' American competition. To comply with federal standards, companies need to invest in research and development, which often yields to new products and systems that both solve public policy problems and, often, boost business. The result? A brighter idea emerges."

It is important to note that such regulations give companies lengthy lead times to comply and, under the daily sandpapering of corporate lobbyists, regulations issued lose much of their early industry-controlling reach.

Here are the report's five innovation-spurring products or processes that at their outset encountered significant industry resistance and inflated estimates of complying with the regulations. Before, that is, the companies came to their senses, responded and found that such changes were not just good for the people but for their own bottom line.

1. Protecting workers from poisonous vinyl chloride.

2. Reducing sulfur dioxide emissions.

3. Preventing ozone-layer-destroying CFC emissions from aerosols.

4. Improving the energy efficiency of home appliances.

5. Utilizing energy-efficient light bulbs.

For the full report go to and search on nader.org.

Here is a suggestion, maybe some "kids"—between the ages of ten and twelve—having learned from their parents the importance of telling the truth, can start a Kiddy Corps for a Truthful Congress drawn from the internet-savvy children all over the US. What a wonderful expression of grassroots truth-telling directed toward the Great Prevaricators on Capitol Hill. Yes-job-producing, life-saving, economy-stimulating, innovation-producing regulations for a more secure future for our children.

Interested parents may contact us at info@ csrl.org.

Congressional Tea Party Downgrades America

August 8, 2011

The Boston Tea Party in December 1773 threw the East India Company's tea overboard. The Republican Tea Party in August 2011 threw America overboard.

Only in Congress, with its rules for minority rule, can a minority of the Republican Party in the House of Representatives impose its havoc on the American people there, then on the Senate and Obama.

Leaving aside the psychiatric question of why a clutch of Republican Tea Partiers, many of them freshmen, terrify the veteran Republicans who outnumber them in the House, consider what they just pushed through the House against the American people.

For 150 million workers, Tea Partiers pushed through more cuts in the already starved federal programs that are aimed at diminishing the yearly 58,000 fatalities in workplace-related disease and trauma plus larger numbers injured and wounded.

There are 307 million eaters in America. More than 7,000 of them die from contaminated food and more than 300,000 are hospitalized each year. The Tea Partiers pushed cuts through the House to the already underfunded FDA food safety programs. They did this even though last year Congress strengthened the FDA's authority and expanded its responsibilities, including closer inspection of hazardous foodstuffs increasingly coming from communist China.

There are 60 million investors in company stocks in America. The Tea Partiers stomped their feet and cut the House appropriations for law enforcement against Wall Street's frauds by the Securities and Exchange Commission and the Commodity Futures Trading Commission. This cuts the number of federal cops on the Wall Street crime beat, especially on derivative scams.

All Americans breathe air and drink water. The Tea Partiers are cutting the budget of the federal agencies working to get the toxic pollution out of those two necessities for life on Earth. Don't even mention global warming and climate change to Tea Partiers who are willing to die laughing at such a prospect.

There are millions of women and children with special health needs who depend on federal programs for assistance. The House Tea Party members want to slash the modest budgets for these programs.

There are 200 million drivers in America. The Tea Partiers intend to cut the already measly auto safety budget of the Transportation Department. The auto safety budget is less than a third of the budget they allowed for guarding the US embassy in Baghdad!

They have also told others in Congress that they are opposed to last year's auto and bus safety bill which gave long-overdue authority to safety regulators. The bill was supported by Democrats and Republicans but was blocked by one Senator Tom Coburn, a physician no less, in the last December days of the session. Minority rule again blocking the ninety-nine senators who signed off on unanimous consent to get this life-saving legislation through the Senate.

There are 30 million American workers, polls show, who would like to have a trade union represent them in negotiations with giants like Walmart. The Tea Partiers hate unions of workers and were instrumental in blocking the budget for the FAA in late July and early August due to a union organizing mechanism and $16

million in subsidies for a few rural airports. For almost two weeks, the Tea Partiers punished tens of thousands of American workers who had to stop working on airport improvement and repair projects, and, with the law's expiration, the Tea Partiers let the US government lose $30 million in airline ticket taxes.

The Tea Partiers hate taxes, especially on the rich and corporations, even though they are at the lowest rates in twenty years. They are extremists, mindlessly embracing Grover Norquist's no-tax pledge. They are even against giving the IRS funds it needs to collect $15 for every $1 it spends collecting taxes on the ever-more privileged. The number of Treasury auditors focused on these giant global companies is miniscule.

The Tea Partiers don't even care that 50 percent of Tea Partiers back home and 70 percent of Republicans polled thought additional tax revenues should be part of the deficit-reduction program passing through Congress.

You see, these House and Senate Tea Partiers are like mad dogs—at times even beyond control of their political and corporate masters. Fanatics neither think nor blink in their hostage politics. They're scaring Wall Streeters with their brinkmanship. Brandishing a historic moniker that symbolized rebellion against the then monarchial power, the Congressional Tea Partiers are anything but rebels against power— whether against the wars of empire, corporate welfare, sovereignty shedding NAFTA and WTO, corporate crime, the flouted war powers of Congress, or a runaway Wall Street.

Back home last year, Tea Party rhetoric did echo the people's concerns about these matters. It turned out to be just talk by those now in Congress. The other Tea Party in Congress is more interested in wielding the axe against public works programs, education, housing, public health, drug safety, and medical research. But they leave alone the hugely expensive, cost-over-run weapons systems—long after the dissolution of the Soviet Union. Raising money from the fat cats for next year's election, the Tea Partiers aren't about to challenge tax favoritism—officially known as tax expenditures—that Reagan's economist, Professor Martin Feldstein recently called the single largest source of wasteful and low-priority spending in the federal budget.

It is one thing for the Tea Party politicians in Congress—already well-to-do and consuming a pretty nice salary and a bevy of benefits—to lack empathy. But America needs to call them out on their downright ideologically-inebriated animosity toward the domestic necessities of the American people. Tea Party extremists in Congress may well sink the Republican Party but in the process take many Americans down with them.

When they took the debt-limit vote to the cliff they set up the Standard and Poor's (S&P) first-ever downgrade of the US government's credit rating, last Friday. Call it the Tea Party downgrade.

It is time to put a firm cap on the kettle.

Retreat, Surrender, Can He At Least Plead?

August 2, 2011

The headlines came quickly after President Obama concluded the deficit-debt deal with the Republicans on Sunday evening. There were few shades of gray. The *New York Times* editorial was titled "To Escape Chaos, a Terrible Deal: Democrats won almost nothing they wanted except avoiding default."

It was truly, as the *Times* pointed out, "a political environment laced with lunacy." But don't blame it all on the Republican "mad dogs" on Capitol Hill playing chicken with the economic plight of the American people and its wobbling economy. It was President Obama who surrendered.

In one of the most inept episodes of presidential-congressional relations, Mr. Obama managed to give the Republicans more than they expected and leave the Democrats with less than the Republicans offered. The Republicans never expected Mr. Obama to give in entirely on tax increases on the wealthy, on the reviled oil industry giants and other corporate tax escapees. The Republicans even agreed to $800 billion in new revenue over ten years. Obama fumbled the ball day after day, and with the August 2 debt ceiling deadline looming, he fell to the extortionists. Unlike Presidents Roosevelt, Truman, Eisenhower, Kennedy, Johnson, Nixon, Ford, Carter, Reagan, Bush, Clinton, and Bush II, who routinely expected and got debt ceilings raised without conditions.

President Obama's disaster began months ago when he agreed to tie raising the debt ceiling to a grand bargain with the Republicans regarding deficits and revenues instead of demanding a debt ceiling raise while he was caving on extending Bush tax cuts for the wealthy. That immediately gave the "fanatic" Republicans a veto power over the "establishment" Republicans in Congress. And fanatics don't blink. Especially those fanatics who, elected last year, say they don't care about being re-elected.

So Obama accepted about $2.5 trillion in spending cuts over the next decade, got no revenue producing tax increases and therefore made it nearly impossible to create a public works jobs program to uplift a sliding economy.

With economic indicators registering more trouble in recent days for American workers, Mr. Obama has no cards left. Interest rates cannot be driven any lower by the Federal Reserve. He didn't get even a renewal of the extension of unemployment benefits. Consumer spending—two-thirds of the economy, is stagnant. Without consumer demand, new investment is sluggish. Unemployment is rising, and without jobs, workers can't increase their consumer spending. State, local and federal government spending cannot increase under the yoke of the just agreed-upon cuts. The weaker dollar may increase exports a little, but the US still has a continuing massive trade deficit, especially with China. Europe's financial problems will curb orders for US goods and services.

So what can Mr. Obama do? He can propose a public works program, paid for by the tax increases on the wealthy and the corporations. Both are getting richer. The large corporations are reporting very good second quarter profits further disconnecting their affluence from that of their workers and labor in general. He could, if he wanted, make a very strong case for repairing America's infrastructure and bringing the soldiers back from Iraq and Afghanistan, as a majority of the American people and most of the mayors of our cities desire.

First, however, he has to take the offensive by showing that the bulk of the deficits since 2002 were caused by the Bush tax cuts, mostly for the wealthy, and Bush's two wars. Obama also has to hold the Republicans accountable for their hostage-taking of the American economy so they cannot impede public works proposals in an election year.

Amazingly, as a Harvard-trained lawyer, he was quick to compromise from the get-go. Consequently, he painted himself into a corner. So,

since he is not a leader, maybe he can become a pleader.

Given that non-financial companies are sitting on two trillion dollars of inert cash and other liquid assets, maybe he can appeal to these companies to disgorge ten percent in immediate special dividends to their long-parched shareholders who are, after all, their owners. Loosening the executive locks on this hoard of money would provide $200 billion for more likely spending in the market place. Companies like Apple, Google, Cisco, Intel, and Microsoft alone are sitting on well over $200 billion cash. To these coddled, indentured US companies he can invoke President John F. Kennedy's challenge—"Ask not what your country can do for you, ask what you can do for your country."

Second, he can plead with those very profitable corporations that have benefited from the government bailout and pay little or no federal income taxes to voluntarily contribute to a public works fund in their community.

Companies like GE, Verizon, Exxon Mobil, Boeing, IBM, Wells Fargo, DuPont, American Electric Power, FedEx, Honeywell, Yahoo, United Technologies as a group made $171 billion in US profits over three years and paid zero federal income tax with a $2.5 billion negative advantage. And that, says Bob McIntyre, director of Citizens for Tax Justice, is "just the tip of an iceberg of widespread corporate tax avoidance."

Is such pleading just Pollyanna-ish? Maybe. But it will resonate with the American people's sense of injustice. Those feelings of indignation can reverberate and cause members of Congress to start remembering who sent them to Washington. Last I heard, corporations don't have a single vote.

Taking Progressives for Granted

April 12, 2011

When liberals and progressives have nowhere to go, New York's new Democratic Governor Andrew Cuomo can move toward the corporatist-right of the political spectrum with impunity. Brandishing an inherited $10 billion state deficit, Cuomo has earned the following description in the April 7th edition of the *New York Times*:

> He has clashed with unions, who he believes have helped drive the state toward bankruptcy. He has been praised by prominent conservatives like Sarah Palin and Rudolph W. Giuliani. And he has taken thousands of dollars in campaign money from the New York billionaire David H. Koch, who with his family has helped finance the Tea Party movement....
>
> The man who began public life advocating for homeless people won passage of a state budget that makes steep cuts to schools, healthcare and social services. In a year when Wall Street posted record profits, Mr. Cuomo finally rejected a politically popular income tax surcharge on the wealthy.

Praised by the *Wall Street Journal* and the Republican raptor, New Jersey Governor Chris Christie, who calls Andrew Cuomo "my soulmate," the son of moral vision orator, former Governor Mario Cuomo, is on a roll unchallenged by his fellow Democrats and the media. Using the deficit—which is far less per capita than Connecticut's deficit—he revels in being "Cuomo the cutter." "I am a realist . . . Forget the philosophy. Here are the numbers."

Mr. Cuomo picks his numbers so that the cuts fall on the lower economic classes, the powerless along with the reviled public employee unions. Granted, there is waste, fraud or ineffectiveness in many social service programs, but Governor Cuomo is cutting the programs indiscriminately without cutting them by squeezing out the waste and eliminating ineffective programs directly.

What results is that the wasteful practitioners know how to fight to preserve their programs better than the efficient ones do. The former have allies like well-connected corporate vendors with their procurement contracts.

But there is a more blatant misfocus by Cuomo. It is his fear of Wall Street whose crooks, speculators and self-enrichment pros collapsed the economy, looted or drained savings and pensions in 2008–09 leading to much unemployment and many closed businesses that, through the loss of tax revenue, expanded the state deficit. He refuses even to speak about holding these spoiled, back-to-business-as-usual financial giants responsible.

On the contrary he is rejecting an extension of the tax surcharge on New Yorkers and residing foreigners who make over $200,000 dollars in income a year, which expires this December. It is so much easier to tax the faceless masses. Already, lower income New Yorkers pay a slightly higher percentage of their income in all taxes imposed than do the wealthy. Regressive!

It gets worse. During his campaign for Governor, Mr. Cuomo refused to even contemplate keeping the $14 billion (some estimate higher amounts) a year that the state collects from a century-old stock transfer tax, which is really a sales tax and instantly rebates back to the stock brokers. New York used to keep this tax revenue until the early 1980s, when Wall Street pressure finally prevailed. Green Party candidate for Governor, Howie Hawkins, argued during a public debate that keeping these revenues would eliminate the deficit and prevent the reduction of necessary programs. On that stage, Mr. Cuomo refused to engage. Mum's the word on Wall Street's fair share.

Cuomo calls himself "a progressive Democrat who's broke." A progressive Democrat would push for sacrifice at the wealthy top and work down if necessary. Many of the wealthy derived their billions and millions from many favored policies like tax leniency and other privileges and immunities including violation of the law (a few of whom Cuomo pursued as Attorney General).

After all, corporate lobbyists work hard to produce many layers of favoritism, including selling products and services to the state government, that are as profitable as they are often wasteful. Consider, for example, the immense gouging in the outsourcing of CityTime—a large ongoing contract to computerize the New York City payroll (http://www.nyc.gov/html/opa/html/about/city_time.shtml).

The costs of healthcare reflect big time fraud in billing practices. Should a Governor just cut benefits across the board—stranding indigent patients to suffer or die—or should he crack down on the cheating and stealing that too many vendors have perfected?

To be sure it is quicker to slice arbitrarily, but there is no indication that key cost-beneficial law enforcement budgets against business crime are going to increase on Governor Cuomo's watch.

Mr. Cuomo did relent on one budget provision, which would have enriched the hospital and insurance lobbies placing a lifetime $250,000 cap on serious baby injuries from malpractice. That was too much to defend by this "progressive Democrat" in Albany. Credit the Center for Justice and Democracy for urging that good deed (www.centerjd.org).

How far will elected Democrats from the White House on down go in capitulating to the insatiable corporate dominators if their liberal/progressive base continues to signal that they politically have nowhere to go? These voters seem to have few visible breaking points on the dark horizon of over-reaching corporatism.

Institutional Insanity
December 6, 2010

If there was a mental health hospital for institutions the Republican Party and its top leaders would be admissible as clinically insane. Their bizarre wackopedia seems to contain no discernible boundaries. Repeatedly, these corporate supplicants oppose any measure, any regulation, any legislation that will directly help workers, consumers, the environment, small taxpayers, and even investor-shareholders.

There are some exceptions. Since these Republican politicians eat, some did vote for the long-delayed food safety bill last week so that e-coli does not enter their intestines to disrupt the drivel drooling from their daily repertoire.

The Republicans get away with countless absurdities for at least two reasons. One is that their nominal opponents are the spineless, clueless, gutless Democrats (with a few notable exceptions) who present themselves as uncertain waverers, dialing for the same corporate dollars as the Republicans chase. The other is the political reporters who dwell on questions directed toward tactics and horseraces that the dimmest of Republicans can easily handle.

Take the evasive next Speaker of the House, Ohio Republican John Boehner. I've lost count of the times he said the recent healthcare law would "kill jobs in America, ruin the best healthcare system in the world, and bankrupt our country." I don't recall one reporter asking him to be specific on these claims. Instead, the questions focused on Capitol Hill timing and tactics.

Mitch McConnell, the Republican leader in the Senate, makes similar declarations such as, "I've said over and over again, you don't raise taxes in a recession." Really? Of all previous presidents, only Only George W. Bush did not raise taxes but actually reduced them in wartime. But don't expect a reporter to ask McConnell whether he thinks the children and grandchildren should be sent the bill for the Iraq and Afghanistan wars. Or if he thinks repealing the Bush tax cuts on the rich would help reduce the deficit.

How many times have you heard the Republicans demand cutting the national deficit? Probably as often as they did nothing when George W. Bush piled up trillions of dollars in red ink. Now that Obama is president, they rarely get specific about just how they are going to do this, other than jumping on Medicare (where corporate fraud is indeed rampant and untreated by them) or Social Security which is solvent for another thirty years.

For most Republicans, it is never about cutting the bloated military budget—ridden with corporate crime and fraud and burdened with massive redundancies that keep the military-industrial complex that President Eisenhower warned about deep in profitable government contracts.

Nor do the Republicans go after the corporate welfare budget—the hundreds of billions of dollars per year of subsidies, giveaways and handouts to domestic and even foreign corporations. Except for Ron Paul and a very few others, that is. (See: http://www.taxpayers.org and http://www.goodjobsfirst.org)

Another assertion made in this year's midterm elections by Republican candidates for Congress all over the country is that: "Government does not create jobs, only the private sector does." Let's see, government not only creates jobs, taxpayers have paid trillions of dollars for research, development and tax credits that are given over to build entire industries. These include the semi-conductor, computer, aerospace, pharmaceutical, biotech, medical device and containerization industries, to name a few.

The Pentagon created the job-producing internet, for example. When the government funds public works or expands the armed forces, millions of jobs are created.

Will there be one reporter who challenges this Republican nonsense, often expressed in press interviews on *cell phones* while driving on *highways* in cars with *seat belts* and *air bags* either based on taxpayer-funded research, directly paid for, or regulated into being through the government?

Mute Democrats and mindless reporters make insane Republicans possible. Bringing these cruel descendants of Lincoln's Party down their ladder of generalities is to become concrete, to give substantiating examples that will either show that they have no clothes or that they prefer mink.

The American people deserve to have reporters ask one question again and again: "Senator, Representative, Governor, President, would you be specific, give examples and cite your sources for your general assertions?"

For instance, Republicans especially regularly roar their demand for "tort reform." A reporter could ask for clarification such as: "Sir, do you mean by 'tort reform' giving more access to the courts to millions of excluded Americans who get nothing for injuries and illnesses recklessly caused by manufacturers, hospitals, and other wrongdoers, or do you mean further restricting the law designed to afford these people compensation for their harms?" (See: http://www.centerjd.org)

The same demand for concreteness can be directed to the dittoheads who cry out against "over-regulation." Where? Over Wall Street? For health and safety requirements that are either weak when issued, technically obsolete or rarely enforced? (See: http://www.progressivereform.org)

Bringing these well-greased pontificators down their abstraction ladder to where people live, work, overpay, bleed and suffer is a major step forward so the sovereignty of the people can begin exercising itself.

My Friend Barack
November 22, 2010

After nearly two years out, I can imagine George W. Bush writing his successor the following letter:

Dear President Obama:

As you know I've been peddling my book *Decision Points* and while doing interviews, people ask me what I think of the job you're doing. My answer is the same: he deserves to make decisions without criticism from me. It's a tough enough job as it is.

But their inquiries did prompt me to write to you to privately express my continual admiration for the job you are doing. Amazing! I say "privately" because making my sentiments public would not do either of us any good, if you know what I mean.

First, I can scarcely believe my good fortune as to how your foreign and military policies— "continuity" was the word used recently by my good friend, Joe Lieberman—have protected my legacy. More than protected, you've proven yourself just as able—and I may say sometimes even more so—to "kick ass" as my Daddy used to say.

My pleasant surprise is darn near limitless. Your Justice Department has not pursued any actions against my people—not to mention Dick Cheney and me—that the civil liberties and human rights crowd keep baying for you to do.

Overseas, all I see are five stars. You are roaring in Afghanistan, dispatching our great special forces into Yemen, saying, like me, that you'll go anywhere in the world to kill those terrorists. When you said you would assassinate American citizens abroad suspected of "terrorism"—that news came over the radio during breakfast when I was eating my Shredded Wheat and I almost choked with amazement. You got cajones, buddy. I was hesitant about crossing the border into Pakistan—but you, man, are blasting away. Even Dick, who would never say it publically, told me he is impressed.

The Leftists are always trying to have your policies show me up negatively. Hah—they're having one hell of a tough time, aren't they?

Me state secrets, you state secrets. Me executive privilege, you executive privilege. Me stop the release of torture videos, you backed me up. Me indefinite detention, you indefinite detention. Me extraordinary rendition, you extraordinary rendition. Me sending drones, you sending tons more, flying 24/7. Me just had to look the other way on collateral damage, you doing the same and protecting our boys doing it. Me approving night time assassination raids, you're upping the ante especially since General Petraeus took over. Me beefing up Defense, you not skipping a beat. Me letting the CIA loose, you told them operate at large. Me demanding no pictures of our fallen troops, you doing the same, but allowing the families to go to Dover which I should have done.

There is one big difference. I never cracked a law book. You are a top Harvard lawyer and teacher of constitutional law. So when you do what I did, man, it's—what's the word—legitimization!

Domestically, sure you rag Wall Street, but you continued the big bail out of the bankers and their supporting cast. Sure, you're tougher with your words, but they deserve it—remember I said that the Wall Streeters "got drunk" and "got a hangover."

What I get such a kick out of is how you handled the unions and libs who backed you with dreams of Hope and Change. How smoothly you let them learn they've got nowhere to go, just as we used to tell our conservative wing the same thing (though now they've been reborn as growling Tea Partiers). So, cardcheck, single-payer, rolling back my party's passage of legislation in Congress—you made them forget it!

You have been such a great president—backing me on so many things—keeping most tax cuts and shelters, support for my oil and gas buddies (my base), big loan guarantees for nukes, keeping Uncle Sam from bargaining down pharma, expanding free trade, not going tough on China (my Daddy especially liked this one), avoiding class struggle rhetoric and so on.

You want to know how confident I am about you? Even though you called waterboarding "torture," I proudly admitted approving its use to protect our country and its freedoms. Isn't that really what the presidency is all about, along with honoring our troops and the entire national defense efforts?

Semper fi—

George W. Bush

P.S. My mother, Barbara, is a big fan. She calls your term so far *Obamabush*. Cute, aye, for someone who was never a wordsmith.

Democrats Squander the Swing Vote
November 5, 2010

The mid-term 2010 Congressional elections are over and the exaggerations are front and center. "A tidal wave," "an earthquake," "a tsunami," cried the Republican victors and their media acolytes.

Wait a minute! No more than 7 percent of the actual voters switched sides to create a fourteen point spread. This amounts to about 3 percent of all the eligible voters who produced this "tidal wave." That is what happens in our winner-take-all system. So when it is said that "the people have spoken," chalk it up to 7 percent or so switcheroos. The rest voted the way they did in the previous presidential and congressional election (and about 28 million voters stayed home).

Such sweeping descriptions gave incoming House Speaker, John Boehner, even more leeway than usual to play with words when he declared, without further elaboration, that "the peoples priorities and agenda are our priorities." Mr. Boehner is the consummate corporate logo-man masquerading as a Congressman. If someone drew the logos of all the big companies that have marinated his career and put them on his suit coat, they would run into each other.

How then did the Democrats lose against the most craven Republican party in modern history—a Party that opposes again and again the fair rights of workers, consumers, investors, savers, and patients.

Regarding patients, Boehner's oft-repeated view of the modest, non-single-payer health insurance changes by Congress and Obama—"it will kill jobs, destroy the best healthcare system in the world and bankrupt our country." Reporters listen to Mr. Boehner say this repeatedly and do not ask him to explain his wild rhetoric.

So, in listing some of the ways the Democrats failed to defend the country against such Republicans, put near the top not rebutting the crisp lies and abstract assertions that Republican candidates uttered while campaigning or "debating" their Democratic opponents. Listening to debate after debate on C-SPAN radio, I was amazed at how infrequently the Democrats demanded examples from their Republican opponents each time the words "cut spending," "cut taxes," "reduce the deficit," "deregulate" and "create jobs," were uttered.

In elections, one side is either chronically on the offensive or on the defensive. The offense creates momentum unless it is countered and driven back. Since the Democrats are furiously dialing for the same corporate campaign dollars, it is difficult for them to stand for the people. That is why the Democrats are wishy-washy, reticent, and reluctant to put major subjects of abusive power on the table.

Rarely did one hear Democrats state their position on corporate crime law enforcement, huge vendor fraud on the taxpayer (Medicare), anti-collective-bargaining laws for labor, the bloated military budgets, the wars in Afghanistan and Iraq, the flood of corporate subsidies, handouts, giveaways and bailouts, or the grotesque tax escapes for the multinational corporations and the super-wealthy.

They did not want to talk about consumer rip-offs, or the hundreds of thousands of unprotected Americans who lose their lives every year from un-regulated workplace-related diseases/traumas, medical malpractice, air, water, and food contamination, or from having no health insurance.

Too many Democrats are cowering candidates. Speaker Nancy Pelosi told incumbent Democrats that they could criticize her if necessary to get elected and preserve their majority in the House. Since Republicans made a practice of assailing Pelosi in almost every debate or on every occasion, many Democrats did not rebut their Republican opponents. Some Democrats stated they would not vote for Pelosi as Speaker in 2012. Unrebutted political attacks often influence voters who wonder at mixed messages from members of a Party.

A key Democratic failure was not to keep on Howard Dean as Chairman of the Democratic National Committee. Between 2005 and 2009, Dr. Dean, with his fifty state strategy, energized both the DNC and state Democratic Committees. He knew what it took to go on the offensive against Republicans. He produced victories in 2006 and 2008 before his bête noire, Obama's Rahm Emmanuel, pushed him out.

Dr. Dean would have challenged the Tea Party and slowed its momentum. When the Democrats saw this self-styled conservative/libertarian rebellion receive the first of its vast mass media coverage (especially by Fox News and Fox Cable) in August 2009, when Tea Partiers loudly showed up at town meetings of incumbent Congresspersons, there should have been a Democratic response. A "Coffee Party" of progressives and deprived workers rebelling against the corporate control, that 75 percent of Americans believe is excessive, might have caught on.

Instead, the Tea Partiers, in all their disparate strands and wealthy right-wingers trying to take them over, became the daily feature and news of the 2010 campaign year.

Obama came out of his 2008 victory with 13 million names of donors and supporters, along with great enthusiasm from young voters. The Democrats squandered this support. This astonishing blunder happened, in no small part, because Obama turned his back on his supporters and denied their leaders White House access that he so often afforded corporate CEOs—e.g., the health insurance giants, drug companies, and banking behemoths. That's one reason so many of his 2008 supporters stayed home in 2010 and did not vote. They felt betrayed.

With twenty-three Democratic senators up in 2012, as compared with ten Republican senators, the Democrats may lose both Houses of Congress. Voters shouldn't only have the barren choice of voting for the least worst of the two parties. Here we go again. Or as F. Scott Fitzgerald wrote: "So we beat on, boats against the current, borne back ceaselessly into the past."

Why Say Yes to the Party of No?

September 24, 2010

How does the Big Business-indentured Republican Party get away with expectations of a runaway election victory this November? If such a victory should occur in Congress and in many governorships and state legislatures, it will be due to a ten percent or less shift in voters who voted Democratic in 2008 and are expected to vote Republican this year or will stay home in despair or disgust. The rest of the voters who do vote will still stay with their hereditary Republican or Democratic candidates.

So what is accounting for a possible ten percent shift? Let's briefly review some of the Congressional Republicans' voiced positions.

1. They don't want to do anything about unfair Chinese trade practices that lure jobs away from our country through huge factory subsidies where workers are repressed and counterfeit products abound. Imagine, Republicans coddling a communist regime, luring the auto parts, electronic, solar and drug ingredients industries away from America, often in violation of the World Trade Organization rules. And, in turn, China is exporting to the US impure food, faulty tires, toxic drywall, lead-tainted toys and medicines which are contaminated, defective or harmful. And, don't forget the dumping violations.

2. Republicans, led by Senator Richard Shelby and his banking friends, declared their adamant opposition to Professor Elizabeth Warren becoming head of the new consumer financial regulation agency (to avoid a confrontation with them, President Obama made her a special assistant to organize this consumer watchdog). Ms. Warren has a solid record of exposing and communicating clearly to families the tricks and traps of credit card companies, mortgage firms, and intermediaries that have taken so many billions of consumer dollars with impunity.

3. The Republicans, led by their House leader John Boehner (R-Ohio), a total toady of the gouging student loan companies, opposed the Democrats successful reform of this taxpayer boondoggle that guaranteed obscene profits and had the taxpayers absorb any student defaults. Boehner's lobbying should upset millions of parents who had to foot the bill for so many years.

4. The Republicans are opposed to raising the federal minimum wage to what it was, adjusted for inflation, in 1968! They opposed an adequate budget for health and safety enforcement by OSHA to diminish the 58,000 Ameri-

382 Told You So

can workers who die every year from workplace toxics and trauma. They are now even blocking protections for coal miners pending in the Senate after the Massey mine disaster.

5. Republicans oppose doing anything about "too big to fail" even after Wall Street's reckless, avaricious collapse of the economy, costing 8 million jobs and trillions of lost pension and mutual fund dollars.

Moreover, they do not support genuine enforcement of the anti-trust laws which are supposed to break up monopolization efforts, monopolies or oligopolies like Monsanto (seeds) or the big five banks—bailed out by taxpayers and secure in their domination of well over 50 percent of all bank assets, deposits and the credit card business. This is by far the highest concentration of financial power in modern US history. With few exceptions, the GOP want very few federal cops on the corporate crime beat.

6. Fighting for the last billionaire and multimillionaire, Republicans are blocking ending Bush's tax cuts on incomes beyond $250,000 per year. Yes, Republicans want to reduce the deficit yet they want to end revenues of over 700 billion dollars over ten years of restored super-rich taxes. They are blocking the renewal of the estate taxes after their expiration on December 31, 2009. (Over 99 percent of estates were already exempt from the federal estate tax.)

7. Republicans supported the health insurance industry's blaming the federal government, no less, for this month's latest sharp hike in insurance premiums by Aetna and others largely on the policies of individuals and small business. The Republicans did this after blocking the "public option" that would have given consumers both a choice and the benefit of some competition to the big insurance firms.

8. Have the Congressional Republicans ever challenged the bloated, wasteful, contractor-corrupt military budget that makes up half of the entire government's discretionary budget?

Even Congress's own auditing agency—the Government Accountability Office (GAO) declares the Pentagon budget unauditable. Many Pentagon audits document the abuses of Halliburton, KBR, Blackwater, and other firms in the deficit-driving, bloody Iraq and Afghanistan wars (both Republican espoused). The Pentagon's burgeoning budget, now nearing $800 billion a year, is deemed untouchable. (A few Republicans, like Senators Charles Grassley and John McCain sometimes object to contracting abuses.)

9. President Obama says he wants a counter-recessionary public works program renovating airports, bridges, highways, rail, and mass transit, drinking water and sewage treatment facilities and other infrastructures. Republicans sneer at this local job creation for much needed facilities.

10. Unlike any Republican Party since its creation in 1854, it has misused the filibuster threat, and any one of its Senators misuse the rules and block measures even going to a floor discussion or a nomination vote. The party is earning its moniker as the Party of NO. Republicans have turned the US Senate into America's graveyard.

There is much more, but enough has been cited to ask again—how are Republicans seen by the polls as front runners in the upcoming election?

The answer my friends, is not in the stars. The answer is in the clueless, gutless and spineless Democrats, busily dialing for the same corporate campaign dollars.

The other answer is in the ten percent of the actual voters who need to seriously avail themselves of the facts and a modicum of thought.

For if they don't, they will continue to pay bills handed to them and their children by their ruling corporatists in Republican clothing.

Democrats' Corporate Cocoon
September 10, 2010

It is astonishing how many Democrats in the past three months have been discussing the worst case scenario for their prospects in the November mid-term congressional elections. Do they believe that the most craven Republican Party in history needs their help in such a self-fulfilling prophecy?

The arguments that the Democratic pundits, along with some elected lawmakers, are giving focus on the recessionary economy and the "natural giveback" to the Republicans of the hitherto safe seats that they lost to the Democrats in 2008.

The mass media-exaggerated aura of the Tea Party, pumped by Limbaugh, Hannity and the histrionic Glenn Beck, has put the Democrats in a defensive posture. It is giving the puzzled Republicans an offensive image. I say puzzled because they can't figure out the many disparate strands of the Tea Party eruption which includes turning on the Republicans and George W. Bush for launching this epidemic of deficits, debt, bailouts and unconstitutional military adventures.

Being on the defensive politically becomes a nightmarish self-replicating wave among that 10 percent slice of swing voters who can make the difference between a big win or a big loss. These are also the non-hereditary party voters whose philosophy is to "throw the bums out" again and again until they get the message.

Gallup's most recent poll predicted the Republicans taking the House of Representatives.

While political scientist, Larry Sabato, with a 98 percent predictive accuracy in congressional races over ten years, sees the House gone and the Senate as a toss-up. But it is still early.

The Democratic Party's problems are much deeper than the Sunday talk shows indicate. First the Democrats do not have a progressive political philosophy. They could learn from a four-time winner—Franklin Delano Roosevelt—when it comes to being perceived as the friend of working families.

One has only to listen to the debates on C-SPAN between Democrats and Republicans running for Congress or the governorships. Too often, apart from a Libertarian or Green in the mix, there are very few bright lines or contrasts between the Republicans and Democrats however much they try to magnify personal differences. Indeed, the freshman Blue Dog Democrats, who won in 2008, go out of their way to criticize their own congressional leaders and President Obama, with the full encouragement of the national Democratic Leaders. The latter stayed away from the hustings during the long congressional recess. The Democrats lost August to the Republicans and the right-wing radio and cable yahoos who speak of the stimulus, the healthcare law and the proposed restoration of Bush's tax cuts for the wealthy as "job-killing agendas" and a disaster "for families and small businesses." Such Republican false statements fill the congressional record.

What keeps the Democrats from making their case? Is it their desire to keep raising big money from big business at the cost of muzzling a far more effective political message than their post-Labor Day offerings of more small business tax cuts and a ten year $100 billion tax credit for corporate research and development?

Do they believe those two actions are vote-getters or balm for getting more campaign money from business? Indeed, the tax credit mainly goes to super-profitable computer companies (Cisco, Intel, Microsoft) and big drug companies that already have outsourced their production to China and India.

And small business, which is receiving eight tax cuts under Obama, is waiting for consumer spending to increase. President Obama should fulfill his campaign pledge in 2008 to raise the federal minimum wage to $9.50 per hour by 2011, which would increase that buying power. Even that increase, while worthwhile, still wouldn't equal the minimum wage of 1968, adjusted for inflation.

The Democrats might listen to some of the articulate callers to C-SPAN radio or WPFW in Washington, DC to catch the powerful vernacular of protest. One caller succinctly made the case for policies, including using the tax code, to encourage companies to bring back industry and outsourced jobs that were shipped to China and other repressive or low-wage countries. With Washington's help, no less.

People are really upset about where corporate globalization, one-sided trade treaties, and costly foreign wars have taken our country. Working Americans who have lost their jobs can stay at home in November and cost the Democrats elections as they did in 2004. Voters look for politicians who take a stand, who know who they are and can show they side with the people, not global companies that have no allegiance to the country that bred, subsidized and defended them.

How did Reagan, even as a big business apologist, hold the fifty-four GOP Senate seats and only lose twenty-six House seats in the midterm election of 1982? Reagan was, in the words of Jim Kessler, "facing 10.8 percent unemployment, 6 percent inflation, a declining GDP, an approval rating barely above freezing and the indignity of having drastically increased the budget deficit over the previous year after running as a fiscal hawk." Maybe it is because enough voters saw the "Gipper" as knowing what he stood for and showing steadfastness and better times coming soon, in comparison to the wavering, concessionary posture of the then-majority Democrats in the Congress.

California Enshrines the Duopoly

July 23, 2010

Last month, Big Business interests shamelessly dealt our already depleted democracy a devastating blow by misleading California voters into approving Proposition 14, without opponents to the measure being able to reach the people with rebuttals. This voter initiative provides that the November elections in that state for members of Congress and state elective offices are reserved only for the top two vote-garnering candidates in the June primary.

There are no longer any party primaries per se, only one open primary where voters can vote for any candidate on the ballot for any office. Presidential candidates are still under the old system that allows all candidates who win their primary to go to the November general elections.

Since the two major parties are the wealthiest and have the power of incumbency and favored rules, the "top two" as this "deform" is called, will either be a Republican and a Democrat or, in gerrymandered districts, two Republicans or two Democrats.

Goodbye to voter choices for smaller third party and independent candidates on the ballot in November who otherwise would qualify, with adequate signature petitions, for the ballot. Goodbye to new ideas, different agendas, candidates and campaign practices. The two-party tyranny is now entrenched in California to serve the barons of big business who outspent their opponents twenty to one for TV and radio ads and other publicity.

To seal this voter incarceration by the two-party duopoly, Proposition 14 decreed that even write-in votes in November by contrarian citizens could no longer be counted.

The Democratic and Republican Parties nominally opposed it, devoting very little money or staff to show their seriousness. Their principal complaint is that the proposition opens a larger door for known celebrities to jump into the race and disrupt the parties' command-and-control systems.

The prior public debate over Proposition 14, for those who noticed the measure, was strange. First, the *Ballot Book*, sent to voters, misled voters by describing the initiative as one that "Increases Right to Participate in Primary Elections." In fact, it wipes out all other candidates on other lines but the top two vote-getters to get to November, thereby decreasing the right to participate in the general election.

Second, many of the state's largest newspapers, except for the conservative *Orange County Register*, editorially endorsed Proposition 14, saying it would reduce "partisan bickering."

As detailed in *Ballot Access News*, Richard Winger, the *San Jose Mercury News* claimed the measure would not harm minor party candidates. Their one example of a Green Party legislator was erroneous. The *Monterey County Herald* inaccurately claimed the League of Women Voters had endorsed the initiative. The *Sacramento Bee*, supported it, saying that the Green

Party could well place first or second in San Francisco. The Greens never placed first or second in blanket primary years, according to the super-accurate Mr. Winger.

Indeed, the smaller Parties all opposed Proposition 14. These included the Peace & Freedom Party, the Libertarian Party, and the Green Party. The energetic ballot-access group Free & Equal developed the leading web page (freeandequal.org) against the measure, and along with Californians for Electoral Reform used their tiny budgets to organize lightly covered press conferences to inform the public.

The final vote was 53.7 percent for and 46.3 percent against. The pro side advertisements, distorted as they were, reached millions more voters than did the penurious opposition.

Curiously, if the by-mail voters were taken out of the equation, more voters who went to the polls on Election Day voted against Prop 14 (52 percent) than for it (48 percent). Winger suggests this difference may reflect the fact that Election Day voters benefited from a more public discussion of the Proposition 14, including its negatives, in the two weeks before Election Day.

Supporters of a "top two" scheme want to spread it throughout the country, with Michigan as the next stop. Already, Washington state enacted "top two" for the 2008 election. Predictably, it resulted in a "Democratic-Republican monopoly on the ballot [in November] for all congressional and all statewide state offices," reports Winger.

The Washington state law is being challenged in the courts. Opponents of Proposition 14 assert they too will file a lawsuit challenging this censorious law, on constitutional grounds, in the federal courts.

The constant squeeze plays keep tightening on the peoples' democratic procedures to have a voice; to participate, challenge, and dissent.

Ballot access obstacles are not enough for the monetized minds of corporations. Better, they say, to abolish election day altogether for minor parties and independent candidates.

What's next for the corporate supremacists, who misled and lied to the people to get their vote for Prop 14? When will the people awake and repeal it?

Washington: Theater of the Absurd

June 18, 2010

The festering corporate government in Washington, DC, is a theater of the absurd. Some of the acts of this tragedy follow:

1. Start with the often hapless Center for Medicare and Medicaid Services (CMS), the agency that administers Medicare. Medicare pays $1,593 per injection of Lucentis for wet age-related macular degeneration as well as $42 per dose for Avastin, a drug that has a similar molecular structure, used by ophthalmologists.

Both drugs are made by Genentech. Lucentis is FDA approved for the vision problem and the other, Avastin, is approved to treat cancer. Doctors can also use Avastin for vision treatment. A study by three officials of CMS and Dr. Philip Rosenfeld, a retina specialist at the University of Miami, reported that for Medicare patients 60 percent of eye injections were Avastin, while 40 percent used Lucentis. Note this: Medicare paid $537 million for Lucentis in 2008 and only $20 million for Avastin!

2. Saving about half a billion a year by using Avastin is small potatoes to another CMS shortcoming. For fiscal year 2010, *CMS paid $65 billion in erroneous payments*—to deceased doctors, fraudsters, delinquent or imprisoned contractors and other suspended or debarred firms.

Organized fraud of Medicare is becoming more systemic. President Obama wants CMS to use a new fraud-detection program. Professor Malcolm Sparrow of Harvard University, the nation's leading expert on healthcare billing fraud, told them how to do this many years ago, but they were not listening.

The president wants to reduce throughout the government "payments in benefits, contracts, grants and loans to ineligible people or organizations," according to the *Washington Post*. Better trillions of dollars late over the decades than never!

3. Five oil company executives, including BP, admitted at a congressional hearing this week that they did not have contingency plans worked out for catastrophic failures. What is, by comparison, the worst case scenario for offshore windfarms or solar/thermal conservation, or passive solar architecture? Energy Secretary Stephen Chu still does not note such a criteria to differentiate between energy supply priorities.

4. President Obama now, belatedly, recognizes that the notorious oil industry patsy, the Minerals Management Service (MMS) in the Department of Interior, was a washout non-regulator of offshore drilling inherited from the Bush and Clinton Administrations. Well he also better take a hard look at the Federal Railroad Administration (FRA), the Office of Pipeline Safety (OPS), and the Nuclear Regulatory Commission (NRC), which are variously pleased with being captured by the very industries they are supposed to regulate. Too many agencies, in essence, allow the companies to "self-regulate"—an oxymoron.

Each of these agencies may wake up some day to witness a catastrophic hazardous materials disaster or meltdown that they should have prevented with stronger standards, inspection and law enforcement. Heed this caution, Mr. President!

5. Another $50 billion request by the White House just whisked through Congress for the brutal, spreading, futile war in Afghanistan—the historic graveyard of empires. Republicans loved to vote for this raid on the taxpayers.

But this week, a united Republican cabal, joined by Senators Joseph Lieberman (D-Conn.) and Ben Nelson (D-Neb.), blocked a $120 billion package (the threat of filibuster again) to extend unemployment benefits, preserve Medicare payments, extend tax credits for corporate research, raise taxes on oil companies, other big companies and investment partnerships. The bill also includes $24 billion to aid state governments in preventing thousands of state layoffs, including teachers.

The point here is not arbitrarily to decry Republican questioning of this domestic bill. It is to show how an overall ignorant, rubberstamping Congress is not heeding the lessons from Vietnam and Iraq—the immense casualties, the destruction and poisoning of these countries by detonations, and laying waste to the environment, and the imperialist policies that also harmed our country in so many tangible and intangible ways.

6. Dana Milbank, the *Washington Post* reporter-satirist, was at the House of Representatives' hearing this week where Congressman Joe Barton (R-Texas) apologized to BP's CEO, Tony Hayward, saying the White House's demand that BP set aside $20 billion for its huge toxic contamination to the Gulf coast and its people was "a shakedown." He added, for good supplicant measure, that he doesn't "want to live in a country" that treats a private corporation this way. He later apologized for his apology, at the behest of Republican House leaders.

The Barton outburst illustrates why it should be easy for the Democratic Party to landslide the Republicans in the 2010 Congressional elections. Probably the most craven version of the Republican Party ever, this team takes huge slurries of corporate money while blocking any safeguards for workers, consumers, small taxpayers, and the environment. They even defeated investor rights for shareholders, who own these companies, but whose bosses pay themselves obscenely to control them.

The Democrats have their hand out to the same commercial interests. But if they want to win, they'd better *formulate the language of standing with the people over big business by November*. And, if the Democrats don't want November to mark their curtain call, their language of standing with the people needs to be followed by action.

The Filibuster Flim Flam
March 16, 2010

The US Senate has become the graveyard of Congress! Dozens of bills passed by the Democratically-controlled House of Representatives—to improve the health, safety, and economic well-being of Americans—are locked up in the Senate month after month.

This was not always the case. In the sixties and seventies, legislation affecting consumers, workers and the environment often started in the Senate and was sent to the House in the hope that that body would not weaken or defeat these bills.

Committee chairs like Senators Warren Magnuson, Gaylord Nelson, and Walter Mondale would move legislation after great public hearings open to the citizenry. Auto safety, product safety, meat and poultry inspection, gas pipeline safety in the late sixties, followed by the sweeping air and water pollution control bills in the early seventies, were examples of senatorial initiatives.

Today, the Senate lies paralyzed even as it is controlled by fifty-nine Democrats—usually enough for comfortable passage of legislation sought by a majority party that also controls the presidency.

A combination of a few reactionary Democratic Senators, a unified pro-corporate Republican opposition, anti-democratic Senate rules and the decades-long weakening of citizen and trade union groups have combined to produce a constipated Senate.

The usually mild House Democratic Caucus Chairman, John Larson (CT) showed his irritation recently when he said that people are tired of the House passing legislation that stalls in the Senate.

Some of the bills passed by the House include the financial reform bill regarding Wall Street's abuses, the omnibus energy bill, a long overdue adjustment of Postal Service pension payments, vision care for children, a job security act for wounded veterans, a paycheck fairness bill, an elder abuse victims bill, a water use efficiency and conservation research bill, an act to prohibit the importation of certain low-level radioactive waste into the US, an imposition of additional taxes on executive bonuses awarded by financial companies under bailout salvation, a mortgage reform and anti-predatory lending bill, food safety legislation, stronger enforcement authority for the Securities and Exchange Commission (SEC), and a student aid and fiscal responsibility bill.

These are some of the 290 bills already passed in the House—many of them minor to be sure—that House Speaker, Nancy Pelosi (D-Calif.)

has noted. (See: http://thehill.com/homenews/senate/83057-290-bills.)

Granted the major House bills are not as strong as some citizen groups would like, which is why they try to get them strengthened in the Senate. Fat chance, as long as Rule 22—the notorious filibuster mechanism—exists, and as long as the Senators remain marinated in corporate campaign cash and prospective jobs for them or their relatives.

The filibuster is now virtual, unlike the traditional filibuster where its practitioners would have to go on the Senate floor for hours straining their bladders and the patience of the public.

Presently, all Minority Leader Senator Mitch McConnell (R-Ky.) has to do is merely notify Majority Leader, Senator Harry Reid (D-Nev.) of the intent to extend debate and, voila, a minority of forty-one Senators defeats the majority rule of fifty-nine Senators.

So Senator Reid bewails, "We had to file cloture some seventy times last year, seventy times. That's remarkably bad. Let's change that."

So why don't the Democrats "change that?" In 1975, Vice President Nelson Rockefeller, in his role as president of the Senate, ruled that fifty-one Senators could amend Senate rules. Senator Tom Udall has a resolution to do just that—predictably languishing in the Senate without even a hearing.

Moreover, Senator Tom Harkin proposed a resolution that would require a series of votes to cut off a filibuster. The first stage would need sixty votes, the second would need fifty-seven, then fifty-four and finally a simple majority over a period of weeks. That proposal is going nowhere.

Obviously, the Democrats could end the filibuster with a majority vote but choose not to because they may wish to use this tool of obstruction should they be in the minority some-day. In fact, Harry Reid has ruled out any fili-buster reform. Well then, why not end the "vir-tual" filibuster and make the Republicans hit the floor with round-the-clock debate televised around the nation. People are waiting and suf-fering from corporate-desired inaction.

Chicago lawyer and scholar, Thomas Geoghe-gan, wrote an open letter to Senator Reid (See: http://www.thenation.com/doc/20100222/geoghegan_editors) urging that he make the Re-publicans actually filibuster. Either make them stall the Senate on a minor bill to generate public ire or generate public outrage by making them filibuster a popular bill aimed at curbing corpo-rate crime, waste and abuse or one that would save people money or their health.

Still, no response, other than debilitating talk by the Democrats about seeking bi-partisan support for their bills.

Face it—the Senate is breaking an already broken Congress into little pieces which are then sold for a mess of pottage. People: organize Congress Watch Locals in every state, folks, for nobody will save you but yourselves!

Barney Frank and the Planet of the Banks

October 16, 2009

What planet is Congressman Barney Frank on, anyway? It is the planet of the banks and other financial firms that keep his campaign coffers humming, as their powerful chairman of the House Financial Services Committee.

On his extraterrestrial perch, camouflaged by his witty and irreverent observations, he sees the agony of gouged, debt-ridden consumers and homeowners, but his actions do not measure up.

As of this writing before the final set of hear-ings, Mr. Frank has dropped key provisions from a proposal to establish an independent Con-sumer Financial Protection Agency (CFPA).

The banks did not want a consumer right of action against companies violating standards for their mortgages, credit and debit cards, or pay-day and installment loans. Barney said sure!

In addition, the banks want a weak oversight panel consisting of their toady regulators, who failed repeatedly and miserably in the past de-cade to stave off the collapse of Wall Street and its economically lethal consequences for work-ers and consumers. Barney said sure!

The banks want their buddies in Congress to drop the standard of reasonableness by which the new consumer protection agency can go af-ter wildly gouging fees and deceptive practices, such as the check overdraft racket that rakes in $40 billion for the banks. Barney said sure, sure!

The American Bankers Association is crow-ing like a thousand roosters. The five biggest banks—now even bigger after the collapse, their taxpayer bailout and their acquisitions—are crowing the loudest.

And why not? They speculated with retire-ment and other savings of the American peo-ple. Trillions of dollars were drained from the accounts and looted from these innocents. Yet, the banks have every expectation that the *Glass-Stegall Act*—repealed by Clinton, Citigroup and the Congress in 1999—will not be reinstated to separate retail banking from investment bank-ing and block the conflicts of interest that rav-age investors.

The banks will still have their protective Federal Reserve which, though empowered by a 1994 law to crack down on predatory lend-ing, did nothing to stop the subprime mortgage rackets that submarined the housing economy.

Smelling a concessionary Barney Frank, other businesses want exemptions from the new consumer agency's authority, including auto dealers, realtors, merchants, retailers and other assorted players in the fine print game of financial services.

Possessed by the sneering arrogance of the corporate state, these big banks are still granting huge bonuses to their management and top bosses, while the taxpayers of America are subsidizing them and bailing them out. Their chosen Secretary of the Treasury, Timothy Geithner, conceded that the US government is now insuring not just the deposits of big banks but their capital as well.

Most stunning to Americans, right or left, who follow these big money boys is that they are developing more speculative derivative packages, loaded with luscious fees, such as securitized bets on life insurance policies. Does this remind you of the kind of financial wheeling and dealing that sank Wall Street and the economy last year?

Naturally, consumer groups like the National Community Reinvestment Coalition (fairlending.com) and the US Public Interest Research Groups (USPIRG) (uspirg.org) who have provided excellent testimony in recent months about what the exploited consumers and savers need at long last, are disappointed. But they and the Consumer Federation of America (consumerfed.org) are facing an overwhelming resource mismatch with the financial businesses. These businesses are deploying armies of lobbyists on Capitol Hill and hosting hundreds of campaign cash parties.

In an excellent article in the *New York Times*, regular columnist Joe Nocera asks the question—"Have the Banks No Shame?" He starts his reply by quoting Simon Johnson, a former economist with the International Monetary Fund: "They can't pay what they owe!" he began angrily. Then he paused, collected his thoughts and started over: "Tim Geithner saved them on terms extremely favorable to the banks . . . What gets me is that the banks have continued to oppose consumer protection. How can they be opposed to consumer protection as defined by a man who is the most favorable Treasury secretary they have had in a generation . . . It is unconscionable."

Well said, but not enough. As long as the top banking bosses get their huge bonuses and their mismanaged, corrupted banks get their taxpayer bailouts, because they are too big to fail, they will continue pushing their devastating greed with impunity.

The issue is not only shame. The issue is guilt and for that prosecution, conviction and incarceration are the remedies. That is the only prospect that sobers up the corporate crooks.

Adequate prosecution budgets, tougher corporate criminal laws and a government going for law and order—none of these are in any legislative proposals or in the hearts and minds of our Washington representatives.

So, sovereign citizens everywhere, if you don't organize to have the say, you'll continue to pay, pay and pay. Time to make apathy boring!

"Now Make Me Do It"
August 14, 2009

Never much of a fighter against abusive corporate power, Barack Obama is making it increasingly clear that right from his start as president, he wanted the kind of health insurance reform that receives the approval of the giant drug and health insurance industries.

Earlier this year he started inviting top bosses of these companies for intimate confabs in the White House. *Business Week* magazine, which proclaimed recently that "The Health Insurers Have Already Won" reported that the CEO of UnitedHealth, Stephen J. Hemsley, met with the president half a dozen times.

These are the vendors. They and their campaign slush funds cannot be ignored in the power struggle over the legislation percolating in the Congress. One public result of these meetings was that the drug industry promised $80 billion in savings over ten years and the health insurance moguls promised $150 billion over the same decade. Mr. Obama trumpeted these declarations without indicating how these savings would be guaranteed, how the drug companies could navigate the antitrust laws and what was given to the healthcare industry by the White House in return.

We have now learned that one Obama promise was to continue the prohibition on Uncle Sam from bargaining for volume discounts on drugs that you the taxpayer have been paying for in the drug benefit program enacted in 2003.

Unknown is whether the health insurance companies were also promised continuation of Medicare Advantage with its 14 percent added taxpayer subsidy to induce the elderly to make the move out of public Medicare. Also unknown is whether the Medicare public option that Mr. Obama formerly espoused but since has wavered on has been put on the concession table.

The whole secret process is seedy and demonstrates cruel disregard for the millions of American who, whether in dire need of medical services or not, voted in "change we can believe in."

By stark contrast, President Obama has never invited to the White House the leading consumer-patient champions in this country who favor full Medicare and free choice of physician and hospital—often called "a single-payer" system. Open to the corporate barons who have failed decade after decade to deliver what patients need, the White House door is closed to the likes of Dr. Quentin Young—a founder of the Physicians for a National Health Program and an old Chicago friend of Obama's, Dr. Sidney Wolfe, who heads Public Citizen's Health Research Group, Drs. Marcia Angell, Stephanie Woolhandler, and David Himmelstein, who are nationally known and accomplished single-payer advocates or Rose Ann DeMoro, executive director of the fast-growing California Nurses Association.

Mr. Obama even tried to exclude any advocate of a single-payer system—previously favored by Obama and still favored by a majority of the American people, doctors and nurses—from his roundtable meetings convened to receive the views of different constituencies.

"Make me do it" was the advice of Franklin Delano Roosevelt to reformers when faced with legislation he desired but did not have the votes for in Congress. Mr. Obama is not exerting that plea for people power. Were he to do that, he would be encouraging daily public hearings in the Senate and the House on the bureaucratic waste, greed, overbilling, collusion, and fraud that many in the corporate world have inflicted with their costly, pay or die healthcare marketeering.

Such publicized hearings would keep him on the offensive. It would arouse the public and focus energies on the main problem—the corporatization of medicine. This commercialism has left tens of millions of people without health insurance, caused 20,000 fatalities a year, and cost Americans twice or more per capita than have full Medicare systems in western countries, which have universal coverage and better health outcomes than the US.

Further indication of Obama's corporate dealings is that he never identified himself with a specific bill with a House and Senate number that he could rally the people around. No wonder people are confused, frustrated and angry. President Obama did not stand for an unambiguous proposal.

He thereby emboldened both the cash and carry Blue Dog Democrats to rebel and the Republican yahoos to launch their lies and distortions via Rush Limbaugh and similar trash media.

Obama is about to make his biggest mistake to date by favoring the bipartisan deal his assistants are working out with Blue Dog Senator Max Baucus and his Republican counterparts on the Senate Finance Committee. This proposal has no public option, no consumer protections or restraints on the mayhem and skyrocketing charges of the so-called healthcare industry.

Already the less corporate-indentured bills being reported from the House Committee by Rep. Henry Waxman (D-Calif.) and his allies are getting short-shrift from a White House that clearly views the forthcoming Baucus-Grassley "compromise" as the "more practical" go-to legislation.

There is reliable word that the AFL-CIO will endorse whatever Obama approves, with the exceptions of the California Nurses Association and the Sheet Metal Workers' union. The latter, through their president, Michael J. Sullivan, announced in late July that it was suspending all future campaign contributions to any candidate for Congress or the Presidency.

Already over sixty progressive members of the House, headed by Congresswoman Lynn Woolsey (D-Calif.) have declared opposition to these unacceptable compromises moving forward in both the House and the Senate.

So is gridlock around the corner? Will there be a health insurance reform of any stripe signed into law this year? It depends on the alliances that agree to block the lowest corporate denominators led by the unyielding principled stands of the progressives who want something that puts patients above the failed profiteering vendors.

The guess here is that Obama will sign anything which squirms through a cowardly Congress that cannot give the American people in 2009 the healthcare system Congress stopped President Harry Truman from establishing in 1950.

It is up to the people of our country to "make him do it" whether this year or next. A mere one million immediate calls to members of Congress by one million assertive citizens will start sobering up these legislators who think they can get away with another sale of our public trust.

The Congressional switchboard is 202-224-3121. The full Medicare, single-payer bill (backed by nearly ninety legislators) is H.R. 676. The go-to citizen group for your sustained engagement is singlepayeraction.org. The rest is up to you, the majority, who want to put the people first.

Ignoring Prophethic Predictors

July 2, 2009

I've wondered often why people who go to "town meetings" held by campaigning politicians rarely ask fundamental questions.

Here is one that should have been asked of presidential candidate Barack Obama: "If you get to the White House, will you appoint to top positions Americans who have a track record of making the right decisions in their respective fields?"

"Of course, I will," Obama would have undoubtedly replied.

Of course, he did not when it came to the collapse of the corrupt Wall Street casinos and the bailout of these gamblers by the American people. Obama chose the very Wall Streeters and Wall Street servants who were involved in, condoned, or profited from the speculative binges that led to the biggest government bailout scheme in world history.

The president's explanation is that he wants experienced people who know how Wall Street works. Yeah, right! In reality, he wanted political cover.

Something very important is missing when even people who are part of the ruling establishment are ignored, marginalized, or ridiculed even though their detailed, public warnings prove to be all too accurate.

Consider billionaire, Ross Perot. Back in the 1980s and 1990s, Ross, as everyone calls him, was right on General Motors, right on NAFTA trade, and right on the federal deficits.

In 1984, he joined the Board of Directors of GM after selling his successful company, EDS, to the auto giant. He could scarcely believe how stodgy, bureaucratic, and insensitive GM executives were in running the company. He tried to shake up the boys at the top to meet the fast-growing competition from Asia and Europe.

The GM brass couldn't stand Ross "at large" probing up and down the company, so in 1986 they bought out his shares in return for him leaving the Board.

Two years later, reflecting on his experience at GM with a reporter from Fortune, Perot called the "General Motors system a blanket of fog that keeps people from doing what they know needs to be done."

Warming up, Perot continued: "One day I made a speech to some senior executives. I said, 'Okay, guys, I'm going to give you the whole code on what's wrong. You don't like your customers. You don't like your dealers. You don't like the people who make your cars. You don't like your stockholders. And, to a large extent, you don't like one another. For this company to win, we're going to have to love our customers. We're going to have to stop fretting about dealers who make too much money and hope they make $1 billion a year though us. The guys on the factory floor are the salt of the earth—not mad-dog, rabid, burn-the-plant-down radicals. And all this sniping at one another—the financial guys vs. the cars guys—is terribly destructive.'"

GM didn't listen to Ross. Now, after a long, relentless slide, GM is bankrupt, abandoning their workers, two thousand of their dealers, and their customers' grievances, including insured victims of its defective cars. Moreover, GM is into the US taxpayers for over $70 billion.

Perot devoted much of his 1993 published book *Save Your Job, Save Our Country* to NAFTA and trade. Looking back, he was right most of the time. NAFTA cost more US jobs than it created, generated a huge US trade deficit with Mexico, and mainly benefited the "36 businessmen who own Mexico's 39 largest conglomerates or over half of Mexico's Gross National Product."

The border-located maquiladora factories have high worker turnover and squeeze the laborers in often unsafe conditions for little pay.

Here is how Perot described the scene behind the boasting of Washington, DC, and corporations about the large increase in trade after NAFTA:

Most of the goods produced in the maquiladoras are shipped into the US market. Consequently, most of the so-called trade between the US and Mexico is not trade as trade is commonly understood. Rather, it is primarily US companies shipping their own machinery, components, and raw materials across the border into their Mexican factories and then shipping their finished or semi-finished goods back over the border into the US.

A good deal of the US auto industry went south after NAFTA, leaving workers and communities stranded in Michigan and other states. Bankrupt Chrysler is planning to move a modern, award-winning engine plant in Wisconsin to Mexico after receiving billions of dollars in taxpayer bailouts.

On Perot's nationally-televised deficit warnings (with charts), what more need be said? Even he did not envision what would pile up after his clarion calls. The burden on the next generation and the tax dollars diverted from our country's needs to pay the interest on these trillions of dollars of debt were pointed out again and again nearly twenty years ago by the Texas entrepreneur. He even has a website (perotcharts.com) updating the red ink.

In Bush's and Obama's Washington, there is no room for Perot to gain visibility and recognition.

It is one thing for the Washington politicians to ignore prescient progressive commentators, like William Grieder, who have been prophetically right on. It is quite another escape from reality to turn their backs on leaders within the business establishment itself.

There are many like Perot who must be watching the day's news and saying "we told you so, but you didn't listen then and you are not listening now."

Financial Reform, Words and Deeds

June 26, 2009

It's good that Barack Obama is an agile basketball player because on financial regulatory reform he's having to straddle an ever widening chasm between his words and his deeds.

Obama said: "Millions of Americans who have worked hard and behaved responsibly have seen their life dreams eroded by the irresponsibility of others and by the failure of their government to provide adequate oversight. Our entire economy has been undermined by that failure."

"Over the past two decades, we have seen, time and again, cycles of precipitous booms and busts. In each case, millions of people have had their lives profoundly disrupted by developments in the financial system, most severely in our recent crisis."

Strong words, even though he didn't include "corporate crime, fraud and abuse" to replace the euphemism "irresponsibility." One would think that his 88 page reform proposal to Congress would be up to his words. Instead he provides Washington aspirins for Wall Street brain cancer.

The anemic nature of these reforms ostensibly designed to prevent or deter another big bust on Wall Street and its hostage grip on the nation's savings and investments immediately drew the ire of well-regarded business columnists.

Joe Nocera of the *New York Times* wrote "the Obama plan is little more than an attempt to stick some new regulatory fingers into a very leaky financial dam rather than rebuild the dam itself." Nocera asserts that the reforms do not "attempt to diminish the use" of the customized type of derivatives which trillions of risky dollars generated "enormous damage to the financial system" ala A.I.G's collapse. He notes President Roosevelt's far more fundamental reforms, including the Glass-Steagall Act, which "separated banking from investment." It prevented a lot of banking mischief until Clinton, his Treasury Secretary Robert Rubin and Citigroup got Glass-Steagall repealed in 1999. Obama is not proposing to re-instate this critical safeguard. Nocera said firms "will have to put up a little more capital, and deal with a little more oversight, but. . . . in all likelihood, [it will] be back to business as usual."

Star business reporter, Gretchen Morgenson, ripped into the Obama plan in the *Sunday New York Times* for doing too little to eliminate systemic risks posed by financial firms that are "too big to fail." She writes, "Rather than propose ways to shrink these companies and the risks they pose, the Geithner plan argues instead for enhanced regulatory oversight of the behemoths." She implies that taxpayers will be on the hook for even greater bailouts in the future.

A measure to prevent the "too big to fail" bailouts was suggested by none other than Obama's current economic advisor, former Federal Reserve Chairman, Paul Volcker. Speaking in China, no less, Volcker recently said the Federal government could simply prevent these big banks from trading for their own accounts. But Obama is not listening to Volcker these days. Instead Treasury Secretary Timothy Geithner and White House advisor, Larry Summers, who played important roles in the past decade facilitating the enormous speculation on Wall Street, have got Obama's ear.

The president's plan omits (1) strong anti-trust enforcement, (2) tough corporate crime prosecution, and (3) more authority for shareholders, who own their companies, to control their hired bosses. The plan should have included giving shareholders the decisive power to set executive compensation—the perverse compensation incentives that Warren Buffet believes helped push companies to wild speculation.

The reform plan's defaults go on and on. There are no mechanisms to encourage millions of investors to voluntarily band together in Financial Consumer Associations. In 1985 then Congressman Chuck Schumer (D–N.Y.) introduced such an amendment to the savings and loans bailout legislation. It did not pass.

What about sub-prime mortgage securities? Banks would be required to retain just a five percent stake before handing them off to other syndicates. This is hardly enough to induce prudence by banks selling these mortgages to impecunious home buyers.

Obama does propose a new financial consumer regulatory agency. But unless he appoints someone as chair, like tough-minded Harvard Law Professor, Elizabeth Warren, who advanced the idea, the regulated financial firms will, as usual, take over the agency.

The *Washington Post's* Steven Pearlstein, derided the Obama proposals for not being "grounded, first and foremost, in a thorough and independent analysis of how the crisis was allowed to develop and what regulators did and didn't do to prevent it. . . ." He was disappointed by the lack of controls over "hedge funds, private-equity funds or structured investment vehicles."

Obama did strengthen the fiduciary duties to investors by stock brokers. But he did not give these defrauded investors any better civil action rights in court beyond what they were left with by the hand-tying securities law passed in 1995.

So now it is up to Congress and its hordes of banking and insurance lobbyists. Good luck, savers and investors. Unless, that is, you're doing your business with credit union cooperatives which don't gamble with your money.

Blundering Into Bankruptcy
May 29, 2009

Dear President Obama and GM Chairman Henderson,

The hour is late. You seem bent on an orchestrated bankruptcy for General Motors on June 1, 2009. Before any irreversible moves are made—the GM/task force reorganization plan should be submitted to Congress for deliberative review and decision. There are several major concerns with a precipitous bankruptcy declaration that have emerged over the last several days.

First, the previously understood rationale for bankruptcy—namely obstinate bondholders—no longer applies. Recent developments indicate that GM and the auto task force have revised the proposed allocation of equity in a restructured GM, and reached agreement with at least the most prominent bondholders. Although a June 1 bond payment is due, it certainly seems that that payment could easily be wrapped into the new bondholder offer, as effectively will be the case if GM enters bankruptcy.

With the bondholder problem moving toward resolution, or at least now clearly resolvable, there is no evident rationale for bankruptcy other than an unstoppable momentum of some hidden agendas. Given the high stakes, including job losses, communities devastated, the effects on consumer confidence in the GM brand and the socio-economic impacts of potentially excessive downsizing, this is a last chance to avoid the tyranny against the weak that is a Chapter 11 bankruptcy court.

Second, the matter of how GM's holdings in China will be treated in bankruptcy continues to demand attention before any filing. Kevin Wale, president and managing director of GM China, told CNN that "Our business is run as separate joint-ventures here in China in partnership with SAIC . . . so we're profitable, we fund our own investment and we would be largely independent of any action that took place in the US." Yet the GM assets and profits in China must be included in any bankruptcy proceeding, and available to creditors, claimants and litigants who could, conceivably, petition to take the company into Chapter 7 liquidation.

Has GM clearly presented to the government its valuable holdings, large profits and contractual obligations in China as part of its assets in any bankruptcy? The task force has indicated some uncertainty about these questions.

Third, proceedings in the Chrysler bankruptcy have highlighted the manifold injustice being perpetrated on victims of defective Chrysler products—and likely also to be perpetrated on victims of GM products. In the Chrysler proceeding, top Chrysler officials have acknowledged that they were ready and able to do a deal with Fiat that established successor liability for the emergent Fiat "good Chrysler" company. In the course of bankruptcy or in preparing for bankruptcy, however, they reversed course, apparently just because they could. Now, hundreds of Chrysler victims are on track to have their claims extinguished unless the bankruptcy judge or other court overrules this element of the bankruptcy plan.

There are many differences between the bankruptcy of the private company, Chrysler and the pending GM bankruptcy, but the GM restructuring plan is similar to Chrysler in the anticipated creation of a bad/old GM and a good/new GM that emerges without liabilities. Does the government as the major owner of GM plan to follow the Chrysler approach? Has President Obama and his Task Force given consideration to the suffering of real adults and children that will follow from such a move?

Not to mention the political backlash.

One such real person is Amanda Dinnigan, a 10-year-old girl from Long Island, New York. Amanda was injured by an allegedly faulty seatbelt in a GMC Envoy that snapped her neck in a crash. Her father, an ironworker, estimates her healthcare costs at $500,000 a year. Her lost quality of life will obviously be tragic. Will a discretionary decision not to establish successorship liability in a discretionary (voluntary) bankruptcy leave Amanda and her family—and thousands of others like them stranded with no access to justice?

If the Obama officials intend to proceed with maneuvers that effectively extinguish their claims, they should at least talk to some of them first, and confront the human consequences of such actions.

The GM/task force bankruptcy plans appear geared to saving the General Motors entity—but at a harsh and often avoidable cost to laid-off workers, communities, suppliers, consumers, dealers, and the nation's auto manufacturing capacity which might move faster, post-bankruptcy, to China.

At this late stage we again urge President Obama to reconsider the bankruptcy filing plans, and to enable deliberative and meaningful Congressional review—as many Members of Congress are seeking—of the restructuring plans before irreversible steps are taken.

After all, Congress is more than a potted plant. The "first branch" legislated, after public hearings, the 1979 Chrysler bailout and the complex Conrail restructuring a few years later.

Where's My Change?

April 24, 2009

"No more fine print; no more confusing terms and conditions." This is what Barack Obama told a White House gathering of leading credit card issuers this week.

Right afterward, President Obama told the press that "there has to be strong and reliable protections for consumers, protections that ban unfair rate increases and forbid abusive fees and penalties."

This soaring rhetoric places a heavy burden on Mr. Obama to stand up to the giant power of the credit card bosses and their monetized allies on Capitol Hill. Yet he has shown little interest in re-instating a presidential consumer advisor compared to Lyndon Johnson appointing the formidable Betty Furness or Jimmy Carter bringing on the legendary Esther Peterson.

Deep recession times are tough for the nation's over 200 million consumers. Still there is no consumer voice in the White House, though consumer groups asked Mr. Obama to move promptly on this tiny advocacy office months ago.

The corporate chieftains have easy access to the White House and the new president, whether these bosses come on missions demanding power or missions of beggary for bailouts. When will he meet with the leading heads of consumer protection groups with millions of dues-paying members who could give him the base to hold accountable and regulate the democracy-denying, economy-wrecking corporate supremacists?

"Where's the Backbone?" asked Ruth Marcus, the usually-restrained lawyer-columnist for the *Washington Post*. On April 15, 2009 she wrote: "When will President Obama fight, and when will he fold? That's not entirely clear—and I'm beginning to worry that there may be a little too much presidential inclination to crumple." Ms. Marcus asserts that "for all the chest-thumping about making hard choices and taking on entrenched interests, there has been disturbingly little evidence of the new president's willingness to do that." This is the case even with his allies in Congress, never mind his adversaries.

Just four days later, the *New York Times* weighed in with a page one news article that said President Obama "is well known for bold proposals that have raised expectations, but his administration has shown a tendency for compromise and caution, and even a willingness to capitulate on some early initiatives. . . . His early willingness to deal or fold has left commentators, and some loyal Democrats, wondering: 'Where's the fight?'" Like the *Post*, the *Times* gave examples.

It is not as if Mr. Obama is lacking in public opinion support. Overall he has a 65 percent approval rating. People know he inherited a terrible situation here and abroad from the Bush regime and they want action. Large majorities believe America is declining, that there is too much corporate control over their lives, and that the two parties have been failing the American people.

But the president's personality is not one to challenge concentrated power. A Zogby poll reports that only six percent of the public supports the financial bailouts for Wall Street. The vast majority of people do not think the bailouts are fair.

The upcoming 100 day mark for the Obama administration is a customary time for evaluations by the politicos, the pundits, and the civic community. While his supporters can point to the pay-equity law for women, more health insurance for poor children, and a $787 billion economic stimulus enactment, the general appraisal by the liberal-progressive intelligentsia is decidedly mixed and gentle with undiluted hope.

Mr. Obama nourishes these mixed feelings. He showed some courage when he agreed, as part of an ongoing court case, to release the four torture memos written by Bush's Justice Department. Graphic photos of prisoner treatment in Iraq and Afghanistan are to be released next week. Yet Obama came out against a Truth Commission regarding the alleged crimes of the Bush regime and said he would "look forward and not look back." For Obama that means immunity for anyone from the Bush Administration who may have violated the criminal laws of the land.

It is remarkable to read those oft-repeated words by lawyer Obama. Law enforcement is about looking back into the past. Investigation and prosecution obviously deals with crimes that have already occurred. That's the constitutional duty of the president.

After 100 days it is far too early to render many judgments about Obama. One can, however, evaluate his major appointments—heavily Clintonite and corporate. One can also look at what he hasn't gotten underway at all—such as labor law reform, a living wage, and citizen empowerment.

Next Monday, the Institute for Policy Studies (www.ips-dc.org) releases a detailed report card on Obama's first 100 days titled "Thirsting for a Change." While the *Nation* magazine held a panel discussion on April 22 in Washington, DC, the panelists largely gave Obama the benefit of the doubt so far, and declared that only grassroots mobilizing will move him forward on such matters as "single-payer" healthcare, corporate abuse, and the demilitarization of our foreign policy and our federal budget.

Panelist William Grieder coined the phrase "independent formulations" to describe the citizen action needed.

It is important to note that a transforming president has to ask for and encourage this pressure from the citizenry, much as Franklin Delano Roosevelt did in the 1930s.

Bailout Indignation
April 17, 2009

How about a test of your injustice barometer?

You might think that the reckless, avaricious, giant corporations, having shrunk the economy, cost millions of jobs and then demanded that taxpayers be dunned for years into the future for multi-trillion dollar bailouts, would show contrition, regret, or self-restraint of their power over Washington.

Forget it. They're baaack! Their greed and power are revving up big time to bring Washington and you the taxpayer, you the parent, you the consumer, you the worker, to your knees.

Here is a sample of the appalling dynamics of corporate greed and continuing over-reach each day in your nation's capital.

1. Just when people thought the taxpayer-subsidized corporate student loan racket was ended by the Democrats, its cohorts and lobbyists, like Jamie S. Gorelick of FannieMae notoriety, are descending on Congress. The non-partisan Congressional Budget Office concluded that replacing these subsidized loans with direct Department of Education lending will save $94 billion over the next ten years.

It is long overdue to end this gouging, college-payola-giving, obscenely overcompensated industry, and give students an efficient and reasonable lending system. Still, Sallie Mae, Citigroup, Bank of America and others are swarming over Congress to retain a big piece of the action. "Why do we even need private lenders?" correctly asks Congressman Timothy H. Bishop, a former provost of Southampton College.

2. ABC News reports that banks are hiking already high credit card rates and other bank-related fees: "The Banks have been given billions of dollars of tax money and only lend it out if customers are willing to pay extortion rights," said Tony Cesnik, a Concord, California, resident. Cesnik adds: "The banks need a legal spanking. They are acting like spoiled brats!" Elizabeth Warren, Harvard law professor and chair of the Congressional Oversight Panel agrees: "We're asking taxpayers to pay twice."

3. The big oil and gas companies are saturating the airwaves with ads warning about the Obama Administration's alleged desire to tax them $400 billion. This will cost jobs and reduce the discovery of more oil and gas, they say. Where is this $400 billion figure from? Obama's ambition is not much beyond repealing the tax breaks George W. Bush gave his oily friends for drilling in the Gulf of Mexico when oil was selling at less than $40 per barrel. Some of the oil industry's own spokespersons admitted last year that their argument doesn't hold water any more with such high oil prices and profits since then.

So what are the big oil corporations like Exxon doing with their excess profits that totaled a record $45 billion just for Exxon last year? They're not even drilling on two-thirds of the acreage they have rights to explore. Instead Exxon is spending $35 billion to buy back its stock and hold in cash. When the next oil shock comes, Exxon will demand more tax breaks and other dispensations to fund its drilling. We've seen that game played out before at the gas pump.

4. Now comes *Newsweek*'s Michael Hirsh to report a private meeting recently between six senators and Obama in the White House where the president heard complaints that his proposed regulatory reforms were too weak and were being devised by his appointed officials who were part of the problem in Wall Street. Well, are you surprised that a new powerful lobby created by the likes of Citigroup, JPMorgan, and Goldman Sachs is gearing up to stop adequate regulation of "over the counter" derivatives, to keep these transactions secret, and to continue to permit what Hirsh called the "systemic risk that led to the crash"? This brazen move by the incorrigible banks is underway after they received huge bailout money from Washington. Beware they may yet demand and receive another big bundle.

5. With workers losing millions of jobs, the US Chamber of Commerce, the National Association of Manufacturers, and virtually the entire business juggernaut are amassing tens of millions of dollars to stop the union-facilitating "card-check" legislation and any effort to bring the federal minimum wage up to what is was back in 1968, no less, adjusted for inflation. It is now about three dollars short of that modest goal for hard-pressed laborers, many without health insurance.

6. And oh, how these company bosses are fighting to keep their big bonuses going as a reward for tanking many of their own companies. Call it hubris, arrogance, disdain for the common decencies of the American people, it all reflects too much corporate power over our lives—a judgment over 75 percent of Americans share.

All this lobbying of Congress and the White House year after year pays off. A study by three Kansas University professors found that a single tax break in 2004 earned drug, manufacturing, and other companies $220 for every dollar they spent on their cash register politicking. Presently, Lockheed Martin is spending millions of our taxpayer dollars to oppose Obama, Defense Secretary Robert Gates, and many other defense experts who want to finally shut down the price-skyrocketing F-22 fighter extravaganza designed for combat during the Soviet Union era of hostilities.

So, are you more upset than when you started reading this column? Feel frustrated and powerless? With your friends, ask your Senators and Congressperson during their frequent recesses for a three-hour public accountability session. If you can assemble 300 or more residents, after you rev up your community, you're likely to have your elected Congressional representatives come to an auditorium where you live and work. If they think 500 people will show up, it is even more likely. Especially if you are organized and tell them this is just the beginning. Just the beginning!

Without the rumble from the people back home, a majority of the 535 members of Congress will continue to kowtow to about 1500 corporations and you'll pay the price again and again. So, rumble, rumble, rumble!

The Ones Who Got It Right
April 3, 2009

Why is it that well regarded people working the fields of corporate power and performance who repeatedly predicted the Wall Street bubble and its bursting receive so little media and attention?

Instead, the public is still being exposed to the comments and writings of people like Alan Greenspan, Robert Rubin, James Glassman (of Dow 36,000 notoriety) while others like Timothy Geithner, Larry Summers, and Gary

Gensler are newly-appointed at high levels in the Obama Administration. These men were variously architects, rationalizers and implementers of the massive de-regulation and non-regulation that unleashed the epic forces of greed, speculation and ruination of millions of livelihoods and trillions of dollars of other peoples' money worldwide.

Here are some of the people who got it right—early and often:

1. William Greider—author and columnist with the *Nation* magazine—wrote books (including *Secrets of the Temple*, 1988) and articles warning about the Federal Reserve and the anti-democratic consequences of rampant corporate globalization.

2. Robert Kuttner whose books (e.g. *Everything for Sale*, 1999) and articles predicted what will happen to workers and pensions when the regulatory state is tossed aside by the corporatists operating inside and outside of government.

3. Jim Hightower whose books (*If the Gods Had Meant Us to Vote, They Would Have Given Us Candidates*, 2000) and the monthly mass circulation *Hightower Lowdown* newsletter pointed out again and again the abuses of the "greed-hounds" and vastly overpaid corporate bosses that have run consumers of healthcare, credit, cars and their own banks into the ground.

4. Nomi Prins (*Other People's Money*, 2004) a former managing director of Goldman Sachs, quit in disgust and began disclosing how these giant Wall Street firms deal and how, with their ideological backers, they wove their webs of deception and fraud against investors, students borrowing money for college, taxpayers ripped off by corporate contractors, sick people gouged and insurance companies denying legitimate claims. (See her book *Jacked: How "Conservatives" Are Picking Your Pocket*, 2008)

5. John R. MacArthur, author (*The Selling of "Free Trade"*, 2001) columnist and publisher of Harpers, authored a sharp, prophetic criticism of NAFTA's effect on US and Mexican workers. Finally, on March 24, 2009 the *New York Times* featured a report titled "NAFTA's Promise, UNfulfilled."

6. Robert A.G. Monks—the leading shareholder rights advocate in our country warned for years in books (latest *Corpocracy*, 2008), articles, testimony and standup challenges at corporate annual meetings that keep investors—the owners of these companies—powerless and dominated by corporate executives, would lead to big trouble. Every day, you can now see the ways that avaricious abuses of executive compensation by Wall Street led to cooking the books, hiding the debts and wildly losing other peoples' money.

7. Tom Stanton, whose 1991 book *State of Risk*, exposed the dangerously undercapitalized condition of Fannie Mae and Freddie Mac and predicted coming disaster if this reckless leveraging continued. By comparison, a year ago Fannie and Freddie's federal regulator, James B. Lockhart III backed by Treasury Department Secretary, Henry Paulson called fears of a bailout "nonsense" and amazingly further lowered the required capital levels months before their collapse and takeover a few months later. Mr. Lockhart is still in his job heading a new regulatory entity over these two goliaths.

8. Republican Kevin Phillips, (latest book *Bad Money: Reckless Finance, Failed Politics, and the Global Crisis of American Capitalism*, 2007) whose numerous writings on Wall Street power and money and the dictatorial rule of the plutocracy were wise, historically-rooted premonitions of future collapse.

9. Dean Baker (latest *Plunder and Blunder*,

2004) Washington-based economist, warned repeatedly earlier in this decade of the housing bubble and the calamitous consequences once it burst. He even sold his own home in 2004 and became a tenant, so convinced was he of the housing precipice.

10. Then there is Naomi Klein who has been documenting how economic disasters produced by corporations and their governmental cohorts end up not with reforms but with further increasing the power of the corporate state. (See *The Shock Doctrine: The Rise of Disaster Capitalism*, 2007)

Chances are that, outside the independent media and an occasional public TV-radio interview, you have not seen or read them in the mass media. But they were right, so why haven't you? Well, first of all, they took on commercial interests and called them out by name and specific misdeeds. Take it from one who knows, big advertisers do not hesitate to let their media outlets know about their displeasure. Publishers, editors and producers will deny being affected by such realities of the bottom line but money talks; not always, but enough to screen out or marginalize the provocative early warners.

Second, these early warners are not like their counterparts such as the market fundamentalists and other active corporatists in the world of writers and commentators. The latter meet and plan often and ferociously attach themselves to political and corporate leaders. While the progressive forecasters do not connect as much either with each other or with their policy allies on Capitol Hill. The media likes to see growing power like that of the intertwined Heritage Foundation with the Reagan regime and their supporters in Congress.

Third, there is this sense that these progressives are exposing conditions that the report-

ers themselves should be revealing. So why not publish staff-driven magazine-style features instead of publicizing outsiders and covering an unfolding story as reportage. Journalistic prizes go to the former. But, they're not the same either in reader impact or for change.

Finally, there are establishment figures who tried, in their own way, to blow the whistle—James Grant, Henry Kaufman and, twenty five years ago, Felix Rohatyn come to mind. Their astute alarms regarding excessive risk-taking were ignored. They are not getting much media play either.

Maybe it's also a cultural thing. Big book deals, radio talk shows, promotions and quotable celebrity status go to the rogues, the grossly negligent, the suppressors of truth and the wrongdoers. They're just so much more exciting!

This is a fast road to a state of decay.

What Can Bush Teach Us?
March 20, 2009

George W. Bush is hitting the lecture circuit. Represented by the Washington Speakers Bureau, Mr. Bush, for a fee of at least $150,000, flew up to Calgary, Canada and spoke to a conservative business audience amidst street protests.

He also has signed a book contract with Crown Publishers tentatively titled *Decision Points* about a dozen personal and presidential decisions ranging from giving up booze to choosing Dick Cheney to invading Iraq.

Now that he is becoming a lecturer and an author, why not also be a teacher? The 43rd president has much to teach Americans about how weak their democracy is—rights, institutions, processes and the sovereignty of the people.

His first lecture to students could be how he and Cheney violated, circumvented and trampled our Constitution. It was as if they replaced the opening preamble of "we, the people" with "we, George W. Bush and Dick Cheney."

Early in his Administration, Mr. Bush showed a determination to pick up on King George III and root himself in something called "the inherent powers of the Presidency," often called the "unitary Presidency." With that, King George IV was establishing his unilateral kingdom, though instead of invoking his divine right, his mantra was the "War on Terror."

He became the most recidivist criminal president, the most variously impeachable president on a regular day-to-day basis in American history. Repeatedly violating our Constitution, laws and treaties, Mr. Bush warred, terrorized, tortured, imprisoned many people without charges, illegally snooped on masses of Americans and set a record for signing statements saying he "the decider" would determine which laws he signed that he would obey and when. And that's just what is public knowledge so far from a very secretive regime.

The ways this outlaw president devastated the rule of law has been well documented in many firsthand accounts of former members of his government in the military, intelligence, and diplomatic service. The lies and deceptions that took our country to war, with immense loss of life and limb, and turned the rights and lives of millions of families upside down have been the material of many books, public hearings and admissions. Even the conservative American Bar Association condemned the Bush White House three times for unconstitutional practices.

Mr. Bush taught us how cowardly the Congress could be in not defending its constitutional authorities and the crucial checks and balances to hold the White House accountable. He taught us the degree of abdication by the major opposition Democratic Party which allowed him and his ilk to do what they did and to leave office on January 20, 2009 without being subjected to impeachment and trial, without even being subjected to a Congressional censure resolution.

He taught us that the courts, with few exceptions, cannot be counted on to defend the constitution from the marauding president—avoiding doing so by excuses that these seizures of power are "political questions." Bush going to war without a declaration of war is too political? Tell that to Jefferson, Madison and other founding fathers who made a big matter out of taking away the war-making authority from any future would-be monarch and decisively repositing it with the Congress.

He taught us how easily you could fool, manipulate, delay or intimidate the mainstream media into becoming a cheerleader for war and a collaborator in covering up what a few intrepid reporters uncovered.

He showed that truth is indeed the first casualty of war and that lies have no consequences for him other than a 70 percent disapproval rating.

He did tell the truth, however, when he announced to a big business audience in Texas early in his first term that they were "his base." Acting like a corporation masquerading as a human in the White House, Mr. Bush pursued policies unleashing the greed and control of Wall Street that tanked the economy and destroyed trillions of dollars of the people's money in an orgy of reckless speculation.

As Jamal Simmons wrote recently, "Unlike the story of King Midas, everything Bush touched turned to coal."

Mr. Bush threw the gauntlet down to 800,000 American lawyers and unlike the marching Pakistani lawyers, only a handful such as Michael Greco, Ramsay Clark, David Cole and Jonathan Turley took up his challenge. The vast majority of lawyers went about their own business, shrugging off what it means to be "officers of the court."

Bush, former American Caesar, tore the pretense off our democratic pretensions. By not holding him and his top collaborators responsible for violating the constitutional, criminal and civil laws of the land, those persons, entrusted with their observance, took a holiday. These outrageous practices—still unchecked—are becoming institutionalized as illustrated in the several (but not all) ways that President Obama is continuing Bush's legacy of license.

Democracies when they are eroded must show resiliency to recover and strengthen what was lost by way of freedom and justice. Otherwise the erosions fester and deepen. Who, you might ask, must be the tribunes of such resiliency? You will not find them now in officialdom.

The wise early twentieth century judge, Learned Hand, gave us the compass. He wrote these words: "Liberty lies in the hearts of men and women; when it dies there, no constitution, no law, no court can save it."

The More Things Change The More They Stay The Same

November 20, 2008

While the liberal intelligentsia was swooning over Barack Obama during his presidential campaign, I counseled "prepare to be disappointed." His record as a Illinois state and US Senator, together with the many progressive and long overdue courses of action he opposed during his campaign, rendered such a prediction unfortunate but obvious.

Now this same intelligentsia is beginning to howl over Obama's transition team and early choices to run his Administration. Having defeated Senator Hillary Clinton in the Democratic Primaries, he now is busily installing Bill Clinton's old guard. Thirty one out of forty seven people that he has named so far for transition or appointments have ties to the Clinton Administration, according to *Politico*. One Clintonite is quoted in the *Washington Post* as saying—"This isn't lightly flavored with Clintons. This is all Clintons, all the time."

Obama's "foreign policy team is now dominated by the Hawkish, old-guard Democrats of the 1990," writes Jeremy Scahill. Obama's transition team reviewing intelligence agencies and recommending appointments is headed by John Brennan and Jami Miscik, who worked under George Tenet when the CIA was involved in politicizing intelligence for, among other officials, Secretary of State Colin Powell's erroneous address before the United Nations calling for war against Iraq.

Mr. Brennan, as a government official, supported warrantless wiretapping and extraordinary rendition to torturing countries. National Public Radio reported that Obama's reversal when he voted for the revised FISA this year relied on John Brennan's advice.

For more detail on these two advisers and others recruited by Obama from the dark old days, see Democracy Now, November 17, 2008 (http://www.democracynow.org/2008/11/17/headlines#7) and Jeremy Scahill, AlterNet, Nov. 20, 2008 "This is Change? 20 Hawks, Clintonites and Neocons to Watch for in Obama's White House."

The top choice as White House chief of staff is Rahm Emanuel—the ultimate hard-nosed corporate Democrat, military-foreign policy hawk and Clinton White House promoter of corporate globalization, as in NAFTA and the World Trade Organization.

Now, recall Obama's words during the bucolic "hope and change" campaign months: "The American people . . . understand the real gamble is having the same old folks doing things over and over and over again and somehow expecting a different result." Thunderous applause followed these remarks.

"This is more 'Groundhog Day' then a fresh start," asserted Peter Wehner, a former Bush adviser who is now at the Ethics and Public Policy Center.

The signs are amassing that Barack Obama put a political con job over on the American people. He is now daily buying into the entrenched military-industrial complex that President Eisenhower warned Americans about in his farewell address.

With Robert Rubin on his side during his first photo opportunity after the election, he signaled to Wall Street that his vote for the $750 billion bailout of those speculators and crooks was no fluke (Rubin was Clinton's financial deregulation architect in 1999 as Secretary of the Treasury before he became one of the hugely paid co-directors tanking Citigroup.)

Obama's apologists say that his picks show he wants to get things done, so he wants people who know their way around Washington. Moreover, they say, the change comes only from the president who sets the priorities and the courses of action, not from his subordinates. This explanation assumes that a president's appointments are not mirror images of the boss's expected directions but only functionaries to carry out the Obama changes.

If you are inclined to believe this improbable scenario, perhaps you may wish to review Obama's record compiled by Matt Gonzalez at Counterpunch (see: http://counterpunch.org/gonzalez10292008.html).

Debatable Debates
October 20, 2008

The three so-called presidential debates—really parallel interviews by reporters chosen by the Obama and McCain campaigns—are over and they are remarkable for two characteristics: redundancy and avoidance.

A remarkable similarity between McCain and Obama on foreign and military policy kept enlarging as Obama seemed to enter into a clinch with McCain each time McCain questioned his inexperience or softness or opinions on using military force.

If anyone can detect a difference between the two candidates regarding belligerence toward Iran and Russia, more US soldiers into the quagmire of Afghanistan (next to Pakistan), kneejerk support of the Israeli military oppression, brutalization and colonization of the Palestinians and their shrinking lands, keeping soldiers and bases in Iraq, despite Obama's use of the word "withdrawal," and their desire to enlarge an already bloated, wasteful military budget which already consumes half of the federal government's operating expenses, please illuminate the crevices between them.

This past spring, the foreign affairs reporters, not columnists, for the *New York Times* and the *Washington Post* concluded that Barack Obama and Hillary Clinton are advancing foreign and military policies similar to those adopted by George W. Bush in his second term.

Where then is the "hope" and "change" from the junior Senator from Illinois?

Moreover, both Obama and McCain want more nuclear power plants, more coal production, and more offshore oil drilling. Our national priority should be energy efficient consumer technologies (motor vehicles, heating, air conditioning and electric systems) and renewable energy such as wind, solar and geothermal.

Both support the gigantic taxpayer funded Wall Street bailout, without expressed amendments. Both support the notorious Patriot Act, the revised FISA act which opened the door to spy on Americans without judicial approval, and Obama agrees with McCain in vigorously opposing the impeachment of George W. Bush and Dick Cheney.

What about avoidance? Did you see them speak about a comprehensive enforcement program to prosecute corporate crooks in the midst of the greatest corporate crime wave in our history? Did you see them allude to doing anything about consumer protection (credit card gouging, price of medicines, the awful exploitation and deprivation of the people in the inner city) and the ripoffs of buyers in ever more obscure and inescapable ways?

Wasn't it remarkable how they never mentioned the poor, and only use the middle class when they refer to "regular people?" There are one hundred million poor people and children in this nation and no one in Washington, DC associates Senator Obama, much less John McCain, with any worthy program to treat the abundant poverty-related injustices.

What about labor issues? Worker health and safety, pensions looted and drained, growing permanent unemployment and underemployment, and outsourcing more and more jobs to fascists and communist dictatorships are not even on the peripheries of the topics covered in the debates.

When I was asked my opinion about who won the debates, I say they were not debates. But I know what won and what lost. The winners were big business, bailouts for Wall Street, an expansionary NATO, a boondoggle missile defense program, nuclear power, the military-industrial complex and its insatiable thirst for trillions of taxpayer dollars, for starters.

What lost was peace advocacy, international law, the Israeli-Palestinian peace movement, taxpayers, consumers, Africa and We the People.

The language of avoidance to address and challenge corporate power is spoken by both McCain and Obama, though interestingly enough, McCain occasionally uses words like "corporate greed" to describe his taking on the giant Boeing tanker contract with the Pentagon.

Funded by beer, tobacco, auto and telecommunications companies over the years, the corporation known as the Commission on Presidential Debates features only two corporate-funded candidates, excludes all others and closes off a major forum for smaller candidates, who are on the ballots in a majority of the states, to reach tens of millions of voters.

In the future, this theatre of the absurd can be replaced with a grand coalition of national and local citizen groups who, starting in March, 2012 lay out many debates from Boston to San Diego, rural, suburban and urban, summon the presidential candidates to public auditoriums to react to the peoples' agendas.

Can the Democratic and Republican nominees reject this combination of labor, neighborhood, farmer, cooperative, veteran's, religious, student, consumer and good government with tens of millions of members? It will be interesting to see what happens if they do or if they do not.

Politics of Avoidance

August 26, 2008

The "politics of avoidance" is receiving a great deal of media attention during this period of national political conventions. Unfortunately, the newspapers and television programs do not use the phrase: "the politics of avoidance." Together with John McCain and Barack Obama, members of the press have become used to living the "politics of avoidance" every day by *not* asking, talking or reporting about the essential core of what politics should be about—power!

Power! Who has it? Who doesn't have it? Who should have less of it and who should have more of it? What does concentrated power do to the everyday life of the people as workers, patients, consumers, taxpayers, voters, shareholders and citizens?

Just use these and other power yardsticks and watch how thin and superficial daily political reporting, even by the best of the press, can become.

In the August 25th edition of the *New York Times*, a long analysis by Michael Powell is titled "Tracing the Disparate Threads in Obama's Political Philosophy." There was no mention of corporate misbehavior—as in corporate crime, corporate corruption, corporate governance, corporate accountability, or cracking down on corporate abuses from the contractors in Iraq to the speculators on Wall Street.

Bear in mind, the *New York Times* and other newspapers often report about corporate crime and misdeeds. Sometimes reporters do such a good job that they win the Pulitzer and other prizes. Yet, strangely, these reporters do not carry over from the reporting of their own paper to their questioning of the presidential candidates.

Since there are no reporters challenging the candidates on what they would do about this continual corporate crime wave and the miniscule prosecution budgets, or the limited enforcement and regulatory efforts, the candidates can remain mum, very mum.

In Powell's article, Obama's economics are described as "a redistributionist liberalism but [he] is skeptical of too much government tinkering. His most influential advisors hail from the University of Chicago, a bastion of free-marketers." This is Obama's way of saying to corporations that he is a safe bet not to trouble them with his earlier experience as a community organizer in neighborhoods that were up against a variety of corporate predators, including redlining banks and insurance companies, supermarkets that dumped contaminated food products, landlords who rented apartments with asbestos and lead contaminations, CEOs who close plants, and street-corner, payday-lending sharks.

The same day—August 25, 2008, the *Wall Street Journal* had an entire special section devoted to "Debating the Issues" described as 'Healthcare,' 'Energy & the Environment,' 'The Economy' and 'Trade.' The Healthcare headline is sub-titled: "How Involved Should the Government Be?

Once again the same paradox. The *Journal* prints some of the best exposes of corporate greed and power in all of mainstream journalism. Yet one strains to detect any of this power analysis when it comes to the paper's political coverage or campaign features.

Conventional political journalism is all about palliative descriptions, such as governmental involvement primarily as an issuer of dollars to the recipients in presumed need. It is about symptoms, rarely about causes, and even less often about the need to curb or displace corporate control.

About 75 percent of the American people believe corporations have too much control over their lives. Yet reducing such control or holding it accountable is not part of electoral or political discourse.

A majority of the American people, and fifty-nine percent of physicians in an April poll, favor single-payer or full government health insurance (as in full Medicare for all) with free choice of hospital and doctor, private delivery of care, and far less administrative costs and billing fraud. The health insurance companies would be displaced.

John McCain and Barack Obama have never had to debate this majoritarian preference along with their piecemeal, concessionary heathcare plans that please these same insurance companies.

The pollsters also reflect, embody and are saturated with this politics of avoidance. They do not poll the various impacts of concentrated corporate power on the various roles people play in the workplace, marketplace, and their communities.

The *New York Times/CBS News* Poll of delegates to the Democratic Convention asked about the condition of the economy, healthcare, going into Iraq, energy, abortion and gay marriage.

Not one question was asked about big business—the most dominant power over government, elections, politics, the federal operating budget, and our political economy.

Whoever asks the questions, whoever controls the yardsticks controls the agenda of public dialogue. The politics of avoidance is designed to avoid the politics of corporate power.

Presidents Jefferson, Lincoln, Theodore Roosevelt, and Franklin Delano Roosevelt and leading Supreme Court Justices, Louis Brandeis and William Douglas understood and warned about the menace of unbridled corporate domination.

Today multinational corporations are more powerful then ever, especially over workers and the government. And politics is more about avoiding this central topic than ever before. Discussions about corporate power are off the table.

So much for the Preamble to our Constitution which reads, "We the People . . ."

Fabricator-in-Chief
March 21, 2008

On the occasion of the fifth anniversary of Bush's illegal war of aggression in Iraq, the Fabricator-in-Chief made a speech at the Pentagon, whose muzzled army chiefs had opposed his costly, ruinous adventure from the start for strategic, tactical and logistical reasons.

As benefits the dictatorial monarch of yesteryear, evicted by America's first patriots, this modern-day King George blistered the truth, somersaulted the facts and declared that a "strategic victory" in Iraq is near. He called the war "a just and noble cause." Sugarcoating the terrible, impoverished sociocidal state of daily life in Iraq, he acknowledged "the high cost in lives and treasure," but said the recent situation in Iraq made it all worthwhile. "Worth the sacrifice" is how he put it often in previous statements.

At the same time, his V.P., his Prince Regent, Dick Cheney was having this exchange with ABC's Martha Raddatz:

Raddatz: "Two-thirds of Americans say it's not worth fighting, and they're looking at the value gain versus the cost in American lives, certainly, and Iraqi lives."

Cheney: "So?"

Raddatz: "So—you don't care what the American people think?"

Cheney: "No," who then inaccurately wrapped Abraham Lincoln's stand during the Civil War around his relentless illegal warmongering in Iraq.

In an article called "Defining Victory Downward: No, the surge is not a success," columnist Michael Kinsley exposed the fatuous standards of comparison used by Bush and took his readers to standards back in 2003. Kinsley observed how Bush spouts success against conflicts and conditions that never existed before March 2003. There were no al-Qaeda fighters in Iraq, no large scale sectarian carnage. There were modicum rudimentary public facilities and necessities, notwithstanding severe Clinton-Bush propelled economic sanctions, under dictator Saddam Hussein, instead of a devastated, riven nation of 4 million refugees and violent street anarchy.

At the same time that the rancidly redundant fictionalizations of reality in Iraq by Bush and Cheney were once again receiving front page attention at the *New York Times* and the *Washington Post*, protests on the downtown streets of Washington, DC and in scores of cities and communities around the country received subdued short articles deep inside these newspapers. Both remarked on the smaller turnout of marchers compared to the large demonstrations in 2003.

This decline should not be surprising. Most people are trying to communicate their concerns and their repeatedly accurate warnings about the impacts of this war of aggression to a wider audience. But the mainstream media, often hardly working on weekends, never gave these outpourings the attention they deserved (even

though American public opinion was behind their call to end the war-occupation and said that the war was not worth the cost to America in lives and dollars).

Fortunately, along came a Nobel Prize-winning economist, Joseph Stiglitz, with a new detailed book titled *The Three Trillion Dollar War* to inform the American people just how right they are about the long term cost of Bush's messianic reckless pursuit launched on a platform of lies, distortions and cover-ups.

The twisted defiance of Bush, the cowardliness of the majority Democrats in Congress and the frustration and powerlessness felt by sensitive Americans who see no light at the end of the Iraq tunnel leaves little room for citizens to gain control of their runaway government.

There is a possible way to turn the tide in favor of ending this illusion of "victory" and the occupation that breeds its own opposition in Iraq.

Unlike before or during any other war in our nation's history, hundreds of former high military, national security-intelligence and diplomatic officials have spoken, written, testified and some even marched against Bush's tragic folly—before and after the March 2003 invasion.

These retired public servants include generals and anti-terrorism specialists who worked inside the Bush Administration. Taken as a whole, were they to aggregate their standing and influence before the American people by banding together as a group, their cumulative impact on Congress, on galvanizing and focusing public opinion during this election year could well turn this deteriorating situation around.

These patriotic Americans, with their experience in battles, conflicts and geopolitical tensions, coupled with their desire to wage peace for a change in Washington's policies, could be the catalyst that spells the difference. Compared with Bush and Cheney, successful draft-dodgers during their Pro-Vietnam war past, they make for quite a credible contrast.

Will they mobilize themselves for the common good and provide the new dynamic needed?

Time will tell.

What the Candidates Avoid

January 14, 2008

Here is a short list of what you won't hear much of from the front-runners in this presidential primary season. Call them the candidate taboos.

1) You won't hear a call for a national crackdown on the corporate crime, fraud, and abuse that have robbed trillions of dollars from workers, investors, pension holders, taxpayers and consumers. Among the reforms that won't be suggested are providing resources to prosecute executive crooks and laws to democratize corporate governance so shareholders have real power. Candidates will not shout for a payback of ill-gotten gains, to rein in executive pay, or to demand corporate sunshine laws.

2) You won't hear a demand that workers receive a living wage instead of a minimum wage. There will be no backing for a repeal of the anti-union Taft-Hartley Act of 1947, which has blocked more than 40 million workers from forming or joining trade unions to improve wages and benefits above Wal-Mart or McDonald's levels.

3) You won't hear for a call for a withdrawal from the WTO and NAFTA. Renegotiated trade agreements should stick to trade while labor, environmental, and consumer rights are advanced by separate treaties without being subordinated to the dictates of international commerce.

4) You won't hear a call for our income tax system to be substantially revamped so that workers can keep more of their wages while we tax the things we like least, such as pollution, stock speculation, addictive industries, and energy guzzling technologies. Nor will you hear that corporations should be required to pay their fair share; corporate tax contributions as a percent of the overall federal revenue stream have been declining for 50 years.

5) You won't hear a call for a single-payer health system. Almost sixty years after President Truman first proposed it, we still need health insurance for everyone, a program with quality and cost controls and an emphasis on prevention. Full Medicare for everyone will save thousands of lives a year while maintaining patient choice of doctors and hospitals within a competitive private healthcare delivery system.

6) There is no reason to believe that the candidates will stand up to the commercial interests profiting from our current energy situation. We need a major environmental health agenda that challenges these entrenched interests with major new initiatives in solar energy, doubling motor vehicle fuel efficiency, and other quantified sustainable and clean energy technologies.

Nor will there be adequate recognition that current fossil fuels are producing not just global warming, but also cancer, respiratory diseases, and geopolitical entanglements. Finally, there will be no calls for ending environmental racism that leads to more contaminated water, air, and toxic dumps in poorer neighborhoods.

7) The candidates will not demand a reduction in the military budget that devours half of the federal government's operating expenditures

at a time when there is no Soviet Union or other major state enemy in the world. Studies by the General Accounting Office and internal Pentagon assessments support the judgment of many retired admirals and generals that a wasteful defense weakens our country and distorts priorities at home.

8) You won't hear a consistent clarion call for electoral reform. Both parties have shamelessly engaged in gerrymandering, a process that guarantees reelection of their candidates at the expense of frustrated voters. Nor will there be serious proposals that millions of law-abiding ex-felons be allowed to vote.

Other electoral reforms should include reducing barriers to third-party candidates, same day registration, a voter verified paper record for electronic voting, run-off voting to insure winners receive a majority vote, binding none-of-the-above choices and most important, full public financing to guarantee clean elections.

9) You won't hear much about a failed war on drugs that costs nearly $50 billion annually. And the major candidates will not argue that addicts should be treated rather than imprisoned. Nor should observers hope for any call to repeal the "three strikes and you're out" laws that have needlessly filled our jails or to end mandatory sentencing that hamstrings our judges.

10) The candidates will ignore the diverse Israeli peace movement whose members have developed accords for a two state solution with their Palestinian and American counterparts. It is time to replace the Washington puppet show with a real Washington peace show for the security of the American, Palestinian, and Israeli people.

11) You won't hear the candidates stand up to business interests that have backed changes to our civil justice system that restrict or close the courtroom to wrongfully injured and cheated individuals, but not to corporations. Where is the vocal campaign against fraud and injury upon innocent patients, consumers, and workers? We should make it easier for consumers to band together and defend themselves against harmful practices in the marketplace.

Voters should visit the webpages of the major party candidates. See what they say, and see what they do not say. Then email or send a letter to any or all of the candidates and ask them why they are avoiding these issues. Breaking the taboos won't start with the candidates. Maybe it can start with the voters.

The Next Step Not Taken
December 28, 2007

The conscientious quest for turning around our fragile democracy can usefully turn its attention to a widespread but sub-visible phenomenon that can be called "The Next Step Not Taken."

Let's look at three areas that need fundamental reforms where the people who can get them in place are not taking the next step.

1. Call them small investors, savers or shareholders—corporate crimes, frauds and abuses have battered them in the past decade. Think Enron, Worldcom, Wall Street's brokerage and investment giants and now the big shaky banks. Trillions of dollars have been drained or looted by these corporate bosses while they pay themselves handsomely with other people's money.

Speaking, writing and testifying against these massive unregulated rip-offs of defenseless Americans are two former chairmen of the Securities and Exchange Commission (SEC)—Arthur Levitt and William Donaldson. Openly sharing their urgent pleas for reform are John

Bogle, founder of mutual fund indexing and severe critic of excessive, often hidden, mutual fund fees, and Lynn Turner former chief accountant of the SEC.

These men are well known and respected in their fields, have ready access to the mass business media, possess great rolodexes of supportive people all over the country and could raise substantial sums of money. They are part of the monied classes themselves.

And for what? To start a large investor protection and action organization to represent the 60 million powerless and individual investors in our country. Individual investors really have no organized voice, either in Washington, DC, or the state and local level where public sentiment and demand for action generates the rumble for change.

These experienced, superbly connected men, who have respected each other for years and are frustrated over inaction by those in authority, are not taking the next step.

To demonstrate their credentials, see their books *Take on the Street: How to Fight Your Financial Future* and *Take on the Street: What Wall Street and Corporate America Don't Want You to Know* by Arthur Levitt, and *The Little Book of Common Sense Investing and The Battle for the Soul of Capitalism* by John Bogle. To document the broader urgency of their concerns, see veteran shareholder rights leader, Robert Monks' new book *Corpocracy*.

2. It would not take you very long, searching the internet, to come up with scores of retired high military officers, from Generals and Admirals on down, high-ranking former diplomats and national security officials, who have spoken and written against the invasion of Iraq and the continuing quagmire and casualties that have cost our country so much and destroyed so much

of Iraq and its people. They include retired generals William Odom and Anthony Zinni and key advisers to the first President Bush, Brent Scoweroft and James Roker.

These outspoken, stand-up Americans, include former cabinet secretaries, agency chiefs, and White House special assistants, who have served under both Republican and Democratic administrations.

No one can question the experience and service of these straight-talk, former public officials. They have seen it all. Wealthy, like-minded funders would return their calls.

Organized together into a powerful, well-funded advocacy organization, these Americans can have a decisive impact on Congress and the White House, because they would be able to reach the American people through the mass media and public hearings with the truth, and the strategies for peace and justice.

Although active in their pursuit of a sound foreign and military policy that does not jeopardize and bankrupt America, they have not taken this next step.

3. Can you possibly count all the progressives—elected, academic, authors and columnists—who are tearing into the Democratic Party for how often they caved in Congress this year to George W. Bush and his minority Republicans in the Senate and House?

There is nothing new about their complaints. Whether on foreign or domestic policy, whether on the domination of giant corporations over elections, legislatures, regulatory agencies and mass media, whether on the destructive results and portents of corporate globalization and autocratic trade regimes (WTO and NAFTA), progressives have been criticizing the Democrats for years now.

Hear it from Bob Herbert of the *New York*

Times, John Nichols of the *Nation* magazine, the duos of James Carville and Paul Begala, Mark Crispin Miller and Jim Hightower, Bill Moyers and Anthony Lewis, Senators Bernie Sanders and Sherrod Brown, and Congressman John Conyers and Ed Markey—to name just a very few of the grossly disappointed and outraged critics of the establishment Democrats, their Democratic Leadership Council and their corporate financiers.

But they do not take the next step. Or steps. Either organize into a powerful counter-weight inside the Democratic Party to make progressive demands that cannot be shrugged off, or move to a progressive third party that can either lever its messages to the Democrats or compete with them.

How many years can the bad Republicans and their corporatist allies keep pulling the mainstream Democratic Party toward them and leave progressives with the futility of the least worst form of disastrous corporate government?

There are many influential and knowledgeable people in our country who know what causes are critical to pursue, what redirections are necessary for present and future generations, what assets of persuasion and change to amass. But they are stalled in this state of *the next step not taken*.

Taking the next step is the difference between talking and acting, between promise and performance, between autocracy and democracy!

Destroying the Rule of Law

October 26, 2007

Every law student promptly learns the national ideal that our country is governed by the rule of law, not the rule of men. Today, the rule of law is under major attack.

Such activities have become a big business and, not surprisingly, they have involved big business.

On October 25th, Secretary Condoleeza Rice officially recognized before a House Oversight Committee that, remarkably, there was no law covering the misbehavior of Blackwater Corporation and their private police in Iraq.

Any crimes of violence committed by Blackwater and other armed contractors commissioned by the Defense and State Departments to perform guard duty and other more ambitious tasks, fell into a gap between Iraqi law, from which they have been exempted by the US military occupation and the laws of the United States.

Since the United States government is ruled by lawless men in the White House who have violated countless laws and treaties, Bush and Cheney clearly had no interest in placing giant corporate contractors operating inside Iraqi jurisdiction under either the military justice system or the criminal laws of the United States.

Presidential power has accumulated over the years to levels that would have alarmed the Founding Fathers whose constitutional framework never envisioned such raw unilateral power at the top of the Executive Branch. Accordingly, they only provided for the impeachment sanction. They neither gave citizens legal standing to go to court and hold the presidency accountable, or to prevent the two other branches from surrendering their explicit constitutional authority-such as the war-making power-to the Executive Branch.

The federal courts over time have refused to adjudicate cases they deem "political conflicts" between the Legislative and Executive branches or, in general, most foreign policy questions.

Being above the law's reach, Bush and Cheney

can and do use the law in ways that inflict injustice on innocent people. Politicizing the offices of the US Attorneys by the Justice Department, demonstrated by Congressional hearings, is one consequence of such presidential license. Political law enforcement, using laws such as the so-called PATRIOT Act, is another widespread pattern that has dragneted thousands of innocent people into arrests and imprisonment without charges or adequate legal representation. Or the Bush regime's use of coercive plea bargains against defendants who can't afford leading, skilled attorneys.

Books and law journal articles have been written about times when government violates the laws. They are long on examples but short on practical remedies of what to do about it.

Corporations and their large corporate law firms have many ways to avoid the laws. First, they make sure that when Congress writes legislation, the bills advance corporate interests. For example, numerous consumer safety laws have no criminal penalties for willful violations, or only the most nominal fines. The regulatory agencies often have very weak subpoena powers or authority to set urgent and mandatory safety standards without suffering years or even decades of corporate-induced delays.

If the laws prove troublesome, the corporations make sure that enforcement budgets are ridiculously tiny, with only a few federal cops on the beat. The total number of Justice Department attorneys prosecuting the corporate crime wave of the past decade, trapping investors, pensioners and workers into trillions of dollars of losses and damaging the health and safety of many patients and other consumers, is smaller than just one of the top five largest corporate law firms.

Out in the marketplace, environment and the workplace, the corporations have many tools

forged out of their unbridled power to block aggrieved people from having their day in court or getting agencies or legislatures to stand up for the common folk.

Companies can wear down or deter plaintiffs from obtaining justice by costly motions and other delaying tactics. When people get into court and obtain some justice, the companies move toward the legislature to restrict access to the courts. This is grotesquely called "tort reform"—which takes away the rights of harmed individuals but not the corporations' rights to have their day in court.

Lush amounts of campaign dollars grease the way for corporations in the legislatures of the fifty states and on Capitol Hill.

As if that power to pass their own laws is not enough, large corporations become their own private legislatures. You've been confronted with those fine-print standard form agreements asking you to sign on the dotted line if you wish to secure insurance, tenancy, credit, bank services, hospital treatment, or just a job.

Those pages of fine print are corporations regulating you! You can't cross any of them out.

You can't go across the street to a competitor—say from Geico to State Farm, or from Citibank to the Bank of America—because there is no competition over these similar fine-print contracts with their dotted signature lines. Unless, that is, they compete over how fast they require you to give up your rights to go to court or to object to their unilaterally changing the terms of the agreement, such as in changing the terms of your frequent flier agreement on already accumulated miles

Oh, for the law schools that provide courses on the rule of men over the rule of law.

Oh, for the time when there will be many public interest law firms working just on these portentous dominations of concentrated power to deny open and impartial uses of the laws to achieve justice and accountability.

Dodging Impeachment
October 12, 2007

The meeting at the Jones Library in Amherst, Massachusetts on July 5, 2007 was anything but routine. Seated before Congressman John Olver (D-Mass.) were twenty seasoned citizens from over a dozen municipalities in this First Congressional District which embraces the lovely Berkshire Hills.

The subject—impeachment of George W. Bush and Richard B. Cheney.

The request—that Rep. Olver join the impeachment drive in Congress.

More than just opinion was being conveyed to Olver, a then 70-year-old Massachusetts liberal with a Ph.D. in chemistry from the Massachusetts Institute of Technology. These Americans voted overwhelmingly during formal annual town meetings in 14 towns and two cities in the First District endorsing resolutions to impeach the president and vice president.

Presented in the form of petitions to be sent to the Congress, the approving citizenry cited at least four "high crimes and misdemeanors."

They included the initiation of the Iraq War based on defrauding the public and intentionally misleading the Congress, spying on Americans without judicial authorization, committing the torture of prisoners in violation of both federal law and the UN Torture Convention and the Geneva Convention, and stripping American citizens of their Constitutional rights by jailing them indefinitely without charges and without access to legal counsel

or even an opportunity to challenge their imprisonment in a court of law.

Forty towns in Vermont and the State Senate had already presented their Congressional delegation with similar petitions.

Impeachment advocates reported the results to Olver from each town meeting. Leverett's vote was 339-1; Great Barrington was 100-3. No vote in any of the towns or cities was less than a two-third majority "yes" in favor of impeachment, according to long-time activist, Attorney Robert Feuer of Stockbridge, Massachusetts.

With three fourths of reports completed Olver, who voted against the war, raised his hand and said, "Spare me, I know full well the overwhelming majority of my constituency is in favor of impeachment." He then told them he would not sign on to any impeachment resolution whether against Bush or against Cheney (House Resolution 333 introduced by Rep. Dennis Kucinich (D-Ohio)). He was quite adamant.

In taking this unrepresentative position, Rep. Olver's position was identical to that of the House Democratic leadership and many of his Democratic colleagues.

The Democratic Party line on impeachment is that Bush and Cheney are the most impeachable White House duo in American history (they believe this privately). The Democrats do not want to distract attention from their legislative agenda, and need Republican votes for passage. Moreover, they do not have the votes to obtain the requisite two-thirds of the members present for conviction in the Senate.

Strangely, none of these excuses bothered Republicans when they impeached Bill Clinton in the House for lying under oath about sex and proceeded to a full trial in the Senate where they failed to get the required votes. Can Clinton's "high crimes and misdemeanors" begin to compare with this White House crime wave?

The last question to Olver was from a young veteran back from Iraq and Afghanistan. "What could we possibly do to bring you around to our way of thinking?" he asked.

Olver's response, after several seconds of silence, was "You have to prove to me that impeachment will not be counterproductive."

Members of Congress should apply the same standard to themselves that they like to apply to members of the Executive and Judicial branches—namely to honor their oath to uphold and defend the Constitution. That Oath is supposed to transcend political calculations.

Maybe the Democrats think that Bush and Cheney are such wild and crazy guys that a serious impeachment drive in Congress would provoke the two draft-dodgers to launch a military emergency, strike Iran or otherwise generate a crisis, based on their continual fulminations about the "war on terror," that would engulf the Democrats and throw them on the defensive for 2008.

In short, the Democrats may be viewing Bush and Cheney as being so defiantly, aggressively impeachable on so many counts as to be unimpeachable. That is, with the White House harboring so much political nitroglycerine, don't even try to remove it.

Such a cowardly position would make quite a precedent for future presidents who want to illegally elbow out the other two branches of government and our Constitution.

Make them Sweat the Big Stuff

September 25, 2007

A society reveals its values, priorities and distribution of power in the way its rulers punish deviant behavior. Here are some examples for you to ponder:

Members of Congress were in an uproar recently over a MoveOn.org political advertisement in the *New York Times* titled "General Petraeus or General Betray Us?" The following copy alerted readers to their belief that he may likely testify before Congress as a political General reflecting the rosy views on the Iraq War-quagmire by his commander-in-chief, George W. Bush.

How dare MoveOn.org criticize a general in the midst of Bush's war of choice, growled Republicans and some Democrats as the Senators rushed to overwhelmingly vote for a resolution condemning the ad?

How dare those many past Americans who criticized Civil War Generals, World War II Generals, Korean War Generals (remember General Douglas MacArthur) and Vietnam War Generals (remember General William Westmoreland)?

This kind of criticism inside Army, inside the Congress and among the citizenry has been as American as apple pie.

How come a similar uproar has not come forth about the many female US soldiers in Iraq raped or sexually harassed by male soldiers who are often their superiors? Where are the generals to crack down on these outrages? This story was documented in a long cover story in the *New York Times* magazine some months ago, citing numerous sources, including the Pentagon.

Senators demanded the resignation of Senator Larry Craig (R-Idaho) caught in a toilet sting operation at Minneapolis airport. Senator Craig—he now says foolishly so—pleaded guilty to a charge of disorderly conduct. For doing what? As Frank Rich described the situation in the *New York Times*: "He didn't have sex in a public place. He didn't expose himself. His toe tapping, hand signals and 'wide stance' were at most a form of flirtation."

Conservative columnist, George Will expressed similar views.

The penalty for Senator Craig may be termination of his Senate career but not one required by law. Just by pressure from his "pure" Senate colleagues.

Now contrast what should be required of George W. Bush by our Constitution, laws and international treaties to which the US is a signatory nation.

Plunging our nation into an unconstitutional war of massive carnage and cost, and committing numerous, repeated crimes along the way, from widespread torture in violation of US law and the Geneva conventions to spying on Americans without court approval (a felony), does not agitate the Senators as did the airport toilet tapping.

Added to the Bush presidency's serial and continuing crimes are his bungling and incompetence. He has enriched crooked corporations, burned tens of billions of taxpayer dollars and most seriously, deprived soldiers of sufficient body and humvee armor year after year, which has cost the lives and limbs of thousands of American GIs.

In a US court of law, such behavior would be judged criminal negligence.

Yet, there has been no demand from Congress for his impeachment, or his resignation, or even any support for Senator Russ Feingold's modest resolution of censure (S.Res. 302 and 303).

Bush's Justice Department has thrown the book at several plaintiff lawyers for paying people to be lead plaintiffs in securities fraud cases while not pursuing the corporate crooks who actually stole big money from investors and shareholders while paying themselves compensation beyond their dreams of avarice.

If the Department needed a bigger budget to go after this corporate crime wave, they should have requested it from Congress. The resulting fines and restitutions alone would have more than paid for such an enlarged law and order drive.

I am sure you can cite many examples of public hypocrisy, double standards and inverted priorities from your knowledge and experience. There are many explanations about why and how these powerbrokers and powerholders get away with such behavior.

But let us remember Abraham Lincoln's observation about the power of "public sentiments." We need to inform, focus and deliver a different quality and quantity of "public sentiments" directly to our allegedly public servants.

So that they start to sweat the big stuff.

Acting on Impeachment
July 27, 2007

Most readers of the *Washington Post* probably missed it. But probably not Attorney General Alberto Gonzales. Fifty-six of his law school classmates (Harvard Law School, class of 1982) bought space for an open letter in mid-May that excoriated his "cavalier handling of our freedoms time and again."

It read like an indictment, to wit:

Witness your White House memos sweeping aside the Geneva Conventions to justify torture, endangering our own servicemen and women;

Witness your advice to the president effectively reading habeas corpus out of our constitutional protections;

Witness your support of presidential statements claiming inherent power to wiretap American citizens without warrants (and the Administration's stepped-up wiretapping campaign, taking advantage of those statements, which continues on your watch to this day); and

Witness your dismissive explanation of the troubling firings of numerous US Attorneys, and their replacement with other more "loyal" to the president's politics, as merely "an overblown personal matter."

In these and other actions, we see a pattern. As a recent editorial put it, your approach has come to symbolize "disdain for the separation of powers, civil liberties and the rule of law."

By now you're expecting something like a conclusion by his classmates, such as a demand for resignation or a call for Gonzales' impeachment. No such logic.

Instead, these intrepid classmates punted, urging Gonzales and President Bush "to relent from this reckless path, and begin to restore respect for the rule of law we all learned to love many years ago."

Just this week, four Democratic Senators called for a special prosecutor to investigate their belief that Gonzales gave false testimony about the regime's warrantless domestic surveillance program. They criticized the Attorney General for possessing an instinct "to dissemble and to deceive."

Four of Gonzales' top aides have already resigned. The head of the FBI, Robert Mueller, just testified before Congress and contradicted Gonzales' statements which were made under oath.

It is not often that an Attorney General of the United States is treated with bi-partisan inferences of perjury before a major Senate Committee (the Senate Judiciary Committee). Senator Patrick J. Leahy, the soft-spoken Chairman, said to him: "I just don't trust you."

His counterpart, Republican Senator Arlen Specter, the ranking minority member of the Committee, extended his fellow Senator's remark, adding, "Your credibility has been breached to the point of being actionable."

Why don't these and other Democratic and Republican Senators say plainly what they say privately day after day: that they believe that the Attorney General has lied under oath, and not just once.

Again, they avoid the logical conclusion.

But then the Democrats have been doing this dance of evasion with George W. Bush on a far larger scale for four years. After all, Gonzales' impeachable offenses are his superiors'. Gonzales took the orders; Bush-Cheney gave the orders. The litany of Bush-Cheney impeachable abuses extends far beyond those associated with Gonzales, foremost among them of course Bush plunging the nation into a bloody, costly war-quagmire on a platform of fabrications, deceptions and cover-ups again and again, year after year. And Gonzales took the orders; Bush-Cheney gave the orders, providing a more serious basis for a Congressional demand for their resignation or the commencing of impeachment proceedings in the House of Representatives.

Compare the many impeachable offenses of Bush-Cheney with the certain impeachment of President Richard M. Nixon that was rendered moot by his resignation in 1974. Compare the actual impeachment of President William Jefferson Clinton by a Republican-controlled House of Representatives in 1998 for lying under oath about sex.

Granted, Nixon became ensnared in the criminal laws and Clinton was caught by the tort laws. But Bush-Cheney's "high crimes and misdemeanors" tower in scope and diversity over those earlier presidents.

Instead of a burglary and cover-up, as with Nixon, it is the horrific ongoing war (longer than either the Civil War or World War II) with hundreds of thousands of lost lives and many more injuries and sicknesses.

Instead of a sex scandal, as with Clinton, there is a serial ongoing constitutional scandal oozing ongoing repeated constitutional crimes. For which, alas, there is only one constitutional remedy arranged by the framers—impeachment.

And that remedy the Democrats took "off the table" after they won the Congress last November and before they even took office. Just what the White House recidivists needed to know to keep at it. What a lesson for future generations.

Most Americans do not want their members of Congress to practice rushing to judgment. Nor do they want their members to rush away from judgment. The Democrats, with very few exceptions, are very good at escaping from their constitutional responsibilities.

It is time to hold the Bush-Cheney-Administration responsible for their indefensible acts.

Hillary's Hypocrisy

June 18, 2007

Is Hillary Clinton a political weather vane or a political compass?

Consider her latest detour from the NAFTA

and WTO policies of her husband. Last week she announced her opposition to the proposed trade agreement between the US and South Korea. The place for her remarks was a town hall meeting in Michigan organized by the AFL-CIO.

She described the agreement between Bush and the South Koreans, requiring Congressional approval, as "inherently unfair." "It will hurt the US auto industry, increase our trade deficit, cost us good middle-class jobs and make America less competitive."

No kidding! Where has she been for the past fifteen years? For those words could have described the consequences of both NAFTA and the WTO. The US auto industry has been emigrating to Mexico and China. The trade deficit has gone off the charts, nearing nine hundred billion dollars in 2007 and is four times greater than what it was ten years ago. Industrial job loss is being joined by the outsourcing of white collar jobs in even larger numbers.

About 90 percent of the products sold in the L.L. Bean catalogue are imports or produced by foreign manufacturers.

Corporate managed trade—misnamed free trade—is draining our country's competitiveness, as US corporations take their factories and jobs abroad to authoritarian or dictatorial nations, especially China. Imagine modern capital equipment, and 50¢ an hour for workers who are making things for the US market, without fair labor standards, pollution controls and other standards that companies have to comply with in the US.

Senator Clinton felt reassured with her opposition. Ford Motor Company and the Chrysler group of DaimlerChrysler came out against the Korea deal before Hillary did.

A politician like Hillary Clinton has her finger to the wind. The workers and domestic companies are providing her with the wind. Still, she has not supported the renegotiation of NAFTA and WTO which the US can force by utilizing the Treaties' six-month notice of withdrawal from each of these autocratic systems of transnational governance and secret courts known as NAFTA and WTO. Not enough organized citizen wind power compared to the corporate power behind those trade pacts.

If Senator John F. Kennedy's best-selling book *Profiles in Courage* was updated, nothing Hillary Clinton has done in the Congress would come close to being a footnote.

As a member of the Senate Armed Services Committee, she has not challenged the many GAO documented boondoggle military contracts. One gigantic weapon system—the F-22 aircraft—has been privately denounced by people in the Office of the Secretary of Defense who believe this aircraft is clearly unnecessary and saturated with cost over-runs.

Whether the causes are wasteful, corrupt military contracts or generally the corporate crime wave from Enron to Wall Street, Senator Clinton has not been there in the Congress to advance comprehensive corporate crime legislation and larger enforcement resources.

Nor has she taken on the hundreds of billions of dollars in corporate welfare—subsidies, giveaways, handouts and bailouts for big business—that consume the contributions of millions of small taxpayers.

Even in New York City, have you heard Senator Clinton object to taxpayer-funded corporate sports stadiums, while health clinics, schools, libraries and public works decay for lack of public investment? Tax dollars for entertainment are ok by her.

Some of her paucity of candor is not going unnoticed, however. In explaining why she voted for George Bush's Iraq War resolution in 2002, she said she believed that it called for an attempted diplomatic solution. There were no words in that resolution to support that belief. She is a lawyer. She also knows that an amendment by Senator Carl Levin, a fellow Democrat, demanded just such a prior diplomatic effort. She voted against the Levin proposal.

Still, Hillary, with Bill right there, is the frontrunner for the Democratic Party's nomination. The money from commercial interests, which the Clintons have favored and coddled for years, is pouring into her campaign coffers.

So she travels around the country with her twofer strategy—pandering to powerful audiences and flattering gatherings of Democratic voters. She has watched Bill's lack of political fortitude win elections in this two-party, elected dictatorship against the hapless Republicans. Why should she be any different?

If she wins the primary and the November elections the country will get another kind of twofer in the White House. Here they'll go again.

President Bush Owes Troops an Apology

November 3, 2006

The baying pack of belligerent draft dodgers—Messrs. Bush, Cheney and Limbaugh—were out in verbal force this week against John Kerry. The Senator miscued a joke about Bush by reading without the "us" in the line, "You end up getting us stuck in a war in Iraq. Just ask President Bush." The missing of the "us" word gave the messianic militarists an opening to demand that Kerry apologize to the US troops for his "insulting" and "shameful" remarks.

Interesting isn't it, how a misreading of a word can be seen as cause for apology when thousands of illegal and destructive deeds and tortures constitute the Bush regime's "business as usual."

There will likely be no apologies from Bush/Cheney for putting US soldiers into a fabricated war-quagmire—a disastrous, costly boomeranging invasion. But to set the record straight about who should apologize, here are on the ground reasons for nine Bush/Cheney *mea culpas.*

1. FAILURE TO PROVIDE ADEQUATE BODY ARMOR AND TRUCK ARMOR IN A TIMELY FASHION.

A Pentagon study found that "as many as 80 percent of the marines who have been killed in Iraq from wounds to the upper body could have survived if they had had extra body armor," according to a *New York Times* report. Hundreds of soldiers died who could have been saved.

The *Washington Post* reported "that in some places in Iraq the US military could provide only one Interceptor vest with protective plates for every three US soldiers."

2. FAILURE TO ACCURATELY REPORT CASUALTIES.

The Bush administration has undercounted injuries to soldiers in Iraq to hold down opposition to the war. Injuries that were not incurred in the middle of battle are not part of the official casualty count by the Bush Administration. Cases of diseases, such as thousands of Sand Fly afflictions, are not even counted. This disrespects these soldiers and their families to bolster a cynical political calculation.

3. FAILURE TO PROVIDE SUFFICIENT TROOP STRENGTH IN IRAQ

The *Washington Times* reports that retired military leaders who served in Iraq said that Secretary of Defense Donald Rumsfeld "ignored advice for more troops, failed to make a post-invasion plan or equip troops properly and hid information from the public."

"I believe that Secretary Rumsfeld and others in the administration did not tell the American people the truth for fear of losing support for the war in Iraq," retired Army Maj. Gen. John R.S. Batiste told the panel. Mr. Batiste, a self-described Republican who has been criticizing Mr. Rumsfeld for months, said the secretary "forbade military planners from developing plans for securing a postwar Iraq" and helped create the current insurgency by ignoring the potential for one, though it was "an absolute certainty."

Retired Army Maj. General Paul D. Eaton, who criticized Mr. Rumsfeld in the *New York Times* last spring, said the post-invasion effort in Iraq is about 60,000 troops short of what it needs for success and that the Army "is in terrible shape," lacking proper equipment and resources.

President Bush should never have invaded Iraq, but whenever troops are deployed they should be at levels which are necessary to protect the civilian population—an obligation military occupiers are required, under international law, to fulfill. Hundreds of thousands of innocent Iraqi women, men and children have become the casualties of incompetent planning.

4. FAILURE TO PROVIDE TROOPS IN IRAQ WITH SAFE DRINKING WATER.

Former Halliburton employees and army officials have testified before Congress that Halliburton provided our troops in Iraq with very contaminated water, which the troops used to shower, wash their hands and their faces, brush their teeth, wash their clothes, and sometimes even make coffee.

5. FAILURE TO CARE FOR TROOPS.
Sending part-time soldiers from the Reserves and National Guard on dangerous missions—such as roadside mine searches—without anything resembling adequate training.

6. FAILING TO CARE FOR RETURNING TROOPS.
The Knight Ridder News Service reported that the Government Accountability Office found that the Veterans Administration "badly underestimated how many soldiers returning from Iraq and Afghanistan might seek medical and other services, in part because of problems in getting accurate information from the Pentagon." Consequently many returning troops have had difficulty getting prompt medical attention.

7. FAILURE TO HELP VETERANS WITH POST-TRAUMATIC STRESS DISORDER (PTSD).
The *Washington Post* reports that a Government Accountability Office report concluded: "Nearly four in five service members returning from the wars in Iraq and Afghanistan who were found to be at risk for post-traumatic stress disorder (PTSD) were never referred by government clinicians for further help. . . ."

8. FAILURE TO PROTECT SOLDIERS AND VETERANS FROM OFF-BASE SCAMS.
The *New York Times* reports that "several financial services companies or their agents are using questionable tactics on military bases to sell insurance and investments that may not fit the needs of people in uniform." *USA Today* reports that a Defense Department report said "the average borrower pays $827 on a $339 loan and called the lending predatory." A recently passed law will cap interest rates at 36 percent. The De-

fense Department should have cracked down on the corporate and economic predators that prey on military personnel and their families.

9. FAILURE TO ADEQUATELY PAY TROOPS WHEN ABROAD AND WHEN INJURED.
The *Baltimore Sun* reports that deployment in Iraq is "taking a financial toll on part-time soldiers who make up about half of the 150,000 troops there. Forty-one percent of National Guard and Reserve soldiers are losing thousands of dollars through a 'pay gap' between their civilian salary and military pay . . ."

These inexcusable, contemptuous indifferences to the well-being of the soldiers, combined with the rush to wage an unnecessary, immoral and unconstitutional war, characterized by corrupt, wasteful contracting debacles of unprecedented proportions, should compel President George W. Bush and Vice President Dick Cheney not only to apologize, but to resign.

Bill Moyers for President?
October 27, 2006

How does "Bill Moyers for president" sound to you? The long time Democrat and special assistant to President Lyndon B. Johnson would surely widen the political debate inside the Democratic Party and its primaries in 2008.

For over a year, since leaving Public Television and his luminous Friday night program NOW, Moyers has been completing a book about President Johnson. His periodic lectures on the politics of progressive populism and the dangers of corporate power and abuses have thrilled large civic audiences and circulated widely on the internet.

A few months ago, columnists Molly Ivins

and John Nichols wrote about the desirability of Moyers' tossing his hat into the ring. In his private conversations with friends, I am told, he has not ruled out a run. On the contrary he showed some interest in an exchange with an old Texan friend.

Moyers brings impressive credentials beyond his knowledge of the White House-Congressional complexes. He puts people first. Possessed with a deep sense of history relating to the great economic struggles in American history between workers and large companies and industries, Moyers today is a leading spokesman on the need to deconcentrate the manifold concentrations of political and economic power by global corporations. He is especially keen on doing something about media concentration about which he knows from recurrent personal experience as a television commentator, investigator, anchor and newspaper editor.

As millions of viewers and readers over the decades know, Bill Moyers is unusually articulate and authentic in evaluating the unmet necessities and framing the ignored solutions in our country.

He has interviewed hundreds of authors, scholars, politicians and activists demonstrating his penchant for being well prepared in advance.

Moyers would bring to the Democratic Party a much needed understanding of the South, its political, populist and religious history and contemporary dynamics. His Baptist, Texas background would help his Party understand how to stop writing off the South to the Republicans from the presidential to the state and local levels and how to become engaged in this fastest growing region of the nation.

Few people can bridge the perceived gaps between political regions. His books demonstrate that unique and calm ability to persuade people to come to grips with fundamentals. His presence in the presidential primary debates would not be marginalized.

Moyers has done compelling television programs on the corruption of money in politics—commercial money given to incumbents and candidates with the understanding that there is a quid pro quo. He wouldn't follow those paths. Still he would have to raise money without strings attached to be credible to the media and the pollsters.

This is where Moyers has an advantage over other progressive candidates either within the Democratic Party, like Dennis Kucinich, or in the Green Party, like Peter Camejo and Howie Hawkins.

Moyers has the best contacts among well-to-do progressive Americans of anyone I know. People, who want nothing in return but clean politics, responsive government and more power to the people to make corporations the servants, not masters, respect Moyers.

My guess is that with a good campaign staff he could raise $30 million during the primary season and receive millions more in federal matching funds. Such a sum would not come close to the cash that Hillary Clinton or John Kerry could raise. But carefully spent and connected to a community based movement of new leaders to freshen and redirect the Democratic Party, something of a breakthrough could happen.

At the least Moyers would quicken the pulse of his Party and give it some moxy.

If you have any interest in this proposal contact me at P.O. Box 19312, Washington, DC 20036.

Wrecker-in-Chief

October 20, 2006

On October 17th, George W. Bush, signed into law a bill he bulldozed through Congress that, in Senator Patrick Leahy's prophetic words, would suspend "the writ of habeas corpus, a core value in American law, in order to avoid judicial review that prevents government abuse." This law, whose constitutionality is in doubt and will be reviewed by the Supreme Court in due time, puts so much arbitrary and secret unilateral power in the hands of the Presidency that the ghost of King George III must be wondering what all the fuss was about in 1776.

If you want more evidence of how obsessive-compulsive George W. Bush is about his wars, their fabrications, budgets and cover-ups, consider his cue card statement on the legislation at the White House signing ceremony. "It is a rare occasion when a president can sign a bill he knows will save American lives," he declared.

Hello! He has rejected all kinds of occasions to save American lives here at home. He has refused to do anything about the widespread and preventable mayhem known as medical and hospital malpractice, while fanatically pushing for restrictions on the right of such victims or their next of kin to have their full day in court. Close to 100,000 Americans die from malpractice just in hospitals every year, according to the Harvard School of Public Health.

The same presidential pen could have saved thousands of more lives and prevented many more injuries were it used to sign safety legislation and larger budgets for reducing job-related sickness and trauma (58,000 lost lives a year) and air pollution (65,000 lives a year)—to name a few categories of preventable violence. But he signaled from the onset of his presidency that such bills would be opposed from the get-go.

And once again remember his incompetence in letting US soldiers—hundreds of them die in Iraq from the lack of adequate body armor.

At the signing event, Mr. Bush called the legislation "a way to deliver justice to the terrorists we have captured." To him all captured subjects are *ipso facto* convicted terrorists. It is not as if his record gives any credence to such fantasies. But he persists in his deception none the less. Out of nearly 700 prisoners in Guantánamo Bay, he has charged only ten after over four years of detention. Ten! Why? Mostly, as military, civilian lawyers and other monitors have said, because the vast majority of these abused or beaten prisoners were innocent from the day of their apprehension—victims of bounty hunters in Afghanistan and its surroundings.

It served Bush's political purposes to say to the American people that Guantánamo Bay contained the most evil of all people, so long as he could deny the innocents any opportunity to challenge their incarceration (habeas corpus) in an impartial tribunal. Until the Supreme Court ordered him to stop denying the "detainees" due process.

Here in the US, Bush has imprisoned over 5,000 people as terror suspects without charging them. Ninety nine percent turned out to be innocent of accusations that they were engaged in terrorist activities. Given this batting average, it is troubling that Mr. Bush has the unchecked power to deprive those he imprisons, with or without charges and without attorneys, of habeas corpus. In these tribunals established by the new law, the defendants' have no right to review evidence against them and cannot challenge Bush's unbridled power to determine the definition of torture.

So vague are the law's words that what constitutes "terrorist activity" and whether it can be used against US citizens remain within the monarchical power of George W. Bush to decide.

Anyone who doubts the assertion that the new law will be used to remove any boundaries—constitutional, statutory or treaty—from restraining Mr. Bush and his subordinates should read the celebratory article by a former Bush Administration official, law professor John Yoo, in the *Wall Street Journal.* He reads the law as removing the courts—including the Supreme Court—from any judicial review of Bush's "war on terror". Mr. Yoo left out the obvious conclusion, which is that Mr. Bush is now, in this area, the legislative and the judicial authority—the dominator of checks and balances.

To Bush allies, such as Mr. Yoo, the boundless inherent power of the presidency, does not ever include any recommendation that these poor, innocent souls, swept up by wasteful, boomeranging dragnet practices, be compensated for their brutalization and confinement.

Bush's belligerent policies after 9/11, which caught him napping in Crawford, Texas have served to provide recruitment grounds for more and more trained terrorists. Look at Iraq and Afghanistan. Pursuing policies against terrorism that create more terrorists have been noted by Bush's own military and civilian officials, not to mention scores of ex-military, diplomatic and intelligence retirees who served in past Republican and Democratic administrations.

One would think, with such backing, the Congressional Democrats would have moved to block his rampages which have so lowered his public approval to below 40 percent.

None of this fazes or affects the messianic militarist in the White House. He continues his ways of endangering our nation, weakening its moral and political influence abroad, turning off more and more of the American people disgusted with the huge costs in lives and money, and deep-sixing his Republican Party. Even the latter achievement cannot rescue history's description as an all-purpose, self-inflicted Wrecker-in-Chief.

"Options for Revision"
October 6, 2006

Imagine the US military—from the soldiers on the ground to the generals—saying publicly what they are saying and thinking privately about their two draft-dodging but bellicose rulers in the White House.

Sometimes, reporters have gathered a few excoriating statements from the frustrated, beleaguered, often body armor-less GIs. One even demanded Bush's resignation from his barracks in Iraq, which was shown on national television.

There is also the under-reported Zogby poll released in January 2006—the only scientifically sampled field poll in Iraq—which showed over 70 percent of the soldiers thought the United States should withdraw in a time period ranging from six months to a year. And this opinion in the war zone was registered when the situation was not as bad as the quagmire is today.

As for the Generals, their dissatisfaction with Don Rumsfeld, Secretary of Defense, goes well beyond his brusque personality into the rigid and mistaken policies from the beginning of this fabricated, illegal war.

Now comes the *New York Times* reporter, Michael R. Gordon, with a page-one story about a forthcoming Army and Marine Corps field manual with a "new counterinsurgency doctrine that draws on the hard learned lessons from Iraq and makes the welfare and protection of civilians a bedrock element of military strategy."

Some might view this manual—drawing from the experiences of bottom to top military personnel—to be an indirect rebuke of the failed brute force military policies of the Bush White House. Some may also wonder what took the Pentagon so long to rediscover old knowledge about what succeeded and failed in foreign military occupations. Old knowledge that says reliance on sheer military power, mistreating prisoners, and not safeguarding civilians and essential public services fails again and again.

Well, better late than never. This particular field manual went through many comments, consultations, and drafts before distilling nine "representative paradoxes" of counterinsurgency operations. Their theme is that the more force used, the less effective it is. Staying in touch with the civilian population, instead of staying in compounds, is more effective than a brute force and firepower approach. Dollars and ballots have more impact than sheer weaponry because they strengthen the host country's restoration of basic services like police, electricity, drinking water, food, health and schools.

Other paradoxes include one that says "tactical success guarantees nothing," and that "most of the important decisions are not made by generals," but by troops at all levels.

By now you are probably saying, "Isn't that just repeating the obvious?" Why, yes, but when your dogmatic, messianic commanders are Bush and Cheney, shorn of history, common sense, and critical reactive thinking, the "obvious" has to be conveyed as something new, lest it be seen as what it is—a repudiation of disastrous policies from design to supply to logistics.

Col. Conrad C. Crane (Ret.), the director of the Military History Institute at the Army War College and a principal drafter of the new doctrine told the *New York Times*: "In many ways, this is a bottom-up change. The young soldiers who had been through Somalia, Haiti, Bosnia, Kosovo, and now Iraq and Afghanistan, understood why we need to do this."

But the drafters of this "new" approach know that applying it on the ground requires more soldiers, more smarts and fewer profiteering, bungling corporate contractors. They might have added that protecting the civilian population—in contrast to the violent chaos and anarchy brutalizing the Iraqi people daily—is a requirement of international law. Invaders who occupy another country are obligated under international treaties to keep order and to safeguard the rights and safety of civilians.

By engaging in sectarian politics in Iraq and playing favorites, among their publicized blunders, the Bush occupation sowed the seeds of the upheavals that are tearing the country apart at an increasing pace.

So when this field manual reaches President Bush's desk, with the requisite cue card summaries, the findings will likely be rejected. After all, a failed war that keeps failing can at least point to the growth of the terroristic forces in Iraq as the circular rationale for "staying the course."

Mr. Bush's own intelligence reports, and not just the most recent highly publicized National Intelligence Estimate, have concluded that the war-occupation is providing recruitment and training grounds for terrorists.

Daddy Bush should take his son and have him repeat after him again and again—"options for revision," "options for revision," "options for revision." Unless, that is, Bush and Cheney both do the country a favor and resign.

The No-Fault President

September 1, 2006

The chronically no-fault White House and its no-fault president were on their no-fault roll again around the country. George W. Bush, the Commander-in-Chief of the politics of no-faultism—went on another redundant symbolic trip to Katrina land. There, near the wreckage that even now is much of New Orleans, he announced: "I take full responsibility for the federal government's response."

Politicians often resort to such "full responsibility" language when they know no one can impose any real accountability—in this case for a continuing cascade of Bush's governmental blunders, incompetence, corrupt contracting and fundamental dereliction of duty. All these abysmal failures are occurring in spite of the many billions of dollars made available by Congress for rebuilding and critical services.

Month after month, the same pictures of huge swaths of the devastated city dominate television news programs. Half of the population of New Orleans has not returned because there is still nothing to return to. Most of the hospitals are still closed.

Thousands of trailers purchased for the people who lost their homes are still parked, undistributed along the affected Gulf regions, in Hope, Arkansas—the hometown of Bill Clinton. Your 400 million tax dollars at work.

If George W. Bush heard one message from the bone-weary residents during his trip again and again, it was the question, "Mr. President, are you going to turn your back on me?" "Not again," he replied to one witness. And then off he flew to the ranch at Crawford before taking off again to visit cities sounding his anti-terrorism theme. A theme he is hoping will win for the Republicans in the November mid-term elections.

Polls and other indicators show that he is losing ground. More and more Americans are going with the majority who don't believe him on Iraq and not just his fabricated arguments for the boomeranging invasion of 2003. They don't believe the Iraq War is worth the cost; worth the distraction from the problems here at home, or has anything to do with the terrorism he invokes when he speaks of 9/11.

This past week the president—obsessively-compulsive with his disastrous war policies—chose assemblies of veteran groups to reach new depths of historical hysteria. He compared the struggle against "Islamic extremists" to the battles against Nazism and Communism.

Consider this grotesque exaggeration. The Nazis launched an expansionist world war against numerous countries with what was then the most powerful military machine in the world. They slaughtered many millions of civilians. The Soviet communists possessed multiple nuclear capabilities which could destroy the United States in an hour—as the US could do to them. Does George W. Bush have any idea what his prepared cue cards are telling him to utter?

The thrust of the opposition to the US in the Middle East is to get the US out of their land, their oil resources, and to stop backstopping the Israeli occupations of Arab land and control of precious Arab water in Palestine and Syria. Many in the Middle East want an end to the decades long military, political and diplomatic support of what they see as dictatorships over their own people.

As Mr. Bush, Secretary of State Colin Powell and Secretary of Defense Donald Rumsfeld each said once in the aftermath of 9/11, dictatorships, destitution, poverty and hopelessness are breeding grounds for the emergence of terrorists. But Mr. Bush, Mr. Cheney and Mr. Rumsfeld are not following the logic of such a recognition in perpetuating their failed and perilous policies overseas.

Inside the Bush Administration—from General Casey to then CIA Director, Porter Goss—to outside the government among prominent former Generals, Ambassadors and intelligence officials, there is the realization that our military presence in Iraq is a recruiting magnet for training more and more young men for violent sabotage.

Many of the retired government officials, who have served under Republican and Democratic Administrations, have spoken out. They have written articles, given media interviews, co-signed letters, testified and some have marched in protest. But they're not yet ready to say publicly that Bush and Cheney should resign for their disastrous performances against the interests of the United States and its position in the world.

The Bush regime simply has no standards for failures in its operations because it has no intention of ever admitting their failures and then changing course. No-fault-Bush and Cheney have every intention of continuing the loss of the lives of American soldiers and the bloody casualties among Iraqis until they hand the situation in Iraq over to their successors in January 2009. Mr. Bush has said as much a few weeks ago.

He will never withdraw our troops and close our military bases no matter what the cost to our country and its ignored critical necessities here at home.

So, taking the lead in full page advertisements in the *New York Times* is a new group by the name of The World Can't Wait (www.worldcantwait.org). They are not waiting for Congress to impeach Bush. They want a mass mobilization to make Bush/Cheney resign. Richard Nixon resigned and Vice President, Spiro Agnew, resigned for causes far less momentous than the crimes of these stubborn recidivists in control of our federal government.

In one of his desperate rhetorical reaches last week, Mr. Bush assailed his critics as "blaming America first." No, Mr. Bush, a growing majority of Americans are blaming you—George W. Bush—not America. Every day you demonstrate how you are ruining America.

Accept your responsibility at long last and retire to Texas along with Mr. Cheney, as an act of mercy.

George the Foolish

July 21, 2006

British Kings used to be described with an epithet after their name, as with Richard-the Lion Hearted. Events on the warring grounds of the Middle East—from Iraq to Palestine to Lebanon—that Bush, by his aggressive choice is mired in—warrant him being called "George-the War Criminal" or "George-the Patron Saint of Elected Islamic Theocracies," or "George-the Foolish." Take your pick.

Consider the little, defenseless country of Lebanon—so friendly to the United States—being "torn to shreds," in the words of its desperate Lebanese Prime Minister, Fouad Siniora, by Israel's American-built warplanes, missile and artillery.

Bush's asserted foreign policy theme has been to spread democracy in the Middle East (while he daily weakens democracy in America), and all he has done so far is to destroy or injure hundreds of thousands of innocent people, leaving the chaos and utter destruction that strengthens the power of grassroots Islamists and trains more stateless terrorists in Iraq. In other words, to use the CIA's phrase, "blowback" against our country's interests is breaking out all over.

But Lebanon was supposed to be the exception. With US pressure, Syrian troops—originally invited in with US support during the Lebanese civil war to provide stability—were pressured to leave last year. The "Cedar Revolution" was peaceably proclaimed in Lebanon by a US friendly government composed of the various religious denominations. Finally, independent of both Israeli and Syrian troops for the first time in twenty-three years, the Lebanese started to pull themselves and their economy together.

See Lebanon, see the future in the Middle East, cried George W. Bush—the American Caeser with his advisors in the White House.

Now see Lebanon. In a matter of days, the country is in ruins, its economy shattered, roads, bridges, airports, wheat silos, trucks with medical supplies, new ambulances rushing into service and whole families fleeing north in packed vehicles blown up.

The horrific stillness is in the civilian neighborhoods mostly populated by the innocent poor and their children. The *New York Times* reports "In Srifa, a neighborhood was wiped out—15 houses flattened, 21 people killed, 30 wounded—in an Israeli air strike. The town's mayor, Afif Najdi called it a massacre." Half-a-million civilians and growing are homeless.

In the Palestinian refugee camp of Al Bourj holding 20,000 people, Israeli bombers unleashed explosives. In a frantic appeal for help to anyone on the global internet a charitable rescue

organization entered the area and described a scene of "total devastation with all the buildings and roads totally smashed. There was the smell of death and destruction everywhere."

And so the rain of Israeli terror fell over this utterly defenseless country, while Bush does nothing but emit "go" signals to the fifth most powerful military in the world. He repeats again and again that "Israel has a right to defend itself." Of course, but not "collective punishment" against millions of people (including tens of thousands of Arab-Americans and other US citizens living or visiting there) who had nothing whatsoever to do with the border raid by Hezbollah.

The Israeli practice of collective punishment, a war crime under the Geneva Convention, is standard against the Palestinians, who lost 78 percent of their land in the 1940s and want to preserve the 22 percent that is left to them (the 1967 boundaries). More collective punishments against the Lebanese now, just like during the unprovoked Israeli invasion of 1982.

In that year, Israel broke an 11 month truce with the PLO and smashed their way to Beirut, destroying 20,000 Lebanese lives and injuring many more. The *New York Times* reported "indiscriminate" bombing of Beirut. Israeli planes dropped deadly cluster bombs all over the country including four clearly marked hospitals, as reported in the *Washington Post* and the *Philadelphia Inquirer.*

Who took the brunt of these war crimes? The Shiites who make up the bulk of the population of south Lebanon. And what emerged to defend these defenseless human beings who were not part of the PLO resistance that was the alleged object of the invasion? Hezbollah. A product of Israel's collective punishment.

Since the Israelis withdrew from southern

Lebanon in 2000—after 18 years of oppression over the natives—the still land-mined border has been porous. Far more for the well-equipped Israelis than to Hezbollah. Israel also routinely violated Lebanon's airspace and coastal waters, terrorized the area with abductions and damage, retained control over Lebanese territory called Shebaa Farms and generally got away with it without international news coverage. Since 2000, Israeli soldiers and Hezbollah fighters would ritually eye each other over the border and sometimes engage in skirmishes. Still, Hezbollah and Israel wisely negotiated some prisoner exchanges. Israel had 100 times more prisoners to exchange than did Hezbollah.

So on July 12, Hezbollah went for another prisoner exchange by capturing two Israeli soldiers in a firefight, and thought the result would be another such exchange. Big mistake. Even Hezbollah under-estimated the need for each new Israeli Prime Minister to demonstrate his capability for massive mayhem.

Among other towns, he is destroying the ancient coastal town of Tyre where the carpenters have run out of wood for the coffins. The fleeing inhabitants of this municipality of approximately 25,000 people wonder whether they will survive the flight to who knows where from Israeli shelling and aircraft.

So George W. Bush, who knows that Hezbollah's rockets were fired after Israel started its mass bombing and shelling of Lebanon, willfully rejects a truce, typical of his refusal for five years to overcome Israel's opposition to an adequate multinational peacekeeping force on the Lebanese-Israeli border.

Finally, did you know that Hezbollah is one of the largest employers in Lebanon—schools, clinics, stores, farming, transport? It has 14 elected members in the Lebanese Parliament.

It is militantly determined to defend its nearly 2 million Shiites—the downtrodden of Lebanon—from all aggressions. It receives weapons from Iran and the international weapons markets, while Israel receives weapons from the United States within an overall annual aid program of $4 billion.

Israel has 175,000 soldiers and another 400,000 ready reservists. It totally controls the skies, the seas and the ground forces with its advanced precision armaments. It is backed up by the United States to whose Congress it will send the bill for this war. Hezbollah has anywhere from 2,000 to 3,500 fighters, according to US press reports, with small arms and short to medium range rocket launchers.

This is a relevant comparative reality, which should replace the apoplectic exaggerations so that sane voices and powers—Israeli, Arab, American and European—can stop the battles, stabilize the border with an effective international guard and move toward a broader Israeli-Palestinian peace agreement.

The powerful parties and their allies can make this happen far easier than the weaker parties to the conflict. Meanwhile, George W. better stop "losing Lebanon," and fast.

The South Central Farm Showdown

June 5, 2006

South Central Farm, Los Angeles—The showdown is likely here this week over the preservation of this nation's largest urban farm worked by 350 families for 13 years to feed themselves and their neighbors a dazzling variety of organic produce.

Will the Sheriff of Los Angeles County

move on this 14 acre farm with dozens of squad cards to enforce an eviction notice on behalf of its developer-owner?

Or will the Mayor of Los Angeles, Antonio R. Villaraigosa, come up with the private benefactors to match what has already been raised in order to meet the hefty selling price of about $16 million by its present owner, Ralph Horowitz?

Wednesday seems to be the day of decision. The Sheriff is focusing on eviction and has laid elaborate battle plans featuring overwhelming force in the early dawn hours and hoping for a minimum of injuries. He proudly swears that this is not going to be "another Seattle," meaning a prolonged, out of control, media-saturated struggle.

At the same time, the mayor, desiring to let the farmers continue their urban community gardens and farmers' market, is racing to raise the over $1 million per acre price tag. He wants to avoid what could become a very ugly confrontation between determined residents, practicing organized non-violent civil disobedience against police with clubs, tear gas and other eviction tools. The Mayor knows that he could become either the hero of this vast, impoverished area of the city or its memorable villain.

Yesterday, I visited South Central Farm and felt the energy of its people—creative energy brimming with plans to make their acres a "hub of a city-wide green movement, a learning center for schoolchildren, a demonstration garden for home gardeners, a community space for art and performance, a plaza for our farmers' market, a commons for all of us." Mr. Horowitz wanted the land for use as a warehouse.

The South Central Farm is fast becoming a cause célèbre and earning the designation—"The Whole World is Watching." Celebrities from Hollywood, the musical and political are-

nas have visited. The stalwart of stalwarts, Julia Butterfly Hill—of Redwood Tree Residence fame—is living in a tree there and is in her 20th day of fasting. Contributions and expressions of support are coming in from many countries.

Walking through the gardens felt like the two meanings of the word *verdure* "the greenness of growing vegetation and a condition of health and vigor." The corn was shoulder high, vines, vegetable and fruit plants of large varieties were coming to fragrant fruition. The seeds are a big deal. People here talk about them lovingly. Many came from Mexico and none are the kind that are subjected to a regular payment to Monsanto. They are passed from one small farmer to another.

A dualistic sense of impending doom or victory is everywhere. Having experienced a series of legal defeats, due to a bizarre history of City Hall dealings with this land, there appear to be more pessimists than optimists. At least a foreboding pessimism. To people here the law is seen as an instrument of oppression instead of a mechanism for justice.

A little history will frame the present conflict. In 1986, the City of Los Angeles took over this scarred, debris-ridden tract by eminent domain for the purpose of building a waste incinerator. The city paid a developer, Horowitz, $5 million with the proviso that if the land was ever resold he would have the right to buy it back. Attorneys for the farmers assert this is an illegal proviso and there is a trial date to litigate the question on July 12th.

Local opposition to the incinerator stopped the project. In 1992 after the upheavals in the wake of the Rodney King verdict, then Mayor Tom Bradley let the farmers move onto the land under the aegis of the L.A. Food Bank. They cleaned up the area and in their words, "made the soil live again."

In 1995, the city shifted the property to the L.A. Harbor Department as part of the Alameda Corridor plan—a commercial zone set up for development.

In 2002, Mr. Horowitz sued the city alleging that the transfer violated his earlier buy back agreement with the city. Attorneys for Los Angeles won three separate motions to dismiss his case but Mr. Horowitz persisted. Suddenly city officials agreed to sell the land back to him for the same $5 million, in secrecy, even though these officials knew the land was worth over twice that sum. The developer received the title in December of 2003.

The next month, Mr. Horowitz told the farmers to get out immediately. A flurry of lawsuits followed—the farmers have good, conscientious attorneys—but the court ruled for the developer and issued an order of eviction on May 24th 2006.

After I spoke with a well-placed city official, my prediction is that South Central Farms will be like its soil. It will continue "to breathe, drink and sweat. It will continue to harbor life and dreams."

It will not be destroyed because its people are indomitable. People who are indomitable, who stay together and take a stand in a righteous cause with overwhelming public support, often can end political careers. For more, see www.southcentralfarmers.com.

The whole world is watching.

The Bush-Cheney Cabal

March 24, 2006

Attention please, good people! Adjust your routines and come to the aid of your country, and your children with your thoughtful patriotism. Don't just hope for impeachment, demand the resignation now of the mad hatters in the White House—George W. Bush and Richard Cheney.

Already, a large majority of you do not consider this shifty duo trustworthy. By more than two to one you disapprove of Bush's war in Iraq. Similar majorities believe this is also a president whose administrative incompetence—note the post-Katrina debacles compared to his promises last September in that devastated New Orleans—nearly matches his penchant for daily fabrications.

The precipitous drop in Bush's polls (Cheney's are even lower) is not coming from liberals who long ago registered negative in these national surveys. The drop is coming from millions of erstwhile Bush supporters, Bush voters, Bush-loving conservatives.

Why? Just look at or read the news every day. There goes Bush and Cheney insisting that conditions in Iraq are getting better and better, when they are getting worse and worse. And Americans also know this because hundreds of thousands of soldiers and other personnel are rotating from Iraq back into every state and community and telling millions of people the truth.

Repeated reports from diverse official, media and eyewitness accounts say that there is less electricity, more disease, less drinkable water, less housing, far less street security, less healthcare, less gasoline, fewer jobs and far more violence against civilians after the Bush-Cheney-Rumsfeld invasion in March 2003 than before the sanctioned, tottering, besieged dictator, Saddam Hussein, was toppled.

With Bush's own ambassador to Iraq warning of a possible civil war and Bush's handpicked interim Iraqi prime minister, Ayad Allawi saying "We are in a terrible civil conflict now," the serial delusionists, Bush and Cheney, having lied five ways into their war, go around daily as smarmy pollyannas spouting what Bush calls "a strategy that will lead to victory in Iraq".

Why, didn't you know about all the progress in Iraq? If only the media would report it, they both say again and again. Really! What about all the corruption by the many contractors, all the brutal militias that now often do their work wearing Iraqi soldier or police uniforms, all the bogus reconstruction, paid with billions of American taxpayer money? What about the spreading chaos that Bush has no intention of confronting, as international law requires any invading occupiers to remedy. Remember Colin Powell's tight phrase, "We broke it, we own it," that sums up the global law on this subject.

Massive separation from reality frequently involves ordinary personalities with psychotherapy. Read the words of the *Washington Post's* respected columnist, Eugene Robinson:

The people running this country sound convinced that reality is whatever they say it is. And if they've actually strayed into the realm of genuine self-delusion—if they actually believe the fantasies they're spinning about the bloody mess they made in Iraq over the past three years—then things are even worse than I thought.

He described Bush as "divorced from reality".

Worse still is the delusion that claims the Bush-Cheney War is not generating more terrorists. Mr. Bush doesn't listen to intelligence, military and diplomatic officials, or even to his CIA Director Porter Goss. Mr. Goss has testified that the US occupation is a magnet and a training ground for even more terrorists from outside and inside Iraq. Thereby, setting up a boomerang against our national security in the future.

One area, however, in Iraq is proceeding on schedule—the building of four massive, permanent super-bases, complete with American suburban amenities such as Pizza Hut, Burger King, miniature golf courses, theaters, swimming pools and even a football field. There is almost a news blackout about Balad Air Base, al-Asad Airbase and others, though not quite the blockage that the two White House draft-dodgers have placed on reporters trying to cover the return of the fallen US soldiers to Dover, Delaware.

Senator Joe Biden (D-Del.) spoke about the growing opposition by both Republican and Democratic Senators to what can deliberately be called disinformation coming out of the Bush administration. Not to mention the refusal to respond at all to serious inquiries by members of Congress.

Unlike the presidential ordering of military invasions that violate our domestic laws, our Constitution and international treaties to which the US is a signatory, massive delusion in the White House is not an impeachable offense. But it should be a cause for resignation driven by popular bipartisan demand. Bush and Cheney have arrayed their no-fault power, their political egos against the interests of our country. They are obsessive-compulsive.

Bush recently traveled to West Virginia and did not speak to the poverty among some of the hardest workers in America. He went to Ohio on Air Force One and ignored the huge loss of manufacturing jobs there to Mexico, China and other authoritarian nations. No, instead, he brings his gigantic sign, "Plan for Victory", stands in front of it and, as befits the Mayor of Baghdad, talks about his delusions in that oil-rich, devastated country.

Reality, good citizens, can fairly describe the dictatorial Bush and Cheney as psychiatrically challenged. Send them to the unemployment lines, where Halliburton and Exxon will certainly pick them up.

The DNC's "Grassroots Agenda"

March 17, 2006

I just received a letter from Howard Dean, Chairman of the Democratic National Committee, describing me as a "Democratic Leader" and "an active and engaged member of our Party in your community." He asks for my "opinions" which "will help shape the future direction of the Democratic Party and make us more effective in building grassroots support for our agenda."

Dr. Dean attaches a survey "registered in your name and intended exclusively for your use." How nice! He made me feel even more exclusive when he called me "the strength and soul of the Democratic Party," along with other "local leaders."

Well, with such encomiums, how could I not peruse the lengthy questionnaire so that I can meet Mr. Dean's expectations. Especially with his personal instructions "Ralph, please turn the page to begin your survey."

The questions covered some important topics. They include one asking whether I support "new tax cuts targeted at working families." But no request for my opinion on removing the massive Bush tax reductions for the wealthy and their unearned income of capital gains and dividends, and for large corporations now making rocket profits.

Another inquiry asked about raising the minimum wage of $5.15 per hour, but no higher figure was listed. Nor was there a question about labor law reform assisting workers in our concentrated industrial, commercial and retail economy (eg. Walmart) to establish or expand

trade unions. The present system is rigged in favor of giant companies.

Down further in the survey, there is the question about allowing Medicare to bring in less expensive drugs from Canada, but nothing about controlling sky-high drug prices, including drugs developed by your federal taxpayer research dollars or drugs purchased without Uncle Sam having the right to bargain under the new notoriously nutty drug benefit concoction.

Question seven asks quite properly my opinion about "healthcare for all Americans." Three choices: tax credits for employers, medical savings accounts or "a government-run system where everyone is guaranteed health coverage." Who gave them these last words—the HMO industry? Why didn't the Democratic National Committee simply say "full Medicare for everyone?" Besides, the DNC should have said "a government-funded" system, which is what I believe they and "single-payer" advocates understand those words to mean. Not a takeover of the entire medical and health industry by the government. One would have thought Dr. Dean would have caught this miswording.

Two questions relate to withdrawal of US troops from Iraq. Various time frames are offered. But there is no question about whether a survey of Democratic leaders want to impeach Bush and Cheney or in any way hold these documented, serial outlaws accountable.

No inquiries on the corporate crime epidemic, so well described in the *Wall Street Journal*, *Fortune* and *BusinessWeek* magazines. No question about the massive corporate welfare payouts, directly and indirectly by the US Government, including the eminent domain controversy of seizing homes to raze them and give away the land to corporations.

Mississippi, for instance, wants to allocate

$240 million in hurricane-related federal tax escapes to a Korean auto company to build an assembly. The nearly $1 billion package of corporate welfare amounts to giving Kia Company $500,000 per job created, declared *Automotive News* in a critical editorial recently.

The survey also ignored the bloated, wasteful, redundant military budget, denounced as such by many Congressional and Executive branch reports, which now absorbs over one half of your entire federal discretionary budget. And there is no Soviet Union to provoke any more continual building of the Cold War era of weapons systems ala Lockheed Martin's endless wish list.

Of course, no Democratic Party survey ever includes a question on the need for much more consumer protection to avert harms and fraud, eating mightily into the standards of living, health and safety.

Sure, you can't keep adding questions for a survey like this but omitting questions relating to corporate crime, fraud and abuse of power is a telling commentary on the heavily business-funded Democratic Party. Which may explain why there is no question on getting dirty private money out of our public elections.

I was just getting going with my private critique of this survey when it occurred to me that I could not, in good conscience, reply to it. After all, I am not "an active and engaged Democratic Party leader."

Oh how indiscriminate and indiscreet computers have become, Dr. Dean!

Shredding the Constitution
March 10, 2006

George W. Bush and Dick Cheney, two top outlaws smashing our country's rule of law and democratic liberties, are testing the American people's resistance. Every day they are testing. Every day they think by flaunting the words, "war on terror", they can get Americans to concede more and more of what makes the United States a constitutionally-abiding government under the rule of law.

You know what? With not enough exceptions, they are right. Day by day, we're giving up what our forefathers fought to bequeath us since that famous Declaration of Independence of 1776. They were determined that people in this country would not be arrested without charges and jailed indefinitely, that they would not be tortured, or sent to be tortured in dictatorial regimes, or deprived of habeas corpus to take their incarceration to our courts of law, or be snooped on at the whim of the president and his deputies or that people in faraway lands would be destroyed in the tens of thousands due to a fabricated war-invasion-quagmire.

They instituted a constitution so that people would not be jailed without "probable cause", or be lied to about taking this country and its soldiers to war, or have shoved aside the checks and balances represented by American courts and the Congress. All these are being done by two earlier pro-Vietnam war draft dodgers!

What does all this tell you about all of us out there in the great United States of America? A giant yawn of "who cares" by citizens, nearly two-thirds of whom now have turned against these two White House fabricators in poll after poll regarding the war, the surrender to Big Business, the gross incompetence in managing taxpayer dollars and the Katrina disaster.

But listen, the rumble of resistance and opposition is getting louder and not just from the increasing number of public demonstrations around the country.

A new Zogby poll reports that 72 percent of American soldiers serving in Iraq think the US should get out within the next year, including 58 percent of the Marines! Three-quarters of National Guard and Reserve units support withdrawal within 6 months. Every month, more former high-ranking military officers, intelligence officials and diplomats are declaring their opposition to the war.

For a few examples of many: Retired four-star General, Joseph P. Hoar, who commanded the US forces in the Persian Gulf after the 1991 war, described the Iraq War as "wrong from the beginning". Similar tough criticism has come from John Deutch, former head of the CIA, Zbigniew Brzezinski, national security advisor to President Carter and Brent Scowcroft, national security advisor to the first President Bush.

Retired General William Odom, former head of the National Security Agency and security adviser to Ronald Reagan, wrote that the Iraq War "is serving the interests of Osama bin Laden, the Iranians, and is fomenting civil war in Iraq." He describes the Iraq War as "the most strategic foreign policy disaster in US history."

More recently, internal memos of criticism or dissent, Inspector General reports from Defense the Justice Department, and former highly-positioned staff within the Bush Administration, like Colonel Lawrence Wilkerson, chief of staff to Colin Powell, are taking apart the public relations sheen concocted by the Bush/Cheney/Rumsfeld triad.

Now comes the conservative American Bar Association—400,000 lawyers—whose House of Delegates has overwhelmingly approved a task force report accusing President Bush, in polite legal language, of violating both the Constitution and federal law. ABA President Michael S. Greco sent it to Mr. Bush with a cover letter dated February 13, 2006 (see americanbar.org for the full report).

The mass media, which has finally produced many exposes of the Bush war, ignored the significance of this condemnation by the nation's largest body of lawyers, written in part by attorneys who have served in the FBI, CIA and NSA. It should have been page one news.

There comes a tipping point, however, when the opposition of the establishment, the public opinion of the citizenry, the disgust of the soldiers—their spreading casualties, diseases and mental traumas—and the corruption of the large corporate contractors to whom much of the military's functions have been outsourced, all congeal and overcome the cowardliness of most members of Congress. Then a surge of Congressional followers and allies of Rep. John Murtha (D-Pa.), war veteran and leading voice against the Bush Iraq policies, may come to the forefront.

The illegal, disastrous (to both Iraqis and Americans) Iraq War is now almost three years of quagmire old. The chaos and bloodshed are worsening.

It is time to make the spring of 2006 the tipping point period for constitutionalism, justice and a sane foreign and national security policy. More yawns must turn into growls from outside Washington, DC. (See DemocracyRising.US for more information.)

Bush and Katrina: "Situational Information?"

March 3, 2006

Dear President Bush,

I saw you on the CBS television evening news the other day using a new phrase—"situational information." You were referring to the conditions just before and during the Katrina hurricane-Levee disaster in New Orleans. The "situational information" was not what it should have been, you declared. This was your way of saying that you did not receive prompt information about the risk the giant hurricane posed for the breaching of the city's levees.

Now it appears that you were given advance warning. This was the thrust of the CBS television news report by Bob Orr. Anchor Russ Mitchell introduced the segment with these words: "In the days following hurricane Katrina, President Bush insisted that no one in his administration anticipated the failure of the levees protecting New Orleans. But newly released videotape shows that as the huge storm approached the Gulf Coast, the president and his top advisors WERE warned it posed just such a threat to the low-lying city." (emphasis in the original).

These advisors included National Hurricane Center Director Max Mayfield and FEMA Director Michael Brown, who told top administration officials, including Homeland Secretary Michael Chertoff, of the "looming danger" "a day before landfall."

These tapes caused the *Wall Street Journal*'s article on March 2 to have this headline: "Tape of Pre-Katrina Briefing Shows Bush Was Warned of Dangers." Sounds like you received quite explicit "situational intelligence" which you still decline to acknowledge getting. Maybe the White House has a problem with "situational credibility".

Since that day when Hurricane Katrina struck the city of New Orleans and surrounding coastal areas, tens of thousands of displaced people—the survivors—have felt abandoned by the federal government. Scores of newspaper, television and radio eyewitness reports record

this abandonment in places like Ward 9 in New Orleans and Pearlington, Mississippi. The level of failure under your presidential watch is massive, ringed with private corporate contracting graft, corruption and waste. Prime Ministers in parliamentary nations would have fallen by now.

Recall your dramatic, nationally-televised choreographed assurance, standing near the French Quarter, that the federal government would take the lead in rebuilding New Orleans for its desperate residents and the return of those who fled. Get that videotape out and watch it, over six months of little action later. Maybe it will teach you something about the price that a destroyed area of America and its people are paying because you are expensively preoccupied being the Mayor of Baghdad.

Your regime's debacle after Katrina continues to leave tens of thousands of people without their homes. They are either in some motels temporarily, with friends or relatives or simply just homeless.

Yet next to the little-used municipal airport in Hope, Arkansas—Bill Clinton's home town—ten thousand or more FEMA mobile homes/trailers are sitting immobile week after week. The trailers were delivered to that staging area by the manufacturer, awaiting shipment to the needy, displaced families down south around New Orleans and the Gulf Coast communities. These families wait day after day, week after week.

You always tell reporters that the federal government's response could have been better. What about your response from late August to now? You are supposed to lead the federal government, so start leading directly by example.

Why not call up your friend Bill Clinton, with whom you and your father often have been seen together at social, ceremonial and charitable occasions? The telephone conversation can go like this:

GWB—"Hey Bill, how about you and me hopping on Air Force One pronto and heading down to your old stomping grounds around Hope. Let's show we can break up that bureaucratic log jam and leave Hope with 10,000 fewer trailers. I'm the president, you were the president. You were the governor of Arkansas. Hometown boy comes home to do good. What a great photo opportunity for bipartisanship?"

WJC—"Not a bad idea, George. But the bureaucracy starts in Washington, DC so there will have to be some bureaucracy-busting advance work done to make the visit a success. Then there is the matter of getting floodplain rules waived and all the other state and local rules which Washington has not confronted for months."

GWB—"Hmmm, Bill, you've been doing your homework."

WJC—"Not really, George, just reading the newspapers."

GWB—"Ok, ok, I get the snide remark. But I've been running a war for freedom."

WJC—"Didn't mean it that way, George. Sure, let's go down and get those trailers on the road. Where do you want to meet up . . . in Hope?"

GWB—"Very funny, Bill, like you are summoning me. We meet at the White House, get on the presidential helicopter and head for Andrews Air Force base. You know the protocols".

WJC—"What do you think our chances of success will be?"

GWB—"Well, heh, heh, Bill, what's that phrase—'Hope Springs Eternal.'"

Bush's Energy Escapades

February 3, 2006

It was, to use Yogi Berra's phrase—*déjà vu* all over again. George W. Bush's energy program in his State of the Union speech echoed the many similar promises made by his presidential predecessors going back to Ronald Reagan. Promises that were either vague or if specific, distant from realization. What irony to pledge to become energy independent, as we become ever more dependent on imported oil—imports are now reaching 60 percent of total US oil consumption.

"America is addicted to oil," exclaimed the president. No one more so than the president himself, a former oil industry executive who appointed over three dozen oil men like himself to high posts in his Administration—a regime marinated in oil.

The results have been, to say the least, oily. Although he has started to talk about renewable forms of energy, his actions speak louder. Last year, Bush's energy bill passed with billions of dollars in new subsidies for gas and oil, as if a staggering price for $60 or $70 a barrel is not enough to provide incentives to profit-glutted oil companies to produce.

Before reaching his desk, Bush made sure that some of the legislation's provisions were cut out. The renewable portfolio standard that was to require electric companies to obtain a certain percentage of their fuel from renewable sources was dropped. Bush also rejected an "oil savings amendment" to reduce oil use. And, of course, he adamantly refused to support any higher federal standards for motor vehicle fuel efficiency which has reached its lowest dismal level since 1980. Going backward into the future—GM style!

Moreover, he never uses the onset of global warming as a reason for more fuel efficient vehicles—even as Alaska melts down in ice and permafrost more and more each year.

Unwilling to push the auto companies, presently subsidized by your tax dollars in a boondoggle joint program with Uncle Sam, George W. Bush turns his back on what specialists inside and outside the industry know. Namely, that, as MIT's *Technology Review* documented in November 2002, "if it chose to, Detroit could manufacture a 40-mpg SUV by the end of the decade." Using existing or readily available technology, cars could go to an average of 46 mpg, that is, from the present level of about 21 mpg.

Imagine if the auto companies started to move, during the first oil crises in the mid-'70s. Your old vehicle would have reached the above-noted levels of efficiency, as the then U. S. Department of Transportation predicted could be the case.

Nice and warm in the White House, Mr. Bush did not throw his powerful lobbying crew late last year against the reduction of the already inadequate low-income home fuel assistance program for impoverished Americans. This reduction occurred in pouting retaliation to the Senate's defeat of Senator Ted Stevens' (Rep. Alaska) demand to drill in the Arctic National Wildlife Refuge.

Drained long ago of any empathy, Bush did not even react to the stupendous profit reports last week by the big oil companies, led by Exxon Mobil corporation's $10.71 billion for the fourth quarter of 2005 and $36.13 billion for the entire year.

Mind you, Exxon did not make this profit through its own innovation or bold marketing expertise. It received an undeserved windfall born of cartel-determined supplies and growing demand, the customary special tax breaks,

expanding taxpayer subsidies from Washington, and the gas guzzling motor vehicles that the stubborn auto giants deliver to the marketplace.

With his big business uber-allies mentality, Mr. Bush would not even go along with his fellow Republican, Senator Chuck Grassley's written request last November to the oil and gas moguls that they give 10 percent of their profits to help low-income Americans get through a cold winter.

Americans who do not qualify for low-income assistance are finding their budgets busted. David Harb of Redford, Michigan writes as a 58 year-old adult who stays home to take care of his elderly mother fulltime: "Regarding the prices of oil, natural gas and home heating costs, I am shocked, sickened & disgusted by their continually escalating utility bills that have gone through the roof and are driving the citizens, voters, taxpayers and homeowners of this state into bankruptcy and the poorhouse."

There needs to be a consumer uprising, with each gouged citizen pouring their demands on their members of Congress, on talk radio shows, newspaper editors and talking it up in their neighborhood. Nothing is faster and more credible than word of mouth between friends and relatives. At least make the oil giants give some of it back while the winter is here.

For more information, visit www.USPIRG.org.

Aggregate the Travesties to Hold Bush and Cheney Responsible
January 27, 2006

What will it take for George W. Bush and Dick Cheney to be held responsible for a multitude of political crimes, recklessness, prevarications and just plain massive ongoing mismanagement of the taxpayers' government?

The first step is to aggregate these travesties so they add up to a more comprehensive judgment. Then, together they confront us with an awful truth—that our present system of constitution, law and checks and balances have failed to be invoked by the elected and appointed officials of our Congress and our Courts. This is happening even though the polls have been dropping on the Bush regime for over a year and are now quite negative on many important questions.

Consider the following sample of irresponsibility and flouting of the law and then ask yourself how much more will it take to start holding the Bush/Cheney crowd of serial fibbers and dictacrats accountable? Is there ever to be a tipping point in the Washington world of spineless Democrats and supine Congressional Republicans worried about Bush losing the 2006 elections?

1. The drug benefit boondoggle, starting January 1, 2006, has been by all reports maelstrom of confusion, deprivation, gouging and misadministration, leaving many sick people in a frightening limbo. That is Bushland messing up big time while giving the gouging, long-subsidized profit-glutted drug companies hundreds of billions of dollars over the next decade paid by the taxpayer.

2. Katrina! The breaching of the levees was predicted at least over a year before and warned about just before the Hurricane hit by federal officials but ignored by the Administration. Bush's super-natural complex let him give the public the impression that the destruction was an unavoidable Act of God, when it was an avoidable disaster by Bush. The White House earlier had cut the Army Corps of Engineers budget designed for hurricane defense in the New Orleans area. The Corps itself is not blameless, but its commander in chief is, after all, George W. Bush.

3. Bush-Cheney plunged our country into an endless war-quagmire in Iraq on an often repeated platform of falsehoods, cover-ups and deliberate distractions from the ignored necessities here at home. Tens of thousands of American have lost their lives, their limbs and their health over there and the casualties of innocent Iraqi adults and children are much, much more numerous. Already costing hundreds of billions of dollars, the mismanagement of this war of choice is the material of hundreds of Pentagon audits, Congressional reports, official admissions, firsthand press reports and Congressional condemnations by the respected Government Accountability Office (GAO).

"Iraq Rebuilding Badly Hobbled", *US Report* finds, "is a recent front page headline in the *New York Times*—one of many such headlines in recent months. The corporate contractors, such as Halliburton, will set records for waste and worse as the facts spill out to the people.

4. The impeachable George W. Bush imperiously asserts that he will continue to violate federal law and place the American people under any surveillance without ever using a Congressionally-approved procedure requiring a quick and secret court warrant that is even permitted to be retroactive.

He and his pitchmen claim that they are pursuing terrorists. But the National Security Agency's (NSA) electronic dragnets are enveloping millions of people, flooding the FBI with what that agency says is mountains of indiscriminate undigested data that are useless.

Besides, as of the end of 2004, Bush and John Ashcroft, his then Attorney General had arrested 5,000 people on suspicion of terrorism, jailed them, most without charges, and then proceeded to strike out. Two were convicted and those convictions were overturned in Michigan. The Bush scorecard, according to Georgetown Law professor David Cole was 0 for 5000! Does this record qualify for chronic abuse of legal process or is it just sloppy law enforcement designed to produce political press releases?

5. Bush pumps "the ownership society" and opposes attempts to give investors the power that should accrue to them as owners over the self-enriching managers of the giant corporations. As a result, big time corporate executives keep vastly overpaying themselves through their rubber-stamp Boards of Directors (starting at $7200 an hour in 2002 and upward for the CEOs of the top 300 corporations). Warren Buffet called runaway executive compensation and stock options a central cause of cooking corporate books and undermining jobs and their own companies' financial stability.

6. Cutting life-sustaining programs for needy children, sick adults and regulatory health-safety protections for most Americans while reducing the taxes of the richest one percent, including his own and Cheney's taxes, invites Biblical condemnation. He has left many Americans defenseless from preventable hazards here at home, while he plays the providential Viceroy of Iraq. At the same time, Bush's forked tongue touts "the safety of the American people" as his highest responsibility.

7. He encumbers young children with taxes (who will have to pay the debt) through massive federal deficits brought about significantly by huge numbers of corporate handouts, giveaways, subsidies and tax escapism. That's one way of leaving children behind.

8. Mismanagement and underfunding im-plode his educational distraction called No Child Left Behind. Just ask the Republican state of Utah or millions of teachers beset with constant, vapid standardized multiple choice tests created by corporate consultants.

9. He huffs and puffs about spreading democracies around the world while condoning and encouraging the shipment of whole American industries and jobs to the communist Chinese dictatorship, and other dictatorships on which he continues to lavish such globalized policies.

However, his boomeranging foreign policy may yet turn him into an unintended patron saint of elected Islamic theocracies.

These and many other documentations of his tortured tenure can demonstrate what their aggregation can contribute to motivate the American people toward holding him and Cheney accountable to them under the rule of law. But don't count on the Democrats leading. They blew another election—congressional and presidential—against the worst Republicans in American history.

Aggregation, my fellow citizens, is up to your independent minds and judgments to absorb and act upon.

For a sample of *aggregation*, see DemocracyRising.us.

Congressional Ethics Reforms Miss Corporate Welfare

January 20, 2006

The Abramoff scandal has spurred one of the episodic "reform" moments on Capitol Hill. Republicans and Democrats are competing to offer ethics reform packages that ignore entirely their past entanglement in the very activities they now seek to regulate or eliminate. Not all of these reforms are toothless, and if enacted and enforced, some may, perhaps, reduce the scale and scope of corruption that has reached a zenith in the Congress.

But there is far too little attention being devoted to what exactly is provided in exchange for the favors that lobbyists bestow on members of Congress.

Those gifts—the campaign contributions, the airplane rides, the visits to resorts disguised as speech opportunities—are not really gifts as such to lawmakers. They are more like investments (or quasi-bribes). And they are investments that pay back beyond the dreams of the greediest Wall Street prospector, in the form of corporate welfare: grants and direct subsidies, government giveaways, bailouts, tax subsidies, loopholes and other escapes, below-market loans and loan guarantees, export and overseas marketing assistance, pork for defense, transportation and other companies, regulatory removals, immunities from civil justice liability, and a host of other government-provided benefits.

To take one example of note: the *Washington Post* reported on December 31 how Jack Abramoff helped arrange the payment of half a million dollars from textile firms in the Mariana Islands in the Pacific, to a front group controlled by Tom DeLay. In exchange, they "solicited and received Rep. DeLay's public commitment to block legislation that would boost their labor costs, according to Abramoff associates," the *Post* reported. Textiles made in the Mariana Islands may be labeled "Made in the USA," the factories there are exempt from US labor law, and working conditions are appalling.

The goodies bestowed by Congress on their patrons are too numerous and diverse to be addressed with any single reform approach.

But good legislation could go a long way to-

ward reducing corporate welfare doled out in the form of giveaways, subsidies, and cheap loans.

In one sweeping bill, Congress should decree that every federal agency shall terminate all below-market-rate sales, leasing or rental arrangements with corporate beneficiaries, including of real and intangible property; shall cease making any below-market-rate loans or issuing any below-market-rate loan guarantees to corporations; shall terminate all export assistance or marketing promotion for corporations; shall cease providing any below-market-rate insurance; shall terminate all fossil fuel or nuclear power research and development efforts; shall eliminate all liability caps; and shall terminate any direct grant, below-market-value technology transfer or subsidy of any kind. The bill should also amend the Internal Revenue Code to eliminate all corporate "tax expenditures" (Beltway talk for loopholes and gimmicks for corporate taxpayers) listed in the president's annual budget.

Some of what gets cancelled in such a bill might be good public policy. If so, Congress should reauthorize it. But there's too much accumulated contribution/lobbyist-driven institutionalized graft for a case-by-case review to eliminate what's in place. What's needed is a clean slate.

Other steps should be taken to complement a clean-sweep bill:

Citizens should be given standing to sue to challenge corporate welfare abuses—to restrain agencies that reach beyond their statutory powers to dole out corporate welfare.

Automatic corporate welfare sunsets should be established, with every corporate welfare program automatically phasing out in four years after initial adoption, and every five years thereafter.

Annual agency reports should be required on corporate welfare, with each federal agency listing every program under its purview which confers below-cost or below-market-rate goods, services or other benefits on corporations—and identifying the recipients. The president's budget already does this for tax giveaways, though the beneficiaries are not identified.

A ban on corporate welfare for corporate wrongdoers. Corporations convicted of serious wrongdoing should not be eligible to receive the government's largesse.

Corporate welfare cuts to the core of political self-governance, because it is perpetuated in large measure through campaign contributions and the subversion of open procedural and substantive democracy. Also, because the perpetuation of corporate welfare itself misallocates public and private resources and exacerbates the disparities of wealth, influence and power that run counter to a functioning political system in which the people rule. The current reform moment is the time to address the problem.

Confirming, Not Confronting Alito

Janyary 15, 2006

The right wing columnist for the *Wall Street Journal*, Daniel Henninger, in a mocking column on the Democrats' performance during the Samuel A. Alito Jr. nomination hearings called them "intellectually exhausted and politically befuddled." Overall, with some exceptional moments, his description was not that far off the mark, though he also could have applied this description to the Democrats letting through now Justices Scalia and Thomas in years past.

Justice Scalia was confirmed 98-0 with every Democrat voting for him. The two absentees were Republicans. Justice Thomas was confirmed 52-48 in a Senate controlled by Democrats when eleven Democratic Senators crossed over and voted for him, despite a record either mediocre or terrible.

It was not always this way. The Democrats rejected Nixon's nominees Judge Carswell and Judge Haynesworth and then confirmed Justice Harry Blackmun who wrote the majority opinion in Roe v. Wade. The Democrats blocked Judge Bork and then confirmed Justice Kennedy who has turned out more recently to be comparatively moderate.

Not so anymore. Judge Alito's record is clearly one that has favored in most instances big government and big business against the little guys. His judicial philosophy tends toward downgrading the role of Congress. His belief in a very powerful "unitary Presidency" should send shivers up the spines of self-described conservatives in the age of King Bush. But then they have their own version of political befuddlement these days.

When it comes to law enforcement against individuals, he has come down for extreme police power and snooping into people's privacy. Don't bet on any Justice Alito to side often with consumers and workers who are defrauded and abused by corporations. His positions on the environment have turned environmental groups against him.

When asked which sitting justice would a Justice Alito most closely resemble, Harvard Law Professor Lawrence Tribe said—somewhere between Justices Scalia and Thomas. Not much mind room in that crevice. Before the Alito hearings were over, some anonymous Democratic Senators and their aides were already telling the reporters that he would be confirmed, that there would be no filibuster and that once again the Republicans would prevail.

Such comments take the heat off the liberal Republican Senators from more politically liberal states such as Maine or Rhode Island. Such comments deflate the efforts of the progressive citizen and labor groups fighting the nomination. Such comments make it easier for a Democratic Senator, Den Nelson, from Nebraska, to indicate he's voting for Judge Alito.

So now the Democrats will be saddled with what Kevin Zeese, who is running as an independent for the US Senate from Maryland, called the "four horses of the apocalypse"—four partisan justices who favor executive power, corporate power, expansive law enforcement authority [but not against corporate or governmental violators], co-mingling of religion and government and minimal individual rights." "Justices Roberts, Scalia, Thomas and Alito will provide the foundation for right wing extremism for decades to come," he said.

If they were disciplined, the Democrats could have blocked all of them. Hoist by their own petards, to use the law school phrase, the Democrats continue to berate the Republicans for these Justices whom they let through by default, disorganization and lack of conviction.

The very format of the hearings helps the Republicans. Even though they obviously control the Judiciary Committee, it is a narrow majority. The Democrats should demand longer hearings—three days and short times for follow-up questioning regarding a lifetime position on the Supreme Court are ridiculous. Further, many Democrats damage their chances for longer hearings when they spend too much time talking and too little time getting more questions to and replies from Supreme Court nominees.

The panels of citizen witnesses should come before the nominee's testimony so as to provide broader and deeper frameworks for the public and the Congress. Instead, these testifiers have become an anti-climax after the nominee finishes and leaves, along with more than a few other absent Judiciary Committee Senators. It is not a little rude to invite Law Professors, Practitioners and others from long distances and treat them so curtly and cavalierly.

Chairman Arlen Specter and Senator Patrick Leahy—the senior Republican and Democrat on the Committee present themselves as impeccably fair. Yet persons who wrote and faxed requests to be witnesses, including myself, never received so much as an acknowledgment of rejection.

Moreover, the witnesses selected were not known for raising issues of corporate power, regulatory policies and the Constitution. These are major, serious and telling omissions that must gladden the omnipresent corporate lobbyists. Nor do the Senators pose questions relating to access-to-justice, such as tort law, nor to the generic constitutional questions relating to NAFTA and the World Trade Organization and their dubious authority to side-step the sovereignty of our three branches of governments with their mandatory decisions.

Before the Judge Roberts' hearings last year, I submitted over two dozen questions relating to corporate power and corporate status to the members of the Senate Judiciary Committee. There was bi-partisan *disinterest* in seeking Judge Roberts' views on the most powerful institutions in our country.

If you are interested, you can download a copy of these and other questions from the website www.Nader.org.

Speak Up Military!

December 30, 2005

Civilian control over the military is a long established democratic tradition in our country. It was the military that was believed by our founding fathers to be susceptible to plunging our country into foreign adventure. Presently, however, the boondoggles, crimes and recklessness of draft-dodging George W. Bush, Dick Cheney and former Air Force pilot, Donald Rumsfeld, together with their draft-dodging neo-con associates, have turned this expectation upside down. The civilians are the war-mongers.

Probably the least told story of the Iraq War-quagmire is the extent to which the Pentagon military, especially the US Army brass, disagrees with and despises these civilian superiors. Donald Rumsfeld, one of the most disliked of the Secretaries of Defense, has spent much energy making sure that high level dissent in the military is muzzled and overlayered by his loyalists.

Just last week Rumsfeld demoted three military service chiefs in the Pentagon hierarchy and replaced them with three loyalists who previously worked for his buddy Dick Cheney.

Right from the beginning the US Army brass opposed the invasion of Iraq for both military and strategic reasons. They believed such an attack would absorb massive human and material resources that would divert from the chase after the 9/11 terrorists and the resolution of the Palestinian-Israeli conflict. They disagreed with the paucity of soldiers that Bush/Cheney and Rumsfeld were to send there. They were appalled by the lack of post-war planning directives by the Administration.

At the 4 star general level, the Army brass knew Saddam Hussein was a tottering dictator, embargoed, surrounded and contained by the US, Britain, Turkey, and Israel, and unable to field an army equipped with minimum loyalty and equipment. They also knew that going to Iraq would be the gigantic equivalent of batting a large beehive. To this day Army commanders in Iraq, most recently General George Casey, recognize that the US military occupation is a magnet for more and more terrorists from inside and outside Iraq. CIA Director Porter Goss was more explicit before Congress last February testifying that occupied Iraq is a recruiting and training ground for more terrorists who will return to their countries for more disruption.

When Colin Powell was at the Pentagon, he developed what came to be known as the Powell Doctrine—know clearly what your military and political objectives are, follow up with overwhelming force and have a clear exit plan. Bush/Cheney and Rumsfeld violated this Doctrine. Their only objective was to topple their former ally, in the '80s, Saddam Hussein. After that, they were clueless and surprised by the insurgency.

To top Army officers, the worst of all worlds is Iraq. Their Chief of Staff, General Eric Shinseki, after testifying before Congress about the need for over 300,000 soldiers for any such invasion, found his retirement accelerated. Draft-dodger Paul Wolfowitz, then number two in the Pentagon, rejected his estimate and recommended less than half that number.

Retired high military officers, diplomats and intelligence officials, with good sources inside the Department of Defense, say that the military is furious with Bush/Cheney. The latter orders torture with thinly veiled instructions and dubious legal memos and when disclosed, as at Abu Gharib, the Army takes the rap to its reputation.

Bush/Cheney/Rumsfeld start these so-called

commando groups, which included ex-Saddam toughs, and their predictable atrocities against young Sunni men become the US Army's headache to restrain. The idea behind these outlaw, death squads, reported the *New York Times* magazine last year, was to enable summary destruction of arbitrary 'suspects' and terrorization of the Sunni population. The Army kept telling Bush/Cheney/Rumsfeld that such Administration-approved mayhem was backfiring and fueling more hatred by the Sunnis against the US, its soldiers, and these hired gangs.

The Administration finally responded by telling the Army to assign more men to advise and monitor these gangs which the US is equipping and paying.

Other sources of irritation within the military is Bush/Cheney making sure that the fallen and injured soldiers are returned in stealth fashion at Dover Air Force base and Andrews Air Force base outside of Washington, DC. Bush/Cheney do this for political reasons, knowing opposition to the war increases as US casualties mount.

Bush/Cheney/Rumsfeld still refuse to count officially US soldiers who are injured outside a combat situation, again for political reasons. This keeps the official injury count at about one third of the real total. Career Army officers do not like their solders being used this way.

The Army is also upset over the loss of some of their senior officers and non-commissioned officers to the giant corporate contractors operating in this cost-plus environment of maximum profit for less than maximum service. These companies are hiring away these experienced soldiers with offers that double or triple their salaries to do the very privatized jobs which the Army used to do for itself. In a tight skilled manpower situation, the Army finds this drain to be undermining its mission.

On the surface, Bush/Cheney/Rumsfeld are heavy on their photo opportunities with the troops, heavy with the flattery that these political tricksters heap on the soldiers but alert to any potential public dissent.

There was a recent slip up though. At a Pentagon news conference, November 29th, a reporter asked General Peter Pace, the chairman of the Joint Chiefs of Staff, what should American soldiers in Iraq do if they witness Iraqi security forces abusing prisoners. The General's reply: "It is absolutely the responsibility of every US service member, if they see inhumane treatment being conducted, to intervene and stop it."

Standing next to him, the calculating conniver, Donald Rumsfeld tried to distort the words of the forthright Pace by saying that American soldiers only had an obligation to report any mistreatment.

In a nutshell, that is the difference between the Pentagon military and their arrogant civilian superiors who have disrespected their judgment and ordered them to shut up and follow unlawful policies. Meanwhile the quagmire bleeding Iraq continues in its way to bleed America. Speak up military. Remember the Nuremberg principles.

Stand With The People
November 18, 2005

With the Bush regime reeling from its own derelictions and falling in the national polls, the question most frequently put to the leading Democrats is, "What do the Democrats stand for?"

This is the question that Tim Russert asked Howard Dean, Chairman of the Democratic National Committee, on "Meet the Press" recently. Mr. Dean responded that the Democrats do not control the House, the Senate or the White House and that, "right now it's not our job to give out specifics. . . . it's our job to stop this . . . corrupt and incompetent administration from doing more damage to America." He added that the Democrats had "plenty of time to show Americans what our agenda is and we will long before the '06 elections".

This is Mr. Dean strapped to the mast by his superiors in the Congress, where fear of the Republicans supercedes the Democrats' loathing of them. When their most senior member on the House military appropriations committee, Rep. John Murtha (D-Pa.), a double-decorated Vietnam veteran and their most untouchable member by the Republican smear machine, came out last week for "immediate withdrawal" (meaning over six months) of US soldiers from Iraq, the Democratic Party caucus did not come out in support of his position. This is the case even though most Democrats privately agree with Rep. Murtha, as does a growing majority of the American people.

The Republicans continue to taunt the cowardly Democrats by making them vote on a resolution for immediate termination without explaining what it means. The Democrats watch the Republicans implode, but by not advancing their own agenda for America they find themselves also low in the polls.

Last month, the Democratic Party and its political consultants came up with their proposed new slogan: "Together, America Can Do Better." That's reassuring, given the Republican mess of huge deficits, rising job exports, runaway corporate militarism, pounding the poor and re-enriching the rich and generally leaving Americans defenseless against concentrated greed and power.

Why not cast aside this slogan and replace it with a program that signifies that the Democrats "Stand With The People"? Stand with them for full Medicare for all. Stand with them for quality public services from schools to public transit to environmental protection to libraries.

Stand with them for an end to diverting their taxes into huge programs that subsidize, bailout and give away peoples' assets to large corporations.

Stand with them for consumer protection from rip-offs, from shredding traditional consumer rights to take companies to court who cheat or hurt them, from taking the government cops off the corporate crime, fraud and abuse beats.

Stand with them and their rights vis-à-vis large corporations like Walmart that exploit them and block their right to organize and fight back.

Stand with them in their desire to nurture their children's childhoods in decent, affordable housing, safe neighborhoods and good schools and clinics.

Stand with them with a people's budget directed to necessities of the American people receiving the benefits of tax dollars under a fair system of taxation.

I can hear some Democrats now saying, "I have said this," or, "the Party passed a resolution on that." That doesn't pass muster. Has the Democratic Party as a force in politics launched a serious drive against commercial crimes focused on minorities in the urban ghettos? These are the daily commercial crimes against tenants, consumers and patients.

Has the Democratic Party aggressively challenged as a party the notorious Patriot Act and its further abuse by the Bush regime? To the contrary, the Bush people in Congress are making most of the worst provisions permanent and adding a few more erosions of liberty.

Lastly, the Democratic Party is clueless when it comes to a party's declared responsibility to continually strengthen the power of the people to direct and hold their government accountable through clean elections and facilities that make it easy to band together as workers, consumers and taxpayers.

Come on, Democratic Party, "Stand With The People." Corporatist Democrats cannot defeat corporatist Republicans.

All Fizzle, No Sizzle at Big Oil Hearing

November 13, 2005

It was Wednesday, November 10th, 2005 and the Senators had the five bosses of the largest oil conglomerates in the world facing them and the media in a large hearing room. Millions of Americans are indignant over gouging gasoline and natural gas prices and want action.

So what did the two Senate Committees do? They blew it.

As Dana Milbank wrote in the *Washington Post*, "instead of calling oil executives on the carpet yesterday, senators gave them the red-carpet treatment." Not quite. Senator Barbara Boxer, among a few, gave the oil tycoons a hard time. But generally, by the end of the hearing, none of the executives broke a sweat.

There was at least a high expectation for some tough rhetoric and demands for information, though nobody thought there would be any action whether for an excess profits tax, tougher anti-gouging legislation or antitrust crackdowns. But surely some table thumping. After all, it was the people-frightened Republicans who called the hearing to expose, in their majority leader, Senator Bill Frist (R-Tenn.)'s words "those who abuse the free-enterprise system to advantage themselves and their businesses at the expense of all Americans."

Instead, what the public saw was the astonishing workings of corporate power, ideology and campaign money on Capitol Hill. Senators, like Mary Landrieu (D-La.), were tossing soft questions and deep praise on the oil moguls, after receiving big time campaign money from their oil and gas paymasters. Landrieu took $249,155 over the past five years.

Observing the moguls, one got no sign that any of them were at all worried about the hearing. Many of the Senators were marinated in oil. The rest were frustrated or not courageous enough to come adequately prepared to take apart the all-purpose response that these oil companies were merely reacting to the global marketplace. It is always the impersonal market, the all-encompassing ideology that leaves these oil giants so powerless—just so many profit-gushing buoys on the ocean of market determinism.

When Senator Maria Cantwell (D-Wash.) wanted the moguls to be sworn in at the onset of the hearing (an almost routine formality in many hearings), Chairman Senator Ted Stevens (R-Alaska) repulsed the suggestion. Later he rejected Senator Barbara Boxer's large chart showing the huge salaries and bonuses of each of the five oil executives by name, from being entered into the hearing record as irrelevant to the subject matter of the hearing.

Steven Pearlstein of the *Washington Post* was disgusted. In his column, he described Stevens as "so cloyingly deferential to his corporate witnesses one had to wonder if he was auditioning for the job of headwaiter at the grille room of the Petroleum Club in Houston."

The testimony by the executives was so similar to one another that their words became metaphors for the structural collusiveness of this ever tighter corporate cartel. The market makes them behave as they do. They just want lower taxes, more subsidies, more freedom from environmental regulations and more access to the public lands onshore and offshore. They denied the lower taxes bit, but their lobbyists pushed through another multi-billion dollar tax break bill through Congress a few weeks earlier.

Some of the executives made the same assertion that they have reinvested the identical amount that they earned into larger facilities and exploration, but didn't they send much of those earnings to their shareholders? No one asked this question.

Here is the game the big companies are playing. Blame the helpless gas stations if you are pushed to explain why gas prices are so high.

Never mind that ExxonMobil made 79 percent more profit this last quarter than a year earlier, which was also very profitable. That 79 percent amounted to almost $10 billion after modest taxes in just one quarter! By way of comparison, the first company to make $1 billion in one quarter was AT&T twenty years ago.

They had to admit that refinery capacity was tight but refused to take responsibility for the industry shutting down half of the refineries in the US since 1980. The oil companies have long played this game of raising prices by tightening refinery capacity or shipping refined products to other countries.

Given the internal industry documents showing this strategy, one would have thought some Senators would have probed more. But the oil Senator, Ted Stevens, held each senator to five minutes and refused to have a multi-day hearing examination as Senators used to do back in the '60s and '70s. After all, tens of billions of dollars out of the family budgets could have justified a lengthier investigative hearing.

There was little mention of the oil companies taking out useless newspaper ads urging consumers to conserve, while having avoided over the years pressuring the auto and appliance industries to sell more consumers energy efficient products. But then, the oil and gas companies would sell less of their fuel, wouldn't they?

Meanwhile, ex oil men, Bush and Cheney, continue to push for lower taxes on corporations and their affluent executives, while pressing for large cuts in programs benefiting the middle class and the poor. Bush is pushing to liquidate Amtrak and replace it with pieces of private companies. Last week, Amtrak's Board, picked by Bush, fired Amtrak's competent CEO, David Gunn who opposed scuttling a passenger railroad system—crucial to energy conservation and national security—that is starved for capital funds while the airlines and auto companies benefit from huge taxpayer subsidies for airports and highways.

The *Post*'s Pearlstein titled his column, "Oil's Bigwigs Enjoy a Rigged Market." It is more than that. The antitrust laws no longer stop mergers of the big companies. The big oil companies have learned to profit from the overseas producers' oil cartel. And the Mercantile Exchange in New York daily turns oil into a speculative commodity to further enhance the dominant rule of Big Oil.

As for ExxonMobil and their brethren paying some of these rigged profits into a fund, earlier urged by Republican Senator Charles Crassley, to help poor families pay their fuel bills this winter, forget it. Not a single Senator pressed them each for answers. Corporate greed has reached new depths, because our indentured government has left the American people defenseless.

Democratic Haplessness

September 30, 2005

With all of the troubles surrounding George W. Bush and the Republican leadership in Congress—from the life-costing bungling of Hurricane Katrina responses to the deepening quagmire in Iraq to the front page stories of corruption, self-dealing and national security leaks—you would think the Democrats would be in the ascendancy.

Not so. The polls are plummeting for George W. Bush on a whole variety of questions, including the key approval rating being at a record low for him. But the Democrats seem to be sinking right along with the besieged Republicans. Stan Greenberg, a leading Democratic Party pollster, declares that "feelings about Democrats are at a 54 month low." Another pollster, John Zogby, reports that the Democrats are floundering because people do not perceive them as having any credible national leaders.

Instead of drawing bright and bold lines with the Republicans about the nation's future directions, leaders in the Democratic Party have persuaded themselves to just stand by and let the Republicans sink themselves. By standing by, the Democrats are feeding the "pox on both your houses" mindset of many citizens.

Apart from protecting Social Security, what do the Democrats fight for these days? As a Party they are headless regarding the Iraq War-occupation. Their leaders cannot even follow some of their own members in Congress and propose a responsible but definitive exit strategy. This passivity is the norm even though there are former leading retired military, diplomatic and intelligence officials around the country who have done just that.

I and others have called on the Democrats to raise the roof on Bush's grotesque dereliction in still not providing adequate protective armor for the military vehicles in Iraq. Billions for the Halliburtons; lethal excuses for the soldiers.

Also, deliberately undercounting US casualties in Iraq because thousands of serious injuries and sicknesses were not incurred directly in combat is a monumental display of disrespect by Bush for these soldiers and their families. Low-balling the human casualties keeps the public's political opposition lower than if the truth were told about the injury and sickness toll being triple the official false figures.

To this day, in criticizing Mr. Bush, even the anti-war Democrats like Rep. Dennis Kucinich use the false official lowball figure of injuries.

To this day, Democratic House Leader, Nancy Pelosi, with arguably the most anti-war constituents in the nation residing in her California district, is not leading the Democrats with even comparable statements that some outspoken Republicans are making.

Consider the following:

From Vietnam war veteran, Republican Senator Chuck Hagel, who, after returning from one of several trips to Iraq, said: "We should start figuring out how we get out of there . . . our involvement there has destabilized the Middle East. And the longer we stay there, I think the further destabilization will occur."

From Rep. John Duncan, Jr., conservative Republican from Tennessee, who urges conservatives to oppose the "undeclared and unnecessary war" not only because of the deaths but because "there is nothing conservative about this war; . . . it . . . mean[s] massive foreign aid, [and] huge deficit spending."

From CIA Director Porter Goss, who told the Senate in February that the war in Iraq has become a recruitment and training ground for more and more terrorists who will go back to other countries.

From Walter B. Jones, Jr., Republican Congressman from North Carolina, comes the declaration that he wants out of Iraq—a war he once prominently supported but does no longer because the president did not tell him the truth when invading that country.

These legislators come from regions where a much larger percentage of the people support the war than in Nancy Pelosi's San Francisco district. There is a growing majority of Americans who believe that war was a costly mistake and want out.

On other major matters affecting and afflicting the American people, the Democrats, dominated by their corporate connectors, are not up front.

On defending our civil justice system from the corporate attack on injured or defrauded people's right to their full day in court, the Democratic Party is gutless.

On moving serious corporate reforms to stop corporate crimes that have drained trillions from workers, investors and pensioneers, the Democrats are spineless.

On challenging the huge waste, fraud and corruption in government contracts and programs under the Republicans, the Democrats are hapless.

On raising the impoverished minimum wage to give working Americans a living wage, the way Senator Ted Kennedy has been calling for, the Democratic Party is clueless.

The Democratic Party will continue sliding into serial haplessness until a new breed of "jolters" comes to take over.

For more information, see DemocracyRising. US.

Four Days For Forty Years
September 16, 2005

If only corporations could laugh . . . if only corporations could laugh during the Senate Judiciary Committee's hearings on Judge John Roberts' nomination for Chief Justice of the Supreme Court, they would head for the nearest champagne closet in their executive suites.

What a triumph for the most dominant powers in and around our nation. Judge Roberts got away without having important questions asked regarding the interface between corporations, the Constitution, the election laws, the regulatory agencies as they relate to workers, consumers, the environment, manipulated communities, the double standard justice system and the pertinent practices of corporate law firms.

It is not for lack of trying by various citizen groups, including our own, who beseeched one Senator after another to ask this former corporate lawyer about widely reported contemporary conflicts between unusually deceptive or reckless large corporations and real human beings. The US Chamber of Commerce and the National Association of Manufacturers came out big time with big publicity budgets for Judge Roberts. They had not done this for previous nominations for the High Court. That ought to tell you something.

Since these two giant business lobbies swarm over Capitol Hill, together with other similar lobbies, and finance many campaigns there, the prediction was that Judge Roberts would not be asked penetrating questions about the federal regulatory role, the federal pre-emption of state laws protecting consumers and injured people, the questionable authority given NAFTA and the World Trade Organization to make decisions overriding our judicial and regulatory institutions or the unequal status under our Constitution, as interpreted by Supreme Court decisions, between corporations and real people.

Much has been written about the growing and varied power of global corporations. Recently, the Justice Department has been signing "deferred prosecution" agreements with companies that admitted criminal guilt. The reasons given: prosecution could seriously damage the company or, more quietly, going to full trial would drain the limited resources of the federal government devoted to pursuing trillions of dollars of corporate crime, fraud and abuse.

Corporations, like giant banks, have long been on Washington's list as being "too big to be allowed to fail" no matter how badly these corporations behave. So the federal government has bailed them out, because they were too large a factor in the economy to fail. Well then, why weren't the antitrust laws enforced to preclude such massive concentration in our economy? And isn't it unfair competition against smaller companies, smaller banks, who have the freedom to fail all on their own without a federal taxpayer rescue?

Corporate attorney, now Judge Roberts, should have been asked to respond to such questions before the millions of Americans who were watching or listening to these hearings.

For some eleven years, John Roberts worked at the large corporate law firm, Hogan & Hartson, in Washington, DC. He should have been asked whether he believes in the positions he took on behalf of his major corporate clients. Prominent corporate attorneys like the late Lloyd Cutler pride themselves on asserting that they do believe what they argue for their clients.

Much was made of Judge Roberts' integrity and character. But no one tested them. He was not asked about a widespread and well-docu-mented practice of billing abuses by corporate lawyers. What did he know? Did he openly disapprove of these practices by corporate law firms? Did he know of any such billing frauds in his firm or in his own practice?

Judge Roberts made two troubling declarations during his roughly three days of public hearings about which more needs to be made. He was asked whether he regretted or changed his mind about any of the positions he took in hundreds of memos on many significant legal issues which he wrote for the Reagan White House or the positions taken at the Justice Department years ago. He did not name any. Maybe that is understandable for an advocate, but not for a judge repeatedly referring to his "open mind" and judicial temperament.

The other assertion was simply not credible. He stated that when deciding cases he leaves his values and personal philosophy at home. No human being, short of robotic status, can so detach himself or herself. Later in his testimony, Judge Roberts himself acknowledged widely differing "philosophies" on the Supreme Court now. He was simply not being forthright.

As has been my practice with Supreme Court nominations, I requested to testify early on, sensing that corporate power subjects would not be given much attention. My request was turned down by Senator Patrick Leahy, who filled his 15 permitted witness slots with good people mostly concentrating on non-corporate issues of law and justice. I was permitted to submit testimony for the hearing record, which is on Democracyrising.us or Nader.org in its entirety.

To emphasize the gravity of his nomination, several Senators noted that, given decent health, Judge Roberts could be Chief Justice for 40 years or until 2045. So then what was the rush with the hearings which started Monday and ended by Thursday afternoon? In fact, Chairman Senator Arlen Specter announced a short recess to let some Senators catch planes.

The Committee called 30 witnesses, many of them from long distances, and gave them 5 minutes each to speak. Most Senators who remained that last Thursday afternoon and early evening did not even bother questioning them, thereby losing an opportunity to make important points, elicit more insights and further inform the millions of people paying attention to these proceedings.

Quite disappointing was that during Panel Six, featuring such significant witnesses as former Secretary of Labor, Robert Reich, and president of the National Association of Manufacturers, John Engler, the ranking Democrat on the Committee, Senator Patrick Leahy remarked, when his turn came to ask questions, "I'm sorely tempted, but no."

In the future, it would improve the process for such nominations to have some witnesses go first, then receive the nominee, then have some witnesses follow. For forty years of projected tenure to head the Supreme Court, four rushed days were grossly insufficient and reckless in both quality and quantity.

Cindy Sheehan
August 19, 2005

While George W. Bush keeps saying that the United States is at war, for most of the United States, apart from the soldiers and military families, the people seem detached from the daily devastation in Iraq. Reporters and anti-war activists have made this observation repeatedly over the past months.

To be sure, the polls are showing a growing majority opposed to the war believe it was a costly mistake to invade Iraq, and 61 percent disapprove of how Bush is handling "the situation in Iraq." Yet most people find their daily lives at work and play untouched by any unusual sacrifices or inconveniences that go with being at war.

There is no draft to roil through the population those anxieties that tie more people to the feeling of war. No products are being rationed or restricted because of the conflict. The grown children of the corporate oligarchs and the political rulers are not sweating it out in the Sunni Triangle, thereby lending more media notice and gravity to the fighting in Iraq.

No extra taxes are being imposed to pay nearly $2 billion a week that the war is costing Americans. Rather, the reverse is the case. Mr. Bush, unlike all previous "wartime" presidents, has cut the taxes on the wealthy twice, including himself, Cheney and Rumsfeld, and is financing the war on the backs of children who will have to pay off this huge debt later.

Granted, there are economic impacts, such as reductions in funding for many health, safety and economic necessities of those Americans in dire need, but they are not attributed to the war. Cuts in housing assistance are not accompanied by the message to poor tenants saying—"sorry, nation at war."

Still the times may be changing on this score. The galvanizing effect of the fallen Casey Sheehan's mother Cindy down in Crawford, Texas has been a rallying point which is spreading around the country. Cindy Sheehan has made her grief a personal appeal to see the president, thus sweeping aside his flacks, handlers and PR buffers and leaving him exposed to judgments of his character day after day.

Mother Cindy has personalized this automated war and its scripted presidential promoter who lowballs US casualties and prevents families and reporters from going to Dover, Delaware, where the deceased are returned from Iraq.

It is the nature of civic movements that sparks tend to make what is simmering erupt. For the civil rights drive, it was Rosa Parks' refusal to go to the rear of the bus in Montgomery, Alabama. Cindy Sheehan is performing this role of arousing people, if not to act, at least to start conversing and arguing about the war-occupation—its purpose, its impact on our country and how to end it.

We need additional sparks so that, in the words of one military mother, "the architects of this war, who have no children at risk, start listening to those families who do."

There are hundreds of pastors who are opposed to this violent quagmire in which our country has been plunged. Every morning their churches could toll their bells for each US soldier lost the previous day—one bell for each ultimate sacrifice. And one long bell for the Iraqis who lost their lives that day.

On Sunday, the bells could be rung at the same time everywhere in the memory of the weeks' total casualties. The National Council of Churches, outspoken before the war with compassionate prescience, can lead this effort with rapid effectiveness.

These bells of sorrow and reminder will get millions of Americans thinking and talking with one another where it counts—in communities North, South, East and West.

People would transcend the bromides and slogans that the Bush people trumpet daily over the television and radio and give themselves a daily opportunity to ask and contemplate the fundamental question—for whom does the bell toll?

Asking this question puts our society on the road to finding the answers, as if people matter here and in Iraq first and foremost.

Karl Rove's Campaigning in the White House

July 29, 2005

Remember the day after the election last November, a triumphant newly elected (for the first time) President George W. Bush introduced to a national television audience a beaming Karl Rove as "The Architect" of his winning campaign. Did you know that you, the taxpayers, paid for his salary and benefits while he was running George W. Bush's political campaign day after day inside the White House?

Isn't this illegal, you may properly ask? It would be if it were a staff member of a Senator or Representative in the Congress. Any such staffers would have to take an unpaid leave of absence, leave their office and set up shop somewhere else to work on their boss's re-election campaign. To do this on the Congressional payroll would be illegal.

So what about Rove? Well, back in 1993, the two Parties got together and assured the passage of amendments to the Hatch Act (5 USC 7521 et seq.) to decriminalize such behavior for presidential appointees who work outside normal business hours. Karl Rove is one of those privileged employees paid by the taxpayer to run a political campaign while on the job because there is no objection from the out of power party that wants the same privilege when it occupies the White House.

Neither party bothered to ask the taxpayers for their opinion. But the politicos had to concede one obligation imposed on this political freeloading. People like Karl Rove can only do politics while on the job in a government building or in a government vehicle "if the costs associated with that political activity are not paid for by money derived from the Treasury of the United States." Sec. 7324(b)(1).

Some official has to be able to show that Karl Rove allocated costs between his political activity and his non-political activity and that these expenses were not paid for by the government (i.e. you, the taxpayer).

It is not clear in the statute or the regulations what official is supposed to get Mr. Rove's accounting. Calls and letters to the White House resulted only in a response citing those vague regulations. The office of Special Counsel which implements the Hatch Act does not collect this accounting as a matter of course.

There is one pertinent prohibition in the regulations. Cutting through the verbiage, it is apparent that Karl Rove cannot engage in campaign fund-raising unless he quits his government job. Imagine someone in a public or news-gathering capacity accessing all those thousands of phone calls and e-mails made by Karl Rove and whomever assisted him in the White House.

The White House is not subject to the Freedom of Information Act (FOIA). Therefore a citizen or reporter cannot file a request for documents or reports under that important law.

So what can be done? A reporter could ask the question at a White House press briefing. For whatever it is worth, a complaint can be filed with the Office of Special Counsel. A request can be made of the Counsel to the President, Harriet Miers, for an allocation separating his expenditures in time and resources on political activity from the time spent as a staff assistant to President Bush. We made such a written request two weeks ago.

Or members of Congress can ask the Government Accountability Office to investigate and report back to them.

Meanwhile, Karl Rove continues his very political activities and travels around the country raising money for upcoming Congressional campaigns. It is a very convenient career, so long as you can get away with it. The self-described conservatives in the White House are on welfare in the midst of their warfare against the American worker.

For more information, log onto DemocracyRising.US and help get Karl Rove off of welfare and out of the White House.

The Perfect Political Trap
June 10, 2005

The horrific Republicans had another two weeks of victories over the hapless Democrats. After seven Republican and seven Democratic Senators forged the compromise that averted a showdown against the filibuster, the Republicans moved the confirmation of the worst nominees for the federal circuit courts of appeals which the Democrats had vigorously opposed before they were gulled. Or frisked by Frist, the Senate Republican leader.

Then came the Howard Dean dust-up over his comments saying that many Republicans leaders "have never made an honest living in their lives," and that Republicans are "pretty much a white Christian party." The "media circus", as Dean called it, erupted further when Senator Joe Biden, ex-Senator John Edwards, House Minority Leader Nancy Pelosi and New Mexico Governor Bill Richardson sharply distanced themselves from their Party Chairman. Republicans chortled and chuckled over their opponents' imbroglio.

Meanwhile, down in Oklahoma, the state Republican Party was unveiling its 2005 platform. The editor of the Oklahoma Observer, Frosty Troy, described the document as "written for the greedy, not the needy; for special interests, not the people's interest."

Similar to the 2002 Texas Republican Party platform, the latest Oklahoma version would make the Bush Republicans blush and run. That is, *if* the hapless Democrats would make an issue out of what the Republican Parties in several southern and mountain states stand for that the Washington Republicans cannot accept but also cannot openly reject.

A perfect political trap for the Republicans awaits the clueless Democrats if they had half of Karl Rove's brain and instinct for the jugular. Only this trap would be about substance and the livelihoods of the American people, not a Swift Boat maneuver.

Devolving under the national media's radar is a retrograde Republican political ideology, mixed with some positive policies, that can cause relentless and diverse embarrassment between the corporate Republicans dominating the nation's capitol and the self-described conservative, red-state Republicans who make Bush-type election victories possible.

Take the Oklahoma platform, typical of several other state Republican Parties. It wants to privatize Social Security, eliminate the minimum wage, the income tax, all toll roads, institute a national sales tax, get rid of the US Department of Education, and repeal much corporate regulation that protects consumers, workers and the environment.

The Oklahoma Republican Party wants to get the US out of the UN, eliminate funding for PBS and National Public Radio, and repeal the state tax on business inventory. They want to post the Ten Commandments in all public schools, oppose monetary foreign aid, and government credits with which to buy US goods.

On the other hand, the Oklahoma Party wants to abolish many forms of corporate welfare such as tax holidays to attract industry and other subsidies and giveways so dear to the hearts and pockets of corporate Republicans. The state Party is opposed to Bush's No Child Left Behind's budgets, testing, national teacher and student standards.

Similar to their Texas counterparts, they want the US out of the World Trade Organization, an end to the Office of Surgeon General, no limits on campaign contributions and no national health insurance. Lots of treaties they do not like, including the ones limiting nuclear proliferation and environmental devastation. They cannot stand the EPA, or the National Endowment for the Arts and the Endangered Species Act.

The Republican Sooners do not offer ways to replace much of the revenue most Americans believe supply necessities, such as maintaining highways or paying off turnpike bondholders.

In October 2003, I wrote President George W. Bush (see nader.org/releases) a letter outlining the 2002 Texas Republican Party Platform, his own launching political organization. I asked where he stood on many positions of his state Party that were directly opposed to his own Administration's policies and programs. Would he, for example, stop funding the International Monetary Fund, oppose all unfunded mandates by the federal government and repeal NAFTA?

He never replied. So I sent a copy of the letter to the Democratic National Committee and spoke to a high level official there. No follow up by the Democrats. On the contrary, a top Texas Democratic Party official provided an irritated response to a reporter for my bringing up the subject of Republican extremisms.

Call one for the Republicans. They are neither squeamish about their off-the-wall declarations nor worried about their internal contradictions from the state to the national level. And they intimidate the Democrats so much that the national Democratic Party Platforms refuse to adopt any plans to reduce poverty, crack down on corporate crime and corporate subsidies, make the income tax less loop-holed, stand for a living wage, and specifically push for environmentally efficient motor vehicles and other technologies, to list a few abdications.

The Democrats fear the Republicans, while the Republicans mock the gutless Democrats.

Meanwhile the Democrats, largely on the defense against the most craven Republicans in a century, are busy trying to cool down the hot seat beneath Howard Dean.

Democratic Offensive

May 19, 2005

As President George W. Bush rushes around the country frantically trying to find acceptance of his exaggerated, deceptive and sometimes deliberately inaccurate (note his use of the word "bankrupt") plan for a social insecurity system, the pundits and the polls say he is not gaining traction. A large majority still opposes his proposals for private investment accounts. Yet, Bush and his political brain, Karl Rove, are winning in another way; their ongoing, successful strategy of distraction puts the Democrats in a chronic postion of playing defense.

Bush's politics of distraction has made the Republicans take command of the offense, of the agendas, and of the media coverage of Washington, DC.

The drumbeat to war, invasion and then the occupation of Iraq crowded out the Democrats and was a significant factor in tipping the 2002 Congressional and 2004 presidential elections to Bush. It took the spotlight away from the domestic necessities of the American people. It shoved aside the entry of the corporate crime issue into the political arena where it could have engulfed the Bushies and their big donor buddies who were enmeshed in many big time scandals and thefts.

Bush's social insecurity gambit pleases his Wall Street. It distracts attention from the present, real-time crisis of the private corporate pension system, which is collapsing on the hopes and dreams of millions of active and retired American workers. There are $450 billion of unfunded private pension liabilities in the corporate sector.

Pension plans have been looted or drained during the dot.com years of both boom and bust. The federal government's Pension Benefits Guaranty Corp. that is supposed to bail out failing corporate pension plans is already nearly $30 billion in the red. United Airlines, in bankruptcy but still operating and paying handsome salaries to its top executives, has just dumped its gigantic pension plan onto the Pension Benefits Guaranty Corp.

Since corporate bankruptcy is now considered as a competitive strategy against other companies in an industry, there may be a rush by beleaguered companies to unload their pension liabilities on the backs of a potential taxpayer bailout. Only raising the premiums paid into this fund by companies can avert that possibility. Companies have more lobbyists inside Congress than do individual taxpayers.

If you landed from Mars and had one question to ask to determine which of the two parties is prevailing over the other, that question would be: Which Party is on the offensive and which party is on the defensive?

The Republicans are on the offensive with a most offensive, sugar coated agenda against

America, against workers, consumers, justice and the environment. While the Democrats have no countering agenda as a party.

Here are some suggestions for an offensive against the Republicans. The Democrats should come out clearly for a living wage. There are 47 million American workers laboring full time who make between $5.15 (not counting illegal sweatshop workers) and $10.00 per hour. The federal minimum wage at $5.15 is much less than it was in 1968 adjusted for inflation. Meanwhile the rich have gotten richer.

The Democrats should advance a comprehensive corporate reform agenda (as described in the new book *The People's Business* by Drutman and Cray) which includes a much tougher crackdown on corporate crooks who destroy the health, safety and economic savings of millions of Americans.

The Democrats should stand for fundamental tax and labor law reforms to make the tax system less rigged and to give workers in companies like Walmart a chance to establish trade unions.

Abolishing the outrageous forms of corporate welfare , subsidies, handouts, giveaways and bailouts of largely big business, should become a trademark of the Democratic Party. This approach will not only lift burdens on small taxpayers but also free monies for good job-producing public works repair and modernization projects in communities' schools, libraries, drinking water systems, clinics, public transit and parks.

Democrats should stand for shifting more power to the people by electoral reforms so that dirty money elections badly counted will be replaced and so that regular people can pursue their grievances in courts and before agencies more readily.

A determined national fuel efficiency and solar energy movement should be spearheaded by the Democratic Party. Imagine all the good arguments and support for that timely initiative.

Well, I've run out of space to suggest more Offense. Are the Democrats too distracted dialing for corporate dollars to listen to these urgings from the few progressives in their Party?

Conservative and Liberal Alliances
April 1, 2005

The on-again-off-again alliances between conservative and liberal groups is on again, but not without its contradictions. Back in the early Eighties, during the Reagan years, conservatives joined with anti-nuclear power groups to end the multi-billion tax dollar boondoggle called the Clinch River Breeder Reactor in Tennessee. Their joint lobbying in Congress overcame the opposition of both the nuclear industry and the White House.

In subsequent years, "corporate welfare" began to be critically noticed by such right-wing groups as the Heritage Foundation and the Cato Institute. They viewed it as an unacceptable disruption of market forces and a drain on taxpayers.

In 1999, I called arch-conservative Grover Norquist to inform him that my exchanges with House Budget Committee Chair, Rep. John Kasich (R-Ohio), had born-fruit. Mr. Kasich held the first hearings on corporate subsidies, giveaways and bailouts ever in Congress. Mr. Norquist joined with a mixed panel of liberals and conservatives that raised corporate eyebrows. But Rep. Kasich's superiors—Newt Gingrich and others—were distinctly cool to any follow-up legislation. They were corporatists first.

More recently, in 2003, the Federal Communications Commission was flooded with about a half a million messages from the likes of Common Cause and the NRA against its proposal to allow further ownership of more radio and television stations by giant media conglomerates. Although the FCC commissioners passed the measure by a narrow three-to-two vote, the jolted House of Representatives overwhelmingly overruled it and the Senate rejected one segment of the ruling. Unfortunately, this very rare Congressional rebuff to giant media companies like Clear Channel and Murdoch was blocked in the House-Senate Conference.

Dependence by our country on foreign oil has brought together environmental groups and right-wing leaders concerned about national security. What the *Washington Post* called "strange bedfellows," people like ex-Senator Gary Hart and Senator John Kerry have joined with former CIA director James Woolsey and conservative lawyer-lobbyist C. Boyden Gray, in sympathy with a group called Set America Free.

Forget about stronger fuel-efficiency regulation with this group. Instead they are into subsidizing both the auto companies (investment tax credits for example) and car buyers to provide GM, Ford and Chrysler with "incentives" to make the kind of hybrid vehicles that Toyota and Honda are already selling in the US. So their choice is guess-what: more corporate welfare and an aversion to technology-forcing regulation similar to the 1975 legislation which propelled the auto companies to nearly double their average duel efficiency over the next quarter-century.

There is still no serious talk within these groups of a national solar energy conversion mission that would over time displace the fossil fuel-nuclear economy.

The latest convergence of liberal and conservative activity involves selective opposition to the renewal of the Patriot Act in Congress before the year's end.

The ACLU, Center for Constitutional Rights and prominent liberal law professors and scholars have opposed various provisions since its hasty passage, without public hearings, by a panicked Congress in October 2001. Since then, the Act has been championed and abused by both Bush and his attorney general John Ashcroft, who retired with a record of zero victories from five thousand arrests for terrorist activity, according to Georgetown Law Professor David Cole.

In an open letter, dated March 22, 2005 and posted on www.checksbalances.org, twenty of the more prominent leaders of conservative organizations, led by the ex-CIA official, ex-Republican Congressman, Bob Barr, called on President George W. Bush to drop his support for renewing "the most intrusive, unchecked powers temporarily granted by the Patriot Act."

The signers, who include David Keene, Grover Norquist, Paul M. Weyrich, and John Snyder, specifically listed Section 213, which allows government agents to "secretly search through people's homes and business and seize their personal property without notice for days, weeks, months or perhaps ever."

Also, they opposed Section 215, which "allows government agents to collect personal data on law-abiding Americans—such as the books they buy or borrow, their personal medical history, or even records of goods they purchase," without the probable cause of connections to the "commission of a crime or to a foreign terrorist agent."

They also objected to Section 802, which defines "terrorism" so broadly as to give unbridled discretion to government agents at the expense of judicial review for constitutional compliance.

Liberal anti-Patriot Act groups also oppose arrests without charges and imprisonment without attorneys, even of material witnesses, indefinitely. Both groups decry a government that destroys the liberties of law-abiding Americans in the name of protecting them.

How effective will these alliances be? On paper, the right-left coalitions jar many members of Congress. But if they stay on paper and do not move to a coordinated stage of civic action that has lasting power, unlike the FCC episode, Congress and the two major Parties will feel they can wait them out and let Mr. Bush unleash once again his scare tactics that send members of Congress running for cover.

Terri is dehydrating. Time is running out.

Keep The Hammer

March 18, 2005

The Republican majority leader in the House of Representatives, Cong. Tom DeLay of Texas, and I agree on one issue dear to his mind and heart. We do not want him to resign from Congress in the midst of deepening scandal surrounding his aggressive political and fundraising activities.

Stay put, Tom. The Republican Party needs you a whole lot longer so that the media can expand its coverage of the Party's corrupt rule on Capitol Hill and its dancing with corporate lobbyists bent on greed and harm to the interests of the people.

Tom DeLay came to Congress in 1984 because he was outraged at environmental regulations that applied to his pest extermination business. He rose up the ladder because he would

do things and say things that other Republicans shied away from. He was a ruthless arm twister and soon earned the name "The Hammer."

In a page one story a few years ago, the *Washington Post* described how K Street corporate influence-peddlers would shudder at the prospect of visiting his office because he would demand campaign contributions, while discussing their agendas, in too direct a manner. Companies like a little subtlety and indirection attached to their buying our national legislators. DeLay came across as an abrupt shakedown-artist, a cash-register political extortionist.

The *Post*'s expose didn't make DeLay skip a beat. Soon thereafter, he was demanding from Washington's numerous trade associations that if they did not dump their managers, who were Democrats, and replace them with Republicans, they would not be very welcome when it came to give them a hearing. He got his way quite often on this unprecedented interference.

Like other arrogant politicians, before him, who became inebriated with their own power and capacity to corral large amounts of campaign riches and hand it out to expand their sway, DeLay outpaced them with his brazenness. He began to enrich his former staffers who would set up lobbying firms in Washington representing corporations that wanted DeLay to help give their lucrative clients more privileges and immunities, more government contracts and appointments at high levels in the Executive Branch.

DeLay became the House dictator, shutting down dissent, twisting or changing House rules to seal off the Democrats in House committees and conference committees with the Senate on crucial legislation. He finally dumped his own Republican Ethics Chair, Cong. Joel Hefley, after the evenly divided House Ethics Committee reprimanded DeLay on three occasions.

While stacking the Ethics Committee, he pushed a rule through the House Republican Conference that the Party's congressional leaders could keep their leadership positions even if they were under indictment for a crime. The ensuing political uproar against DeLay led to a reversal of the rule, but he kept one intact that requires a vote by one Republican on the House Ethics Committee to initiate an investigation of an ethics violation charge.

Although DeLay has been caught taking junkets and campaign money in Washington that violate House rules or the campaign laws themselves, "The Hammer" is most worried about a Travis County District Attorney by the name of Ronnie Earle. Earle, a Democrat, who prosecutes Democrats, turned his attention to the DeLay crowd during the notorious Delay-led drive to take control of the Texas state legislature and thereby redraw Congressional Districts to defeat six incumbent Democrats. DeLay believes that redistricting lets politicians pick the voters rather than reverse the process.

Big money was collected from corporations through a maze of routes that found their way into the 2002 state elections in Texas. Such corporate money cannot be spent in political campaigns in that state. Earle has already indicted eight corporations and three politicos described by the press as part of "DeLay's network in Washington, DC."

More indictments are expected later this spring and DeLay fears he may be one of the indictees. His allies in the state legislature are trying to cut the D.A.'s budget or even enact legislation to take the case away from him. That would really generate a huge backlash.

Meanwhile, DeLay has asked fellow Republicans and admiring corporations, like R.J. Reynolds and Reliant Energy, to expand his legal defense fund. However, he has had to return some of the money that came from registered lobbyists because such contributions violate House ethics regulations.

As more incriminating evidence pours out from Washington to Texas, Cris Feldman, one of the plaintiff's attorneys in a civil case, told National Public Radio reporter Wade Goodwyn, "Tom DeLay was up to his eyeballs in it. It was Tom DeLay's people, all the way down to his daughter, helping to run Texans for a Republican Majority Political Action Committee (TRMPAC)."

DeLay claims all this is a rumor and innuendo. Ok, Tom, more time and evidence are needed for more law enforcement and more implications of Republicans and grasping corporate lobbyists until a critical mass is reached.

DeLay can become the garb of the Republican Party's greed and power, the poster man for millions of Americans to turn against in disgust and give the House of Representatives back to the Democrats in 2006. Who needs Howard Dean when the Democrats have Tom DeLay so long as he stays on the job and does not cut and run too soon.

Maintaining the Duopoly

February 13, 2005

The phrase "participant-observer" comes from social science literature to mean someone who writes about an event or process while having participated in it. I'm going to have to do a little of that to make the following remarks.

Bob Herbert is one of my favorite columnists. Writing twice a week in the *New York Times* op-ed page, he regularly expresses factually based indignation about widespread poverty in America, about its criminal injustice system, about human rights violations, about the failed war on drugs, about the other failed war-occupation in Iraq. He is one of the few major media columnists who goes after corporate crooks and their craven and crummy politicians.

Last year, Herbert asked again and again why the presidential candidates did not take positions or speak out on these matters. After the November elections he continued his forceful outcries. On January 17th, he asked: "Where are today's voices of moral outrage? Where is the leadership willing to stand up and say: Enough! We've sullied ourselves enough."

Bob, this is what I and veteran human rights advocate, Peter Camejo, thought we were doing throughout 2004 in all fifty states with our campaigns for social and economic justice, for peace, for clean politics and a strengthened democratic society. You never mentioned our efforts once. Nor did you mention initiatives by former Attorney General Ramsey Clark who reflects your views on the illegal Iraq War.

You write that "effective leadership can come from anywhere at any time." Then why not give it a little visibility? If Nader/Camejo's decades of standing tall and speaking out is too outside your Democratic Party to mention, give some print space to other national and regional big picture advocates who daily have to work anonymously due to their being shut out by the commercial media. You're much better at publicizing victims of criminal injustice than adding to their proper recognition by writing about those civic activists or small party/independent political candidates trying to change the system.

In your recent column, you end with these words: There was a time when no one had heard of Dr. King. Or Oscar Arias Sanchez. Or Martin O'Brien who founded the foremost human

rights organization in Northern Ireland, and who tells us: "The worst thing is apathy, to sit idly by in the face of injustice and to do nothing about it."

There is another kind of abdication. That is when a progressive columnist, who reaches millions of readers, sits idly by and watches the Democratic Party spend millions of dollars with corporate law firms to file phony lawsuits to push Nader/Camejo off one state ballot after another, and unleash torrents of lies about this candidacy. Denying candidates' right to freedom of speech and assembly, which is what running for elective office comprises, might have been seen by a consistent Bob Herbert as an important violation of civil liberties, if not for the candidates, at least for the voters who were corruptly denied their choice of candidates.

When progressive writers turn progressive candidates into non-persons because the former have signed on to the "Anybody but Bush, Leave Kerry alone, Make no demands on him" Club, they are undermining their own scripted desires. The widespread reporting of corporate power, crime, fraud and abuse in the independent and mass media is hitting two stone walls blocking their disclosures from moving into the political arena for attention and reform. Those two stone walls are the Republican and Democratic Parties (subject to a very few exceptions among Democratic incumbents).

Herbert is not alone among progressive writers. The *Nation* and *Progressive* magazines, and the *Washington Monthly*, proceeded to demonstrate their policies of non-personhood, once they came out against the Nader/Camejo or other progressive candidacies. Almost all other liberal/progressive syndicated columnists were like Herbert.

Back in the 19th century, when the two party

duopoly began to congeal, progressive or reform publications did not come out against slavery, women's suffrage, the industrial workers' rights to form trade unions, the farmers need for federal regulation of banks and railroads and then decline to support or even write about candidates and small parties who were championing vigorously these same issues inside the electoral arena.

Those early journalists knew that positions of justice had to be moved into election contests, no matter how uphill was the struggle. They believed in small starts rather than least worst. And guess what, eventually measured by decades, the small starts continued to lose elections but their agendas took hold.

The current crop of progressives need to rethink their imprisonment by a two centuries old, two party monopolized winner take all electoral college system. Do they want to break out of jail? Or do they want to continue sliding into the political pits with their least-worse corporatized Party that takes them for granted because it knows these liberalized progressives have put out the "nowhere to go" sign?

Duke historian Larry Goodwyn, author of books on American political populism, wrote in the Texas Observer last December that "To corral the minions of entrenched corporate power, one needed to possess the rhetorical power to be clear; and one additionally needed to be a long-distance runner." Guess who Larry Goodwyn did not support?

The BBB's

January 16, 2005

The controversy over going ahead with the nine Inaugural balls' huge fireworks and party bashes, to which mostly the rich and powerful have been invited, has not been restricted to talk radio shows. Deep in the White House deliberations last year, some of the BBBs (the brainy big backers), who are selected to give policy advice, counseled cancellation of all but the formal inaugural proceedings, as some previous presidents, such as Franklin Delano Roosevelt, have done.

These BBBs made the argument that in a time of war, with our soldiers dying in Iraq, enormous and growing human casualties from Iraq to South Asia, it would be an expression of respect to cool off the often-garish festivities and use the $40 million or more to help those in need.

There was actually some support in the White House for this view, but "the Texans prevailed," said a participant. However, one Texan who dissented from Dallas way was Mark Cuban, owner of the Mavericks and a strong Bush voter. He thought the Tsunami catastrophe should warrant such a sobering decision.

Some of Bush's defenders on Talk Radio called to say that since the millions of dollars are coming from private sources, what's the big deal? First, it is costing almost that much again in federal and District of Columbia police, helicopters, surveillance staff and other requirements of the Inaugural security state. Second, and more consequential, this private or corporate money is a very costly deal for regular Americans who don't get their calls returned.

It is not that these Americans are asked to contribute. Not while the corporate fat cats are falling all over themselves writing out $100,000 to $250,000 checks to the Bush bash. In return these companies get favors, privileges, tax breaks, subsidies, lax law enforcement for which the people pay dearly in health, safety and economic burdens. But then with Bush it has always been about Big Business.

An example is the atomic power industry that wants Bush to give them huge taxpayer guarantees to create the next generation of nuclear plants and freeze out the public even more from challenging their location and emergency standards. So John E. Kane, the industry lobbyist, says that its $100,000 donation is a way of supporting the president.

The *Washington Post* summarized this cash register politics: "Wall Street investment firms seeking to profit from private Social Security accounts; oil, gas and mining companies pushing the White House to revive a stalled energy-subsidy bill; and hotels and casinos seeking an influx of immigrant labor are among the 44 interests that have each given $250,000 and the 66 that have donated $100,000 to $225,000. And the money keeps pouring in."

Corporations are free to give as much as they want to the Inaugural, unlike elections where they are prohibited from direct contributions (there are many indirect ways, of course). The Bush people placed a top limit of $250,000 to restrain those straining to add more for this lavish potlatch.

No industry has benefited more monetarily from George W. Bush than the drug companies. So they are reciprocating for all those massive taxpayer subsidies, free giveaways of government research, and weaker regulations for which they are so indebted.

Ameriquest, a mortgage company working the high interest fields of minority neighborhoods, got around the $250,000 limit by adding another $500,000 from its two subsidiaries. This company wants weaker federal pre-emption of tougher laws that states have been passing against predatory lending.

There is another contract that is unsavory in this modern version of Marie Antoinette's "let

them eat cake" posture. In the next few days, there will be reports leaking about the forthcoming Bush Budget. They will describe how those most in need and all Americans who require good public services and safety will see such programs further reduced. These will include environmental, transportation, health, poverty, housing and other essential services.

Already Bush intends to end a rural housing program and other anti-poverty efforts, while giving more money to the staggeringly wasteful and often misdirected Defense and Homeland Security Budgets.

For all the excess, one might think that regular Americans at least would be able to sit in the bleachers. Sure, just fork over $100 to $150 dollars and prove you're a Bush partisan and you'll be there.

The merchants naturally are taking full advantage of this invasion by the grasping affluent. Hotels are marking up room prices. The good ones go for $2000 a night. For those willing to pay more, the Ritz-Carlton offers a four day $150,000 package starting with private jet transportation from wherever for the couple, caviar and Dom Perignon 24 hours a day and endless other perks.

Want to rent a fur coat? That'll be $15,000 down for a deposit (presumably to be returned) plus the rental. "No problem," said one visitor who did not want his own fur coat to go through the hassle at the airport, reports public radio.

When will the organized people be heard from?

Political Bigotry
January 9, 2005

Webster's Collegiate Dictionary defines a "bigot" as "One obstinately or intolerantly devoted to his own church, party, belief or opinion."

George W. Bush has not turned, overtly at least, his war on Iraq and America's civil justice system into his religion. But he has folded his "party, belief and opinion" into a relentless pattern of bigotry.

Just about every day, the newspapers report reality that is removed from this president. The massive failure to document his reasons for invading Iraq, an unconstitutional war launched on a platform of fabrications, deceptions and fulminations, continue to be subject to his am-. nesia.

Inside and outside his Administration, full-blooded American military, intelligence and diplomatic officials have rejected Bush's assertions that Iraq was tied into al-Qaeda (and by inference 9/11), that Iraq possessed weapons of mass destruction or was about to and that Iraq's dilapidated army was a threat to its neighbors such as the vastly more powerful Israel, Turkey and Iran. That the violent situation in Iraq is worsening and the troops are under armed and under equipped are received with denials by all the president's men.

Both Bush and Cheney proceed with the war as if these facts should not affect their permanent occupation of Iraq, its oil resources, under a puppet regime, costing our country hundreds of billions of dollars, casualties and further enmity of people who never harmed any Americans.

Here is where the "bigotry" enters the political realm. Bush never listens to anyone who tells him what he doesn't want to hear. Apropos the book title *Bush's Brain,* the omnipresent filter, Karl Rove, is Bush's brain because Bush doesn't want to give any other "belief or opinion" a chance to make its case.

A brief review of the mistakeless president is in order. Before Bush's invasion of Iraq, his father's key advisers, Brent Scowcroft and James Baker, in private and publicly in articles, warned against falling into this trap.

Thirteen groups representing millions of Americans, church, veterans, business, labor, student, peace, intelligence specialists, and other associations—wrote their president asking for a chance to meet and present their knowledge and experience. He boorishly never bothered to send them a letter saying no. They received no response from the White House.

White House reporters rarely get a chance to ask him questions. When they do they fear being cut off in the future and avoid the tough ones. Moreover, after November 2, Bush has initiated a no follow-up question policy, freeing him to indulge in televised evasion without challenge.

Before the Iraq invasion, Bush used to say that he makes decisions "in my gut." This visceral temperament is not reassuring. Last week, Bush spent much of his time going outside of Washington to cast aspersions on state judges and jurors whom he implies let lawyers bring frivolous suits on behalf of injured and sick people. Apparently, his "gut" tells him that he can say anything he wants, however wild, and proceed on the grounds that judges, most of whom were former business lawyers, are not in control of their courtroom.

Again and again, the White House has refused to document his allegations of frivolous medical malpractice lawsuits causing healthcare costs to spiral and physicians to leave their practices. He has refused to respond to the insurance company's premium gouging of physicians or to organized medical societies doing very little about the minority of bad, incompetent doctors who cause a large number of malpractice deaths and injuries among defenseless patients.

Not once has he bewailed the deadly toll

of close to 100,000 Americans who lose their lives annually due to medical-hospital malpractice, according to the Harvard School of Public Health study conducted by M.Ds. He has often afforded photo opportunities with physicians but never with victims of medical malpractice, like the woman who received a mastectomy that was supposed to be given to the woman in the next hospital room.

Bush is on a drive to take away legal rights that American who are harmed or cheated have had for decades, including going back to our founding fathers providing for the right of trial by jury not controlled by absentee legislators. His contempt for one of America's proudest constitutional pillars is unabashed because he is so ignorant.

Bush's goal is to have Congress usurp the states' jurisdiction over the laws of personal injury and class actions. He uses phrases like "junk lawsuits", caps on "non-economic damages" (meaning disability, pain and suffering) and "greedy lawyers" to absolve corporations, like asbestos and chemical manufacturers, negligent drug companies, hospitals and doctors, from full responsibility in courts of law where the evidence can be cross-examined in public, under rights of appeal.

During his traveling week of presidential jury-tampering, Bush made no mention of curbing corporations' right to have their full day in court or to cap their damages or to go after their "junk lawsuits" or to excoriate their corporate attorneys who tie up, delay and subject the courts to their tactics of cover-up and attrition.

How many times have you heard Bush say, "The safety of the American people is my top priority?" He says these words when he speaks of terrorism. Not when safety is destroyed by dangerous products, workplaces, environments and healthcare locations. Millions of Americans die or are seriously injured or sickened from causes that are preventable to which he has paid no regulatory attention for four years.

But Bush's "gut" does not signal alarms and concerns. Instead his "gut", and his desire for business campaign contributions, tells his brain to further obstruct the need for the injured, sick and next of kin to secure justice in the courts, which in turn generates deterrence against unsafe practices outside the courts.

That is how "political bigotry" works, "don't give me the facts, my mind is made up." Corporate power reigns and the people and children suffer. Interested readers can visit citizen.org or CenterJD.org.

Giant Tsunami Strikes and Bush Goes AWOL for 3 Days
December 30, 2004

This commander in chief of the carnage fields in Iraq calls himself a "compassionate conservative." But when one of the world's greatest natural disasters, the giant tsunami's waves of destruction, struck South Asia's millions of human beings on Sunday morning, George W. Bush was AWOL for over three days.

On vacation again, Bush had delegated the representation of our country to a second string press man who announced that the US government would give a paltry $15 million to the relief effort. That was our nation's immediate image as the death toll soared over 100,000 souls in the midst of unimaginable devastation and looming infectious diseases.

When the Iraq-obsessed Bush finally emerged from his ranch in Crawford, Texas, the assistance sum was upped to $35 million (little

Spain is giving $68 million). Bush, bristling before public criticism of his belated mini-start, did what he usually does. He hid behind the American people. "We're a very generous, kind-hearted nation," he declared.

It is not the American peoples' generosity we're worried about, Mr. Bush, it is your failed leadership to take the helm of the world's relief effort. Great humanitarian missions are historic opportunities to bring the best out of our country and its people as they rush to the aid of the innocents. The victims, both residents and tourists, came from 40 countries.

Unparalleled opportunities for solidarity among a wide expanse of the world's peoples elevate the best instincts of humanity and its governors. Divisions, tensions, bigotries, and violent conflicts are submerged by these common expressions of care, love and rescue. For Bush, since many of the victims were Muslim, it would have softened the daily belligerence that they see him emitting for many months. Such sensibilities seem to escape both the president and his hard-nosed advisers.

Then there is the matter of our nation's readiness for natural calamities. A gigantic earthquake, registering 9.0 on the Richter scale, opened a fissure the length of California off the coast of Sumatra. The quake had an estimated force of one million Hiroshima-size atomic bombs, which propelled tsunami waves at 500 mph in many directions. With sudden impact, they slammed into Indonesia, Sri Lanka, Thailand, India, and Malaysia, and as far away as Somalia in Africa. Waves rising 60 feet high and reaching up to 10 miles inland struck with no advance notice, because such waves are invisible until they hit shallow coastal waters.

But in an age of instant communications and precise seismic instruments, there should have been advance warnings for millions of people. What nature did not do, technology could have done. Yet these populations at risk were treated as if they were living in the 19th century, given the multiple breakdowns that occurred that Sunday.

Instantly, the Pacific Tsunami Center in Honolulu, among other stations, registered the earthquake's intensity and location. It was the biggest earthquake in the world since 1964 when Alaska was struck. The ensuing waves of these tsunamis took 7 1/2 hours to reach Somalia, crushing hundreds of coastal communities in their wake.

The first populated areas were flooded within an hour, yet for hours there were no alarms sounded either by radio, television, internet, or any other telecommunications technologies for the soon-to-be inundated areas. Australian embassies were warned by their country but diplomatic protocols and other bureaucratic reasons stalled the news inside those stately edifices.

So, in spite of all these electronic technologies that its innovators and promoters have told us would change the world, human and institutional failures rendered them inoperative for those critical hours. Compounding the tragedy, unlike big hurricanes, people can quickly run away from tsunamis to higher ground and save themselves.

Early explanations of these failures don't wash. One is that the watchdogs did not think the Indian Ocean experienced such tsunamis as did the Pacific Ocean. It is not a function of oceans, it is a function of powerful undersea earthquakes.

The United States spends a good deal of money on earthquake research, both on land and sea, and their consequences. California and western Tennessee, alone, require such attentiveness.

But the United States has stations around the world as well. Maybe George W. Bush should order a real readiness plan for homeland security on natural disasters, even if he is told there are no terrorists behind them.

Party-Party

July 30, 2004

The Democratic Party-Party Convention in Boston is over and its singular memory will be its predictable banality and the commercialism that mostly financed it.

Historically, conventions were newsworthy because there was a struggle over who would receive the nomination and what the Parties would stand for in their platforms.

Today there is a coronation for the nominee amidst delegates' inquiries about what would be on the menus of the 250 parties that corporations and their smooth-tongued lobbyists were throwing for their favorably-positioned congressional bigwigs.

Inside the festooned Convention Center there were dozens of speeches all pre-viewed, sanitized and edited down to the last minute on teleprompters by the standby Kerry censors. When Al Sharpton departed from the script for a couple of minutes, you would have thought their wedding cake was burning.

Fifteen thousand reporters spent five days looking for stories—any stories—that qualified as news or soft features from the Party, its 4000 plus delegates and the swarm of corporate backslappers. It was not difficult to describe the wine, whiskey, music and obvious temptations, in return for the implicit political favors, that the drug, insurance, banking, chemical, oil, media and computer companies presented to the attending politicians.

For this business bacchanalia the taxpayers were required to pay the Democratic party thirteen million dollars (and later the same amount for the Republican Party Convention). A few years ago Congress—namely the two Parties—decided that these political Conventions were "educational" in nature and worthy of your tax dollars.

Around, over and under the Convention premises hovered a security army of police, detectives, troops and armed, airborne and land-based technology worthy of a Marine division. Thwarting a possible terrorist attack was one reason for spending over tens of millions of dollars—the other objective was to keep the people from protesting anywhere near the Fleet Center Convention.

The people- voters, taxpayers, workers—were detained in a "free speech zone" (catch the irony) that looked like an ad hoc concentration camp encirclement. The intimidating zone was distant enough not to be convenient to the electronic media placements. In a phrase, the Democratic Party did what it does so regularly in Washington—it shut out the people who resigned themselves to social justice gatherings elsewhere in Boston.

But the "people" should have been smarter. They should have had contrasting parties held by dispossessed workers, defrauded consumers, medical malpractice victims, fleeced taxpayers, small farmers, and polluted communities with open invitations for the politicians to attend. The media likes contrasts, especially when very few of these Congressional delegates would have left their lavish business bashes to greet the American voters they court and flatter only at election time from distant stages and 30 second television ads.

The Democratic Convention did have its amusing moments. Bill Clinton didn't charge his $200,000 per speech fee for his speech to the convention and the viewing public. The National Association of Broadcasters—representing those television stations who use your public airwaves free and decide 24 hours a day what is allowed to air on our property—held a huge party for Congressman Ed Markey. Mr. Markey started his congressional career as a major outspoken critic of the broadcasting industry. He has been much quieter in recent years.

Open Debates

February 20, 2004

Last week, Open Debates (see Opendebates. org), a nonprofit, non-partisan organization, whose purposes I support, filed a complaint with the Federal Election Commission (FEC) against the Commission on Presidential Debates (CPD) which was created and controlled by the Republican and Democratic Parties. Open Debates charged, with documentation, that the CPD is not non-partisan but is deeply bi-partisan, serving and obeying the dictates of the two major Parties.

Open Debates argues that such control is a violation of FEC debate regulations. Corporate contributions which could go only to an educational association are instead going to a bi-partisan political organization which is unlawful.

A new, non-partisan Citizens Debate Commission (CDC) has been established by Open Debates with a Board of Directors composed of conservative, liberal and moderate representatives. The CDC is not under the control of any candidates or any parties. It advances an educational function by urging rigorous debates with exciting third party or independent candidates participating.

This entry criteria is not easy but it is possible, unlike the CPD's mountainous hurdle, required in 2000, of averaging 15 percent voter support in 5 national polls in September. Even Ross Perot, who got on the debates in 1992 and received 19 million votes, did not come close to reaching a 15 percent level in September of that year.

The new Debate Commission's criteria are that a candidate must be on enough states' ballots to be able theoretically to win the electoral college, and must either garner 5 percent voter support or be supported by a majority of citizens in polls who want him/her to be on the presidential debates.

Open Debates had a news conference on February 19th at the National Press Club (carried by C-SPAN) where directors of the Citizen Debate Commission spoke their mind on the necessity to open up the debate process to vital issues and differing views by more than two major party candidates. In 2000, candidates Bush and Gore set a debate record for agreeing with one another.

All the speakers, Paul Weyrich, Alan Keyes, Kert Davies and Rob Richie provided their unique elaborations for the benefits to the voters, their vital issues, and voter turnout from more diverse debates and more flexible debate formats. The existing CPD debate formats are really parallel interviews by one chosen questioner, and not really debates.

There is an additional importance. The debates are overwhelmingly the only major way candidates, without big money and television ads, can reach the American people. Indeed, even with the big-money candidates it is presently the only way that any positions or rebuttals can be communicated apart from sound bite journalism on television. The major nominees usually do not like to give long interviews to the press or go on radio.

My nephew, Tarek Milleron, while thinking about this debate subject, came up with a sterling idea. The CPD stonewalls all criticisms and challenges (although a new book-length exposé by George Farah may flush it out soon). So Milleron proposes tens of thousands of proxy debates all over the country—in schools, universities, Elks Clubs, union halls, chambers of commerce, forums by the League of Women Voters, the Junior League Civic and neighborhood associations. People would volunteer to stand in for the presidential candidates, under cross-questioning debate formats. The internet can help find these proxies. National sponsors can offer user-friendly debate manuals, prizes and other incentives that bring the better debates beyond their auditoriums to websites with larger audiences.

High school and college debate teams should pick this idea up readily on a national scale. They are already in debating trained and ready to go. The point is not an occasional debate here and there which probably goes on, but a large number of debates everywhere in the country with a national focus. His proposal would be a great educational mechanism to inform and animate voters and bring them to the polls in greater numbers. It would also help to diversify the issues and broaden the subject matter and solutions to our problems which are deserving of attention by those presidential candidates on the ballot.

Usually, presidential contests between the two major parties narrow the number of repeated disagreements, however rhetorical, to a half dozen or less. This cul-de-sac campaign shortchanges the many matters that are left out. Also excluded are the many people, whose on the ground innovations, for example, in education, tax reform, energy, public transit, healthcare, civil and criminal justice, childhood nurturing, recycling, consumer rights, workplace conditions and more effective foreign policy and defense call out for attention and diffusion.

Milleron's proposal is very cost-effective; but it needs a new level of voter will power to participate in the upcoming presidential election and not just accede to a spectator role. Should these mini-debates proliferate, the Citizens Debate Commission will be on its way to displacing the stagnant, arrogant corporate funded, corporation known as the Commission on Presidential Debates.

Golden Oldies

Gore Vidal once said the four most beautiful words in our common language are "I told you so."

In many ways they are also the four most unfortunate words in our common language.

Reading through my past columns going back to the early 1970s, I was impressed by how many of our society's deprivations and remedies have been brought to public attention by citizen activists and public advocates. I have often said that our country has far more problems than it deserves and far more solutions than it applies.

For example, many of the warnings presented in my weekly column, if heeded, could have prevented or at least mitigated the damage inflicted on our society. And, many of the suggested reforms might have significantly improved our environment and quality of life.

In the following selection of columns, I detail the various conditions harming our society and point to some promising innovations.

One column from 1976 reports on the petitions, protests, read-ins and demonstrations that confronted the announcement by the financially-pressed New York City Public Library that eight branch libraries would be promptly closed with still others to be shut down within the next two years. Other branches and the great central library at Fifth Avenue and 42nd Street had their hours and services curtailed. There was something both noble and sad about the neighborhood people who protested. The elderly and the young explained what libraries meant to them—solace, a place to reflect, study, research a school paper, let the imagination roam, or obtain self-help guidance or civic information.

The destruction of libraries, whether by war or dictatorship, has been viewed as a serious blow to freedom and democracy. In New York it was seen merely as a way to save some money.

Then, in another column, there is the explanation of the devastation of our land using dangerous energy such as coal and more importantly, nuclear, which is too loosely regulated, costly and capable of causing mass destruction if safety measures fail. Take a look at what happened in Japan post-tsunami. Nuclear power is a lasting, dangerous source of energy that we don't need to use.

Another column in this section deals with the woes of privatization. Inside the offices of the Heritage Foundation—the nonprofit policy cheerleader for the Reagan Administration—a handful of zealots were in constant touch with the Office of Management and Budget (OMB). Their mission: privatize a large array of governmental services and assets. The President's Commission on Privatization, whose official adviser was none other than Stuart M. Butler of the Heritage Foundation, recommended to Mr. Reagan that significant government assets be privatized—that is, sold off to private businesses—which is often done at bargain basement prices.

If you think holding government officials accountable is difficult, try making the privatizers or corporatizers responsive to taxpayers when they are once removed and can lavish their campaign contributions on elected officials.

Just as privatization harms the economy, over-commercialization poisons American culture. Years ago, the word "overcommercialized" used to apply to highway billboards marring the landscape. Look what rampaging commercialism is like now. Commercials are embedded in every aspect of daily life, inundating us with loud messages to buy from the moment we wake up until the moment we go to sleep. The separation between commerce and culture continues to blur as corporatism subordinates the well-being of men, women and their children.

How about the theology of labor and capital-shifting globalization? It is time for some humility from the proponents of unregulated markets and intensified economic globalization. It is no longer plausible for their proponents to contend that the solutions to the problems caused by deregulation, marketization and globalization are more deregulation, marketization and globalization.

US corporations aren't even subtle about it. Waving a flag and carrying a big shovel, corporate interests scoop up government handouts and taxpayer money in an unprecedented fashion while the public is preoccupied with the undeclared and boundless war on terrorism.

Reckless financial institutions on Wall Street brought down the economy on Main Street. If prudent regulations had been properly enforced we might have limited the financial devastation to worker pension funds, shareholders and taxpayers, who paid for the costly bailouts. The savings & loan industry, Enron, and the wild and crazy Wall Street gamblers engaged in activities that should have been checked. There continue to be official complaints about "crime in the suites." Imagine if the federal cop on the corporate crime beat had adequate prosecutorial resources.

Modern societies specialize in a dazzling number of indicators that mark the ups and downs of various activities, especially economic, health and audience ratings. But when it comes to signs of societal decay that cannot easily be reduced to numbers, there is a void. So let's look at the "decays" of our society that are trending downward, and see how they could have been prevented. Let's also look forward to actually put these deteriorations in the past rather than the present.

Then saying an "I told you so" might be less necessary.

Why Can't Voters Be as Diligent Voters as they are Sports Fans?

November 12, 2004

Whenever I hear sports fans chatting on talk radio shows or when I personally chat with people about sports—both spectator and participatory games—the depth and breadth of the conversations are not surprising. As a teenager fan, I knew the batting averages of half the players in the American League. It is the American way to know your sports.

This mental diligence does not carry over, by and large, into their role as voters. Let's compare the differences:

1. Sports fans do their homework. They know the statistics of the players and teams, and they are deeply involved in analyzing strategies and tactics on the playing field. To them the game is a study and not just a matter of chance or luck. The looks, smiles, big salaries and rhetoric of

the players mean nothing unless they are based on performance. Fans think about foreseeing and forestalling their opposing team's adjustments and responses, always looking forward and analyzing.

The same cannot be said about most voters. Half of them do not even know the name of their member of Congress. Half of them do not even come to the "game" on Election Day to register their opinion.

2. Fans hold the hierarchy responsible—from the players to referees (umpires), to the coaches, managers and owners.

Voters, on the other hand, have allowed top-down forms of no-fault government. This is true even when votes are not properly counted or elections are stolen. Presidents, governors and senators, representatives are rarely held accountable for their most series boondoggles, failures or wrongheaded policies. Smiles and rhetoric go a long way on the likeability index in contrast to studying their actual voting records. Voting records recede into the dark mists while the propaganda materials of the politicians shine in the bright lights.

3. Fans analyze reasons for defeat or victory not just on what happened in the ninth inning or in the last two minutes of the final quarter. They understand that the seeds of winning or losing are planted throughout the game.

Voters just look at the final voting count at the end of Election Day. As a result, they miss the dynamics before elections to understand what were the influential factors. Focusing on the latter had led some scholars to conclude that Al Gore cost me more votes than I cost Al Gore in the 2000 election.

4. Fans evaluate the dual performance of the teams—offensive and defensive. They know that both who made it happen and who let it

happen are keys to grasping the game. They know when a team beats itself.

Voters almost always focus on which Party or elected officials proposed a policy or a nomination. Rarely do they criticize their favorite Party for not stopping bad bills or judicial nominees.

5. Fans understand that chronically losing teams need different players and managers. Beyond just booing loudly at their home team, they have many specific ideas about replacements and which positions need fresh talent.

Voters, many of whom are on automatic because they are hereditary Republicans or hereditary Democrats, seem resigned to the same field year after year. After ten years of losses to the Republicans at the local, state and federal level, Democratic voters still meekly go to the polls sensing they are voting for the least worst choices. Instead of asking "why not the best?," voters too often appear resigned, not demanding a new game plan, new players and managers.

6. Sports fans complain loudly and engage in robust arguments with opposing fans. They have a long memory. I know because my small Connecticut home town was split down the middle—Red Sox fans on one side and Yankee fans on the other. The Red Sox fans never let us forget that their team gave the Yankees their best early players, including Babe Ruth.

Except for one or two fervent issues, voters tend to give politicians a free ride about dozens of other positions that may affect them adversely in their daily lives and dreams of a better future for their children. Single-issue voters are easily captured by politicians who support them on that issue and are allowed to escape accountability for dozens of other subjects.

7. Fans are never satisfied. Take a look at Yankee fans for example, home to a legacy of wins. Voters settle for very little and let their expecta-

tion levels run down year-by-year. Their cynicism makes them say that they're not turned on politics which is why politics has been turning onto them very disagreeably. And the golden rule of this brand of politics becomes, "he who has the gold, rules."

One thing is for certain. If fans were as serious about politics as they are about sports they, as taxpayers, would not be paying for stadiums and arenas that should be paid for by private capitalists and the wealthy owners of professional sports teams.

Poletown, Michigan

August 6, 2004

Better later than never. More than two decades after Michigan's Supreme Court upheld an egregious abuse of government's power of eminent domain, that same court acknowledged the error of its ways.

The Fifth Amendment to the United States Constitution permits government to seize private property for a "public use," such as a highway, railroad, or military facility, provided it give the owner "just compensation." Many state constitutions have similar provisions. But in modern times it has become common for the government, usually at the state or local level, to seize property and transfer it to another private party rather than maintaining it for public use.

Neglecting their role as guardian of the Constitution and individual rights, courts across the country have rubber-stamped these illegal actions, claiming that private-to-private transfers satisfy the "public use" requirement as long as the new recipient's use of the land provides a "public benefit."

Which brings us back to Michigan. In 1980,

in the teeth of a recession, Detroit was desperate for economic revitalization. General Motors took advantage. Having announced plans to shut down two plants in the city, GM offered to build a new complex if a suitable site could be found and given to GM on favorable terms. Detroit and GM eventually agreed that the best site was Poletown, a close-knit residential neighborhood consisting primarily of second-generation Polish-Americans and African-Americans.

To make room for GM, the city of Detroit told innocent Poletown residents to accept the city's offer of modest compensation and get out. Many protested, insisting that no amount of money was "just compensation" for their cherished homes and neighborhood. But the Michigan Supreme Court didn't care, upholding the seizure of hundreds of homes, a half-dozen churches, an array of schools, a hospital, and dozens of small businesses. In all, 4,200 persons were forced to relocate, and a thriving community was destroyed.

Sadly, this abuse of power yielded no net gain for Detroit. GM fell 3,500 short of its promise to create 6,500 new jobs. In the end, more people were displaced than employed and the sweetheart deal cost taxpayers more than $300 million in federal, state, and local subsidies for GM.

Hundreds of similar abuses of eminent domain have occurred during the last few decades, with municipalities playing reverse Robin Hood—taking from ordinary citizens and giving to powerful individual developers or corporations. In many cases, the alleged public benefit is a transparent cover for what amounts to legal bribery. Those who fill campaign coffers expect rewards, and eminent domain is used to produce rewards. Some new, unneeded sports stadiums result from such a process. A regulatory agency even sought to seize an elderly woman's home and turn it over to tycoon Donald Trump to expand the parking lot and limousine waiting station at one of his casinos (fortunately a lower level court ruled against Mr. Trump).

Now, at last, a prominent court has said enough is enough. The case of *Wayne County v. Hathcock* bore obvious similarities to Poletown. A county in Michigan planned to seize 1,300 acres of land, encompassing scores of homes, and transfer it to private developers and businesses to create an industrial park. Just as in Poletown, the county justified the seizure with wholly speculative, extravagant predictions about future economic benefits. A dozen brave homeowners refused to yield, and took the county to court. Citing Poletown as precedent, the trial court and court of appeals upheld the proposed transfer.

Perhaps chastened by the way things turned out after Poletown, or enlightened by a body of commentary criticizing the use of eminent domain to enrich private businesses, the Michigan Supreme Court announced its intention to reconsider its Poletown decision. Several public interest groups weighed in with friend-of-the-court briefs urging the Court to rectify its tragic error in the earlier case. On July 30, the Court handed down a momentous decision. In a holding endorsed by all seven justices, the Court explicitly overruled Poletown and said that henceforth eminent domain may not be used to transfer property to a private party except in very unusual circumstances.

In the single most important sentence in its lengthy opinion, the Court rejected the suggestion, central to Poletown, that "a vague economic benefit stemming from a private profit-maximizing enterprise is a 'public use.'" Rather, land may be seized and transferred to a private party only if

"public necessity of the extreme sort" so requires and "the property remains subject to public oversight after transfer to a private entity."

This decision makes good sense as a matter of constitutional law and fundamental fairness. Under Michigan law, people's homes can no longer be seized to achieve speculative benefits or to reward usually large corporate welfare kings. Courts nationwide should follow Michigan's lead and reestablish their rightful role in our constitutional system.

Corporate UNPATRIOTIC BEHAVIOR

July 2, 2004

During this 4th of July weekend, why not assess the behavior of giant US chartered multinational corporations by the yardsticks of patriotism to the supportive country of their birth? These standards for the corporate entities themselves are important for the moral, legal and political persuasion necessary to improve their patriotic performance.

Let a few examples do for many.

1. During the Vietnam War the Department of Defense learned that the second leading cause of hospitalization for the troops was malaria. Fed up by the refusal of the profit glutted drug companies to research for new medicines, the Department established its own in-house, first-class drug research division at Walter Reed Institute of Health. Many new medicines to treat malaria and other tropical diseases were discovered and made available to the world with staggering efficiency compared to the private drug companies. Even today

these drug companies continue to avoid investing their money in vaccines or other related medicines needed for Americans and natives in tropical regions. This is the same industry that receives billions of dollars each year in NIH research and development (e.g. Taxol, AZT) and tax credits. UNPATRIOTIC BEHAVIOR.

2. US corporations, with your taxpayer subsidies, are selling weapons of rapid destruction to regimes all over the world—many of which are dictatorships and oligarchies oppressing their people and reshipping these weapons wherever they please. Moreover, for years these corporations have been pressing to override export controls and sell advanced computer technologies to countries hostile or potentially hostile to our country. These arms sales range from fighter planes to lethal "anti-personnel" weapons that slice into innocent children and adults. UNPATRIOTIC BEHAVIOR.

3. Wal-Mart systematically pushes wages, standards and benefits downward in the US—below the level required by Western countries where Wal-Mart is operating. They treat American workers worse than Western European workers. Moreover, they advise their low-wage workers how to qualify for federal welfare like food stamps. Wal-Mart is demanding more and more that their US suppliers meet the "China Price"—meaning that they either cut their workers wages and benefits or close down and open up in China with its government's dictatorial repression of workers. UNPATRIOTIC BEHAVIOR.

4. US multinationals export industries (e.g., auto parts) and jobs to oppressive regimes utilizing an assortment of tax and other governmental incentives and promotions. Attempts in Congress to end these subsidies for fleeing America to tax havens in Bermuda, etc., have been defeated by corporate lobbyists and President Bush who loses no sleep over such callous behavior that hollows our communities and leaves families in desperate straits while some worry about their sons and daughters in the Iraq quagmire. UNPATRIOTIC BEHAVIOR.

5. Pentagon and Government Accountability Office audits have repeatedly found Halliburton and other companies ripping off Uncle Sam in their contracts with the Pentagon—even selling contaminated water and overcharging for meals for the soldiers. Many more gouges and profiteering will be disclosed with further audits and, it is hoped, Congressional investigations. UNPATRIOTIC BEHAVIOR.

6. Chemical, nuclear power, bio-labs and other vulnerable "ports of call" for potential stateless terrorism have been resisting federal demands and certifications for upgrading security. These firms call these upgrades "over-regulation." The EPA has pointed to 100 chemical plants in the US where the sabotage of one could cause a million casualties. This resistance is broad and deep, as the Department of Homeland Security knows full well. UNPATRIOTIC BEHAVIOR.

7. For many decades corporate polluters

have been relentlessly using our air, water and soil as their private, toxic sewers. Despoiling, poisoning and ruining the natural and inhabited land of our country has made large swaths of America uninhabitable due to deeply toxic territory. Year after year, with lobbyists and campaign cash, oppose or undermine the laws, regulations and enforcement to reduce the sources of cancer, respiratory ailments, genetic damage and other diseases and property damage on innocent Americans. UNPATRIOTIC BEHAVIOR.

Has corporate globalization ended our expectations to demand allegiance to the country that has bred and raised these large companies, subsidized these companies and has defended them abroad with the lives of American soldiers for over a century?

At stake is whether the constitutional sovereignty of the people can prevail and subordinate the imposed sovereignty of multinational corporations in the interests of our country and posterity. Let the debate expand.

Signs of a Societal Decay

October 24, 2003

Modern societies specialize in a dazzling number of indicators that mark the ups and downs of various activities, especially economic, health and audience ratings. But when it comes to signs of societal decay that cannot easily be reduced to numbers, there is a void. So let's look at four "decays" that are trending downward:

1. Gluttony literally is rapidly becoming a competitive sport. In fact, over-gorging has become a contest with the self-proclaimed gorgers traveling around the country performing in what its euphemists call "competitive eating." No longer one of the seven deadly sins in this field, "Crazy Devin" Lipsitz, winner of the 2000 year United Carnegie International Pickle Eating Contest in New York City, describes his skill as "a sport" played by "athletes." There is even an International Federation of Competitive Eating which presides over dozens of events a year where contestants inhale hot dogs (the champion swallowed 50 hot dogs in 12 minutes), matzo balls, chicken wings and who knows what's next—mayonnaise? The voyeuristic audience for such gluttony battles is growing fast. It may be only a matter of time before the first cable TV show is launched. By the way, according to the rules, if an "Athlete" vomits, he/she is disqualified. So much for the Peter the Great maneuver.

2. Next on the decay derby is Tyco, under CEO L. Dennis Kozlowski, presently the defendant in a criminal trial. He held a $2 million 40th birthday party for his wife in faraway Sardinia that featured a shrunken model of Michelangelo's David with vodka streaming from its penis into crystal glasses. Videotapes also showed an exploding birthday cake with a replica of a woman's breast. Government prosecutors charge that Tyco paid for much of this party as a deductible business entertainment expense. Parents cannot deduct their children's college tuition as educational expenses. Yet corporations can and do deduct liquor, lurid entertainment

and expensive, luxurious gifts as "ordinary and necessary" business expenses. They, thereby, reduce the revenues going to the US Treasury which could have been used to provide grants and loans to America's deserving students. Call this the decay of inverted priorities.

3. A third decay comes from the electoral arena. There was a time in our history when a resurgent citizenry gave itself the right to vote. So the oligarchs devised a "wealth election" when dollars began voting in ever greater numbers. But buying elections was not enough for the power brokers in the two major parties. Lately they are determined to pick their voters by increasingly precise computer-driven legislative redistricting. In the past, redistricting came once every ten years after the decennial census. Now Republicans and Democrats cannot resist the lure of more frequent redistricting because, depending on who controls the state government, the reward of making their one-party districts are obvious. In Texas, the state Republicans have broken cynical new ground in passing legislation that carves new zigzag Congressional districts in order to pick the voters that would replace almost certainly up to five Congressional House Democrats with Republicans. These elections are over before they start. The courts have been too lenient in permitting such blatant electoral map-making that is turning most of House of Representative districts into areas of one-party domination. Both parties now believe that over 90 percent of House districts in the country are not competitive, meaning that the other major party doesn't try to contest the incumbents seat. This is worsening decay for voter choice and political competition in a weakening democracy.

4. The fourth "decay" is occurring in the midst of the nation's largest corporate crime wave (remember Enron, WorldCom, Health South, etc.) that has drained or looted trillions of dollars from millions of workers, their pension funds and small investors. Well, it seems that the corporate crooks so vastly outnumber the federal cops on the corporate crime beat that "accommodations" have become necessary. Faced with a tiny enforcement budget and the "soft on corporate crime" attitude of the Bush Administration, the Justice Department has developed ways to avoid traditional, straight out indictment, prosecution and conviction approaches of the past. Presently, the Department initiates a criminal prosecution of a company and then settles for a probation plus a modest fine. Or, the Department criminally prosecutes companies but then enters into a "deferred prosecution" agreement stipulating that the case will be dropped if the company shows good behavior over a year or two. Another lax approach is to file criminal charges but then not prosecute the company and instead enter into a "memorandum of understanding."

Large corporations with their giant corporate law firms skilled in battles of attrition and delay can routinely bring the small number of state and federal prosecutors to such levels of concessions, if they do not escape prosecution filings entirely in the first place. Congressional and state legislators know this, as they raise money from these companies for their campaign treasuries. So these lawmakers return the favor to their business benefactors by starving the budgets of these federal and state anti-corporate crime task forces. And you the consumers, workers and investors of America continue to pay the big price. Discerning more yardsticks of decay is a way for people to arouse themselves to reverse course.

Enron and the Consumer Empowerment Imperative

February 26, 2002

Enron, Enron, Enron—front page and center, top of the network television news and the biggest criminally-derived bankruptcy in US history. A "gargantuan pyramid scheme," says Republican Senator Peter G. Fitzgerald. Proposals for reform are gushing forth from congressional minds of varying sincerities. Tougher regulations to protect investors, and pension holders from crooked self-dealing corporate executives and their compliant outside auditors.

No one is yet speaking of helping investors and pension holders organize themselves in order to defend themselves and provide the grass roots power to get the laws enforced. Last week the new Chairman of the Securities and Exchange Commission, a former big time attorney for the large accounting firms, Harvey L. Pitt, told a House of Representatives investigating committee about his concern for ordinary defrauded people who trust their companies: "It is these Americans whose faith fuels our markets, who have no lobby and no trade associations,

whose interests are, and must be, paramount. I am appalled at what happened to them as a result of Enron's collapse."

Ergo? Is Chairman Pitt implying that these ordinary people should continue to trust members of Congress to enact strong laws with enough funds for dutiful regulators to strongly enforce them. The lessons of history do not provide assurances for such trust. Does Chairman Pitt have a proposal to see that these faithful Americans have their own lobby? Do members of Congress have a bill in the works now? Not to my knowledge.

In his small, but important book, *Here the People Rule,* Harvard constitutional law professor Richard Parker argues that the federal government has an affirmative constitutional duty to facilitate the political and civic energies of the people. His point certainly finds resonance in Lincoln's words "government of the people, by the people and for the people."

In 1974, I wrote my first article on the need to redress the imbalance between consumers and large companies, the latter who were recipients of governmental privileges such as legal monopolies or taxpayer subsidies. I suggested the idea of putting mandatory inserts in company billing envelopes inviting consumers to band together in groups with full-time consumer advocates to right this imbalance. The immediate occasion for this proposal was rising electricity rates, weak regulation and powerless residential ratepayers.

But in the '80s, the savings and loans scandals started piling up. Corporate looters, mismanagers and their speculators put at risk or devoured tens of billions of dollars of ordinary peoples' savings. In September 1985, Rep. Charles E. Schumer of New York, then perhaps more idealistic than today's Senator Schumer, introduced the Consumer Banking Act of 1985. A key provision of the legislation, Rep. Schumer wrote, is establishing state-level Financial Consumers' Boards with a voluntary membership bases.

These self-funded, private boards "would act as an institutional watchdog for consumers' interests; representing citizens in financial services matters before regulatory agencies, legislatures, and the courts, and informing bank customers of these actions," Schumer declared. These boards would also conduct surveys, disseminate information such as shoppers' guides to financial services, as well as assist citizens in resolving consumer complaints.

Four years later, with an avalanche of collapsing S&Ls demanding a Congressional bailout, Schumer's proposal was turned down in 1989, 1990 and 1991 by a large majority of the House Banking Committee members as they were passing massive taxpayer bailouts of these once-fiduciary institutions. These boards would not have cost the taxpayer a penny, as the projected millions of members would become members after paying modest annual dues. An Illinois Board, representing utility ratepayers, attracted over 150,000 members in that state within eighteen months of its establishment. In one negotiation, nine years ago, this board, without filing a lawsuit, persuaded Commonwealth Edison to refund $1.3 billion in overcharges to northern Illinois families.

Now comes Enron, capping a decade of casino capitalism and corporate crime fraud and abuse, chronicled in the *Wall Street Journal*, *Business Week*, the *New York Times* and other mainstream publications. How will investors and pension holders be able to protect their savings and retirement funds? By dusting off Rep. Schumer's proposal and extending it across the entire financial industry to start Financial Consumer Associations in every state.

Let those who would be ripped off more easily organize themselves through facilities such as inserts in these companies' statements and bills that go out at least once a month to customers and beneficiaries.

For more information on this proposal, during these momentous Congressional hearings about what to do after Enron, contact Theresa Amato at Citizen Works, PO Box 18478, Washington, DC 20036 or visit Citizenworks.org.

Corporate Patriotism
November 9, 2001

US corporations aren't even subtle about it. Waving a flag and carrying a big shovel, corporate interests are scooping up government benefits and taxpayer money in an unprecedented fashion while the public is preoccupied with the September 11 attacks and the war in Afghanistan.

Shamelessly, the Bush Administration and Congress have taken advantage of the patriotic outpouring to fulfill the wish lists of their most generous corporate campaign donors. Not only is the US Treasury being raided, but regulations protecting everything from personal privacy to environmental safeguards are under attack by *Wall Street Journal* editorials and well-heeled lobbyists who want to stampede Congress to act while the media and citizens are distracted.

Only a handful in Congress—members like Senator Russell Feingold of Wisconsin and Representatives Peter DeFazio of Oregon and Barbara Lee of California—have shown the courage to question the giveaways and the quick wipeout of civil liberties and other citizen protections. In most cases, such as the $15 billion airline bailout and corporate tax breaks, legislation has been pushed to the forefront with little or no hearings and only fleeting consideration on the floor of the Senate and the House of Representatives.

One of the boldest grabs for cash has been by corporations seeking to eliminate the Alternative Minimum Tax (AMT), which was enacted during the Reagan Administration to prevent profitable corporations from escaping all tax liability through various loopholes. Not only do the corporations want relief from the current year's AMT taxes, but they are seeking a retroactive refund of all AMT taxes paid since 1986.

This giveaway, as passed by the House of Representatives, would make corporations eligible for $25 billion in tax refunds. Just fourteen corporations would receive $6.3 billion of the refund. IBM gets $1.4 billion; General Motors, $833 million; General Electric $671 million; Daimler-Chrysler $600 million; Chevron-Texaco $572 million. The fourteen biggest beneficiaries of the minimum tax repeal gave $14,769,785 in "soft money" to the national committees of the Democratic and Republican parties in recent years.

Soon to join the bailout parade is the nation's insurance industry, which is lobbying the Congress to have the federal government pick up the tab for future losses like those stemming from the attack on the World Trade Center. Proposals are on the table for taxpayers to either pick up losses above certain levels or to provide loans or loan guarantees for reinsurance.

The insurance companies want federal bailouts, but they continue to insist on regulation only by underfunded, poorly staffed state insurance departments, most of which are dominated by the industry. Any bailout or loan program involving the insurance companies must in-

clude provisions which ensure that insurance companies cannot refuse to write policies and make investments in low, moderate and minority neighborhoods. Allegations about insurance company "redlining" or discrimination against citizens in these areas have been prevalent for many years. It would be a terrible injustice for citizens to be forced to pay taxes to help bail out insurance companies that discriminate against them. Congress needs to address this issue before it even considers public assistance for the industry.

The concerns of the people have been missing in all the bailouts. When the airline companies walked off with $15 billion plus in bailout money, the thousands of laid-off employees—airline attendants, maintenance crews, baggage handlers and ticket counter employees—received not a dime. Attempts to include health benefits and other help for these employees were shouted down on the floor of the House of Representatives.

Last month, more than 400,000 employees lost their jobs nationwide and the national unemployment rate rose to 5.4 percent, the highest level since 1996. The Bureau of Labor Statistics said roughly a fourth of the lost jobs were the direct result of the terrorist attacks of September 11. Bailouts, benefits or other aid for these victims of the attacks? No, that's reserved just for the corporations under the policies of the Bush Administration and the present Congress.

Yet it is the workers in the low-wage jobs—like those in restaurants, hotels, retailing and transportation—who are bearing the brunt of the layoffs in the aftermath of the attacks on the World Trade Center, according to a report from the New York State Department of Labor. Almost 25,000 people told the department that they lost their jobs because of the Trade Center disaster. An analysis by the department of the first 22,000 of the claims found that 16 percent worked at bars, 14 percent worked at hotels, 5 percent worked in air transportation and 21 percent in a category termed "business services." Only 4 percent worked at Wall Street brokerage firms.

While more workers lose jobs, the Administration is pushing for authority to expand the North American Free Trade Agreement (NAF-TA) under new "fast-track" authority. The Department of Commerce concedes that at least 360,000 jobs have been lost under NAFTA, and private research groups estimate the total may be twice that number. Now, with unemployment rising to alarming levels, the Administration decides to cave to pro-NAFTA corporate demands which will only make the labor picture worse. No bailout for laid off workers, just a hard crack across the knees.

As Bill Moyers, the author and national journalist, commented, "They (the corporations) are counting on your patriotism to distract you from their plunder. They're counting on you to stand at attention with your hand over your heart, pledging allegiance to the flag, while they pick your pocket."

The present crisis cries out for shared sacrifice—not the opportunism so blatantly displayed by the nation's corporate interests. President Bush and the Congress must summon the courage to resist the self-serving demands—the kind of courage and shared sacrifice that guided the brave rescue workers on September 11.

The Commission on Presidential Debates: Not the Unpartisan Organization It Appears

January 11, 2000

On January 6, 2000, the Commission on Presidential Debates (CPD) announced that there would be three presidential debates and one vice-presidential debate in October 2000 at different locations around the country.

The Commission has an official sounding name, but it is, in fact, a private organization run by the Republican and Democratic Parties, led by co-chairmen Paul G. Kirk, Jr. (Democrat) and Frank J. Fahrenkopf, Jr. (Republican) and heavily funded by corporate money, which in 1996 included the tobacco and auto companies.

Both Mr. Kirk and Mr. Fahrenkopf represent corporate clients and the latter is well known as a chief lobbyist for the gambling industry.

The Commission laid down three criteria for determining which candidates are invited onto the debates that are sure to be nationally televised on several networks.

These criteria are (1) the candidate must meet the constitutional requirements of being at least thirty-five years of age, a natural born citizen and resident of the US for fourteen years; and is otherwise eligible under the Constitution;

(2) The candidate must be on enough state ballots to have "at least a mathematical chance of securing an Electoral College majority in the 2000 general election;"

(3) The candidate must have "a level of support of at least 15 percent of the national electorate as determined by five selected national public opinion polling organizations, using the average of those organizations' most recent publicly-reported results at the time of the determination."

The five polling groups include the joint ventures between newspapers such as the *Washington Post*, the *New York Times, Wall Street Journal* and the television networks—NBC, CBS, ABC and CNN.

Mr. Kirk and Mr. Fahrenkopf declared themselves satisfied that their "non-partisan" commission has established an approach which "is both clear and predictable." Unfortunately, it is too clear and predictable for smaller party presidential candidates who will be excluded from the debates leaving only the two major party candidates having the field to themselves. The Commission is really not "non-partisan," it is "bi-partisan" and designed to protect as it did in 1996 the debates for its dominant two-party system.

These exclusionary rules are nothing new. For years the Republican and Democratic Parties have conspired in one state legislature after another to enact laws that create huge barriers (often tens of thousands of signatures on petitions plus other harassments) to make sure that smaller political candidates never have a chance to have a chance. These barriers are unique in comparison to the easy ballot access requirements in Canada and several other western nations.

So the two parties are acting in their grand exclusionary tradition—one which in the business world would subject them to antitrust prosecution.

There is yet another convoluted complication to the Commission's year 2000 criteria—the reliance on polling organizations whose news and editorial bureaus can determine whether or not to cover third-party candidates. If a near news blackout prevails, then the polling arm can report that the candidates don't register much in the polls.

Why would the commercial news media agree to such an arrangement and expose itself to legitimate charges that it is compromising its alleged detachment or objectivity? The Commission's arrangement inexorably draws these media organizations into a partisan pit. Indeed, some of the moderators for the debates may come from these same news organizations. The matrix becomes more intricate.

When the Commission was asked at the news conference "why 15 percent?" the reply was that this number was their fairest judgment in order to keep the debates manageable. No one representing the executive suites of the mass media was around to answer "why do these giant media corporations leave the number of nationally televised debates up to the two major parties?"

After all the time devoted to soap operas, sports, game shows and advertisements, is there no time within these very profitable television and radio stations, which use our public airwaves free of charge, to air more accessible debates in the fall?

Hardly had Mr. Kirk and Mr. Fahrenkopf left their heavily attended news conference when Anheuser-Busch company announced that it had been selected by the Commission as "a national sponsor of the four presidential debates . . . as well as the sole sponsor of the debate schedules for October 17 at Washington University in St. Louis." (The latter will be paid for with a contribution of $550,000.)

Imagine a beer company financing the presidential debates in the world's longest lasting, richest democracy. Will Anheuser-Busch haul out the free kegs at Saint Louis' bars in celebration?

Economic Globalization

September 4, 1998

It is time for some humility from the proponents of unregulated markets and intensified economic globalization. It is no longer even superficially plausible for their proponents to contend that the solutions to the problems caused by deregulation, marketization, and globalization are more deregulation, marketization, and globalization.

Wall Street's wild swings, the collapse of the Russian economy, and the phenomenon of the Asian economic contagion suggest important lessons that we can no longer ignore.

- All advocacy for Social Security privatization should cease and realize the absurdity of these requests. Irrespective of the Wall Street trajectory over the next few days and weeks, the myth that the stock market provides a relatively risk free, high-return investment outlet—a safe place for the nation's accumulated savings for retirees—has been re-shattered. Unless proponents wish for more government bailouts of stock markets, as some Asian countries have attempted, en route to a full corporate socialism, they might as well redirect their efforts to proposals that give more Americans a stake in capital, as suggested in Jeff Gates' new book, *The Ownership Solution*.

Senior citizens banking on Social Security cannot afford a two-week 15 percent drop in their retirement lifeline. Their daily anxiety factor alone is enough to disqualify Wall Street's self-serving Social Security privatization proposals. After all, some large listed companies make big money selling "peace of mind" products and services.

- Financial globalization entails massive, unsupportable risks; controls are needed. While it may reflect underlying problems of overvaluation, the most recent Wall Street plunge was touched off by economic anarchy in Russia, now a country with a shrunken economy. Globalization brings with it an excessive interdependence that can ricochet isolated problems into worldwide slides. Unregulated globalization in finance—far looser than in the real economy—must be reversed. National and international legal controls are needed to cool the foreign investments and short-term loans that pour too fast into oligarchic countries that appear attractive and evaporate as soon as economic indicators start to sour. Too often, this foreign money is taken from the savings of ordinary people in US mutual funds.

- The International Monetary Fund (IMF) has worsened the economic crisis and should be denied any new money. The IMF multibillion dollar bailout of Russia has been completely frittered away. This money, like that which was lent in Asia, has gone to rescue foreign investors and the domestic super-rich. Rather than bridging countries through troubled times, the IMF loans have spread economic contagion.

On the one hand, the IMF has encouraged foreign investors to make additional risky investments around the world without the discipline of the fear of failure. On the other hand, the IMF has pressured countries to further open up to short-term loans and investments, making their economies even more vulnerable to sudden investor withdrawal.

- The international pull-down model (subordinating health, safety, and other standards of living to the supremacy of international trade) of the IMF and World Trade Organization (WTO) should be discarded. IMF austerity measures—imposed on borrower countries as a condition for receiving loans—depress domestic demand, and have transformed acute financial crises in Asia into chronic recessions and depressions.

Meanwhile, the WTO sets countries against one another in a global race to the bottom in wages, environmental standards and health and safety protections—all for the purpose of promoting exports and attracting foreign investment. The combined effect of these pull-down strategies weakens global demand and creates a worldwide overcapacity problem. The United States, as buyer of last resort, has absorbed the worldwide excess, but there is a limit to how much our debt-loaded consumers can spend.

- With financial uncertainty high, now is the wrong time to act on misnamed financial modernization proposals now pending in the Senate. This proposal, H.R. 10, would permit common corporate ownership of banks, insurance companies and securities firms, and foreshadows many future injustices. With a big bank merger binge bringing radical change to the US financial landscape, and world markets in turmoil in Asia and Russia—where major US banks have significant investments—there is no

basis for the Senate to rush forward with a largely corporate-drafted deregulatory bill that will add to the uncertainty that huge concentrations of power bring.

Under the guiding hand of the Clinton administration and Treasury Secretary Robert Rubin, formerly a partner at Goldman Sachs, economic policy is increasingly crafted to benefit the US financial sector, even at the expense of corporate manufacturers. The result has been a casino economy, where speculative capital reigns supreme, where criminal capitalists of Russia are viewed as worthy business partners, where big investors often win big, but where the game is rigged against small investors, workers, consumers, and the environment.

Critics of the model of unregulated globalization have issued dire warnings for some time now, with much of their analysis rejected by powerful corporate interests and their allies in academia and the punditocracy. With the critics' warnings increasingly borne out, it is time to consider their proposals for a global economy more oriented to serve workers and consumers' needs under the rule of law, rather than those of financial speculators and a national corporations that have no allegiance even to a nation that created, domiciled, and enriched them.

WTO—"Pull Down" Trade Agreement
July 21, 1994

The intense struggle, yet to be reported by the press, over the United States becoming a member of the 120 nation World Trade Organization (WTO) has produced some strange alliances. I find myself, for example, having a joint press conference with Pat Buchanan to denounce the way the WTO damages our democratic practices and impermissibly undermines our sovereignty.

Whether one is liberal, conservative, or just commonsensical, joining an international entity with the power to judge, to legislate and to impose sanctions that leaves the largest economy in the world with just one vote and no veto raises interesting yellow lights.

The US belongs to a number of international organizations and all provide either weighted voting or a veto to our country. In stark contrast, under the WTO, St. Kitts or any other tiny country, whether a dictatorship or mostly democratic, has the same vote as does the US.

The WTO has teeth. Its tribunals can rule for a foreign country challenging our food safety, motor vehicle safety, pollution and other laws as disguised trade barriers against products they want to export to the US. Our country would then either have to repeal the law or pay perpetual trade fines.

These tribunals are secret to all except the national government representatives. There is no press permitted, no citizen groups, no public transcript and no independent public appeal from its decisions. The tribunals' judges are three trade specialists who do not have to meet any conflict of interest standards.

We do not operate this way in the US. Why then do we subjugate our democratic practices, to such an over-ride, and our domestic laws to such risks by an international autocratic regime called the WTO?

Yellow lights go off when one reads three recent reports by the European Community (EC), Japan and Canada literally describing the federal and state laws—consumer, environmental and others—that these countries intend to take to the tribunals in Switzerland as illegal trade barriers.

These are, for example, food labeling, fuel efficiency, asbestos-ban, recycling, food safety, and nuclear nonproliferation laws. The EC wants to force us to change the nuclear law because it requires proof of how countries buying our nuclear materials are going to use these materials. The EC maintains that a "process" requirement is illegal should the US join the WTO.

The revealing bias of the WTO agreement is that member nations do not violate its terms by treating their people too harshly as consumers, workers or allow massive poisoning of their environments. Oh, no, it is only the nations whose safety protections are deemed too advanced (read too humane) who can be charged with impeding trade. Other countries can say your food standards regarding pesticides are too stringent, your cars have too strong safety standards and haul the US off to Geneva.

This is why I call the WTO a "pull down" trade agreement, pulling down our standards. Certainly, enough yellow lights have been going off among state officials in recent days. Forty-two Attorneys General, thirty state treasurers, many state tax officials and the National Association of Counties have called for an immediate consultation summit with the Clinton Administration. Their concern: state and local laws and how the federal government intends to defend them from foreign nations' attack.

Mickey Kantor, Clinton's trade representative, wants to rush this gigantic trade agreement through Congress this year under "fast-track" procedures that permit no amendment.

A number of influential fellow Democrats in Congress think this would be political suicide for some shaky legislators up for re-election. Almost thirty senators want Clinton to postpone the vote on the WTO until next year.

The remaining senators need to hear from

the folks back home. These are the same folks who have enough problems with their state and federal governments without giving more control to a secret autocratic international regime in Switzerland, under the influence of global corporations looking for the cheapest and most permissive place on the globe.

Overcommercialism

July 18, 1993

Years ago, the word "overcommercialized" used to apply to highway billboards marring the landscape. Look what rampaging commercialism is now like.

Item: Governor Branstad of Iowa is opening the state tax instruction booklet to advertisements by accounting firms, banks, and other companies eager to reach 1.3 million individual taxpayers. He wants to solicit ads for placement in tax refund envelopes. The price for a full page in the instruction manual is $38,000. He expects to raise $500,000 for the state's treasury. A Des Moines advertising executive says that advertisers will benefit from association with official state publications.

Item: State and federal court decisions are disappearing from published records. If the parties to a lawsuit settle after a court decision—say a business lawsuit or a product defect lawsuit—they can ask the trial judge or the appeals court to vacate the decision. It is no longer in the published court reports nor can it be used as a precedent.

Soon the Supreme Court will rule on this issue, but for some years, the situation has been what Arthur Bryant, director of Trial Lawyers for Public Justice, described as "court decisions [that] can be purchased and destroyed by those with the money to do so."

Item: Capital Centre, the twenty-year-old arena that is home to the Washington Capitals hockey team and the Washington Bullets basketball team, has lost its name. The place is now called "USAir Arena." For this logo, USAir is paying the owners $1 million a year for ten years.

Most, but not all, people would react to these stories with some uneasiness or displeasure. They would feel that a boundary between good taste and commercialism has been crossed. But just what intangibles have been lost in this mercantile mania?

Well, take the Iowa governor's bazaar. A state tax instruction manual is not an advertising manual. It is supposed to have a certain integrity of purpose—to give taxpayers clear information about the law. Selling ads amounts to a political action contribution to state officials. Will these agencies be evenhanded in their treatment of companies that do not advertise? Will this become a worse shakedown in the future? Suspicions and doubts are raised where they have no business being raised in what should be commercial free zones.

How can the Governor Branstad—ten years in office—be taught that public service should not be so commercialized? I have an idea. The governor can turn himself into a human billboard whenever he walks around in public. Hanging on his chest and on his back would be considerable space for two corporate ads.

He would raise his $500,000 a year easily, being seen at state fairs, social functions at the mansion, shaking hands in numerous Iowan communities and, above all, conducting press conferences. Think how avidly interested companies, such as John Deere, Inc., the tractor manufacturer, or DuPont, the pesticide producer, would be in being plastered all over the governor's torso. Why there might be a bidding war.

Seeing their governor so displayed would spark critical or patronizing reactions from the citizens. They would tell him in so many diverse ways why exhibiting himself in this manner is wrong and compromising of his integrity. The governor would learn about boundaries to commercialism.

When commerce can expunge judges' decisions, the record of the courts can be distorted. Companies can brag about how many court decisions they have won, not noting the ones that money has caused to disappear. Taxpayers pay judges and courts to produce these decisions; merchants agreeing between themselves can nullify these taxpayer assets from public use and judicial precedent and history.

Instead of USAir using that million dollars a year to hire more telephone operators so that possible customers don't have to wait so long on the line and be compelled to listen to canned advertisements, the money for an airline that says it will lose money this year goes to cover a sports arena. Image instead of customer service is one of the costs of mindless commercialism. People need to demand that such costly frolics and detours be rebuked and that taste, decorum and integrity be reasserted to put commerce back in its place.

Cesar Chavez
April 27, 1993

Senator Robert Kennedy (D-N.Y.) called him "one of the heroic figures of our time." He was Cesar Chavez, the founder of the United Farmworkers of America (UFWA) who passed away in his sleep in San Luis, Arizona, doing what he has been doing for over forty years—organizing

and defending the migrant farm workers who harvest much of the nation's food.

Untiring, incorruptible, unassuming, almost "spiritual," the man who once was a migratory farm laborer with his parents and siblings, placed before the nation's conscience the health, safety, and economic plight of the farm laborers as no one has ever done in our history. During the '60s, migrant workers went on strike, sang and organized their way upward to minimum levels of wages and rights, led by Chavez and his legions of $5-per-week-plus-room-and-board associates.

Early on, Chavez read the non-violent philosophy of Mahatma Gandhi and the Indian leader's consumer boycott strategies. Starting in California, with the help of many celebrities and some national political figures, Chavez began his grape boycott against the growers. The growers became nasty but could not provoke the farm workers into anything other than peaceful marches and demonstrations.

The growers then invited the Teamsters to sign what Chavez called "sweetheart" contracts for farm workers in order to undermine the UFWA. This was one of the most worrisome periods for Chavez, but the Teamsters abandoned the efforts after the AFL-CIO used its good offices to help Chavez in this situation.

Although Chavez showed organized labor how a labor leader should lead—by example and by reaching out to the media, consumer and civil rights groups and anyone who could help—most of the traditional unions were cool to the farm workers cause.

In 1975, Governor Jerry Brown got through the California state legislature a collective bargaining law for farmworkers (who had been exempted from the nation's labor law coverage). There followed an expansion of farmworkers in the UFWA. But in the '80s, with a hostile governor and president and a loss of interest in the farmworkers' causes among former constituencies, especially the media, membership declined. Grape boycotts were not working as well.

Undeterred, Chavez developed a fundraising operation through the mails, purchased two radio stations to communicate with farmworkers directly and fought on. Frustrated by the growers' intransigence and their expanded use of illegal immigrants whom they exploited, three years ago Chavez announced he was fasting for a period in protest.

The media was not interested anymore in his fasts. Losing weight and strength by his twenty-ninth day without food, Chavez refused to listen to his closest friends and stop. I called a television network to ask them to give Chavez's fast and cause a few minutes on the evening news. The producer said: "call me back when he reaches thirty-seven days."

Friends of Cesar Chavez are convinced he damaged his health seriously with that final fast. It may well have contributed to his death this month. It will also contribute to the legacy of self-sacrifice and commitment to his life's mission that will inspire future generations. Someone like Cesar Chavez does not come along very often in the labor movement. But, his personal style of leadership and strategies will endure.

Civic Memorabilia

March 28, 1991

There are those times when large farces meet great performances. One of those unique events occurred a few days ago at Sotheby's, the New York City auction house. A 1910 Honus Wagner baseball card in multicolor, mint condition was auctioned for a record $451,000. For those of you who collected baseball cards years ago, put some on the spokes of your bicycle wheels and then let your parents throw them out during an attic cleaning after you lost interest in them, the sales price needs repeating—yes $451,000!!

The buyers were hockey star, Wayne Gretzky and his boss, Bruce McNall, owner of the Los Angeles Kings. In inflated adjusted dollars, this Honus Wagner baseball card, with the Piedmont cigarette advertisement on the reverse side, sold for five times the year's salary that this great Pittsburgh shortstop and Hall of Famer earned at his peak performance.

Once worth just a few cents, this card is considered a rarity because Wagner, who opposed smoking asked that his name be taken off the card.

The same Sotheby's auction sold a 1952 Mickey Mantle Topps baseball card for $49,500. The auctioneer expected to get no more than $15,000, but the bidding became very active and competitive. A complete set of 1952 Topps cards went for about $60,000.

Clearly, the market for baseball sports memorabilia is going into orbit. One baseball, autographed in 1939 by twelve famous players, sold for $20,900. There are price guides, weekend sales and 10,000 baseball card shops, up from about 200 such outlets tens years ago.

Just as clearly, the value of these memorabilia is entirely in the speculative expectation level of the traders. There is no artistic or aesthetic appeal and certainly no utilitarian value.

What determines price is not only supply—the number of similar baseball cards in existence or a famous players baseball bat in the final World Series game. There are 19th century baseball cards that have few buyers, for example. Rather, the market is determined in ever so micro focus. The Honus Wagner cards, for instance, are their own market, just as a rare stamp becomes its own craved and envied market.

When an athlete, such as Wayne Gretzky (and his partner), can pay for one baseball card with dollars that amount to five times the peak annual salary of the baseball player whose picture is on the card, not only creative economists but also perceptive psychologists need to be called upon for their analysis.

These collectors' markets do need to be studied in order to see whether the same kind of micro demand and active trading can be developed for civic activity. Imagine civic memorabilia becoming a staple of Sotheby's and other venerable auction houses.

The auction room setting would be tense, filled with aficionados of various legendary civic struggles and victories in American history. The chairs upon which sat the six women in an upstate New York farmhouse in 1846 to start the successful drive for women's right to vote could be auctioned. The bus in Montgomery, Alabama, that Rosa Parks refused to go to the rear of prior to her arrest that sparked the civil rights movement might go for a tidy sum.

Other potential items come to mind. Rachel Carson's typewriter out of which came her celebrated book, *Silent Spring*, which launched the modern environmental movement. A few weeks ago, 100-year-old, George Seldes, gave away his lifelong typewriter to a neighbor along with its memories of his pioneering weekly, *In Fact*, which critiqued the press during the 1940s. There was no market for this super-productive typewriter that had traveled the world with Seldes, not even in a museum.

How about the posters of the sit-down strikers in the automobile plants of Michigan during the 1930s that launched the United Auto Workers? Wouldn't they be worth the venue of some low-priced baseball cards? And imagine the interest that could be directed toward those internal company memoranda by whistleblowers exposing consumer product defects or industrial hazards. Some of them must be in mint condition.

Well, don't hold your breath for a Sotheby's auction of civic memorabilia anytime soon. But it is worth keeping in mind someday when a few collectors' micro markets start moving from farce to performance.

Anita Roddick and the Body Shop
June 15, 1990

Bursting out of England to encircle the globe is a chain of stores that primarily sells shampoo and skin lotion and is shaking the conventional assumptions of the business world. So much so that *Inc.* magazine put founder, Anita Roddick, on its cover this month with the headline, "This Woman Has Changed Business Forever."

The closest phrase that can describe what is going on in the Body Shops is what she calls "electricity and passion," or doing business as a byproduct of other values and goals. There is no set philosophy in one of Britain's fastest growing businesses with 500 stores there and in thirty-seven countries. There are only illustrations that give people an idea of what is going on.

One can start with the "causes." The Body Shop is against animal testing for cosmetics and stores and signs remind customers of that position. Body Shop employees demonstrated in front of the Brazilian Embassy in London to help save the Amazon rainforest and the natives who "are the custodians of the rainforests," said one sign.

Body Shop trucks ride the highways with their long sides covered with signs urging stronger environmental values such as recycling (the stores use refillable bottles and biodegradable materials).

Fourteen years ago, Anita Roddick, then a thirty-three-year-old mother of two young daughters, started the first Body Shop with her husband, Gordon, who now runs the chain with a fine managerial hand. Gordon frees Anita to travel all around the world picking up sources of materials and anecdotal ideas that fuel this electricity and passion.

There is Anita in the Atlas Mountains of Morocco to find a traditional mud which has astringent and toning properties. Result: Rhassoul Mud Shampoo. There is Anita in the Amazon jungle with the indigenous people learning how they use their local materials and urging upon them what patent rights come from these applications in her business. There is Anita before a large conference in Minneapolis full of hardboiled, idealistic environmental types dazzling the audience with a torrent of true tales about what she has done, is doing and plans to do with her business. From defending the whales and dolphins to speaking out on behalf of native peoples and their customs in developing countries to starting (her latest project) an informal British Peace Corps of young people to go to Romania to help the orphan babies being discovered in warehouse conditions of shocking deprivation, Anita is here, there, everywhere.

She reads, absorbs, observes, listens, speaks, gestures and, all the while, there is a very discernible clarity of purpose and direction which includes experimenting, risking and, above all, doing, doing, doing. She intensely dislikes meetings of the bureaucratic stripe in her company, business jargon, and what she calls "a fat-cat mentality."

At age forty-seven, she is on a faster rising sales and profit curve that is stunning stock market analysts. For the past ten years, sales and profits have continued to grow an average of 50 percent a year! In five years the Body Shop expects a billion dollars in sales.

A clue to her success is the way she views consumers and employees. The latter are expected to inform and educate their customers, if asked, about the properties, sources, history, and lore of the quietly but attractively displayed products. She does not use pictures of models. She does not hype the consumer. To her, standard marketing techniques are increasingly less effective because the customer is hyped out, over-marketed, and overwhelmed with the din of pitch and promotion and advertising.

Employees are there to answer questions with humor, anecdotes, videos, graphics, and the light touch. Anita expects them to choose how they are going to be civically active outside of work and then tries to help them or march with them or protest with them.

By humanizing the company's stores and by creating conversation instead of branding, the Roddicks let the customers do the word of mouth with their friends and neighbors. The Body Shop has never spent a shilling on advertising and does not even have a marketing department—this is an industry that spends over 30 percent of its revenue in advertising and promotion.

Employees go through a training process that "trains for knowledge," says Anita, not for "a sale." The company newsletter often reads like a counter-culture publication with space given to the company's campaigns against ozone-depleting chemicals and snippets of poetry, environmental tidbits and anthropological observations.

She tells her husband, Gordon, that the company should have a Department of Surprises to keep it loose, creative, and different in order to "rewrite the book on business." Watch her—the climb of her can-do vision is just beginning. With twenty Body Shops operating already in the US, the process of opening new stores as franchises is accelerating to further meet what Anita calls the Body Shop's "global responsibility." Skin lotions and shampoos are just a means to Anita's horizons.

The Savings and Loan Bailout Pledge

April 4, 1989

In all that has been written about the gigantic savings and loan bank scandals, one observation is uniformly held by all parties and positions in Washington—criminal fraud and insider abuse were the overwhelming factors in the insolvencies. Two weeks ago, the General Accounting Office (GAO), an investigative arm of the Congress, reported that twenty-six out of twenty-six insolvent S & Ls that it studied involved white collar crime.

Since the federal government has guaranteed all deposits up to the $100,000 limit to be insured, you may wonder what all this looting has to do with you. The answer is plenty. Under the bailout plan submitted to Congress by the Bush Administration, you are going to pay for the wreckage wrought by these crooks—an average of $500 for every man, woman and child in the US, at the very least.

The Bush plan, which contains some good regulatory reforms, violates the principles of fairness and deterrence when it comes to answering the question, Who pays? The general answer should be those entities who are most

culpable and most able to pay, not those small depositors and small taxpayers who are the most innocent and least able to pay. These Americans did not cause the scandals, did not benefit from the scandals, and should not pay for them.

Time and time again when big companies or powerful industries get into trouble through their own greed or fault, they go to Washington for bailouts. None have been more at fault in this use of Uncle Sam as the all-purpose bailout man than the commercial banks and the savings and loans. Making the banking industry pay and then, next in line, the corporate taxpayers generally, will send a message that there is a limit beyond which they cannot socialize their crimes on the backs of innocent working people.

In 1967, Chase Manhattan Bank, which was a key lobbyist along with Citicorp in successfully pushing for federal bank de-regulation a decade ago, earned $650 million and paid less than 2 percent federal income tax. Let those who pushed Washington into taking the federal cop off the bank beat and letting savings and loans invest in junk bonds and speculative real estate—let them soak up the red ink they helped to spill.

This month the Senate and House Banking Committees will write the legislation heavily guided by the Bush plan. One House Banking Committee member told me that the differences are not along Republican and Democratic lines, nor even liberal and conservative lines; they are between "those members who are in the pockets of the banks and those who are not."

Well, judging by early indications, many lawmakers are peering out at you from the pockets of the powerful savings and loan lobby. Most of the amendments to the Bush plan point toward further weakening the bailout safeguards. Senator Donald Riegle, chairman of the Senate Banking Committee, certainly has no stomach to block the Bush plan's intent to stick the bill to the small taxpayer and, by raising insurance deposit premiums, to the small depositor on whose back most of the pass-along will be placed.

But there is still hope. A coalition of consumer groups with effective grassroots presence is mobilizing to inform and arouse the American people as they did two months ago against the Reagan salary-grab proposal that Congress was trying to adopt. We know what happened to that one once the people flexed their collective outrage in protests.

Now a new wave of protests is necessary, centering on the arguments of simple justice and deterrence. The centerpiece of this citizen drive is the Savings and Loan Bailout Pledge form which Public Citizen is distributing all over the country.

This pledge is to be sent to your senators and representative. Your members of Congress are asked to pledge that "the responsible parties pay" to ensure that a similar scandal will not happen again. They are asked to pledge in writing that (1) they will not support a bailout which sends the bill to depositors and small taxpayers; (2) they will support legislation to prudently re-regulate the financial industry; and (3) they will support the creation of Financial Consumer Associations to give the customers a permanent voice.

Readers interested in obtaining an information kit and the pledge can send a self-addressed, stamped, business-size envelope to Public Citizen.

Privatization

March 24, 1988

Inside the offices of the Heritage Foundation–the nonprofit policy advocate for the Reagan Administration, a handful of zealots are in constant touch with the Office of Management and Budget (OMB). Their mission: privatize a large array of governmental services and assets. The Heritage list was reflected in the recent report of the President's Commission on Privatization whose official adviser was none other than Stuart M. Butler of the Heritage Foundation. The Commission recommended to Mr. Reagan that all or part of the following be privatized—that is sold off to private business or serviced by private contractors:

Low-Income Housing (or what is left of it under Reagan), housing finance, federal loan programs, Postal Service, Air Traffic Control, prisons, military commissaries, Amtrak, the Naval Petroleum Reserves, Medicare, and urban mass transit.

The privatizers left out the federal lands and federal dams, knowing that selling off one third of America and less expensive electricity would cause an instant public furor. But their list is ignoble enough to warrant some observations about their claims that privatization would be more efficient and provide Americans with more choice.

First, there is ample experience with privatization. One can start with the privatizing of the manufacture of military weapons, aircraft and ships. Only a joker can assert that this has been efficient. The cost over-runs of the military contracting companies have set world records. The long delayed B-1 bomber now comes in at $2.8 billion per plane–over ten times what it was originally expected to cost and still it is full of bugs.

At the municipal level, privatizing garbage collection and meter collections have provided some of the worst excesses of corruption and bribery. Local and state government procurement and construction scandals have kept many a prosecutor busy with grand juries and, yet, these laws enforcers say they are only scratching the surface.

The Postal Service offers a presort discount for commercial mailers. There is a thriving private presort industry which is being given an extra $430 million a year as an outright subsidy above and beyond the amount that presorting saves the Postal Service.

This presort industry is now a powerful lobby preserving and extending a subsidy that is indirectly paid by postal users such as residential first-class mailers. Ending this subsidy would easily restore the closing of post offices for half a day (estimated saving-$20 million a year) and the stopping of Sunday pickup and sorting (estimated savings of about $50 million a year.)

One of the bizarre recommendations of the Presidential Commission was the private operation of prisons, including maximum security facilities. These private prison corporations would make the profits, but the government would still incur any liability for the misoperation of these penitentiaries. Just think of the problems which would arise when massive coercion starts mixing with bottom line-trade secrecy corporatism.

With oil prices near a ten year low, the Commission urges the "immediate" selling of the federal government's naval petroleum reserves in California and Wyoming. These wells were set aside for national security purposes, not for the further enrichment of Exxon or Mobil Oil.

In an incisive critique of the privatization ideologues, Professor Paul Starr of Princeton University points out the erosion of services (where profits cannot be maximized) the loss of accountability and the removal of essential services that formerly were considered a public service. If you think making government accountable and legislators responsive is difficult, try making the privatizers heed you when they are once removed and have their campaign contributions and other lobbying grips on their governmental patrons to pay them even more.

Independents, Third Parties Need Greater Ballot Access
July 22, 1985

Why do so many state laws make it so difficult and costly for independent and minor party candidates to get on the ballot? The official reason for such restrictions is that voters must be protected from frivolous candidates. The real reasons are: the Republican and Democratic Parties. They want to monopolize ballot access to the greatest degree possible and deprive voters of wider choices.

In Canada, a few dozen dollars and a few dozen signatures on a petition are sufficient to get a candidate's name on the printed ballot. In California it takes about 125,000 valid petition signatures for an independent or minor party candidate to run for a federal office from that state. Arizona requires 7,264 signatures to be collected within a specified ten day period. In New York, Missouri, and Virginia, you not only have to collect a substantial number of signatures, but they have to come from all over the state, such as from each county in New York. West Virginia forbids petitioners from voting in its primary, while New York and Nebraska void the signatures of citizens who have already participated in a primary.

South Carolina requires citizens to write down both their precinct and voter registration numbers—the kind of information that most people do not carry with them. Kansas mandates that the petition circulator live in the same neighborhood as the petition signers even if the candidate is running for the US Congress.

To run on a party label is even more difficult. In California a minor party has to register 81,000 voters into the party to get on the ballot. In Georgia, a minor political party needs 60,000 people to sign eleven petitions each to obtain a party designation on the ballot.

These nasty obstructions are fostered by a Tweedledee and Tweedledum two-party system which is not satisfied with constitutionally protected winner-take-all elections that entrench its dominance and undermine third party challenges. A minor party in the United States could get 25 percent of the vote in a state and end up with nothing, unlike many European countries where there is proportional representation.

Historically, third parties espoused numerous pioneering proposals which were later adopted by the major parties In their recent book, *Third Parties in America*, authors Rosenstone, Behr and Lazarus list women's right to vote, the graduated income tax and the direct election of Senators by the voters as illustrations. They quote scholar Fred Haynes as arguing that third parties in the nineteenth century "were pioneers in the conversion of American politics from almost exclusive attention to constitutional and governmental matters to the vital needs of the people." Historian John Hicks writes that, as regards a third-party voter, "[A] backward glance through American history would seem to indicate that his kind of vote is after all probably the most powerful vote that has ever been cast."

The proper shift to the secret "Australian ballot" by most states late in the 19th century ironically set the stage for the deplorable barriers of state ballot access laws, with their widely different filing deadlines and restrictions. Court challenges by George Wallace, Eugene McCarthy and John Anderson have resulted in decisions moderating some state rules. Governor Wallace won a case against the state of Ohio, with the US Supreme Court holding Ohio's requirement for 433,100 signatures on a petition nine months before the general election to be unlawful.

Against this dismal anti-democratic behavior wrought by the two major parties, corrective legislation has been introduced by Congressman John Conyers, Jr. (D-Mich.) in the form of H.R. 2320. This bill would create fairer and more uniform standards for ballot access and ballot status in all federal elections. Conyers believes that the "labyrinth of state-enacted restrictions" deprives independent candidates and parties, together with the great number of voters who would otherwise vote for them, "of their constitutional rights of freedom of political expression and equal protection under the law."

H.R. 2320 is simplicity itself. In four pages this legislation sets two uniform standards for all states to observe. One allows an individual candidate and his/her party to be placed on the ballot after submitting a petition with either 1,000 signatures or a number of signatures equal to one-tenth of one percent of the number of registered voters during the previous election. The other allows a political party to remain on the ballot if during the prior election that party received the lesser of 20,000 votes or one percent of the votes cast for president or senator in that state.

With anywhere from 50 to 60 percent of all eligible voter not voting, our federal elections need all the political choices that H.R. 2320 can help give them.

Postal Consumer Group Urged

March 21, 1981

On March 22, 1981, the cost of mailing a first-class letter will go up to eighteen cents from the current fifteen cents. But the stamp will be a non-denominational "B" postage stamp. This indicates that the postal service's board of governors is not satisfied. It wants at least twenty cents to be the price you pay and is asking the Postal Rate Commission to raise first-class mail to that level. In 1973, first-class postage was eight cents.

Service continues to deteriorate. There is no longer any door delivery at new housing projects. The mailman delivers to a cluster of mailboxes and residents have to go there to pick up their mail, rain or shine. In many areas mail pickups have been reduced to one a day. Mailboxes have been removed from many residential areas. Saturday window service has been cut back. Saturday delivery may be dropped.

The board of governors of the postal service is run by business executives with a sprinkling of academics. For years, the chairman was M.A. Wright, the top executive of Exxon USA. Now the chairman is Robert Hardesty, a vice chancellor at the University of Texas. There are no representatives of first class household users or of the neighborhoods where the postal service's historic function of binding together the nation occurs.

I asked the Postmaster General William F. Bolger about this gap. He replied that he thought he represented the neighborhood people on the board. I asked whether he would support a regular public session between the board of governors during their monthly meeting in Washington and members of the mail-using public who could come and sit in the room.

Presently, the board meets partly in private and partly in public where several dozen chairs for observing visitors are available.

Bolger strongly opposed, contrary to management principles, what I believe would be good sensitivity sessions providing citizen feedback to the excessively unknown board. (How many Americans scoffing at the postal service in the '70s knew that an Exxon executive was the chairman of its board, for example?)

In December, I submitted to Bolger a proposal to facilitate the informed organization of postal customers who are interested in responsive delivery service and reasonable rates. Such a consumer organization would have local chapters around the country and a professional staff to deal with immediate and far-range postal problems and opportunities. A grass-roots awareness and knowledge would be built up around this essential but declining mass communications system.

Let's call this organization the Post Office Consumer Action Group (POCAG). It could be funded by voluntary contributions solicited on a regular basis by a mailing sent to all residential postal addresses. Presently, Bolger is considering a mailing to all such addresses to explain the nine-digit ZIP code. An invitation to join POCAG (for, say, $5 annual dues) could be included in this mailing at very nominal cost. Or a special annual mailing could be conducted through the postal service. POCAG members could vote for their local and national council of directors, who, in turn, would retain skilled advocates and specialists.

US postal policy decisions are presently shaped by management, labor unions and lobbyists for mass mailers. The household-small business, first-class user has no organization and no advocates.

Besieged by the competition of the telephone, new electronic mail transmission systems and private companies competing for package deliveries, the postal service needs help. Its management and top personnel are too introverted to recognize that values, other than strict mercantile ones, must measure the adequacy and future of mail service. Postal service spokesmen, for instance, receive their priorities from mail-volume percentages. Household users mail less than 18 percent of the annual postal service delivery volume. Yet they make up the vast proportion of all the people who use the service and their messages are qualitatively different than, say, a third-class, mail-order seller.

A postal users group can present these other values effectively from Elm Street to Main Street to Washington.

The Effectiveness of Presidential Speeches

November 26, 1977

Last spring, before President Carter's energy speech to the nation, General Motors was worried about the slow sales of its Chevette. After the speech, which emphasized the need for energy conservation, Chevette sales significantly improved. GM makes a direct connection between Carter's remarks and the sales upsurge.

Clearly, when presidents speak, some Americans listen. But of all the analysis done on the use of presidential powers, the speechmaking power, informal as it is discretionary, has received little attention. How much effect do such speeches have on people's attitudes, their motivation, and their behavior?

Much depends on what kinds of speeches are delivered and their purpose. Historically, presidential speeches have tried to (a) rally the country around proposed legislation or controversial federal programs, (b) directly assist the re-election chances of the incumbent, (c) defend the incumbent against criticism, (d) send indirect messages to foreign adversaries or allies on national security or economic matters, or (e) ingratiate the president with an important special interest bloc at their annual convention.

President Roosevelt's speeches often served several of these purposes together and inspired a depression-weary nation to recover some hope. President Kennedy sensed that eloquent words from the White House, followed by a program like the Peace Corps, could change the careers and directions of many young and older Americans.

Judging by the record to date, President Carter does not place much value on domestic speechmaking. He has made speeches on foreign affairs but very few major speeches on domestic matters and those were largely related to energy legislation.

Some of his associates believe that domestic addresses are largely rhetoric and a waste of presidential time and capital. Other, more cautious advisers believe that they could generate misunderstandings that the White House does not need.

This is unfortunate and not only because President Carter is known to be upset over the way his schedule is filled every day. It is unfortunate because properly focused presidential addresses can have highly beneficial effects on various groups in our society. A president needs to speak to these groups in the context of sharpening appreciation of their rights and enlarging their ability to engage in self-government and other citizen initiatives.

Take three kinds of speeches that President Carter can make, without burdening the Treasury. The students of America have not heard from the president. He has much to tell them that is constructive, wholesome, and motivating beyond mere rhetoric. It is a particularly auspicious time to speak to students, many of whom lack a sense of mission for themselves and for their country. The tandem advance of educational achievement and citizen training is ripe for presidential recognition. His associates, particularly aide Greg Schneiders, have much to suggest in this area.

Second, not many yards from the White House, there labors a team on Carter's government reorganization plans. These plans will try to make government become more efficient, produce more effective policies, and be more accountable to citizens. The accountability recommendations are the most important of this triad and a significant precondition for the other two goals.

A well-structured presidential address on governmental accountability, with specific reference to protecting ethical whistle-blowers inside government and providing remedies for aggrieved citizens outside government vis-a-vis officials who behave unlawfully, would be in accord with Carter's campaign statements. Such remarks would uplift the conscientious civil servants who hold dear the public trust and generate broad public discussion about this little-noticed but crucial issue.

Third, across the country, the neighborhood and block association movement is growing. In New York, Baltimore, Pittsburgh, and other cities, the neighborhoods are organizing to protect their interests and redirect government along more just pathways.

They are waiting for an indication of presidential understanding and creativity. They are not looking for an expression of "neighborhood confidence," as the industrial community keeps demanding from the White House with its code phrase "business confidence." Instead, they want the instruments and opportunities for greater self-reliance and self-determination at the community and national level.

What presidential addresses can do immediately is to take local developments and give them national visibility. Presidents can also take unglamorous but essential subjects, neglected by the media, and make even *Time* magazine sit up and take notice.

President Carter should not neglect using this important White House resource. Words endure. Words that are meant endure more. And words that quicken the pulse of the citizenry can last for generations. History meaningfully has shown us the truth of such an observation.

The Student Loan Scandal
September 4, 1976

AUSTIN, Texas—John L. Hill is angry at the Department of Health, Education, and Welfare (HEW). As attorney general of Texas, he has his lawyers looking into the mushrooming scandal of federally insured student loans (FISL) involving proprietary schools and banks. The more they investigate, the more they believe that HEW officials bear a heavy complicity in a nationwide consumer fraud that will end up costing taxpayers about a billion dollars. Approximately ten years ago, Congress recognized that students need to borrow money to finance their education and made the federal government a guarantor of loans extended by banks to students. It was accurately believed without Uncle Sam lending his credit and an interest subsidy, the banks would not loan money to students.

In the past decade nearly five million students received over $8 billion of federally guaranteed loans. But, as is often the case in subsidy programs, Congress neglected to write into the law safeguards against abuse, mismanagement and fraud. It also failed to provide anything other than ridiculously small funding for HEW to hire investigators and adjustors to protect both taxpayers and students.

Whenever the taxpayer is made the payer of last resort, the seeds for business crime are sown. Abuses in the student loan program arose heavily out of the fast growing world of vocational training at private for-profit business or trade schools.

In recent Senate testimony, Hill said:

"These students, rather than becoming the beneficiaries of the FISL program, became its unwitting victims. They became easy prey for an all too statistically significant number of knowledge hucksters whose deceptive and fraudulent business practices were directly subsidized by the federal government through the US Office of Education."

Cases investigated by state and federal law enforcement agencies in various states have pinpointed the following patterns:

- Proprietary or vocational schools going bankrupt, leaving students with the obligation to repay loans for education they never or only partially received. Advance Schools, Inc., a Chicago-based giant in this industry, filed for bankruptcy over a year ago with about $100 million in government guaranteed student loans outstanding.

- Proprietary schools that lure students by false or misleading claims of employment and salary opportunities.

- Banks that take incentive payments for purchasing the note paper from the schools or charging illegally high interest rates, engaging in illegal discounting or kickbacks to bank officials.

Under prodding by such units as the Texas Attorney General's office, HEW began, in 1975, tightening its regulations governing participating schools and banks in student loan programs. The scandal-ridden local HEW office administering the program in Dallas was closed. Several former employees of this office are now facing charges.

The picture which emerges from HEW's role is one of serious negligence with the taxpayers' money. Former HEW Secretary Caspar Weinberger, who liked to tout his determination to cut federal spending, was quite willing to overlook the need to stop the massive criminal fraud effecting the billions of Medicare and Medicaid disbursements as well as the student loan fiasco, A new office of investigations, headed by John Walsh, a former congressional prober, is a modest improvement.

Much more remains to be done. Last week, as a start, the Senate passed and sent to the House amendments that stiffen penalties.

Hill and the US Attorney in Texas believe the indictment trail will lead to HEW officials in Washington. Hill's office is also going to sue HEW for not honoring, as it should, valid student defenses in cases of defaulted loans, in order to protect the banks which are reaping great profits from this no-risk program. Hill's attorneys believe HEW is ignoring the fact that in many instances, the banks are not independent third parties but are really the undisclosed principals, with the schools acting as agents or credit arrangers.

Gobbledygook is Growing

July 31, 1976

Gobbledygook is a growth industry. Verbal obscurity, gigantic, intertwined sentences, semantic blahs, bureaucratese, and legal esoterica put people to work.

There are people who produce Gobbledygook, people who interpret Gobbledygook and people hired to help other people adversely affected by insensitive Gobbledygook. It's all part of the GNP.

There are even people working to make fun of Gobbledygook. Take the *Washington Star* staffer who collects the daily Gobbledygook examples from government agency documents. People from around the country submit examples (write to Gobbledygook '76, Metro Desk, The Washington Star, 225 Virginia Ave. SE, Washington, DC 20061) and collect $10 if they are printed. That little column is working a renewable resource; it may be the closest thing to infinity that journalism possesses. It also needs no explanation because, standing alone, Gobbledygook is, well, Gobbledygook.

But Gobbledygook does not often stand alone. In its fertile context it displays a versatile perniciousness. One-upmanship, for example. Gobbledygook turns people who can't fathom the fog into functional illiterates. It makes them feel inferior, weak, "out of sync." It leads them to think that if they can't understand, that is because they are not lawyers or highly-educated.

Well, illiterates, take heart, there is a counterinsurgency (oops) brewing against Gobbledygook. The first active insurgent was probably Herb Denenberg who began to admit quietly to himself, while he was Pennsylvania's insurance commissioner, that he could not comprehend the meaning of insurance policies sent to him

for approval. The next ingredient in the rebellion was Denenberg's self-confidence. It didn't shatter. He is both a lawyer and has a PhD in insurance. If he didn't understand the policies, millions of policyholders couldn't, either.

So Denenberg went to work. In May 1973, he turned down an insurance company's policy that contained one sentence of 120 words. Then he devised a readability scale of zero to one hundred on that scale. Time Magazine scored 52.30; The Wall Street Journal, 13.39; Einstein, 17.72; the standard auto policy, 10.31, and homeowners policies had zero or negative scores.

Gradually, companies began to discover the joys of readability. Insurance agents, adjusters, lawyers and judges began freely to admit that Gobbledygook was not their mother tongue. Enlightenment followed admissions of incomprehensibility.

The wave reached Citibank—that towering pillar of Gobbledygook in New York City. Why, someone exclaimed, our customers may not understand our installment loan contracts, even assuming they can see the tiny print. So, an expert in primitive English was hauled out to rewrite the instrument. Out came a one-page, simple consumer loan note clearly stating the terms of indenture between consumer and Citibank.

A short while later, Kemper Insurance Companies in Chicago put out simplified homeowners policies in large print with bright blue sectionheadings—"Agreement," "Definitions," "Coverages," "Perils Insured Against," "Exclusions" (such as nuclear power hazards) and "Conditions." A few other insurance companies are doing the same.

Something else is also helping. It seems that some judges believe that what consumers cannot reasonably understand in a form contract they should not he held to. Imagine what could happen if Their Honors began applying similar guidelines to the tomes of tax regulations and forms.

Even that caricature of federal bureaucracy, the Department of Health, Education, and Welfare, announced last week an immediate change of procedures. According to Secretary F. David Mathews, one thousand agency employees who write the rules will take special classes in English to help these regulations be more easily understood.

Readability is not yet a mass movement in executive suites, however. Neither in Washington nor on Wall Street. You see, Gobbledygook is an instrument of power. By confusing the consumer or citizen, it can deplete the will to resist. By seeming to offer many meaningless choices (as among insurance policies), it can lead to indiscriminate consumer surrender. By obscuring language, it can obscure bureaucratic accountability.

So Gobbledygook is not about to become a historic memory. As any exercise that concentrates power and provides employment, it has a certain momentum. But if people demand clarity, the juggernaut will slow down. And if people demand justice, Gobbledygook's rout will begin.

Save the Public Libraries

January 31, 1976

Petitions, protests, read-ins, and demonstrations confronted the announcement by the financially pressed New York Public Library that eight branch libraries would be promptly closed with still others to be shut down within the next two years. Other branches and the great central library at Fifth Avenue and 42nd Street have had their hours and services curtailed. There

was something both noble and pathetic about the neighborhood people who protested. The elderly and the young told some of what libraries mean to them—solace, a place to reflect, study, research a school paper, let the imagination roam, or obtain self-help guidance or civic information.

One man, who described himself simply as "a citizen of the city of New York," donated $315,000 to help keep a branch library in the Bronx open for a few more months until the community could organize longer term support.

Over history's time, the destruction of libraries, whether by war or dictatorship, has been viewed as a serious blow to freedom and democracy. In New York it is seen merely as a way to save some money.

One can make a long list of waste, fraud, or institutional crimes that deserve higher priority for budget slashing in the city's accounts. But libraries are relatively easy pickings.

What politicians ever won or lost an election over their stand on libraries? The protesters were noble, but their cries had the echo of pathos about them.

Around the country, libraries are witnessing growing and varied demand for their services amidst shrinking budgets. The prices of books, video equipment, fuel and electricity are zooming upward while our political leaders' recognition of what libraries mean to millions of Americans declines.

People do not associate Gerald Ford with books, but he did not have to go to such lengths to intensify the image. In his latest annual budget proposal to the Congress, President Ford provided nothing for the nation's 8,500 public libraries.

Last year he asked for 10 million dollars and Congress appropriated about $52 million under the Library Services and Construction Act. In the overall yearly expenditure of about $1 billion for public libraries (mostly raised locally), $52 million is not that much. But without this sum services at libraries will be squeezed further, especially the bookmobile and outreach programs that have been developing.

To highlight the needs and benefits of libraries, Congress passed legislation in 1974 for a White House conference on library and information services to be held in 1978. President Ford has done nothing to put the machinery in motion for this conference and its parallel state gatherings.

But Congress has had its brusque moments as well. Until the Senate indicated its stern opposition, the leaders of the House of Representatives wanted to take over the nearly completed annex to the overstuffed Library of Congress as another office building for their colleagues.

What will it take to develop a power base from the grassroots to Washington behind libraries and their emerging role as community information centers? Certainly it will take more than data about the alarming percentage of functional illiterates (20 percent) in the country and what expanded library teaching classes could do for them.

It will take more than conveying testimonials by library consumers or scenarios of what modern technology can do for library services of the future—such as instantly connecting them to the country's leading libraries.

The stimulating force must come from the communities directly in the form of organized "Friends of the Library" groups. It would not take a large number of people or a great amount of time to assess the needs and weaknesses of local libraries and galvanize the community into at least arresting their worsening plight.

If enough of these groups work together, the impact on Congress to reassess its library support policy and its spending priorities will be stronger.

The connection between the crumbling of local institutions in this country and their causes has received too little attention at the local level. If the torch of knowledge employed at the local level can help begin the process of reconstruction, the library could be its pilot light.

Send us your suggestions about how to help library services to PO Box 19312, Washington DC 20036, and we will select the best ideas for a later report.

Subsidizing the Banks
July 28, 1974

Back in December 1970, law professor John A. Spanogle sat down and wrote a letter to Hampton Rabon, deputy assistant secretary of the Treasury Department, about a very large subsidy which the Treasury was providing hundreds of banks.

Spanogle, who was working with us at the time, wanted to know why the Treasury was leaving billions of dollars of its tax deposits and other funds, known as tax and loan accounts, in non-interest-bearing demand deposits.

He believed that the banks were reaping a massive windfall at the expense of taxpayers, whose payments should have been earning interest for the Treasury.

Rabon replied, two weeks later:

> I must take exception to your categorical statement that the earning value of balances in tax and loan accounts is much greater than the value of services performed by banks.

These facts . . . clearly show, in my opinion, that the balances maintained in tax loan accounts with some 12,700 banks throughout the country are not surplus to our needs and, therefore, no part of the balances should be invested.

Spanogle was not satisfied. He pressed on and his cause was taken up in 1971 and 1972 by another law professor, Fairfax Leary, who was on leave with us. Congressman Wright Patman, chairman of the House Banking and Currency Committee, renewed his longstanding criticism of this bank subsidy with a staff report in May 1972 that denounced these non-interest bearing accounts.

These accounts are not small. The average tax and loan account balances by the Treasury in banks ranged from $6.9 billion in 1970 to $8.4 billion in 1973.

More than four-fifths of these sums could be invested in short term money market instruments. At present interest rates, the Treasury could be earning more than $600 million a year instead of being a sugar daddy for banks already reporting record profits.

Other voices spoke up against this tax and loan windfall. Sen. Thomas McIntyre, went to the Senate floor in June 1973 calling for Congressional hearings. Congressman John Seiberling (D-Ohio) introduced a bill to require the payments on interest on these balances.

In the meantime, there were stirrings at the Treasury Department. A study was ordered in 1972 and a draft questionnaire was developed for banks to answer about what services they believed they were providing the government.

My associate, attorney Tommy Jacks, submitted detailed suggestions on the inadequacy of this draft questionnaire, some of which were adopted.

Last month, the force of fact and reason prevailed and the Treasury Department changed its mind.

In a public report, the department concluded that the nation's banks, based on the 1967–72 average interest rate on ninety-one-day Treasury bills (5.5 percent) reaped a $300 million benefit each year by investing idle tax and loan accounts. At current interest rates the windfall in 1974 will be over $600 million.

That amount of money would have funded in fiscal 1974 all the following federal agencies: the Small Business Administration, Civil Aeronautics Board, Consumer Product Safety Commission, Equal Employment Opportunity Commission, Federal Power Commission, Federal Trade Commission, Occupational Safety and Health Review Commission, Securities and Exchange Commission, and the Selective Service System.

There was one more hurdle to overcome, said the Treasury: "Congress should consider legislation authorizing the Treasury to invest in money market instruments for cash management purposes." Pending such legislation, the Treasury says it is limited in what it can do to reduce this unjust bank enrichment.

So everyday that the Congress delays, the Treasury is losing almost two million dollars in interest.

Congress has been known to move very quickly in favor of a special interest, such as the present loan guarantee program for banks lending to the cattle industry. If the Treasury is sincere in its desire for congressional authority, its emissaries will move quickly on Capitol Hill in cooperation with Rep. Pitman and Sen. McIntyre.

Our experience with this matter, however, indicates that citizens cannot take anything for granted when it comes to Congress and the Treasury actually doing something for the public interest, even when they agree about what should be done. So let them hear from you.

Nuclear Power Plant Risks

December 3, 1973

When Richard Nixon was promoting the safety of nuclear power plants before the Associated Press editors last month, he asserted reassuringly that his San Clemente residence was only a few miles from one such nuclear facility. What he didn't tell the editors is that this plant at San Onofre, California, had closed down on October 21 for several months due to a serious and costly accident.

The Atomic Energy Commission (AEC) was notified that day of the damage by Southern California Edison but, contrary to regulations, kept the matter secret. Public disclosure came on November 22 through a story in the *Los Angeles Times*. Reporter Lee Dye asked an AEC official why the secrecy and was told, "I just don't have an answer for that."

Not having answers to key questions about nuclear plants, as well as the transportation and disposal of their deadly wastes, is nothing new at the AEC. In recent months, the agency has learned more about how its vaunted standards were either inadequate or unobserved by the reactor manufacturers and utilities who build these "nukes".

AEC internal memoranda and reports refer to "near misses" or the presence of "good luck" to describe how design defects or operating errors were close to causing a catastrophic chain reaction which would release radioactivity into the environment.

Here are some recent plant hazards acknowledged by AEC officials:

1. The critical emergency core cooling system (ECCS) in these plants (thirty-nine are now operating with varying degrees of unreliability) is deficient. The ECCS is the fail-safe system that is supposed to prevent the doomsday class melt-down accident and the massive civilian casualties, property damage and the cancerous contamination of an area the size of Pennsylvania.

2. A uranium fuel densification (shrinkage) problem took the AEC by surprise and led it to admit that such a defect can seriously aggravate accidents. This risk illustrates how much remains to be understood about reactor operation by those officials who so glibly assure the public about nuclear power safety.

3. Earthquake risks, which are slowing licensing of "nukes" in California, have presented themselves in Virginia where a nearly completed $1 billion nuclear plant forty-five miles from Richmond was belatedly discovered by a "Who, us worry?" AEC to be right over a geological fault. The agency also discovered that the Millstone Plant in Connecticut and other plants contained inoperative equipment designed to control excessive vibrations in the event of an earthquake.

4. Another recently discovered defect affects certain reactors manufactured by General Electric and the adequacy of reactor cooling.

5. The AEC's regulatory staff has issued a report casting doubt even on the reliability of the emergency shutdown systems at nuclear plants.

Add to these troubles the warnings to the AEC by the General Accounting Office which reported laxness in the AEC's supervision of the transportation of nuclear waste materials. More recently the GAO told Congress that it found little security at three commercial facilities handling special nuclear materials which could be stolen or diverted to make nuclear weapons. The AEC had previously given these plants ok ratings.

More radioactive wastes—in the thousands of gallons—have leaked from their temporary storage sites in Richland, Washington. Nuclear power plant wastes must be contained from the environment for nearly a half million years. An amount of the lethal Plutonium 239 not exceeding twenty pounds could, if efficiently dispersed, give lung cancer to everyone on earth. In calling for a nuclear fission plant phase-out, a leading cost benefit economist, Allen Kneese of Resources for the Future, called it a "moral problem" and "one of the most consequential that has ever faced mankind."

In the light of these and other developments, more scientists are favoring short term energy alternatives through pollution controlled fossil fuels, the reduction of vast energy waste in our economy and the development of solar, geothermal and other clean, inexhaustable forms of energy for the longer future.

Is any of this penetrating the AEC hardliners? Certainly not Chairperson Dixy Lee Ray who fervently advocates with all the force of ignorance an even more dangerous and uneconomical design—the breeder reactor.

What of the Joint Committee on Atomic Energy in Congress? Ridicule of the nuclear critics pours from the uninformed lips of Congressmen Holifield and Hosmer who equate doubts about the "nukes," which they have nourished with 30 billion taxpayer dollars, with blasphemy. Committee Chairman Melvin Price has delayed announcing hearing dates for the critics to present their case.

After twenty years such hearings may be described as overdue.

Let's Go After the Crime in the Suites
December 25, 1972

The US attorney for the Southern District of New York, Whitney North Seymour, is distributing a sixty-four-page booklet entitled "Fighting White-Collar Crime" to corporations and other business groups. This effort is a follow-up to a Seymour speech last July in which he stated,

> Let there be no mistake about it, there is extensive crime in the business world. Our office currently is prosecuting scores of cases involving the payment of bribes, securities abuses, tax frauds, and numerous other violations. Virtually every single one of these cases was developed without any cooperation from the business community. In fact, most of these cases came about because of a look-the-other-way attitude by businessmen who could have prevented the crimes from ever happening in the first place.

In that address before the Rotary Club of New York City, Seymour was clearly indignant. He complained that business crimes receive favored treatment in the courts, which give much lighter sentences, frequently suspended, than to individuals prosecuted for petty stealing. "Businessmen," he noted sharply, "too often tend to smile understandingly at illegal conduct by their colleagues—while loudly complaining about 'crime in the streets.' We must set these things right."

Official complaints about "crime in the suites" are increasing. The acting FBI director, L. Patrick Gray, told another business group in Cleveland recently that, among other lawbreakers, corporate executives who conspire to fix prices in violation of the antitrust laws "attack the society of law from within."

State and local governmental units, recognizing that business crime costs consumers billions of dollars yearly, are stepping up their enforcement. California, for example, has brought suit under the antitrust laws against snack food manufacturers for alleged price-fixing. Washington state has sued major dairy companies for fixing the prices of milk and milk products sold to school districts. Illinois has cases in the courts over alleged statewide coal price-fixing and tie-in sales of milk and ice cream, milk price-fixing in Chicago, and beer price-fixing in Decatur. New York has charged a large oil company with price-fixing and price discrimination.

In addition to the increasing number of suits brought by state attorneys general, consumer fraud offices are being expanded or opened at state and local levels in cities such as New York City, Cleveland, Pittsburgh and Los Angeles. The New York Department of Consumer Affairs, led by Bess Myerson, believes that catching business violators is not enough. She says full refunds with interest must be repaid to defrauded consumers. In Maryland, unprecedented prison sentences of six and 10 years were meted out to the operators of an auto repair store which systematically fleeced motorists.

What is clear from a survey of business crime prosecutions brought by federal and state authorities in recent years is that the defendants represent a wide diversity and cross-section of industry and commerce. They are not just fly-by-night outfits. Price-fixing or other economic crimes have been located in such varied industries as companies selling pharmaceuticals, bread, heavy electrical equipment, steel sheets, plumbing fixtures, cranberries, and chrysanthemums.

What such depredations do to the consumer dollar in the marketplace is similar to what a pay-cut or traditional inflation does to individuals' purchasing power. Sen. Philip Hart's antitrust and monopoly subcommittee, for example, reports that consumers spend about $10 billion annually on auto repairs and parts that are improperly done, unnecessary or not performed at all. A House subcommittee estimates that elderly citizens are swindled out of $1 billion yearly through medical quackery. The Michigan Department of Agriculture found shortages in 15 percent of 50,000 food packages that it examined.

Given these and many other similar surveys and cases, what is the reply to the Indiana official who stated at a recent antitrust meeting of state attorneys general, "We have no money and we have no staff. But we have a healthy interest." The best advice for state attorneys general is to vigorously apply for grants from the justice Department's Law Enforcement Assistance Administration (LEAA). According to LEAA's General Counsel's office, funds can be made available for corporate crime and consumer fraud law enforcement purposes. In fiscal 1973, LEAA will have almost $850,000,000 for distribution to law enforcement agencies. Some of these funds can be wisely used to combat the corporate crime wave.

This Land is Your Land

August 14, 1972

A controversy is brewing over the ownership and use of underdeveloped and agricultural land in the US. The cries of land fraud, land dispossession and the need for land reform are uttered frequently from a wide diversity of groups. On one side are small farmers and landowners, conservationists, elderly retired people, and officials who take their law enforcement duties seriously.

The trends feeding this struggle over the land are:

- A growing concentration of land ownership, particularly in agricultural areas such as California and Florida, by giant agri-business corporations. The US Department of Agriculture has information on land ownership concentration but refuses to make it public.

- Corporate speculators are buying up large land tracts, and by legal and political maneuvers, are jacking up development land prices that increase housing and other development costs. There's a lot of secrecy about these purchases, thereby depriving nearby residents from learning what the corporation plans to do that might drastically upset their way of life. International Telephone & Telegraph, for example, is quietly buying up tens of thousands of acres in northwest Maine and isn't saying why. Attention is focusing on the gigantic land holdings of the railroads obtained free from the US government in the 19th Century. A group headed by Senator Fred Harris (D-Okla.) has demanded that Southern Pacific Railroad give up these surplus lands, claiming they are not being used for railroad purposes as required under the original land grants.

- Public interest lawyers in Appalachia are studying the notorious broad-form deed used decades ago by corporate lawyers to fleece innocent mountain folk of valuable coal and other minerals on their land.

- Property tax reformers are documenting their charges that large timber, coal, and oil and gas companies are among those who are vastly underpaying their taxes through politically inspired low assessments. Schools and other services suffer as a result. Small businesses and homeowners pay higher taxes as well.

- Interstate land sales frauds directed at retired people who want to settle in Florida, Arizona or other retirement areas, are mushrooming. High-pressure tactics and deception have often cost elderly people their entire investments in misrepresented acreage. Federal law enforcement agencies are paying too little attention to these abuses.

- Congress is now deliberating a national land use policy to prod the states into establishing planning programs for such major land uses as highways, parks, mass transit systems, airports, utilities, and other large developments. The chief sponsor of this legislation is conservative Sen. Henry Jackson (D-Wash.).

All this adds up to a recognition of just how limited the nation's land resources are becoming, and the potential loss to future generations. It is the present and future duty of all Americans to keep the land from being seriously polluted. Our founding fathers recognized this in the great decisions they made. The early conservationists in Teddy Roosevelt's days met the challenges new to that period. It is time now to stop the drive to monopolize and despoil the land by a few in order to profiteer from the many.

Index

About the Author

RALPH NADER is America's leading consumer and citizen advocate. As a result of his efforts, cars are safer, food is healthier, our environment is less polluted, and our democracy is more robust. A lawyer and author, Nader has co-founded numerous public interest groups including Public Citizen, the Center for Auto Safety, Clean Water Action Project, the Disability Rights Center, the Pension Rights Center, Commercial Alert, the Public Interest Research Group (PIRG), and the Center for Study of Responsive Law. For the past forty-five years he has challenged abuses by corporate and government officials and urged citizens to use their time, energy, and democratic rights to demand greater institutional accountability. In 1965, Nader's landmark book *Unsafe at Any Speed* changed the face of the automobile industry. *The Atlantic Magazine* named Nader as one of the hundred most influential figures in American history, and *Time* and *Life* magazines honored him as one of the most influential Americans of the twentieth century.

About Seven Stories Press

Seven Stories Press is an independent book publisher based in New York City. We publish works of the imagination by such writers as Nelson Algren, Russell Banks, Octavia E. Butler, Ani DiFranco, Assia Djebar, Ariel Dorfman, Coco Fusco, Barry Gifford, Martha Long, Luis Negrón, Hwang Sok-yong, Lee Stringer, and Kurt Vonnegut, to name a few, together with political titles by voices of conscience, including Subhankar Banerjee, the Boston Women's Health Collective, Noam Chomsky, Angela Y. Davis, Human Rights Watch, Derrick Jensen, Ralph Nader, Loretta Napoleoni, Gary Null, Greg Palast, Project Censored, Barbara Seaman, Alice Walker, Gary Webb, and Howard Zinn, among many others. Seven Stories Press believes publishers have a special responsibility to defend free speech and human rights, and to celebrate the gifts of the human imagination, wherever we can. In 2012 we launched Triangle Square *books for young readers* with strong social justice and narrative components, telling personal stories of courage and commitment. For additional information, visit www.sevenstories.com.

INTO FILM